THE
CONTEMPORARY
ESSAY

BOOKS BY DONALD HALL

Books of Poetry

Exiles and Marriages, 1955
The Dark Houses, 1958
A Roof of Tiger Lilies, 1964
The Alligator Bride: Poems New and Selected, 1969
The Yellow Room: Love Poems, 1971
The Town of Hill, 1975
Kicking the Leaves, 1978
The Happy Man, 1986
The One Day, 1988

Books of Prose

String Too Short to Be Saved, 1961
Henry Moore, 1966
Writing Well, 1973, 1976, 1979, 1982, 1985, 1988
Playing Around (with G. McCauley et al.), 1974
Dock Ellis in the Country of Baseball, 1976
Goatfoot Milktongue Twinbird, 1978
Remembering Poets, 1978
Ox-Cart Man, 1979
To Keep Moving, 1981
The Weather for Poetry, 1982
Fathers Playing Catch with Sons, 1985
The Ideal Bakery, 1987
Seasons at Eagle Pond, 1987
Poetry and Ambition, 1988

Edited Works

New Poets of England and America (with R. Pack and
    L. Simpson), 1957
The Poetry Sampler, 1961
New Poets of England and America (Second Selection) (with R. Pack),
    1962
Contemporary American Poets, 1962, 1971
A Concise Encyclopedia of English and American Poetry and Poets (with
    Stephen Spender), 1963
Poetry in English, 1963, 1970 (with Warren Taylor)
The Faber Book of Modern Verse (New Edition with Supplement), 1965
The Modern Stylists, 1968
A Choice of Whitman's Verse, 1968
Man and Boy, 1968
American Poetry, 1970
A Writer's Reader (with D. L. Emblen), 1976, 1979, 1982, 1985, 1988
Oxford Book of American Literary Anecdotes, 1981
To Read Literature, 1981, 1982, 1987
Claims for Poetry, 1982
Oxford Book of Children's Verse in America, 1985

THE CONTEMPORARY ESSAY

SECOND EDITION

EDITED BY

Donald Hall

A Bedford Book

ST. MARTIN'S PRESS • NEW YORK

For Nan and Dick Smart

Publisher: Charles H. Christensen
Associate Publisher: Joan E. Feinberg
Managing Editor: Elizabeth M. Schaaf
Developmental Editor: Ellen Darion
Production Editor: Mary Lou Wilshaw
Copyeditor: Barbara G. Flanagan
Text Design: Anna Post
Cover Design: Robert L. Barry, Barry Design

Library of Congress Catalog Card Number: 88–70428

For information, write: St. Martin's Press, Inc.
175 Fifth Avenue, New York, NY 10010
Editorial Offices: Bedford Books of St. Martin's Press
29 Winchester Street, Boston, MA 02116

ISBN: 0–312–00346–3

ACKNOWLEDGMENTS

Edward Abbey, "Aravaipa Canyon." From *Down the River* by Edward Abbey. Copyright © 1982 by Edward Abbey. Reprinted by permission of the publisher, E. P. Dutton, a division of NAL Penguin Inc.

Margaret Atwood, "Canadian-American Relations: Surviving the Eighties." From *Second Words: Selected Critical Prose*, copyright © 1982 O. W. Todd Limited. Reprinted by permission of Beacon Press and House of Anansi Press.

Acknowledgments and copyrights are continued at the back of the book on pages 598–600, which constitute an extension of the copyright page.

Preface
for Instructors

The Contemporary Essay is intended for composition instructors who believe, as I do, that much of the best recent writing in America is nonfiction — and who regret that more of this excellent writing does not appear in composition anthologies because it defies rhetorical or thematic classification. Instructors who use this book will demand from their students sustained attention to essays that are longer and more challenging than usual. But good prose and good thinking require each other; a composition course that demands more attentive and thoughtful reading will encourage attentive and thoughtful writing.

The Introduction that follows speaks to the diversity of the writers assembled here. This anthology could have been three times as long without lowering its standards; my final selection of fifty-one essays was necessarily arbitrary. I arrived at the mix by seeking diversity in tone, in level of difficulty, in strategy, and in subject matter: *The Contemporary Essay* entertains matters of economics and fashion, dinosaurs and eclipses, torture, and Wyoming.

For the second edition of this book I decided to take my title literally. Because we live in an age of the essay, we can assemble a collection which is both contemporary and high in quality. Thus a few of these essays derive from the 1970s but most were published within the decade of the 1980s. There is much to be said for studying old models of prose; but when students of composition look for the templates of a modern style, there is more to be said for using the best work of our own literary moment.

In the second edition we collect fifty-one essays, seventeen more than last time. The book is larger, but this time we have included a number of brief essays. Many teachers told us that they wanted the options provided by shorter texts among the longer ones. Other teachers suggested new essays by some of our old writers. Thus, thirteen essays in the second edition are different choices from the work of writers previously included. All in all, thirty-nine essays are new to this edition, many by women: Margaret Atwood, Carol Bly, Gretel Ehrlich, Francine Du Plessix Gray, Vicki Hearne, Maxine Kumin, Jan Morris, Joyce Carol Oates, Cynthia Ozick, and Phyllis Rose join the company of Joan Didion, Annie Dillard, Frances FitzGerald, Diane Johnson, Maxine Hong Kingston, Alison Lurie, Adrienne Rich, Barbara W. Tuchman, Alice Walker, and Eudora Welty.

The alphabetical arrangement of the essays makes for arbitrary juxtaposition. But any rhetorical or thematic organization would belie the actual range and variety of these essays. Very few could easily associate under one topic heading; no essay exemplifies only one rhetorical device.

In both its choice of selections and its editorial apparatus, *The Contemporary Essay* tries to avoid the condescension to students endemic to so many composition anthologies. I assume that students have dictionaries; I assume that the class uses a rhetoric or a handbook. Therefore, I do not footnote words easily available in dictionaries or gloss common rhetorical terms. The Introduction gives advice about reading in general, and the headnotes supply help toward reading each essay. After each selection I have written a brief Afterword, notes on the essay just read which may prove useful for some students and some teachers. These Afterwords are deliberately nonparallel: Some focus on one trick of style; others examine larger issues of structure; many center on the different strategies available to the essayist. Each tries to point out something useful; none attempts to respond to a whole essay.

Suggestions for teaching the works included in *The Contemporary Essay*, Second Edition, along with questions for every selection appear in *Resources for Teaching the Contemporary Essay*, which is bound with the Instructor's Edition of this text. Because the selections in the text are rich enough to accommodate multiple approaches, and in response to suggestions from instructors who used the first edition, I have chosen not to limit instructors' options by including the conventional editorial apparatus in the text itself. Instead, the questions and suggestions appear in the *Resources*, where they can be used entirely at the instructor's discretion. These resources, prepared by Diane Elizabeth Young of Stanford University, include Questions on Meaning, Questions on Strategy, Questions on Language, and at least two writing assignments for every essay. Each question is followed by a lengthy discussion, which includes suggested answers to the question. (Questions are also available separately upon request. See the Note to Instructors in *Resources for Teaching The Contemporary Essay* for ordering information.)

My debts in assembling this collection are many. I am indebted to writers and editors, to my old teachers and to colleagues at the University of Michigan where I taught for many years. I am indebted to students. In recent years, I have talked about teaching exposition with composition staffs at many colleges and universities, from Lynchburg College in Virginia to the University of Utah in Salt Lake City, from the University of New Hampshire to Pacific Lutheran in Tacoma, Washington. I wish to express my gratitude to more people than I can name. By name, I would like to thank the following instructors, who used the first edition and generously took the time to share their ideas about it: Flavia Bacarella, Herbert H. Lehman College; Eileen Barrett, Boston College; Dante K. Cantrill, Idaho State University; Marlene Clarke, University of California, Davis; David Cohen, State University of New York at Buffalo; Robert Cohen, State University of New York at Stony Brook; Patty S. Derrick, University of Maine at Fort Kent; C. Annette Ducey, Rhode Island College; Kathleen Estrada-Palma, University of Maine-Orono; Michael Friedlander, Sacramento City College; Joan Garrett-Goodyear, Smith College; Marcia Gealy, Northwestern University; Paul Gianoli, School of the Ozarks; Joseph Green, Western Washington University; Henry Hahn, Modesto Junior College; Robert J. Hall, College of Sequoias; Ed Harkness, Shoreline Community College; D. Scott Hinson, University of North Carolina at Charlotte; Nora C. Jaffe, Smith College; Sabrina Kirby, Virginia Polytechnic Institute; Steve Klepetar, St. Cloud State University; Barbara Lakin, Colorado State University; Leslie Lawrence, Boston University; Ruth Lepson, Boston College; Carol S. Long, Willamette University; Catherine Lupori, College of St. Catherine; Candice Matzhe, College of Sequoias; Robert Miles, California State University, Sacramento; Jacqueline A. Mintz, University of California, Berkeley; Diane Molberg, San Francisco State University; Alice P. Nunnery, Middle Tennessee State University; Kevin Oderman, Iowa State University, Ames; Suzanne Owens, Ohio State University; George Peranteau, College of DuPoye; Ruth Perkins, Linn-Benton Community College; Raymond C. Phillips, Jr., Western Maryland College; Libby Schlagel, Adelphi University; Jocelyn A. Sheppard, State University of New York at Buffalo; Thomas Simmons, University of California, Berkeley; Bill Siverly, Portland Community College; Patricia L. Skarda, Smith College; Roger Sorkin, South-eastern Massachusetts University; Karyn Sproles, State University of New York at Buffalo; Paul Strong, Alfred University; Joan Taylor, University of South Carolina at Beaufort; Wayne Ude, Mankato State University; Anmarie Wagstaff, University of California, Davis; Eileen M. Ward, College of Dupage-Alpha; Kathleen M. Ward, University of California, Davis; Alice F. Worlsey, California State University, Stanislaus; Betsy R. Zimbalist, Washington University; John N. Zneimer, Indiana University Northwest.

More locally, I am indebted to Jane Kenyon who proofread, to Lois Fierro who typed (and retyped, and re-retyped). At Bedford Books, I am always indebted to Charles Christensen and Joan Feinberg, who approached me about this book remembering my wistful notion of years ago. For this edition I have relied grossly on the resourceful, mighty, but gentle intelligence of Ellen Darion. I am grateful to Diane Elizabeth Young, who has done the excellent Instructor's Manual. I am grateful to Matthew Carnicelli, Erin Curtiss, Sarah Royston, Steve Scipione, and Julie Shevach for many specific chores, and to Elizabeth Schaaf and Mary Lou Wilshaw for taking this book through production. I am grateful to Barbara Flanagan who copyedited this immense manuscript. Robert Atwan gave knowledgeable advice, especially in recommending essays for this edition; all who care for the literature of the essay owe Atwan a debt for his annual collection, *Best Essays*.

D.H.
Wilmot, New Hampshire

Contents

> "As Thoreau found a universe in the woods around Concord, any person whose senses are alive can make a world of any natural place, however limited it might seem, on this subtle planet of ours."

> "Americans get discouraged when they can't get instant results; they vacillate between romantic idealism and black humor, its opposite. Canadians on the other hand think any change will probably be for the worse. Consequently they are less easily stampeded, less extreme in their trends."

appear to ape this usage, although down there thin is seldom a matter of choice."

"Beyond his devotion to work, however, he is also well spoken, tolerant of disagreement, disposed always to negotiate — for that is how he spends his time — and otherwise given to persuasion rather than to command."

"The speeding reader guts a book the way the skillful clean fish. The gills are gone, the tail, the scales, the fins; then the filet slides away swiftly as though fed to a seal."

"The best scientific hypotheses are also generous and expansive: they suggest extensions and implications that enlighten related, and even far distant, subjects. Simply consider how the idea of evolution has influenced virtually every intellectual field."

"What exactly would happen if we women remodeled our concepts of ideal human bonding on the ties of friendship and abandoned the premises of enchantment and possession?"

"What [my dog] Belle has is an ability to act with moral clarity, and this is a result of having qualities that have to do with real love, love with teeth."

"She waits and blinks, pumping her throat, turning her head, then sets off like a loping tiger in slow motion, hurdling the jungly lumber, the pea vine and twigs."

"Women sense — indeed, are carefully taught to feel — that the institution of rape is mysteriously protected by an armor of folklore, Bible tales, legal precedents, specious psychological theories."

CONTENTS

xiv

CONTENTS

CONTENTS

THE
CONTEMPORARY
ESSAY

Introduction for Students: On These Writers and Their Work

Often one literary form dominates an era. In Shakespeare's time the play was the thing, and lyric poets and pamphleteers wrote for the stage when they turned aside from their primary work. A few decades ago, American novelists wrote novels when they could afford to but paid their bills by writing short stories for *Colliers* and the *Saturday Evening Post*. Today novelists of similar eminence and ability — Joan Didion, James Baldwin, Walker Percy, Cynthia Ozick, Alice Walker, Robert Stone, Paul Theroux — become masters of the essay, for we live in the age of the essay.

In part, our age needs the essay because it requires exposition. We live in a time bewildered by the multiplicity of information; we cherish the selection and organization of information by our best writers. We live in a time that allows writers freedom to choose what they investigate, to follow their thoughts wherever they lead, and to use a variety of styles and strategies. Therefore the essay thrives, and many of our best essayists are writers for whom, as Annie Dillard puts it, the essay is "the real work." In our age, we are also fortunate to read essayists whose real work is science. Stephen Jay Gould and Lewis Thomas write brilliant prose in the service of paleontology and medicine. For most of us — who are specialists, or generalists with many gaps of knowledge — the exposition of technology by gifted writers is a major necessity.

But the essay of our moment is not only exposition of information. Annie Dillard's real work is personal narrative that contains exact description of the natural world. This kind of writing, with opinions argued or suggested, belongs to the older tradition of the essay. Although a few classical writers — like Plutarch in Greek, Cicero in Latin — wrote brief historical or philosophical meditations which resemble the genre, it was Michel de Montaigne in sixteenth-century France who invented the form that we know. He also invented the name, *essais*, which is modest but not *too* modest — for its suggestion of attempt or trial allows the writer freedom of tentative exploration; because the essayist does not pretend to speak the final word, she or he is at liberty to extend over unknown or speculative territory. Typically the classic essay combines personal experience with thought or opinion leading to tentative generalization — like Samuel F. Pickering, Jr., as he identifies "An Occupational Hazard."

The contemporary essay is a house with many rooms. Trying to define "essay" so as to include everything offered in this collection, we could collapse into the negative: An essay is something in paragraphs (not poetry) which is true or supposed to be true (not fiction). But the negative is not good enough. For that matter, the contemporary essay when it is narrative and dramatic sometimes resembles a short story; look at Maxine Hong Kingston and Tom Wolfe.

It is better to talk of three main traditions that make the contemporary essay.

There is the essay of personal experience and opinion, where the author is center stage, which can extend from the extremely personal (Paul Zweig on confronting cancer) to the almost-objective (Pickering); see Joan Didion on water and her feelings about water. Other examples of the personal essay abound in this book: Looking at the table of contents, we can list Abbey, Atwood, Berger — and keep going.

Another category of essay is primarily philosophical, intellectual, or critical — an essay that examines, argues, thinks, and makes decisions. Clearly this form resembles the essay of personal opinion, but Walker Percy wants not to suggest the opinion of one author but the truth of experience. The difference in tone is considerable. Other criticial or intellectual essays here include work by William H. Gass, Adrienne Rich, Diane Johnson, Francine Du Plessix Gray, and Joseph Brodsky.

A third type of essay is the magazine article of our day — information or exposition arranged so that we can take it in. This essay means to report on *what is there*, without apparent reference to the writer's life or opinion.

2

See John McPhee, Frances FitzGerald, and Calvin Trillin, for instance. However, when we read work that seems purely objective, we must remember that the instrument that measures distorts the measuring: The author chooses only a tiny proportion of the details available, and this choice expresses opinion even when the writer tries to remain out of it.

The moment we divide the essay into three parts like Caesar's Gaul, we face the fact that the largest number of essays in this book must belong to another category: NONE OF THE ABOVE, or maybe ALL OF THE ABOVE. Malcolm Cowley writes from personal experience, from opinion, but also with research and information in pursuit of a critical objectivity. In the category of humor — Russell Baker, Garrison Keillor, Ian Frazier — we find opinion, ethics by way of satire, and personal narrative or perhaps mockery of personal narrative. In Jonathan Schell we might seem to discover pure exposition — but Jonathan Schell's writing conveys personal passion and belief.

The editor's burden in making this anthology has been to choose wisely and representatively among a dazzling variety of the best. We have tried for diversity of author, style, and subject. After reading more than a thousand essays, after making a short list of a hundred and fifty, we have finally arrived at this collection. We may hope that we have chosen a range of topics and attitudes to suit and to offend practically everybody, for contemporary factual writing explores the universe, and its manners of procedure are as various as its subject matters: Writers explain, describe, narrate, argue, and reminisce about childhood, wolves, corporate men, rape, torture, habits of the civilized mind, dinosaurs, education, the fourteenth century, snobbishness, clothing, murder, mothers, and nuclear holocaust. Nothing human is alien to the essay, nor is any method or length or degree of difficulty alien. On the one hand Walker Percy's philosophical ideas make reading him difficult, and equally rewarding for the effort. On the other hand Frances FitzGerald on a retirement community or Eudora Welty on a neighborhood store does not tax the philosophical mind: With these topics, difficulty would be inappropriate.

Typical strategies vary from essay to essay, partly by type — one wouldn't construct a narrative by means of analogy or definition — but also within a type. In a critical essay, Alison Lurie speaks of clothing by constructing a long and ingenious analogy to language. In an essay of argument, Richard Rodriguez describes his growing up, using personal narrative for purposes of persuasion as he discusses ethnicity and bilingualism. It pleases Calvin Trillin to use his skill partly in self-effacement; his talent renders the author invisible behind his subject matter. On the other hand, Scott Russell Sanders has no interest in invisibility even when

3

he writes like Calvin Trillin about the culture of violence in America. Differences in strategy derive partly from subject matter but also from diverse abilities and obsessions. Some writers, like Tom Wolfe, leave their personal histories out of their stories but fly the flag of personality by flaunting an idiosyncratic style.

In subjects and strategies, this book offers a diversity for study. Yet when we look at the prose of these writers from a distance — for instance, from the vantage point of another century's style — we realize that certain agreements about writing unite the distinct minds of Gretel Ehrlich and Alastair Reid, Barry Lopez and Barbara W. Tuchman. These writers agree, by and large, to use the concrete detail in place of the abstraction; to employ the active, not the passive, mood; to withhold the adjective and search for the verb. They agree to pursue clarity and vigor. And most would agree with Robert Graves (English poet, novelist, and essayist), who said some years ago: "The writing of good English is . . . a moral matter."

Graves wrote these words in the late 1930s, shortly before George Orwell (novelist and pamphleteer, author of *Animal Farm* and *1984*) wrote "Politics and the English Language," an essay which introduced or codified many assumptions about modern prose style. Orwell noted that the vices of vagueness, triteness, jargon, and pomposity are often not merely errors; often they serve the purposes of deceit. A clear prose style will not deceive others and will help the writer to avoid self-deceit. Even earlier, the American poet Ezra Pound had talked about closing the "gap between one's real and one's declared meaning." Bad writers are vague ones. The novelist Ernest Hemingway said: "If a man writes clearly, anyone can see if he fakes." These writers reached a consensus which emphasized, in Pound's words, that "good writers are those who keep the language efficient . . . accurate . . . clear."

Much good nonfiction works the way an efficient machine works, by directness that matches energy to production. A sentence is good the way an ax handle is good. Order and organization move from writer's mind to reader's by the ethics of clarity in sentence structure and transition. For good prose to aid us, both socially and psychologically, it need not speak of society or psyche; for good style, all by itself, *is* good politics and good mental hygiene. Thus John McPhee, who writes without revealing his values, contributes to ethics by the lucidity, clarity, and vigor of his exposition.

But efficiency and clarity are not the only values we derive from good style. It is true that sentences show us around the surface of the globe, lead us from one place to another; but sentences also dig beneath the earth's surface. The subjectivity of much contemporary writing — private feelings publicly exposed — provides a model for self-examination. Thus we find

4

room not only for John McPhee but also for Annie Dillard, with whom we explore underworlds of feeling. If she did not write with the efficiency and clarity of a John McPhee, her self-exploration would reveal nothing. But because she writes with intense clarity about matters seldom regarded as clear, the light of the imagination blazes in a dark place.

On Reading Essays

We read to become more human. When we read *Gilgamesh* — the oldest surviving narrative, a Babylonian epic from 2000 B.C. — we connect with other human beings. We raise a glass across four thousand years of time and drink with our ancestors the old wine of friendship, courage, loss, and the will to survive. And in *The Contemporary Essay*, when we read Wendell Berry on national defense or William H. Gass on speedreading or Vicki Hearne on pit bulls or Alice Walker on her mother, we find another kind of linkage. We connect not across chasms of millennia but across contemporary gaps of knowledge and experience. We read for information and pleasure together. We read to understand, to investigate, to provide background for decision, to find confirmation, to find contradiction.

We also read to learn how to write. If we study architecture, we learn in part by studying structures already designed and built. If we study basketball, we learn in part by watching other players dribble, drive to the left, and shoot. Although in learning anything we add our own flourishes, develop our talents, and overcome our drawbacks, we build on things that others did before us. For the writer of essays today, the things done are

7

the essays written yesterday. We build on others' work and add our own uniqueness. Many professional writers, not only students in composition classes, prepare for the day's work by reading an admirable example of the kind of prose they undertake — for the example of excellence, the encouragement of brilliance, the stimulation of achievement.

Reading is as various as writing is. If we read well we read differently according to what we read. Suppose when we eat breakfast we look at a daily paper; later in the day we take on a philosophical essay, a poem, a chemistry assignment, *People* magazine, and the instructions in a box of film. If we try reading the newspaper as we should read the poem, nightfall will find us halfway through the first section. If we try reading the philosophy essay as we read *People*, the essay passes us by. Every piece of print requires a different level of attention; good readers adjust their speed automatically when they read the first words of anything. Something tells them: "Slow down or you'll miss out!" or "Speed up or you'll bore yourself to death!"

In our education, in the culture that shapes us, we acquire unconscious habits of reading. Some habits are good, some bad. It helps to become conscious of how we read; it helps to learn appropriate reading.

A century ago, even sixty years ago, silent reading was noisier to the mental ear because people were used to hearing books read aloud. Long church services included much reading of scripture. Home entertainment was reading aloud from novels, scripture, or poetry. Public entertainment — before radio, films, or television — was lectures, debates, and dramatic recitation. In school, students memorized pieces for speaking and read aloud to their classmates. Because students practiced recitation themselves, they could not read a text in silence without considering how they would say it out loud. Unconsciously, as they read alone, they decided in what tone or with what feeling they would enunciate each word.

Mental mimickry makes for *active* reading. We cannot supply the tone of a word unless we understand its meaning. Nowadays, most of us grow up passive readers. Our passivity is encouraged by television, which provides everything for us, even a laughtrack to tell us when to laugh. This collection of essays is intended for students who want more than printed television. These essays require active reading.

A few years ago I taught a composition class in which I assigned an article by Richard Rhodes called "Packaged Sentiment." This essay about greeting cards came out in *Harper's*, addressed to an audience which would expect to find that magazine contemptuous of prefabricated emotions. But the sophisticated author took pains to explore the opposite of the preconception; he made a limited, reasonable defense of the greeting card industry.

At the end of his argument, he quoted an English novelist's qualified praise of a political institution: "I celebrate [greeting] cards as E. M. Forster celebrated democracy, with a hearty two cheers." When my students came to class that morning I wrote on the blackboard: "Five minutes. Why *two* cheers?" I expected them to tell me why Rhodes's praise was incomplete. They told me something different: They told me what Rhodes found to praise about greeting cards, as if I had asked, "Why two *cheers*?"

My students were victims of passive reading. They read Rhodes's essay and accepted "two cheers" without asking themselves, "Why two rather than twelve, or one, or ten million?" When I said this much at the next meeting of the class, three or four students slapped their palms on their foreheads — the classic gesture: "How *could* I have missed that one?" These students learned a lesson; they had neglected to read actively and to note that Richard Rhodes withheld one third of the normal tribute: "Three Cheers! Hip Hip Hooray! Hip Hip Hooray! Hip Hip Hooray!"

Those students who got the point should never again forget that three is the normal number for cheers. But how would they keep from making the same kind of mistake in further reading? How would they learn to read actively, engaging the text, requiring the text to make sense? Here is a series of answers to these questions.

1. *Learn the model for active reading.* Put the author on the witness stand and make him tell not only the truth but the whole truth. Give the author the benefit of the doubt — expect him to reveal himself if you work hard at it — but be prepared on occasion to discover that the author, rather than the reader, is at fault (illogic, missed step in an argument, unfairness, lack of support).

2. *Adjust the speed of your reading.* Learn to adjust your reading to an appropriate speed. Most of these essays ought to be read slowly, but their demands will vary. It should take twice as long to read a page of Joseph Brodsky as it does to read a page by Raymond Carver. (I refer to the essays by these writers in this book. Raymond Carver is sometimes, appropriately, slower reading, and Joseph Brodsky faster.) If you tend to read quickly, learn to slow down when it is appropriate. If you tend to read slowly, make sure that your slowness results from close attention to the text, not from a wandering mind. But be neither a slow reader nor a fast one: Be an appropriate reader, adjusting your speed to the text you are reading.

3. *Take notes as you read.* Everyone should take reading notes; they help to make sure that you understand *as* you read. Pause regularly, perhaps at the end of each paragraph, at least at the end of every page or two, to inspect yourself and your text. Underline the most crucial sentences, passages with which you tentatively disagree, and phrases you need to return

to. Ask yourself: Do I know where we are and how we got there? Why are we entertaining *this* subject, in *this* essay? Try to answer yourself, in a note. Write in a notebook or on the margin of the page. When you commit yourself by writing a note, often you recognize that your understanding is less secure than you had considered it.

4. *Look up what you need to know.* Learn what it is appropriate to know exactly and what you can understand approximately. If an essayist on medicine refers to "the etiology of disease," we need to understand the word *etiology* to follow the sense. We turn to the dictionary. On the other hand, the essayist may refer to a particular disease by a long Latinate name, in a context where we understand that the word is an example and that the exact nature of the disease (which we could discover scurrying from definition to definition in a dictionary) is irrelevant to our understanding of the sentence. Learn what to look up and learn what not to look up; this knowledge resembles social tact. If you are in doubt, look it up, but mature readers when they read Lewis Thomas need not trace down *corpus callosum* in a medical dictionary. They know by the context of the essay what is happening; they know that scientific terminology suits the essayist's purpose — and that the message is the choice of scientific language, not its definition.

5. *Read and reread.* Most important: Read, reread, and reread again. When your teacher assigns an essay, read it through the first time as soon as you can. Read the headnote first; read the essay at an appropriate speed, pausing to interrogate it; take notes and underline; use a dictionary. Then read the afterword that follows the essay. Think the essay over. Consult your notes, look back at the text for difficult points, think about the whole essay — and then sleep on it. It is useful to come back to *anything* a second time after an interval, especially after sleepwork. Never write a paper or read an essay once only, at one sitting, even if it is a long sitting.

When you return to the essay a day later, reread the headnote, which should be more useful the second time. Reread the essay more slowly, now that you know its plot, and take further notes. Reread the afterword. Take notes on your notes.

6. *Make your own list.* Finally, there are problems that vary from reader to reader. Think about your *own* problems in reading, before you begin to read each essay assigned. Study your own reading to identify mistakes made in the past. ("How did I manage *not* to notice that 'two cheers' is a diminution of 'three cheers'?") When a neighbor in class finds more in an essay than you found, interrogate yourself. What in your reading prevented you from getting it all?

Keep a list, at the front of a reading notebook, of injunctions that you need to remember. "Pause after every page to summarize." "Watch for transitions." "Look up words." Toward the end of the term, maybe you can cross some injunctions out.

Everyone assigned this textbook knows how to read. Everyone can improve as a reader.

When we improve as readers we improve as writers. By observing Malcolm Cowley or Joyce Carol Oates or James Baldwin solve a problem in writing, be it as small as a transition or as large as any essay's whole shape, we add to our own equipment for solving problems of style and construction. By reading we also improve as human beings; we increase our ability to absorb the history of our species, preserved in the language of the tribe through time and in the language of our contemporaries in an age of the essay.

EDWARD
ABBEY

*B*ORN IN PENNSYLVANIA (1926), Edward Abbey has lived for the past forty years in the Southwest, in love with the desert and with places of wild rough beauty like Aravaipa Canyon. Abbey discovered the West in 1948 when he arrived fresh from the East to study at the University of New Mexico.

In politics he calls himself "agrarian anarchist." While he loves the land and its natural flora and fauna with a passion, anger as well as love gives energy to Edward Abbey's writing. His best-known novel, with a large underground following, is The Monkey Wrench Gang (1975), which tells about eco-vigilantes who sabotage polluters and developers. His best work is done in the essay, beginning in the collection Desert Solitaire (1968) and continuing through Abbey's Road (1979), Down the River (1982), from which we take "Aravaipa Canyon," and Beyond the Wall (1984). Slumgullion Stew (1984) is a reader which brings fiction and essay together. Abbey's most recent book is the essay collection One Life at a Time, Please (1988). His love of the natural world attacks exploiters and developers and engineers and scientists; his passion for mystery finds its enemy in the scientific mind that denies multiplicity. At times he writes out of passion for the natural world, almost like Solomon singing his Song; at times he denounces the destroyers like Jeremiah.

The great celebrators of place in literature are rarely native to the places they celebrate; they are aliens who discover and choose the beloved place. Often they look back contemptuously on a younger self. When he arrived in New Mexico as a student, Abbey tells us in an essay, he considered, "like most simpleminded easterners," that "a cowboy was a kind of mythic hero." He no longer idolizes the cowboy. Nor the cow. He tells us that if he were rich enough now to buy a cattle ranch, he would shoot the cattle. "Shoot them all, and stock the place with real animals, real game, real protein: elk, buffalo, pronghorn antelope, bighorn sheep, moose. And some purely decorative animals, like eagles. We need more eagles. And wolves. We need more wolves. Mountain lions and bears. Especially, of course, grizzly bears. Down in the desert, I would stock every watertank, every waterhole, every stock pond, with alligators."

Images, anecdotes, details, and exact description locate us in the loved places. Although Abbey gives us the look of things, he does not leave us with snapshots: Language embodies the precision of his looking and the passion of his advocacy.

Aravaipa Canyon

Southeast of Phoenix and northeast of Tucson, in the Pinal Mountains, is a short deep gorge called Aravaipa Canyon. It is among the few places in Arizona with a permanent stream of water and in popular estimation one of the most beautiful. I am giving away no secrets here: Aravaipa Canyon has long been well known to hikers, campers, horsemen, and hunters from the nearby cities. The federal Bureau of Land Management (BLM), charged with administration of the canyon, recently decreed it an official Primitive Area, thus guaranteeing its fame. Demand for enjoyment of the canyon is so great that the BLM has been obliged to institute a rationing program: no one camps here without a permit and only a limited number of such permits are issued.

Two friends and I took a walk into Aravaipa Canyon a few days ago. We walked because there is no road. There is hardly even a foot trail. Twelve miles long from end to end, the canyon is mostly occupied by the little river which gives it its name, and by stream banks piled with slabs of fallen rock from the cliffs above, the whole overgrown with cactus, trees, and riparian desert shrubbery.

Aravaipa is an Apache name (some say Pima, some say Papago) and the commonly accepted meaning is "laughing waters." The name fits. The stream is brisk, clear, about a foot deep at normal flow levels, churning its way around boulders, rippling over gravelbars, plunging into pools with bright and noisy vivacity. Schools of loach minnow, roundtail chub, spike dace, and Gila mudsuckers — rare and endemic species — slip and slither past your ankles as you wade into the current. The water is too warm to support trout or other varieties of what are called game fish; the fish here live out their lives undisturbed by anything more than horses' hooves and the sneaker-shod feet of hikers. (PLEASE DO NOT MOLEST THE FISH.)

The Apaches who gave the name to this water and this canyon are not   4 around anymore. Most of that particular band — unarmed old men, women, children — huddled in a cave near the mouth of Aravaipa Canyon, were exterminated in the 1880s by a death squad of American pioneers, aided by Mexican and Papagos, from the nearby city of Tucson. The reason for this vigilante action is obscure (suspicion of murder and cattle stealing) but the results were clear. No more Apaches in Aravaipa Canyon. During pauses in the gunfire, as the pioneers reloaded their rifles, the surviving Indians could have heard the sound of laughing waters. One hundred and twenty-five were killed, the remainder relocated in the White Mountain Reservation to the northeast. Since then those people have given us no back talk at all.

Trudging upstream and over rocky little beaches, we are no more troubled by ancient history than are the mudsuckers in the pools. We prefer to enjoy the scenery. The stone walls stand up on both sides, twelve hundred feet high in the heart of the canyon. The rock is of volcanic origin, rosy-colored andesites and buff, golden, consolidated tuff. Cleavages and fractures across the face of the walls form perfect stairways and sometimes sloping ramps, slick as sidewalks. On the beaches lie obsidian boulders streaked with veins of quartzite and pegmatite.

The walls bristle with spiky rock gardens of formidable desert vegetation. Most prominent is the giant saguaro cactus, growing five to fifty feet tall out of crevices in the stone you might think could barely lodge a flower. The barrel cactus, with its pink fishhook thorns, thrives here on the sunny side; and clusters of hedgehog cactus, and prickly pear with names like clockface and cows-tongue, have wedged roots into the rock. Since most of the wall is vertical, parallel to gravity, these plants grow first outward then upward, forming right-angled bends near the base. It looks difficult but they do it. They like it here.

Also present are tangles of buckhorn, staghorn, chainfruit, and teddy-bear cholla; the teddybear cholla is a cactus so thick with spines it glistens under the sun as if covered with fur. From more comfortable niches in the rock grow plants like the sotol, a thing with sawtooth leaves and a flower stalk ten feet tall. The agave, a type of lily, is even bigger, and its leaves are long, rigid, pointed like bayonets. Near the summit of the cliffs, where the moisture is insufficient to support cactus, we see gray-green streaks of lichen clinging to the stone like a mold.

The prospect at streamside is conventionally sylvan, restful to desert-   8

15

weary eyes. Great cottonwoods and sycamores shade the creek's stony shores; when we're not wading in water we're wading through a crashing autumn debris of green-gold cottonwood and dusty-red sycamore leaves. Other trees flourish here — willow, salt cedar, alder, desert hackberry, and a kind of wild walnut. Cracked with stones, the nuts yield a sweet but frugal meat. At the water's edge is a nearly continuous growth of peppery-flavored watercress. The stagnant pools are full of algae; and small pale frogs, treefrogs, and leopard frogs leap from the bank at our approach and dive into the water; they swim for the deeps with kicking legs, quick breaststrokes.

We pass shadowy, intriguing side canyons with names like Painted Cave (ancient pictographs), Iceberg (where the sun seldom shines), and Virgus (named in honor of himself by an early settler in the area). At midday we enter a further side canyon, one called Horsecamp, and linger here for a lunch of bread, cheese, and water. We contemplate what appears to be a bottomless pool.

The water in this pool has a dark clarity, like smoked glass, transparent but obscure. We see a waterlogged branch six feet down resting on a ledge but cannot see to the bottom. The water feels intensely cold to hand and foot; a few tadpoles have attached themselves to the stony rim of the pool just beneath the surface of the water. They are sluggish, barely animate. One waterbug, the kind called boatman, propels itself with limp oars down toward darkness when I extend my hand toward it.

Above the pool is a thirty-foot bluff of sheer, vesiculated, fine-grained, monolithic gray rock with a glossy chute carved down its face. Flash floods, pouring down that chute with driving force, must have drilled this basin in the rock below. The process would require a generous allowance of time — ten thousand, twenty thousand years — give or take a few thousand. Only a trickle of water from a ring of seeps° enters the pool now, on this hot still blazing day in December. Feels like 80°F; a month from now it may be freezing; in June 110°. In the silence I hear the rasping chant of locusts — that universal lament for mortality and time — here in this canyon where winter seldom comes.

The black and bottomless pool gleams in the shining rock — a sinister 12 paradox, to a fanciful mind. To any man of natural piety this pool, this place, this silence, would suggest reverence, even fear. But I'm an apostate Presbyterian from a long-ago Pennsylvania: I shuck my clothes, jump in, and touch bottom only ten feet down. Bedrock bottom, as I'd expected, and if any Grendels° dwell in this inky pool they're not inclined to reveal themselves today.

---

seeps Small pools formed by water oozing from underground to the surface.
Grendels In the Old English epic *Beowulf*, Grendel is the monster slain by the hero, Beowulf.

We return to the Aravaipa. Halfway back to camp and the canyon entrance we pause to inspect a sycamore that seems to be embracing a boulder. The trunk of the tree has grown around the rock. Feeling the tree for better understanding, I hear a clatter of loose stones, look up, and see six, seven, eight bighorn sheep perched on the rimrock a hundred feet above us. Three rams, five ewes. They are browsing at the local, salad bar — brittlebush, desert holly, bursage, and jojoba — aware of us but not alarmed. We watch them for a long time as they move casually along the rim and up a talus slope beyond, eating as they go, halting now and then to stare back at the humans staring up at them.

Once, years before, I had glimpsed a mountain lion in this canyon, following me through the twilight. It was the only mountain lion I had ever seen, so far, in the wild. I stopped, the big cat stopped, we peered at each other through the gloom. Mutual curiosity: I felt more wonder than fear. After a minute, or perhaps it was five minutes, I made a move to turn. The lion leaped up into the rocks and melted away.

We see no mountain lions this evening. Nor any of the local deer, either Sonoran whitetail or the desert mule deer, although the little heart-shaped tracks of the former are apparent in the sand. Javelina, or peccary, too, reside in this area; piglike animals with tusks, oversized heads, and tapering bodies, they roam the slopes and gulches in family bands (like the Apaches), living on roots, tubers, and innards of barrel cactus, on grubs, insects, and carrion. Omnivorous, like us, and equally playful, if not so dangerous. Any desert canyon with permanent water, like Aravaipa, will be as full of life as it is beautiful.

We stumble homeward over the stones and through the anklebone- 16 chilling water. The winter day seems alarmingly short; it is.

We reach the mouth of the canyon and the old trail uphill to the road-head in time to see the first stars come out. Barely in time. Nightfall is quick in this arid climate and the air feels already cold. But we have earned enough memories, stored enough mental-emotional images in our heads, from one brief day in Aravaipa Canyon, to enrich the urban days to come. As Thoreau found a universe in the woods around Concord, any person whose senses are alive can make a world of any natural place, however limited it might seem, on this subtle planet of ours.

"The world is big but it is comprehensible," says R. Buckminster Fuller. But it seems to me that the world is not nearly big enough and that any portion of its surface, left unpaved and alive, is infinitely rich in details and relationships, in wonder, beauty, mystery, comprehensible only in part. The very existence of existence is itself suggestive of the unknown — not a problem but a mystery.

We will never get to the end of it, never plumb the bottom of it, never know the whole of even so small and trivial and useless and precious a place as Aravaipa. Therein lies our redemption.

AFTERWORD

This essay is a classic of description. Without Abbey's visual images, his assertions would flatten themselves on to a banal page. In paragraph 17, he cites Thoreau and continues, "any person whose senses are alive can make a world of any natural place, however limited it might seem, on this subtle planets of ours." When he gives us these common words — only "alive" and "subtle" ascribe value — he has already performed for us, with exquisite skill and invention, two thousand words of acute seeing, making alive a "natural place."

At the end of an essay fertile in joyous evocation of Aravaipa Canyon, he finds and names his enemy of the day: the engineer and inventor R. Buckminster Fuller, creator of the geodesic dome, who found this world "comprehensible." For Abbey only the incomprehensible, not to mention the unpaved, survives contempt. Abbey's "wonder, beauty, mystery" — three abstract sisters — could sound naive were it not for his earlier density of detail and image. He ends his descriptive essay with the earned diction of religious thought.

BOOKS AVAILABLE IN PAPERBACK

Abbey's Road: Take the Other. New York: Dutton. *Essays*.

Beyond the Wall. New York: Henry Holt. *Essays*.

Black Sun. New York: Avon. *Novel*.

The Brave Cowboy. New York: Avon. *Novel*.

Confessions of the Barbarian. Santa Barbara: Capra Press. *Nonfiction*.

Desert Solitaire: A Season in the Wilderness. New York: Ballantine. *Essays*.

Down the River. New York: Dutton. *Essays*.

Fire on the Mountain. New York: Avon. *Novel*.

Good News. New York: Dutton. *Novel*.

The Journey Home: Some Words in Defense of the American West. New York: Dutton. *Nonfiction*.

The Monkey Wrench Gang. New York: Avon. *Novel*.

One Life at a Time, Please. New York: Henry Holt. *Essays*.

MARGARET
ATWOOD

*B*ORN IN OTTAWA, *Ontario (1939), Margaret Atwood did not attend school for a full year until she was eleven years old. Her father was an entomologist who worked for the Canadian government (her mother was a dietitian), and the family moved every April into the backwoods of Quebec, where her father studied insects until November. A good deal of the bush works itself into Atwood's writing.*

At sixteen she decided that writing would be her life: "It was suddenly the only thing I wanted to do." Best known as a novelist — The Edible Woman *(1969),* Surfacing *(1972),* Lady Oracle *(1976),* Life Before Man *(1979),* Bodily Harm *(1982), and* The Handmaid's Tale *(1985) — she first published as a poet, and in 1987 Houghton Mifflin published a new* Selected Poems *in two volumes. Like many freelance writers, Margaret Atwood has tried her hand at other genres as well: children's books, collections of short stories (*Dancing Girls, *1977;* Bluebeard's Egg, *1983), anthologies of Canadian poetry, television plays — and of course the essay. The collection* Second Words *(1982) includes this lecture-essay, "Canadian-American Relations," originally delivered at Harvard, where years earlier she had attended graduate school in her first exile from Canada.*

When she decided to become a writer, Atwood remembers, she "was scared to death for a couple of reasons. For one thing, I was Canadian, and the prospects for being a Canadian and a writer, both at the same time, in 1960, were dim. The only writers I had encountered in high school had been dead and English . . . but it was more complicated than that, because, in addition to being a Canadian, I was also a woman." In her life's work, she has of course converted these prospective limitations into a double blessing. Prejudice invited energetic response. From the vantage point of a Canadian woman, she writes books that leave modifiers behind (adjectives like Southern poet or Swiss novelist are diminutives; subcategories, small pools) for the largest ocean of literature.

In 1972, she published a book on Canadian letters, Survival, which provoked controversy; certainly her feminist novels have engendered the same. Firsthand perceptions of oppression and bias have widened in later work into concern about more general political repressiveness. One critic suggests that Atwood's bias against bias is inherited: "Before Margaret Atwood's ancestors emigrated to Canada, one of them — a certain Mary Webster of Connecticut — was accused of witchcraft and hanged. But when the town fathers came around the next day to cut her down, Webster was still alive (either miraculously or thanks to the ineptitude of her accusers); because of the principles of double jeopardy, she was allowed to go free. . . . As a writer who has managed both to make a devastating attack on contemporary American political trends and to get critical acclaim for it, Atwood apparently inherited old Mary's neck."

The United States has been important in Margaret Atwood's life not only as enemy or potential enemy. Her writing is popular here as it is in England. When she went to Massachusetts after her Canadian college, she learned about her own country by living outside it. Ten thousand writers, exiled by choice, for study, or for pleasure, have learned who they were only by leaving the place that made them — and by returning with new eyes.

Canadian-American Relations: Surviving the Eighties

I am always pleased to be able to return to the scene of my youthful debaucheries — which were of course purely intellectual in nature — especially since it is also the land of my ancestors. My ancestors would have been pleased to return to it as well, I suspect, once they'd found out what

Canada was really like, but there had been a slight disagreement over who should rule this country — divinely constituted law and order in the person of George III or a lot of upstart revolutionaries — and my ancestors had departed for the north in search of some place where you could still get a decent cup of tea, thus becoming part of the brain drain; a drain, according to my father, from which the States has never entirely recovered. Canadian-American relations were a frequent topic of conversation in my grand-mother's house. There were the Canadian relations and then there were the American relations, who lived mostly in Boston. That's what makes Canadian-American relations somewhat touchy at times: they *are* relatives. There's nothing that rankles more than a cousin, especially one with a Rolls-Royce.

I'll preface this speech by saying that if you really feel you have to bring me all the way down from the frozen north to tell you how all of us are going to make it through the next ten years, you're in deep trouble. The fact is that nobody knows, least of all me. What you are about to hear is merely the fruit of idle speculation.

I have two things to say in defense of idle speculation. First, it's what universities are for. Where else could one devote three months of one's life to an investigation of whether John Keats did or did not have syphilis? Second, I'm a novelist, and idle speculation is what novelists do. How odd to spend one's life trying to pretend that nonexistent people are real: though no odder, I suppose, than what governmental bureaucrats do, which is trying to pretend that real people are nonexistent. However, when you invite a novelist to speak to you, what you get is a novelization.

I'll warn you right at the beginning that although this is a slightly mean   4
speech, I do know the difference between an individual and a foreign policy. Americans as individuals can be enthusiastic, generous, and optimistic in ways undreamt of by your average Canadian. How could I think otherwise when the Americans so consistently give me better reviews than do my begrudging, dour, and suspicious fellow countrymen? Americans worship success; Canadians find it in slightly bad taste. In fact, Canadians find Canadians in slightly bad taste, which is probably why Texas is currently cornering the market on Canadian studies. This does not startle the Cana-dians: they always knew Texans had bad taste. (They'll collect *anything*.)

No Canadian ever made a speech in the United States without beginning with an apology, and that was mine. Having now fulfilled the obligations which politeness and protocol demand, I'll proceed to the speech proper, which is supposed to be about Canadian-American relations, and what the future holds for them.

Canadian-American relations sounds like a dull subject, and it is, unless you've ever tried explaining them to an American. What you get in return is usually a version of "You're so cute when you're mad, honey." Americans don't usually *have* to think about Canadian-American relations, or, as they would put it, American-Canadian relations. Why think about something which you believe affects you so little? We, on the other hand, have to think about you whether we like it or not.

Last month, during a poetry reading I was giving, I tried out a short prose poem called "How to Like Men." It began by suggesting that one might profitably start with the feet and work up, the toes being an innocuous enough part of the body, one would think. Unfortunately the question of jackboots soon arose, and things went on from there. After the reading I had a conversation with a distressed young man who thought I was being unfair to men. He wanted men to be liked, not just from the soles to the knees, but totally, and not just as individuals but as a group. He found it negative and inegalitarian of me to have alluded to war and rape. In vain did I point out to him that as far as any of us knew these were two activities not widely engaged in by women, the first perhaps from lack of opportunity, the second for what we might delicately call lack of interest. He was still upset. "But we're both in this together," he protested. I had to admit that this was so; but could he, maybe, see that our relative positions might be a little different?

This is the kind of roadblock one runs into with Americans, when one 8 has been unable to prevent the dinner-table conversation from veering around to Canadian-American relations. Americans are quite happy to claim that we're both in this together when it comes to a discussion of continental energy resources; in fact, they sometimes talk as if they'd be more than willing to share the benefits of the American system with us, by having us join them. A Texan once put this proposition to Pierre Berton, one of our larger writers. Berton retorted that he thought this would be a dandy idea. The Americans could get back the Queen, whom they've always coveted, and revert to constitutional monarchy, and do away with the FBI and receive the much more colorful Royal Canadian Mounted Police in return, and change to a three-party system and become officially bilingual. Well, that wasn't exactly what the Texan had in mind.

Such unconscious imperialism is not confined to Texas. During an early '70s feminist "international" conference being held in Toronto, the Canadian sisters ended up locking themselves in the john because they felt that the American sisters were being culturally imperialistic. They claimed to be speaking for Woman, capital W, universal, but as far as the Canadian sisters could tell they thought Woman, capital W, was not only white and middle-class but American as well. Then there's the history of the Canadian labor movement, which was annexed to the American labor movement in the thirties in the name of the United Front. Then, too, Canadians succumbed to that most seductive of slogans, "We're all in this together," and they've been finding ever since that their fellow workers have been quite happy to collect their dues but not all that interested in hearing about such boring items as wage parity and the alarming tendency of American companies to close down their Canadian branch plants whenever there's a slump in trade. The discussion has a tendency to break down into a version of afternoon soap opera, those scenes in which the puzzled man says, "What are you trying to tell me?" and the woman, wringing her hands, says, "You haven't been listening! You don't understand!" One could sum up the respective stances by saying that the typical American one is unthinkingly and breezily aggressive and the Canadian one peevishly and hesitantly defensive, and there's even some accuracy in such a generalization, but that doesn't help us much if we want to know why.

Why and how are often closely related, and how in this case is historical. I won't go back to the war of 1812 and the Fenian raids,° as it is bad manners to remind one's hosts of their failure to invade and conquer one's country by military means. ("We won't do that again," an American once said to a friend of mine. "We don't need to, we own it anyway.") I'll skip the two World Wars as well, merely pointing out in passing that if Americans thought Canadians were sitting back and sucking their thumbs and watching it all on television during the Vietnam years, meanwhile benefiting from arms manufacture, it was a mere nothing to what happened between 1939 and Pearl Harbor. I'll go to the postwar years, when I began to have a memory, and trace for you my own progress from wild colonial girl to the person who gives these kinds of speeches, because I think that progress is typical of my generation, the generation of 1960s literary nationalism.

I was born in 1939, which means that I was ten in 1949 and twenty in 1959. I spent a large part of my childhood in northern Quebec, surrounded by many trees and few people. My attitude towards Americans was formed by this environment. Alas, the Americans we encountered were usually pictures of ineptitude. We once met two of them dragging a heaving metal boat, plus the motor, across a portage from one lake to another because they did not want to paddle. Typically American, we thought, as they ricocheted off yet another tree. Americans hooked other people when they tried to cast, got lost in the woods, and didn't burn their garbage. Of course, many Canadians behaved this way too; but somehow not *as* many. And there were some Americans, friends of my father, who could shoot a rapids without splintering their canoe and who could chop down a tree without taking off a foot in the process. But these were not classed as

---

war of 1812 . . . Fenian raids In the early stages of the War of 1812, ill-prepared U.S. forces engaged the British along the Canadian border but failed to capture any Canadian territory. In the mid-1800s, a group of Irish-American Fenians, rebels fighting for Irish independence from Great Britain, unsuccessfully attempted to invade Canada.

Americans, not *real* Americans. They were from Upper Michigan State or Maine or places like that, and were classed, I blush to admit, not as Americans but as honorary Canadians. I recognize that particular cross-filing system, that particular way of approving of people you as a rule don't approve of, every time a man tells me I think like a man; a sentence I've always felt had an invisible comma after the word *think*. I've since recognized that it's no compliment to be told you are not who you are, but as children we generalized, cheerfully and shamelessly. The truth, from our limited experience, was clear: Americans were wimps who had a lot of money but did not know what they were doing.

That was the rural part of my experience. The urban part was somewhat   12
different. In the city I went to school, and in the early years at any rate the schools I went to were still bastions of the British Empire. In school we learned the Kings of England and how to draw the Union Jack and sing Rule Britannia, and poems with refrains like "Little Indian, Sioux or Cree, Don't you wish that you were me?" Our imaginations were still haunted by the war, a war that we pictured as having been fought between us, that is, the British, and the Germans. There wasn't much room in our minds for the Americans and the Japanese. Winston Churchill was a familiar figure to us; Theodore Roosevelt was not.

In public school we did not learn much about Americans, or Canadians either, for that matter. Canadian history was the explorers and was mostly brown and green, for all those trees. British history was kings and queens, and much more exciting, since you could use the silver and gold colored pencils for it.

That era of Canadian colonialism was rapidly disappearing, however. One explanation for the reason it practically vanished during the postwar decade — 1946 to 1957, say, the year I graduated from high school — is an economic one. The Canadians, so the theory goes, overextended themselves so severely through the war effort that they created a capital vacuum in Canada. Nature and entrepreneurs hate a vacuum, so money flowed up from the United States to fill it, and when Canadians woke up in the sixties and started to take stock, they discovered they'd sold their birthright for a mess. This revelation was an even greater shock for me; not only was my country owned, but it was owned by the kind of people who carried tin boats across portages and didn't burn their garbage. One doubted their competence.

Looking back on this decade, I can see that the changeover from British cultural colony to American cultural colony was symbolized by what happened after school as opposed to in it. I know it's hard to believe in view of my youthful appearance, but when I was a child there was no television. There were, however, comic books, and these were monolithically American. We didn't much notice, except when we got to the ads at the back, where Popsicle Pete reigned supreme. Popsicle Pete would give you the earth in exchange for a few sticky wrappers, but his promises always had a little asterisk attached: "Offer good only in the United States." International world cynics may be forgiven for thinking that the same little asterisk is present invisibly in the Constitution and the Declaration of Independence and the Bill of Rights, not to mention the public statements of prominent Americans on such subjects as democracy, human dignity and freedom, and civil liberties. Maybe it all goes back to Popsicle Pete. We may all be in this together, but some of us are asterisked.

Such thoughts did not trouble our heads a great deal. When you were finished with Donald Duck and Mickey Mouse (and Walt Disney was, by the way, a closet Canadian), you could always go on to Superman (whose creator was also one of ours). After that it would be time for Sunday night radio, with Jack Benny and Our Miss Brooks. We knew they talked funny, but we didn't mind. Then of course there were movies, none of which were Canadian, but we didn't mind that either. Everyone knew that was what the world was like. Nobody knew that there had once been a Canadian film industry.

After that I went to high school, where people listened to American pop music after school instead of reading comic books. During school hours we studied, among other things, history and literature. Literature was still the British tradition: Shakespeare, Eliot, Austen, Thomas Hardy, Keats and Wordsworth and Shelley and Byron; not experiences anyone should miss, but it did tend to give the impression that all literature was written by dead Englishmen, and — this is important — by dead English*women*. By this time I wanted to be a writer, and you can see it would be a dilemma: being female was no hindrance, but how could one be a writer and somehow manage to avoid having to become British and dead? The generation before mine compromised; they settled for the British part and emigrated to England, taking their chances on the death. My generation, in ways I'll come to in a minute, took another road.

In history it was much the same story. We started with Ancient Egypt and worked our way through Greece, Rome, and medieval Europe, then the Renaissance and the birth of the modern era, the invention of the steam engine, the American revolution, the French revolution, the Civil War, and other stirring events, every single one of which had taken place outside Canada.

Finally, in the very last year, by which time many future citizens had dropped out anyway, we got a blue book called *Canada in the World Today*. It was about who grew the wheat, how happy the French were, how well the parliamentary system worked for everybody, and how nice it was that the Indians had given us all their land in exchange for the amenities of civilization. The country we lived in was presented to us in our schools as colorless, dull, and without much historical conflict to speak of, except for a few massacres, and nobody did *that* anymore. Even the British war of conquest was a dud, since both of the generals died. It was like a hockey game in which both teams lost.

As for Canada in the World Today, its role, we were assured, was an 20 important one. It was the upper northwest corner of a triangle consisting of Canada, the United States, and Britain, and its position was not one to be sneezed at: Canada, having somehow become an expert at compromise, was the mediator. It was not to be parochial and inward-looking anymore but was to be international in outlook. Although in retrospect the role of mediator may shrink somewhat — one cannot quite dispel the image of Canada trotting back and forth across the Atlantic with sealed envelopes, like a glorified errand boy — there's a little truth to be squeezed from this lemon. Canadians, oddly enough, *are* more international in outlook than Americans are; not through any virtue on their part but because they've had to be. If you're a Canadian traveling in the United States, one of the first things you notice is the relative absence of international news coverage. In Canada, one of the most popular news programs ever devised has two radio commentators phoning up just about anyone they can get on the line, anywhere in the world. Canadians live in a small house, which may be why they have their noses so firmly pressed to the windows, looking out.

I remember *Canada in the World Today* with modified loathing — "Canada comes of age," it trumpeted, not bothering to mention that what happened to you when you came of age was that you got pimples or a job or both — and still not a year passes without some politician announcing that Canada has finally grown up. Still, the title is significant. Canada sees itself as part of the world; a small sinking Titanic squashed between two icebergs, perhaps, but still inevitably a part. The States, on the other hand, has always had a little trouble with games like chess. Situational strategy is difficult if all you can see is your own borders, and beyond that some wispy brownish fuzz that is barely worth considering. The Canadian experience was a circumference with no center, the American one a center which was mistaken for the whole thing.

A few years ago I was in India and had occasion to visit both the Canadian and American enclaves in New Delhi. The Canadian there lived in a house decorated with Indian things and served us a meal of Indian food and told us all about India. One reason for going into the foreign service, in Canada anyway, is to get out of Canada, and Canadians are good at fitting in, partly because they can't afford to do otherwise. They could not afford, for instance, to have the kind of walled compound the Americans had. We were let in to do some shopping at the supermarket there, and once the gate had closed you were in Syracuse, N.Y. Hot dogs, hamburgers, Cokes, and rock music surrounded you. Americans enter the outside world the way they landed on the moon, with their own oxygen tanks of American air strapped to their backs and their protective spacesuits firmly in place. If they can't stay in America they take it with them. Not for them the fish-in-the-water techniques of the modern urban guerilla. Those draft dodgers of the sixties who made it as far as Canada nearly died of culture shock: they thought it was going to be like home.

It's not their fault, though. It's merely that they've been oddly educated. Canadians and Americans may look alike but the contents of their heads are quite different. Americans experience themselves, individually, as small toads in the biggest and most powerful puddle in the world. Their sense of power comes from identifying with the puddle. Canadians as individuals may have more power within the puddle, since there are fewer toads in it; it's the puddle that's seen as powerless. One of our politicians recently gave a speech entitled "In the Footsteps of the Giant." The United States of course was the giant and Canada was in its footsteps, though some joker wondered whether Canada was in the footstep just before or just after the foot had descended. One of Canada's problems is that it's always comparing itself to the wrong thing. If you stand beside a giant, of course you tend to feel a little stunted. When we stand beside Australia, say, or the ex-British West Indies, we feel more normal. I had lunch recently with two publishers from Poland. "Do Canadians realize," they said, "that they live in one of the most peaceful, happy, and prosperous countries on earth?" "No," I said.

Back to my life story. We've reached 1960. I was at University, in the City of Toronto — which had not yet become the Paris of the Northeast, the place where people from Buffalo go for the weekend, clean, safe, glitzy, filled with restaurants of high quality, and up to its eyeballs in narcissism. Instead it was known as Hogtown; it was a synonym for essence of boredom, and the usual joke about it was "I spent a week in Toronto last night." Very funny if you didn't want to be a writer, but what if you did? Some of us did, and there we were, living in a city in which there was one theater, no ballet, one art gallery, and no literature that a serious person would take seriously, or so we thought. Being young snobs, we declined to know much about it. Although we wanted to become writers, we certainly didn't want to become *Canadian* writers. It was the period of late existentialism, and we wore long black stockings (those of us who were female) and no makeup (male and female alike) and read Sartre and Beckett. Canadian writers were associated in our minds with the damp unromantic vestibules of United Churches in March, smelling of damp wool. "Canadian writer" for us was an oxymoron.

And no wonder. For statistics fans, here's a batch: all the novels and books of poetry by Canadians, published in Canada, in the year 1961, could be and were reviewed in part of one issue of the *University of Toronto Quarterly*. I think there were about five novels and under twenty books of poetry, but that included the mimeo jobs and the flatbed press numbers which were not yet dignified by being called "little press books." Poets of my generation published their own work because nobody else would. It was not an activity born of heroism or the desire to appear artistic. Our publishing activities, tiny and futile as they were, were motivated by one thing: desperation. Even the "established" writers were doing well if they sold 200 copies of a book of poetry, countrywide. A novel that sold a thousand was a raving best-seller. Needless to say, you could hardly expect us to make a living at it, and anything resembling the American notion of literary success was out of the question. Canadian books were routinely not taught in schools and universities. I myself have never taken a course on Canadian literature.

The reason for this deplorable state of affairs was not that Canadians didn't read books. They just didn't read *Canadian* books. Colonies breed something called "the colonial mentality," and if you have the colonial mentality you believe that the great good place is always somewhere else. In those days you could walk into a bookstore, any bookstore, and find it (not surprisingly) full of books; but they would all be *imported* books. Down at the back there would be a shelf labeled *Canadiana*, and there would be the Canadian novels, along with the Canadian cookbooks and the coffee-table books entitled *Our Magnificent North*. No self-respecting young writer wanted to end up as *Canadiana*.

So some of us went to England, which was where I was headed, intending to work as a waitress and write great literature in garrets in my spare time. I was intercepted however by a Woodrow Wilson Fellowship, back in the days when there were any, and found myself at Harvard.

One of the exciting things that happened to me at Harvard was that I 28 helped to corner a lurking sexual pervert upon the roof of the graduate women's dormitory. The other exciting thing, some might say entirely unrelated, was that I was requested at the beginning of my first year by the graduate advisor to fill in my gaps. As it turned out, I had only one gap, the others having been adequately filled in by the University of Toronto. My gap was American literature, and so, to my bemusement, I found myself reading my way through excerpts from Puritan sermons, political treatises of the time of the American revolution, and anguished essays of the early nineteenth century, bemoaning the inferiority not only of American literary offerings but of American dress design, and wondering when the great American genius would come along. It sounded familiar. Nobody pretended that any of this was superb literature. All they pretended was that it was necessary for an understanding of the United States of America, and it was. As we huddled in the front parlor of Founders' House on the

Appian Way, in the fall of '62, just after President Kennedy had announced the Cuban Missile crisis,° drinking tea and wondering whether the human condition was about to become rapidly obsolete, it was possible to look back through three hundred years of boring documents and see the road that had led us to this nasty impasse. The founding Puritans had wanted their society to be a theocratic utopia, a city upon a hill, to be a model and a shining example to all nations. The split between the dream and the reality is an old one and it has not gone away.

Canada suffers from no such split, since it was founded not by idealists but by people who'd been kicked out of other places. Canada was not a city upon a hill, it was what you had to put up with. Americans think anything can be changed, torn down and rebuilt, rewritten. Canadians tend to think nothing can. Both are wrong, of course. Americans get discouraged when they can't get instant results; they vacillate between romantic idealism and black humor, its opposite. Canadians on the other hand think any change will probably be for the worse. Consequently they are less easily stampeded, less extreme in their trends. Americans have riots; Canadians have panel discussions on riots. Which may be why they won't invest in things like the telephone. Alexander Graham Bell was one of ours, once.

But I digress. There I was, at one of the greatest universities in the world, studying third-rate poems and dreary journals and the diaries of Cotton Mather,° and why? Not because they were great world literature, but because they could tell me something about the society that produced them. Believe it or not, this was an amazing and dangerous insight. If old American laundry lists were of interest at Harvard, why should not old Canadian laundry lists be of interest in Toronto, where they so blatantly weren't? Everyone who was anyone in Toronto dismissed Canadian literature as second-rate and therefore not worth studying; but here before my very eyes were reams and reams of second-rate, and I had to write exams on it in order to fill my gap.

It was at Harvard then that I first began to think seriously about Canada. Even the idea of thinking seriously about Canada had something shocking about it: seriousness and Canada just didn't seem to go together. It was almost revolutionary. Unknown to me, other members of my generation were beginning to do the same thing. Then, as a generation, we did something very odd: instead of staying where we were and becoming part of the brain drain, we went back to Canada. Then we did something even

---

Cuban Missile crisis   A short-lived but tense episode in 1962 in which the United States discovered Soviet missile sites being constructed in Cuba and demanded their removal.
Cotton Mather   (1663–1728), a New England Puritan preacher and writer.

odder. Instead of trying to publish in New York or London, or Paris (for this movement back to the indigenous was occurring at an even greater speed in the province of Quebec) we started thinking in terms of Canadian publication for a Canadian audience. Because the few established publishers were reluctant to publish work that was too experimental or too nationalist — the two were, strangely enough, sometimes equated — writers became involved in setting up their own publishing companies. Nobody expected the results. The growth of both audience and industry between 1965 and 1970 was phenomenal. To our surprise, people, even Canadian people, wanted to read what we wanted to write. Most of us were apolitical art-for-art's-sakers when we set out, but the lesson was clear. American branch plants and our own conservatives wouldn't publish us. If we wanted to be heard, we had to create the means of production and maintain control over it.

One of the things that quickly became apparent to us was that Canadians 32 were remarkably ignorant about their own history and literature. For the most part they didn't know they had any, and lots of them were resistant to hearing anything about it. They'd been trained to think of themselves as international, and for them that term meant not national. It did not occur to them that in order to have international relationships you have to have nations first, just as in order to have interpersonal relationships you have to have persons.

About this time it became fashionable to talk about the absence of a Canadian identity. The absence of a Canadian identity has always seemed nonsense to me, and the search for it a case of the dog chasing its own tail. What people usually mean by a national identity is an advertising gimmick. Everything has an identity. A stone has an identity, it just doesn't have a voice. A man who's forgotten who he is has an identity, he's merely suffering from amnesia, which was the case with the Canadians. They'd forgotten. They'd had their ears pressed to the wall for so long, listening in on the neighbors, who *were* rather loud, that they'd forgotten how to speak and what to say. They'd become addicted to the one-way mirror of the Canadian-American border — we can see you, you can't see us — and had neglected that other mirror, their own culture. The States is an escape fantasy for Canadians. Their own culture shows them what they really look like, and that's always a little hard to take.

The cultural nationalism of the early '70s was not aggressive in nature. It was a simple statement: we exist. Such movements become militant only when the other side replies, in effect, No you don't. Witness feminism.

In 1972, I wrote and published a book about Canadian Literature. It was called *Survival*, and was an introductory guide to the subject, for the average reader. One of the reasons I wrote it was that nobody else had. Within it, the revolutionary seed planted at Harvard many years before burst into full flower, producing, in the minds of some, a large crop of thistles. Canadian critics felt it owed much to the noxious influence of Northrop Frye, under whom I'd studied up there, but they overlooked the noxious influence of Harvard's own Perry Miller, under whom I studied down here. Canadians tend to be touchy about imported noxious influences: they want all noxious influences to be their very own. They feel the same way for instance about acid rain. If we want our lakes killed we'd rather do it ourselves; not that you folks aren't doing a good job.

As far as I could see, *Survival* merely belabored the obvious. Everyone, 36 surely, would agree that the literature produced by a society has some connection with the society. It follows that by reading the literature you can get a bearing on the society. After a quick scan of classic Canadian literature — that is, anything written before 1970 — I concluded that Canadian literature had certain *leitmotifs* running through it. Victims abound; the philosophy is survivalism, the typical narrative a sequence of dire events which the hero escapes from (if he does escape) not with triumph or honor or riches but merely with his life. I talked about the difference between being a genuine victim and being one by choice. I drew certain conclusions relating to Canada in the World Today, and I prefaced the whole thing with a few reasons why people should read their literature and not just everybody else's. Worst of all, I said that Canada was a cultural colony and an economic one as well.

Some people thought these were the most important words set down since Moses went up the mountain. Others thought no such thing. Canadian nationalism is by no means homogeneous in nature or even thickly spread. The ultra left thought I was being petit bourgeois. The merely left thought I hadn't put in enough about the songs of the people. Another branch of the left (whom I hesitate to call national socialists because it gives entirely the wrong idea) thought I was showing a historical perspective and was being dialectical. In case you're unsure, that was good. The paranoid ethnic center thought I was being national socialist. The conservative right thought I had written a book on something that didn't exist at all, like a medieval theologian debating how many angels could dance on the head of a pin. The feminists took the five basic victim positions I'd outlined — something like the five basic positions of ballet — and applied them to women. Critics fast on their feet said the book was an interesting expression of my artistic sensibility. Eighty thousand ordinary Canadians bought the book; a large market penetration, as they say in the trade. The Americans however did not publish it; as my editor in New York said, "Listen sweetie, Canada is *death* down here."

Having an identity is one thing, having a negative one is another. Some objected to the victim motif; others said that people died all over world literature, not just in Canada. Survivalism, of course, is not the same as

31

tragedy or existential despair or even pessimism about the human condition. It's being stuck in a blizzard with one match; a kind of minimalism, fine, but if you get that fire lit it's a triumphant event, considering the odds. Nor is the stance purely negative. In a world where there seems to be increasingly less and less of more and more, it may be a more useful as well as a more ethical attitude towards the world than the American belief that there is always another horizon, a new frontier, that when you've used up what's in sight you only have to keep moving.

Survival was part of the English-Canadian cultural nationalism that peaked in about 1975. Meanwhile, the Liberal economic nationalists under Walter Gordon had been defeated and so had the NDP ones under the Waffle:° the government was against nationalism; continentalism was their favored phrase. The writers and artists, having made certain gains, wandered off to their private cabbage patches or settled down to the dogwork of such organizations as the newly formed Writers' Union, and newspaper headlines turned their attention elsewhere. One could be forgiven for thinking that fighting the nationalist fight was like rolling a big stone up a hill time after time, only to have it kicked down again by one's very own government.

On both cultural and economic fronts, regionalism replaced nationalism 40 as something to feel self-righteous about. To the jaundiced viewer, regionalism was merely the thesis of *Survival* writ small, with Ottawa replacing the States as the overbearing giant and the provinces competing with each other for the position of chief victim. There seemed to be a contest going on as to which one could outwhine the others. "Centralist thinking" became a bad word.

Then, out of the blue, what to our wondering eyes should appear but the National Energy Policy? Canada, it seems, was going to get back its own oil. It would have cost less if they'd done it earlier or never sold it in the first place, but why quibble? "Canada comes of age," someone predictably announced, and the United States reacted as though someone had just seduced its sister.

Which is where we are now.

The United States does not think of its own nationalism as being anything out of the ordinary, but it has never cherished warm feelings for other peoples'. Reaction to the current Canadian wave has ranged from anger, to squeeze plays of the If-you-don't-let-us-buy-you, We-won't-let-you-buy-us variety, to jocular condescension. I give you an example of the

---

NDP . . . Waffle The New Democratic Party (1961–1974), a democratic socialist party in Canada. The Waffle was a nationalist caucus group within the NDP.

latter from the Toronto *Star*, June 20, 1981. The headline reads, U.S. PA-
TRONIZES US WITH NELSON EDDY TAG, and the copy explains:

> George Ball, ex-diplomat and ambassador and now a New
> York investment banker, said yesterday: "At the moment the
> current (Ottawa) government is going through one of those
> spasms of nationalism such as happened in the 1960's when
> Walter Gordon was finance minister. I think they'll get over
> it. It's a political issue. It comes and goes."
>
> That patronizing assessment was nothing compared with
> a day earlier, when witnesses at a merchant marine committee
> hearing were slashing Canada for winning away too much
> seaport business. "I like to think of Canada as a Nelson Eddy,"
> remarked Democrat Barbara Mikulski, recalling the American
> actor who played a Mountie in the 1936 movie *Rose Marie*.
> "What we need here is a legislative Jeanette Macdonald," she
> added; presumably to lure Canada away from its ardent pur-
> suit of trade.
>
> "No, No," said committee chairman Mario Biaggi, "Can-
> ada can be Jeanette Macdonald because in the movies Eddy
> always gets the girl."

I guess a little verbal castration is better than getting a bomb dropped 44
on you, but let us remember there has always been more than one way of
getting the girl. Are we talking about a proposal of marriage, in which case
the States would proclaim, "With all my worldly goods I thee endow" in
exchange for Canada's adopting the missionary position? Are we talking
about proposition, in which case Canada is to assume the same position in
exchange for a few roses and a box of chocs? It doesn't sound like a love
affair, somehow. There's a fourth alternative which is not mentioned in
polite company — every girl's got her price, say the cynics, and Canada
has always been a cheap lay — and even a fifth, in which Nelson Eddy
gets the same thing without having to pay anything at all, justifying his
actions by believing that Canada was behaving provocatively and secretly
loves it anyway. You'll notice that in each case Canada gets screwed; we've
just been haggling a little about the out-of-pocket expenses. What it all goes
to show, I suppose, is the danger of metaphors. In any case, it looks as if
Canada doesn't want to play the female lead, not at the moment and maybe
not any more. Someone once said that Canada is ruled by men with crystal
balls, referring to Mackenzie King's° habit of consulting his mother's spirit
before deciding what not to do. Perhaps the fellows in Ottawa are changing
to a more reliable method of decision-making.

Mackenzie King   Canadian Liberal prime minister, 1921–1930, 1935–1948.

Ah, say the futurists. But surely the nation state is obsolete. Even national governments are fast-fading archaisms; it's really international big business that's running things, and by the 21st century it's going to be one world, one way or another. Think of fiber optics and the imminent demise of the postal system; think of satellite transmission, ready and able to beam anything anywhere any time. National borders, those little moats countries build around themselves, their ability to determine what will be seen and heard within and what will stay without, will have become ineffectual in a few decades. Let's not try to turn back the clock. Open it up and let everything slosh back and forth from brain to brain, and then we won't have any nasty little pockets of nationalists who want to retain their own language and customs and blow up mailboxes or each other to prove it.

But of course it won't be a question of back and forth. It will only be forth, an expansion outward of the boundaries of whoever controls the technology for information transmission. I hate to say it, but it probably won't be Canada. The fight over who gets a pay TV license, going on in Canada right now, is only the tip of the tip of the iceberg. Control what goes into people's heads and you control what comes out.

If you think that's unduly pessimistic, listen to this one. You hear the most amazing things on the Canadian Broadcasting Corporation; just the other day there was a program on new weapons technology. The neutron bomb is already old-fashioned. The Russians, apparently, are working on something involving ultrasound. They send a sort of amplified disco overhead in rockets, and it frazzes out the brain cells of everyone who hears it and turns them into smiling docile idiots. It doesn't damage property or genetic material, just your ability to think and therefore to protest. The ever-present satirist among us commented that it probably wouldn't make that much difference to the Canadians anyway, as they are already smiling docile idiots, but that was a little unfair. If the neutron bomb is the ultimate capitalist weapon, antipersonnel without being anti–real estate, ultrasound is the ultimate totalitarian one. The lumpen proletariat will become truly lumpen at last.

I've just given you two ways in which nationalism can be transcended. 48 Neither sounds very attractive, but maybe I'm just being a little Luddite about it and docile idiocy of one kind or another is the wave of the future. Both suggest that there may be things to worry about that are more important than who gets to be Nelson Eddy.

There's a third way to transcend nationalism, and for that I'll go back for a moment to 1962. Perry Miller, in his lectures on American Romanticism, suggested that there was not one America but two: the America of Thoreau and Lincoln, the articulators of human dignity and human values and true democracy, and the other America which is opposed to them. I suggest that there are not only two Americas but two Canadas as well, and two Englands and two Russias; that, in fact, no country has a monopoly on any human characteristic, good or evil. The most lethal weapon on earth is the human mind; but on the other hand it is only the mind that is capable of envisioning what is humanly desirable and what is not. Totalitarian control of any kind is not. The world is rapidly abandoning the nineteenth-century division into capitalist and socialist. The new camps are those countries that perform or tolerate political repression, torture, and mass murder and those that do not. Terrorism of the hijacking and assassination variety is now international; so is the kind practiced by governments against their own citizens. The most important field of study at the moment is not Canadian literature or even old American laundry lists, delightful as these may be. It's the study of human aggression. I seem to recall that a revolution was once fought on the slogan "No taxation without representation." For 1981 there's a more appropriate slogan: "No annihilation without represen-tation." The only drawback is the lack of any one mad king to rebel against, and I expect the sense of futility felt by many Americans in face of the sick and gargantuan and apparently uncontrollable power struggle that's going on makes them in a way honorary Canadians. I say apparently uncontroll-able because I am, after all, an optimist. Power corrupts, but it has never managed to corrupt everybody.

Americans and Canadians are not the same; they are the products of two very different histories, two very different situations. Put simply, south of you you have Mexico and south of us we have you.

But we *are* all in this together, not just as citizens of our respective nation states but more importantly as inhabitants of this quickly shrinking and increasingly threatened earth. There are boundaries and borders, spiritual as well as physical, and good fences make good neighbors. But there are values beyond national ones. Nobody owns the air; we all breathe it.

AFTERWORD

Talking is talking, and writing is writing — except when a lecture like "Ca-nadian-American Relations" is printed after delivery.

When we put a lecture into print we often make changes required by the differences between the two forms of publication, or making public. Gesture, inton-ation, smiles, and frowns create tone in public delivery; on the page we supply the equivalents in a thousand ways: A pause is a period, a dash, a new paragraph — depending on its length; punctuation and syntax supply changes of pitch and rhythm; capitalization and italic type provide emphasis which the voice supplies in volume. Speaking, we sometimes get away with a word that is only approximately right, adding definition by performance. When we alter a talk for print, we search for the exact word to replace the approximate one.

When we read a speech, it helps us to know to whom it was addressed and under what circumstances. As when we read a play, it can be useful to imagine scene and speaker, to put ourselves as we read into the place of the audience. Here Margaret Atwood interrupts her opening sentence by an aside, between dashes, which provides the joke obligatory at the start of all lectures, relaxing both audience and speaker. There's more humor at the beginning of her talk than there is later, perhaps because the speaker — more than the writer — needs to make herself acceptable to an audience before she can persuade them of her convictions. In the circumstances of this lecture, Atwood begins by establishing her special relationship to the visible throng, something an essayist can seldom do.

BOOKS AVAILABLE IN PAPERBACK

Bluebeard's Egg and Other Stories. New York: Fawcett Books. *Short stories*.

Bodily Harm. New York: Bantam. *Novel*.

The Circle Game. Toronto: University of Toronto Press-Anansi. *Poetry*.

Dancing Girls and Other Stories. New York: Bantam. *Short stories*.

The Edible Woman. New York: Warner. *Novel*.

The Handmaid's Tale. New York: Fawcett Books. *Novel*.

Journals of Suzanna Moodie: Poems. New York: Oxford University Press. *Poetry*.

Lady Oracle. New York: Fawcett Books. *Novel*.

Life Before Man. Orlando: Holt, Rinehart & Winston. *Novel*.

Power Politics. Toronto: University of Toronto Press-Anansi. *Nonfiction*.

Second Words: Selected Critical Prose. Boston: Beacon Press. *Nonfiction*.

Selected Poems, 1965–1975. Boston: Houghton Mifflin. *Poetry*.

Selected Poems II: Poems Selected and New, 1976–1986. Boston: Houghton Mifflin. *Poetry*.

Surfacing. New York: Fawcett Books. *Novel*.

Survival: A Thematic Guide to Canadian Literature. Toronto: University of Toronto Press-Anansi. *Nonfiction*.

True Stories. New York: Simon & Schuster. *Poetry*.

Two-Headed Poems. New York: Simon & Schuster-Touchstone. *Poetry*.

RUSSELL
BAKER

I *'VE HAD AN UNHAPPY LIFE, thank God," Russell Baker told someone in 1976. In* Growing Up *(1983) he wrote about his childhood and youth during the Depression, through army service, his first job, and marriage. Baker was born in 1925 in the mountains of Virginia and later lived in New Jersey and Baltimore, where he went to college at Johns Hopkins University and began his newspaper career on the Baltimore* Sun. Growing Up *is affectionate, melancholy, and striking in its portrait of Baker's mother from her vigorous middle years — Baker's father died when he was five — into her senility, which Baker treats with gentle, exact observation. You would not think, if you read* Growing Up *without knowing Russell Baker the columnist, that his work for the New York* Times *(since 1962) has made him a leading contemporary humorist.*

He has collected his columns into many books, including Poor Russell's Almanac *(1972),* So This Is Depravity *(1980), and* The Rescue of Miss Yaskell and Other Pipe Dreams *(1983), from which we take "Through a Glass Darkly." Author as well of a novel, a children's book, a musical, and dozens of magazine articles, he has won two Pulitzer Prizes. Like the best American humorists before him — S. J. Perelman of course, James Thurber with his obsessions about language,*

E. B. White, not to mention Mark Twain the father of us all — Baker is a stylist, not only in his careful attention to his own writing but in his scrutiny of the language of others. By the words we use, especially by the absurdities of our clichés, euphemisms, and evasions, ye shall know us.

Another less obvious matter unites the humorists. "I'm basically a guy with a yearning for the past," says Baker. "Life was better when there were trains." He mocks himself, of course, but satirists are always conservative, not as the term is used in contemporary politics, but in satire's continual discovery of new human foolishness for mocking.

Through
a Glass Darkly

What is the Situation?

The Situation is bad. The crisis has become acute. Time is running out. The outlook is grave. This may be our last opportunity.

What must we do when the Weather Bureau says the air quality is unacceptable?

Avoid breathing and all other exercise until the All Clear is sounded. If   4
it is 10 P.M., find out where your children are. Curb your dog. Fight drug addiction. Watch out for deer. No littering or spitting. Don't be fuelish. Use your ashtray.

What are the origins of the present Situation?

Violence on television. Cigarette smoke. Sex education in the schools. Cholesterol. Drought. The Warren Commission.

How can we survive?

Get a regular dental checkup. Give to muscular dystrophy. Do not park   8
unless you have diplomatic license plates. Support your police. Get a chest X-ray. Check tire pressure twice a month. Fasten seat belt. Don't walk. Give to the Heart Fund. No left turn. Avoid wetness twice as long. Make love not war. Check blood pressure once a month.

What about the big oil companies?

The oil companies and the Arabs are in it up to their necks. This is because they were raised by permissive parents. As a result, the supply of big oil companies will be exhausted before the year 1996 and the last of the Arabs will be used up before the year 2010.

Is there hope in science's recent discovery of rings around Uranus?

It is too soon to tell. Some scientists believe the Uranian rings may 12 provide a rich new source of ionospheric patching material to plug holes around the earth caused by aerosol sprays. Most students of science, however, believe science will discover that the rings cause cancer in mice.

What is the immediate outlook?

For America's forgotten senior citizens, grim. For the permanently unemployed, bleak. For disadvantaged minorities, oppressive. For the young, higher taxes. For Social Security, bankruptcy. For the middle-aged, despair. The only hope is a dramatic breakthrough in solar energy, or new sugar-substitute research — and, in the long run, lasers or development of synthetic pets with sharply reduced nutritional requirements.

Would the Situation improve with a drop in coffee prices?

Not unless it were accompanied by a sharp drop in the consumption of 16 cream, sugar, fried foods, marbled beef, gravy, big automobiles, cigarettes, alcohol, barbiturates, candy, chemical sprays, carbon monoxide, heroin, asbestos fiber, cocaine, pistols, shotguns, bald eagles, pornography, welfare funds, mugging victims, and stolen Indian lands.

In the moment of crisis, what can the individual do to help?

File by April 15. Avoid mediciney breath and baggy panty hose. Don't carry cash.

Where is the safest place to be when time runs out?

There is no safe place, but some places are safer than others. Federal 20 crisis analysts say it is better to be in the Sun Belt at the critical moment than to be a hostage in a hijacked airplane. Do not be on the streets when disgruntled snipers are struggling to achieve television stardom. Stay a safe distance from careering oil companies, nursing homes run by racketeers, large corporations fleeing to the suburbs, and lawyers of all varieties.

What is Federal policy on the Situation?

It is bold, imaginative, new, and dynamic, as well as timid, devoid of new ideas, stale, and tired. The Government has at last met the challenge, although it is too little and too late. In his dramatic appearance before the Congress, the President declared that the Situation had become almost as complex as the tax law. Congress is moving swiftly to add new complexities to the tax law so that it will maintain its present lead over the Situation.

How much time is left?

It depends on the Russians and insecticides. A breakthrough in pothole- 24 patching technology could also give us more time, as could a solution of the African problem, a sudden decline in greed, easier-to-understand insurance policies, a rise in reading skills among high-school students, or development of a horse capable of cruising eight hours at 55 miles per hour to replace the automobile. Otherwise, as the Babylonians were the first to point out, it's all going to be over almost any day now.

AFTERWORD

Something like the form of this essay was used by Frank Sullivan in his New Yorker *pretend-interviews with Dr. Arbuthnot the cliché expert. Say "home" to Dr. Arbuthnot and he spewed out: "Gracious living . . . A man's is his castle . . . Home Sweet Home . . . No home without one . . ." with witless fecundity. Russell Baker is more surreal or zany as he pokes fun at the clichés of punditry, as he randomly lists signs and warnings, as he mocks dire statistics, as he invents improbable new statistics, and as he mixes up commonplaces, making monstrous impossible new commonplaces. This essay denounces, by means of humor, sloppy devices of bad thinking through bad language. Consider the sentence "It is bold, imaginative, new, and dynamic, as well as timid, devoid of new ideas, stale, and tired." Within the self-canceling sentence — self-canceled by contradiction and ineptitude — Baker makes his judgment and his humor at the same time.*

BOOKS AVAILABLE IN PAPERBACK

Growing Up. New York: New American Library. *Nonfiction.*

The Rescue of Miss Yaskell and Other Pipe Dreams. New York: New American Library. *Essays.*

So This Is Depravity. New York: Washington Square Press. *Essays.*

JAMES
BALDWIN

*W*HEN JAMES BALDWIN *died of cancer in 1987, in France where he lived much of his adult life, his death was front-page news. For decades he had been a leading literary spokesman of American black experience, without modification one of our leading writers. One critic said that Baldwin, "more than any other writer, . . . can make one begin to feel what it is really like to have a black skin in a white man's world; and he is especially expert at evoking, not merely the brutally overt physical confrontations between black and white, but the subtle unease that lurks beneath all traffic between the colors."*

He was born (1924) in Harlem, a native son of the American black ghetto. He was also born a writer, as near as anybody can be. "I began plotting novels at about the time I learned to read," he once wrote. "My first professional triumph . . . occurred at the age of twelve or thereabouts, when a short story I had written about the Spanish Revolution won some sort of prize in an extremely short-lived church newspaper. I remember the story was censored by the lady editor, though I don't remember why, and I was outraged."

A series of fellowships supported Baldwin when he was young — a Saxton when he was only twenty-one in 1945, a Rosenwald in 1948, a Guggenheim in 1954, a

Partisan Review *fellowship in 1956, and support from the Ford Foundation in 1959. His first novel was the autobiographical* Go Tell It on the Mountain *(1953), followed by the essay collection* Notes of a Native Son *(1955). Many novels followed, and many essays.* The Fire Next Time *(1963) was a crucial document in the struggle for civil rights that occupied the sixties before the Vietnam War took center stage. Although he felt fiction to be his calling, outrage led James Baldwin into nonfiction. "One writes out of one thing only — one's own experience," he said. "Everything depends on how relentlessly one forces from this experience the last drop, sweet or bitter, it can possibly give. This is the only real concern of the artist, to recreate out of the disorder of life that order which is art."*

Baldwin was also a playwright, notably of Blues for Mr. Charlie *(1964), and author of short stories. His second novel was* Giovanni's Room *(1956), followed by* Another Country *in 1962. Black with a large white readership, homosexual, an American frequently domiciled in France, Baldwin lived in many worlds. In the sixties he was criticized by black leaders; Eldridge Cleaver spoke of his "agonizing, total hatred of blacks." Langston Hughes, the great writer of the Harlem Renaissance, did not agree with Cleaver but said of Baldwin — what has become almost a commonplace — that "he is much better at provoking thought in an essay than he is in arousing emotion in fiction."*

This essay appeared in the New York Times *in 1979.*

If Black English
Isn't a Language,
Then Tell Me, What Is?

The argument concerning the use, or the status, or the reality, of black English is rooted in American history and has absolutely nothing to do with the question the argument supposes itself to be posing. The argument has nothing to do with language itself but with the *role* of language. Language, incontestably, reveals the speaker. Language, also, far more dubiously, is meant to define the other — and, in this case, the other is refusing to be defined by a language that has never been able to recognize him.

People evolve a language in order to describe and thus control their circumstances, or in order not to be submerged by a reality that they cannot articulate. (And, if they cannot articulate it, they *are* submerged.) A Frenchman living in Paris speaks a subtly and crucially different language from that of the man living in Marseilles; neither sounds very much like a man living in Quebec; and they would all have great difficulty in apprehending what the man from Guadeloupe, or Martinique, is saying, to say nothing of the man from Senegal — although the "common" language of all these areas is French. But each has paid, and is paying, a different price for this "common" language, in which, as it turns out, they are not saying, and cannot be saying, the same things: They each have very different realities to articulate, or control.

What joins all languages, and all men, is the necessity to confront life, in order, not inconceivably, to outwit death: The price for this is the acceptance, and achievement, of one's temporal identity. So that, for example, though it is not taught in the schools (and this has the potential of becoming a political issue) the south of France still clings to its ancient and musical Provençal, which resists being described as a "dialect." And much of the tension in the Basque countries, and in Wales, is due to the Basque and Welsh determination not to allow their languages to be destroyed. This determination also feeds the flames in Ireland for among the many indignities the Irish have been forced to undergo at English hands is the English contempt for their language.

It goes without saying, then, that language is also a political instrument, means, and proof of power. It is the most vivid and crucial key to identity: it reveals the private identity, and connects one with, or divorces one from, the larger, public, or communal identity. There have been, and are, times, and places, when to speak a certain language could be dangerous, even fatal. Or, one may speak the same language, but in such a way that one's antecedents are revealed, or (one hopes) hidden. This is true in France, and is absolutely true in England: The range (and reign) of accents on that damp little island make England coherent for the English and totally incomprehensible for everyone else. To open your mouth in England is (if I may use black English) to "put your business in the street": You have confessed your parents, your youth, your school, your salary, your self-esteem, and alas, your future.

Now, I do not know what white Americans would sound like if there had never been any black people in the United States, but they would not sound the way they sound. *Jazz*, for example, is a very specific sexual term, as in *jazz me, baby*, but white people purified it into the Jazz Age. *Sock it to me*, which means, roughly, the same thing, has been adopted by Nathaniel Hawthorne's descendants with no qualms or hesitations at all, along with *let it all hang out* and *right on! Beat to his socks*, which was once the black's most total and despairing image of poverty, was transformed into a thing called the Beat Generation, which phenomenon was, largely, composed of *uptight*, middle-class white people, imitating poverty, trying to *get down*, to get *with it*, doing their *thing*, doing their despairing best to be *funky*, which we, the blacks, never dreamed of doing — we *were* funky, baby, like *funk* was going out of style.

Now, no one can eat his cake, and have it, too, and it is late in the day to attempt to penalize black people for having created a language that permits the nation its only glimpse of reality, a language without which the nation would be even more *whipped* than it is.

I say that this present skirmish is rooted in American history, and it is. Black English is the creation of the black diaspora. Blacks came to the United States chained to each other, but from different tribes: Neither could speak the other's language. If two black people, at that bitter hour of the world's history, had been able to speak to each other, the institution of chattel slavery could never have lasted as long as it did. Subsequently, the slave was given, under the eye, and the gun, of his master, Congo Square, and the Bible — or, in other words, and under these conditions, the slave began the formation of the black church, and it is within this unprecedented tabernacle that black English began to be formed. This was not, merely, as in the European example, the adoption of a foreign tongue, but an alchemy that transformed ancient elements into a new language: *A language comes into existence by means of brutal necessity, and the rules of the language are dictated by what the language must convey.*

There was a moment, in time, and in this place, when my brother, or my mother, or my father, or my sister, had to convey to me, for example, the danger in which I was standing from the white man standing just behind me, and to convey this with a speed, and in a language, that the white man could not possibly understand, and that, indeed, he cannot understand, until today. He cannot afford to understand it. This understanding would reveal to him too much about himself, and smash that mirror before which he has been frozen for so long.

Now, if this passion, this skill, this (to quote Toni Morrison) "sheer intelligence," this incredible music, the mighty achievement of having brought a people utterly unknown to, or despised by "history" — to have brought this people to their present, troubled, troubling, and unassailable and unanswerable place — if this absolutely unprecedented journey does not indicate that black English is a language, I am curious to know what definition of language is to be trusted.

A people at the center of the Western world, and in the midst of so hostile a population, has not endured and transcended by means of what is patronizingly called a "dialect." We, the blacks, are in trouble, certainly, but we are not doomed, and we are not inarticulate because we are not compelled to defend a morality that we know to be a lie.

The brutal truth is that the bulk of the white people in America never had any interest in educating black people, except as this could serve white purposes. It is not the black child's language that is in question, it is not his language that is despised: It is his experience. A child cannot be taught by anyone who despises him, and a child cannot afford to be fooled. A child cannot be taught by anyone whose demand, essentially, is that the child repudiate his experience, and all that gives him sustenance, and enter a limbo in which he will no longer be black, and in which he knows that he can never become white. Black people have lost too many black children that way.

And, after all, finally, in a country with standards so untrustworthy, a   12
country that makes heroes of so many criminal mediocrities, a country unable to face why so many of the nonwhite are in prison, or on the needle, or standing, futureless, in the streets — it may very well be that both the child, and his elder, have concluded that they have nothing whatever to learn from the people of a country that has managed to learn so little.

AFTERWORD

Among the old rhetorical patterns of language — devices for thinking that include comparison and contrast, cause and effect, example, process analysis, classification and division — maybe none sounds so boring as definition: "An apple is a spheroid fruit consisting of skin, pulp, and core with seeds. . . ."

But definition can be used for argument, even for polemic, as James Baldwin shows in this essay. To begin with, he defines language by asserting that a language enacts itself by its purposes: "People evolve a language in order to describe and thus control their circumstances, or in order not to be submerged by a reality that they cannot articulate." Utility, not history, provides definition.

The linguist and traveler Baldwin supplies examples from other cultures, within francophone and anglophone cultures, to develop ideas and values intrinsic to his definition. Definition becomes argument as the role of black English supports an indictment of racism. Language is experience, and "It is not the black child's language that is . . . despised: It is his experience."

BOOKS AVAILABLE IN PAPERBACK

Another Country. New York: Dell. *Novel.*

Blues for Mister Charlie. New York: Dell. *Play.*

The Evidence of Things Not Seen. New York: Henry Holt. *Nonfiction.*

The Fire Next Time. New York: Dell. *Essays*.

Giovanni's Room. New York: Dell. *Novel*.

Go Tell It on the Mountain. New York: Dell. *Novel*.

Going to Meet the Man. New York: Dell. *Short stories*.

If Beale Street Could Talk. New York: Dell. *Novel*.

Just Above My Head. New York: Dell. *Novel*.

No Name in the Street. New York, Dell. *Nonfiction*.

Nobody Knows My Name. New York: Dell. *Essays*.

Notes of a Native Son. Boston: Beacon Press. *Essays*.

Tell Me How Long the Train's Been Gone. New York: Dell. *Novel*.

JOHN
BERGER

*J*OHN BERGER'S MIND *investigates and creates, using his many talents as painter, art critic, novelist, and poet. Born in London (1926), he served in the British army at the end of World War II, then attended art school in London. He has worked as a painter and as a teacher of drawing, exhibiting his own work in many English galleries. In periodicals, on television, and in many books and collections of essays — among them* Permanent Red: Essays in Seeing *(1960),* The Success and Failure of Picasso *(1965),* The Moment of Cubism *(1969),* The Look of Things *(1972),* The Sense of Sight *(1985) — he has developed a Marxist criticism of art that derives and values painting in relation to society and history.* Ways of Seeing *was a television series that became a book in 1972. He has written books of poems and three screenplays and has translated from the German. He has also published novels, beginning with* A Painter of Our Time *(1958), most notably* G *(1972), which won both the Booker Prize and the James Tait Black Memorial Prize. He has also made books of social documentation with the aid of photographer Jean Mohr:* A Fortunate Man *(1982) records the life and work of a physician in rural England, with observations on politics and society.* A Seventh Man *(1975)* mixes Mohr's photographs and Berger's prose on the subject of migrant workers in Europe.

In his art criticism, fiction, and essays Berger's Marxism continually investigates the impact of society and economics on the individual life. This autobiographical essay about his mother and her death is more personal, less argumentative, than most of his work. We found it in the Threepenny Review.

Her Secrets

FOR KATYA

From the age of five or six I was worried about the death of my parents. The inevitability of death was one of the first things I learnt about the world on my own. Nobody else spoke of it yet the signs were so clear.

Every time I went to bed — and in this I am sure I was like millions of other children — the fear that one or both my parents might die in the night touched the nape of my neck with its finger. Such a fear has, I believe, little to do with a particular psychological climate and a great deal to do with nightfall. Yet since it was impossible to say: You won't die in the night, will you? (when Grandmother died, I was told she had gone to have a rest, or — this was from my uncle who was more outspoken — that she had passed over), since I couldn't ask the real question and I sought a reassurance, I invented — like millions before me — the euphemism: See you in the morning! To which either my father or mother, who had come to turn out the light in my bedroom, would reply: See you in the morning, John.

After their footsteps had died away, I would try for as long as possible not to lift my head from the pillow so that the last words spoken remained, trapped like fish in a rock-pool at low tide, between my pillow and ear. The implicit promise of the words was also a protection against the dark. The words promised that I would not (yet) be alone.

Now I'm no longer usually frightened by the dark and my father died ten years ago and my mother a month ago at the age of ninety-three. It would be a natural moment to write an autobiography. My version of my life can no longer hurt either of them. And the book, when finished, would be there, a little like a parent. Autobiography begins with a sense of being alone. It is an orphan form. Yet I have no wish to do so. All that interests me about my past life are the common moments. The moments — which if I relate them well enough — will join countless others lived by people I do not personally know.

Six weeks ago my mother asked me to come and see her; it would be the last time, she said. A few days later, on the morning of my birthday, she believed she was dying. Open the curtains, she asked my brother, so I can see the trees. In fact, she died the following week.

On my birthdays as a child, it was my father rather than she who gave me memorable presents. She was too thrifty. Her moments of generosity were at the table, offering what she had bought and prepared and cooked and served to whoever came into the house. Otherwise she was thrifty. Nor did she ever explain. She was secretive, she kept things to herself. Not for her own pleasure, but because the world would not forgive spontaneity, the world was mean. I must make that clearer. She didn't believe life was mean — it was generous — but she had learnt from her own childhood that survival was hard. She was the opposite of quixotic — for she was not born a knight and her father was a warehouse foreman in Lambeth. She pursed her lips together, knitted her brows as she calculated and thought things out and carried on with an unspoken determination. She never asked favors of anyone. Nothing shocked her. From whatever she saw, she just drew the necessary conclusions so as to survive and to be dependent on nobody. If I were Aesop, I would say that in her prudence and persistence my mother resembled the agouti.° (I once wrote about an agouti in the London zoo, but I did not then realize why the animal so touched me.) In my adult life, the only occasions on which we shouted at each other were when she estimated I was being quixotic.

When I was in my thirties she told me for the first time that, ever since I was born, she had hoped I would be a writer. The writers she admired when young were Bernard Shaw, J. M. Barrie, Compton Mackenzie, Warwick Deeping, E. M. Dell. The only painter she really admired was Turner — perhaps because of her childhood on the banks of the Thames.

Most of my books she didn't read. Either because they dealt with subjects which were alien to her or because — under the protective influence of my father — she believed they might upset her. Why suffer surprise from something which, left unopened, gives you pleasure? My being a writer was unqualified for her by what I wrote. To be a writer was to be able to see to the horizon where, anyway, nothing is ever very distinct and all questions are open. Literature had little to do with the writer's vocation as she saw it. It was only a by-product. A writer was a person familiar with

8

---

agouti   A rodent about the size of a rabbit.

the secrets. Perhaps in the end she didn't read my books so that they should remain more secret.

If her hopes of my becoming a writer — and she said they began on the night after I was delivered — were eventually realized, it was not because there were many books in our house (there were few) but because there was so much that was unsaid, so much that I had to discover the existence of on my own at an early age: death, poverty, pain (in others), sexuality . . .

These things were there to be discovered within the house or from its windows — until I left for good, more or less prepared for the outside world, at the age of eight. My mother never spoke of these things. She didn't hide the fact that she was aware of them. For her, however, they were wrapped secrets, to be lived with, but never to be mentioned or opened. Superficially this was a question of gentility, but profoundly, of a respect, a secret loyalty to the enigmatic. My rough and ready preparation for the world did not include a single explanation — it simply consisted of the principle that events carried more weight than the self.

Thus, she taught me very little — at least in the usual sense of the term: she a teacher about life, I a learner. By imitating her gestures I learnt how to roast meat in the oven, how to clean celery, how to cook rice, how to chose vegetables in a market. As a young woman she had been a vegetarian. Then she gave it up because she did not want to influence us children. Why were you a vegetarian? I once asked her, eating my Sunday roast, much later when I was first working as a journalist. Because I'm against killing. She would say no more. Either I understood or I didn't. There was nothing more to be said.

In time — and I understand this only now writing these pages — I 12 chose to visit abattoirs in different cities of the world and to become something of an expert concerning the subject. The unspoken, the unfaceable beckoned me. I followed. Into the abattoirs and, differently, into many other places and situations.

The last, the largest, and the most personally prepared wrapped secret was her own death. Of course I was not the only witness. Of those close to her, I was maybe the most removed, the most remote. But she knew, I think, with confidence that I would pursue the matter. She knew that if anybody can be at home with what is kept a secret, it was me, because I was her son whom she hoped would become a writer.

The clinical history of her illness is a different story about which she herself was totally uncurious. Sufficient to say that with the help of drugs she was not in pain, and that, thanks to my brother and sister-in-law who arranged everything for her, she was not subjected to all the mechanical ingenuity of aids for the artificial prolongation of life.

Of how many deaths — though never till now of my own mother's — have I written? Truly we writers are the secretaries of death.

She lay in bed, propped up by pillows, her head fallen forward, as if 16
asleep.

I shut my eyes, she said, I like to shut my eyes and think. I don't sleep
though. If I slept now, I wouldn't sleep at night.

What do you think about?

She screwed up her eyes which were gimlet sharp and looked at me,
twinkling, as if I'd never, not even as a small child, asked such a stupid
question.

Are you working hard? What are you writing? 20

A play, I answered.

The last time I went to the theater I didn't understand a thing, she said.
It's not my hearing that's bad though.

Perhaps the play was obscure, I suggested.

She opened her eyes again. The body has closed shop, she announced. 24
Nothing, nothing at all from here down. She placed a hand on her neck.
It's a good thing, make no mistake about it, John, it makes the waiting
easier.

On her bedside table was a tin of handcream. I started to massage her
left hand.

Do you remember a photograph I once took of your hands? Working
hands, you said.

No, I don't.

Would you like some more photos on your table? Katya, her grand- 28
daughter, asked her.

She smiled at Katya and shook her head, her voice very slightly broken
by a laugh. It would be *so* difficult, so difficult, wouldn't it, to choose.

She turned towards me. What exactly are you doing?

I'm massaging your hand. It's meant to be pleasurable.

To tell you the truth, dear, it doesn't make much difference. What plane 32
are you taking back?

I mumbled, took her other hand.

You are all worried, she said, especially when there are several of you.
I'm not. Maureen asked me the other day whether I wanted to be cremated
or buried. Doesn't make one iota of difference to me. How could it? She
shut her eyes to think.

For the first time in her life and in mine, she could openly place the
wrapped enigma between us. She didn't watch me watching it, for we had
the habits of a lifetime. Openly she knew that at that moment her faith in
a secret was bound to be stronger than any faith of mine in facts. With her
eyes still shut, she fingered the Arab necklace I'd attached round her neck
with a charm against the evil eye. I'd given her the necklace a few hours
before. Perhaps for the first time I had offered her a secret and now her
hand kept looking for it.

She opened her eyes. What time is it? 36

Quarter to four.

It's not very interesting talking to me, you know. I don't have any ideas any more. I've had a good life. Why don't you take a walk.

Katya stayed with her.

When you are very old, she told Katya confidentially, there's one thing 40 that's very very difficult — it's very difficult to persuade other people that you're happy.

She let her head go back onto the pillow. As I came back in, she smiled.

In her right hand she held a crumpled paper handkerchief. With it she dabbed from time to time the corner of her mouth when she felt there was the slightest excess of spittle there. The gesture was reminiscent of one with which, many years before, she used to wipe her mouth after drinking Earl Grey tea and eating watercress sandwiches. Meanwhile with her left hand she fingered the necklace, cushioned on her forgotten bosom.

Love, my mother had the habit of saying, is the only thing that counts in this world. Real love, she would add, to avoid any factitious misunderstanding. But apart from that simple adjective, she never added anything more.

AFTERWORD

"Truly we writers are the secretaries of death."

John Berger's prose is straightforward, a glass of water compared with the rich, complex, personal styles of writers like Annie Dillard and Edward Abbey, who multiply metaphors and visual images. But when Berger requires it, he invents the metaphor or analogy that situates tone or value by its comparison. It is ordinary to note how writers speak often about death; Berger does not say anything so watery. He makes the writer an amanuensis taking down the spoken words of death the dictator.

Other examples, in this essay almost without metaphor, make themselves equally prominent by adding excellence to rarity: when he was a child thinking in bed of his parents' potential deaths, "fear . . . touched the nape of my neck with its finger," or "the most personally prepared wrapped secret was her own death."

BOOKS AVAILABLE IN PAPERBACK

About Looking. New York: Pantheon. *Nonfiction.*
And Our Faces, My Heart, Brief As Photos. New York: Pantheon. *Nonfiction.*

Art in Revolution. New York: Pantheon. *Nonfiction.*

Corker's Freedom. New York: Writers & Readers Publishing Inc. *Novel.*

The Foot of Clive. New York: Writers & Readers Publishing Inc. *Novel.*

G. New York: Pantheon. *Novel.*

A Painter of Our Time. New York: Writers & Readers Publishing Inc. *Novel.*

Permanent Red: Essays in Seeing. New York: Writers & Readers Publishing Inc. *Essays.*

Pig Earth. New York: Pantheon. *Novel.*

The Sense of Sight. New York: Pantheon. *Nonfiction.*

A Seventh Man. New York: Writers & Readers Publishing Inc. *Nonfiction.*

The Success and Failure of Picasso. New York: Pantheon: *Nonfiction.*

Ways of Seeing. New York: Penguin. *Nonfiction.*

WENDELL
BERRY

WENDELL BERRY *was born (1934) in Kentucky, where he attended college before teaching in New York and California for several years and then returning to his native soil. Over many years he farmed and wrote while he commuted to teach at the University of Kentucky. For a decade he stopped teaching in order to farm, write, and lecture. In 1987 he returned to the University of Kentucky part-time; lecturing had taken him away from his farm more than teaching had. He described his self-sustaining farm life:* "We produce our own meat and vegetables, milk and butter. We grown our own fuel, firewood. We have a small farm, which is farmable with horses, so we grow our own traction power."

Berry has written three novels: The Memory of Old Jack *came out in 1974; the earlier* Nathan Coulter *was revised and reissued by North Point Press in 1985 and* A Place on Earth *in 1983; he collected his short stories in* The Wild Birds *(1986). He began publishing books of poems with* The Broken Ground *in 1964; a* Collected Poems *in 1985 was followed in 1987 by his tenth major collection,* Sabbaths. *All along, Berry has written essays, collecting them in many books, from* The Long-Legged House *(1969) through* A Continuous Harmony *(1972),* The Unsettling of America *(1977),* Recollected Essays *(a selection, 1981),* The

Gift of Good Land *(1981),* **Standing by Words** *(1983), and* **Home Economics**
(1986), from which we take "Property, Patriotism, and National Defense."

*To his essays Berry brings the images of a lyric poet, the narrative line of a
novelist, and the thought of a moralist. Reading him we feel his attachment to the
Kentucky land we see through his careful eyes; we are caught by the desires and
goals that occupy and drive him. We become aware of values attached to particulars
and deriving from them, beliefs that form a system both local and general. He exacts
his morality from literature and the land together, and his ideas cohere through the
many genres in which he works. "Unconsciously perhaps from the beginning, and
more and more consciously during the last . . . years, my work has been motivated
by a desire to make myself responsibly at home in this world and in my native and
chosen place. As I have come to understand it, this is a long-term desire, proposing
not the work of a lifetime but of generations."*

Property, Patriotism, and National Defense

Man cannot so far know the connexion of causes and events, as that
he may venture to do wrong in order to do right.
                                        – SAMUEL JOHNSON, *Rasselas*

If it were a question of defending rivers, hills, mountains, skies,
winds, rains, I would say, "Willingly. That is our job. Let us fight.
All our happiness in life is there." No, we have defended the sham
name of all that.
                                        – JEAN GIONO, *Blue Boy*

The present situation with regard to "national defense," as I believe that
we citizens are now bidden to understand it, is that we, our country, and
our governing principles of religion and politics are so threatened by a
foreign enemy that we must prepare for a sacrifice that makes child's play
of the "supreme sacrifices" of previous conflicts. We are asked, that is, not
simply to "die in defense of our country," but to accept and condone the
deaths of virtually the whole population of our country, of our political and
religious principles, and of our land itself, as a reasonable cost of national
defense.

That a nation should purchase at an exorbitant price and then rely upon
a form of defense inescapably fatal to itself is, of course, absurd; that good

55

citizenship should be defined as willing acceptance of such a form of defense can only be ruinous of the political health of that nation. To ask intelligent citizens to believe an argument that in its essentials is not arguable and to approve results that are not imaginably good (and in the strict sense are not imaginable at all) is to drive wedges of disbelief and dislike between those citizens and their government. Thus the effect of such a form of defense is ruinous, whether or not it is ever used.

The absurdity of the argument lies in a little-noted law of the nature of technology — that, past a certain power and scale, we do not dictate our terms to the tools we use; rather, the tools dictate their terms to us. Past a certain power and scale, we may choose the means but not the ends. We may choose nuclear weaponry as a form of defense, but that is the last of our "free choices" with regard to nuclear weaponry. By that choice we largely abandon ourselves to terms and results dictated by the nature of nuclear weapons. To take up weapons has, of course, always been a limiting choice, but never before has the choice been made by so few with such fatal implications for so many and so much. Once we have chosen to rely on such weapons, the only *free* choice we have left is to change our minds, to choose *not* to rely on them. "Good" or "humane" choices short of that choice involve a logic that is merely pitiful.

In order to attack our enemies with nuclear weapons, we must hate 4 those enemies enough to kill them, and this hatred must be prepared in advance of any occasion or provocation. In order to work this hatred must be formalized in devices, systems, and procedures before any cause for the hatred exists.

And this hatred must be complete; there can be nothing selective about it. To use nuclear weapons against our enemies, we must hate them all enough to kill them. In this way, the technology dictates terms to its users. Our nuclear weapons articulate a perfect hatred, such as none of us has ever felt, or can feel, or can imagine feeling. In order to make a nuclear attack against the Russians, we must hate the innocent as well as the guilty, the children as well as the grown-ups. Thus, though it may be humanly impossible for us to propose it, we allow our technology to propose for us the defense of Christian love and justice (as we invariably put it) by an act of perfect hatred and perfect injustice. Or, as a prominent "conservative" columnist once put it, in order to save civilization we must become uncivilized.

The absurdity does not stop with the death of all of our enemies and all of our principles. It does not stop anywhere. Our nuclear weapons articulate for us a hatred of the Russian country itself: the land, water, air, light, plants, and animals of Russia. Those weapons will enact for us a perfect political hatred of birds and fish and trees. They will enact for us, too, a perfect hatred of ourselves, for a part of the inescapable meaning of those weapons is that we must hate our enemies so perfectly that in order to destroy them we are willing to destroy ourselves and everything dear that belongs to us.

The intention to use nuclear weapons appears to nullify every reason to use them, since there is no ostensible or imaginable reason for using them that could hope to survive their use. They would destroy all that they are meant to protect. There is no peace in them, or hope, or freedom, or health, or neighborliness, or justice, or love.

Except in the extremity of its immediate threat, nuclear weaponry is 8 analogous to the inflated rhetoric of factional and political quarrels. It is too general and too extreme to be meant by any individual person; belief in the propriety of its use requires personal abandonment to a public passion not validated by personal experience. Nuclear behavior is thus like the behavior of the prejudices of race, class, or party: it issues a general condemnation for a cause that cannot prove sufficient.

As against political and factional rhetoric, the only defense against nuclear weaponry is dissent: the attempt to bring the particularizing intelligence to the real ground of the problem.

Since I am outlining here the ground of my own dissent, I should say that I am not by principle a passive man, or by nature a pacific one. I understand hatred and enmity very well from my own experience. Defense, moreover, is congenial to me, and I am willingly, sometimes joyfully, a defender of some things — among them, the principles and practices of democracy and Christianity that nuclear weapons are said to defend. I do not want to live under a government like that of Soviet Russia, and I would go to considerable trouble to avoid doing so.

I am not dissenting because I want the nation — that is, the country, its lives and its principles — to be undefended. I am dissenting because I no longer believe that the standing policy on national defense can defend the nation. And I am dissenting because the means employed, the threatened results, and the economic and moral costs have all become so extreme as to be unimaginable.

It is, to begin with, impossible for me to imagine that our "nuclear 12 preparedness" is well understood or sincerely meant by its advocates in the government, much less by the nation at large. What we are proposing to ourselves and to the world is that we are prepared to die, to the last child, to the last green leaf, in defense of our dearest principles of liberty, charity, and justice. It would normally be expected, I think, that people led to the brink of total annihilation by so high and sober a purpose would be living lives of great austerity, sacrifice, and selfless discipline. That we are not doing so is a fact notorious even among ourselves. Our leaders are not doing so, nor are they calling upon us or preparing us to do so. As a people, we are selfish, greedy, dependent, and negligent of our duties to our land and to each other. We are evidently willing to sacrifice our own lives and the lives of millions of others, born and unborn — but not one minute of pleasure. We will have more arms, but not more taxes; we will aggrandize the military-industrial establishment, but not at the cost of self-aggrandizement. We will have defense and self-indulgence, which is to say, defense and debt. Surely not many nations before us have espoused bankruptcy and suicide as forms of self-defense.

This policy of national defense by national debt, so ruinous to the country as a whole, is exploited for profit and power by a subversive alliance of politicians, military officers, industrialists, and financiers — who, secure in their assumption that they will be the last to suffer or die as a result of their purposes, shift the real burden of industrial militarism onto the livelihoods of working people and onto the lives of young recruits.

Our alleged willingness to die for high principles, then, is all whitewash. We are not actually prepared to die for anything; we are merely resigned to the sham piety and the real greed of those in power.

What would make this willingness, this "state of nuclear preparedness," believable? It is easy enough to suggest some possible measures, both reasonable and necessary:

1. Forbid all taking of profit from military industries. Put an end to the possibility that anyone could get rich from any military enterprise. If all are asked to sacrifice their lives, why should not a few be asked to sacrifice their profits? If high principle is thought a sufficient motive for many, why should the profit motive be considered indispensable for a few?

2. Recognize that the outbreak of war in any form is a *failure* of government and of statesmanship. Let those who make or allow any war be the first into battle.

3. Require *all* the able-bodied to serve. Old and young alike have fought before in wars of national defense, such as the American Revolution, and they should be expected to do so again; "able-bodied" should mean "able to walk and to work." So far as possible, exemptions should be granted to the young, who have the greatest number of useful years still to live and have had the least time to understand the principles we wish to defend.

Let us assume, for the moment, that the argument of our present defense policy is valid, that our country, our lives, and our pinciples are indeed under threat of absolute destruction, and that our only possible defense against this threat is to hold the same absolute threat over our enemies — let us assume, in other words, that we have no choice but to accede to and pay for, the industry, the bureaucracy, and the politics of nuclear war. Let us assume that nuclear war is survivable and can be won and that the credibility of our will to wage such war might be established 16 beyond suspicion. *Then* would those of us who care about the defense of our country, its lives, and its principles have anything to worry about?

We would still have a great deal to worry about, for we still would not have shown that the present version of national defense could really defend what we must mean when we speak of "the country, its lives, and its principles." We must ask if the present version of national defense is, in fact, national defense.

To answer that question, we must ask first what kind of country is defensible, militarily or in any other way. And we may answer that a defensible country has a large measure of practical and material independence: that it can live, if it has to, independent of foreign supplies and of long distance transport within its own boundaries. It must also rest upon the broadest possible base of economic prosperity, not just in the sense of a money economy, but in the sense of properties, materials, and practical skills. Most important of all, it must be generally loved and competently cared for by its people, who, individually, identify their own interest with the interest of their neighbors and of the country (the land) itself.

To a considerable extent, that is the kind of country we had from the Revolution through World War II — and, to an even more considerable extent, that is the kind of country a great many people *hoped* to have during that time — which largely explains why the country was then so well defended. The remains and relics of that country are still scattered about us. The ideal or the fact of local independence is still alive in some individuals, some communities, and some small localities. There remain, here and there, a declining number of small farms, shops, stores, and other small enterprises that suggest the possibility of a broad, democratic distribution of usable property. If one hunts for them, one can still find small parcels and plots of our land that have been cared for and safeguarded in use, not by the abstract political passion that now disgraces the name of patriotism, for such passion does not do such work, but by personal knowledge, affection, responsibility, and skill.

And even today, against overpowering odds and prohibitive costs, one does not have to go far in any part of the country to hear voiced the old hopes that stirred millions of immigrants, freed slaves, westward movers, young couples starting out: a little farm, a little shop, a little store — some kind of place and enterprise of one's own, within and by which one's family could achieve a proper measure of independence, not only of economy, but of satisfaction, thought, and character.

That our public institutions have not looked with favor upon these hopes is sufficiently evident from the results. In the first twenty-five years after World War II, our farm people were driven off their farms by economic pressure at the rate of about one million a year. They are still going out of business at the rate of 1,400 farm families per week, or 72,800 families per year. That the rate of decline is now less than it was does not mean that the situation is improving; it means that the removal of farmers from farming is nearly complete. Less than 3 percent of the population of our country is left on the farms; that tiny percentage is presently declining and, if present conditions continue, will certainly decline further. Of that tiny percentage, a percentage still tinier now owns most of the land and produces most of the food. *Farming*, the magazine of the Production Credit Association, told farmers in its issue for March/April 1984: "Projections are that within the next 10 to 15 years, there'll be 200,000 to 300,000 of you farming big enough to account for 90% of the nation's gross farm receipts."

But this is not happening just on the farm. A similar decline is taking place in the cities. According to Joel Havemann, in the Los Angeles *Times*, 10 December 1983, "The percentage of households that own their own homes fell from 65.6 percent in 1980 to 64.5 at the end of 1982." Those percentages are too low in a country devoted to the defense of private ownership, and the decline is ominous. The reasons were the familiar ones of inflation and usury: "During the 1970s, the value of a median-priced home nearly tripled, while family income only doubled and mortgage interest rates rocketed to a peak of more than 16 percent in late 1981." And in the *Atlantic Monthly* of September 1984, Philip Langdon wrote: "Most families are priced out of the new-home market and have been for years. In April the median price of a new single-family house rose above $80,000 — an increase of 24 percent since 1979. . . . "

Those of us who can remember as far back as World War II do not need statistics to tell us that in the last forty years the once plentiful small, privately owned neighborhood groceries, pharmacies, restaurants, and other small shops and businesses have become endangered species, in many places extinct. It is this as much as anything that has rotted the hearts of our cities and surrounded them with shopping centers built by the corporate competitors of the small owners. The reasons, again, are inflation and usury, as well as the legally sanctioned advantages of corporations in their competition with individuals. Since World War II, the money interest has triumphed over the property interest, to the inevitable decline of the good care and the good use of property.

As a person living in a rural, agricultural community, I need no statistics 24 to inform me of the decline in the availability of essential goods and services in such places. Welders, carpenters, masons, mechanics, electricians, plumbers — all are in short supply, and their decline in the last ten years has been precipitous. Because of high interest rates and inflation, properties, tools, and supplies have become so expensive as to put a small business out of reach of many who would otherwise be willing. High interest works directly to keep local capital from being put to work locally.

When inflation and interest rates are high, young people starting out in small businesses or on small farms must pay a good living every year for the privilege of earning a poor one. People who are working are paying an exorbitant tribute to people who are, as they say, "letting their money work for them." The abstract value of money is preying upon and destroying the particular values that inhere in the lives of the land and of its human communities. For many years now, our officials have been bragging about the immensity of our gross national product and of the growth of our national economy, apparently without recognizing the possibility that the national economy as a whole can grow (up to a point) by depleting or destroying the small local economies within it.

The displacement of millions of people over the last forty or fifty years has, of course, been costly. The costs are not much talked about by apologists for our economy, and they have not been deducted from national or corporate incomes, but the costs exist nevertheless and they are not to be dismissed as intangible; to a considerable extent they have to do with the destruction and degradation of property. The decay of the inner parts of our cities is one of the costs; another is soil erosion, and other forms of land loss and land destruction; another is pollution.

There seems to be no escape from the requirement that intensive human *use* of property, if it is not to destroy the property, must be accompanied by intensive — that is, intimate — human care. It is often assumed that ownership guarantees good care, but that is not necessarily true. It has long been understood that absentee ownership is a curse upon property. Corporate ownership is plagued by the incompetence, irresponsibility, or antipathy of employees. And among us, at least, public ownership, as of waterways and roads, amounts virtually to an invitation to abuse. Good use of property, then, seems to require not only ownership but personal occupation and use by the owner. That is to say that the good use of property requires the widest possible distribution of ownership.

When urban property is gathered into too few hands and when the division between owners and users becomes therefore too great, a sort of vengeance is exacted upon urban property: people litter their streets and destroy their dwellings. When rural property is gathered into too few hands, even when, as in farming, the owners may still be the users, there is an inevitable shift of emphasis from maintenance to production, and the land deteriorates. People displaced from farming have been replaced by machines, chemicals, and other technological "labor-savers" that, of themselves, contribute to production, but do not, of themselves, contribute to maintenance, and often, of themselves, contribute to the degradation both of the land and of human care for it. Thus, our extremely serious problems of soil erosion and of pollution by agricultural chemicals are both attribut-

28

61

able to the displacement of people from agriculture. The technologies of "agribusiness" are enabling less than 3 percent of our people to keep the land in production (for the time being), but they do not and cannot enable them to take care of it.

Increasing the number of property owners is not in itself, of course, a guarantee of better use. People who do not know how to care for property cannot care for it, no matter how willing they may be to do so. But good care is potential in the presence of people, no matter how ignorant; there is no hope of it at all in their absence. The question bearing ever more heavily upon us is how this potential for good care in people may be developed and put to use. The honest answer, at present, seems to be that we do not know how. Perhaps we will have to begin by answering the question negatively. For example, most people who move from place to place every few years will never learn to care well for any place, nor will most people who are long alienated from all responsibility for usable property. Such people, moreover, cannot be taught good care by books or classroom instruction, nor can it be forced upon them by law. A people as a whole can learn good care only by long experience of living and working, learning and remembering, in the same places generation after generation, experiencing and correcting the results of bad care, and enjoying the benefits of good care.

It may be, also, that people who do not care well *for* their land will not care enough *about* it to defend it well. It seems certain that people who hope to be capable of national defense in the true sense — not by invading foreign lands but by driving off invaders of their own land — must love their country with the particularizing passion with which settled people have always loved, not their nation, but their *homes*, their daily lives, and daily bread.

An abstract nationalist patriotism may be easy to arouse, if the times offer a leader sufficiently gifted in the manipulation of crowds, but it is hard to sustain, and it has the seed of a foolishness in it that will become its disease. Our great danger at present is that we have no defensive alernative to this sort of hollow patriotic passion and its inevitable expression in nuclear warheads; this is both because our people are too "mobile" to have developed strong local loyalties and strong local economies and because the nation is thus made everywhere locally vulnerable — indefensible except as a whole. Our life no longer rests broadly upon our land but has become an inverted pyramid resting upon the pinpoint of a tiny, dwindling, agricultural minority critically dependent upon manufactured supplies and upon credit. Moreover, the population as a whole is now dependent upon goods and services that are not and often cannot be produced locally but must be transported, often across the entire width of the continent or from the other side of the world. Our national livelihood is everywhere pinched into wires, pipelines, and roads. A fact that cannot have eluded our military experts is that this "strongest nation in the world" is almost pitifully vulnerable on its own ground. A relatively few well-directed rifle shots, a relatively few well-placed sticks of dynamite could bring us to darkness, confusion, and hunger. And this civil weakness serves and aggravates the military obsession with megatonnage. It is only logical that a nation weak at home should threaten abroad with whatever destructions its technology can contrive. It is logical, but it is mad.

Nor can it have eluded our military experts that our own Revolution 32 was won, in spite of the gravest military disadvantages, by a farmer-soldiery, direct shareholders in their country, who were therefore, as Jefferson wrote, "wedded to its liberty and its interests, by the most lasting bonds." The Persian Wars, according to Aubrey de Sélincourt, "proved to the Greeks what a handful of free men, fighting for what they loved, could achieve against a horde of invaders advancing to battle 'under the lash. . . . '" And though the circumstances are inevitably different, we should probably draw similar conclusions from our experience in Vietnam, and from the Soviet Union's in Afghanistan. People tend to fight well in defense of their homes — the prerequisite being, of course, that they must have homes to defend. That is, they must not look on their dwelling places as dispensable or disposable campsites on the way to supposedly better dwelling places. A highly mobile population is predisposed to retreat; its values propose no sufficient reason for anyone to stay anywhere. The hope of a defensive *stand* had better rest on settled communities, whose ways imply their desire to be permanent.

I have been arguing from what seems to me a reasonable military assumption: that a sound policy of national defense would have its essential foundation and its indispensable motives in widespread, settled, thriving local communities, each having a proper degree of independence, living so far as possible from local sources, and using its local sources with a stewardly care that would sustain its life indefinitely, even through times of adversity. But now I would like to go further, and say that such communities, where they exist, are not merely the prerequisites or supports of a sound national defense; they *are* a sound national defense. They defend the country daily and hourly in all their acts by taking care of it, by causing it to thrive, by giving it the health and the satisfactions that make it worth defending, and by teaching these things to the young. This, to my mind, is *real* national defense, and military national defense would come from it, as if by nature, when occasion demanded, as the history of our Revolution suggests. To neglect such national defense, to destroy the possibility of it, in favor of a highly specialized, expensive, unwieldy, inflexible, desperate, and suicidal reliance on nuclear weapons is already to be defeated.

It is not as though the two kinds of national defense are compatible; it is not as though settled, stewardly communities can thrive and at the same time support a nuclear arsenal. In fact, the present version of national defense is destroying its own supports in the land and in human communities, for not only does it foster apathy, cynicism, and despair, especially in the young, but it is directly destructive of land and people by the inflation and usury that it encourages. The present version of national defense, like the present version of agriculture, rests upon debt — a debt that is driving up the cost of interest and driving down the worth of money, putting the national government actively in competition against good young people who are striving to own their own small farms and small businesses.

People who are concerned with the work of what I have called real national defense will necessarily have observed that it must be carried out often against our national government, and unremittingly against our present national economy. And our political and military leaders should have noticed, if they have not, that, whereas most of the citizenry now submit apathetically or cynically to the demands and costs of so-called national defense, works and acts of real national defense are being carried out locally in all parts of the country every day with firm resolve and with increasing skill. People, local citizens, are getting together, without asking for or needing governmental sanction, to defend their rivers, hills, mountains, skies, winds, and rains. They are doing this ably, peaceably, and many times successfully, though they are still far from the success that they desire.

The costs of this state of affairs to our instituted government are many 36 and dangerous; perhaps they may best be suggested by questions. To what point, for instance, do we defend from foreign enemies a country that we are destroying ourselves? In spite of all our propagandists can do, the foreign threat inevitably seems diminished when our air is unsafe to breathe, when our drinking water is unsafe to drink, when our rivers carry tonnages of topsoil that make light of the freight they carry in boats, when our forests are dying from air pollution and acid rain, and when we ourselves are sick from poisons in the air. Who *are* the enemies of this country? This is a question dangerous to instituted government when people begin to ask it for themselves. Many who have seen forests clear-cut on steep slopes, who have observed the work of the strip miners, who have watched as corporations advance their claims on private property "in the public interest," are asking that question already. Many more are going to ask.

Millions of people, moreover, who have lost small stores, shops, and farms to corporations, money merchants, and usurers, will continue to be asked to defend capitalism against communism. Sooner or later, they are going to demand to know why. If one must spend one's life as an employee, what difference does it make whether one's employer is a government or a corporation?

People, as history shows, will fight willingly and well to defend what they perceive as their own. But how willingly and how well will they fight to defend what has already been taken from them?

Finally, we must ask if international fighting as we have known it has not become obsolete in the presence of such omnivorous weapons as we now possess. There will undoubtedly always be a need to resist aggression, but now, surely, we must think of changing the means of such resistance.

In the face of all-annihilating weapons, the natural next step may be the use of no weapons. It may be that the only possibly effective defense against the ultimate weapon is no weapon at all. It may be that the presence of nuclear weapons in the world serves notice that the command to love one another is an absolute practical necessity, such as we never dreamed it to be before, and that our choice is not to win or lose, but to love our enemies or die.

40

AFTERWORD

The first nine paragraphs of Berry's argument reduce to absurdity the propositions of nuclear war. Logic proceeds in orderly outrage. This lover of the natural world shows how "those weapons will enact for us a perfect political hatred of birds and fish and trees." Line by line he sets up his fierce case against the use — and therefore the threat of the use — of nuclear weapons.

Then Berry tells us that he is not a pacifist, that he believes in defense. He outlines a conservative case against nuclear weapons based on agrarian values set against bigness, greed, agribusiness, and usury. He defends the small — Jefferson against Hamilton, farmers against bankers. Moral passion drives Berry, passion connected to the proper use of the land, but his moral vision includes ideas for cities, for economics and politics, for the military, for all society. In this essay, as in many essays by Wendell Berry, his language works for a water-clarity, for an overtness of logical discourse. It looks at us, saying: If you find these arguments faulty, break one link.

BOOKS AVAILABLE IN PAPERBACK

Clearing. San Diego: Harcourt Brace Jovanovich-Harvest. *Poetry*.

The Collected Poems of Wendell Berry. San Francisco: North Point Press. *Poetry*.

A Continuous Harmony: Essays Cultural and Agricultural. San Diego: Harcourt Brace Jovanovich-Harvest. *Essays*.

The Country of Marriage. San Diego: Harcourt Brace Jovanovich-Harvest. *Poetry*.

Farming: A Hand Book. San Diego: Harcourt Brace Jovanovich-Harvest. *Poetry*.

The Gift of Good Land: Further Essays Cultural and Agricultural. San Francisco: North Point Press. *Essays*.

Home Economics. San Francisco: North Point Press. *Essays*.

The Memory of Old Jack. San Diego: Harcourt Brace Jovanovich-Harvest. *Novel*.

Openings. San Diego: Harcourt Brace Jovanovich-Harvest. *Poetry*.

A Place on Earth. San Francisco: North Point Press. *Novel*.

Recollected Essays, 1965–1980. San Francisco: North Point Press. *Essays*.

Sabbaths: Poems of Wendell Berry. San Francisco: North Point Press. *Poetry*.

Standing by Words: Essays. San Francisco: North Point Press. *Essays*.

The Unsettling of America. New York: Avon. *Essays*.

The Wheel. San Francisco: North Point Press. *Poetry*.

CAROL
BLY

C *AROL BLY was born in 1930, grew up in Duluth, Minnesota, and in Virginia, went to boarding school in New England, and graduated from Wellesley College. After graduate work at the University of Minnesota, she married and raised four children in a small farming town at the western edge of Minnesota. Out of these years she made her first book,* Letters from the Country *(1981), essays, most of which were written for the* Minnesota Monthly *issued by Minnesota Public Radio. "Chin Up in a Rotting Culture" comes from this magazine and this book. A New York* Times *reviewer said that Bly "wants the farmers and small town merchants of America to live with passion, to have a sense of greatness in their lives, to take themselves as seriously as a Beethoven or a Thoreau."*

Her essays are passionate, often funny, exaggerated, and energetic in their moral intelligence. The same moral passion informs Carol Bly's marvelous short stories collected in Backbone *(1985). Besides a writer, Carol Bly has been a lecturer and a teacher, most recently at the University of Minnesota.*

Chin Up
in a Rotting Culture

I am going to propose a way for rural Minnesota to participate in our rotting national culture.

Minnesota country life is more agreeable than most twentieth-century American life of late; Minnesota itself is still more beautiful than most places where Americans have to live. So we don't write many letters to Congressmen. When the priest asks us to pray for those in agony in Nicaragua and Rhodesia and to pray for the Whole State of Christ's Church I notice we all look a little vague. We do not participate actively in the general rot or in the general pain.

But it participates in us. Sadness from its sadness has been flung into our hearts even if we are only spasmodically conscious of it. This sadness is in our unconscious hearts, even here where we walk in the October basswoods and emerge on the lake's harsh edge, where everything ventures to say: the world is absolutely lovely! it is absolutely lovely — what else?

No need to complain where complaint isn't due. Indeed, the surface life 4
of America, if you've any sort of financial security, is marvelous. It is plainly fun. By the millions, we get to drive around in strong cars, wherever we like — although we are running out of fuel. We visit and live in heated places although we are running out of fuel; we hear cellists from countries in sore pain under communism. We pig up joyfully on food imported from countries wrecking the dollar. And nearly everyone gets to go nearly everywhere: Freddy Laker° is going to haul people over to London's Stanstead and Gatwick Airports who twenty years ago would have considered Kansas City, as in the musical, "about as far as a person oughta go."

At certain points in decay most cultures do offer pleasure in the surface life. The Merovingians'° judicial system was such that people opted for death rather than their idea of *habeas corpus* — yet the populace lived generally well. On the eve of the Turkish takeover, relatives of crusaders and relatives of Constantine XIII° enjoyed profitable investments.

Freddy Laker   In the late seventies, Laker started an airline that provided frequent flights and cheap fares between the United States and Europe.

Merovingians   First dynasty of French kings (A.D. 481–751).

Turkish takeover . . . Constantine XIII   Constantine, last emperor of the Eastern Roman Empire, succumbed to the Turks in 1453.

Now, it isn't true that Americans, or Minnesotans, are lying around like the later Romans, being handed around grapes by *famuli bene dependeti*° — but it is nearly true. I allow myself hours and hours every day in which not to think about the creeping rot in our culture. Whole days, too. In truth, months go by when I don't. Others must be doing the same. The surface of American life is variegated and genial.

If the part of life acknowledged by conscious thought and feeling is both genial and amusing, then why stir up grief? In law, of course, grief must be stirred up. If egg shampoos are found not to have eggs they must be recalled. When our principal intelligence service is found to have imprisoned a man alone in a concrete room for three years, he must be released and Americans must be informed as the Minneapolis *Tribune* did on September 16, 1978. The question is not will we correct social evils, because of course we will, and rotting culture or no, we still have dozens of agencies both inside and outside the government devoted to doing so. Americans are still terrific at exposing and punishing violations of public trust. The question here is why should anyone try to remain *conscious* of our rotting culture from day to day?

Each year the Chambers of Commerce in Minnesota towns plan their activities. In my town, Madison, the area Chamber duly convened its publicity committee for 1978. The publicity committee had drawings of a thirty-six- to forty-foot-long lutefisk (lye-drenched codfish — a Norwegian *Vestlandets specialitet*), to be about six feet high of aluminum tubing and green-gold cloth stretched about. Five guys, the chairman explained, would walk along inside the lutefisk at parades in Madison and neighboring towns. (This would show the flag a little: Madison, Minnesota, consumes more lutefisk per capita than any city in the world except Bergen.°) After a lot of delay I got my part of the job done — handing in an estimate of square yardage of cloth needed for fish skin and fins. Then the publicity committee never met again and, so far as I know, never built the lutefisk. This in a town which in years past has put on entire melodramas directed by Lutheran intern clergymen, written by high school faculty members. One year the baker baked two hundred cookies to make the tiled roof of the witch's house for a street production of Hansel and Gretel, and refused any payment. The Catholic priest bought the gingerbread house at auction, and for years, St. Michael's School first graders got to play in it after Reading. So why did nothing come of the lutefisk and of much else we have planned recently?

8

---

famuli bene dependeti   Devoted slaves.
Bergen   City in Norway.

There are the usual explanations why things don't get done — inflation, for one. But under these lies a sharper reason, which interests me here. The conscious mind of Minnesota small towns has always shouted: Our life is still all right! We do not have to live in impersonal cities. We still have fun together — look at the county fair. Our teenagers are not destructive. These remarks presuppose the old Midwest genius for locking out the outside world and being good and worthy by ourselves. The unconscious, however, is always inviting in information from beyond town walls, and beyond the fields: it drinks up everything offered by television and news heads. However hastily a skilled isolationist turns the pages of the Minneapolis *Tribune,* the unconscious, with its speed of light, picks up all the awful news and hurries back down inside ourselves with it, like a dwarf hiding a treasure of poison. What is carried down there, and which we must carry about inside us, is grief over our rotting culture. It gives us just enough general malaise so we don't get around to building forty-foot lutefisk floats.

I would like to list four examples of national-level rot which are all known about but too seldom consciously considered by rural Minnesotans:

Example	*Meaning*
1. Egg shampoos without eggs	1. Willingness to cheat others for profit
2. Trebling of advertising by firms discovered to be producing toxic or radioactive items	2. Willingness to hurt or kill for profit
3. Excessive numbers of academic talk conferences in elegant surroundings, grant-supported, on major moral issues	3. Willingness to do psychological displacement of anxiety, at public expense, for the geniality of it
4. The fate of Yuri Nosenke	4. Willingness to torture a foreigner for three years, our opinion of Nazi and Soviet methods notwithstanding.

The above four examples, standing for dozens more like them, lie in the unconscious of the most robust and thickheaded local boosters.

Yet some towns — most engagingly, perhaps, Olivia, Minnesota — are actually increasing their voluntary recreational life together. They most succeed when they are not trying to play while Rome burns, but rather trying to be serious together. Olivia brought in two poets-in-residence, Nancy and Joe Paddock. Nancy and Joe never gave them a lovely poem about quilt making or the land or birds without adding the swift cry, though all this is lovely, it needs an ethic! Everything needs an ethic! So they worked to do what Chamber publicity committees work *not* to do: they worked to fasten together conscious and unconscious morality.

Small-town conscious morality involves fair and permanent sexual pat- 12 terning, fair and generous work for the day's wage, and generous serving of one another at death and during pain. Those are conscious. We like talking about how well we perform them, too.

I would like to propose that small-town Minnesota participate in our national griefs in the following way. I propose that the city council or the Chamber or some major group meet every Feast of Nicholas (December 6) and decide upon five or six figures who have done marvelous service to the American people at large. Any date for this would do. I commend St. Nicholas's Feast because he was patron saint of just about everybody, especially people of disparate social station, such as pawnbrokers and of course children, and his feast is at the end of the year, a logical time.

In 1962, Dr. Frances Kelsey, a medical officer of the FDA, received the President's Award for Distinguished Federal Civilian Service because she refused to let two companies, Merrill and National Drug, market thalidomide° in this country. Dr. Kelsey received thanks from her own community, and many thanks from individual people, but no citations from towns in the United States, community groups as such. None, although we all saw the photographs of the children whose mothers had taken the drug made in Ansbach-an-See. It would have been marvelous if ten thousand city councils in America — or churches, even (churches! where were they?) — had written to Dr. Kelsey and said:

> Of course this is hopelessly inadequate but we are grateful for your action so we are sending you this plaque [quilt, mittens, hand-italic-printed copy of St. Matthew's Gospel with decorations swiped from Dürer's woodcuts]. (Or if the town or group is rich it could send an encyclopedia of world art with really good plates in it, or season tickets to the Arena Theatre: Dr. Kelsey lives in Kenwood, Maryland — she might like that.)

I want to add quickly that this would not mean much to Dr. Kelsey. In late September this year I talked to her on the phone. I was breathless with admiration left over from 1962. I cannot describe how indifferent she was to my chattering praise or to the proposal I make here. Apparently you cannot change unegotistical people: if they don't learn to crave flattery when they are young, they don't develop a taste for it later.

---

thalidomide A drug used as a sedative and found to cause severe deformities in infants whose mothers took the drug during pregnancy.

The value in the deliberate, yearly praise of public figures would lie in 16 enabling rural people to participate in morality, not just locally at the fair stand, but nationally, and to relate to serious issues. Killing and maiming people is something we must think about. As Marianne Moore wrote:

> quiet form upon the dust, I cannot
> look and yet I must.

Finally, there will be a lovely side effect if we do it: it means once a year we argue about very good people. We won't agree on who should get our praise. We will lose sight of how unimportant our praise is; we will lose sight of ourselves a bit. We will be thinking about national-scale virtues.

We could do some condemnations, too. I like a fight.

AFTERWORD

"Everything needs an ethic!" Carol Bly cries out to us, and surely she is asked the question a thousand times a year: "If the part of life acknowledged by conscious thought and feeling is both genial and amusing, then why stir up grief?" Most of us would prefer not to recognize suffering that is not our own, or evil that is not our responsibility — or for which we deny responsibility. Surely "I like a fight," as Bly ends her essay, is a portion of every moralist's character, unacknowledged by many. But Bly's moral energy derives from more than the joy of combat. Bly believes that, no matter how passive we wish to be, there is an ear inside us that hears the screams of others when they suffer. She writes to take the wax out of that ear.

Bly's moral argument displays itself by real examples. There's no other way, because exhortation without example sounds like the Boy Scout oath. Moral urgency in abstraction is fine if you already agree with it; if you don't know about it, you will learn only from examples. Her anecdotes here come from a decade past, and many are out of date; Freddy Laker got clobbered. But anyone reading this essay can supply examples from our own moment, or from any moment. Her good examples never date because they suggest parallel examples. Alas.

BOOKS AVAILABLE IN PAPERBACK

Backbone: Short Stories. Minneapolis: Milkweed Editions. *Short stories.*
Letters from the Country. New York: Penguin. *Essays.*

JOSEPH
BRODSKY

*J*OSEPH BRODSKY *was born in Leningrad (1940) and learned tyranny firsthand. He left school at fifteen, worked at menial jobs — and wrote poems
acclaimed by the great poet Anna Akhmatova. But in 1964 Brodsky was judged a
"social parasite" because he refused to work at a regular job like other Soviet citizens.
It was charged against him in court that between 1956 and 1964 he held thirteen
jobs.*

*Brodsky was sentenced to five years of hard labor on a prison farm, giving rise
to more Western criticism of Soviet oppression against Jews, dissenters, and artists.
Brodsky's father had been dismissed from the Russian navy, as the son put it, "in
accordance with some seraphic ruling that Jews should not hold substantial military
rank." Brodsky was released from prison after a mere eighteen months of carrying
manure and chopping wood, but he continued to suffer official harassment. Finally,
in 1971 the Soviet authorities found him incorrigible enough: He was invited to
emigrate to Israel, and it was suggested that he would regret it if he did not. He
moved to the United States instead, taking a professorship at the University of
Michigan (he has taught at several universities) and has lived here ever since. In
1981 the MacArthur Foundation granted him five years of financial support; in
1987 he received the Nobel Prize for literature.*

Brodsky's poems do not read well in English. Russian to English appears a difficult trip for poetry; the great Pushkin won't make the journey, and the extraor-dinary Russian modernist poets (Mandelstam, Akhmatova, Tsvetayeva) tantalize us by the difficulties and approximations of their English translations. In our language, we find Brodsky best in his magnificent essays, collected in Less Than One *(1984), of which "On Tyranny" is an example. This book contains essays in literary criticism — about English, Russian, and Greek poets — in political thought, and most notably in reminiscence.*

On Tyranny

Illness and death are, perhaps, the only things that a tyrant has in common with his subjects. In this sense alone a nation profits from being run by an old man. It's not that one's awareness of one's own mortality necessarily enlightens or makes one mellow, but the time spent by a tyrant pondering, say, his metabolism is time stolen from the affairs of state. Both domestic and international tranquilities are in direct proportion to the num-ber of maladies besetting your First Secretary of the Party, or your President-for-Life. Even if he is perceptive enough to learn that additional art of callousness inherent in every illness, he is usually quite hesitant to apply this acquired knowledge to his palace intrigues or foreign policies, if only because he instinctively gropes for the restoration of his previous healthy condition or simply believes in full recovery.

In the case of a tyrant, time to think of the soul is always used for scheming to preserve the status quo. This is so because a man in his position doesn't distinguish between the present, history, and eternity, fused into one by the state propaganda for both his and the population's convenience. He clings to power as any elderly person does to his pension or savings. What sometimes appears as a purge in the top ranks is perceived by the nation as an attempt to sustain the stability for which this nation opted in the first place by allowing the tyranny to be established.

The stability of the pyramid seldom depends on its pinnacle, and yet it is precisely the pinnacle that attracts our attention. After a while a specta-tor's eye gets bored with its intolerable geometrical perfection and all but demands changes. When changes come, however, they are always for the worse. To say the least, an old man fighting to avoid disgrace and discom-fort, which are particularly unpleasant at his age, is quite predictable. Bloody and nasty as he may appear to be in that fight, it affects neither the pyramid's inner structure nor its external shadow. And the objects of his struggle, the rivals, fully deserve his vicious treatment, if only because of the tautology of their ambition in view of the difference in age. For politics is but geometrical purity embracing the law of the jungle.

Up there, on the head of the pin, there is room only for one, and he 4 had better be old, since old men never pretend they are angels. The aging tyrant's sole purpose is to retain his position, and his demagoguery and hypocrisy do not tax the minds of his subjects with the necessity of belief or textual proliferation. Whereas the young upstart with his true or false zeal and dedication always ends up raising the level of public cynicism. Looking back on human history we can safely say that cynicism is the best yardstick of social progress.

For new tyrants always introduce a new blend of hypocrisy and cruelty. Some are more keen on cruelty, others on hypocrisy. Think of Lenin, Hitler, Stalin, Mao, Castro, Qaddafi, Khomeini, Amin, and so on. They always beat their predecessors in more ways than one, and give a new twist to the arm of the citizen as well as to the mind of the spectator. For an anthropologist (an extremely aloof one at that) this kind of development is of great interest, for it widens one's notion of the species. It must be noted, however, that the responsibility for the aforesaid processes lies as much with technological progress and the general growth of population as with the particular wickedness of a given dictator.

Today, every new sociopolitical setup, be it a democracy or an authoritarian regime, is a further departure from the spirit of individualism toward the stampede of the masses. The idea of one's existential uniqueness gets replaced by that of one's anonymity. An individual perishes not so much by the sword as by the penis, and, however small a country is, it requires, or becomes subjected to, central planning. This sort of thing easily breeds various forms of autocracy, where tyrants themselves can be regarded as obsolete versions of computers.

But if they were only the obsolete versions of computers, it wouldn't be so bad. The problem is that a tyrant is capable of purchasing new, state-of-the-art computers and aspires to man them. Examples of obsolete forms of hardware running advanced forms are the Führer resorting to the loudspeaker, or Stalin using the telephone monitoring system to eliminate his opponents in the Politburo.

People become tyrants not because they have a vocation for it, nor do 8 they by pure chance either. If a man has such a vocation, he usually takes a shortcut and becomes a family tyrant, whereas real tyrants are known to be shy and not terribly interesting family men. The vehicle of a tyranny is a political party (or military ranks, which have a structure similar to that of the party), for in order to get to the top of something you need to have something that has a vertical topography.

Now, unlike a mountain or, better still, a skyscraper, a party is essentially a fictitious reality invented by the mentally or otherwise unemployed. They come to the world and find its physical reality, skyscrapers and mountains, fully occupied. Their choice, therefore, is between waiting for an opening on the old system and creating a new, alternative one of their own. The latter strikes them as the more expedient way to proceed, if only because they can start right away. Building a party is an occupation in itself, and an absorbing one at that. It surely doesn't pay off immediately; but then again the labor isn't that hard and there is a great deal of mental comfort in the incoherence of the aspiration.

In order to conceal its purely demographic origins, a party usually develops its own ideology and mythology. In general, a new reality is always created in the image of an old one, aping the existing structures. Such a technique, while obscuring the lack of imagination, adds a certain air of authenticity to the entire enterprise. That's why, by the way, so many of these people adore realistic art. On the whole, the absence of imagination is more authentic than its presence. The droning dullness of a party program and the drab, unspectacular appearance of its leaders appeal to the masses as their own reflection. In the era of overpopulation, evil (as well as good) becomes as mediocre as its subjects. To become a tyrant, one had better be dull.

And dull they are, and so are their lives. Their only rewards are obtained while climbing: seeing rivals outdone, pushed away, demoted. At the turn of the century, in the heyday of political parties, there were the additional pleasures of, say, putting out a haywire pamphlet, or escaping police surveillance; of delivering a fervent oration at a clandestine congress or resting at the party's expense in the Swiss Alps or on the French Riviera. Now all that is gone: burning issues, false beards, Marxist studies. What's left is the waiting game of promotion, endless red tape, paper work, and a search for reliable pals. There isn't even the thrill of watching your tongue, for it's surely devoid of anything worth the attention of your fully bugged walls.

What gets one to the top is the slow passage of time, whose only comfort 12 is the sense of authenticity it gives to the undertaking: what's time-consuming is real. Even within the ranks of the opposition, party advancement is slow; as for the party in power, it has nowhere to hurry, and after half a century of domination is itself capable of distributing time. Of course, as regards ideals in the Victorian sense of the word, the one-party system isn't very different from a modern version of political pluralism. Still, to join the only existing party takes more than an average amount of dishonesty.

Nevertheless, for all your cunning, and no matter how crystal-clear your record is, you are not likely to make it to the Politburo before sixty. At this age life is absolutely irreversible, and if one grabs the reins of power, he unclenches his fists only for the last candle. A sixty-year-old man is not likely to try anything economically or politically risky. He knows that he has a decade or so to go, and his joys are mostly of a gastronomical and a technological nature: an exquisite diet, foreign cigarettes, and foreign cars. He is a status quo man, which is profitable in foreign affairs, considering his steadily growing stockpile of missiles, and intolerable inside the country, where to do nothing means to worsen the existing condition. And although his rivals may capitalize on the latter, he would rather eliminate them than introduce any changes, for one always feels a bit nostalgic toward the order that brought one to success.

The average length of a good tyranny is a decade and a half, two decades at most. When it's more than that, it invariably slips into a monstrosity. Then you may get the kind of grandeur that manifests itself in waging wars or internal terror, or both. Blissfully, nature takes its toll, resorting at times to the hands of the rivals just in time; that is, before your man decides to immortalize himself by doing something horrendous. The younger cadres, who are not so young anyway, press from below, pushing him into the blue yonder of pure Chronos. Because after reaching the top of the pinnacle that is the only way to continue. However, more often than not, nature has to act alone and encounter a formidable opposition from both the Organs of State Security and the tyrant's personal medical team. Foreign doctors are flown in from abroad to fish your man out from the depths of senility to which he has sunk. Sometimes they succeed in their humanitarian mission (for their governments are themselves deeply interested in the preservation of the status quo), enough to enable the great man to reiterate the death threat to their respective countries.

In the end both give up; Organs perhaps less willingly than doctors, for medicine has less in the way of a hierarchy which stands to be affected by the impending changes. But even the Organs finally get bored with their master, whom they are going to outlive anyway, and as the bodyguards turn their faces sideways, in slips death with scythe, hammer, and sickle. The next morning the population is awakened not by the punctual roosters but by waves of Chopin's *Marche Funèbre* pouring out of the loudspeakers. Then comes the military funeral, horses dragging the gun carriage, preceded by a detachment of soldiers carrying on small scarlet cushions the medals and orders that used to adorn the coat of the tyrant like the chest of a prize-winning dog. For this is what he was: a prize- and race-winning dog. And if the population mourns his demise, as often happens, its tears are the tears of bettors who lost: the nation mourns its lost time. And then appear the members of the Politburo, shouldering the banner-draped coffin: the only denominator that they have in common.

As they carry their dead denominator, cameras chirr and click, and both 16 foreigners and the natives peer intently at the inscrutable faces, trying to pick out the successor. The deceased may have been vain enough to leave a political testament, but it won't be made public anyway. The decision is to be made in secrecy, at a closed — that is, to the population — session of the Politburo. That is, clandestinely. Secretiveness is an old party hang-up, an echo of its demographic origin, of its glorious illegal past. And the faces reveal nothing.

They do it all the more successfully because there is nothing to reveal. For it's simply going to be more of the same. The new man will differ from the old man only physically. Mentally and otherwise he is bound to be the exact replica of the corpse. This is perhaps the biggest secret there is. Come to think of it, the party's replacements are the closest thing we've got to resurrection. Of course, repetition breeds boredom, but if you repeat things in secret there is still room for fun.

The funniest thing of all, however, is the realization that any one of these men can become a tyrant. That what causes all this uncertainty and confusion is just that the supply exceeds the demand. That we are dealing not with the tyranny of an individual but with the tyranny of a party that simply has put the production of tyrants on an industrial footing. Which was very shrewd of this party in general and very apt in particular, considering the rapid surrender of individualism as such. In other words, today the "who-is-going-to-be-who" guessing game is as romantic and antiquated as that of bilboquet, and only freely elected people can indulge in playing it. The time is long since over for the aquiline profiles, goatees or shovel-like beards, walrus or toothbrush mustaches; soon it will be over even for eyebrows.

Still, there is something haunting about these bland, gray, undistinguished faces: they look like everyone else, which gives them an almost underground air; they are similar as blades of grass. The visual redundance provides the "government of the people" principle with an additional depth: with the rule of nobodies. To be governed by nobodies, however, is a far more ubiquitous form of tyranny, since nobodies look like everybody. They represent the masses in more ways than one, and that's why they don't bother with elections. It's a rather thankless task for the imagination to think of the possible result of the "one man, one vote" system in, for example, the one-billion-strong China: what kind of a parliament that could produce, and how many tens of millions would constitute a minority there.

The upsurge of political parties at the turn of the century was the first 20 cry of overpopulation, and that's why they score so well today. While the individualists were poking fun at them, they capitalized on depersonalization, and presently the individualists quit laughing. The goal, however, is neither the party's own nor some particular bureaucrat's triumph. True, they turned out to be ahead of their time; but time has a lot of things ahead, and above all, a lot of people. The goal is to accommodate their numerical expansion in the nonexpanding world, and the only way to achieve it is through the depersonalization and bureaucratization of everybody alive. For life itself is a common denominator; that's enough of a premise for structuring existence in a more detailed fashion.

And a tyranny does just that: structures your life for you. It does this as meticulously as possible, certainly far better than a democracy does. Also, it does it for your own sake, for any display of individualism in a crowd may be harmful: first of all for the person who displays it; but one should care about those next to him as well. This is what the party-run state, with its security service, mental institutions, police, and citizens' sense of loyalty, is for. Still, all these devices are not enough: the dream is to make every man his own bureaucrat. And the day when such a dream comes true is very much in sight. For bureaucratization of individual existence starts with thinking politics, and it doesn't stop with the acquisition of a pocket calculator.

So if one still feels elegiac at the tyrant's funeral, it's mostly for autobiographical reasons, and because this departure makes one's nostalgia for "the good old days" even more concrete. After all, the man was also a product of the old school, when people still saw the difference between what they were saying and what they were doing. If he doesn't deserve more than a line in history, well, so much the better: he just didn't spill enough of his subjects' blood for a paragraph. His mistresses were on the plump side and few. He didn't write much, nor did he paint or play a musical instrument; he didn't introduce a new style in furniture either. He was a plain tyrant, and yet leaders of the greatest democracies eagerly sought to shake his hand. In short, he didn't rock the boat. And it's partly thanks to him that as we open our windows in the morning, the horizon there is still not vertical.

Because of the nature of his job, nobody knew his real thoughts. It's quite probable that he didn't know them himself. That would do for a good epitaph, except that there is an anecdote the Finns tell about the will of their President-for-Life Urho Kekkonnen which begins as follows: "If I die . . ."

AFTERWORD

The poet turned essayist argues, thinks, and persuades by means of images. If the writer does his persuading honestly, we watch thought's structure develop; we are free to accept or reject the analogies placed openly before us. (The adroit propagandist or advertiser, on the other hand, seeks our advocacy by euphemism, which gives lowly things prestigious names, or by the loaded word, which pretends objectivity while carrying a surplus of subjective baggage; missiles become peacekeepers.) Describing the vertical topography of tyranny, Brodsky speaks of pyramids, mountains, and skyscrapers; he speaks of the dictator "climbing"; "What gets one to the top"; "the blue yonder"; "the top of the pinnacle." Implicit underneath this tyrannical tower we understand the horizontal mass of a trodden people.

It is typical of Brodsky's individualism that, even in an essay rich in abstract thought, the imaged tyrant is not a principle, an idea, an order, a structure — but a single old evil man. Brodsky begins with allusions to the illness and old age of tyrants Brodsky has known firsthand; he ends with a contemporary leader's wonderfully ill-chosen words.

BOOKS AVAILABLE IN PAPERBACK

Less Than One: Selected Essays. New York: Farrar, Straus & Giroux. *Essays*.

A Part of Speech. New York: Farrar, Straus & Giroux. *Poetry*.

RAYMOND CARVER

*B*ORN IN CALIFORNIA *in 1938, Raymond Carver is as responsible as anyone for the recent resurgence of the American short story. The literature of the short story virtually begins with Poe and Hawthorne, and in the twentieth century Americans have continued to serve the genre: Hemingway, Faulkner, Welty, Porter, Flannery O'Connor, Updike. But until recently it had become axiomatic among publishers that even the best book of stories would find no readers. Carver helped to change things; his collections of stories have been best-sellers in America, England, and all over the world — translated into Japanese, French, and half a dozen other languages. His collections are* Will You Please Be Quiet, Please? *(1976),* What We Talk About When We Talk About Love *(1981), and* Cathedral *(1983) followed in 1988 by a volume of new and selected stories,* Where I'm Calling From. *In 1983 he collected a miscellany,* Fires: Essays, Poems, Stories. *"My Father's Life" appeared in* Esquire *in 1984. Always a poet, Carver in 1987 published* In a Marine Light, *a selection of his best poems.*

As a writer of fiction, Carver is called a minimalist, for his stories are usually lean, spare, and bleak. Many stories narrate moments in the lives of people who have failed, often passive and depressed; many of his characters are heavy drinkers, out of work, out of love, separated, or divorced. From this relentless material Carver makes his art; his ear for the way people speak is devastating: "Will you please be quiet, please?"

Himself an alcoholic for many years — he stopped drinking in 1977 — Carver started writing when he was nineteen or twenty and began taking classes with the late novelist John Gardner at Chico State College in northern California. His successes were rare, occasional stories in Esquire *or in annual anthologies, until late in the seventies. Despite his sudden international celebrity, he has never wavered from his dedication to the art of writing. Most of the year he and Tess Gallagher — also a poet, essayist, and short-story writer — live in the small town of Port Angeles in the state of Washington, where they write and Carver fishes for salmon.*

My Father's Life

My dad's name was Clevie Raymond Carver. His family called him Raymond and friends called C. R. I was named Raymond Clevie Carver Jr. I hated the "Junior" part. When I was little my dad called me Frog, which was okay. But later, like everybody else in the family, he began calling me Junior. He went on calling me this until I was thirteen or fourteen and announced that I wouldn't answer to that name any longer. So he began calling me Doc. From then until his death, on June 17, 1967, he called me Doc, or else Son.

When he died, my mother telephoned my wife with the news. I was away from my family at the time, between lives, trying to enroll in the School of Library Science at the University of Iowa. When my wife answered the phone, my mother blurted out, "Raymond's dead!" For a moment, my wife thought my mother was telling her that I was dead. Then my mother made it clear *which* Raymond she was talking about and my wife said, "Thank God. I thought you meant *my* Raymond."

My dad walked, hitched rides, and rode in empty boxcars when he went from Arkansas to Washington State in 1934, looking for work. I don't know whether he was pursuing a dream when he went out to Washington. I doubt it. I don't think he dreamed much. I believe he was simply looking for steady work at decent pay. Steady work was meaningful work. He picked apples for a time and then landed a construction laborer's job on the Grand Coulee Dam. After he'd put aside a little money, he bought a car and drove back to Arkansas to help his folks, my grandparents, pack up for the move west. He said later that they were about to starve down there, and this wasn't meant as a figure of speech. It was during that short while in Arkansas, in a town called Leola, that my mother met my dad on the sidewalk as he came out of a tavern.

"He was drunk," she said. "I don't know why I let him talk to me. His eyes were glittery. I wish I'd had a crystal ball." They'd met once, a year or so before, at a dance. He'd had girlfriends before her, my mother told me. "Your dad always had a girlfriend, even after we married. He was my first and last. I never had another man. But I didn't miss anything."

They were married by a justice of the peace on the day they left for Washington, this big, tall country girl and a farmhand–turned–construction worker. My mother spent her wedding night with my dad and his folks, all of them camped beside the road in Arkansas.

In Omak, Washington, my dad and mother lived in a little place not much bigger than a cabin. My grandparents lived next door. My dad was still working on the dam, and later, with the huge turbines producing electricity and the water backed up for a hundred miles into Canada, he stood in the crowd and heard Franklin D. Roosevelt when he spoke at the construction site. "He never mentioned those guys who died building that dam," my dad said. Some of his friends had died there, men from Arkansas, Oklahoma, and Missouri.

He then took a job in a sawmill in Clatskanie, Oregon, a little town alongside the Columbia River. I was born there, and my mother has a picture of my dad standing in front of the gate to the mill, proudly holding me up to face the camera. My bonnet is on crooked and about to come untied. His hat is pushed back on his forehead, and he's wearing a big grin. Was he going in to work or just finishing his shift? It doesn't matter. In either case, he had a job and a family. These were his salad days.

In 1941 we moved to Yakima, Washington, where my dad went to work as a saw filer, a skilled trade he'd learned in Clatskanie. When war broke out, he was given a deferment because his work was considered necessary to the war effort. Finished lumber was in demand by the armed services, and he kept his saws so sharp they could shave the hair off your arm.

After my dad had moved us to Yakima, he moved his folks into the same neighborhood. By the mid-1940s the rest of my dad's family — his brother, his sister, and her husband, as well as uncles, cousins, nephews, and most of their extended family and friends — had come out from Arkansas. All because my dad came out first. The men went to work at Boise Cascade, where my dad worked, and the women packed apples in the canneries. And in just a little while, it seemed — according to my mother — everybody was better off than my dad. "Your dad couldn't keep money," my mother said. "Money burned a hole in his pocket. He was always doing for others."

The first house I clearly remember living in, at 1515 South Fifteenth Street, in Yakima, had an outdoor toilet. On Halloween night, or just any night, for the hell of it, neighbor kids, kids in their early teens, would carry out toilet away and leave it next to the road. My dad would have to get somebody to help him bring it home. Or these kids would take the toilet and stand it in somebody else's backyard. Once they actually set it on fire. but ours wasn't the only house that had an outdoor toilet. When I was old enough to know what I was doing, I threw rocks at the other toilets when I'd see someone go inside. This was called bombing the toilets. After a while, though, everyone went to indoor plumbing until, suddenly, our toilet was the last outdoor one in the neighborhood. I remember the shame I felt when my third-grade teacher, Mr. Wise, drove me home from school one day. I asked him to stop at the house just before ours, claiming I lived there.

I can recall what happened one night when my dad came home late to find that my mother had locked all the doors on him from the inside. He was drunk, and we could feel the house shudder as he rattled the door. When he'd managed to force open a window, she hit him between the eyes with a colander and knocked him out. We could see him down there on the grass. For years afterward, I used to pick up this colander — it was as heavy as a rolling pin — and imagine what it would feel like to be hit in the head with something like that.

It was during this period that I remember my dad taking me into the 12 bedroom, sitting me down on the bed, and telling me that I might have to go live with my Aunt LaVon for a while. I couldn't understand what I'd done that meant I'd have to go away from home to live. But this, too — whatever prompted it — must have blown over, more or less, anyway, because we stayed together, and I didn't have to go live with her or anyone else.

I remember my mother pouring his whiskey down the sink. Sometimes she'd pour it all out and sometimes, if she was afraid of getting caught, she'd only pour half of it out and then add water to the rest. I tasted some of his whiskey once myself. It was terrible stuff, and I don't see how anybody could drink it.

After a long time without one, we finally got a car, in 1949 or 1950, a 1938 Ford. But it threw a rod the first week we had it, and my dad had to have the motor rebuilt.

"We drove the oldest car in town," my mother said. "We could have had a Cadillac for all he spent on car repairs." One time she found someone's else's tube of lipstick on the floorboard, along with a lacy handkerchief. "See this?" she said to me. "Some floozy left this in the car."

Once I saw her take a pan of warm water into the bedroom where my 16 dad was sleeping. She took his hand from under the covers and held it in the water. I stood in the doorway and watched. I wanted to know what was going on. This would make him talk in his sleep, she told me. There were things she needed to know, things she was sure he was keeping from her.

Every year or so, when I was little, we would take the North Coast Limited across the Cascade Range from Yakima to Seattle and stay in the Vance Hotel and eat, I remember, at a place called the Dinner Bell Cafe. Once we went to Ivar's Acres of Clams and drank glasses of warm clam broth.

In 1956, the year I was to graduate from high school, my dad quit his job at the mill in Yakima and took a job in Chester, a little sawmill town in northern California. The reasons given at the time for his taking the job had to do with a higher hourly wage and the vague promise that he might, in a few years' time, succeed to the job of head filer in this new mill. But I think, in the main, that my dad had grown restless and simply wanted to try his luck elsewhere. Things had gotten a little too predictable for him in Yakima. Also, the year before, there had been the deaths, within six months of each other, of both his parents.

But just a few days after graduation, when my mother and I were packed to move to Chester, my dad penciled a letter to say he'd been sick for a while. He didn't want us to worry, he said, but he'd cut himself on a saw. Maybe he'd got a tiny sliver of steel in his blood. Anyway, something had happened and he'd had to miss work, he said. In the same mail was an unsigned postcard from somebody down there telling my mother that my dad was about to die and that he was drinking "raw whiskey."

When we arrived in Chester, my dad was living in a trailer that belonged to the company. I didn't recognize him immediately. I guess for a moment I didn't want to recognize him. He was skinny and pale and looked bewildered. His pants wouldn't stay up. He didn't look like my dad. My mother began to cry. My dad put his arm around her and patted her shoulder vaguely, like he didn't know what this was all about, either. The three of us took up life together in the trailer, and we looked after him as best we could. But my dad was sick, and he couldn't get any better. I worked with him in the mill that summer and part of the fall. We'd get up in the mornings and eat eggs and toast while we listened to the radio, and then go out the door with our lunch pails. We'd pass through the gate together at eight in the morning, and I wouldn't see him again until quitting time. In November I went back to Yakima to be closer to my girlfriend, the girl I'd made up my mind I was going to marry.

He worked at the mill in Chester until the following February, when he collapsed on the job and was taken to the hospital. My mother asked if I would come down there and help. I caught a bus from Yakima to Chester, intending to drive them back to Yakima. But now, in addition to being physically sick, my dad was in the midst of a nervous breakdown, though none of us knew to call it that at the time. During the entire trip back to

20

Yakima, he didn't speak, not even when asked a direct question. ("How do you feel, Raymond?" "You okay, Dad?") He'd communicate if he communicated at all, by moving his head or by turning his palms up as if to say he didn't know or care. The only time he said anything on the trip, and for nearly a month afterward, was when I was speeding down a gravel road in Oregon and the car muffler came loose. "You were going too fast," he said.

Back in Yakima a doctor saw to it that my dad went to a psychiatrist. My mother and dad had to go on relief, as it was called, and the county paid for the psychiatrist. The psychiatrist asked my dad, "Who is the President?" He'd had a question put to him that he could answer. "Ike," my dad said. Nevertheless, they put him on the fifth floor of Valley Memorial Hospital and began giving him electroshock treatments. I was married by then and about to start my own family. My dad was still locked up when my wife went into this same hospital, just one floor down, to have our first baby. After she had delivered, I went upstairs to give my dad the news. They let me in through a steel door and showed me where I could find him. He was sitting on a couch with a blanket over his lap. *Hey*, I thought. *What in hell is happening to my dad?* I sat down next to him and told him he was a grandfather. He waited a minute and then said, "I feel like a grandfather." That's all he said. He didn't smile or move. He was in a big room with a lot of other people. Then I hugged him, and he began to cry.

Somehow he got out of there. But now came the years when he couldn't work and just sat around the house trying to figure what next and what he'd done wrong in his life that he'd wound up like this. My mother went from job to crummy job. Much later she referred to that time he was in the hospital, and those years just afterward, as "when Raymond was sick." The word *sick* was never the same for me again.

In 1964, through the help of a friend, he was lucky enough to be hired on at a mill in Klamath, California. He moved down there by himself to see if he could hack it. He lived not far from the mill, in a one-room cabin not much different from the place he and my mother had started out living in when they went west. He scrawled letters to my mother, and if I called she'd read them aloud to me over the phone. In the letters, he said it was touch and go. Every day that he went to work, he felt like it was the most important day of his life. But every day, he told her, made the next day that much easier. He said for her to tell me he said hello. If he couldn't sleep at night, he said, he thought about me and the good times we used to have. Finally, after a couple of months, he regained some of his confidence. He could do the work and didn't think he had to worry that he'd let anybody down ever again. When he was sure, he sent for my mother.

He'd been off from work for six years and had lost everything in that time — home, car, furniture, and appliances, including the big freezer that had been my mother's pride and joy. He'd lost his good name too — Raymond Carver was someone who couldn't pay his bills — and his self-respect was gone. He'd even lost his virility. My mother told my wife, "All during that time Raymond was sick we slept together in the same bed, but we didn't have relations. He wanted to a few times, but nothing happened. I didn't miss it, but I think he wanted to, you know."

During those years I was trying to raise my own family and earn a living. But, one thing and another, we found ourselves having to move a lot. I couldn't keep track of what was going down in my dad's life. But I did have a chance one Christmas to tell him I wanted to be a writer. I might as well have told him I wanted to become a plastic surgeon. "What are you going to write about?" he wanted to know. Then, as if to help me out, he said, "Write about stuff you know about. Write about some of those fishing trips we took." I said I would, but I knew I wouldn't. "Send me what you write," he said. I said I'd do that, but then I didn't. I wasn't writing anything about fishing, and I didn't think he'd particularly care about, or even necessarily understand, what I was writing in those days. Besides, he wasn't a reader. Not the sort, anyway, I imagined I was writing for.

Then he died. I was a long way off, in Iowa City, with things still to say to him. I didn't have the chance to tell him goodbye, or that I thought he was doing great at his new job. That I was proud of him for making a comeback.

My mother said he came in from work that night and ate a big supper. 28 Then he sat at the table by himself and finished what was left of a bottle of whiskey, a bottle she found hidden in the bottom of the garbage under some coffee grounds a day or so later. Then he got up and went to bed, where my mother joined him a little later. But in the night she had to get up and make a bed for herself on the couch. "He was snoring so loud I couldn't sleep," she said. The next morning when she looked in on him, he was on his back with his mouth open, his cheeks caved in. *Graylooking,* she said. She knew he was dead — she didn't need a doctor to tell her that. But she called one anyway, and then she called my wife.

Among the pictures my mother kept of my dad and herself during those early days in Washington was a photograph of him standing in front of a car, holding a beer and a stringer of fish. In the photograph he is wearing his hat back on his forehead and has this awkward grin on his face. I asked her for it and she gave it to me, along with some others. I put it up on my wall, and each time we moved, I took the picture along and put it up on another wall. I looked at it carefully from time to time, trying to figure out some things about my dad, and maybe myself in the process. But I couldn't. My dad just kept moving further and further away from me and back into time. Finally, in the course of another move, I lost the photograph. It was then that I tried to recall it, and at the same time make an attempt to say something about my dad, and how I thought that in some important ways we might be alike. I wrote the poem when I was living in an apartment house in an urban area south of San Francisco, at a time when I found myself, like my dad, having trouble with alcohol. The poem was a way of trying to connect up with him.

Photograph of My Father in His Twenty-Second Year

October. Here in this dank, unfamiliar kitchen
I study my father's embarrassed young man's face.
Sheepish grin, he holds in one hand a string
of spiny yellow perch, in the other
a bottle of Carlsberg beer.

In jeans and flannel shirt, he leans
against the front fender of a 1934 Ford.
He would like to pose brave and hearty for his posterity,
wear his old hat cocked over his ear.
All his life my father wanted to be bold.

But the eyes give him away, and the hands
that limply offer the string of dead perch
and the bottle of beer. Father, I love you,
yet how can I say thank you, I who can't hold my liquor
    either
and don't even know the places to fish.

The poem is true in its particulars, except that my dad died in June and not October, as the first word of the poem says. I wanted a word with more than one syllable to it to make it linger a little. But more than that, I wanted a month appropriate to what I felt at the time I wrote the poem — a month of short days and failing light, smoke in the air, things perishing. June was summer nights and days, graduations, my wedding anniversary, the birthday of one of my children. June wasn't a month your father died in.

After the service at the funeral home, after we had moved outside, a woman I didn't know came over to me and said, "He's happier where he is now." I stared at this woman until she moved away. I still remember the little knob of a hat she was wearing. Then one of my dad's cousins — I didn't know the man's name — reached out and took my hand, "We all miss him," he said, and I knew he wasn't saying it just to be polite.

I began to weep for the first time since receiving the news. I hadn't been able to before. I hadn't had the time, for one thing. Now, suddenly, I couldn't stop. I held my wife and wept while she said and did what she could do to comfort me there in the middle of that summer afternoon.

I listened to people say consoling things to my mother, and I was glad that my dad's family had turned up, had come to where he was. I thought

I'd remember everything that was said and done that day and maybe find a way to tell it sometime. But I didn't. I forgot it all, or nearly. What I do remember is that I heard our name used a lot that afternoon, my dad's name and mine. But I knew they were talking about my dad. *Raymond,* these people kept saying in their beautiful voices out of my childhood. *Raymond.*

AFTERWORD

The poet Marianne Moore talked about poetry written "in plain American that dogs and cats can read" — though she did not succeed in writing it. Raymond Carver, whether he writes story, poem, or essay, chooses the common and unpretentious word, the demotic over the literary. Nineteen out of twenty writers in this book would have used "father's" for the second word of this essay. Few of them would have said, five sentences into the story, "which was okay."

Now, the avoidance of affectation can be affectation itself, but Carver is too good a writer to catch himself in any beartrap. Two lines after "okay" he tells us that he "announced" something to his father, where "said" would have done the job: Carver controls an ironic tone by elevating the diction, attributing a touch of pomposity to his younger's self's speech.

With his spare, bare, demotic style, Carver does wonders: The precision of the death date makes its own announcement at the end of the first paragraph, and the second paragraph introduces difficult themes — duplication of father and son, relations of wife and mother — by means of a laconic, bizarre anecdote.

BOOKS AVAILABLE IN PAPERBACK

Cathedral. New York: Random House-Vintage. *Short stories.*

Fires: Essays, Poems, Stories. New York: Random House-Vintage.

Ultramarine. New York: Random House-Vintage. *Poetry.*

What We Talk About When We Talk About Love. New York: Random House-Vintage. *Short stories.*

Will You Please Be Quiet, Please? New York: McGraw-Hill. *Short stories.*

MALCOLM
COWLEY

*M AYBE MALCOLM COWLEY (b. 1898) looks back on "The View from 80"
as youthful work. Vigorous essays have continued to emerge from his
Connecticut house, often in commemoration of younger writers, now dead, whom
Cowley befriended at the beginnings of their careers. His affectionate, acute remi-
niscence of the novelist and short-story writer John Cheever appeared in the
Sewanee Review in 1983.*

*Cowley has much to look back on. He drove an ambulance during World War
I, interrupting his studies at Harvard, and when he graduated in 1920 he returned
to France, where literary Americans lived as expatriates in those days. Cowley
published his first book of poems, Blue Juniata, in 1929 — and almost forty years
later he used the same title for his collected poems. Back in the United States he
became an editor at the New Republic and a freelance writer, professions he has
combined ever since. He was literary advisor for the Viking Press and edited Viking
Portables of Hemingway and Faulkner. He has written many books about writers
and writing. Exile's Return is the best known, chronicling the expatriate generation
Cowley belonged to. It appeared first in 1934 and, extensively revised, in 1951.*

*Age has not slowed him down Who's Who lists five books published by Cowley
after the age of seventy, almost as many as he published before the age of seventy.*

His most recent books, criticism and literary reminiscence, include A Second Flowering *(1973),* And I Worked at the Writer's Trade *(1978), and* The Dream of the Golden Mountains *(1980). In 1981 he received the Gold Medal of the American Academy of Arts and Letters.*

It was appropriate. Cowley has been an old-fashioned man of letters — poet, essayist, editor — which is what he set out to be. "I believed, first of all, that the only respectable ambition for a man of letters was to be a man of letters — not exclusively a novelist, an essayist, a dramatist, but rather one who adopts the whole of literature as his province. . . . I believed that the man of letters, while retaining his own point of view, which was primarily that of the poet, should concern himself with every department of human activity, including science, sociology, and revolution."

It made good sense for the editors of Life *magazine to ask him in 1978 to write about turning eighty — a commission that prompted "The View from 80." Later the essay became the first chapter of a book with the same title, which makes a metaphor of age as vantage point. Cowley writes as a traveler reporting on a landscape many of us will not live to visit. As a writer he knows how to gather and assemble varied material. In this essay Cowley includes research on the literature and scholarship of old age as well as his personal experience of the phenomenon. His attitude toward old age shows itself both in direct statement and, by implication, in the mountaintop he writes from.*

The View from 80

They gave me a party on my 80th birthday in August 1978. First there were cards, letters, telegrams, even a cable of congratulation or condolence; then there were gifts, mostly bottles; there was catered food and finally a big cake with, for some reason, two candles (had I gone back to very early childhood?). I blew the candles out a little unsteadily. Amid the applause and clatter I thought about a former custom of the Northern Ojibwas when they lived on the shore of Lake Winnipeg. They were kind to their old people, who remembered and enforced the ancient customs of the tribe, but when an old person became decrepit, it was time for him to go. Sometimes he was simply abandoned, with a little food, on an island in the lake. If he deserved special honor, they held a tribal feast for him. The old man sang a death song and danced, if he could. While he was still singing, his son came from behind and brained him with a tomahawk.

That was quick, it was dignified, and I wonder whether it was any more cruel, essentially, than some of our civilized customs or inadvertences in disposing of the aged. I believe in rites and ceremonies. I believe in big parties for special occasions such as an 80th birthday. It is a sort of belated bar mitzvah, since the 80-year-old, like a Jewish adolescent, is entering a new stage of life; let him (or her) undergo a *rite de passage*, with toasts and a cantor. Seventy-years-olds, or septuas, have the illusion of being middle-aged, even if they have been pushed back on a shelf. The 80-year-old, the octo, looks at the double-dumpling figure and admits that he is old. That last act has begun, and it will be the test of the play.

He has joined a select minority that numbers, in this country, 4,842,000 persons (according to Census Bureau estimates for 1977), or about two percent of the American population. Two-thirds of the octos are women, who have retained the good habit of living longer than men. Someday you, the reader, will join that minority, if you escape hypertension and cancer, the two killers, and if you survive the dangerous years 75 to 79, when half the survivors till then are lost. With advances in medicine, the living space taken over by octos is growing larger year by year.

To enter the country of age is a new experience, different from what 4 you supposed it to be. Nobody, man or woman, knows the country until he has lived in it and has taken out his citizenship papers. Here is my own report, submitted as a road map and guide to some of the principal monuments.

The new octogenarian feels as strong as ever when he is sitting back in a comfortable chair. He ruminates, he dreams, he remembers. He doesn't want to be disturbed by others. It seems to him that old age is only a costume assumed for those others; the true, the essential self is ageless. In a moment he will rise and go for a ramble in the woods, taking a gun along, or a fishing rod, if it is spring. Then he creaks to his feet, bending forward to keep his balance, and realizes that he will do nothing of the sort. The body and its surroundings have their messages for him, or only one message: "You are old." Here are some of the occasions on which he receives the message:

- when it becomes an achievement to do thoughtfully, step by step, what he once did instinctively
- when his bones ache
- when there are more and more little bottles in the medicine cabinet, with instructions for taking four times a day
- when he fumbles and drops his toothbrush (butterfingers)
- when his face has bumps and wrinkles, so that he cuts himself while shaving (blood on the towel)
- when year by year his feet seem farther from his hands
- when he can't stand on one leg and has trouble pulling on his pants

- when he hesitates on the landing before walking down a flight of stairs
- when he spends more time looking for things misplaced than he spends using them after he (or more often his wife) has found them
- when he falls asleep in the afternoon
- when it becomes harder to bear in mind two things at once
- when a pretty girl passes him in the street and he doesn't turn his head
- when he forgets names, even of people he saw last month ("Now I'm beginning to forget nouns," the poet Conrad Aiken said at 80)
- when he listens hard to jokes and catches everything but the snapper
- when he decides not to drive at night anymore
- when everything takes longer to do — bathing, shaving, getting dressed or undressed — but when time passes quickly, as if he were gathering speed while coasting downhill. The year from 79 to 80 is like a week when he was a boy.

Those are some of the intimate messages. "Put cotton in your ears and pebbles in your shoes," said a gerontologist, a member of that new profession dedicated to alleviating all maladies of old people except the passage of years. "Pull on rubber gloves. Smear Vaseline over your glasses, and there you have it: instant aging." Not quite. His formula omits the messages from the social world, which are louder, in most cases, than those from within. We start by growing old in other people's eyes, then slowly we come to share their judgment.

I remember a morning many years ago when I was backing out of the parking lot near the railroad station in Brewster, New York. There was a near collision. The driver of the other car jumped out and started to abuse me; he had his fists ready. Then he looked hard at me and said, "Why, you're an old man." He got back into his car, slammed the door, and drove away, while I stood there fuming. "I'm only 65," I thought. "He wasn't driving carefully. I can still take care of myself in a car, or in a fight, for that matter."

My hair was whiter — it may have been in 1974 — when a young 8 woman rose and offered me her seat in a Madison Avenue bus. That message was kind and also devastating. "Can't I even stand up?" I thought as I thanked her and declined the seat. But the same thing happened twice the following year, and the second time I gratefully accepted the offer, though with a sense of having diminished myself. "People are right about me," I thought while wondering why all those kind gestures were made by women. Do men now regard themselves as the weaker sex, not called upon to show consideration? All the same it was a relief to sit down and relax.

A few days later I wrote a poem, "The Red Wagon," that belongs in the record of aging:

For his birthday they gave him a red express wagon
with a driver's high seat and a handle that steered.
His mother pulled him around the yard.
"Giddyap," he said, but she laughed and went off
to wash the breakfast dishes.

"I wanta ride too," his sister said,
and he pulled her to the edge of a hill.
"Now, sister, go home and wait for me,
but first give a push to the wagon."

He climbed again to the high seat,
this time grasping that handle-that-steered.
The red wagon rolled slowly down the slope,
then faster as it passed the schoolhouse
and faster as it passed the store,
the road still dropping away.
Oh, it was fun.

But would it ever stop?
Would the road always go downhill?

The red wagon rolled faster
Now it was in strange country.
It passed a white house he must have dreamed about,
deep woods he had never seen,
a graveyard where, something told him, his sister was buried.

Far below
the sun was sinking into a broad plain.

The red wagon rolled faster.
Now he was clutching the seat, not even trying to steer.
Sweat clouded his heavy spectacles.
His white hair streamed in the wind.

Even before he or she is 80, the aging person may undergo another identity crisis like that of adolescence. Perhaps there had also been a middle-aged crisis, the male or the female menopause, but the rest of adult life he had taken himself for granted, with his capabilities and failings. Now, when he looks in the mirror, he asks himself, "Is this really me?" — or he avoids the mirror out of distress at what it reveals, those bags and wrinkles. In his new makeup he is called upon to play a new role in a play that must be improvised. André Gide, that long-lived man of letters, wrote in his journal, "My heart has remained so young that I have the continual feeling of playing a part, the part of the 70-year-old that I certainly am; and the infirmities and weaknesses that remind me of my age act like a prompter, reminding me of my lines when I tend to stray. Then, like the good actor I want to be, I go back into my role, and I pride myself on playing it well."

In his new role the old person will find that he is tempted by new vices, that he receives new compensations (not so widely known), and that he may possibly achieve new virtues. Chief among these is the heroic or merely obstinate refusal to surrender in the face of time. One admires the ships that go down with all flags flying and the captain on the bridge.

Among the vices of age are avarice, untidiness, and vanity, which last 12 takes the form of a craving to be loved or simply admired. Avarice is the worst of those three. Why do so many old persons, men and women alike, insist on hoarding money when they have no prospect of using it and even when they have no heirs? They eat the cheapest food, buy no clothes, and live in a single room when they could afford better lodging. It may be that they regard money as a form of power; there is a comfort in watching it accumulate while other powers are dwindling away. How often we read of an old person found dead in a hovel, on a mattress partly stuffed with bankbooks and stock certificates! The bankbook syndrome, we call it in our family, which has never succumbed.

Untidiness we call the Langley Collyer syndrome. To explain, Langley Collyer was a former concert pianist who lived alone with his 70-year-old brother in a brownstone house on upper Fifth Avenue. The once fashionable neighborhood had become part of Harlem. Homer, the brother, had been an admiralty lawyer, but was now blind and partly paralyzed; Langley played for him and fed him on buns and oranges, which he thought would restore Homer's sight. He never threw away a daily paper because Homer, he said, might want to read them all. He saved other things as well and the house became filled with rubbish from roof to basement. The halls were lined on both sides with bundled newspapers, leaving narrow passageways in which Langley had devised booby traps to catch intruders.

On March 21, 1947, some unnamed person telephoned the police to report that there was a dead body in the Collyer house. The police broke down the front door and found the hall impassable; then they hoisted a ladder to a second-story window. Behind it Homer was lying on the floor in a bathrobe; he had starved to death. Langley had disappeared. After some delay, the police broke into the basement, chopped a hole in the roof, and began throwing junk out of the house, top and bottom. It was 18 days before they found Langley's body, gnawed by rats. Caught in one of his own booby traps, he had died in a hallway just outside Homer's door. By that time the police had collected, and the Department of Sanitation had hauled away, 120 tons of rubbish, including, besides the newspapers, 14 grand pianos and the parts of a dismantled Model T Ford.

Why do so many old people accumulate junk, not on the scale of Langley Collyer, but still in a dismaying fashion? Their tables are piled high with it, their bureau drawers are stuffed with it, their closet rods bend with the weight of clothes not worn for years. I suppose that the piling up is partly from lethargy and partly from the feeling that everything once useful, including their own bodies, should be preserved. Others, though not so many, have such a fear of becoming Langley Collyers that they strive to be painfully neat. Every tool they own is in its place, though it will never be used again; every scrap of paper is filed away in alphabetical order. At last their immoderate neatness becomes another vice of age, if a milder one.

The vanity of older people is an easier weakness to explain, and to   16
condone. With less to look forward to, they yearn for recognition of what they have been: the reigning beauty, the athlete, the soldier, the scholar. It is the beauties who have the hardest time. A portrait of themselves at twenty hangs on the wall, and they try to resemble it by making an extravagant use of creams, powders, and dyes. Being young at heart, they think they are merely revealing their essential persons. The athletes find shelves for their silver trophies, which are polished once a year. Perhaps a letter sweater lies wrapped in a bureau drawer. I remember one evening when a no-longer athlete had guests for dinner and tried to find his sweater. "Oh, that old thing," his wife said. "The moths got into it and I threw it away." The athlete sulked and his guests went home early.

Often the yearning to be recognized appears in conversation as an innocent boast. Thus, a distinguished physician, retired at 94, remarks casually that a disease was named after him. A former judge bursts into chuckles as he repeats bright things that he said on the bench. Aging scholars complain in letters (or one of them does), "As I approach 70 I'm becoming avid of honors, and such things — medals, honorary degrees, etc. — are only passed around among academics on a *quid pro quo*° basis (one hood capping another)." Or they say querulously, "Bill Underwood has ten honorary doctorates and I have only three. Why didn't they elect me to . . . ?" and they mention the name of some learned society. That search for honors is a harmless passion, though it may lead to jealousies and deformations of character, as with Robert Frost in his later years. Still, honors cost little. Why shouldn't the very old have more than their share of them?

To be admired and praised, especially by the young, is an autumnal pleasure enjoyed by the lucky ones (who are not always the most deserving). "What is more charming," Cicero° observes in his famous essay *De Senectute*, "than an old age surrounded by the enthusiasm of youth! . . . Attentions which seem trivial and conventional are marks of honors — the morning call, being sought after, precedence, having people rise for you, being escorted to and from the forum. . . . What pleasures of the body can

---

Quid pro quo   Something given for something received.
Cicero   Roman orator and philosopher, 106–43 B.C.

be compared to the prerogatives of influence?" But there are also pleasures of the body, or the mind, that are enjoyed by a greater number of older persons.

Those pleasures include some that younger people find hard to appreciate. One of them is simply sitting still, like a snake on a sun-warmed stone, with a delicious feeling of indolence that was seldom attained in earlier years. A leaf flutters down; a cloud moves by inches across the horizon. At such moments the older person, completely relaxed, has become a part of nature — and a living part, with blood coursing through his veins. The future does not exist for him. He thinks, if he thinks at all, that life for younger persons is still a battle royal of each against each, but that now he has nothing more to win or lose. He is not so much above as outside the battle, as if he had assumed the uniform of some small neutral country, perhaps Liechtenstein or Andorra. From a distance he notes that some of the combatants, men or women, are jostling ahead — but why do they fight so hard when the most they can hope for is a longer obituary? He can watch the scrounging and gouging, he can hear the shouts of exultation, the moans of the gravely wounded, and meanwhile he feels secure; nobody will attack him from ambush.

Age has other physical compensations besides the nirvana of dozing in 20 the sun. A few of the simplest needs become a pleasure to satisfy. When an old woman in a nursing home was asked what she really liked to do, she answered in one word: "Eat." She might have been speaking for many of her fellows. Meals in a nursing home, however badly cooked, serve as climactic moments of the day. The physical essence of the pensioners is being renewed at an appointed hour; now they can go back to meditating or to watching TV while looking forward to the next meal. They can also look forward to sleep, which has become a definite pleasure, not the mere interruption it once had been.

Here I am thinking of old persons under nursing care. Others ferociously guard their independence, and some of them suffer less than one might expect from being lonely and impoverished. They can be rejoiced by visits and meetings, but they also have company inside their heads. Some of them are busiest when their hands are still. What passes through the minds of many is a stream of persons, images, phrases, and familiar tunes. For some that stream has continued since childhood, but now it is deeper; it is their present and their past combined. At times they conduct silent dialogues with a vanished friend, and these are less tiring — often more rewarding — than spoken conversations. If inner resources are lacking, old persons living alone may seek comfort and a kind of companionship in the bottle. I should judge from the gossip of various neighborhoods that the outer suburbs from Boston to San Diego are full of secretly alcoholic widows. One of those widows, an old friend, was moved from her apartment into a retirement home. She left behind her a closet in which the floor was covered wall to wall with whiskey bottles. "Oh, those empty bottles!" she explained. "They were left by a former tenant."

Not whiskey or cooking sherry but simply giving up is the greatest temptation of age. It is something different from a stoical acceptance of infirmities, which is something to be admired. At 63, when he first recognized that his powers were failing, Emerson wrote one of his best poems, "Terminus":

> It is time to be old,
> To take in sail: —
> The god of bounds,
> Who sets to seas a shore,
> Came to me in his fatal rounds,
> And said: "No more!
> No farther shoot
> Thy broad ambitious branches, and thy root.
> Fancy departs: no more invent;
> Contract thy firmament
> To compass of a tent."

Emerson lived in good health to the age of 79. Within his narrowed firmament, he continued working until his memory failed; then he consented to having younger editors and collaborators. The givers-up see no reason for working. Sometimes they lie in bed all day when moving about would still be possible, if difficult. I had a friend, a distinguished poet, who surrendered in that fashion. The doctors tried to stir him to action, but he refused to leave his room. Another friend, once a successful artist, stopped painting when his eyes began to fail. His doctor made the mistake of telling him that he suffered from a fatal disease. He then lost interest in everything except the splendid Rolls-Royce, acquired in his prosperous days, that stood in the garage. Daily he wiped the dust from its hood. He couldn't drive it on the road any longer, but he used to sit in the driver's seat, start the motor, then back the Rolls out of the garage and drive it in again, back twenty feet and forward twenty feet; that was his only distraction.

I haven't the right to blame those who surrender, not being able to put 24 myself inside their minds or bodies. Often they must have compelling reasons, physical or moral. Not only do they suffer from a variety of ailments, but also they are made to feel that they no longer have a function in the community. Their families and neighbors don't ask them for advice, don't really listen when they speak, don't call on them for efforts. One notes that there are not a few recoveries from apparent senility when that situation changes. If it doesn't change, old persons may decide that efforts are useless. I sympathize with their problems, but the men and women I envy are those who accept old age as a series of challenges.

For such persons, every new infirmity is an enemy to be outwitted, an obstacle to be overcome by force of will. They enjoy each little victory over themselves, and sometimes they win a major success. Renoir was one of them. He continued painting, and magnificently, for years after he was crippled by arthritis; the brush had to be strapped to his arm. "You don't need your hand to paint," he said. Goya was another of the unvanquished. At 72 he retired as an official painter of the Spanish court and decided to work only for himself. His later years were those of the famous "black paintings" in which he let his imagination run (and also of the lithographs, then a new technique). At 78 he escaped a reign of terror in Spain by fleeing to Bordeaux. He was deaf and his eyes were failing; in order to work he had to wear several pairs of spectacles, one over another, and then use a magnifying glass; but he was producing splendid work in a totally new style. At 80 he drew an ancient man propped on two sticks, with a mass of white hair and beard hiding his face and with the inscription "I am still learning."

Giovanni Papini said when he was nearly blind, "I prefer martyrdom to imbecility." After writing sixty books, including his famous *Life of Christ,* he was at work on two huge projects when he was stricken with a form of muscular atrophy. He lost the use of his left leg, then of his fingers, so that he couldn't hold a pen. The two big books, though never to be finished, moved forward slowly by dictation; that in itself was a triumph. Toward the end, when his voice had become incomprehensible, he spelled out a word, tapping on the table to indicate letters of the alphabet. One hopes never to be faced with the need for such heroic measures.

"Eighty years old!" the great Catholic poet Paul Claudel wrote in his journal. "No eyes left, no ears, no teeth, no legs, no wind! And when all is said and done, how astonishingly well one does without them!"

Yeats is the great modern poet of age, though he died — I am now 28 tempted to say — as a mere stripling of 73. His reaction to growing old was not that of a stoic like Emerson or Cicero, bent on obeying nature's laws and the edicts of Terminus, the god "Who sets to seas a shore"; it was that of a romantic rebel, the Faustian° man. He was only 61 when he wrote (in "The Tower"):

> What shall I do with this absurdity —
> O heart, O troubled heart — this caricature,
> Decrepit age that has been tied to me
> As to a dog's tail?

Faustian   In German legend, Faust sells his soul to the devil in return for ultimate knowledge and eternal youth.

At 68 he began to be worried because he wasn't producing many new poems. Could it be, he must have wondered, that his libido had lost its force and that it was somehow connected with his imagination? He had the Faustian desire for renewed youth, felt almost universally, but in Yeats's case with a stronger excuse, since his imagination was the center of his life. A friend told him, with gestures, about Dr. Steinach's then famous operation designed to rejuvenate men by implanting new sex glands. The operation has since fallen into such medical disfavor that Steinach's name is nowhere mentioned in the latest edition of *The Encyclopaedia Britannica*. But Yeats read a pamphlet about it in the Trinity College library, in Dublin, and was favorably impressed. After consulting a physician, who wouldn't say yes or no, he arranged to have the operation performed in a London clinic; that was in May 1934.

Back in Dublin he felt himself to be a different man. Oliver St. John Gogarty, himself a physician, reports a conversation with Yeats that took place the following summer. "I was horrified," he says, "to hear when it was too late that he had undergone such an operation. 'On both sides?' I asked.

"'Yes,' he acknowledged.

"'But, why on earth did you not consult anyone?'   32

"'I read a pamphlet.'

"'What was wrong with you?'

"'I used to fall asleep after lunch.'"

It was no use making a serious answer to Gogarty the jester. He tells 36 us in his memoir of Yeats that the poet claimed to have been greatly benefited by the operation, but adds, "I have reason to believe that this was not so. He had reached the age when he would not take 'Yes' for an answer." Gogarty's judgment as a physician was probably right; the poet's physical health did not improve and in fact deteriorated. One conjectures that the operation may have put an added strain on his heart and thus may have shortened his life by years. Psychologically, however, Yeats was transformed. He began to think of himself as "the wild old wicked man," and in that character he wrote dozens of poems in a new style, direct, earthy, and passionate. One of them reads:

> You think it horrible that lust and rage
> Should dance attention upon my old age;
> They were not such a plague when I was young;
> What else have I to spur me into song?

False remedies are sometimes beneficial in their own fashion. What artists would not sacrifice a few years of life in order to produce work on a level with Yeats's *Last Poems*? Early in January 1939, he wrote to his friend Lady Elizabeth Pelham:

I know for certain that my time will not be long. . . . I am happy, and I think full of energy, of an energy I had despaired of. It seems to me that I have found what I wanted. When I try to put all into a phrase I say, "Man can embody truth but he cannot know it." I must embody it in the completion of my life.

His very last poem, and one of the best, is "The Black Tower," dated the 21st of that month. Yeats died a week after writing it.

AFTERWORD

In the book that began with this essay, Malcolm Cowley surveyed the literature of aging. The Latin orator and statesman Cicero wrote about old age, in **De Senectute**, *when he was merely middle-aged. He avoided the conditions of advanced age, in a fashion commonplace during the civil wars that established the Roman Empire, by having his head cut off. Another essayist of the aging process was Michel de Montaigne, four hundred years ago the inventor of the essay as we know it, who wrote about old age when he was forty-seven. Montaigne's* essais *emphasized by their name (from the French for "trial" or "test") the tentative, modest, and personal: a prose composition on a subject, setting forth the author's opinion or experience; an endeavor or an attempt (in gesture) without the manner of deeming itself the last word on the subject.*

Malcolm Cowley's essay is classic in form — but it does not appear so. It appears informal, personal ("They gave me a party . . ."); it carries its considerable information with a light touch. Even the beginning example of the Northern Ojibwas, a zinger of an opening, drops into place with a modest if dreadful humor. From this example he is able to move into consideration of our own culture's treatment of the old and deftly deposit some useful statistics. These numbers are useful: They also provide a stone foundation of apparent objectivity upon which the essay can construct the frailer house of private testimony. For Cowley the analogy is not architectural but geographical, "the country of old age."

Beginning with paragraph 5, the heart of this essay is personal observation, experience wittily recounted: the feeling *of growing old. A personal voice addresses us; readers with imagination or compassion responds to the voice that touches them. The first anecdote of paragraph 5 gives a new habitation and a name to an old insight. Then Cowley lists messages, as he calls them, visually isolating them as if they were telegrams. Or the list resembles a free verse poem, each line rhythmically distinct and grammatically variant, each beginning with a parallel "when." This is the device of the list, notes of detail and experience spread out on the page. Paragraph 6 alludes to a vivid anecdote of aging's effects, then uses it as a transition from the* internal sensations of age to the sensations of the outside world's response to the old.

The structure of a good essay appears casual, like a person talking, while it executes the designs of art. Between Gide and the painters and writers who triumph over the adversity of aging — positive models — Cowley inserts a series of bad models, terrors, and warnings. He uses a trinity of abstractions — avarice, untidiness, vanity — and specifies or particularizes by different methods — by example, by anecdote, and by allusion — generalized stories of greed or miserliness, the Collyer brothers, and vanity in several forms, including a reference to the aging Robert Frost.

When we finish the essay — or more likely when we finish it a second time, sleep on it for two nights, and glance at it again to refresh our minds — we understand that we have been manipulated and we are happy about it: The apparently rambling ruminations of an agreeable old sort turns out to be the art of a scrupulous writer.

BOOKS AVAILABLE IN PAPERBACK

And I Worked at the Writer's Trade: Chapters of Literary History, 1918–1978. New York: Penguin. Nonfiction.

Blue Juniata: A Life. New York: Penguin. Poetry.

The Dream of the Golden Mountains: Remembering the 1930s. New York: Penguin. Nonfiction.

Exile's Return: A Literary Odyssey of the 1920s. New York: Penguin. Nonfiction.

The Faulkner-Cowley File: Letters and Memories, 1944–1962. New York: Penguin. Nonfiction.

The Flower and the Leaf. New York: Penguin. Nonfiction.

Many-Windowed House: Collected Essays on American Writers and American Writing. Carbondale: Southern Illinois University Press. Essays.

A Second Flowering: Works and Days of the Lost Generation. New York: Penguin. Nonfiction.

Think Back on Us: A Contemporary Chronicle of the 1930s. 2 vols. Carbondale: Southern Illinois University Press. Nonfiction.

GUY
DAVENPORT

*G*UY DAVENPORT *is a poet, short-story writer, essayist, translator, librettist,
and illustrator. Born in South Carolina (1927), he took a B.A. at Duke
University, a B.Litt. at Oxford University (Merton College), where he was a Rhodes
scholar, and a Ph.D. at Harvard University. Since 1963 he has taught at the
University of Kentucky along with (from time to time) Wendell Berry. His translations are mostly from the Greek — Archilochus, Heraclitus, Alcman, Sappho. His
poems are collected in* Flowers and Leaves *(1966) and* Thasos and Ohio *(1986).
He has provided libretti for contemporary composers.* Da Vinci's Bicycle *(1979)
was his first book of short stories — formally innovative or experimental — followed
by* Eclogues *(1981) and* Apples and Pears *(1984). His books of essays are*
Geographies of the Imagination *(1981) and* Every Force Evolves a Form
*(1987), which included "Making It Uglier to the Airport." His drawings have
illustrated his own work and translations from Virgil and Horace.*

*Some of Davenport's essays are as inventive as his stories; others are book
reviews, conventional in appearance, written with unusual wit in a usual form.
Although his work is often innovative, he considers it impersonal; his writing, he
says, comes out of the classroom, and he is "primarily a teacher." "The translations*

. . . are meant to serve the Greekless, as my stories are lessons in history. My poems are lessons in aesthetics. There is room enough for self-expression in even the most rigorously scholarly writing, and thus I have avoided all temptations to use writing for personal expression."

Making It Uglier to the Airport

Every building in the United States is an offense to invested capital. It occupies space which, as greed acknowledges no limits, can be better utilized. This depressing fact can be thought of as a kind of disease of the American city for which the only specific is law, and, to make a wild gesture toward common sense, aesthetics. One might as well say that multiple sclerosis can be cured with cough drops.

In Chicago six years ago they tore down Adler and Sullivan's Old Stock Exchange, a perfectly useful building. That it was bone and blood of Chicago history, that it was an architectural landmark, that its ornamentation was beautiful and irreplaceable were arguments that could not save it. Money has no ears, no eyes, no respect; it is all gut, mouth, and ass. The Heller International Building went up in its place, a glass cracker-box forty-three stories high. Its mortgage payments are $400,000 every first of the month: interest — *interest,* money which bankers earn by tightening their shoelaces, yawning, and testing teakwood surfaces for dust — on a $48,300,000 loan. The building cost $51,000,000, and is up for grabs, as the speculators can't hold on to it. This time nobody cares if, as they shall, they tear it down and put up something more "economically viable," as they say.

Heaps of New York are being torn down because what's left over after property taxes isn't quite what our greedy hearts would like to take to our investment broker. Between the banker and the tax-collector, life can be very hell. But then, they built the cities in the first place. One of the greatest of architects built snowmen for the Medici children (a use of Michelangelo we would have expected of J. Pierpont Morgan° sooner than Lorenzo the Magnificent°); all architects are now sculptors in ice.

J. Pierpont Morgan   (1837–1913), American industrialist-tycoon, notably in steel and banking, and also a patron of the arts.
Lorenzo the Magnificent   (1449–1492), head of the wealthy, influential Medici family

Ada Louise Huxtable, who writes about architecture and city planning 4
for the *Times*, has collected a batch of her terse essays on buildings going
up and coming down, on design, and practically anything else that her
lively eye hits on.[1] Her comments are all arrows of the chase, released when
the aim seemed good, and with some fine hits. Like all such writing, you
can feel the pressure of the deadline on her attention. She turns up many
problems (the war, apparently to the death, between city design and real-
estate adventurers; the coherence of American cityscape; the preservation
of landmarks; the tension between contemporaneity and tradition) that I
would like to have seen her expand and explore.

While I was reading her essays, I happened to run across Manfredo
Tafuri's *Architecture and Utopia: Design and Capitalist Development*, which I
saw in the MIT catalogue when I was ordering Dolores Hayden's fine survey
of American utopian communities.[2] Tafuri traces the decay and disorder of
cities to the rise of commercial centers during the industrial revolution,
causing cities to enter a paranoia of identity. His little book is worth reading
— worth studying with care — but it gleams and blinds with too much
Marxist intellect for me to pretend to discuss it here. The one idea that I
want to take from it is that what we call a city bears little resemblance to
the historical city or to cities outside the United States. Yet our cities still
sit on top of a living archaeological base that used to be a city in the old
sense. The automobile and the truck have shaved the yards to mere margins
in the quiet residential sections; the streets have become freeways all over
every city and town. Automobile exhaust, equal in volume daily to that of
the Atlantic Ocean, has replaced breathable air. The automobile is an insect
that eats cities, and its parking lots are a gangrene.

The simple fact is that cities in America came into being not as the
historical city did, for mutual protection and to be the home of a specific
family of people, but as commercial ports. That is, their model was the
kind of prosperous city Defoe describes in the first inventory the mercantile
class made of itself, his *Tour Thro' the Whole Island of Great Britain* (1724–26).
All important elements were in walking distance of each other; *nearness*
defined the city. If it grew large, each neighborhood (as in Paris and London
today) remained a conglomerate of components within easy reach.

---

in Florence during the height of the Italian Renaissance, patron of Michelangelo and
other Renaissance artists.

[1]Ada Louise Huxtable, *Kicked a Building Lately?* (New York: Quadrangle, 1976). [Num-
bered footnotes are Davenport's notes.]

[2]Manfredo Tafuri, *Architecture and Utopia: Design and Capitalist Development*, trans.
Barbara Luigia La Penta (Cambridge: MIT Press, 1976). Dolores Hayden, *Seven American
Utopias: The Architecture of Communitarian Socialism, 1790–1975* (Cambridge: MIT Press,
1976).

Within the last twenty years the automobile has gradually canceled this definition of the city as a community. And the smaller the city, the larger the inconvenience has grown. When I moved to Lexington, Kentucky, fifteen years ago, I could walk to three supermarkets in my neighborhood, to the post office, and to the mayor's house, which happened to be around the corner. All three markets have moved miles away, to the belt line; God knows where they have put the post office. I have been there but once since they moved it. It took me an hour to get there, and an hour to get back. It is technically in the next county, and is near no habitation of any citizen. Only some desolate warehouses does it have for company. This happened when Nixon and his government of scoundrels, liars, and sneaks had us *scrotum in mano*° and I assumed that sheer hatefulness snatched the post office from downtown and put it out in the horse pastures.

The post office, in any case, was only good for buying stamps at. When I tried to renew my passport there a few years ago, a passport kept functional for thirty years, I was told that if I couldn't show a driver's licence I couldn't renew my passport. (I will not spin out the Gogolian scene that ensued, though it featured my being told that I didn't deserve to live in this country, my pointing out that I could scarcely leave it without a passport, and on around in circles that left the art of Gogol for that of Ionesco,° until I got the State Department on the phone, and had my new passport, together with an apology, in three days.) The point of the anecdote is that the pedestrian is officially a second-rate citizen and definitely an obsolete species.

Where the mayor moved to I do not know. The neighborhood is now zoned for business. Henry Clay's townhouse, part of the neighborhood, sits in a tarred-over parking lot.[3]

I had not realized before reading Dolores Hayden's *Seven American Utopias* that the Civil War marked the end of utopian experimentation in American communities. We now know how very much of modern design derives from Shaker clarity and integrity, and how useful, if only as models to modify or tolerate, the Owenite, Fourierist, Moravian,° and other eccentric societies were.

---

scrotum in mano Literally, in Latin, "scrotum in hand"; in English, a crude expression meaning exerting fierce control over someone.

Gogolian . . . Gogol . . . Ionesco Nikolai Gogol (1809–1852), a Russian essayist, novelist, and satirist, considered the father of realism in Russian literature; Eugène Ionesco (b. 1912), a French playwright and master of the theater of the absurd.

[3]There is an excellent essay on the kinds of cities bequeathed us by history as paradigms, in *Salmagundi* No. 24 (Fall 1973), "The City under Attack" by George Steiner. This is a rich essay, with long historical perspectives. He shows us that much of what we take to be peculiarly modern ills are in fact very old, and that our double tradition, classical and Judaeo-Christian, gives us two distinct ideas of what a city is.

Owenite . . . Fourierist . . . Moravian Related to utopian communities founded,

Acceleration in culture is demonic, and there ought to be periodic recesses to look back and reclaim elements that were ditched along the way. To read Dolores Hayden is to see how much we elbowed aside, or smothered, or deliberately obliterated. Fourier's phalanx seems to be a congenial mode of life that might have forestalled our present alienation of the young, the old, and the lonely. Shaker respect for materials is certainly the corrective we need for our present norm of tacky shoddiness, for mushroom proliferation. Shaker morals wouldn't be amiss, either.

Backward surveys can also turn up some astonishing forks in the road. 12 Alison Sky and Michelle Stone have compiled what amounts to a treasury of American designs, from cities to individual buildings, that never made it from the blueprint into actuality.[4] One purpose of this book was to assess our architectural legacy — designs, for instance, that might still be realized. There is a postmortem career awaiting Frank Lloyd Wright; all great architects are ahead of their times. Sadly, many of these plans have been chucked into the wastebasket. An architect's firm is a business, not an archive. Not even so distinguished a figure as Frederick Law Olmsted was spared this kind of careless destruction. A vigorous society might well build Thomas Jefferson's President's House, if only in Disneyland, where, in effect, Jacques J. B. Benedict's Summer Capitol for President Woodrow Wilson (projected for Mt. Falcon, Colorado) already stands — it looks like an Arthur Rackham drawing for Mad Ludwig of Bavaria. Many of these rejected designs are lugubrious and hilarious: a robber-baron New Versailles for Manhasset Bay, Long Island, that would have been the biggest building in the world, something that Hitler and Albert Speer might have drooled over; art-book cathedrals recapitulating the whole span of the Gothic in Europe, beacons taller than Everest, Babylonian banks, war memorials that would have trivialized the Pyramids, linear towns with highways for halls, space islands, underground metropolises, a New Harmony phalanx that looks like a Victorian penitentiary crossbred with Flash Gordon's spacecraft port. And yet these designs are full of attractive and charming ideas: a Manhattan with separate thoroughfares for pedestrians and traffic, garden cities, beautiful vistas that would have made Chicago as handsome as Paris, and buildings that ought to have existed for the fun of it, William McKinley Xanadus, palaces, follies — outrageous flowers for the granite forest.

The depressing obliteration of communities can sometimes be as thorough as Noah's Flood. New Burlington, Ohio, a town between Dayton and

---

respectively, by Robert Owen in New Harmony, Indiana (1825); Charles Fourier at Brook Farm in Massachusetts (1844); and the Moravian evangelical sect at Bethlehem, Pennsylvania (1740).

[4] Alison Sky and Michelle Stone, *Unbuilt America: Forgotten Architecture in the United States from Thomas Jefferson to the Space Age* (New York: McGraw-Hill, 1976).

Cincinnati, is now at the bottom of a lake created, as it often seems, to keep the Army Corps of Engineers busy. Before New Burlington went under, an extraordinarily sensitive writer, John Baskin, talked with the old-timers and recorded their memories. The resulting book is poignant and, if you're in a reflective mood or of a pessimistic turn, heartbreaking. The obituary of an entire town has the aura of doom all over it. The only horror of death is in waiting for it, and here was a community that knew its doom: not of life, but of so much of it that the difference perhaps is not account-able. The terror of Hektor's death was that, moments before his heart tasted Achilles' blade,° he had to run past places where he had played as a boy. John Baskin carefully avoids dramatics in this book. His business was to hear the past. In the process, however, it dawned on him that American life has changed. What's different is that whereas just a few years ago we all had something to do, now we don't.

It is tempting to believe that New Burlington, Ohio, was built before the Civil War (partly by Methodists, partly by Quakers) by people for whom skill and hard work were as natural a fact as breathing, and that it went underwater because a society had emerged that is neurotic with idleness and pointlessness. (The Red River Gorge in Kentucky was saved from flooding by the Corps of Engineers because when our governor asked the corps *why* they wanted to obliterate so much natural beauty, they could not give an answer.)

It is good to know, on the other hand, that a small community can fight and can win against the restless greed of investment capital and botchers of all breeds. A nameless town in California has so far held out over a sudden influx of developers and do-gooders working together. The do-gooders noticed the town when it was gunked up by an oil spill (halt and give some time to the ironies that crisscross here). During the cleanup it was noticed that the community had an inadequate sewer system. This attracted the money boys from a water company, who convinced the state that vast sums must be spent to get everybody onto a flushing toilet. This alerted the osmagogue° bankers, who alerted the real-estate gang. As long as this community — half retired folk, largely hermits, half young utopians who had fled the city — was to be modernized, so thought the developers, let's pop in resort hotels, Burger Kings, miniature golf, redwood-shingle condominiums, and let's see these old geezers and hippies clear the hell out.

The struggle and triumph of this community (not named, for its own 16

Hektor . . . Achilles' blade In the *Iliad*, Hektor is the Trojan hero slain in his own Troy by Achilles, the Greek hero.
osmagogue Stimulating to the sense of smell.

protection) is presented in a thoroughly good book.[5] Orville Schell, who has written well and humanely about Chinese communes, shows how a community that is eccentric, almost centerless, and even casual, can knit together and drive away the bulldozer, sanitary engineer, and real-estate shark. He presents his problem in a paragraph that it would be brutal to paraphrase:

> A town which is a community is a delicate organism. As yet, it has virtually no legal means at its disposal by which to protect itself from those who choose to search it out. Unlike an individual, it cannot sue for invasion of privacy. It cannot effectively determine how many people can live in it. It cannot even decide for itself the number of visitors with which it feels comfortable. The roads are there; anyone may travel on them. A commercial establishment is free to advertise the town's name and its desirable attributes in the hopes of attracting people to it in order to make money. If the people who call that town home find the influx of people, cars, and money unsettling, they have little recourse.

If those words were attributed to a New England Conservative complaining about Italian immigrants, or to Robert Moses° complaining about the influx of Puerto Ricans, they would outrage Liberal ears. Paradoxically they illustrate how accurately we must understand a writer's point of view. "Organism" is the word to hold on to. Schell's words are true, and astutely stated. The nature of the organism determines what kind of turbulence it can tolerate.

Poland survived the Second World War better than my hometown in South Carolina. Main Street has rotted into a wasteland. Gracious old homes came down to make way for used-car lots, tacky little finance companies, and drive-in hamburger pavilions. The seven ancient oaks that stood around the house where Thomas Wolfe's sister lived fell to the power saw, and the house itself, deporched, hoked up with neon and Coca-Cola signs, was islanded in a desolation of tar paving and converted into an eatery called, with that genius of the destroyer for taunting, The Seven Oaks. Some two miles of magnolia shade became a glare of festooned light bulbs, and all the used-car dealers are named Shug and Bubber, a semiology I am not equipped to explore. The ugliness of it all is visual migraine. And yet a mayor and his councilmen let it happen. The American politician may

---

[5]Orville Schell, *The Town That Fought to Save Itself*, with photographs by Ilka Hartmann (New York: Pantheon Books, 1976).
Robert Moses (1888–1981), powerful New York City planner who wielded a far-ranging influence over the urban environment from the thirties through the sixties.

be a psychological type, like the kleptomaniac, peeping tom, or exhibition-ist. He is the only professional who may apply for a job and present as his credentials the blatant and unashamed fact that he has none. (Lincoln Steffens° was surprised to discover that city management throughout Europe requires a college degree.) But the explanation of why our cities are being uglified is not to be found wholly in political venality, capitalistic exploitation, greed, carelessness, or any one force.

The history of a city ought to disclose how it came to be what it is. John and LaRee Caughey have put together a composite "history" of that monster metropolis Los Angeles.[6] The apologies for the word *history* are because the book is an anthology of short passages from over a hundred writers. The method seems appropriate for a sprawling subject, the locale of such contrasts (Hollywood and Watts, UCLA and Sunset Boulevard). I suspect the book is of greatest interest to Angelenos themselves, though it is a marvelous book to read around in. It makes the tacit assumption that no American city of such size can be got between the pages of a book. The word *history* is wonderfully tricky when applied to a city. One can write the history of England better than the history of London. In another sense, the history of Los Angeles can be written sometime in the next century, but not now.

A more thorough and integral history of a city is Roger Sale's of Seattle.[7] 20 This is a model of how city histories should be written. Seattle is a perfect example of the American city in that it was not an accidental pooling of settlers in its beginning, but a deliberate act by stalwart citizens who had come to found a city. The university, the neighborhoods, the businesses, the bank, practically all the elements were decided on as the first buildings went up. We think of the westward expansion as so many pioneers clearing the wilderness for *farms*; that's mythology — they were colonists who had the plans of cities in their heads, the first since Greeks and Romans set out from *mother cities* (*metropolites*) to reproduce examples of the model they came from.

Professor Sale, a highly skilled and spirited writer, gives us each epoch of Seattle's history in fine detail. He knows that cities are really so many people, and inserts full biographies throughout. He gives a lucid account of the city's economic and sociological history; he knows its institutions and newspapers. Most importantly, he knows the city's lapses and false

---

Lincoln Steffens (1886–1936), American author and muckracking journalist at the turn of the century.

[6]John and LaRee Caughey, *Los Angeles: Biography of a City* (Berkeley: University of California Press, 1976).

[7]Roger Sale, *Seattle, Past to Present* (Seattle: University of Washington Press, 1976).

steps; not a syllable of chauvinism or whitewashing mars these pages. The book is therefore vigorous in its honesty and in the range of its considerations; it is as good on labor leaders (Dave Beck) as on intellectuals (Vernon Parrington). It is a speculative book that can discuss the benefit of good high schools and parks, and can explain how the American labor movement, which by rights ought to have emerged as leftist and radical (as the Seattle friend of Mao, Anna Louise Strong, urged), became rightist and conservative.

A city's history can be done in finer and finer detail. You can zone off a decade, as Michael Lesy has done with the twenties in Louisville, or study neighborhoods family by family, as Roslyn Banish has done with a London and a Chicago neighborhood, or trace a single family through six generations.[8] Lesy, who began his method of composite history with *Wisconsin Death Trip*, repeats that work with Louisville in Prohibition times. Using photographs from the commercial firm of Caulfield and Shooks, police and insane-asylum records, he constructs, with what seems to me like morbidity and gratuitous cynicism, a sustained surrealistic picture of the period. His point, of course, is that's the way they chose to see themselves — Masons in all their gaudy trappings, blacks at lodge banquets, society folk looking superior, T-Model wrecks, prehistoric Gulf stations, promotion photos by go-getter salesmen. A lot of the surrealism is, I'm afraid, mere psychological tone. Similar photographs of the 1860s we would perceive as History. These things come in phases: today's junk is tomorrow's antique, etc., but the process has some subtle quality one can't pin down. Lesy makes the age seem indecent; I grew up in it, and don't remember it that way at all. The present moment is far tackier (he would probably agree), and it is true, as he claims, that newspapers speak in a tongue all their own. And all documents in a neutral voice (police recorder, case histories from the asylum) tell us more about the institution keeping such files than about the subject. It is Lesy's hope that raw documents speak for themselves, and that captionless photographs are powerfully meaningful. I have my doubts. The method seems to me to be a bit cocky and fraudulent. The truth of a period cannot be summoned by a few eloquent photographs and a batch of newspaper clippings. It is the equivalent of trying to understand the Second World War from newsreels alone.

Roslyn Banish supplements her photographs of London and Chicago families with responsible statistics and with commentaries by the subjects

[8]Michael Lesy, *Real Life: Louisville in the Twenties* (New York: Pantheon Books, 1976). Roslyn Banish, *City Families: Chicago and London* (New York: Pantheon Books, 1976). Dorothy Gallagher, *Hannah's Daughters: Six Generations of an American Family: 1876–1976* (New York: Crowell, 1976).

themselves. She also allowed the subjects to choose their setting (almost invariably the best-looking room, as they thought) and pose. Ms. Banish is a canny photographer, giving us in splendid light just enough detail to complete the portraits (a coat hanger inexplicably in a living room, a dime-store Gainsborough over a policeman's mantel), and an even cannier sociologist to have conceived and carried out her project. She has made a book from which one learns about people in a particular and piquant way without any violation of their privacy, without condescension, and with gentleness toward their vulnerability. There is more respect for human beings in these photographs than I have ever seen a photographer achieve. One falls in love with the eighty-year-old Alice Williams in the first photograph (lovebirds, electric heater, paper flowers) and remains in awe of the dignity of these homefolks right up to a smiling Irish Chicago police sergeant in the last. I liked Douglas Humphreys (butler, Buckingham Palace), who looks like the Hon. Gally Threepwood in Wodehouse,° part of whose interview recalls a buffet supper for heads of state after Churchill's funeral: "I was entertaining myself a few moments with Mr. Khrushchev. Oh yes, now he had two bodyguards and an interpreter with him. I took off his greatcoat and I felt the eyes of those burly guards. I hung his greatcoat up and I said to the interpreter, 'Just tell your two men to relax. I'm on duty on the occasion of Her Majesty's Royal Household.' And I added, 'One day I should like to pay a visit to your country, sir.' He . . . actually shook hands." One feels that Humphreys was *comforting* Comrade K., and not even Trollope° could have thought of such a wonderful moment.

Dorothy Gallagher's *Hannah's Daughters* is an oral history, taken down in a series of interviews, of six generations of a Washington family of Dutch descent, members of all of them being alive in August 1973, a chain of daughters reaching from the ninety-seven-year-old Hannah to her two-year-old great-great-great-granddaughter. The hundred photographs illustrating the narratives progess from tintype to Polaroid. The text has the interest of good talk, and covers a great deal of American history in very American voices: ". . . everybody was kissing everybody. It was really something. That was V-E Day. It was absolutely wild. I didn't think there *were* that many people." Gertrude Stein° would have liked this book, and even tried to write it, the wrong way round, in *The Making of Americans*. Family history has traditionally been a woman's preserve. And what a

24

Wodehouse   P. G. Wodehouse (1881–1975), British-born writer of light fiction set in Edwardian society.

Trollope   Anthony Trollope (1815–1882), British writer of novels depicting the social life of ordinary people, mostly in the English countryside.

Gertrude Stein   (1874–1946), American writer whose book, *The Making of Americans* (1925), is a history of her family.

distance there is from "They'd kill a hog and I'd get the fat cleaned off the hog intestines to make lard. I was quick at that" to "Even if Tony had an affair, if it was a quickie affair, I'm sure we'd still be together. If it was a long one, I'm sure we'd get a divorce."

The inner life of the city — voices, children, baths, meals — has not undergone any substantial change since Jericho, the oldest city still inhabited. When Odysseus was finally united with Penelope,° they talked all night in a cozy bed, under sheepskin covers. Children and the old are the same the world over. Only public lives are different: the automobile and airplane have made us nomads again. The city seems to be obsolete; a sense of community evaporates in all this mobility and stir. As persuasion is impotent in so distracted a world, and as our legislators seem to be mere pawns of lobbies, their hands hourly open to bribes, we must socially wait out whatever awful hiatus there is to be between the technological destruction of the only known unit of civilization, the city, and its logical and natural reinvention, however that is to come about. Meanwhile, as a voice says in Zukofsky's *"A"-18,*

> . . . all
> their world's done to change the world is
> to make it more ugly to the airport.

AFTERWORD

Davenport's curiosity is boundless. Here he writes a collective review, a variation on the essay-review in which he touches on many different books — with brief, unpretentious remarks and judgments on each — in order to put forward his ideas about cities and architecture. The books reviewed become vehicles for Davenport's ideas.

Davenport's prose makes use of the apothegm, the brief and pithy sentence, the homemade proverb, the prose epigram. Apothegms are witty, memorable, often funny, and dangerous for the neophyte: If you try to make one and fail, you look foolish, like someone showing off with unfunny jokes or inept imitations. Speaking of the life span of contemporary buildings, Davenport tells us: "All architects are now sculptors in ice." Elsewhere "The automobile is an insect that eats cities," he tells us, and balances it: "and its parking lots are a gangrene."

Odysseus . . . Penelope Odysseus, the wandering hero of the *Odyssey*; Penelope, his faithful wife who waited ten years for his return.

BOOKS AVAILABLE IN PAPERBACK

Da Vinci's Bicycle: Ten Stories by Guy Davenport. Baltimore: Johns Hopkins University Press. *Short stories.*

Eclogues: Eight Stories by Guy Davenport. San Francisco: North Point Press. *Short stories.*

The Geography of the Imagination. San Francisco: North Point Press. *Essays.*

The Jules Verne Steam Balloon. San Francisco: North Point Press. *Short stories.*

JOAN
DIDION

*J*OAN DIDION *is a fifth-generation Californian, born in Sacramento (1934),*
who took her B.A. at Berkeley and lives in Los Angeles. Between college and
marriage to the writer John Gregory Dunne, she lived in New York for seven years,
where she worked as an editor for Vogue *and wrote essays for the* National Review
and the Saturday Evening Post. *In California, Didion and Dunne separately write*
novels and magazine articles and collaborate on screenplays. Didion's novels are
Run River *(1963),* Play It as It Lays *(1970),* A Book of Common Prayer
(1977), and Democracy *(1984). Her collections of essays are* Slouching Towards
Bethlehem *(1968) and* The White Album *(1979), from which we have taken this*
selection. She published Salvador *in 1983, and in 1987* Miami.

Joan Didion is one of our best nonfiction writers. She describes the alien, simple
California she grew up in and the southern California where she now lives — a
landscape of drive-ins and orange groves, ocean and freeway, the Manson murders
and ordinary, domestic, adulterous homicide. She has done witness to the turmoils
of the decades, especially the sixties — drugs, Vietnam, and personal breakdown.
Expertly sensitive and inventive with language, she is most talented in the repre-
sentation of hysteria. While her book about El Salvador mentions politics, it is

essentially the record of a sensibility, sensitive to fear, exposed to an atmosphere that engenders it: "Terror is the given of the place."

Much of Didion's journalism derives from interviews. She has written of herself: *"My only advantage as a reporter is that I am so physically small, so temperamentally unobtrusive, and so neurotically inarticulate that people tend to forget that my presence runs counter to their best interests. And it always does. That is one last thing to remember: writers are always selling somebody out."*

In an essay called "Why I Write," she remembers how she tried to think in abstractions when she was an undergraduate at the University of California. *"I failed. My attention veered inexorably back to the specific, to the tangible. . . . I would try to contemplate the Hegelian dialectic and would find myself concentrating instead on a flowering pear tree outside my window."* She was a particularist, not an abstractionist; finally, her particulars are not the world outside the window but the words she puts on the page. She is a writer, obsessed by the language she manipulates: *"Grammar is a piano I play by ear. . . . All I know about grammar is its infinite power. To shift the structure of a sentence alters the meaning of that sentence, as definitely and inflexibly as the position of a camera alters the meaning of the object photographed."*

Holy Water

Some of us who live in arid parts of the world think about water with a reverence others might find excessive. The water I will draw tomorrow from my tap in Malibu is today crossing the Mojave Desert from the Colorado River, and I like to think about exactly where that water is. The water I will drink tonight in a restaurant in Hollywood is by now well down the Los Angeles Aqueduct from the Owens River, and I also think about exactly where that water is: I particularly like to imagine it as it cascades down the 45-degree stone steps that aerate Owens water after its airless passage through the mountain pipes and siphons. As it happens my own reverence for water has always taken the form of this constant meditation upon where the water is, of an obsessive interest not in the politics of water but in the waterworks themselves, in the movement of water through aqueducts and siphons and pumps and forebays and afterbays and weirs and drains, in plumbing on the grand scale. I know the data on water projects I will never see. I know the difficulty Kaiser had closing the last two sluiceway gates on the Guri Dam in Venezuela. I keep watch on evaporation behind the Aswan in Egypt. I can put myself to sleep imagining the water dropping a thousand feet into the turbines at Churchill Falls in Labrador. If the Churchill Falls Project fails to materialize, I fall back on waterworks closer at hand — the tailrace at Hoover on the Colorado, the surge tank in the Tehachapi Mountains that receives California Aqueduct water pumped higher than water has ever been pumped before — and finally I replay a morning when I was seventeen years old and caught, in a military-surplus life raft, in the construction of the Nimbus Afterbay Dam on the American River near Sacramento. I remember that at the moment it happened I was trying to open a tin of anchovies with capers. I recall the raft spinning into the narrow chute through which the river had been temporarily diverted. I recall being deliriously happy.

I suppose it was partly the memory of that delirium that led me to visit, one summer morning in Sacramento, the Operations Control Center for the California State Water Project. Actually so much water is moved around California by so many different agencies that maybe only the movers themselves know on any given day whose water is where, but to get a general picture it is necessary only to remember that Los Angeles moves some of it, San Francisco moves some of it, the Bureau of Reclamation's Central Valley Project moves some of it, and the California State Water Project moves most of the rest of it, moves a vast amount of it, moves more water farther than has ever been moved anywhere. They collect this water up in the granite keeps of the Sierra Nevada and they store roughly a trillion gallons of it behind the Oroville Dam and every morning, down at the Project's headquarters in Sacramento, they decide how much of their water they want to move the next day. They make this morning decision according to supply and demand, which is simple in theory but rather more complicated in practice. In theory each of the Project's five field divisions — the Oroville, the Delta, the San Luis, the San Joaquin, and the Southern divisions — places a call to headquarters before nine A.M. and tells the dispatchers how much water is needed by its local water contractors, who have in turn based their morning estimates on orders from growers and other big users. A schedule is made. The gages open and close according to schedule. The water flows south and the deliveries are made.

In practice this requires prodigious coordination, precision, and the best efforts of several human minds and that of a Univac 418. In practice it might be necessary to hold large flows of water for power production, or to flush out encroaching salinity in the Sacramento–San Joaquin Delta, the most ecologically sensitive point on the system. In practice a sudden rain might obviate the need for a delivery when that delivery is already on its way. In practice what is being delivered here is an enormous volume of water, not quarts of milk or spools of thread, and it takes two days to move such a delivery down through Oroville into the Delta, which is the great pooling place for California water and has been for some years alive with electronic sensors and telemetering equipment and men blocking channels and diverting flows and shoveling fish away from the pumps. It takes perhaps another six days to move this same water down the California Aqueduct from the Delta to the Tehachapi and put it over the hill to Southern California. "Putting some over the hill" is what they say around the Project Operations Control Center when they want to indicate that they are pumping Aqueduct water from the floor of the San Joaquin Valley up and over the Tehachapi Mountains. "Pulling it down" is what they say when they want to indicate that they are lowering a water level somewhere in the system. They can put some over the hill by remote control from this room in Sacramento with its Univac and its big board and its flashing lights. They can pull down a pool in the San Joaquin by remote control from this room in Sacramento with its locked doors and its ringing alarms and its constant print-outs of data from sensors out there in the water itself. From this room in Sacramento the whole system takes on the aspect of a perfect three-billion-dollar hydraulic toy, and in certain ways it is. "LET'S START DRAINING QUAIL AT 12:00" was the 10:51 A.M. entry on the electronically recorded communications log the day I visited the Operations Control Center. "Quail" is a reservoir in Los Angeles County with a gross capacity of 1,636,018,000 gallons. "OK" was the response recorded in the log. I knew at that moment that I had missed the only vocation for which I had any instinctive affinity: I wanted to drain Quail myself.

Not many people I know carry their end of the conversation when I 4 want to talk about water deliveries, even when I stress that these deliveries affect their lives, indirectly, every day. "Indirectly" is not quite enough for most people I know. This morning, however, several people I know were affected not "indirectly" but "directly" by the way the water moves. They had been in New Mexico shooting a picture, one sequence of which required a river deep enough to sink a truck, the kind with a cab and a trailer and fifty or sixty wheels. It so happened that no river near the New Mexico location was running that deep this year. The production was therefore moved today to Needles, California, where the Colorado River normally runs, depending upon releases from Davis Dam, eighteen to twenty-five feet deep. Now. Follow this closely: yesterday we had a freak tropical storm in Southern California, two inches of rain in a normally dry month, and because this rain flooded the fields and provided more irrigation than any grower could possibly want for several days, no water was ordered from Davis Dam.

No orders, no releases.

Supply and demand.

As a result the Colorado was running only seven feet deep past Needles today, Sam Peckinpah's° desire for eighteen feet of water in which to sink a truck not being the kind of demand anyone at Davis Dam is geared to meet. The production closed down for the weekend. Shooting will resume Tuesday, providing some grower orders water and the agencies controlling the Colorado release it. Meanwhile many gaffers, best boys, cameramen, assistant directors, script supervisors, stunt drivers, and maybe even Sam Peckinpah are waiting out the weekend in Needles, where it is often 110 degrees at five P.M. and hard to get dinner after eight. This is a California parable, but a true one.

I have always wanted a swimming pool, and never had one. When it   8
became generally known a year or so ago that California was suffering severe drought, many people in water-rich parts of the country seemed obscurely gratified, and made frequent reference to Californians having to brick up their swimming pools. In fact a swimming pool requires, once it has been filled and the filter has begun its process of cleaning and recirculating the water, virtually no water, but the symbolic content of swimming pools has always been interesting: a pool is misapprehended as a trapping of affluence, real or pretended, and of a kind of hedonistic attention to the body. Actually a pool is, for many of us in the West, a symbol not of affluence but of order, of control over the uncontrollable. A pool is water, made available and useful, and is, as such, infinitely soothing to the western eye.
It is easy to forget that the only natural force over which we have any control out here is water, and that only recently. In my memory California summers were characterized by the coughing in the pipes that meant the well was dry, and California winters by all-night watches on rivers about to crest, by sandbagging, by dynamite on the levees, and flooding on the first floor. Even now the place is not all that hospitable to extensive settlement. As I write a fire has been burning out of control for two weeks in the ranges behind the Big Sur coast. Flash floods last night wiped out all major roads into Imperial County. I noticed this morning a hairline crack in a living-room tile from last week's earthquake, a 4.4 I never felt. In the part of California where I now live aridity is the single most prominent feature of the climate, and I am not pleased to see, this year, cactus spreading wild to the sea. There will be days this winter when the humidity will drop to ten, seven, four. Tumbleweed will blow against my house and the sound of the rattlesnake will be duplicated a hundred times a day by dried

---

Sam Peckinpah   American film director.

bougainvillea drifting in my driveway. The apparent ease of California life is an illusion, and those who believe the illusion real live here in only the most temporary way. I know as well as the next person that there is considerable transcendent value in a river running wild and undammed, a river running free over granite, but I have also lived beneath such a river when it was running in flood, and gone without showers when it was running dry.

"The West begins," Bernard DeVoto wrote, "where the average annual rainfall drops below twenty inches." This is maybe the best definition of the West I have ever read, and it goes a long way toward explaining my own passion for seeing the water under control, but many people I know persist in looking for psychoanalytical implications in this passion. As a matter of fact I have explored, in an amateur way, the more obvious of these implications, and come up with nothing interesting. A certain external reality remains, and resists interpretation. The West begins where the average annual rainfall drops below twenty inches. Water is important to people who do not have it, and the same is true of control. Some fifteen years ago I tore a poem by Karl Shapiro from a magazine and pinned it on my kitchen wall. This fragment of paper is now on the wall of a sixth kitchen, and crumbles a little whenever I touch it, but I keep it there for the last stanza, which has for me the power of a prayer:

> It is raining in California, a straight rain
> Cleaning the heavy oranges on the bough,
> Filling the gardens till the gardens flow,
> Shining the olives, tiling the gleaming tile,
> Waxing the dark camellia leaves more green,
> Flooding the daylong valleys like the Nile.

I thought of those lines constantly on the morning in Sacramento when I went to visit the California State Water Project Operations Control Center. If I had wanted to drain Quail at 10:51 that morning, I wanted, by early afternoon, to do a great deal more. I wanted to open and close the Clifton Court Forebay intake gate. I wanted to produce some power down at the San Luis Dam. I wanted to pick a pool at random on the Aqueduct and pull it down and then refill it, watching for the hydraulic jump. I wanted to put some water over the hill and I wanted to shut down all flow from the Aqueduct into the Bureau of Reclamation's Cross Valley Canal, just to see how long it would take somebody over at Reclamation to call up and complain. I stayed as long as I could and watched the system work on the big board with the lighted checkpoints. The Delta salinity report was coming in on one of the teletypes behind me. The Delta tidal report was coming in on another. The earthquake board, which has been desensitized to sound its alarm (a beeping tone for Southern California, a high-pitched tone for the north) only for those earthquakes which register at least 3.0 on the Richter Scale, was silent. I had no further business in this room and yet I wanted to stay the day. I wanted to be the one, that day, who was shining the olives, filling the gardens, and flooding the daylong valleys like the Nile. I want it still.

AFTERWORD

Somewhere Didion writes: "A place belongs forever to whoever claims it hardest, remembers it most obsessively, wrenches it from itself, shapes it, renders it, loves it so radically that he really makes it in his image." Whatever she speaks of, she will always discover the extreme; *the middle way does not interest her. (Even as a child, "I can recall disapproving of the golden mean. . . .") Surely we can imagine a* middling *essay on water, all statistics and predictions, which would interest nobody. Information in "Holy Water" supplies a frame, and we would miss it if it were not there, but it is not the essay's heart. With Didion, information is the ephemeral flesh; feeling is the skeleton that endures. She will not work herself up to write unless "the extremes show up."*

This extremity is a matter of personal feeling, it requires the letter "I." Feeling requires someone to do *it. In her essay called "Why I Write," Didion says, "in many ways writing is the act of saying I, of imposing oneself on people, of saying* listen to me, see it my way, change your mind."

BOOKS AVAILABLE IN PAPERBACK

A Book of Common Prayer. New York: Washington Square Press. *Novel.*

Democracy. New York: Washington Square Press. *Novel.*

Plays It as It Lays. New York: Washington Square Press. *Novel.*

Run River. New York: Washington Square Press. *Novel.*

Salvador. New York: Washington Square Press. *Nonfiction.*

Slouching Towards Bethlehem. New York: Washington Square Press. *Essays.*

The White Album. New York: Washington Square Press. *Essays.*

ANNIE
DILLARD

A NNIE DILLARD *(b. 1945) grew up in Pittsburgh and attended Hollins*
College in Virginia, where she completed her B.A. and M.A. She has taught
at Western Washington University and currently teaches at Wesleyan University
in Connecticut. But she has worked mostly as a writer. A book of poems, Tickets
for a Prayer Wheel, *appeared in 1974. In the same year she published* Pilgrim at
Tinker Creek, *her first prose — an example of the ecstatic natural observation that*
makes up her best work. The book won a Pulitzer Prize. In 1977 she published Holy
the Firm *and early in 1982 a work of literary theory called* Living by Fiction.
Later in the same year she collected her essays into Teaching a Stone to Talk.
Encounters with Chinese Writers *appeared in 1984. In 1987 she published* An
American Childhood, *her energetic and lively and thoughtful memoir of growing*
up in Pittsburgh; the book is funny and profound, with acute observations of the
beginnings of consciousness and self-consciousness.

Book reviewers often deride miscellaneous collections of work from periodicals,
as if a book that preserves magazine pieces must be ephemeral. Annie Dillard writes
a note at the front of Teaching a Stone to Talk, *to make sure that no one*
misunderstands her own attitude toward this work: "This is not a collection of

occasional pieces, such as a writer brings out to supplement his real work; instead, this is my real work. . . ."

The ellipsis at the quotation's end omits Annie Dillard's last words: "*such as it is.*" Such as it is, Annie Dillard's real work reaches a level of imagination we usually associate not with the essay but with poetry and fiction. Her mind combines qualities not often found together: an almost insatiable curiosity about details of the natural world, science, and thought together with a spiritual appetite, a visionary's or mystic's seeking through religious study and meditation. Combining these qualities, she becomes a major writer of American prose.

Like all writers, Dillard encounters difficulties writing. Every time she tries, she says, "There's just some prohibitive and fatal flaw in the structure. And that's where most people quit. You just have to hang on." Handing essays back to a class of students not long ago, she said, "I hand back these miserable things — that's O.K. I knew they'd be miserable. . . . The assignment was to write a brilliant essay. The assignment is always to write a brilliant essay." It is the assignment she gave herself, and fulfilled, when she wrote "Total Eclipse," from Teaching a Stone to Talk. Dillard's curiosity, observation, narrative, description, and vision bring to this volume a model of the modern essay.

Total Eclipse

I

It had been like dying, the sliding down the mountain pass. It had been like the death of someone, irrational, that sliding down the mountain pass and into the region of dread. It was like slipping into fever, or falling down that hole in sleep from which you wake yourself whimpering. We had crossed the mountains that day, and now we were in a strange place — a hotel in central Washington, in a town near Yakima. The eclipse we had traveled here to see would occur early in the next morning.

I lay in bed. My husband, Gary, was reading beside me. I lay in bed and looked at the painting on the hotel room wall. It was a print of a detailed and lifelike painting of a smiling clown's head, made out of vegetables. It was a painting of the sort which you do not intend to look at, and which, alas, you never forget. Some tasteless fate presses it upon you; it becomes part of the complex interior junk you carry with you wherever you go. Two years have passed since the total eclipse of which I write. During those years I have forgotten, I assume, a great many things I wanted to remember — but I have not forgotten that clown painting or its lunatic setting in the old hotel.

The clown was bald. Actually, he wore a clown's tight rubber wig, painted white; this stretched over the top of his skull, which was a cabbage. His hair was bunches of baby carrots. Inset in his white clown makeup, and in his cabbage skull, were his small and laughing human eyes. The clown's glance was like the glance of Rembrandt in some of the self-portraits: lively, knowing, deep, and loving. The crinkled shadows around his eyes were string beans. His eyebrows were parsley. Each of his ears was a broad bean. His thin, joyful lips were red chili peppers; between his lips were wet rows of human teeth and a suggestion of a real tongue. The clown print was framed in gilt and glassed.

To put ourselves in the path of the total eclipse, that day we had driven   4
five hours inland from the Washington coast, where we lived. When we tried to cross the Cascades range, an avalanche had blocked the pass.

A slope's worth of snow blocked the road; traffic backed up. Had the avalanche buried any cars that morning? We could not learn. This highway was the only winter road over the mountains. We waited as highway crews bulldozed a passage through the avalanche. With two-by-fours and walls of plywood, they erected a one-way, roofed tunnel through the avalanche. We drove through the avalanche tunnel, crossed the pass, and descended several thousand feet into central Washington and the broad Yakima valley, about which we knew only that it was orchard country. As we lost altitude, the snows disappeared; our ears popped; the trees changed, and in the trees were strange birds. I watched the landscape innocently, like a fool, like a diver in the rapture of the deep who plays on the bottom while his air runs out.

The hotel lobby was a dark, derelict room, narrow as a corridor, and seemingly without air. We waited on a couch while the manager vanished upstairs to do something unknown to our room. Beside us on an overstuffed chair, absolutely motionless, was a platinum-blond woman in her forties wearing a black silk dress and a strand of pearls. Her long legs were crossed; she supported her head on her fist. At the dim far end of the room, their backs toward us, sat six bald old men in their shirtsleeves, around a loud television. Two of them seemed asleep. They were drunks. "Number six!" cried the man on television. "Number six!"

On the broad lobby desk, lighted and bubbling, was a ten-gallon aquarium containing one large fish; the fish tilted up and down in its water.

Against the long opposite wall sang a live canary in its cage. Beneath the cage, among spilled millet seeds on the carpet, were a decorated child's sand bucket and matching sand shovel.

Now the alarm was set for six. I lay awake remembering an article I had read downstairs in the lobby, in an engineering magazine. The article was about gold mining. 8

In South Africa, in India, and in South Dakota, the gold mines extend so deeply into the earth's crust that they are hot. The rock walls burn the miners' hands. The companies have to air-condition the mines; if the air conditioners break, the miners die. The elevators in the mine shafts run very slowly, down, and up, so the miners' ears will not pop in their skulls. When the miners return to the surface, their faces are deathly pale.

Early the next morning we checked out. It was February 26, 1979, a Monday morning. We would drive out of town, find a hilltop, watch the eclipse, and then drive back over the mountains and home to the coast. How familiar things are here; how adept we are; how smoothly and professionally we check out! I had forgotten the clown's smiling head and the hotel lobby as if they had never existed. Gary put the car in gear and off we went, as off we have gone to a hundred other adventures.

It was dawn when we found a highway out of town and drove into the unfamiliar countryside. By the growing light we could see a band of cirrostratus clouds in the sky. Later the rising sun would clear these clouds before the eclipse began. We drove at random until we came to a range of unfenced hills. We pulled off the highway, bundled up, and climbed one of these hills.

II

The hill was five hundred feet high. Long winter-killed grass covered it, as high as our knees. We climbed and rested, sweating in the cold; we passed clumps of bundled people on the hillside who were setting up telescopes and fiddling with cameras. The top of the hill stuck up in the middle of the sky. We tightened our scarves and looked around. 12

East of us rose another hill like ours. Between the hills, far below, was the highway which threaded south into the valley. This was the Yakima valley; I had never seen it before. It is justly famous for its beauty, like every planted valley. It extended south into the horizon, a distant dream of a valley, a Shangri-la. All its hundreds of low, golden slopes bore orchards. Among the orchards were towns, and roads, and plowed and fallow fields. Through the valley wandered a thin shining river; from the river extended fine, frozen irrigation ditches. Distance blurred and blued the sight, so that the whole valley looked like a thickness or sediment at the bottom of the sky. Directly behind us was more sky, and empty lowlands blued by distance, and Mount Adams. Mount Adams was an enormous, snow-covered volcanic cone rising flat, like so much scenery.

Now the sun was up. We could not see it; but the sky behind the band of clouds was yellow, and, far down the valley, some hillside orchards had lighted up. More people were parking near the highway and climbing the hills. It was the West. All of us rugged individuals were wearing knit caps and blue nylon parkas. People were climbing the nearby hills and setting up shop in clumps among the dead grasses. It looked as though we had gathered on hilltops to pray for the world on its last day. It looked as though we had all crawled out of spaceships and were preparing to assault the valley below. It looked as though we were scattered on hilltops at dawn to sacrifice virgins, make rain, set stone stelae in a ring. There was no place out of the wind. The straw grasses banged our legs.

Up in the sky where we stood the air was lusterless yellow. To the west the sky was blue. Now the sun cleared the clouds. We cast rough shadows on the blowing grass; freezing, we waved our arms. Near the sun, the sky was bright and colorless. There was nothing to see.

It began with no ado. It was odd that such a well-advertised public 16 event should have no starting gun, no overture, no introductory speaker. I should have known right then that I was out of my depth. Without pause or preamble, silent as orbits, a piece of the sun went away. We looked at it through welders' goggles. A piece of the sun was missing; in its place we saw empty sky.

I had seen a partial eclipse in 1970. A partial eclipse is very interesting. It bears almost no relation to a total eclipse. Seeing a partial eclipse bears the same relation to seeing a total eclipse as kissing a man does to marrying him, or as flying in an airplane does to falling out of an airplane. Although the one experience precedes the other, it in no way prepares you for it. During a partial eclipse the sky does not darken — not even when 94 percent of the sun is hidden. Nor does the sun, seen colorless through protective devices, seem terribly strange. We have all seen a sliver of light in the sky; we have all seen the crescent moon by day. However, during a partial eclipse the air does indeed get cold, precisely as if someone were standing between you and the fire. And blackbirds do fly back to their roosts. I had seen a partial eclipse before, and here was another.

What you see in an eclipse is entirely different from what you know. It is especially different for those of us whose grasp of astronomy is so frail that, given a flashlight, a grapefruit, two oranges, and fifteen years, we still could not figure out which way to set the clocks for Daylight Saving Time. Usually it is a bit of a trick to keep your knowledge from blinding you. But during an eclipse it is easy. What you see is much more convincing than any wild-eyed theory you may know.

You may read that the moon has something to do with eclipses. I have never seen the moon yet. You do not see the moon. So near the sun, it is as completely invisible as the stars are by day. What you see before your eyes is the sun going through phases. It gets narrower and narrower, as the waning moon does, and, like the ordinary moon, it travels alone in the simple sky. The sky is of course background. It does not appear to eat the sun; it is far behind the sun. The sun simply shaves away; gradually, you see less sun and more sky.

The sky's blue was deepening, but there was no darkness. The sun was 20 a wide crescent, like a segment of tangerine. The wind freshened and blew steadily over the hill. The eastern hill across the highway grew dusky and sharp. The towns and orchards in the valley to the south were dissolving into the blue light. Only the thin river held a trickle of sun.

Now the sky to the west deepened to indigo, a color never seen. A dark sky usually loses color. This was a saturated, deep indigo, up in the air. Stuck up into that unworldly sky was the cone of Mount Adams, and the alpenglow was upon it. The alpenglow is that red light of sunset which holds out on snowy mountaintops long after the valleys and tablelands are dimmed. "Look at Mount Adams," I said, and that was the last sane moment I remember.

I turned back to the sun. It was going. The sun was going, and the world was wrong. The grasses were wrong; they were platinum. Their every detail of stem, head, and blade shone lightless and artificially distinct as an art photographer's platinum print. This color has never been seen on earth. The hues were metallic; their finish was matte. The hillside was a nineteenth-century tinted photograph from which the tints had faded. All the people you see in the photograph, distinct and detailed as their faces look, are now dead. The sky was navy blue. My hands were silver. All the distant hills' grasses were finespun metal which the wind laid down. I was watching a faded color print of a movie filmed in the Middle Ages; I was standing in it, by some mistake. I was standing in a movie of hillside grasses filmed in the Middle Ages. I missed my own century, the people I knew, and the real light of day.

I looked at Gary. He was in the film. Everything was lost. He was a platinum print, a dead artist's version of life. I saw on his skull the darkness of night mixed with the colors of day. My mind was going out; my eyes were receding the way galaxies recede to the rim of space. Gary was light-years away, gesturing inside a circle of darkness, down the wrong end of a telescope. He smiled as if he saw me; the stringy crinkles around his eyes moved. The sight of him, familiar and wrong, was something I was remem-bering from centuries hence, from the other side of death: yes, *that* is the way he used to look, when we were living. When it was our generation's

turn to be alive. I could not hear him; the wind was too loud. Behind him
the sun was going. We had all started down a chute of time. At first it was
pleasant; now there was no stopping it. Gary was chuting away across
space, moving and talking and catching my eye, chuting down the long
corridor of separation. The skin on his face moved like thin bronze plating
that would peel.

The grass at our feet was wild barley. It was the wild einkorn wheat 24
which grew on the hilly flanks of the Zagros Mountains, above the Euphrates valley, above the valley of the river we called *River*. We harvested
the grass with stone sickles, I remember. We found the grasses on the
hillsides; we built our shelter beside them and cut them down. That is how
he used to look then, that one, moving and living and catching my eye,
with the sky so dark behind him, and the wind blowing. God save our life.

From all the hills came screams. A piece of sky beside the crescent sun
was detaching. It was a loosened circle of evening sky, suddenly lighted
from the back. It was an abrupt black body out of nowhere; it was a flat
disk; it was almost over the sun. That is when there were screams. At once
this disk of sky slid over the sun like a lid. The sky snapped over the sun
like a lens cover. The hatch in the brain slammed. Abruptly it was dark
night, on the land and in the sky. In the night sky was a tiny ring of light.
The hole where the sun belongs is very small. A thin ring of light marked
its place. There was no sound. The eyes dried, the arteries drained, the
lungs hushed. There was no world. We were the world's dead people
rotating and orbiting around and around, embedded in the planet's crust,
while the earth rolled down. Our minds were light-years distant, forgetful
of almost everything. Only an extraordinary act of will could recall to us
our former, living selves and our contexts in matter and time. We had, it
seems, loved the planet and loved our lives, but could no longer remember
the way of them. We got the light wrong. In the sky was something that
should not be there. In the black sky was a ring of light. It was a thin ring,
an old, thin silver wedding band, an old, worn ring. It was an old wedding
band in the sky, or a morsel of bone. There were stars. It was all over.

III

It is now that the temptation is strongest to leave these regions. We
have seen enough; let's go. Why burn our hands any more than we have
to? But two years have passed; the price of gold has risen. I return to the
same buried alluvial beds and pick through the strata again.

I saw, early in the morning, the sun diminish against a backdrop of sky.
I saw a circular piece of that sky appear, suddenly detached, blackened,
and backlighted; from nowhere it came and overlapped the sun. It did not

look like the moon. It was enormous and black. If I had not read that it was the moon, I could have seen the sight a hundred times and never thought of the moon once. (If, however, I had not read that it was the moon — if, like most of the world's people throughout time, I had simply glanced up and seen this thing — then I doubtless would not have speculated much, but would have, like Emperor Louis of Bavaria in 840, simply died of fright on the spot.) It did not look like a dragon, although it looked more like a dragon than the moon. It looked like a lens cover, or the lid of a pot. It materialized out of thin air — black, and flat, and sliding, outlined in flame.

Seeing this black body was like seeing a mushroom cloud. The heart 28 screeched. The meaning of the sight overwhelmed its fascination. It obliterated meaning itself. If you were to glance out one day and see a row of mushroom clouds rising on the horizon, you would know at once that what you were seeing, remarkable as it was, was intrinsically not worth remarking. No use running to tell anyone. Significant as it was, it did not matter a whit. For what is significance? It is significance for people. No people, no significance. This is all I have to tell you.

In the deeps are the violence and terror of which psychology has warned us. But if you ride these monsters deeper down, if you drop with them farther over the world's rim, you find what our sciences cannot locate or name, the substrate, the ocean or matrix or ether which buoys the rest, which gives goodness its power for good, and evil its power for evil, the unified field: our complex and inexplicable caring for each other, and for our life together here. This is given. It is not learned.

The world which lay under darkness and stillness following the closing of the lid was not the world we know. The event was over. Its devastation lay around about us. The clamoring mind and heart stilled, almost indifferent, certainly disembodied, frail, and exhausted. The hills were hushed, obliterated. Up in the sky, like a crater from some distant cataclysm, was a hollow ring.

You have seen photographs of the sun taken during a total eclipse. The corona fills the print. All of those photographs were taken through telescopes. The lenses of telescopes and cameras can no more cover the breadth and scale of the visual array than language can cover the breadth and simultaneity of internal experience. Lenses enlarge the sight, omit its context, and make of it a pretty and sensible picture, like something on a Christmas card. I assure you, if you send any shepherds a Christmas card on which is printed a three-by-three photograph of the angel of the Lord, the glory of the Lord, and a multitude of the heavenly host, they will not be sore afraid. More fearsome things can come in envelopes. More moving photographs than those of the sun's corona can appear in magazines. But I pray you will never see anything more awful in the sky.

You see the wide world swaddled in darkness; you see a vast breadth 32 of hilly land, and an enormous, distant, blackened valley; you see towns' lights, a river's path, and blurred portions of your hat and scarf; you see your husband's face looking like an early black-and-white film; and you see a sprawl of black sky and blue sky together, with unfamiliar stars in it, some barely visible bands of cloud, and over there, a small white ring. The ring is as small as one goose in a flock of migrating geese — if you happen to notice a flock of migrating geese. It is one 360th part of the visible sky. The sun we see is less than half the diameter of a dime held at arm's length.

The Crab Nebula, in the constellation Taurus, looks, through binoculars, like a smoke ring. It is a star in the process of exploding. Light from its explosion first reached the earth in 1054; it was a supernova then, and so bright it shone in the daytime. Now it is not so bright, but it is still exploding. It expands at the rate of seventy million miles a day. It is interesting to look through binoculars at something expanding seventy million miles a day. It does not budge. Its apparent size does not increase. Photographs of the Crab Nebula taken fifteen years ago seem identical to photographs of it taken yesterday. Some lichens are similar. Botanists have measured some ordinary lichens twice, at fifty-year intervals, without detecting any growth at all. And yet their cells divide; they live.

The small ring of light was like these things — like a ridiculous lichen up in the sky, like a perfectly still explosion 4,200 light-years away: it was interesting, and lovely, and in witless motion, and it had nothing to do with anything.

It had nothing to do with anything. The sun was too small, and too cold, and too far away, to keep the world alive. The white ring was not enough. It was feeble and worthless. It was as useless as a memory; it was as off kilter and hollow and wretched as a memory.

When you try your hardest to recall someone's face, or the look of a place, you see in your mind's eye some vague and terrible sight such as this. It is dark; it is insubstantial; it is all wrong.

The white ring and the saturated darkness made the earth and the sky look as they must look in the memories of the careless dead. What I saw, what I seemed to be standing in, was all the wrecked light that the memories of the dead could shed upon the living world. We had all died in our boots on the hilltops of Yakima, and were alone in eternity. Empty space stoppered our eyes and mouths; we cared for nothing. We remembered our living days wrong. With great effort we had remembered some sort of circular light in the sky — but only the outline. Oh, and then the orchard trees withered, the ground froze, the glaciers slid down the valleys and overlapped the towns. If there had ever been people on earth, nobody knew it. The dead had forgotten those they had loved. The dead were parted one from the other and could no longer remember the faces and lands they had loved in the light. They seemed to stand on darkened hilltops, looking down.

I V

We teach our children one thing only, as we were taught: to wake up. We teach our children to look alive there, to join by words and activities the life of human culture on the planet's crust. As adults we are almost all adept at waking up. We have so mastered the transition we have forgotten we ever learned it. Yet it is a transition we make a hundred times a day, as, like so many will-less dolphins, we plunge and surface, lapse and emerge. We live half our waking lives and all of our sleeping lives in some private, useless, and insensible waters we never mention or recall. Useless, I say. Valueless, I might add — until someone hauls their wealth up to the surface and into the wide-awake city, in a form that people can use.

I do not know how we got to the restaurant. Like Roethke, "I take my waking slow." Gradually I seemed more or less alive and already forgetful. It was now almost nine in the morning. It was the day of a solar eclipse in central Washington, and a fine adventure for everyone. The sky was clear; there was a fresh breeze out of the north.

The restaurant was a roadside place with tables and booths. The other eclipse-watchers were there. From our booth we could see their cars' California license plates, their University of Washington parking stickers. Inside the restaurant we were all eating eggs or waffles; people were fairly shouting and exchanging enthusiasms, like fans after a World Series game. Did you see . . . ? Did you see . . . ? Then somebody said something which knocked me for a loop.

A college student, a boy in a blue parka who carried a Hasselblad, said to us, "Did you see that little white ring? It looked like a Life Saver. It looked like a Life Saver up in the sky."

And so it did. The boy spoke well. He was a walking alarm clock. I myself had at that time no access to such a word. He could write a sentence, and I could not. I grabbed that Life Saver and rode it to the surface. And I had to laugh. I had been dumbstruck on the Euphrates River, I had been dead and gone and grieving, all over the sight of something which, if you could claw your way up to that level, you would grant looked very much like a Life Saver. It was good to be back among people so clever; it was good to have all the world's words at the mind's disposal, so the mind could begin its task. All those things for which we have no words are lost. The mind — the culture — has two little tools, grammar and lexicon: a decorated sand bucket and a matching shovel. With these we bluster about the continents and do all the world's work. With these we try to save our very lives.

There are a few more things to tell from this level, the level of the restaurant. One is the old joke about breakfast. "It can never be satisfied, the mind, never." Wallace Stevens wrote that, and in the long run he was right. The mind wants to live forever, or to learn a very good reason why not. The mind wants the world to return its love, or its awareness; the mind wants to know all the world, and all eternity, and God. The mind's sidekick, however, will settle for two eggs over easy.

The dear, stupid body is as easily satisfied as a spaniel. And, incredibly, 44 the simple spaniel can lure the brawling mind to its dish. It is everlastingly funny that the proud, metaphysically ambitious, clamoring mind will hush if you give it an egg.

Further: while the mind reels in deep space, while the mind grieves or fears or exults, the workaday senses, in ignorance or idiocy, like so many computer terminals printing out market prices while the world blows up, still transcribe their little data and transmit them to the warehouse in the skull. Later, under the tranquilizing influence of fried eggs, the mind can sort through this data. The restaurant was a halfway house, a decompression chamber. There I remembered a few things more.

The deepest, and most terrifying, was this: I have said that I heard screams. (I have since read that screaming, with hysteria, is a common reaction even to expected total eclipses.) People on all the hillsides, including, I think, myself, screamed when the black body of the moon detached from the sky and rolled over the sun. But something else was happening at that same instant, and it was this, I believe, which made us scream.

The second before the sun went out we saw a wall of dark shadow come speeding at us. We no sooner saw it than it was upon us, like thunder. It roared up the valley. It slammed our hill and knocked us out. It was the monstrous swift shadow cone of the moon. I have since read that this wave shadow moves 1,800 miles an hour. It was 195 miles wide. No end was in sight — you saw only the edge. It rolled at you across the land at 1,800 miles an hour, hauling darkness like plague behind it. Seeing it, and knowing it was coming straight for you, was like feeling a slug of anesthetic shoot up your arm. If you think very fast, you may have time to think, "Soon it will hit my brain." You can feel the deadness race up your arm; you can feel the appalling, inhuman speed of your own blood. We saw the wall of shadow coming, and screamed before it hit.

This was the universe about which we have read so much and never 48 before felt: the universe as a clockwork of loose spheres flung at stupefying, unauthorized speeds. How could anything moving so fast not crash, not veer from its orbit amok like a car out of control on a turn?

Less than two minutes later, when the sun emerged, the trailing edge of the shadow cone sped away. It coursed down our hill and raced eastward over the plain, faster than the eye could believe; it swept over the plain and dropped over the planet's rim in a twinkling. It had clobbered us, and now it roared away. We blinked in the light. It was as though an enormous, loping god in the sky had reached down and slapped the earth's face.

Something else, something more ordinary, came back to me along about the third cup of coffee. During the moments of totality, it was so dark that drivers on the highway below turned on their cars' headlights. We could see the highway's route as a strand of lights. It was bumper-to-bumper down there. It was eight-fifteen in the morning, Monday morning, and people were driving into Yakima to work. That it was as dark as night, and eerie as hell, an hour after dawn, apparently meant that in order to *see* to drive to work, people had to use their headlights. Four or five cars pulled off the road. The rest, in a line at least five miles long, drove to town. The highway ran between hills; the people could not have seen any of the eclipsed sun at all. Yakima will have another total eclipse in 2086. Perhaps, in 2086, businesses will give their employees an hour off.

From the restaurant we drove back to the coast. The highway crossing the Cascades range was open. We drove over the mountain like old pros. We joined our places on the planet's thin crust; it held. For the time being, we were home free.

Early that morning at six, when we had checked out, the six bald men 52 were sitting on folding chairs in the dim hotel lobby. The television was on. Most of them were awake. You might drown in your own spittle, God knows, at any time; you might wake up dead in a small hotel, a cabbage head watching TV while snows pile up in the passes, watching TV while the chili peppers smile and the moon passes over the sun and nothing changes and nothing is learned because you have lost your bucket and shovel and no longer care. What if you regain the surface and open your sack and find, instead of treasure, a beast which jumps at you? Or you may not come back at all. The winches may jam, the scaffolding buckle, the air conditioning collapse. You may glance up one day and see by your headlamp the canary keeled over in its cage. You may reach into a cranny for pearls and touch a moray eel. You yank on your rope; it is too late.

Apparently people share a sense of these hazards, for when the total eclipse ended, an odd thing happened.

When the sun appeared as a blinding bead on the ring's side, the eclipse was over. The black lens cover appeared again, backlighted, and slid away. At once the yellow light made the sky blue again; the black lid dissolved and vanished. The real world began there. I remember now: we all hurried away. We were born and bored at a stroke. We rushed down the hill. We found our car; we saw the other people streaming down the hillsides; we joined the highway traffic and drove away.

We never looked back. It was a general vamoose, and an odd one, for when we left the hill, the sun was still partially eclipsed — a sight rare enough, and one which, in itself, we would probably have driven five hours to see. But enough is enough. One turns at last even from glory itself with a sigh of relief. From the depths of mystery, and even from the heights of splendor, we bounce back and hurry for the latitudes of home.

AFTERWORD

A writer can choose to build emotion toward a climax, gradually increasing tempo, but Annie Dillard starts at full throttle with "It had been like dying, that sliding down the mountain pass." She compares moving downhill to the extremity of death. Note, however, that her intensity of feeling and her grandeur of metaphor — fever, falling into a hole; illness and sleep and death; later madness — do not preclude exposition, slipped in like an afterthought: "The eclipse we had traveled here to see. . . ."

The third paragraph contains Dillard's description of the tasteless, horrid, fascinating vegetable-clown, making it into a literary symbol — a device to embody what we lack words to say outright. (A French poet called the symbol "a new word.") The symbolic writer gathers a complex of feelings and sensations into images or narrative. This vegetable-clown horrifies by violating nature; so does the total eclipse, during which (paragraph 23) Dillard looks at her husband: "He was in the film. Everything was lost. He was a platinum print, a dead artist's version of life. I saw on his skull the darkness of night mixed with the colors of day. My mind was going out."

BOOKS AVAILABLE IN PAPERBACK

Encounters with Chinese Writers. Middletown: Wesleyan University Press. *Nonfiction.*

Holy the Firm. New York: Harper & Row. *Nonfiction.*

Living by Fiction. New York: Harper & Row. *Nonfiction.*

Pilgrim at Tinker Creek. New York: Harper & Row. *Essays.*

Teaching a Stone to Talk: Expeditions and Encounters. New York: Harper & Row. *Essays.*

Tickets for a Prayer Wheel. New York: Harper & Row. *Poetry.*

GRETEL
EHRLICH

GRETEL EHRLICH *was born (1946) in Santa Barbara, where her father raised breed mares and rode the professional horse show circuit. Now she rides rough, cowboying in Wyoming. She went to college at Bennington in Vermont, at the UCLA film school, and at the New School for Social Research in New York City. In 1976 when she was thirty, she arrived in Wyoming for the first time, to film a documentary for PBS on sheepherders, while the man she loved, her partner on the film, was dying of cancer in New York. "The tears came and lasted for two years."*

But when the tears ended, Wyoming was still there. Ehrlich fell in love with the land and later married a rancher, with whom she shares a small ranch in the Big Horn Basin ten miles from a paved road. After making films and publishing two collections of poetry, Ehrlich turned to prose. This essay appears in The Solace of Open Places *(1985), which critics have acclaimed. She is writing more essays — a collection to be called* Islands, the Universe, Home — *and recently issued her first novel,* Heart Mountain *(1988). Her work turns up in* Harper's, *the* Atlantic, *and the annual selection* Best Essays. *In 1987 she received a Whiting Award.*

"Landscape does not exist without an observer," she has written, "without a human presence." The vivid language of *"The Solace of Open Places"* makes a landscape palpable for the reader; Ehrlich is also alert to the men and women of her Wyoming, products of the rough indomitable land.

The Solace of Open Spaces

It's May and I've just awakened from a nap, curled against sagebrush the way my dog taught me to sleep — sheltered from wind. A front is pulling the huge sky over me, and from the dark a hailstone has hit me on the head. I'm trailing a band of two thousand sheep across a stretch of Wyoming badlands, a fifty-mile trip that takes five days because sheep shade up in hot sun and won't budge until it's cool. Bunched together now, and excited into a run by the storm, they drift across dry land, tumbling into draws like water and surge out again onto the rugged, choppy plateaus that are the building blocks of this state.

The name Wyoming comes from an Indian word meaning "at the great plains," but the plains are really valleys, great arid valleys, sixteen hundred square miles, with the horizon bending up on all sides into mountain ranges. This gives the vastness a sheltering look.

Winter lasts six months here. Prevailing winds spill snowdrifts to the east, and new storms from the northwest replenish them. This white bulk is sometimes dizzying, even nauseating, to look at. At twenty, thirty, and forty degrees below zero, not only does your car not work, but neither do your mind and body. The landscape hardens into a dungeon of space. During the winter, while I was riding to find a new calf, my jeans froze to the saddle, and in the silence that such cold creates I felt like the first person on earth, or the last.

Today the sun is out — only a few clouds billowing. In the east, where the sheep have started off without me, the benchland tilts up in a series of eroded red-earthed mesas, planed flat on top by a million years of water; behind them, a bold line of muscular scarps rears up ten thousand feet to become the Big Horn Mountains. A tidal pattern is engraved into the ground, as if left by the sea that once covered this state. Canyons curve down like galaxies to meet the oncoming rush of flat land.

To live and work in this kind of open country, with its hundred-mile views, is to lose the distinction between background and foreground. When I asked an older ranch hand to describe Wyoming's openness, he said, "It's all a bunch of nothing — wind and rattlesnakes — and so much of it you can't tell where you're going or where you've been and it don't make much difference." John, a sheepman I know, is tall and handsome and has an explosive temperament. He has a perfect intuition about people and sheep. They call him "Highpockets," because he's so long-legged; his graceful stride matches the distances he has to cover. He says, "Open space hasn't affected me at all. It's all the people moving in on it." The huge ranch he was born on takes up much of one county and spreads into another state; to put 100,000 miles on his pickup in three years and never leave home is not unusual. A friend of mine has an aunt who ranched on Powder River and didn't go off her place for eleven years. When her husband died, she quickly moved to town, bought a car, and drove around the States to see what she'd been missing.

Most people tell me they've simply driven through Wyoming, as if there were nothing to stop for. Or else they've skied in Jackson Hole, a place Wyomingites acknowledge uncomfortably because its green beauty and chic affluence are mismatched with the rest of the state. Most of Wyoming has a "lean-to" look. Instead of big, roomy barns and Victorian houses, there are dugouts, low sheds, log cabins, sheep camps, and fence lines that look like driftwood blown haphazardly into place. People here still feel pride because they live in such a harsh place, part of the glamorous cowboy past, and they are determined not to be the victims of a mining-dominated future.

Most characteristic of the state's landscape is what a developer euphemistically describes as "indigenous growth right up to your front door" — a reference to waterless stands of salt sage, snakes, jack rabbits, deerflies, red dust, a brief respite of wildflowers, dry washes, and no trees. In the Great Plains the vistas look like music, like Kyries° of grass, but Wyoming seems to be the doing of a mad architect — tumbled and twisted, ribboned with faded, deathbed colors, thrust up and pulled down as if the place had been startled out of a deep sleep and thrown into a pure light.

I came here four years ago. I had not planned to stay, but I couldn't   8
make myself leave. John, the sheepman, put me to work immediately. It was spring, and shearing time. For fourteen days of fourteen hours each, we moved thousands of sheep through sorting corrals to be sheared, branded, and deloused. I suspect that my original motive for coming here was to "lose myself" in new and unpopulated territory. Instead of producing the numbness I thought I wanted, life on the sheep ranch woke me up. The vitality of the people I was working with flushed out what had

---

Kyries Short prayers, beginning *Kyrie eleison* ("Lord, have mercy"), often sung or chanted.

become a hallucinatory rawness inside me. I threw away my clothes and bought new ones; I cut my hair. The arid country was a clean slate. Its absolute indifference steadied me.

Sagebrush covers 58,000 square miles of Wyoming. The biggest city has a population of fifty thousand, and there are only five settlements that could be called cities in the whole state. The rest are towns, scattered across the expanse with as much as sixty miles between them, their populations two thousand, fifty, or ten. They are fugitive-looking, perched on a barren, windblown bench, or tagged onto a river or a railroad, or laid out straight in a farming valley with implement stores and a block-long Mormon church. In the eastern part of the state, which slides down into the Great Plains, the new mining settlements are boomtowns, trailer cities, metal knots on flat land.

Despite the desolate look, there's a coziness to living in this state. There are so few people (only 470,000) that ranchers who buy and sell cattle know one another statewide; the kids who choose to go to college usually go to the state's one university, in Laramie; hired hands work their way around Wyoming in a lifetime of hirings and firings. And despite the physical separation, people stay in touch, often driving two or three hours to another ranch for dinner.

Seventy-five years ago, when travel was by buckboard or horseback, cowboys who were temporarily out of work rode the grub line — drifting from ranch to ranch, mending fences or milking cows, and receiving in exchange a bed and meals. Gossip and messages traveled this slow circuit with them, creating an intimacy between ranchers who were three and four weeks' ride apart. One old-time couple I know, whose turn-of-the-century homestead was used by an outlaw gang as a relay station for stolen horses, recall that if you were traveling, desperado or not, any lighted ranch house was a welcome sign. Even now, for someone who lives in a remote spot, arriving at a ranch or coming to town for supplies is cause for celebration. To emerge from isolation can be disorienting. Everything looks bright, new, vivid. After I had been herding sheep for only three days, the sound of the camp tender's pickup flustered me. Longing for human company, I felt a foolish grin take over my face; yet I had to resist an urgent temptation to run and hide.

Things happen suddenly in Wyoming, the change of seasons and 12 weather; for people, the violent swings in and out of isolation. But good-naturedness is concomitant with severity. Friendliness is a tradition. Strangers passing on the road wave hello. A common sight is two pickups stopped side by side far out on a range, on a dirt track winding through the sage. The drivers will share a cigarette, uncap their Thermos bottles, and pass a battered cup, steaming with coffee, between windows. These meetings summon up the details of several generations, because, in Wyoming, private histories are largely public knowledge.

Because ranch work is a physical and, these days, economic strain, being "at home on the range" is a matter of vigor, self-reliance, and common sense. A person's life is not a series of dramatic events for which he or she is applauded or exiled but a slow accumulation of days, seasons, years, fleshed out by the generational weight of one's family and anchored by a land-bound sense of place.

In most parts of Wyoming, the human population is visibly outnumbered by the animal. Not far from my town of fifty, I rode into a narrow valley and startled a herd of two hundred elk. Eagles look like small people as they eat car-killed deer by the road. Antelope, moving in small, graceful bands, travel at sixty miles an hour, their mouths open as if drinking in the space.

The solitude in which westerners live makes them quiet. They telegraph thoughts and feelings by the way they tilt their heads and listen; pulling their Stetsons into a steep dive over their eyes, or pigeon-toeing one boot over the other, they lean against a fence with a fat wedge of Copenhagen beneath their lower lips and take in the whole scene. These detached looks of quiet amusement are sometimes cynical, but they can also come from a dry-eyed humility as lucid as the air is clear.

Conversation goes on in what sounds like a private code; a few phrases imply a complex of meanings. Asking directions, you get a curious list of details. While trailing sheep I was told to "ride up to that kinda upturned rock, follow the pink wash, turn left at the dump, and then you'll see the water hole." One friend told his wife on roundup to "turn at the salt lick and the dead cow," which turned out to be a scattering of bones and no salt lick at all. 16

Sentence structure is shortened to the skin and bones of a thought. Descriptive words are dropped, even verbs; a cowboy looking over a corral full of horses will say to a wrangler, "Which one needs rode?" People hold back their thoughts in what seems to be a dumbfounded silence, then erupt with an excoriating perceptive remark. Language, so compressed, becomes metaphorical. A rancher ended a relationship with one remark: "You're a bad check," meaning bouncing in and out was intolerable, and even coming back would be no good.

What's behind this laconic style is shyness. There is no vocabulary for the subject of feelings. It's not a hangdog shyness, or anything coy — always there's a robust spirit in evidence behind the restraint, as if the earth-dredging wind that pulls across Wyoming had carried its people's voices away but everything else in them had shouldered confidently into the breeze.

I've spent hours riding to sheep camp at dawn in a pickup when nothing was said; eaten meals in the cookhouse when the only words spoken were a mumbled "Thank you, ma'am" at the end of dinner. The silence is profound. Instead of talking, we seem to share one eye. Keenly observed, the world is transformed. The landscape is engorged with detail, every movement on it chillingly sharp. The air between people is charged. Days unfold, bathed in their own music. Nights become hallucinatory; dreams, prescient.

Spring weather is capricious and mean. It snows, then blisters with 20 heat. There have been tornadoes. They lay their elephant trunks out in the sage until they find houses, then slurp everything up and leave. I've noticed that melting snowbanks hiss and rot, viperous, then drip into calm pools where ducklings hatch and livestock, being trailed to summer range, drink. With the ice cover gone, rivers churn a milkshake brown, taking culverts and small bridges with them. Water in such an arid place (the average annual rainfall where I live is less than eight inches) is like blood. It festoons drab land with green veins; a line of cottonwoods following a stream; a strip of alfalfa; and, on ditch banks, wild asparagus growing.

I've moved to a small cattle ranch owned by friends. It's at the foot of the Big Horn Mountains. A few weeks ago, I helped them deliver a calf who was stuck halfway out of his mother's body. By the time he was freed, we could see a heartbeat, but he was straining against a swollen tongue for air. Mary and I held him upside down by his back feet, while Stan, on his hands and knees in the blood, gave the calf mouth-to-mouth resuscitation. I have a vague memory of being pneumonia-choked as a child, my mother giving me her air, which may account for my romance with this windswept state.

If anything is endemic to Wyoming, it is wind. This big room of space is swept out daily, leaving a bone yard of fossils, agates, and carcasses in every stage of decay. Though it was water that initially shaped the state, wind is the meticulous gardener, raising dust and pruning the sage.

I try to imagine a world in which I could ride my horse across uncharted land. There is no wilderness left; wildness, yes, but true wilderness has been gone on this continent since the time of Lewis and Clark's overland journey.

Two hundred years ago, the Crow, Shoshone, Arapaho, Cheyenne, and 24 Sioux roamed the intermountain West, orchestrating their movements according to hunger, season, and warfare. Once they acquired horses, they traversed the spines of all the big Wyoming ranges — the Absarokas, the Wind Rivers, the Tetons, the Big Horns — and wintered on the unprotected plains that fan out from them. Space was life. The world was their home.

What was life-giving to Native Americans was often nightmarish to sodbusters who had arrived encumbered with families and ethnic pasts to be transplanted in nearly uninhabitable land. The great distances, the shortage of water and trees, and the loneliness created unexpected hardships for them. In her book *O Pioneers!*, Willa Cather gives a settler's version of the bleak landscape:

> The little town behind them had vanished as if it had never been, had fallen behind the swell of the prairie, and the stern frozen country received them into its bosom. The homesteads were few and far apart; here and there a windmill gaunt against the sky, a sod house crouching in a hollow.

The emptiness of the West was for others a geography of possibility. Men and women who amassed great chunks of land and struggled to preserve unfenced empires were, despite their self-serving motives, unwitting geographers. They understood the lay of the land. But by the 1850s the Oregon and Mormon trails sported bumper-to-bumper traffic. Wealthy landowners, many of them aristocratic absentee landlords, known as remittance men because they were paid to come West and get out of their families' hair, overstocked the range with more than a million head of cattle. By 1885 the feed and water were desperately short, and the winter of 1886 laid out the gaunt bodies of dead animals so closely together that when the thaw came, one rancher from Kaycee claimed to have walked on cowhide all the way to Crazy Woman Creek, twenty miles away.

Territorial Wyoming was a boy's world. The land was generous with everything but water. At first there was room enough, food enough, for everyone. And, as with all beginnings, an expansive mood set in. The young cowboys, drifters, shopkeepers, schoolteachers, were heroic, lawless, generous, rowdy, and tenacious. The individualism and optimism generated during those times have endured.

John Tisdale rode north with the trail herds from Texas. He was a college-educated man with enough money to buy a small outfit near the Powder River. While driving home from the town of Buffalo with a buckboard full of Christmas toys for his family and a winter's supply of food, he was shot in the back by an agent of the cattle barons who resented the encroachment of small-time stockmen like him. The wealthy cattlemen tried to control all the public grazing land by restricting membership in the Wyoming Stock Growers Association, as if it were a country club. They ostracized from roundups and brandings cowboys and ranchers who were not members, then denounced them as rustlers. Tisdale's death, the second such cold-blooded murder, kicked off the Johnson County cattle war, which was no simple good-guy-bad-guy shoot-out but a complicated class struggle between landed gentry and less affluent settlers — a shocking reminder that the West was not an egalitarian sanctuary after all.

Fencing ultimately enforced boundaries, but barbed wire abrogated space. It was stretched across the beautiful valleys, into the mountains, over desert badlands, through buffalo grass. The "anything is possible" fever — the lure of any new place — was constricted. The integrity of the land as a geographical body, and the freedom to ride anywhere on it, were lost.

I punched cows with a young man named Martin, who is the great-grandson of John Tisdale. His inheritance is not the open land that Tisdale knew and prematurely lost but a rage against restraint.

Wyoming tips down as you head northeast; the highest ground — the Laramie Plains — is on the Colorado border. Up where I live, the Big Horn River leaks into difficult, arid terrain. In the basin where it's dammed, sandhill cranes gather and, with delicate legwork, slice through the stilled water. I was driving by with a rancher one morning when he commented that cranes are "old-fashioned." When I asked why, he said, "Because they mate for life." Then he looked at me with a twinkle in his eyes, as if to say he really did believe in such things but also understood why we break our own rules.

In all this open space, values crystalize quickly. People are strong on scruples but tenderhearted about quirky behavior. A friend and I found one ranch hand, who's "not quite right in the head," sitting in front of the badly decayed carcass of a cow, shaking his finger and saying, "Now, I don't want you to do this ever again!" When I asked what was wrong with him, I was told, "He's goofier than hell, just like the rest of us." Perhaps because the West is historically new, conventional morality is still felt to be less important than rock-bottom truths. Though there's always a lot of teasing and sparring, people are blunt with one another, sometimes even cruel, believing honesty is stronger medicine than sympathy, which may console but often conceals.

The formality that goes hand in hand with the rowdiness is known as the Western Code. It's a list of practical do's and don'ts, faithfully observed. A friend, Cliff, who runs a trapline in the winter, cut off half his foot while chopping a hole in the ice. Alone, he dragged himself to his pickup and headed for town, stopping to open the ranch gate as he left, and getting out to close it again, thus losing, in his observance of rules, precious time and blood. Later, he commented, "How would it look, them having to come to the hospital to tell me their cows had gotten out?"

Accustomed to emergencies, my friends doctor each other from the vet's bag with relish. When one old-timer suffered a heart attack in hunting camp, his partner quickly stirred up a brew of red horse liniment and hot water and made the half-conscious victim drink it, then tied him onto a horse and led him twenty miles to town. He regained consciousness and lived.

The roominess of the state has affected political attitudes as well. Ranchers keep up with world politics and the convulsions of the economy but are basically isolationists. Being used to running their own small empires of land and livestock, they're suspicious of big government. It's a "don't fence me in" holdover from a century ago. They still want the elbow room their grandfathers had, so they're strongly conservative, but with a populist twist.

Summer is the season when we get our "cowboy tans" — on the lower 36 parts of our faces and on three fourths of our arms. Excessive heat, in the nineties and higher, sends us outside with the mosquitoes. In winter we're tucked inside our houses, and the white wasteland outside appears to be expanding, but in summer all the greenery abridges space. Summer is a go-ahead season. Every living thing is off the block and in the race: battalions of bugs in flight and biting; bats swinging around my log cabin as if the bases were loaded and someone had hit a home run. Some of summer's high-speed growth is ominous: larkspur, death camas, and green greasewood can kill sheep — an ironic idea, dying in this desert from eating what is too verdant. With sixteen hours of daylight, farmers and ranchers irrigate feverishly. There are first, second, and third cuttings of hay, some crews averaging only four hours of sleep a night for weeks. And, like the cowboys who in summer ride the night rodeo circuit, nighthawks make daredevil dives at dusk with an eerie whirring sound like a plane going down on the shimmering horizon.

In the town where I live, they've had to board up the dance-hall windows because there have been so many fights. There's so little to do except work that people wind up in a state of idle agitation that becomes fatalistic, as if there were nothing to be done about all this untapped energy. So the dark side to the grandeur of these spaces is the small-mindedness that seals people in. Men become hermits; women go mad. Cabin fever explodes into suicides, or into grudges and lifelong family feuds. Two sisters in my area inherited a ranch but found they couldn't get along. They fenced the place in half. When one's cows got out and mixed with the other's, the women went at each other with shovels. They ended up in the same hospital room but never spoke a word to each other for the rest of their lives.

After the brief lushness of summer, the sun moves south. The range grass is brown. Livestock is trailed back down from the mountains. Water holes begin to frost over at night. Last fall Martin asked me to accompany him on a pack trip. With five horses, we followed a river into the mountains behind the tiny Wyoming town of Meeteetse. Groves of aspen, red and orange, gave off a light that made us look toasted. Our hunting camp was so high that clouds skidded across our foreheads, then slowed to sail out across the warm valleys. Except for a bull moose who wandered into our camp and mistook our black gelding for a rival, we shot at nothing.

One of our evening entertainments was to watch the night sky. My dog, a dingo bred to herd sheep, also came on the trip. He is so used to the silence and empty skies that when an airplane flies over he always looks up and eyes the distant intruder quizzically. The sky, lately, seems to be much more crowded than it used to be. Satellites make their silent passes in the dark with great regularity. We counted eighteen in one hour's viewing. How odd to think that while they circumnavigated the planet, Martin and I had moved only six miles into our local wilderness and had seen no other human for the two weeks we stayed there.

At night, by moonlight, the land is whittled to slivers — a ridge, a river, 40 a strip of grassland stretching to the mountains, then the huge sky. One morning a full moon was setting in the west just as the sun was rising. I felt precariously balanced between the two as I loped across a meadow. For a moment, I could believe that the stars, which were still visible, work like cooper's bands, holding together everything above Wyoming.

Space has a spiritual equivalent and can heal what is divided and burdensome in us. My grandchildren will probably use space shuttles for a honeymoon trip or to recover from heart attacks, but closer to home we might also learn how to carry space inside ourselves in the effortless way we carry our skins. Space represents sanity, not a life purified, dull, or "spaced out" but one that might accommodate intelligently any idea or situation.

From the clayey soil of northern Wyoming is mined bentonite, which is used as a filler in candy, gum, and lipstick. We Americans are great on fillers, as if what we have, what we are, is not enough. We have a cultural tendency toward denial, but, being affluent, we strangle ourselves with what we can buy. We have only to look at the houses we build to see how we build *against* space, the way we drink against pain and loneliness. We fill up space as if it were a pie shell, with things whose opacity further obstructs our ability to see what is already there.

AFTERWORD

Bad writers are niggardly, using in a given essay only what they think they need — holding back, refusing to loosen largess of detail or feeling. On the other hand, the best writers are spendthrift, throwing into the moment's essay (poem, story) everything they know — heaping up details, overwhelming us with their riches and convictions. *The saver loses and the spender gains: Only when the well is emptied may it fill again; the careful conserver waters no meadow but dries the desert.*

Gretel Ehrlich has written many essays about these open spaces; she never holds back and she always has more to tell us. This essay is urgent, written almost entirely in the present tense. (Departures into varieties of past tense explain themselves; nothing is accidental in good prose.) We feel the writer's happy urge to share the gold, to convince us of the wonders of her place and the life lived in it. She has the knack of quick motion from one example — or season or animal — to another, usually without overt transition or development. "Eagles look like small people as they eat car-killed deer by the road," she tells us, giving scene and story we might like more of. But her relentless, quick motion onward excites the reader while it carries Ehrlich's excitement: "Antelope, moving in small, graceful bands, travel at sixty miles an hour, their mouths open as if drinking in the space."

The eagles are "like small people"; we see the look of the antelope's mouth "open as if drinking in the space." Images thrive on comparisons. Elsewhere, with more rapid motion, she glides from music to architecture: "In the Great Plains the vistas look like music, like Kyries of grass, but Wyoming seems to be the doing of a mad architect — tumbled and twisted, ribboned with faded, deathbed colors, thrust up and pulled down as if the place had been startled out of a deep sleep and thrown into a pure light."

BOOKS AVAILABLE IN PAPERBACK

The Solace of Open Spaces. New York: Penguin. *Essays.*

To Touch the Water. Boise: Ahsahta Press. *Poetry.*

FRANCES
FITZGERALD

*F*RANCES FITZGERALD (b. 1940) comes from a notable family. Her maternal
Peabody ancestors include a great-grandfather who founded the Groton School,
an uncle who was governor of Massachusetts, and a series of remarkable women —
poets, abolitionists, sculptors, playwrights, professors, deans, painters, and writers
through a hundred and fifty years of New England history. Her mother (divorced
and remarried) is Marietta Peabody Tree: prominent Democrat, a director of Pan
American Airways and CBS, and the first woman ambassador from the United
States to the United Nations. There were certain perks to her mother's associations:
When FitzGerald was only sixteen, Adlai Stevenson took her to Africa to meet
Albert Schweitzer. Considering FitzGerald's politics, her father's career seems
equally relevant: Desmond FitzGerald abandoned Wall Street brokering for spying
and became deputy director of the CIA. While the daughter was indicting American
policy in Vietnam, the father was in charge of a plot to assassinate Fidel Castro
with a hypodermic needle disguised as a ballpoint pen.

FitzGerald graduated from Radcliffe College in 1962. She wrote profiles for the
New York **Herald Tribune** Sunday magazine and pursued informal studies in
Chinese and Vietnamese history. By 1966 she was reporting from Vietnam. Her

Fire in the Lake *(1972), the book that collected her writing on Vietnam, won a Pulitzer Prize, a National Book Award, and the Bancroft Prize for History. She also reported on Cuba, Northern Ireland, and the Middle East in the* New Yorker, *the* Atlantic, Harper's, Esquire, *and the* New York Review of Books.

Later she wrote America Revised *(1979), which originated as a series of articles in the* New Yorker *on the high school textbook industry and on the changing views of our country which that industry reflects and promotes. She is a historian and a scholar — solid research informs all her work — as well as a reporter.* Cities on the Hill *(1986) is her most ambitious and engrossing work. It began when she was teaching at Berkeley in 1978 and became fascinated by the large homosexual community across the bay in San Francisco, especially a neighborhood called the Castro. She investigated, interviewed, researched, and wrote an article for the* New Yorker. *On a visit to Lynchburg, Virginia, she visited Jerry Falwell's Liberty Baptist Church and eventually wrote about another, contrasting American assemblage. By this time she had discovered the American phenomenon that gives her book its title. She found this image in a speech of John Winthrop's to the Puritans of the Massachusetts Bay Colony: A city on the hill is a community special in its own eyes, self-removed from the greater society, utopian or outcast or religious or whatever it chooses to be.*

She further pursued her subject through Sun City and the Rajneeshpuram commune led by a guru in Oregon. Cities on the Hill *consists of these studies together with parallels out of American history, notably an account of eccentric religious communities that flourished a hundred and fifty years ago in the eastern United States. Americans by their nature, which is to say by their culture, continually reconstitute themselves.*

Sun City — 1983

On Route 301 south of Tampa, billboards advertising Sun City Center crop up every few miles, with pictures of Cesar Romero and slogans that read FLORIDA'S RETIREMENT COMMUNITY OF THE YEAR, 87 HOLES OF GOLF, THE TOWN TOO BUSY TO RETIRE. According to a real-estate brochure, the town is "sensibly located . . . comfortably removed from the crowded downtown areas, the highway clutter, the tourists, and the traffic." It is twenty-five miles from Tampa, thirty miles from Bradenton, thirty-five miles from Sarasota, and eleven miles from the nearest beach on the Gulf Coast. Route 301, an inland route — to be taken in preference to the coast road, with its lines of trucks from the phosphate plants — passes through a lot of swampland, some scraggly pinewoods, and acre upon acre of strawberry beds covered with sheets of black plastic. There are fields where hairy, tough-looking cattle snatch at the grass between the palmettos. There are aluminum warehouses, cinder-block stores, and trailer homes in patches of dirt with laundry sailing out behind. There are Pentecostal churches and run-down cafés and bars with rows of pickup trucks parked out front.

Turn right with the billboards onto Route 674, and there is a green-and-white suburban-looking resort town. Off the main road, white asphalt boulevards with avenues of palm trees give onto streets that curve pleasingly around golf courses and small lakes. White ranch-style houses sit back from the streets on small, impeccably manicured lawns. A glossy four-color map of the town put out by a real-estate company shows cartoon figures of golfers on the fairways and boats on the lakes, along with drawings of churches, clubhouses, and curly green trees. The map is a necessity for the visitor, since the streets curve around in maze fashion, ending in culs-de-sac or doubling back on themselves. There is no way in or out of Sun City Center except by the main road bisecting the town. The map, which looks like a child's board game (Snakes and Ladders or Uncle Wiggily), shows a vague area — a kind of no-man's-land — surrounding the town. As the map suggests, there is nothing natural about Sun City Center. The lakes are artificial, and there is hardly a tree or a shrub or a blade of grass that has any correspondence in the world just beyond it. At the edges of the development, there are houses under construction, with the seams still showing in the transplanted lawns. From there, you can look out at a flat brown plain that used to be a cattle ranch. The developer simply scraped the surface off the land and started over again.

Sun City Center is an unincorporated town of about eighty-five hundred people, almost all of whom are over the age of sixty. It is a self-contained community, with stores, banks, restaurants, and doctors' offices. It has the advertised eighty-seven holes of golf; it also has tennis courts, shuffleboard courts, swimming pools, and lawn-bowling greens. In addition to the regular housing, it has a "life-care facility" — a six-story apartment building with a nursing home in one wing. "It's a strange town," a clinical psychologist at the University of South Florida, in Tampa, told me before I went. "It's out there in the middle of nowhere. It has a section of private houses, where people go when they retire. Then it has a section of condos and apartments, where people go when they can't keep up their houses. Then it has a nursing home. Then it has a cemetery." In fact, there is no cemetery in Sun City Center, but the doctor was otherwise correct.

In his social history of the family in Europe, *Centuries of Childhood*, the 4 French historian Philippe Ariès shows us that "childhood" is a social construct. In medieval France, the concept did not exist, for children were not differentiated from other people. In the twelfth century, children out of swaddling clothes would be dressed as adults, and as soon as they could get about independently they would join the world of adults, participating in their work and their social life as fully as their physical capacities permitted. (The painters of the period depicted children as dwarf adults, ignoring their distinctive physiognomy.) The notion of "childhood" developed very slowly over the centuries. Only gradually did children become specialized people, with their own dress, their own work (schooling), their own manners and games. To travel around Florida these days — and particularly to visit a retirement community such as Sun City Center — is to suspect that a similar kind of specialization is taking place at the other end of the age spectrum: that American society is creating a new category of people, called "the aging" or "senior citizens," with their own distinctive habits and customs. (That the name for these people has not yet been agreed upon shows that their status is still transitional.)

In a sense, the residents of Sun City Center and their peers across the United States are living on a frontier. Not a geographical frontier but a chronological one. Old age is nothing new, of course, but for an entire generation to reach old age with its membership almost intact is something new. Until this century, death had no more relation to old age than it had to any other period of life. In fact, it had less. In seventeenth-century France, for example, a quarter of all human beings died before the age of one, another quarter died before the age of twenty, and a third quarter before the age of forty-five; only ten out of a hundred people reached the age of sixty. In France from the seventeenth century to the nineteenth, the percentage of the population over sixty remained almost constant, at 8.8 percent. In America during the same period, life was probably even shorter for most people, and the population as a whole was much younger. But then in the twentieth century the demographics turned around; they changed more than they had in the six previous centuries. In 1900, the average life expectancy for children born in the United States was 47.3 years. In 1980, it was 73.6 years. This startling increase was due mainly to medical success in reducing the rates of infant, childhood, and maternal mortality. But there was — also as a result of medical advances — some increase in longevity as well. In 1900, white men aged sixty could expect an average of 14.4 more years of life. In 1978, they could expect an average of 17.2 more (And women could expect to do better than that.) As a result of these and other demographic changes, the number of people sixty or sixty-five and over increased both absolutely and relative to the population of the United States as a whole. In 1900, people sixty-five and over represented 4 percent of the population. In 1980, they represented 11.3 percent of it, and there were 25.5 million of them.

The younger generation in this country has grown up with the notion that people should reach the age of sixty-five, and reach it in good health. But Americans now over sixty belong to the first generation to do that.

149

Modern medicine has increased longevity to some degree, but, just as important, it has alleviated some of the persistent, nonfatal maladies of the body. Throughout history, of course, some people have reached their eighties in excellent health, but until this century the majority of Europeans and Americans aged as many people still do in the poorest countries of the world — suffering irreversible physical decay in their forties and fifties. Philippe Ariès reminds us that until recently chronological age had very little meaning in European society; the word "old" was associated with the loss of teeth, eyesight, and so on. The very novelty of health and physical vigor in those past sixty-five is reflected in the current struggle over nomenclature. Since the passage of the Social Security Act, in 1935, demographers have used the age of sixty-five as a benchmark and labeled those at or over it as "the old" or "the elderly." The terms are meant to be objective, but because of their connotations they have proved unacceptable to those designated by them. Sensitive to their audience, gerontologists and government agencies have substituted "older people," "the aging," or "senior citizens." These terms, being relative, could apply to anyone of almost any age, but, by a kind of linguistic somersault, they have come to denote a precise chronological category.

People now over sixty-five live on a frontier also in the sense that the territory is fast filling up behind them. By the end of the century, if current demographic trends hold, one in eight Americans, or slightly more than 12 percent of the population, will be sixty-five or over. The increase will at first be relatively small, because the number of children born in the thirties was a relatively small one; but then, barring catastrophe or large-scale immigration, the numbers will start to climb. In the years between 2020 and 2030, after the baby-boom generation reaches its seniority, some fifty-five million Americans, or nearly 20 percent of the projected population, will be sixty-five or over. How the society will support these people is a problem that Americans are just beginning to think about. Politicians have been considering the implications for Social Security and federal retirement benefits, but they have not yet begun to imagine all the consequences in other realms.

The younger generation assumes that at sixty-five people leave their 8 jobs and spend five, ten, or fifteen years of their lives in a condition called retirement. But here, too, the generation now around sixty-five has broken new ground. Historically speaking, the very notion of retirement — on a mass scale, at any rate — is new, and dates only from the industrial revolution, from the time when a majority of workers (and not just a few professionals) became replaceable parts in organizations outside the family. The possibility of retirement for large numbers of people depended, of course, on the establishment of adequate social-insurance systems, and these were not created until long after the building of industry. In this country, whose industrial revolution lagged behind that of Western Europe, the possibility came only with the New Deal. The Social Security Act of 1935 created an economic floor for those who could not work. More important, it created the presumption that American workers had a right to retire — a right to live without working after the age of sixty-five. This presumption led, in turn, to the establishment of government, corporate, and union pension plans that allowed workers to retire without a disastrous loss of income. But these pension plans did not cover very many people until some time after World War II. Even in 1950, 46 percent of all American men sixty-five and over were still working or looking for work. In 1980, only 20 percent were.

In *The Coming of Age,* published in 1970, Simone de Beauvoir called the treatment of the elderly in Western societies a scandal. Citing 1957 statistics, she pointed out that in the United States a quarter of all couples over sixty-five had incomes below the poverty level; the scandal was far worse in the case of single people, since 33 percent of elderly men and 50 percent of elderly women had less than poverty-level incomes. The de Beauvoir analysis is now way out of date, however. Since the late fifties, the economic situation of older people in this country has improved dramatically. In 1978, only 14 percent of all noninstitutionalized elderly people had incomes below the poverty line — or about the same percentage that existed throughout the society. (Between 1959 and 1978, the numbers of the elderly poor actually declined, not only relatively but absolutely, from 5.5 million people to 3.3 million.) Elderly single women fared far worse than couples or single men (21 percent had incomes below the poverty level), and the older people fared worse than the younger "elderly." But everyone went up with the rising tide. Between 1965 and 1976, the median income for families headed by an elderly person increased by 38 percent in real dollars. In 1960, outlays for the elderly constituted 13 percent of the federal budget. In 1980, the figure was 27.5 percent. This rise reflected not only a growth in the number of elderly people but also a real increase in Social Security and federal-pension benefits. In addition, Social Security benefits and pensions (from the government and also from a few corporations) have been adjusted to the Consumer Price Index. The result is that for the past ten years — the years of high inflation — the economic situation of older people has improved both absolutely and relative to that of younger people. In the seventies, the average Social Security benefit shot up 55 percent faster than the price index, while the average income of wage earners rose less than 2 percent in real terms. Between 1970 and 1976, the median income for younger people increased by only 4 percent, whereas it increased by around 20 percent for those sixty-five and over. Thus, the present generation of people in their sixties and seventies may be the most privileged generation of elderly people in history.

Simone de Beauvoir complained in her book that older people were looked upon mainly as a social problem. In the sense that she was correct at the time, she would be correct today — except that the "problem" has largely reversed itself. In the sixties and seventies, American parents worried about the kids of the Woodstock generation "dropping out of the system"; in fact, as we now discover, it was their fathers who were dropping out, in droves. In 1981, only 68 percent of all men between the ages of fifty-five and fifty-nine had year-round, full-time jobs; of those between sixty and sixty-four, only 49 percent did. By the end of 1981, more than half of all male retirees — 57.1 percent — had gone on Social Security pensions before they were sixty-five. The fact that the median age of retirement rose slightly after the economic downturn of 1974–75 suggests that not all these men were victims of unemployment or of mandatory-retirement policies. According to a Louis Harris poll conducted in 1981, 60 percent of all retirements were voluntary; of the remaining 40 percent the great majority resulted from ill health or disability, with mandatory-retirement policies accounting for only a fifth. What all these statistics indicate is that people are living longer, and are also retiring earlier by choice and maintaining something closer to their old standard of living. The question is whether the society will continue to be able to support this unemployed population in addition to its children. Projecting current trends into the future, demographers calculate that by the year 2000 there will be only three active working people to support every person over sixty-five; in the year 2030, the ratio will be only two to one. Government planners, adding up the cost of federal benefits for these future generations of retirees, estimate that at current rates expenditures for Social Security, government pensions, and other programs benefiting the elderly would claim 35 percent of the federal budget in the year 2000 and 65 percent of it in 2025. Given these statistical projections, a number of commentators have announced the imminent outbreak of a war between the old and the young.

Americans now in their sixties and seventies are surely the first generation of healthy, economically independent retired people in history — and, in the absence of significant economic growth, they may well be the last one. But, whatever the economic arrangements of the future, this generation remains the cultural avant-garde for the increasingly large generations of the elderly which are to follow them. Already, its members have broken with many of the traditions of the past, shattering the conventions of what older people should look like and do. And in the process they have changed the shape of American society. The census statistics describe a part of this transformation. They tell us, for one thing, that this generation has used its economic independence to get out of the house — or to get its children out. In 1900, some 60 percent of all Americans sixty-five and over lived with an adult child. Today, only about 17 percent live with one. The figures do not tell us who initiated the move, but they correlate very well with the increasing wealth of the elderly. Today, a majority of Americans over sixty-five live in the same community as at least one of their children, and live in the place in which they spent most of their lives. However, a significant minority of them have altered the traditional pattern by moving away from their families and out of their hometowns to make new lives for themselves elsewhere. Retired people — so the census shows — have contributed greatly to the general American migration to the Sun Belt; indeed, they have gone in such numbers as to make a distinct impression on the demographics of certain states. New Mexico, Arizona, and Southern California now have large populations of retirees, but it is Florida that has the highest proportion of them. People over sixty-five constitute 17.3 percent of the population of Florida — as opposed to the national average of 11.3 percent. These elderly migrants have not distributed themselves evenly around the state but have concentrated themselves on the coasts and in the area of Orlando. As a result, there are three counties on the west coast where the median age is between fifty and sixty, and eleven counties around the state where it is between forty and fifty.

Before World War II, there was, broadly speaking, no such thing as an 12 age-segregated community and no such concept as "retirement living." Until the mid-fifties, in fact, "housing for the elderly" generally meant church-run homes for the very poor. In 1956, the federal government began to subsidize housing for the elderly in a number of ways — by direct loans to nonprofit developers, by mortgage insurance, by rent subsidies — and the funds translated largely into age-segregated apartment complexes. Around the same time, private developers began to build housing for middle-income retirees. In the early sixties, when credit and housing materials were still relatively cheap, huge developers, such as the Del E. Webb Development Corporation, of Phoenix, began to construct entire new towns for the retired. In the mid-seventies, when housing costs doubled and tripled, the developers grew leery of such grand schemes, but by that time there were — according to one estimate — sixty-nine retirement villages, a number of which has populations of over ten thousand. The sixties and seventies saw a proliferation of mobile-home parks for the elderly — in 1975, one survey indicates, there were 700 of them, housing some 300,000 people — and the creation of various other forms of age-segregated housing, from retirement hotels to luxury condominiums. The most original of these forms was the so-called life-care facility. This offers the buyer a small house or a private apartment, maid service, nursing care, and meals in a common dining room; in addition, it offers nursing-home care when or if it was necessary. Such institutions are expensive, but by the mid-seventies, according to one estimate, some 85,000 Americans were living in them. Gerontologists struggling to create a taxonomy for all these new forms of retirement housing estimate that about 5 percent of Americans sixty-five and over live in age-segregated housing and another unknown but significant percentage live in neighborhoods that are more or less age-segregated.

The twenty-five-year increase in life expectancy, the expansion and growing length of retirement, the migration of elderly people away from their children and hometowns, and the development of age-segregated housing are phenomena that have occurred on a mass scale in such a short time that they are difficult to comprehend, much less to analyze. As Ronald Blythe wrote in the introduction to *The View in Winter,* his book on the elderly in England, "the economics of national longevity apart, the ordinariness of living to be old is too novel a thing at the moment to appreciate." Of course, there are experts, but these experts — the social gerontologists — do not claim to have much information. Social scientists in general have some propensity to conclude articles in academic journals with the announcement that more research on the subject is needed. Social gerontologists often begin and end their articles with this declaration. Robert Atchley, the author of one of the best-known texts on gerontology, concludes his book with the thought that "there is not a single area of social gerontology that does not need more answers to crucial questions."

In the early sixties, the late Professor Arnold M. Rose, a sociologist at the University of Minnesota, published a paper entitled "The Subculture of the Aging: A Framework for Research in Social Gerontology." In it, he listed all the changes in the status and condition of the elderly — greater longevity, improved standards of living, better health, better education, and so on — and deduced from them the growth of a "subculture of the aging." This subculture, according to Rose, would have its own distinctive attitudes toward death and toward marriage, its own style of "interpersonal relationships," its own argot, its own leisure activities, and its own rituals. There was, he said, an "almost complete absence of empirical data" on most aspects of this subculture. But there was evidence that older people were developing "group consciousness" based on "self-conception and mutual identification"; that is, they were beginning to think of themselves as a group and to contemplate group action in social life and in politics. Otherwise, the subculture remained hypothetical.

Since Rose's paper was published, a number of social gerontologists have attacked his thesis, on the ground that race, class, and even generational culture mean a great deal more to people than age, and create more profound divisions in the society. These objections make sense — certainly on a national level. True, organizations representing the elderly — the American Association of Retired Persons, the National Council of Senior Citizens, the National Retired Teachers Association, and others — have combined to fight for Social Security and other federal benefits, and do so most effectively. But these organizations do not always make common cause — and most of them do not take stands — on social, cultural, or political issues. And their lobbying groups do not always speak with a single voice. In St. Petersburg, for example, the oldest retirement town in America, and therefore presumably the most age-conscious, the retired people who live in the old downtown hotels and rooming houses vote differently from those who live in the new high-rise condos on the beach. The first tend to vote Democratic and for government-aid programs; the second vote Republican and against government spending. (Both, however, vote against local bond issues for the schools — this is their only real area of agreement.) Though about three-fifths of the registered voters in St. Petersburg are over sixty, the city has no united "senior citizen" lobby, and it has only one city council member over sixty-five. Furthermore, in all the years that retired people have dominated the city they have not developed a distinctive single "culture." The blacks in St. Petersburg live in neighborhoods segregated by color, not by age, and the white retirees from the North inhabit a variety of different worlds. In St. Petersburg, I met a spry ninety-six-year-old man who was lobbying the city council to build a new auditorium where the state societies could put on dances and minstrel shows without interference from "the coloreds or the kids." There also, I met a sixty-five-year-old woman who divided her time between teaching holistic health care to the elderly, tutoring disturbed children, and growing organic vegetables and herbs in a garden of a house she shared with her ex-husband. "I'm an aging hippie," she told me brightly. And when I asked her about Sun City Center she said, "I wouldn't think of going to a place like that. What, and live with all those old people? I'm sure it's not good for anyone."

To say that there is no national subculture of "the aging" is not, there- 16 fore, to say that subcultures don't exist. Even those gerontologists who have registered objections to Rose's thesis would admit that in certain communities retired people are inventing new kinds of relationships, new ways of spending their time, and new ways of dealing with death. The Sun Cities and Leisure Worlds are without precedent; no society recorded in history has ever had whole villages — whole cities — composed exclusively of elderly people. These communities are not just places where the elderly happen to find each other, as they do in certain rural communities and certain inner-city neighborhoods after everyone else has moved out. They are deliberate creations — places where retired people have gone by choice to live with each other. Most of them, founded in the early sixties, are now old enough to have evolved from mere developers' tracts into communities with traditions of their own. Oddly, however, they remain almost a terra incognita° to gerontologists, despite all the research devoted to them.

---

terra incognita Unknown territory.

The appearance of developer-built retirement villages occasioned a great debate in gerontological circles — indeed, one of the greatest debates ever conducted in that field. In the early sixties, opinion was generally ranged against them. Both professionals and laymen — city planners, journalists, and the like — attacked them as ghettos for ill-adjusted, alienated people or as playgrounds that "trivialized" old age. But there were some who heralded them as an exciting new solution to the problems of physical incapacity and social isolation which so often plagued the elderly. All these early opinions tended to be a priori judgments, by those who had spent little or no time in retirement communities. Then, in the mid-sixties, a number of gerontologists went out to the retirement villages with scientific sampling methods and attitudinal charts. Their investigations produced a new welter of articles in the professional journals. One study showed that the inhabitants of a certain retirement village were better educated and better off than the average retired person — a fact that could have been deduced from the price of houses in that development. Another study showed that the residents of Leisure World, in Laguna Hills, California, had gone there because of the golf; their desire for an "easy-maintenance dwelling unit"; the smog in Los Angeles; and the invasion of their old neighborhood by "minority groups." They had, in other words, gone there for all the reasons overtly and subliminally advertised in the real-estate brochures. The gerontologists had so far discovered what the developers already knew. Measuring the attitudes of residents by "life satisfaction" scales and other tests of their own devising, the researchers also found that the inhabitants of retirement communities were generally satisfied with their communities. This discovery was also less than a scientific break-through, since the householders clearly had the option of moving out if they were dissatisfied. One of the last of these studies, conducted by Gordon L. Bultena and Vivian Wood and published in 1969, reached the conclusion that these communities provided life satisfaction to that self-selected group of people which chose to live in them. This redundancy has become the final considered opinion of most gerontologists today.

The interesting thing about these studies was the near-exclusive concern of the researchers about the happiness of retirement-community residents. "Are you happy?" the researchers would ask in a dozen different ways, and in a dozen different ways the residents would answer, "Yes." More recently, the gerontologists have got around to asking themselves what they mean by happiness. In *Aging in the 1980s*, a new textbook put out by the American Psychological Association, Dr. Joyce Parr writes of "an increasing awareness of the problem of confusion associated with such global concepts [as] life satisfaction, morale, adjustment, and developmental task accomplishment." Dr. Parr continues:

George (1979) expressed the need for reexamining the concept of life satisfaction and the psychometric characteristics of the available instruments. Cutler (1979) demonstrated both the multi-dimensionality of the concept of life satisfaction and that the dimensionality differs substantially across age groups. Larson (1978) presented a review of a variety of measures used to investigate the well-being of older persons. [He] cautions that such measures tell us little about individual informants and notes that "we have little idea how the construct permeates ongoing daily experience."

These are the "crucial questions" that are likely to lack answers for some time to come. Or, as Dr. Parr puts it, "there is an increasing recognition that characteristics of environments interact with characteristics of persons to produce behavior. It is also recognized, however, that much work is needed to develop meaningful ways to describe this interaction." The gerontologists may next begin to ask themselves what they mean by "meaningful."

Among developer-built retirement villages, Sun City Center is middle- 20 sized, conventionally organized, and remarkable only for its isolation. It was founded by the Del E. Webb Development Corporation in 1960. Initial plans called for a development of private houses with communally owned public buildings and recreation centers. That same year, Del Webb also began the development of Sun City, Arizona, near Phoenix. But while Sun City, Arizona, expanded to city size and extends almost to the suburbs of Phoenix, Sun City Center grew slowly and experienced a number of difficulties along the way. The first difficulty was its name. Del Webb wanted to call it Sun City, but a tiny town a few miles away already had the name and refused to give it up, claiming to be the chrysanthemum center of the nation. In 1972, Sun City Center had only about three thousand residents, and Del Webb decided to sell. The purchaser, a Tampa real-estate consortium, formed a new management company for the town, the W-G Development Corporation. Impatient with the pace of sales, W-G broke with the original plan and allowed another development company to build condominiums right next to the housing tract. When it was just under way, the 1974–75 recession hit, the Florida condo market collapsed, and the new development came to a dead stop. W-G and the new development company reverted to their mortgage holders. In 1981, both companies were bought by a partnership supported by corporate pension funds and managed by Victor Palmieri and Company, a large assets-management firm. (Palmieri had been an ambassador-at-large and the Coordinator for Refugee Affairs under the Carter administration.) Sun City Center now comprises the original housing development, with a population of fifty-five hundred (I shall call it Sun City), and the newer condominium development, called Kings Point, with a population of about twelve hundred permanent and eighteen hundred seasonal residents. According to W-G, both developments are now doing very well, and the town has been growing more rapidly in recent years than it grew in the past. The changes of ownership do not seem to have affected the residents adversely, and while some move out after spending some time there, it is usually for reasons of their own; most residents consider W-G a satisfactory landlord.

Twenty-five miles from Tampa, the nearest city, Sun City Center has become a world unto itself. Over the years, the town attracted a supermarket and all the stores and services necessary to the maintenance of daily life. Now, in addition, it has a golf-cart dealer, two banks, three savings and loan associations, four restaurants, and a brokerage firm. For visitors, there is the Sun City Center Inn. The town has a post office. Five churches have been built by the residents, and a sixth is under construction. A number of doctors have set up offices in the town, and a Bradenton hospital recently opened a satellite hospital with 112 beds. There is no school, of course. The commercial establishments all front on the state road running through the center of town, but, because most of them are more expensive than those in the neighboring towns, the people from the surrounding area patronize only the supermarket, the laundromat, and one or two others. The local farmers and the migrant workers they employ, many of whom are Mexican, have little relationship to golf courses or to dinner dances with organ music. Conversely, Sun Citians are not the sort of people who would go to bean suppers in the Pentecostal churches or hang out at raunchy bars where gravel-voiced women sing "Satin Sheets and Satin Pillows." The result is that Sun Citians see very little of their Florida neighbors. They take trips to Tampa, Bradenton, and Sarasota, but otherwise they rarely leave the green-and-white developments, with their palm-lined avenues and artificial lakes. In the normal course of a week, they rarely see anyone under sixty.

Bess Melvin, a resident of Sun City who works part time in public relations for W-G, took me on a tour the first day of a visit I made to Sun City Center. Our first stop was the Town Hall recreation complex — a group of handsomely designed buildings with white columns and low red-tiled roofs. In front were shuffleboard courts and lawn-bowling greens, and in the center was a large, round swimming pool, surrounded by deck chairs and tables with gaily colored umbrellas. The buildings housed a glass-roofed indoor swimming pool, an exercise room, billiard rooms, card rooms, and studios with all the equipment for woodworking, weaving, pottery-making, ceramics, and decoupage. There were shops displaying lapidary work and shell decorations made by the residents, and there was an auditorium with brass chandeliers, and chairs that could be rearranged for a meeting or a formal dance. That morning, there were three or four people working in each of the studios and several people doing laps in the indoor swimming pool.

"Sun City Center isn't like the stereotype of a retirement community," Bess Melvin explained. "The usual thought is that you lose your usefulness. You sit back and rock in your rocking chair, and life slows to a stop. But the people here aren't looking for that. Sun City Center has a hundred and thirty clubs and activities. We've got a stamp club, a poetry club, a softball club, a garden club — I could go on and on — as well as active branches of the Rotary, the Kiwanis, the Woman's Club, and that sort of thing. The residents form their own clubs and run the Civic Association, so if you've got a particular talent or social concern you can always find an opportunity to develop it. Many people take up painting, and we have some really fine artists here."

Possibly some people still imagine retirement communities as board- 24 inghouses with rocking chairs, but, thanks to Del Webb and a few other pioneer developers, the notion of "active retirement" has become entirely familiar; indeed, since the sixties it has been the guiding principle of retire- ment-home builders across the country. Almost all developers now adver- tise recreational facilities and print glossy brochures with photos of gray- haired people playing golf, tennis, and shuffleboard. The "activity centers" in the various developments differ, but the differences have largely to do with the economics of the community.

According to the W-G real-estate agents, a new two-bedroom house in Sun City costs from $60,000 to $90,000. Some of the older houses — the ones on the prettiest of the lakes — now resell for $100,000 or more, though they cost only $20,000 or $30,000 in the mid-sixties. A homeowner can buy membership in the Civic Association for fifty dollars a year and have the use of all the communal facilities. Golf is extra — $850 a year for a couple — and golf is clearly the main attraction of Sun City Center. W-G not only advertises the town's eighty-seven holes of golf prominently but sponsors national golfing tournaments and offers weeks of golfing instruction for seniors across the country. At Kings Point, the arrangements and the eco- nomics are somewhat different. In the early seventies, the developer put up small, flat-roofed buildings with condos costing only about $12,000 each. After the Florida condo bust, however, W-G found that the real market for Kings Point lay among higher-income people. The new condos are thus more luxurious, and cost $40,000 to $60,000 each. Here also golf is the main attraction — that and the huge white Kings Point clubhouse, with indoor and outdoor pools, card rooms, exercise rooms, and so on. The facilities are just as clean and handsome as those in Sun City, but there are certain stylistic differences, in part because many condo owners only winter in

Florida. Whereas at Sun City the residents' Civic Association owns and runs the recreational center, at Kings Point these things are owned by W-G and run by a social director. Whereas Sun City has dance clubs and sports clubs, Kings Point has dance and exercise classes.

Bess Melvin took me to the library in the Town Hall complex at Sun City. The small, bright rooms contained displays of periodicals and a collection heavy on histories, biographies, and novels. Her task there was to photograph the president of the Sun City DAR presenting a book on Early American costumes to the library. A svelte woman in her sixties, the DAR representative had for the occasion dressed in a white jersey dress, stockings, heels, and gloves. She seemed to have no further appointments that morning. I wandered outside to watch the parade of golf carts, bicycles, three-wheelers, and wide American cars proceeding rather slowly along the central boulevard. The traffic was heaviest near the entrance to the golf club. Behind the club, twosomes and foursomes were embarking on the course, the women in golf skirts, the men in Bermuda shorts, Lacoste shirts, and narrow-brimmed straw hats.

Anyone visiting a retirement community for the first time would expect to be impressed by a uniformity of age. But Sun Citians have so much else in common in the realm of appearance that age seems the least of it. On the streets, most people wear golf clothes whether they are golfing or not. At home, the women uniformly wear slacks, with blouses hanging loose outside them. At church on Sunday, it's difficult to recognize a female acquaintance from the back, since all the women have the same neat permanent wave; and in the winter about half of them will have on identical blond fur coats. At Sun City Center Inn on a Saturday night, the women lined up at the well-stocked buffet or dancing to organ music with their husbands wear flowered dresses in pink and green, pearls, and low-heeled sandals. On such occasions, the men — all close-cropped and clean-shaven — dress even more colorfully, in checked trousers and white shoes, red or green linen slacks, pink shirts with blue blazers, madras ties, and the occasional madras jacket.

According to W-G statistics, the people now buying houses in Sun City 28 Center have incomes of between $21,000 and $29,000 a year. ("Some of them are millionaires," Bess Melvin assured me.) The income level of Sun Citians has shifted upward over the past ten years along with the price of the houses. Still, Sun Citians are a remarkably homogeneous group; in particular, those who live in Sun City proper occupy a far narrower band on the spectrum of American society than economics would dictate. To look at the Sun City membership directory is to see that the men are by and large retired professionals, middle-management executives with large corporations, or small businessmen. Among the professionals, there are some retired doctors and lawyers, but these are far outnumbered by school administrators, colonels, and engineers. Most of the women were house-wives, but a surprisingly large number were schoolteachers or registered nurses. Most Sun Citians are Protestants — Episcopalians, Presbyterians, Methodists, Baptists, and Lutherans — but there are some Catholics as well, and a very few Jews. Politically, they are conservative and vote Republican. (The two most prominent visitors to Sun City in recent years were Ronald Reagan and Malcolm Muggeridge. The former came to give a speech in the early days of his 1980 primary campaign, and the latter, unbeknownst to most Sun Citians, stayed almost a month.) A great number of them are Masons or members of such organizations as the Kiwanis, the Shriners, and the Woman's Club. They come from the Northeast and the Midwest, and none of them — it is hardly necessary to say — are black.

One of the earliest settlers in the town, Erna Krauch, a retired school-teacher, explained the homogeneity of the community by the fact that many Sun Citians came here through personal recommendations. Mrs. Krauch and her husband, being one of the first couples to come, found Sun City Center through an advertisement. They had spent winter vacations in Sarasota for a number of years, but when they came to Sun City, in March 1962, they bought immediately. By October of that year, Mr. Krauch had sold his business, a pharmacy in Brentwood, Long Island, and by Thanks-giving the house was finished and they had moved in. "He wanted a warm climate," Mrs. Krauch said. "And a place to play golf. He never worried, as I did, about leaving everything and coming here. He lived only two years after that. I think he knew."

Most of the Sun Citians I talked to had come here in much the same way. They had wintered in Florida for some years. Around the time of the husband's retirement, they had visited Sun City Center — often on the recommendation of a friend or acquaintance — and had made a snap decision to buy. A few months later, they had sold their house in the North and moved in, with all their belongings. The men had initiated the move, and the women had been less than sanguine about it at first. "In the beginning, the people who came were mostly retired schoolteachers and businessmen looking for summer homes," Mrs. Krauch said. "They were people who didn't put on airs, people you could be quite natural with." She dropped the subject, but came back to it later, saying, "They were doctors, lawyers, and professors — that sort of thing — people you didn't have to prove anything to. The people who buy the houses now are finan-cially better off than we were when we came. They are more affluent. They can afford to retire. Whereas for us it was a kind of summer home." Technically, what Mrs. Krauch meant was a winter home, but she was at that moment waving a hand toward her chairs and tables, of white rattan and her sofas, covered in flowered chintz. Still, the distinction she was making was a curious one, since she and her husband had never had a second house. They had sold their house on Long Island before moving here. Mrs. Krauch had lived in her "summer home" continuously for over twenty years.

When I asked why they chose Sun City Center, most of the men I talked to said, "The golf." Ronald Smith, an engineer retired from Western Electric, told me that he had always wanted to live on a golf course but had not been able to afford it while the kids were going to school. When he and his wife, Lora, first arrived here, they had dropped everything — had not even bothered to unpack — and had played golf solidly for two months. Now, fourteen years later, Ronald Smith was still playing every day, and Lora was recovering from a knee operation she had undergone in order to be able to play again.

But for Lora Smith, as for most of the other women I talked to, the main 32 attraction of Sun City was the people. "It's the people who sell the houses, not the real-estate agents," Mrs. Smith said. The Smiths had come at the suggestion of a couple they had met in Florida — he was a banker, Mrs. Smith remembered, and his wife was a schoolteacher, like her. "When I arrived, I looked at all the manicured lawns, and thought perhaps Sun Citians were a lot of conformists," she said. "But then I knocked at five doors, and five different kinds of people came out — all very generous, very pleasant. I could not believe that everybody was that kind of person. There's such a variety of people here — people of achievement, people who talk about ideas, not about their ailments, because that's the kind of minds they have." Lively and gregarious people themselves, the Smiths had no difficulty finding friends. "No one gives a hang here what you did or where you came from," Mrs. Smith said. "It's what you are now that matters." Later, in a different context, her husband said much the same thing, adding that the colonels refused to be called "Colonel."

Sun City Center has age restrictions, of course. For a family to be eligible to live in Sun City, at least one member must be fifty, and neither there nor in Kings Point can residents have children under eighteen. But with one exception no Sun Citian I talked to said he or she had chosen the town because of the age restrictions. When I asked Mrs. Krauch why she and her husband had chosen an age-segregated community she looked startled. "Oh, I didn't feel I would just be with a lot of older people," she said. "And Sun City Center isn't like that!" Sun Citians would certainly be horrified to know that some retirees in St. Petersburg and Tampa look upon their town as an old-age ghetto. When Sun Citians speak of a "retirement community," what they usually mean is a life-care center or a nursing home. They came to Sun City Center for all the amenities spelled out in the advertising brochures and for a homogeneity that had little to do with age. In a country where class is rarely discussed, they had found their own niche like homing pigeons. And once they were home they were happy.

"Lots of fine people," one resident told the community newspaper. "This is a cross section of the better people in the nation."

The notion that Sun Citians do not care about past professional status is a thought often articulated in Sun City. Sun City boosters — and most Sun Citians are boosters when they talk to an outsider — say it almost as regularly as they say that they are always active and on the go. The fact that the Sun City membership directory — it is actually the phone book — lists the residents' past professions along with their addresses suggests, however, that the notion is less a description of the community than a doctrine belonging to it. (Some people list the company or service they worked for, others their calling — "educator," say — and a very few put nothing at all.) Most people, like Mrs. Krauch and Mrs. Smith, have a fairly exact idea of the professional standing of their neighbors. The less exacting say, "We have some doctors and lawyers. We have some millionaires, too." Sun Citians will very often praise the company they are in by saying, "They're people of achievement — people with prestige." That most Sun Citians have the same set of achievements and the same sort of prestige does not seem to worry them; indeed, the contrary is true.

A curious thing about the Sun City Center complex is the lack of parallelism in the rules governing the communal facilities at Sun City and at Kings Point. The Kings Point club — owned by the developer — is open to anyone (or anyone within reason) who wishes to purchase membership. The Sun City Civic Association buildings — owned by the residents — are closed to anyone who does not live in that particular development. More than one resident explained to me that the tax laws were responsible for this restriction. But a community-relations executive for W-G told me that the tax laws had nothing to do with it: the restriction was an arbitrary one, made by Sun City residents. Asking around among Sun Citians, I discovered that when Kings Point was founded, in 1972, a number of Sun Citians had objected to the development, arguing that the cheap condos would attract a new element and ruin the community. Failing to stop it, they had refused to open the Civic Association to Kings Pointers. "It's really foolish," Lora Smith told me. "Sun City has all these clubs established — an Audubon Society Chapter, music groups, and that kind of thing — but the people from over there can't join them if they meet on Civic Association property. I mean, a really good musician from over there wouldn't be able to join a chorus or chamber-music group. There's a sort of a wall between us. People here feel — Well, they feel they arrived a little sooner than people over there. It's a matter of snob appeal, you see."

When I asked Kings Point residents what the people there used to do 36 for a living, the answer was initially "We've got some doctors and lawyers — some millionaires, too." But when I pressed them about the differences between the two developments they said, "Well, they're more affluent over there." The fact is that Kings Point has a much greater variety of people than Sun City. It has former doctors and lawyers and perhaps some millionaires, but it also has retired policemen, retired door-to-door salesmen, and at least one retired commercial fisherman. It used to be impossible to discover the extent of the professional variety, since the Kings Point directory did not list the former employment of its residents. One resident told me he considered the Sun City directory a form of boasting. However, professions are now listed in the Kings Point book. Kings Point also has some Democrats, some Catholics, and some Jews. There are not many Jews — only two hundred in a population of three thousand — but there are more than the handful who live in Sun City. And that is another source of anti–Kings Point feeling. Asked to explain the restriction made by the Civic Association, one long-term resident of Sun City said, "Well, you know, at the beginning some people over there bought six or eight condominiums for speculative purposes, and they rent them out." This woman had told me that she speculated in land elsewhere in Florida, so I thought her objection an odd one to make. But she continued, "I know a lot of Jews I don't think of as being Jewish. But there are just some people I think of as Jewish, because of certain qualities they have."

Dr. Robert Gingery, the pastor of the interdenominational Protestant church in Sun City Center, told me that anti-Semitism was a serious problem in the community. "I do all I can to fight against it," he said. At his invitation, the Jewish congregation holds services and Hebrew classes in the chapel of his church. The Sunday I attended his services, he made a point in his sermon of praising the rectitude and courage of the Jewish people after the Diaspora. "We in the church try to act as a bridge," he said, "but a lot of people were brought up with these attitudes." The Jews in the community are naturally quite conscious of these attitudes, but most of them are anxious to play the issue down. The head of the Jewish congregation said that at Kings Point anti-Semitism was "no worse than it is anywhere in the society"; but he and others admitted that it was one of the reasons for the exclusion of Kings Point people from the Sun City Civic Association.

Kings Point people — Christians as well as Jews — are well aware of Sun City attitudes, and resent them. "There's a strong sense that this is the wrong side of the tracks," one man said. What is more, the Kings Point people retaliate systematically. While I was there, the development voted against sending money and volunteers to the Sun City Emergency Squad, even though the contributions would have meant free ambulance service for Kings Point. Kings Pointers habitually refuse to go along with civic projects initiated by Sun Citians. But they have another, more insidious form of retaliation. At the entrance to Kings Point, there is a large white double archway through which all vehicles must pass. The guards at the gate — some of whom are retired policemen living in Kings Point — will not let anyone though the gate who does not have a sticker or a visitor's pass. The gateway does seem to enhance security in the development. But because the guards are so punctilious about their job, refusing to let even the oldest citizens through without a pass, one function that the gateway serves in the course of a day is to keep Sun Citians out.

What most Kings Point people do not realize is that Sun Citians make distinctions among themselves that are finer but no less finely understood than those between the two developments. Sun Citians are not uniformly "affluent," and people like Mrs. Krauch know exactly where the richer people live and what their houses cost. The newer people have, on the average, higher incomes than those who retired on the Social Security and pension benefits of between ten and twenty years ago. The older people resent this inequity, not only for its own sake but because it makes it seem that the younger people had better jobs than they did. Struggling to make me understand this injustice, one of the older residents said, "No, it's not that the new people are *richer* — it's that they had larger pensions when they retired." There is thus some friction between age groups. But age does not completely determine status; Sun Citians make other distinctions as well. "The golfers are the elite of the community," one man told me. "They're the ones who give the cocktail parties." According to Sun Citians, there are, generally speaking, three social groups: the golfers, the "cultural set," and the people who take craft classes and go to potluck suppers at the Town Hall. The golfers don't mix much with the others. "I went to a party the other day," one of the older residents told me, "and there was a golfer there. He didn't have anyone to talk to. I happened to know him, so finally he came up to me and said, 'I guess golfers are different people.' I'd like to have said, 'Yes, they're the biggest bunch of snobs!'" While the nongolfers tend to categorize all the golfers as "stuffed shirts," the golfers make their own internal distinctions. In 1980, a group of them got together and put up the money for the developer to build a private golf course on the edge of town. Now completed, the Caloosa Club is a private country club inside a semiprivate country club.

In Sun City Center, a few people make serious efforts to break down 40 some of these social barriers. One of them is Lou Ellen Wilson, an attractive and competent woman of forty-four, who is in charge of community relations for W-G. The company has an interest in keeping peace between the developments, and Mrs. Wilson often manages to make them cooperate in spite of themselves. Because of her, the Sun City ambulances do react to emergencies at Kings Point — the fact is simply not advertised. Another such person is Jackie Fenzau, the social director of the Kings Point club. A striking-looking woman of generous enthusiasms, Mrs. Fenzau, who is in her early fifties, has since the beginning organized everything that goes on at the club, including bus trips, classes, and entertainments. She is proudest of her monthly "theme dances," at which people wear costumes and do skits or sing songs. ("You should see the cutups we have!") Her goal is to make people happy with the club and with each other, and in her view the people who are the least happy are the ones who dwell on their past achievements. "Some people are still in competition when they come here," she told me. "A few of the men are very insecure, so they brag about what they have done in their lives. But that doesn't make them any friends. One couple I am thinking about had a terrible time adjusting. He came in here all the time to complain, telling me he was a lawyer. He had a very negative attitude toward everything. With most people, though, you wouldn't know what they did unless you happened to be involved in some activity where their backgrounds could be useful. Most people have reached a time in life when they don't want to worry about what Mr. So-and-So did."

Dr. Gingery has much the same attitude, though he, of course, addresses the problem of community in more global terms. He has served in Sun City Center for over ten years; his church, affiliated with the United Church of Christ, now has over sixteen hundred members and is one of the fastest-growing churches in the denomination. This is something of a personal triumph for Gingery, since there are four other Protestant churches in town and his views are not wholly orthodox for the community. A Methodist by training, he is both a theological liberal, as most Sun Citians are, and a political liberal, as most of them definitely are not. A tall, handsome man of sixty-three, he gives a stylish sermon and could probably get away on charm. But he and his three assistant pastors work very hard. He spends a great deal of time on pastoral work, and he has made his church the cultural and civic center of the town. The most important piece of neutral ground between the two developments, the church has music groups, writing groups, and a "college," which brings in speakers to talk about subjects ranging from medical advances to foreign policy; the "college" also has a weekly forum for the discussion of community affairs. Dr. Gingery worries a good deal about the fact that Sun City Center is an island of wealth in the midst of rural poverty. Recently, he persuaded his church members to put up seed money for a government housing loan so that forty or so very poor families in the area could build houses with indoor plumbing. He is possibly the social conscience of the town. He also likes Sun Citians. "There's a great deal of camaraderie here," he told me. "People know they are in the same boat. When I talk with new arrivals in town, I like to compare them to the Pilgrims crossing the ocean to take up a new life. They have to put their best foot forward, and they do. They work at making friends, and they know what didn't work before."

Dr. Gingery's simile is a powerful one. The story of the Pilgrims' crossing — the creation myth for the United States — suggests an ideal of community, a brotherhood transcending all social distinctions. It evokes the egalitarian strain in the American tradition and the optimism about making a radical break with the past. In the context of Sun City, however, the image is somewhat disturbing, for if Sun Citians were to cast off their past, who or what would they be? They have no jobs, no families around them, and not very much future. Furthermore, the community they have chosen is already so homogeneous as to threaten the boundaries of the self. Writing of the United States in the 1830s, Alexis de Tocqueville as much as predicted the reaction of Sun Citians:

> In democracies where the members of the community never differ much from each other and naturally stand so near that they may at any time be fused in one general mass, numerous artificial and arbitrary distinctions spring up by means of which every man hopes to keep himself aloof lest he should be carried away against his will into the crowd.
>
> This can never fail to be the case, for human institutions can be changed, but man cannot; whatever may be the general endeavor of a community to render its members equal and alike, the personal pride of individuals will always be to rise above the line and to form somewhere an inequality to their own advantage.

Dr. Gingery and Jackie Fenzau would surely consider this a gloomy view of human nature. But Tocqueville did not see it that way at all. His concern was for the integrity of the individual. What worried him about egalitarian systems was their tendency to destroy individual differences, dismantle identity, submerge the individual within the crowd. Had he been able to visit Sun City, he might have felt that by making social distinctions Sun Citians were in an existential sense protecting themselves.

Certainly it is fortunate that Sun Citians can discern the differences between the houses in their development, for an outsider walking or driving around Sun City finds the experience akin to sensory deprivation. The curving white streets — with names like La Jolla Avenue and Pebble Beach Boulevard — lead only back upon themselves, and since the land is flat they give no vistas on the outside world. Turning through the points of the compass, the visitor comes to another lake, another golf course, another series of white houses. The houses are not identical — the developer always gives buyers several models to choose from — but they are all variations on the same theme: white ranch house. Then, too, the whole town looks as if it had been landscaped by the same landscape gardener. Every house has a Bermuda-grass lawn, a tree surrounded by white gravel, and a shrubbery border set off by white stones. Some owners have put white plaster statues of cupids or wading birds in the shrubs. In the newer sections, each house has a wrought-iron fixture with a carriage lamp and a sign reading THE JONESES or THE SMITHS (there are twenty-eight Smiths in Sun City Center, and fifteen Joneses), and, under that, "Bob and Betty" or "Bill and Marge." No toys litter the pathways. The streets and the sidewalks are so clean they looked scrubbed.

The developers have created this world, but they have made no mis-   44 takes. Sun Citians maintain it, and they like it as it is. One woman told me that she had come there at least in part because of the neatness of the lawns. "But I'm afraid I don't take as good care of my lawn as I should," she said. "When the wind blows hard, a palm frond will often blow down, and the next day my neighbor will be angry at me for not picking it up. He wants me to cut the tree down. I don't think I will." Kings Point people often sit outside their houses; Sun City people rarely do, perhaps because they require more privacy, perhaps because they're loath to disturb such perfection.

Sun Citians keep their houses with the same fanatical tidiness: the fibers in the carpets are stiff from vacuuming; the tables reflect one's face. One woman I visited had put a plastic runner across her new white carpeting; another apologized for the mess in her workroom when there was only a pencil and a sheet of paper out of place. But the interiors of Sun City houses are not anonymous, for Sun Citians are collectors; their houses are showcases for family treasures and the bric-a-brac collected over a lifetime. On the walls are oil paintings of bucolic landscapes, pastel portraits of children, Thai rubbings, or Chinese lacquer panels inlaid with cherry blossoms. Almost every living room has a cabinet filled with pieces of antique china and gold-rimmed glass. On the tables are ship models, sports trophies, carved animals, china figurines, or trees made of semiprecious stones. In a week in Sun City, I visited only one house where there was no bric-a-brac to speak of and where the owners lived in a comfortable disarray of newspapers, usable ashtrays, and paperback books. In most Sun City living rooms, the objects seem to rule. China birds, wooden horses, or ivory elephants parade resolutely across coffee tables and seem to have an independent life and purpose of their own.

For all this cleanliness and order, there is something childlike about Sun City. In part, it's that so many people have collections of puppets, animals, pillows, or dolls. In part, it's that everyone is so talkative, so pleasant, so eager to please. The impression also comes from the warm air, the pastel colors, the arbitrary curving of the streets, the white plaster ducks on the lawns and the real ducks that parade undisturbed among them on their way from lake to lake. The very absence of children contributes to this atmosphere, since the people riding around on three-wheelers or golf carts seem to have no parents. Then, too, one associates uniformity of age with camp or school.

The rhythm of life in Sun City comes in some measure from the weekly schedule of events set by the Civic Association. On Mondays from nine to noon, Sun Citians can choose yoga classes, the Table Tennis Club, the Shuffleboard Club, the Lawn Bowlers' Club, or the Men's and Women's Golf Association matches. The studios for the shell-crafters, needlepointers, weavers, and so on are open most weekday mornings and afternoons. On Tuesdays, the Men's Chorus meets from nine to eleven, and the Duplicate Bridge Association meets at one. On Wednesdays and Fridays, the Potter's Wheel Club meets in the mornings, and there is volleyball at two. The decoupage group meets on Thursday mornings, and the Men's Card Club plays gin rummy at twelve-thirty. Most days, a regular bus leaves for Tampa or Bradenton at ten, but there are special trips for dinner theaters once a week in the winter. The Woman's Club has a luncheon once a month, and so do the Investment Club and the Shriners; the Kiwanis Club meets every week. Most of the card clubs — Ladies' Penny Ante Poker, Men's Bridge, and so on — meet at one o'clock or in the evenings from six-thirty to ten. On Tuesday evenings, there is square dancing, on Wednesday evenings there is ballroom dancing, and on Saturday afternoons Sun Citians can practice their rumbas, waltzes, and cha-cha-chas.

To talk with Sun Citians is — necessarily — to hear a great deal about [48] their schedules. With one or two exceptions, all the Sun Citians I met went on at length about the activities, clubs, civic groups, and cultural events in the town. Not just the public relations people but more than one of the residents reminded me that this was "the town too busy to retire." It was not sheer boosterism, for the same people would go on to tell me what activities they participated in and what busy schedules they had. In preparation for an interview, one man went to the trouble of writing out a list of his activities: Emergency Squad, travel abroad, gardening, bicycling, Photo Club, Radio Club. He also wrote out a list of his wife's activities: library, bicycling, cleaning.

So strongly do Sun Citians insist on their activities that after a while the visitor must begin to imagine that there is some unspoken second term of people who are not active at all. And, of course, such people exist. Sun City has its sick and feeble elderly people. It also has some alcoholics — how many it is impossible to tell. Dr. Gingery's pastors counsel only a handful of them, but one of the pastors, Dr. Mark Strickland, believes that there are many more, who go untreated, since their circumstances permit them to live as alcoholics undetected. (A doctor at the University of South Florida who has researched the subject believes that alcoholism is more prevalent among the elderly than is generally supposed.) In addition, there are people who after the loss of a spouse have simply turned their faces to the wall. There are also people who don't know what to do with themselves, and watch an inordinate amount of daytime TV. And there are a great many people who, while active, are not really very busy. When a golf cart breaks down in some public place, a dozen men will collect around it to kick the tires and trade theories about the electrical connections.

But the fact that this second term of people exists does not, perhaps, provide an explanation for Sun City's insistence on busyness. For to stay around Sun City Center for any length of time is to see that some large proportion of the Sun Citians do lead active lives. The Sun City Town Hall and the Kings Point clubhouse are busy places all day long. The craft studios are perhaps not quite as popular as Sun Citians advertise, but there are usually a few people in every one of them. The organized activities — the bingo games, the bus trips, the dances — are well subscribed, and a lot of people swim, play shuffleboard, and work out in the exercise rooms. The golf courses have players on every hole from morning until dusk, and at the Caloosa Club at midday there are sometimes three dozen women playing bridge and gin.

Not all the activities go on at the clubs; many people have private pursuits. The Neubergers, a former meteorologist and his wife, collect replicas of musical instruments of the Renaissance and invite their friends in for musical evenings. (The Neubergers also swim a half mile a day in the lake behind their house. They continue to do this even though Mr. Neuberger was once rather severely bitten by an alligator.) The George Richardses have a dachshund named Gretel who has won numerous prizes for tracking and obedience. Ronald Smith works a ham radio and collects golf balls. (He now has nine hundred golf balls of different makes and markings.) Mrs. Evelyn Schultz swims competitively in the over-seventies division. Colonel Lyle Thomas grows orchids; James Morris carves animals and birds out of wood; and Louis Goodrich collects and rebuilds wall and grandfather clocks. These people are known around town for the interesting hobbies they have.

Frank Minninger is known as the best decoupage artist in Sun City 52 Center. A tall, bronzed, good-looking man in his late seventies, he was wearing, when I met him, red linen slacks and an open shirt. He came here fourteen years ago, when he retired from the Connecticut General Life Insurance Company. Since then, he has made fifty decoupage handbags, half of which he gave away to friends and half of which he could show me, since he had given them to his wife. He had also built five ship models and grown a border of prize red begonias. He had, he said, always loved hobbies. When his boys were growing up, he had built model trains for them. And for some time he was quite serious about photography. He did a series of wildflower photographs which was exhibited around the country. Kodak bought a series of Christmas cards that he and wife did over the years with pictures of their youngest son and their dogs dressed in costume and posed around the fireplace. His wife raised German shepherds, he said, and he was very keen on bird-watching. Minninger described all his hobbies to me in great detail and with enormous pride and enthusiasm. "There's an awful lot of people here who don't do anything," he said. "But if you're not happy it's really your own fault." Frank Minninger seemed to be a happy man. He seemed to be doing what he had wanted to do all his life — and what in fact he might have done for a living if he had not had a certain vision of himself. When I asked why he had chosen Sun City, he said he had come for the golf and the duplicate bridge. "I have all these hobbies," he told me gaily, "but golf is my business."

That many Sun Citians do lead active lives is perhaps not very surprising. Many of them, like Frank Minninger, are not old except by a demographer's measure, and some of the more recent settlers are not old even by that. In the beginning — that is, in the early sixties — most of the people who bought houses were around sixty-five years old. But in recent years people have been coming here in their early sixties and in their late fifties. In 1980, nearly a quarter of the population was under sixty-five. Many of the younger men had been military officers — people who had taken their pensions before retiring. Some of them had been civil servants with similar pension schedules, and some had been executives of companies that, for diverse reasons, encourage retirement before the age of sixty-five. Theodore Peck, for example, a former Air Force Reserve officer and sales manager for a carpet company, bought his house here when he was forty-six and moved in when he reached fifty. (Peck, exceptionally, still works. He deals in local real estate.) Betty Cooper Pierce, the wife of an Air Force officer, has been here almost nine years and is only fifty-nine. To these people, Sun City is certainly not a home for the elderly but, rather, a community desirable for its well-kept grounds, its golf, and its complement of successful people. Furthermore, many of those who are chronologically older have the same attitude. Ronald Smith, for example, plays golf every day, and in the evenings he still has too much energy to sit still for very long. He and his wife told me that they had looked forward to retirement — looked forward to all the things they could do when they were no longer tied down by children and jobs. Now, fourteen years later, they were still enjoying themselves. "It seems as if we'd always been here," Lora Smith said. "It's the long vacation we wished we'd always had."

What surprised me most about Sun Citians was how few of the men seemed to regret leaving their jobs. Civil servants, corporate executives, schoolteachers, independent businessmen — indeed, many of the same people who talked with such pride about the professional success they had had — told me that they had planned their retirement years in advance. A number said they would have retired earlier if they had been able to afford it. One man who had traveled all over the world for the Department of Agriculture, and who appeared enviably fit, said that he had retired at fifty-five, because he was "sick of working." Another man said that he had sold his chemical company "in order to get out of the rat race" and in order to fish and play golf. "I miss the competitiveness of business," he told me. "But I'd hate to go back to work. Pressure, pressure, pressure — I don't want to get involved." He now plays golf five times a week and says, "Don't know what I do but I'm busy all day long." A third man said he had retired from a management position at Kodak. He and his wife had traveled for a year and were now staying in a rented house while deciding whether or not to move to Sun City. "Maybe I shouldn't have retired so early," he said. "But I paid my dues. You work for industry, you work for *x* years, and you retire."

Some Sun Citians told me that they had liked their jobs, and, quite possibly, some who spoke as if they did not miss them were justifying choices that had been made for them. But for many of the men their careers, their professions, seemed only a means of achieving a satisfactory private life — a "life-style," as some put it. And even those who said they had liked their jobs seemed curiously detached from them: they had had jobs, but they had no work in the sense of lifelong interests. There are exceptions. Dr. Harry Skornia, for example, a former professor of communications, is now in his early seventies and continues to read what is being published in his field and to write articles when his health permits. Fred Russell, formerly the president of a construction company and a former city commissioner of public works, has become involved in public works and other civic affairs in Sun City. Then, too, there are some people, such as the Neubergers, who have artistic pursuits or hobbies they care passionately about. But these exceptions were strikingly exceptional. With regard to work, most Sun Citians seemed like castaways on an island of plenty.

Sun Citians' insistence on busyness — and the slightly defensive tone 56 of their town boosterism — came, I began to imagine, from the fact that their philosophies, and, presumably, the beliefs they had grown up with, did not really support them in this enterprise of retirement. Sun Citians are, after all, conservatives and vigorous exponents of the work ethic. They believe that the country is going soft because most Americans don't work hard enough. They complain about the younger generations, and, according to Dr. Gingery, a few of them have threatened to disinherit their grandchildren because "these kids don't know the value of a dollar." Though many of them are former government employees or former executives of large corporations, they believe in free enterprise and rugged individualism. The businessmen quite naturally complain of the "double and triple dippers" in the community, but some of the former government employees — living on indexed pensions — also complain that the government is too big and too paternalistic. A schoolteacher who had taken early retirement in order to move here with her husband told me that she and her friends had backed President Reagan's economic program enthusiastically. "We're old enough and conservative enough to believe that all this spending has to come to a screeching halt," she said. "There are so many boondoggles, so much cheating and crookedness as a result of it. Much of it can be blamed on Johnson and his printing of money. We're just mopping up now after that binge of spending. I can't for the life of me see what's wrong with cutting out the school-lunch program. What's wrong with having a bag lunch from home? We're losing the stuff of which this country was made in the beginning. We want things given to us. We want cradle-to-grave care."

Sun Citians believe in good citizenship, in charity, and in the virtue of volunteer work. They are by temperament joiners, and Sun City has, as Bess Melvin pointed out, a vast array of social, charitable, and civic organizations. Every week, the Sun City Center newspaper announces meetings, fund-raising drives, awards ceremonies, and so forth, held by the Rotary Club, the Woman's Club, the Kiwanis, the Civic and Home Owners associations. The women's groups and national fraternal organizations do raise money for scholarships and other charities; the Shellcrafters and Sawdust Engineers make things to give to the children of the area, or to sell for their benefit. Of course, there is a lot of busywork in these organizations, and a lot of meetings are held for purely social reasons. That is true everywhere. And, as is the case in most volunteer organizations, a few people do the lion's share of the work. What is interesting is that Sun Citians seem to feel somewhat less of a social obligation than they did before they retired. Harry Skornia, who has long been active in community affairs, estimated that only 10 or 20 percent of the Sun Citians took an active role in the various civic organizations. "The rest play golf and bridge, watch TV, and drink at cocktail parties," he said. "They don't come here to be active, they come here to retire." Skornia, being one of the few liberals in the community, had, I imagined, a rather jaundiced view of his fellow citizens. But then Ted Peck, a former president of the Sun City Center Republican Club, told me much the same thing. The club has over six hundred members, but very few of the members are active; they vote in elections but do not otherwise participate. "People are so busy going to cocktail parties," Peck said. "Most of them don't want to work. They feel they've done it all their lives — they feel they've made a contribution." Mrs. Krauch, also a former president of the club and now the head of a cancer drive, gave a similar analysis. "No one wants to take responsibility. They're people who have participated so much that they feel they don't have to anymore. 'I've had it' is what people say. 'I'll help, but I don't want the job.'"

Sun Citians are not Puritans — Dr. Gingery was, in a sense, taking too long a leap with his analogy. "They've never thought their work was socially necessary," Skornia observed. They are private people who enjoy their houses, their friends, their families, and their games. Many of them look upon Sun City as the reward for which they have worked and made sacrifices. Sun City boosters — and there are a lot of them — describe their town as an ideal place to live. But to look upon Sun City Center as an ideal world is to discover something new about the people who live there. Their political philosophy, after all, assumes the wide-open spaces; it is one of unbridled competition, of freedom from social restriction, and even from society itself. Their pleasures, however, are golf and bridge — games for people who love competition but also love rules. They are games for problem-solvers — orderly, conservative people who like to know where the limits are. The harmonious, man-made landscape of a golf course is like a board game writ large — or like Sun City itself. It's not for loners or rugged individualists but for sociable people who value traditions, conventions, and etiquette. It's not "the rat race." There's an aesthetic to it, but it's not that of the open range. Sun Citians think of themselves as quintessentially American, and so, perhaps, they are. But, like President Reagan, they imagine cowboys and live in a world of country clubs. What they value they might themselves associate with the European tradition. What they want is security within a fixed social order. Asked why so many Sun Citians were Republicans, Ted Peck said, "The same reason we feel so comfortable here. It's middle to middle upper class here. There are people who have worked and have prestige. There's comfort in the social status here." The irony is that their golf courses have been carved out for them from Florida swampland, their artificial lakes have alligators in them, and they live in a town without any history on the edge of a social frontier, inventing a world for themselves.

Art Rescorla knows this, but he is an exception, and the organization he heads is also exceptional. The Sun City Emergency Squad is the most important cooperative organization in the town, and the one Sun Citians take most seriously. All those in the housing development contribute to it, and, unlike the Civic and Home Owners associations, it was started by the residents rather than the developers, and has no paid staff. With its fleet of three ambulances, the squad responds to calls for emergency help and drives people to the hospital. For its volunteers — and for many people in the community — the squad has an aura of glamour about it. One woman squad member described it to me in terms of midnight emergencies: a woman with a heart attack, the squad unit responding in five minutes, the victim and her shocked husband being hurried into the ambulance, the rendezvous on the highway with the county paramedical unit, the return home in the middle of the night. And, indeed, the squad does respond to the one real threat to the community — the one thing that bursts through the cocoon of comfort and security.

Art Rescorla spends most of his days in the squad office. When I first 60 went to see him, he was doing the accounts. Excited volunteers kept running in and out of his office with what I first assumed to be emergency business but turned out to be routine bookkeeping questions. Rescorla first referred them to the team head for the day, but they reappeared with the same questions, and then he patiently answered them himself. He described the work of the squad to me in a businesslike fashion. Its main work was transport, he said; only one out of ten calls was an emergency. The squad has 150 volunteers, who go through a twenty-one-hour first-aid course and, in some cases, a driving course; they are then on call for a twenty-four-hour period.

Rescorla had been described to me as "not a very gregarious man," but we talked, initially, for two hours, and he seemed to me to be merely a man who cared less than some others about pleasing. He did not wear resort clothes, and when I went to his house I noticed that he and his wife did not have a collection of animals or dolls. Also, he spoke quite bluntly about the subjects other Sun Citians skirted: illness, old age, and death. He was in many ways the odd man out. He said he had been forced to retire from his job at the American Petroleum Institute when he reached sixty-five. That was in 1975, and he had, he told me, been very resentful — not at the loss of his salary but at the loss of his work. He had taken a volunteer job at the Smithsonian Institution doing research projects, and he had worked without pay for the Virginia town he lived in. But he found that in both places the younger people passed over his ideas and his projects in favor of their own. When I asked him whether this had to do with a lack of respect for age, he said that it had more to do with the fact that younger people were still in the competition — still concerned with furthering their own careers. He could not blame them for that — that was how it was. He had moved to Florida in 1978 because of arthritis. When his doctor told him to go south, he had written away to sixty retirement centers and gone to visit ten or twelve of them. Most of them, he said, were simply apartment complexes or housing tracts built by a promoter and then abandoned with nothing but a sales office. But Sun City Center was a real town, and Rescorla had seen it as an alternative community, a place where he could find work and be useful among his peers.

Rescorla had found work for himself: he served as the managing editor of a publication of the American Chemical Society, he was the academic dean of Dr. Gingery's "college," and he was involved in a number of community projects besides the Emergency Squad. But he had also been in some degree frustrated, because few Sun Citians seemed to share his vision of what a retirement community could be. "What bothers me is that we are losing the brainpower of older people. There's a lot of it around in this area waiting to be tapped. In this job, I look for people with special backgrounds. I found a man who had worked for a telephone company, so I grabbed him, and he helped make a radio hookup for us. He's got the abilities, so I say use them. The trouble is that we push people into senility. A lot of people come here when they're at their peak, and then they drop off." He still, however, believed in the potential of age-segregated communities. "We should put people into areas like this, where they can use their talents. If they're in competition with younger people all the time, they just give up." In his view, what the town needed was a government. It was not likely to get one in the near future, since incorporation would probably mean a rise in the real-estate taxes, but it would have to get one in order to be heard. "When we talk to the county or the state now, we sound like an old-age home," he said.

Rescorla's view of Sun City corresponded to the attitude that the sociologist Arnold Rose labeled "aging-group consciousness." Rose had observed that certain older people were far more conscious than others of their peers; they saw "the aging" as a subsociety and identified with it; they believed that the elderly should organize and demand more rights. These people came from a great variety of backgrounds, but what they had in common was forced retirement. They had not jumped out of the working world and the larger society — they had been pushed.

With the exception of Rescorla, the Sun Citians I talked to had not come 64 here because the town was for older people. On the other hand, they did not seem to object to the age restrictions. When I asked people how they liked living in an age-segregated community, a few said they missed seeing children around. (Some of them then went on to explain that they meant this quite literally: What they missed was seeing children — they didn't miss having them around all the time.) Interestingly, these questions always elicited answers about children — almost never about any other age group. Many Sun Citians, it became clear to me, had simply lost their consciousness of other age groups. They had come to Sun City not to be old but to be young. To put it another way, they were attempting to despecialize old age. "Look at the way we dress," one Sun Citian, a retired minister, said, indicating his own madras shirt. "At a cocktail party the other day, I saw a woman in a miniskirt. She had very nice legs, but she must have been sixty-five or seventy. Her mother would have turned over in her grave!"

Paradoxically, the effort at despecialization seemed to work better in an age-segregated community.

On Thursday nights, the Kings Point club holds an informal dance, with music from an amplified sound system. The night I went, about a hundred people had come. I found a seat at a table with three couples. The men were wearing Western shirts with string ties, the women slacks and flowered cotton blouses. The men handed around drinks from bottles they had brought, and all of them were laughing loudly at each other's jokes. When the music started, the women went to the dance floor to join a half dozen other women, some of whom were certainly in their eighties. Led by a tall woman in a tentlike muumuu, they formed a line and did a kick-step routine to a number called, "Bad, Bad, Leroy Brown." They had learned the routine in dance class, and now they were completely relaxed about performing it in front of an audience. When the dance ended, the men got up, and a few minutes later the floor was filled with couples doing the fox-trot. Through the crowd I could see two diminutive elderly women dancing together.

Actually, there are many ages in Sun City Center. In twenty-some years, the age spectrum has grown almost as large as it is in most new suburban communities: it encompasses four decades, and two generations of certain families. One seventy-three-year-old woman I met had a mother in her nineties living in a house a block away from her. Families with two generations of retired people living in Florida are no longer uncommon; the families tend to consist of a daughter, married or widowed, taking care of her elderly mother. In twenty-odd years, Sun City Center has developed its own life cycle, beginning with people in their fifties and ending with those in their nineties. Carolyn Tuttle, for example, used to be the youngest person on her street when she and her husband moved in, a dozen years ago; now in her seventies, she is, as it were, middle-aged, since some of the earliest settlers are still there and some younger people have moved in. The median age in the whole town is now seventy. When I asked Mrs. Tuttle about age segregation, she told me that she did not miss having young people around. "I love children dearly," she said, "but I don't crave to fall over tricycles on my lawn or see young couples mooning over each other." Later, she said, "When Sun City Center was founded, almost everyone was about sixty-five. Now some of the people are well into their eighties. I know a number of people who are losing their sight, and others who can hardly get about. The next step is the life-care center. I've lost so many friends to retirement homes. It's almost as bad as losing them to death."

Carolyn Tuttle has a bright little dog, a schnauzer, who appears to understand much of what she says. She herself is a greyhound of a woman — tall, lean, attractive, and full of nervous energy. A former English teacher, she uses the language with a playful elegance. Her husband died three and a half years ago. Since then, she has become a member of the Emergency Squad and a vice president of the Civic Association. She does church work, and she directs a poetry workshop, and she belongs to the Woman's Club. A couple of years ago, she took a trip to Australia and the South Pacific with a group. "It's a very fulfilling life here," she said. "Of course, there are people who do nothing but play bridge and golf, but that's their privilege." Though she is a Sun City booster, she finds it difficult to control her irony when she describes the provincial theater groups that come through and the tea-and-cookie meetings of the Woman's Club. She is as demanding of herself as she is of others, and she is also, very obviously, lonely.

In the early sixties, Sun City was a community of couples. The development company pitched its advertisement to couples and built its houses for two. People put up signs that read WORDEN — DOT AND HOW or THE SMITHS — BILL AND MARGE, and the signs signified a good deal. Like many Americans of their generation, Sun Citians had long, stable marriages. On the average, perhaps, their marriages were happier than most, since unhappy couples usually do not decide to pull up roots and leave for a permanent vacation together in a strange town composed of other couples. Then Sun City was a test of these marriages. For social purposes, each couple had to become a united front, an entity. And there were no distractions — no children, no office to go to, no compelling reason for one person to "get out of the house" without the other. Added to that, retirement gradually erased the difference between a man's sphere of activity and a woman's. ("My husband is always the man," one woman told me. "A lot of other men become just people.") Couples that survived these tests grew closer; they became single units, husband and wife joined together like Siamese twins.

But now Sun City is composed of couples and widows. Just how many widows there are it is impossible for a visitor to tell, since most widows do not take down the DOT AND HOW signs or take their husbands' names out of the residents' directory. The 1980 census, however, shows that almost a third of the women in Sun City then were widows living alone. This is about the national average for people their age, since women live an average of 7.7 years longer than men. In Sun City, there are five widows for every widower, which is about the national ratio.

"How," in fact, died three and a half years ago. "Dot" — Dorothy Worden, who is in her seventies and full of life — says she would consider remarrying if she found the right man. But she doubts she ever will, since there are so few men her age around. Of course, she says, some men do lose their wives, and they generally want to remarry, but then there are so many widows with the same thing in mind. "When a man's wife dies, all the widows come around the next day with casseroles," Dot told me. "Some women I know even make a practice of going to funerals. If they like the look of the bereaved husband, they'll go home and make him a casserole even though they've never met him before. Well, it works sometimes. Men aren't very good at living alone. You saw the furniture-sale right down the block? That was put out by a man who just married the widow of a close friend. His wife hasn't been dead a year. That's a fact, but no one really objects. He needed her, and, besides, none of us have all that much time left."

In St. Petersburg, there's a dance hall, called the Coliseum, where for over fifty years retired people have gone to dance to combos and the big bands every Wednesday and Saturday night. Some are couples, but others are single people. The women sit at the tables in groups of four or six with briefcases that open out into bars. The single men stand in a line at the back of the hall, like high-school boys at a prom, passing comments and looking for the prettiest woman to dance with. If a man dances with a woman, and she likes him, she'll invite him for a drink at her table, and sometimes that will be the beginning of something. I asked one man in the line why he came back there night after night, year after year, and he said, "The widows." I said he surely might have found one by then. He turned away slightly and said, "Oh, no, I'm not looking for anything permanent."

At the Kings Point dance, I sat next to a dark-haired woman with dangling silver earrings who seemed to be having a wonderful time. I asked if she and her partner were married, and she said they were not. "My husband died when he was very young," she told me. "He was only fifty-nine years old, but we had been married for thirty-three years. It was shattering. Your friends ask you out, but you're always a fifth wheel. I have children — my oldest son's a doctor in Boston — but I don't want to be a burden to them, so I came to Florida. I met Harry three years ago — his wife had just died, and I adopted him, because I'd been through the same thing. It's like a new life for me. We haven't gotten married, though, because of taxes."

At Kings Point, everyone knows couples like this one, who are not married, and knows the reason for it: if a woman remarries, it is widely (and often erroneously) believed she stands to lose her late husband's pension. Then, too, a couple filing a joint tax return may have to pay more in income tax. The laws are straightforward, but in Florida — particularly in Florida — they have created some strange social circumstances. They have led the most respectable people to the most unconventional behavior. "You can't tell who's married and who's not," a friend of Dot's who lives at Kings Point told me. "People sometimes say they are married, and the woman goes by the man's name. It doesn't matter to us if they're not married, but it seems to bother their children. So sometimes we know and their children don't. Either they tell their children they're married or one of them moves out of the house when the children come down."

Remarriages seem to be more common in Sun City. But then many Sun Citians have enough money to be able to afford the higher taxes. Perhaps for that reason, Sun Citians are far less tolerant than Kings Point people of unconventional living arrangements. Dot, who has lived in Sun City for a decade, knows of only one unmarried couple openly living together there. She does not know of any couples who simply pretend to be married.

Most widows in Sun City Center do not find new partners. The statistics are not in their favor in this town any more than they are nationally. But the statistics are so new that when their husbands die many women face a situation they never anticipated and are not in any way prepared for. According to Dr. Gingery, there are in general two kinds of widows: the dependent ones, who go to life-care centers, and the independent ones, who make a life for themselves. Both Dot and Dr. Gingery know women who actually flourished after their husbands died — who made their own friends for the first time and took up activities they hadn't thought of before. They also know women who do well enough but simply feel that their life has been diminished. Widows at Kings Point seem to be able to have an extensive social life: the neighbors are close, and they can go to dances or on expeditions in groups. Sun City is more of a private place, and thus widows seem to spend more time alone in their houses.

Mrs. Carl Kietzman, who is in her early seventies, has lived alone since her husband died more than three years ago. Formerly an officer in the DAR, she was married to an Army Reserve officer who worked for the automobile insurance division of General Motors. They came here from Ohio, but they had moved around the country a good deal in the course of their lives. A big-boned, strong-looking woman, Mrs. Kietzman has decided opinions on most matters but not on what to do with the stretch of life in front of her. "It's no fun to be alone," she remarked at one point in our conversation, out of the blue. She said it quite simply, and stopped, looking down at her hands. At another point, she said, "This is the first time in my life I've ever lived alone. My family had a big house in Houston. I married young, and I had a happy marriage." When I asked Mrs. Kietzman if she thought of marrying again, she said, "I live on pensions, which would stop if I were married. And I just couldn't live with someone — it's against my principles." Then she said, "But I wouldn't meet anyone here. I don't even see the couples we used to see — or not a lot. You feel like a fifth wheel. I'm in one bridge game because someone's husband died. I miss the company of men. I miss dancing. One night, I went to the single-tons thing they have, but I didn't meet any men there. There were so many women. So I ate dinner and I played bridge and I went home." A year after her husband died, Mrs. Kietzman thought of leaving Sun City and going to live with a woman friend who had a big house in Ohio. She liked the woman — she even liked her eight dogs — but in the end she decided against it, because it would have meant selling most of her furniture, and she couldn't bear to do that.

Mrs. Kietzman took me on a tour of her house, pointing out a handsome walnut four-poster bed and a walnut chest of drawers. "They came from Texas," she said, "and they've been in my family for a hundred years." In the study, she apologized for the terrible mess, though the study was almost as painfully neat at the rest of the house. "I don't like to cook," she said as we went through the small kitchen. "My husband always used to do the cooking after he had his heart trouble." The dining table had a lace tablecloth over it and a set of china angels playing around the centerpiece; it looked as though it was never used. "I swim, and I work on committees," she said as we sat down again. "But there isn't much to do at night. There's a bridge game two or three times a month, and sometimes I go out with my girlfriends. If he'd lived, I might have been better integrated into the community. But it isn't good for widows. My neighbors are kind to me, though. They come over when I need something. The man next door says I should lock the door when I go outside through the carport to the utility room to do the laundry."

Security is something of a preoccupation in Sun City, though the town is safe by the standards of most cities and towns. (There are occasional burglaries, mostly of empty houses, and some years ago there was, very exceptionally, a rape.) Sun Citians discuss crime a great deal. A woman in her seventies told me, "I have a gun, and I would use it." In January of 1982, a committee of residents announced plans to create a security patrol, with volunteers driving two radio cars through the streets from dusk to dawn. Major General Joseph (Smokey) Caldara (U.S. Air Force, retired) was selected to head up the patrol. At the time, there was some feeling that elderly vigilantes driving cars would be more of a hazard than a safeguard, but between three and four hundred people volunteered for service, and General Caldara began the operation in April. By July, there had been six burglaries (making a total of eleven for the year), and there had been one patrol-car crack-up. The patrol continues, but the most effective security system in Sun City is still the neighbors. There are Neighborhood Watch Committees in every section of town, but, more important, the residents all notice what goes on in the streets around them. If something looks amiss at a neighbor's house, a Sun Citian will always go and investigate — particularly if the neighbor is a single person with a health problem. This mutual concern often has nothing to do with friendship; it is impersonal, though unsystematic, and it is generally welcomed, because all Sun Citians feel that one day they may require help of some kind. Art

Rescorla came to Sun City to find work, but there was another reason he and his wife chose this particular town. "I liked the idea that Trinity Lakes" — the life-care center — "was here," he told me. "It was a place to go if we got into trouble. And if things got real bad, this is a place where people work together. So my wife would always have some companionship."

The developers who built Sun City made no provision for sickness or incapacity. Like builders of retirement villages all over the country, they built recreation facilities, not clinics or nursing homes. (The real-estate people are still reluctant to discuss the problems of extreme age. One man told me that the average age in Sun City Center was sixty-two or sixty-three.) But as the years passed and the first Sun City settlers grew older, medical services were established. Doctors set up offices in the town, the Emergency Squad was organized, and in 1975 an independent developer began to build Trinity Lakes. Residents of Sun City worked on the feasibility study for the facility, and when it was finished a number of them moved in. Trinity Lakes eventually had 152 apartments and had 60 beds in the nursing home — almost all of both filled with Sun Citians. In a sense, it completed the community, for it offered residents a place to go when they could no longer take care of their houses, and it meant they could stay in Sun City Center or keep their relatives there for as long as they lived.

Recently, however, Trinity Lakes changed hands, after it was alleged in 80 a lawsuit that several million dollars in membership fees had been used improperly. The suit was eventually dropped, but it shook the faith of Sun Citians not only in Trinity Lakes but in all life-care centers that require a large capital investment in return for lifetime guarantees. There are several such institutions in the Tampa-Bradenton areas, and Sun Citians had heard rumors of financial scandals about some of them. As a result, many Sun Citians, including Art Rescorla, are looking for institutions that do not require an irrevocable commitment of capital. The security they sought has proved elusive.

The fact that many Sun Citians have gone to Trinity Lakes and other such centers in Florida says a good deal about their relationships with their children. Of course, some Sun Citians have no children. (Their age cohort — Americans who came of childbearing age during the Depression — had relatively fewer children, and the Sun Citians probably have even fewer than the average.) And some do rely on their children when they become ill or cannot cope for themselves. But many Sun Citians have made the decision not to depend on their children in sickness any more than in health. In this decision, they are not untypical of middle-class Americans of their generation, and here their generation has broken new ground. Many, perhaps most, Sun Citians took care of their own parents (some of them are still doing so) — and had them living in their houses for years. Art Rescorla was one. "I took care of my mother for fifteen years," he said.

"In the end, I had to put her in a nursing home, because it was either her or my wife. My mother took in her sister, and my father his brother. My kids would take care of me if they had to, but I wouldn't impose that on them."

Whether Sun Citians make this decision for their own sake or for the sake of their children is not at all clear, because they tend to describe it in a perfectly ambiguous manner. Art Rescorla, who has thought about the subject a great deal, said, "If I had a heart condition, I wouldn't want to impose it on my kids — at least, as long as I could afford not to. Why hold children down? It would be an interference. I'm not resentful — they have their own lives to lead. Other people — Negroes and Cubans — all live together, but we've reached the point where we don't have to do it." Rescorla had nonetheless imagined what it would be like to live with his children. "Our life-styles are so different it would be difficult to adjust. I wouldn't have any freedom except in my own room, so in practice I'd be confined there. I might just as well go to a nursing home." He spoke without bitterness — indeed, without any particular emotion. "It's heart-breaking to see people here — terminal cases — put into Trinity Lakes to stay until they die. But it doesn't upset their whole families, and they get better service there."

At the bar in the Sun City Center Inn one night, a man sat alone drinking stingers. He said his name was Lewis Fisher. Sixty-three years old and just retired, he had come down to Sun City with his wife to rent a house for the winter months. His wife was sick in bed with a virus, so he had come out alone — suffering, he said, from "cabin fever." He and his wife were trying to decide whether or not to retire to Sun City. "We have two places up north, but we'd like to move to a warmer climate," he said. "We've thought about it for a long time." When I asked if it would be difficult to leave his family, he replied, "My kids have done well, but there are no strings attached. We are as free as birds now." Later, he said, "Do you want to sacrifice five months of good weather for three days — Thanksgiving, Christmas, and Easter? They have a right to their own lives." Fisher seemed glad to find someone younger — myself — to talk to, explaining, "The youngest person I've talked to in months is the bartender. I look at my wife and I say, 'Are we ready for this?'" Turning away, he continued, "Don't like to admit I'm growing old."

Sun Citians often speak of their children with a great deal of respect [84] and affection, but they do not speak as if their lives and their children's were entwined. A sociologist studying retirement communities found that their members had a marked tendency to disinherit their children in favor of friends in the communities. Because these people did not appear to dislike or disapprove of their children, he called this phenomenon "benevolent disinheritance." Sun Citians do not seem to disinherit their children. Rather, they put up with the distance; they exchange visits with their children, but they often make do without family gatherings on the holidays. (Dr. Gingery now has a breakfast party for his parishioners on Christmas morning, because, as one widow told me, "it is the bluest day of the year.") They make their own independence a virtue. "Our children treat us as friends," Lora Smith said. "They see what full lives we have, and they say we're models for them." Similarly, dependence on children is treated as a weakness. A woman going north to be with her children and grandchildren is said to have "gramma-itis." For many, perhaps, the distance is not entirely unwelcome, since it obviates the inevitable tensions between parents and their grown children. "I've noticed that some people here visit their kids out of charity," Rescorla said. "They think they should, because they're blood relations, but they breathe a sigh of relief when they get back here. People don't dislike younger people, but they don't want to depend on them. They have more confidence in people their own age — they trust them more." Dr. Gingery also thought there had been a general loosening of family ties, but he had a different view of the causes and consequences. "All this moving around since the Second World War has had its deleterious effects. This age group couldn't follow their children, so the kids lose their grandparents. But it's more than that. Kids lose a sense of responsibility to the extended family — not just their grandparents. And they lose a sense of responsibility to the community."

Sun Citians have taken some steps to create a substitute for the extended family. Neighbors do take care of each other in all kinds of emergencies; when someone falls ill they help out by doing errands, bringing food, or just dropping in for a chat. Sun City Center has its own Meals on Wheels unit; it has a blood bank; and it has oxygen tanks strategically placed around the town. Dr. Gingery's church has a guardianship program to take care of those who cannot make decisions for themselves. (The weakness of the program is that people must sign up for it in advance, and not many are willing to do that.) Professional home nursing is readily available, and the churches have volunteers who take care of shut-ins. Sun City is probably one of the best towns in America in which to be sick. Still, the system of caring for the ill and the feeble is far from perfect, and many people worry what they will do when, as Dorothy Worden said, "this nice interlude is over." Rescorla told me that the squad had recently taken a couple to the hospital because the woman had fallen ill and could no longer take care of her husband, who was blind. The hospital, however, could not keep them, and if their son had not come down to put them in a nursing home, they would have had nowhere to go. Rescorla's immediate ambition is to create a cooperative nursing service for the community — a group of volunteers who would do the housekeeping, get the groceries, and so on, at least on a temporary basis. He and other community activists in town believe in extending the network of volunteer organizations, but they worry that the town is getting too big for that, and they worry that the new arrivals do not understand the problems of the very old — or are so well off that they prefer to have things done for them rather than do the work themselves. "We often bring people back from the hospital who can't take care of themselves," Rescorla said. "It's very sad in most cases. People who can't manage and who haven't prepared for this — they're buried, they just die."

Sun City Center has never had a cemetery. The developers of retirement villages make a point of keeping graveyards at a distance. Not long after Del Webb founded Sun City, Arizona, a speculator bought some land near the development and threatened to turn it into a cemetery. Del Webb bought him out at several times the price he had paid. As usual, the developer seems to have understood the trend. At any rate, funeral customs have changed a good deal in Sun City over the past ten years. "When I first came here," Dr. Gingery said, "ninety percent of the people wanted a funeral service with a casket, viewing of the body, and burial in a cemetery. Now ninety percent are cremated and have memorial services."

In shifting from burial to cremation, Sun Citians are a part of a nation-wide trend — only, they are in the avant-garde. Dr. Gingery told me that the preference for cremation in the Sun City was a sign of growing maturity about death. Dr. Strickland explained, more bluntly, that it reflected the decline of pagan thinking about physical resurrection, and this quite naturally took place first among people of a certain class and education. As the ministers suggest, the nationwide trend is in large part a function of changing religious attitudes, particularly among liberal Protestants. It is also, in some part, a judgment on the funeral industry. But Sun Citians have other reasons as well. "I never thought I'd believe in cremation," Verle Modeweg told me. "I'm a Baptist, after all. But we began going to the Presbyterian church down here before the Baptist church was built, and the minister convinced me." Then she said, "Burial is so expensive and such a waste. I'd rather give my money to the church." Cremation is the final act of tidiness, and as such it has appeal for Sun Citians. But it is also quite clearly a function of mobility, of rootlessness. "I don't have anyone," Mrs. Modeweg continued. "And my husband doesn't either, so there's no one to keep up the graves." Many Sun Citians have no hometowns, and their children, if they have any, live in places where they have no attachments. These people ask that their ashes be scattered over the Gulf, or they buy a place for them at Mansion Memorial Park, a cemetery some miles away. Mrs. Modeweg said, "We bought a place at Mansion Memorial, and now friends come up to me and say, 'I've just found out that I'm going to be right next to you!' It seems very neighborly."

Dr. Gingery believes that in ten years Sun Citians have become much [88] more aware of the aging process and much more accustomed to the idea of death than people in general. In this, he is surely correct. Death occurs

185

more frequently in Sun City than it does in most other communities. Yet it is much like death in a wartime army: it is expected, and it happens to comrades, but not (except in the case of a husband or a wife) to somebody one has known all one's life. Sun Citians don't celebrate it with elaborate rituals; they don't talk about it very much, or worry about it in the way they worry about prolonged sickness or incapacity. They are stoics, and they have, in a sense, tamed it.

"Death is less of a tragedy when you're past sixty," Bess Melvin said. She was in her office, but not in her public relations role. "I think people here do have a different attitude toward death from people in a mixed community. There's a greater sense of acceptance. People don't dwell on it so much. They think about how to have fulfilling lives. They say to themselves. 'I enjoy having a big car. I've always wanted a Caddy or a Lincoln. Death — there it is. I'm ready. But in the meantime I'm going to lead the most enjoyable life possible.'"

AFTERWORD

The instrument that measures, we have been warned by analogy from physics, may by its presence distort what it measures. When anthropologists visit primitive tribes, how much do they bring with them that shapes their observations, that informs their reportage? How much does their presence alter the thing observed? In essays parallel to this one in Cities on the Hill, *FitzGerald looked at San Francisco's homosexual community, Jerry Falwell's parish in Virginia, and a guru's commune in Oregon. These communities, in different ways and in different manners, excite suspicion or disapproval from portions of American culture. FitzGerald as reporter keeps as clearly as she can to a tone of nonpartisan or objective description. She seems merely to tell us what is there: She quotes, she describes. "I am a camera," Christopher Isherwood said when he wrote about Berlin between the wars. But FitzGerald and Isherwood understand: The photographer aims the camera, develops, and crops. FitzGerald knows that it is she, finally, who chooses what to notice and record. She keeps as near to a tone of objectivity, to a style of fairness, as her considerable intelligence and talent allow her.*

Communities of the elderly do not raise issues, for the culture as a whole, that are raised by political, religious, or sexual subgroups. Nevertheless, segregation of the old from the young and the middle-aged has provoked criticism. FitzGerald's choice and ordering of detail support, sometimes, a tone of irony. Her language, however, leads not to judgment of the inhabitants of Sun City but to consideration of the American culture they inhabit and represent: "It's not for loners or rugged individualists but for sociable people who value traditions, conventions, and eti-

quette. . . . *Sun Citians think of themselves as quintessentially American, and so, perhaps, they are. But, like President Reagan, they imagine cowboys and live in a world of country clubs."*

BOOKS AVAILABLE IN PAPERBACK

America Revised: History Schoolbooks in the Twentieth Century. New York: Random House-Vintage. *Nonfiction.*

Cities on a Hill. New York: Simon & Schuster-Touchstone. *Nonfiction.*

Fire in the Lake: The Vietnamese and the Americans in Vietnam. New York: Random House-Vintage. *Nonfiction.*

IAN
FRAZIER

IAN FRAZIER has only one absolute rule when it comes to writing. "I quit every day at seven o'clock, buy a quart of beer, and watch TV." He follows this discipline on Canal Street in Manhattan, where he lives these days, having started out from Lake Erie some years ago (b. Cleveland, 1951). As an undergraduate at Harvard University, he wrote for the Lampoon, *which has cradled many American writers: Robert Benchley, Robert Sherwood, George Plimpton, John Updike.*

"Dating Your Mom" is the title essay of Frazier's first collection, which is hysterical and which places him in a grand tradition of American satirists and zanies. For the past fifty years many of these writers, like Frazier, have written for the New Yorker, *where Frazier is also on the staff. A second collection of essays, reportage rather than humor or satire, is called* Nobody Better, Better than Nobody *(1987).*

Dating Your Mom

In today's fast-moving, transient, rootless society, where people meet and make love and part without ever really touching, the relationship every guy already has with his own mother is too valuable to ignore. Here is a grown, experienced, loving woman — one you do not have to go to a party or a singles bar to meet, one you do not have to go to great lengths to get to know. There are hundreds of times when you and your mother are thrown together naturally, without the tension that usually accompanies courtship — just the two of you, alone. All you need is a little presence of mind to take advantage of these situations. Say your mom is driving you downtown in the car to buy you a new pair of slacks. First, find a nice station on the car radio, one that she likes. Get into the pleasant lull of freeway driving — tires humming along the pavement, air-conditioner on max. Then turn to look at her across the front seat and say something like, "You know, you've really kept your shape, Mom, and don't think I haven't noticed." Or suppose she comes into your room to bring you some clean socks. Take her by the wrist, pull her close, and say, "Mom, you're the most fascinating woman I've ever met." Probably she'll tell you to cut out the foolishness, but I can guarantee you one thing: she will never tell your dad. Possibly she would find it hard to say, "Dear, Piper just made a pass at me," or possibly she is secretly flattered, but, whatever the reason, she will keep it to herself until the day comes when she is no longer ashamed to tell the world of your love.

Dating your mother seriously might seem difficult at first, but once you try it I'll bet you'll be surprised at how easy it is. Facing up to your intention is the main thing: you have to want it bad enough. One problem is that lots of people get hung up on feelings of guilt about their dad. They think, Oh, here's this kindly old guy who taught me how to hunt and whittle and dynamite fish — I can't let him go on into his twilight years alone. Well, there are two reasons you can dismiss those thoughts from your mind. First, *every* woman, I don't care who she is, prefers her son to her husband. That is a simple fact; ask any woman who has a son, and she'll admit it. And why shouldn't she prefer someone who is so much like herself, who represents nine months of special concern and love and intense physical closeness — someone whom she actually created? As more women begin to express the need to have something all their own in the world, more women are going to start being honest about this preference. When you and your mom begin going together, you will simply become part of a natural and inevitable historical trend.

Second, you must remember this about your dad: you have your mother, he has his! Let him go put the moves on his own mother and stop messing with yours. If his mother is dead or too old to be much fun anymore, that's not your fault, is it? It's not your fault that he didn't realize his mom for the woman she was, before it was too late. Probably he's going to try a lot of emotional blackmail on you just because you had a good idea and he never did. Don't buy it. Comfort yourself with the thought that your dad belongs to the last generation of guys who will let their moms slip away from them like that.

Once your dad is out of the picture — once he has taken up fly-tying, joined the Single Again Club, moved to Russia, whatever — and your mom has been wooed and won, if you're anything like me you're going to start having so much fun that the good times you had with your mother when you were little will seem tame by comparison. For a while, Mom and I went along living a contented, quiet life, just happy to be with each other. But after several months we started getting into some different things, like the big motorized stroller. The thrill I felt the first time Mom steered me down the street! On the tray, in addition to my Big Jim doll and the wire with the colored wooden beads, I have my desk blotter, my typewriter, an in-out basket, and my name plate. I get a lot of work done, plus I get a great chance to people-watch. Then there's my big, adult-sized highchair, where I sit in the evening as Mom and I watch the news and discuss current events, while I paddle in my food and throw my dishes on the floor. When Mom reaches to wipe off my chin and I take her hand, and we fall to the floor in a heap — me, Mom, highchair, and all — well, those are the best times, those are the very best times.

It is true that occasionally I find myself longing for even more — for things I know I cannot have, like the feel of a firm, strong, gentle hand at the small of my back lifting me out of bed into the air, or someone who could walk me around and burp me after I've watched all the bowl games and had about nine beers. Ideally, I would like a mom about nineteen or twenty feet tall, and although I considered for a while asking my mom to start working out with weights and drinking Nutrament, I finally figured, Why put her through it? After all, she is not only my woman, she is my best friend. I have to take her as she is, and the way she is is plenty good enough for me.

AFTERWORD

An anonymous pamphlet, published in 1729, suggested that the best solution for overpopulation and poverty in Ireland, which would also provide healthy nutrition, was to cook and eat Irish children. Jonathan Swift's "A Modest Proposal for Preventing the Children of Poor People in Ireland from Being a Burden to Their Parents . . . " argued its thesis with a calm logic that fooled, and therefore outraged, some of its readers; others recognized that they read, in the form of satire, a passionate attack on England and its landlords who exploited the "Poor People in Ireland."

Ian Frazier at the end of his essay departs into fiction; at least, one would like to think so. Earlier this essay advances an argument, as logically as Swift, which implies notions about the condition of the male psyche in America. Frazier begins the essay with a string of clichés — "In today's fast-moving, transient, rootless society" — and makes judgment throughout by means of prose style; he parodies the language of self-help, the jargon of pop psychology.

BOOKS AVAILABLE IN PAPERBACK

Dating Your Mom. New York: Penguin. *Nonfiction.*
Nobody Better, Better than Nobody. New York: Penguin. *Essays.*

PAUL
FUSSELL

*A*FTER MANY YEARS *of teaching English at Rutgers University, Paul Fussell (b. 1924) moved to a chair in English literature at the University of Penn-sylvania. Born in California, the son of a millionaire, he did his undergraduate work at Pomona College. He saw combat in World War II as an infantry officer, was wounded, and returned to do his Ph.D. at Harvard. He wrote two books on eighteenth-century literature and* Poetic Meter and Poetic Form *(1965, revised 1979). In* The Great War and Modern Memory *(1975) he investigated the British experience of World War I, especially the books in which that war found its way into literature.* The Great War and Modern Memory *won Fussell the National Book Critics Circle Award and the National Book Award in 1976. He has written many articles and book reviews for magazines, especially for* Harper's *and the* New Republic *(which published "Notes on Class" in 1980). These essays are collected in* The Boy Scout Handbook and Other Observations *(1982); more recently, Fussell edited* The Norton Book of Travel *(1987).*

Paul Fussell is a historian of society and the imagination whose field of inves-tigation is largely literature. In "Notes on Class" he makes ironic commentary on the class structure of our country. Because we lack the rigid social hierarchies of some European countries, with aristocracies of ancient fortunes and inherited titles, we sometimes pretend that our society is classless. Fussell — whose book on the subject, Class: A Guide Through the American Status System, *was published in 1983 — writes about the American class system with wit and sarcasm.*

Notes on Class

If the dirty little secret used to be sex, now it is the facts about social class. No subject today is more likely to offend. Over thirty years ago Dr. Kinsey generated considerable alarm by disclosing that despite appearance one-quarter of the male population had enjoyed at least one homosexual orgasm. A similar alarm can be occasioned today be asserting that despite the much-discussed mechanism of "social mobility" and the constant redistribution of income in this country, it is virtually impossible to break out of the social class in which one has been nurtured. Bad news for the ambitious as well as the bogus, but there it is.

Defining class is difficult, as sociologists and anthropologists have learned. The more data we feed into the machines, the less likely it is that significant formulations will emerge. What follows here is based not on interviews, questionnaires, or any kind of quantitative technique but on perhaps a more trustworthy method — perception. Theory may inform us that there are three classes in America, high, middle, and low. Perception will tell us that there are at least nine, which I would designate and arrange like this:

> Top Out-of-Sight
> Upper
> Upper Middle
>
> —
>
> Middle
> High-Proletarian
> Mid-Proletarian
> Low-Proletarian

—

Destitute
Bottom Out-of-Sight

In addition, there is a floating class with no permanent location in this hierarchy. We can call it Class X. It consists of well-to-do hippies, "artists," "writers" (who write nothing), floating bohemians, politicians out of office, disgraced athletic coaches, residers abroad, rock stars, "celebrities," and the shrewder sort of spies.

The quasi-official division of the population into three economic classes called high-, middle-, and low-income groups rather misses the point, because as a class indicator the amount of money is not as important as the source. Important distinctions at both the top and bottom of the class scale arise less from degree of affluence than from the people or institutions to whom one is beholden for support. For example, the main thing distinguishing the top three classes from each other is the amount of money inherited in relation to the amount currently earned. The Top Out-of-Sight Class (Rockefellers, du Ponts, Mellons, Fords, Whitneys) lives on inherited capital entirely. Its money is like the hats of the Boston ladies who, asked where they got them, answer, "Oh, we *have* our hats." No one whose money, no matter how ample, comes from his own work, like film stars, can be a member of the Top Out-of-Sights, even if the size of his income and the extravagance of his expenditure permit him temporary social access to it.

Since we expect extremes to meet, we are not surprised to find the very lowest class, Bottom Out-of-Sight, similar to the highest in one crucial respect: it is given its money and kept sort of afloat not by its own efforts but by the welfare machinery or the prison system. Members of the Top Out-of-Sight Class sometimes earn some money, as directors or board members of philanthropic or even profitable enterprises, but the amount earned is laughable in relation to the amount already possessed. Membership in the Top Out-of-Sight Class depends on the ability to flourish without working at all, and it is this that suggests a curious brotherhood between those at the top and the bottom of the scale.

It is this also that distinguishes the Upper Class from its betters. It lives on both inherited money and a salary from attractive, if usually slight, work, without which, even if it could survive and even flourish, it would feel bored and a little ashamed. The next class down, the Upper Middle, may possess virtually as much as the two above it. The difference is that it has earned most of it, in law, medicine, oil, real estate, or even the more honorific forms of trade. The Upper Middles are afflicted with a bourgeois sense of shame, a conviction that to live on the earnings of others, even forebears, is not entirely nice.

The Out-of-Sight Classes at top and bottom have something else in common: they are literally all but invisible (hence their name). The façades of Top Out-of-Sight houses are never seen from the street, and such residences (like Rockefeller's upstate New York premises) are often hidden away deep in the hills, safe from envy and its ultimate attendants, confiscatory taxation and finally expropriation. The Bottom Out-of-Sight Class is equally invisible. When not hidden away in institutions or claustrated in monasteries, lamaseries, or communes, it is hiding from creditors, deceived bail-bondsmen, and merchants intent on repossessing cars and furniture. (This class is visible briefly in one place, in the spring on the streets of New York City, but after this ritual yearly show of itself it disappears again.) When you pass a house with a would-be impressive façade addressing the street, you know it is occupied by a mere member of the Upper or Upper Middle Class. The White House is an example. Its residents, even on those occasions when they are Kennedys, can never be classified as Top Out-of-Sight but only Upper Class. The house is simply too conspicuous, and temporary residence there usually constitutes a come-down for most of its occupants. It is a hopelessly Upper- or Upper-Middle-Class place.

Another feature of both Top and Bottom Out-of-Sight Classes is their anxiety to keep their names out of the papers, and this too suggests that socially the President is always rather vulgar. All the classes in between Top and Bottom Out-of-Sight slaver for personal publicity (monograms on shirts, inscribing one's name on lawn-mowers and power tools, etc.), and it is this lust to be known almost as much as income that distinguishes them from their Top and Bottom neighbors. The High- and Mid-Prole Classes can be recognized immediately by their pride in advertising their physical presence, a way of saying, "Look! We pay our bills and have a known place in the community, and you can find us there any time." Thus hypertrophied house-numbers on the front, or house numbers written "Two Hundred Five" ("Two Hundred and Five" is worse) instead of 205, or flamboyant house or family names blazoned on façades, like "The Willows" or "The Polnickis."

(If you go behind the façade into the house itself, you will find a fairly 8 trustworthy class indicator in the kind of wood visible there. The top three classes invariably go in for hardwoods for doors and paneling; the Middle and High-Prole Classes, pine, either plain or "knotty." The knotty-pine "den" is an absolute stigma of the Middle Class, one never to be overcome or disguised by temporarily affected higher usages. Below knotty pine there is plywood.)

Façade study is a badly neglected anthropological field. As we work down from the (largely white-painted) banklike façades of the Upper and Upper Middle Classes, we encounter such Middle and Prole conventions as these, which I rank in order of social status:

Middle

1. A potted tree on either side of the front door, and the more pointy and symmetrical the better.
2. A large rectangular picture-window in a split-level "ranch" house, displaying a table-lamp between two side curtains. The cellophane on the lampshade must be visibly inviolate.
3. Two chairs, usually metal with pipe arms, disposed on the front porch as a "conversation group," in stubborn defiance of the traffic thundering past.

High-Prole

4. Religious shrines in the garden, which if small and understated, are slightly higher class than

Mid-Prole

5. Plaster gnomes and flamingos, and blue or lavender shiny spheres supported by fluted cast-concrete pedestals.

Low-Prole

6. Defunct truck tires painted white and enclosing flower beds. (Auto tires are a grade higher.)
7. Flower-bed designs worked in dead light bulbs or the butts of disused beer bottles.

The Desitute have no façades to decorate, and of course the Bottom Out-of-Sights, being invisible, have none either, although both these classes can occasionally help others decorate theirs — painting tires white on an hourly basis, for example, or even watering and fertilizing the potted trees of the Middle Class. Class X also does not decorate its façades, hoping to stay loose and unidentifiable, ready to relocate and shape-change the moment it sees that its cover has been penetrated.

In this list of façade conventions an important principle emerges. Organic materials have higher status than metal or plastic. We should take warning from Sophie Portnoy's° aluminum venetian blinds, which are also lower than wood because the slats are curved, as if "improved," instead of classically flat. The same principle applies, as *The Preppy Handbook* has shown so effectively, to clothing fabrics, which must be cotton or wool,

---

Sophie Portnoy A character in Philip Roth's novel *Portnoy's Complaint* (1969).

never Dacron or anything of that prole kind. In the same way, yachts with wood hulls, because they must be repaired or replaced (at high cost) more often, are classier than yachts with fiberglass hulls, no matter how shrewdly merchandised. Plastic hulls are cheaper and more practical, which is precisely why they lack class.

As we move down the scale, income of course decreases, but income is less important to class than other seldom-invoked measurements: for example, the degree to which one's work is supervised by an omnipresent immediate superior. The more free from supervision, the higher the class, which is why a dentist ranks higher than a mechanic working under a foreman in a large auto shop, even if he makes considerably more money than the dentist. The two trades may be thought equally dirty: it is the dentist's freedom from supervision that helps confer class upon him. Likewise, a high-school teacher obliged to file weekly "lesson plans" with a principal or "curriculum co-ordinator" thereby occupies a class position lower than a tenured professor, who reports to no one, even though the high-school teacher may be richer, smarter, and nicer. (Supervisors and Inspectors are titles that go with public schools, post offices, and police departments: the student of class will need to know no more.) It is largely because they must report that even the highest members of the naval and military services lack social status: they all have designated supervisors — even the Chairman of the Joint Chiefs of Staff has to report to the President.

Class is thus defined less by bare income than by constraints and insecurities. It is defined also by habits and attitudes. Take television watching. The Top Out-of-Sight Class doesn't watch at all. It owns the companies and pays others to monitor the thing. It is also entirely devoid of intellectual or even emotional curiosity: it *has* its ideas the way it has its money. The Upper Class does look at television but it prefers Camp offerings, like the films of Jean Harlow or Jon Hall. The Upper Middle Class regards TV as vulgar except for the highminded emissions of National Educational Television, which it watches avidly, especially when, like the Shakespeare series, they are the most incompetently directed and boring. Upper Middles make a point of forbidding children to watch more than an hour a day and worry a lot about violence in society and sugar in cereal. The Middle Class watches, preferring the more "beautiful" kinds of non-body-contact sports like tennis or gymnastics or figure-skating (the music is a redeeming feature here). With High-, Mid-, and Low-Proles we find heavy viewing of the soaps in the daytime and rugged body-contact sports (football, hockey, boxing) in the evening. The lower one is located in the Prole classes the more likely one is to watch "Bowling for Dollars" and "Wonder Woman" and "The Hulk" and when choosing a game show to prefer "Joker's Wild" to "The Family Feud," whose jokes are sometimes incomprehensible. Destitutes and Bottom Out-of-Sights have in common a problem involving choice. Destitutes usually "own" about three color sets, and the problem is which three programs to run at once. Bottom Out-of-Sights exercise no choice at all, the decisions being made for them by correctional or institutional personnel.

The time when the evening meal is consumed defines class better than, say, the presence or absence on the table of ketchup bottles and ashtrays shaped like little toilets enjoining the diners to "Put Your Butts Here." Destitutes and Bottom Out-of-Sights eat dinner at 5:30, for the Prole staff on which they depend must clean up and be out roller-skating or bowling early in the evening. Thus Proles eat at 6:00 or 6:30. The Middles eat at 7:00, the Upper Middles at 7:30 or, if very ambitious, at 8:00. The Upper and Top Out-of-Sights dine at 8:30 or 9:00 or even later, after nightly protracted "cocktail" sessions lasting usually around two hours. Sometimes they forget to eat at all.

Similarly, the physical appearance of the various classes defines them fairly accurately. Among the top four classes thin is good, and the bottom two classes appear to ape this usage, although down there thin is seldom a matter of choice. It is the three Prole classes that tend to fat, partly as a result of their use of convenience foods and plenty of beer. These are the classes too where anxiety about slipping down a rung causes nervous overeating, resulting in fat that can be rationalized as advertising the security of steady wages and the ability to "eat out" often. Even "Going Out for Breakfast" is not unthinkable for Proles, if we are to believe that they respond to the McDonald's TV ads as they're supposed to. A recent magazine ad for a diet book aimed at Proles stigmatizes a number of erroneous assumptions about body weight, proclaiming with some inelegance that "They're all a crock." Among such vulgar errors is the proposition that "All Social Classes Are Equally Overweight." This the ad rejects by noting quite accurately:

> Your weight is an advertisement of your social standing. A
> century ago, corpulence was a sign of success. But no more.
> Today it is the badge of the lower-middle-class, where obesity
> is *four times* more prevalent than it is among the upper-middle
> and middle classes.

It is not just four times more prevalent. It is at least four times more visible, as any observer can testify who has witnessed Prole women perambulating shopping malls in their bright, very tight jersey trousers. Not just obesity but the flaunting of obesity is the Prole sign, as if the object were to give maximum aesthetic offense to the higher classes and thus achieve a form of revenge.

Another physical feature with powerful class meaning is the wearing of plaster casts on legs and ankles by members of the top three classes. These casts, a sort of white badge of honor, betoken stylish mishaps with frivolous but costly toys like horses, skis, snowmobiles, and mopeds. They signify a high level of conspicuous waste in a social world where questions of unpayable medical bills or missed working days do not apply. But in the matter of clothes, the Top Out-of-Sight is different from both Upper and Upper Middle Classes. It prefers to appear in new clothes, whereas the class just below it prefers old clothes. Likewise, all three Prole classes make much of new garments, with the highest possible polyester content. The question does not arise in the same form with Destitutes and Bottom Out-of-Sights. They wear used clothes, the thrift shop and prison supply room serving as their Bonwit's and Korvette's.

This American class system is very hard for foreigners to master, partly 16 because most foreigners imagine that since America was founded by the British it must retain something of British institutions. But our class system is more subtle than the British, more a matter of gradations than of blunt divisions, like the binary distinction between a gentleman and a cad. This seems to lack plausibility here. One seldom encounters in the United States the sort of absolute prohibitions which (half-comically, to be sure) one is asked to believe define the gentleman in England. Like these:

> A gentleman never wears brown shoes in the city, or
> A gentleman never wears a green suit, or
> A gentleman never has soup at lunch, or
> A gentleman never uses a comb, or
> A gentleman never smells of anything but tar, or
> "No gentleman can fail to admire Bellini" — W. H. Auden.

In America it seems to matter much less the way you present yourself — green, brown, neat, sloppy, scented — than what your backing is — that is, where your money comes from. What the upper orders display here is no special uniform but the kind of psychological security they derive from knowing that others recognize their freedom from petty anxieties and trivial prohibitions.

"Language most shows a man," Ben Jonson used to say. "Speak, that I may see thee." As all acute conservatives like Jonson know, dictional behavior is a powerful signal of a firm class line. Nancy Mitford so indicated in her hilarious essay of 1955, "The English Aristocracy," based in part on Professor Alan S. C. Ross's more sober study "Linguistic Class-Indicators in Present-Day English." Both Mitford and Ross were interested in only one class demarcation, the one dividing the English Upper Class ("U," in their shorthand) from all below it ("non-U"). Their main finding was that euphemism and genteelism are vulgar. People who are socially secure risk nothing by calling a spade a spade, and indicate their top-dog status by doing so as frequently as possible. Thus the U-word is *rich*, the non-U *wealthy*. What U-speakers call *false teeth* non-U's call *dentures*. The same with *wigs* and *hairpieces*, *dying* and *passing away* (or *over*).

For Mitford, linguistic assaults from below are sometimes so shocking that the only kind reaction of a U-person is silence. It is "the only possible U-response," she notes, "to many embarrassing modern situations: the ejaculation of 'cheers' before drinking, for example, or 'It was so nice seeing you' after saying goodbye. In silence, too, one must endure the use of the Christian name by comparative strangers. . . . " In America, although there are more classes distinguishable here, a linguistic polarity is as visible as in England. Here U-speech (or our equivalent of it) characterizes some Top Out-of-Sights, Uppers, Upper Middles, and Class X's. All below is a waste land of genteelism and jargon and pretentious mispronunciation, pathetic evidence of upward social scramble and its hazards. Down below, the ear is bad and no one has been trained to listen. Culture words especially are the downfall of the aspiring. Sometimes it is diphthongs that invite disgrace, as in *be-yóu-ti-ful*. Sometimes the aspirant rushes full-face into disaster by flourishing those secret class indicators, the words *exquisite* and *despicable*, which, like another secret sign, *patina*, he (and of course she as often) stresses on the middle syllable instead of the first. High-class names from cultural history are a frequent cause of betrayal, especially if they are British, like Henry Purcell. In America non-U speakers are fond of usages like "Between he and I." Recalling vaguely that mentioning oneself last, as in "He and I were there," is thought gentlemanly, they apply that principle uniformly, to the entire destruction of the objective case. There's also a problem with *like*. They remember something about the dangers of illiteracy its use invites, and hope to stay out of trouble by always using *as* instead, finally saying things like "He looks as his father." These contortions are common among young (usually insurance or computer) trainees, raised on Leon Uris° and *Playboy*, most of them Mid- or High-Proles pounding on the firmly shut doors of the Middle Class. They are the careful, dark-suited first-generation aspirants to American respectability and (hopefully, as they would put it) power. Together with their deployment of the anomalous nominative case on all occasions goes their preference for jargon (you can hear them going at it on airplanes) like *parameters* and *guidelines* and *bottom lines* and *funding, dialogue, interface,* and *lifestyles*. Their world of language is one containing little more than smokescreens and knowing innovations.

Leon Uris Popular American novelist, author of *Exodus* (1958) and *Trinity* (1976).

"Do we gift the Johnsons, dear?" the corporate wife will ask the corporate husband at Christmas time.

Just below these people, down among the Mid- and Low-Proles, the complex sentence gives trouble. It is here the we get sentences beginning with elaborate pseudo-genteel participles like "Being that it was a cold day, the furnace was on." All classes below those peopled by U-speakers find the gerund out of reach and are thus forced to multiply words and say, "The people in front of him at the theater got mad due to the fact that he talked so much" instead of "His talking at the theater annoyed the people in front." (But *people* is not really right: *individuals* is the preferred term with non-U speakers. Grander, somehow.) It is also in the domain of the Mid- and Low-Prole that the double negative comes into its own as well as the superstitious avoidance of *lying* because it may be taken to imply telling untruths. People are thus depicted as always *laying* on the beach, the bed, the grass, the sidewalk, and without the slightest suggestion of their performing sexual exhibitions. A similar unconscious inhibition determines that *set* replace *sit* on all occasions, lest low excremental implications be inferred. The ease with which *sit* can be interchanged with the impolite word is suggested in a Second World War anecdote told by General Matthew Ridgway. Coming upon an unidentifiable head and shoulders peeping out of a ditch near the German border, he shouted, "Put up your hands, you son of a bitch!," to be answered, so he reports, "Aaah, go sit in your hat."

All this is evidence of a sad fact. A deep class gulf opens between two [20] current generations: the older one that had some Latin at school or college and was taught rigorous skeptical "English," complete with the diagramming of sentences; and the younger one taught to read by the optimistic look-say method and encouraged to expresss itself — as the saying goes — so that its sincerity and well of ideas suffer no violation. This new generation is unable to perceive the number of syllables in a word and cannot spell and is baffled by all questions of etymology (it thinks *chauvinism* has something to do with gender aggressions). It cannot write either, for it has never been subjected to tuition in the sort of English sentence structure which resembles the sonata in being not natural but artificial, not innate but mastered. Because of its misspent, victimized youth, this generation is already destined to fill permanently the middle-to-low slots in the corporate society without ever quite understanding what devilish mechanism has prevented it from ascending. The disappearance of Latin as an adjunct to the mastery of English can be measured by the rapid replacement of words like *continuing* by solecisms like *ongoing*. A serious moment in cultural history occurred a few years ago when gasoline trucks changed the warning word on the rear from *Inflammable* to *Flammable*. Public education had apparently produced a population which no longer knew *In-* as an intensifier.

That this happened at about the moment when every city was rapidly running up a "Cultural Center" might make us laugh, if we don't cry first. In another few generations Latinate words will be found only in learned writing, and the spoken language will have returned to the state it was in before the revival of learning. Words like *intellect* and *curiosity* and *devotion* and *study* will have withered away together with the things they denote.

There's another linguistic class-line, dividing those who persist in honoring the nineteenth-century convention that advertising, if not commerce itself, is reprehensible and not at all to be cooperated with, and those proud to think of themselves not as skeptics but as happy consumers, fulfilled when they can image themselves as functioning members of a system by responding to advertisements. For U-persons a word's succeeding in an ad is a compelling reason never to use it. But possessing no other source of idiom and no extra-local means of criticizing it, the subordinate classes are pleased to appropriate the language of advertising for personal use, dropping brand names all the time and saying things like "They have some lovely fashions in that store." In the same way they embrace all sub-professional euphemisms gladly and employ them proudly, adverting without irony to hair stylists, sanitary engineers, and funeral directors in complicity with the consumer world which cynically casts them as its main victims. They see nothing funny in paying a high price for an article and then, after a solemn pause, receiving part of it back in the form of a "rebate." Trapped in a world wholly defined by the language of consumption and the hype, they harbor restively, defending themselves against actuality by calling habitual drunkards *people with alcohol problems*, madness *mental illness*, drug use *drug abuse*, building lots *homesites*, houses *homes* ("They live in a lovely $250,000 home"), and drinks *beverages*.

Those delighted to employ the vacuous commercial "Have a nice day" and those who wouldn't think of saying it belong manifestly to different classes, no matter how we define them, and it is unthinkable that those classes will ever melt. Calvin Coolidge said that the business of America is business. Now apparently the business of America is having a nice day. Tragedy? Don't need it. Irony? Take it away. Have a nice day. Have a nice day. A visiting Englishman of my acquaintance, a U-speaker if there ever was one, has devised the perfect U-response to "Have a nice day": "Thank you," he says, "but I have other plans." The same ultimate divide separates the two classes who say respectively when introduced, "How do you do?" and "Pleased to meet you." There may be comity between those who think *prestigious* a classy word and those who don't, but it won't survive much strain, like relations between those who think *momentarily* means in a moment (airline captain over loudspeaker: "We'll be taking off momentarily, folks") and those who know it means for a moment. Members of these two classes can sit in adjoining seats on the plane and get along fine (although there's a further division between those who talk to their neighbors in planes and elevators and those who don't), but once the plane has emptied, they will proceed toward different destinations. It's the same with those who conceive that *type* is an adjective ("He's a very classy type person") and those who know it's only a noun or verb.

The pretense that either person can feel at ease in the presence of the other is an essential element of the presiding American fiction. Despite the lowness of the metaphor, the idea of the melting pot is high-minded and noble enough, but empirically it will be found increasingly unconvincing. It is our different language habits as much as anything that makes us, as the title of Richard Polenberg's book puts it, *One Nation Divisible*.

Some people invite constant class trouble because they believe the offi- 24 cial American publicity about these matters. The official theory, which experience is constantly disproving, is that one can earn one's way out of his original class. Richard Nixon's behavior indicated dramatically that this is not so. The sign of the Upper Class to which he aspired is total psychological security, expressed in loose carriage, saying what one likes, and imperviousness to what others think. Nixon's vast income from law and politics — his San Clemente property aped the style of the Upper but not the Top Out-of-Sight Class, for everyone knew where it was, and he wanted them to know — could not alleviate his original awkwardness and meanness of soul or his nervousness about the impression he was making, an affliction allied to his instinct for cunning and duplicity. Hammacher Schlemmer might have had him specifically in mind as the consumer of their recently advertised "Champagne Recork": "This unusual stopper keeps 'bubbly' sprightly, sparkling after uncorking ceremony is over. Gold electro-plated." I suspect that it is some of these same characteristics that made Edward Kennedy often seem so inauthentic a member of the Upper Class. (He's not Top Out-of-Sight because he chooses to augment his inheritance by attractive work.)

What, then, marks the higher classes? Primarily a desire for privacy, if not invisibility, and a powerful if eccentric desire for freedom. It is this instinct for freedom that may persuade us that inquiring into the American class system this way is an enterprise not entirely facetious. Perhaps after all the whole thing has something, just something, to do with ethics and aesthetics. Perhaps a term like *gentleman* still retains some meanings which are not just sartorial and mannerly. Freedom and grace and independence: it would be nice to believe those words still mean something, and it would be interesting if the reality of the class system — and everyone, after all, hopes to rise — should turn out to be a way we pay those notions a due if unwitting respect.

AFTERWORD

Fussell amuses himself and his readers by hanging this essay on the hook of social class. Although he starts by referring to "the facts about social class," he writes without making use of facts. When he mentions Rockefellers and du Ponts, he could as well speak of Morgans and Vanderbilts; his proper names are exemplary and illustrative. If we hear about welfare on the one hand and unmentionably huge incomes on the other, we hear nothing of numbers or dollar amounts.

Maybe Fussell isn't writing about class at all, but the suggestion of class allows him a structure. Any device that categorizes, even something as foolish as the horoscope, allows us a tentative framework to think with; if we then gather useful insights, we can always deconstruct the framework.

This light essay is about manners or about style; it is not about inherited wealth or power, about accents or clubs — instruments of exclusion that perpetuate families connected by marriage into a system.

For Fussell class is behavior, permissible or derisory. This essay sounds like a feature in a fashion magazine, playing the perpetual game of who's in, who's out. To be sure, there's a difference between people who studied Latin at school and people who didn't, a generation later. But if, say, these generations both attended Choate and Yale, it is questionable to say that the difference between them is class.

BOOKS AVAILABLE IN PAPERBACK

Abroad: British Literary Traveling Between the Wars. New York: Oxford University Press. *Nonfiction.*

The Boy Scout Handbook and Other Observations. New York: Oxford University Press. *Essays.*

Class. New York: Ballantine. *Nonfiction.*

The Great War and Modern Memory. New York: Oxford University Press. *Nonfiction.*

The Rhetorical World of Augustan Humanism: Ethics and Imagery from Swift to Burke. Ann Arbor: University of Michigan, Press. *Nonfiction.*

Samuel Johnson and the Life of Writing. New York: Norton. *Nonfiction.*

JOHN KENNETH GALBRAITH

*J*OHN KENNETH GALBRAITH *was born in 1908 at Iona Station in Ontario, Canada. He took his B.S. at the University of Toronto, then began graduate work by studying agricultural economics and received an M.S. at the University of California. Enlarging his studies into general economics, he took his Ph.D. at the University of California, taught at Harvard late in the 1930s and then at Princeton, until he left the academic world to work for the United States government during World War II. He served as economic adviser to the National Defense Advisory Committee and as deputy head of the Office of Price Administration. His experience in government during the war years was crucial to his development as an economics thinker. After a few years at* Fortune *magazine, he returned to the faculty of Harvard, where he was Paul M. Warburg Professor of Economics when he retired in 1975. On leave from Harvard from 1961 to 1963, he was ambassador to India under President John F. Kennedy.*

Galbraith's vision as an economist has been consistently political and historical, developed especially in a core of four books. The Affluent Society *(1958) criticized the conventional wisdom of classical economics.* American Capitalism *(1972) set forth the ideas that other volumes elucidated in detail.* The New Industrial State

(1967) analyzed things as they are. Economics and the Public Purpose *(1973) set forth Galbraith's notions for an economics adequate for the future.*

His many books have contributed not only to the study of economics but to our understanding of ourselves and our culture. His other economics works include The Great Crash *(1955), which analyzes the 1929 stock market crash that precipitated the Great Depression;* The Liberal Hour *(1960); and* The Nature of Mass Poverty *(1979). Although he is most eminent as an economist, Galbraith does not limit himself to economics: Among his other books are a novel,* The Triumph *(1968), published pseudonymously; and the nonfiction works* The Scotch, *a memoir (1964);* Indian Painting *(1968);* Ambassador's Journal *(1969); and* A China Passage *(1973).* The Galbraith Reader *(1977) is a collection of Galbraith's prose,* A Life in Our Times *(1981) an autobiography. Heading into his ninth decade, retired from teaching, Galbraith does not slow down his productive work.* A View from the Stands *(1986) included "Corporate Man." A year later, he published* Economics in Perspective *(1987).*

Whether Galbraith writes about painting or Scotch ancestry or politics, his general intelligence and his wit bring economics to bear on his subject. This author could wear on his crest the Latin motto from Terence, humani nihil alienum, *which translates "nothing human is alien." The same qualities of wit and intelligence illuminate his prose when he writes on economics. The editors of* The Galbraith Reader *quote him as believing and exemplifying that "there is no mystery in the science of economics that cannot be phrased in good English prose." Throughout his life he has attended to the relationship between economic structures and human character, as in "Corporate Man." This brief essay was commissioned by the New York* Times *for its Sunday magazine feature "About Men." In a note when he reprinted this essay, Galbraith cited its origins: "Thus the sexist tone. But I am compelled to point out that women executives, as and to the extent they emerge, will be bound by the same chains of which I here tell."*

Corporate Man

Any consideration of the life and larger social existence of the modern corporate man — the executive in the reasonably senior ranks of the one thousand largest American corporations — begins and also largely ends with the effect of one all-embracing force. That is organization — the highly structured assemblage of men, and now some women, of which he is a part. It is to this, at the expense of family, friends, sex, recreation, and sometimes health and effective control of alcoholic intake, that he is expected to devote his energies. Every one of us is to some degree the creature of organization and its constraints. The college professor who prides himself on his utter independence of speech and manner gives careful thought in all but the most inconvenient cases to the effect of his voice and behavior on his position in the faculty and perhaps, in some exceptional instances, to their effect on the reputation of his college or university. The business executive, however, is subject to a far more severe and comprehensive discipline. On the job it may not be quite as rigorous as that of a senior army officer, but it embraces a far larger part of his life; he is never off duty.

There are, of course, some notable rewards to society from this circumstance. Principally it provides the larger community with the services of an exceptionally hard-working body of men. Among the many charges that, justly or unjustly, have been brought against the modern corporate executive, one has never been made: not even his most relentless critic suggests that he is lazy. Supply-side economists hold that lower taxes would make him *more* productive. But they never, never suggest the corollary, which is that he is now doing less than his best.

Beyond his devotion to work, however, he is also well spoken, tolerant of disagreement, disposed always to negotiate — for that is how he spends his time — and otherwise given to persuasion rather than to command. In all respects, he is a far more agreeable figure than his predecessor, the great captain of industry, the prototypical entrepreneur.

The counterpart of this disciplined commitment to the job at hand is,   4 unfortunately, a nearly total sacrifice of the right to personal thought and expression. And also of a wide range of personal enjoyments. It is, of course, axiomatic that no responsible corporate executive expresses himself publicly in opposition to the decisions, purposes, social effects, political activities, or malfeasances of his organization. He may dissent in private. But if things get really insupportable, his only choice is to resign and explain that, although all is amicable, he feels that the time has come in his career when he should seek a well-deserved early retirement or look for "new challenges" elsewhere.

The ban on unlicensed expression is not quite the same as silence. Speeches, many speeches, must be made — to stockholders, financial analysts, business organizations, service clubs, church groups, and still, on occasion, to the Boy Scouts. But there is no form of spoken literature, reputable Protestant sermons possibly excepted, that evokes such a profound lack of response. The press and other media ignore entirely such executive communications or, if something is included therein about prospective corporate earnings, subject them to a truly masterly condensation.

Though often offered with no slight vehemence, publicly expressed executive views on public policy are also ignored. Nor should the aspiring corporate leader be in doubt as to the reason. What *he* says is required by the rules and ethics of organization to be both predictable and dull. He does not speak for himself; he speaks for the firm. Good policy is not what he wants but what the organization believes it needs. In the normal case, his speech has been written and vetted by his fellow organization men, and, in the process, it has dropped to the lowest common denominator of novelty. Lindbergh, as has too often been told, could never have flown the Atlantic with a committee. It is equally certain that the General Motors management team could never have written the plays of Shakespeare or a column by Art Buchwald. Executive expression is ignored because, by the nature of organization it must be at an adequately tedious level of stereotype and caution.

This, however, is not the only constraint on the executive. There is a subjective effect that is far more comprehensive and that is also very little noticed in our time. Every year the Harvard Business School graduates some 760 students. They are an extremely bright and diverse convocation, with, as students go, exceptionally high standards of dress and personal hygiene. It has always been a pleasure whenever I have met with them over the years. All, with the rarest exceptions, will enjoy especially ample incomes for the rest of their lives. But only the most ostentatiously eccentric will ever make any personal contribution in music, painting, the theater, films, writing, serious learning, or the lower art of politics. In years past a good income was thought to allow of such diversions; that was its purpose. From the modern business executive the most that can be expected is a check in support of someone else's achievements.

The pay and perquisites accorded the corporate executive in our time 8 are a topic of much comment and some envy. Their size owes a great deal to the convenient circumstance that in the upper reaches of the modern corporation the executive has a key role in setting them both. More attention needs to be accorded, however, to what the executive gives up in return.

This, besides the personal rights and enjoyments already mentioned, now includes even personal identity. Once, we knew the names of the heads of the great corporations — Alfred P. Sloan, Jr., of General Motors, Thomas J. Watson of IBM, Henry Ford of Ford, and, assuredly, John D. Rockefeller of Standard Oil of New Jersey. Today a poll asking who are the chief executive officers of these companies would elicit only an unbroken series of blanks. The organization has taken over; it has the authority and the public recognition; its chairman or president is, perhaps rightly, unknown. The point is emphasized by what happens when he leaves office. While there, he unquestionably commands a considerable measure of respect, often deference, from his fellow executives or when he shows up for high-level meetings in Washington. On the day he steps down, he passes into an oblivion that continues complete until his name finally appears, along with a few dismissing and only approximately accurate lines, in the obituary columns.

I do not suggest that, given his sacrifices, the modern business executive is underpaid. I do note, in a somewhat circumspect defense of his liberal compensation, that to give up so much of the only life one is certain (considering the present state of knowledge on the matter) to have is surely worth something.

AFTERWORD

Galbraith here accepted a commission to fill limited space in a magazine. He picked a subject well known to him, narrowed it down while defining it by comparison and contrast, and sketched a collective portrait. At first he outlines a positive characterization of Corporate Man, using the ploy of fairness, then switches ("unfortunately") to the negative side of this figure he observes or invents. Out of his vast experience of lecturing, arguing, and writing, Galbraith neatly indicts, while praising, an economically derived character common to the contemporary world.

Always he commands an exact, supple syntax that uses tone to locate judgment: "It is, of course, axiomatic that no responsible corporate executive expresses himself publicly in opposition to the decisions, purposes, social effects, political activities, or malfeasances of his organization. He may dissent in private. But if things get really insupportable, his only choice is to resign and explain that, although all is amicable, he feels that the time has come in his career when he should seek a well-deserved early retirement or look for 'new challenges' elsewhere." With an irony gentle but firmly judgmental, with absolute control of managerial jargon, with masterly variation of sentence structure, John Kenneth Galbraith bites where he wishes to bite.

BOOKS AVAILABLE IN PAPERBACK

The Affluent Society, 3rd ed. New York: New American Library. *Nonfiction.*

American Capitalism. Boston: Houghton Mifflin. *Nonfiction.*

The Anatomy of Power. Boston: Houghton Mifflin. *Nonfiction.*

Economics and the Public Purpose. New York: New American Library. *Nonfiction.*

Economics, Peace, and Laughter. New York: New American Library. *Nonfiction.*

The Great Crash of 1929. New York: Avon. *Nonfiction.*

A Life in Our Times. New York: Ballantine. *Nonfiction.*

The Nature of Mass Poverty. Cambridge: Harvard University Press. *Nonfiction.*

The New Industrial State, 4th ed. New York: New American Library. *Nonfiction.*

A Theory of Price Control: The Classic Account. Cambridge: Harvard University Press. *Nonfiction.*

The Triumph. New York: Arbor House. *Novel.*

WILLIAM H. GASS

*W*ILLIAM H. GASS *is a novelist and professor of philosophy at Washington University in St. Louis. His fiction includes* Omensetter's Luck *(1966),* In the Heart of the Heart of the Country *(1968), and* Willie Master's Lonesome Wife *(1971). For decades he has worked on a novel called* The Tunnel *and published excerpts of it in magazines, but he has not yet finished it. In the meantime his philosophical and literary essays have been collected in* Fiction and the Figures of Life *(1970),* On Being Blue *(1976),* The World Within the Word *(1979), and* Habitations of the Word *(1985). This essay appeared in the* New York Times Book Review.

Born in North Dakota (1924), he grew up in Ohio and attended Kenyon College. As an adolescent he found home life insupportable. "I was simply unable to handle my parents' illnesses. My mother was an alcoholic and my father was crippled by arthritis and by his own character." The Second World War interrupted college with naval service, which stationed Gass at the end of the war in China and Japan. He graduated from Kenyon in 1947 and did his Ph.D. in philosophy at Cornell, studying linguistic philosophy and writing a dissertation on metaphor. At Cornell he attended a seminar given by Ludwig Wittgenstein, great of modern philosophers, which remained for Gass "the most important intellectual experience" of his life.

Although he set himself to become a professional philosopher, he always intended to practice literature. His work in fiction is austere and beautiful, the product of obsessive rewriting, sentence by sentence. Perhaps because he thinks for a living, he thinks more clearly than most fiction writers about the nature of what he does. The philosopher Gass cares nothing for ideas, in fiction, but for word, sentence, rhythm — language's body. Writing fiction he makes an object; he wants "to plant some object in the world . . . worthy of love." He goes on: "My particular aim is that it be loved because it is so beautiful in itself, something that exists simply to be experienced."

Of Speed Readers
and Lip-Movers

I was never much of an athlete, but I was once the member of a team. Indeed, I was its star, and we were champions. During high school I belonged to a squad of speed readers in Ohio, although I was never awarded a letter for it. Still, we took on the top 10 in our territory and read as rapidly as possible every time we were challenged to a match, hoping to finish in front of that towheaded punk from Canton, the tomato-cheeked girl from Marietta, or that silent pair of sisters, all spectacles and squints, who looked tough as German script and who hailed from Shaker Heights or some other rough neighborhood full of swift, mean raveners of texts.

We called ourselves the Speeders. Of course. Everybody did. There were the Sharon Speeders, the Steubenville Speeders, and the Niles Nouns. They never won. How could they? I lost a match myself once to a kid with green teeth. And that's the way, I'm afraid, we appeared to others — as creeps with squints, bad posture, unclean complexions, unscrubbed teeth, tousled hair. We never had dates, we only memorized them; and when any real sports team went on the road to represent the high school, we carried the socks, the Tootsie Rolls, the towels for them. My nemesis with the green teeth had a head of thin red hair like rust on a saw; he revolved a suggestive little finger in his large fungiform ears. My God, I thought . . . and the shame of that defeat still rushes to my face whenever I remember it. Nevertheless, even today I possess a substantial, gold-colored medallion on which one sunbeaming eye seems hung above a book like a spider. Both book and eye are open — wide. I take that open, streaming eye to be an omen.

Our reading life has its salad days, its autumnal times. At first, of course, we do it badly, scarcely keeping our balance, toddling along behind our finger, so intent on remembering what each word is supposed to mean that the sentence is no longer a path, and we arrive at its end without having gone anywhere. Thus it is with all the things we learn, for at first they passively oppose us; they lie outside us like mist or the laws of nature; we have to issue orders to our eyes, our limbs, our understanding: Lift this, shift that, thumb the space bar, let up on the clutch — easy! There go the gears! — and don't forget to modify the verb, or remember what an escudo's worth. After a while, we find we like standing up, riding a bike, singing *Don Giovanni*, making puff pastry, puppy love, or model planes. Then we are indeed like the adolescent in our eager green enthusiasms: They are plentiful as leaves. Every page is a pasture, and we are let out to graze like hungry herds.

Do you remember what magic the word *thigh* could work on you, showing up in the middle of a passage suddenly, like a whiff of cologne in a theater? I admit it: The widening of the upper thigh remains a miracle, and, honestly, many of us once read the word *thigh* as if we were exploring Africa, seeking the source of the Nile. No volume was too hefty then, no style too verbal. The weight of a big book was more comforting than Christmas candy, though you had to be lucky, strike the right text at the right time, because the special excitement Thomas Wolfe provides, for instance, can be felt only in the teens. And when, again, will any of us possess the energy, the patience, the inner sympathy for volcanic bombast to read — enjoy — Carlyle?

Repeating was automatic. Who needed Gertrude Stein? I must have rushed through a pleasant little baseball book called *The Crimson Pennant* at least a dozen times, consuming a cake I had already cut into crumbs, yet that big base hit was never better than on that final occasion when its hero and I ran round those bases, and he shyly doffed his hat to the crowd.

No one threatened to whack our rumps if we didn't read another Nancy Drew by Tuesday; no sour-faced virgin browbeat us with *The Blithedale Romance* or held out *The Cloister and the Hearth* like a cold plate of good-for-you food. We were on our own. I read Swinburne and the *Adventures of the Shadow*. I read Havelock Ellis and Tom Swift and *The Idylls of the King*. I read whatever came to hand, and what came to hand were a lot of naughty French novels, detective stories, medical adventures, books about bees, biographies of Napoleon, and *Thus Spake Zarathustra* like a bolt of lightning.

I read them all, whatever they were, with an ease that defies the goat's digestion, and with an ease that is now so easily forgotten, just as we forget the wild wobble in our bikes' wheels, or the humiliating falls we took when we began our life on spokes. That wind I felt, when I finally stayed upright

213

around the block, continuously reaffirmed the basic joy of cycling. It told me not merely that I was moving, but that I was moving *under my own power*; just as later, when I'd passed my driver's test, I would feel another sort of exhilaration — an intense, addictive, dangerous one — that of command, of my ability to control the energy produced by another thing or person, to direct the life contained in another creature.

Yes, in those early word-drunk years, I would down a book or two a day as though they were gins. I read for adventure, excitement, to sample the exotic and the strange, for climax and resolution, to participate in otherwise forbidden passions. I forgot what it was to be under my own power, under my own steam. I was, like so many adolescents, as eager to leap from my ordinary life as the salmon is to get upstream. I sought a replacement for the world. With a surreptitious lamp lit, I stayed awake to dream. I grew reckless. I read for speed. 8

When you read for speed you do not read recursively, looping along the line like a sewing machine, stitching something together — say the panel of a bodice to a sleeve — linking a pair of terms, the contents of a clause, closing a seam by following the internal directions of the sentence so that the word *you* is first fastened to the word *read*, and then the phrase *for speed* is attached to both in order that the entire expression can be finally fronted by a grandly capitalized *When* . . . while all of that, in turn, is gathered up to await the completion of the later segment that begins *you do not read recursively*. You can hear how long it seems to take — this patient process — and how confusing it can become. Nor do you linger over language, repeating some especially pleasant little passage, in the enjoyment, perhaps, of a modest rhyme (for example, the small clause, *when you read for speed*), or a particularly apt turn of phrase (an image, for instance, such as the one that dealt with Green Teeth's thin red hair — like rust on a saw). None of that, when you read for speed.

Nor, naturally, do you move your lips as you read the word *read* or the words *moving your lips*, so that the poor fellow next to you in the reading room has to watch intently to see what your lips are saying: Are you asking him out? For the loan of his Plutarch's *Lives*? And of course the poor fellow is flummoxed to find that you are moving your lips to say *moving your lips*. What can that mean? The lip-mover — O, such a person is low on our skill-scale. We are taught to have scorn for him, for her.

On the other hand, the speeding reader drops diagonally down across the page, on a slant like a skier, cuts across the text the way a butcher prefers to slice sausage, so that a small round can be made to yield a misleading larger oval piece. The speeding reader is after the kernel, the heart, the gist. Paragraphs become a country the eye flies over looking for landmarks, reference points, airports, restrooms, passages of sex. The speeding reader guts a book the way the skillful clean fish. The gills are gone, the tail, the scales, the fins; then the filet slides away swiftly as though fed to a seal. And only the slow reader, whose finger falters in front of long words, who moves the lips, who dances the text, will notice the odd crowd of images — flier, skier, butcher, seal — that have gathered to comment on the aims and activities of the speeding reader, perhaps like gossips at a wedding.

To the speeding reader, this jostle of images, this crazy collision of ideas 12 — of landing strip, kernel, heart, guts, sex — will not be felt, because it is only the inner core of meaning he's after; it is the gist she wants. And the gist is: Readers who read rapidly read only for the most generalized, stereotyped sense. For them, meaning floats over the page like fluffy clouds. Cliché is forever in fashion. They read, as we say, synonymously, seeking sameness; and, indeed, it is all the same to them if they are said in one moment to be greedy as seals, and in another moment likened to descalers of fish. They — you, I, we — "get" the idea.

A speed-reading match had two halves. (I say "had" because I believe these matches long ago lit their last light.) The first consisted of the rapid reading itself, through which, of course, I whizzzzed, all the while making the sound of closing covers in order to disconcert Green Teeth or the silent Shaker Heights sisters, who were to think I had completed my reading already. I didn't wear glasses then, but I carried a glasses case to every match, and always dropped it at a pertinent moment.

Next we were required to answer questions about what we claimed we'd covered, and here quickness was again essential. The questions, however, soon disclosed their biases. They had a structure, their own gist; and it became possible, after some experience, to guess what would be asked about a text almost before it had been begun. Is it "Goldilocks" we're skimming? Then what is the favorite breakfast food of the three bears? How does Goldilocks escape from the house? Why weren't the three bears at home when Goldilocks came calling? The multiple answers we could choose from also had their own tired tilt and, like the questions, gave themselves away. The favorite breakfast foods, for instance, were: (a) Quaker Oats (which this year is paying for the prizes, and in this sly fashion gets its name in); (b) Just Rite (written like a brand name); (c) porridge (usually misspelled); (d) sugar-coated curds and whey. No one ever wondered whether Goldilocks was suffering from sibling rivalry; why she had become a teenie-trasher; or why mother bear's bowl of porridge was cold when baby bear's smaller bowl was still warm and Just Rite.

There were many other mysteries, but not for these quiz masters who didn't even want to know the sexual significance of Cinderella's slipper, or why it had to be made of glass. I won my championship medal by ignoring the text entirely (it was a section from Volume Two of Oswald Spengler's *Decline of the West*, the part that begins, "Regard the flowers at eventide as, one after the other, they close in the setting sun. . . . " But then, of course, you remember that celebrated passage). I skipped the questions as well, and simply encircled the gloomiest alternatives offered. Won in record time. No one's got through Spengler with such dispatch since.

What did these matches with their quizzes for comprehension, their love of literal learning, tell me? They told me that time was money (a speed reader's clearest idea); they told me what the world wanted me to read when I read, eat when I ate, see when I saw. Like the glutton, I was to get everything in and out in a hurry: Turnover was topmost. What the world wanted me to get was the gist, but the gist was nothing but an idea of trade — an idea so drearily uniform and emaciated it might have modeled dresses.

There is another way of reading I'd like to recommend. It's slow, old-fashioned, not easy either, rarely practiced. It must be learned. It is a way of life. What! — I hear your hearts exclaim — is the old wart going to go on some more about reading? Reading? When we can see the rings around his eyes for every year he's worn them out . . . reading? When we are commencing from college, leaving books, book bags, bicycles behind like pretty scenes along the highway? Yes. Just so. That's true. Most of you *are* through. Farewell, chemistry. Farewell, *Canterbury Tales.* Imagine reading *that* again. Or *The Faerie Queene* even the first time. Farewell, Sir Philip Sydney, and your golden lines:

Farewell O Sunn, Arcadias clearest light;
Farewell O pearl, the poore mans plenteous treasure:
Farewell O golden staffe, the weake mans might:
Farewell O joy, the joyfulls onely pleasure.
Wisdom farewell, the skillesse mans direction:
Farewell with thee, farewell all our affection.

Now "Paradise" is "Lost." Who cares if molecular genetics has revolutionized biology? Farewell, philosophy. Farewell, free love. From now on there will be an interest, a carrying, a handling charge. Farewell, *A Farewell to Arms. Goodbye, Columbus.*

You may have noticed that I am now speaking in sentence fragments. The speed reader hates subordination, qualification, refinement, deployment, ritual, decoration, order, mother, inference, country, logic, family, flag, God. Here is a little test: In that last list, what word will the speed reader pick out to stand for the rest of it — to be its gist? *God,* you guess? No. Wrong. Nor *flag,* though that's appealing. *Mother* will be the word we want.

All right. I heard your hearts heave like a slow sea. I'm adaptable. Let's talk about drinking. I belonged to a drinking club once. Defeated the

Fraternal Order of Eagles on their own turf. The Chug-a-lugs, we were called. Inevitably. You don't plan, I'm sure, to give up drinking. Or reading — not altogether — I imagine. Not the letters to *Penthouse*. The inky pages of the *Washington Post*. *TV Guide*. Legal briefs. Medical romances. Business lore.

Well, there is another way of drinking I'd like to recommend. We've already dealt with the first way. Gulp. Get the gist. And the gist is the level of alcohol in your blood, the pixilated breath you blow into the test balloon. It makes appropriate the expression: Have a belt. We can toss down a text, a time of life, a love affair, that walk in the park that gets us from here to there. We can chug-a-lug them. You have, perhaps, had to travel sometime with a person whose passion was that simple: It was *getting there*. You have no doubt encountered people who impatiently wait for the payoff; they urge you to come to the point; at dinner, the early courses merely delay dessert; they look only at the bottom line (that obscene phrase); they are persons consumed by consequences; they want to climax without crescendo.

But we can read and walk and write and look in quite a different way. It is possible. I was saved from sameness by Immanuel Kant. You can't speed-read *The Critique of Pure Reason*. You can't speed-read Wallace Stevens. There is no gist, no simple translation, no key concept that will unlock these works; actually, there is no lock, no door, no wall, no room, no house, no world.

Reading is a complicated, profound, silent, still, very personal, very private, very solitary yet civilizing activity. Nothing is more social than speech — we are bound together by our common sounds more securely than even by our laws. Nevertheless, no one is more aware of the isolated self than the reader, for a reader communes with the word heard immaterially in that hollow of the head made only for hearing, a room nowhere in the body in any ordinary sense. On the bus, everyone of us may be deep in something different. Sitting next to a priest, I can still enjoy my pornography, though I may keep a thumb discreetly on top of the title.

I've grown larger, if not wiser. My vices now are visionary. That baseball 24 book, *The Crimson Pennant*, has become *The Crimson Cancan*. What do I care if Father McIvie is reading about investments? Yet while all of us, in our verbal recreations, are full of respect for the privacy of our neighbors, the placards advertising perfume or footwear invade the public space like a visual smell; Muzak fills every unstoppered ear the way the static of the street does. The movies, the radio, television, theater, music: All run on at their own rate, and the listener or the viewer must attend, keep up, or lose out — but not the reader. The reader is free. The reader is in charge and pedals the cycle. It is easy for a reader to announce that his present run of Proust has been postponed until the holidays.

Reading, that is, is not a public imposition. Of course, when we read, many of us squirm and fidget. One of the closest friends of my youth would sensuously wind and unwind on his forefinger the long blond strands of his hair. How he read — that is how I remember him. Yes, our postures are often provocative, perverse. Yet these outward movements of the body really testify to the importance of the inner movements of the mind; and even those rapid flickers of the eye, as we shift from word to word, phrase to phrase, and clause to clause, hoping to keep our head afloat on a food of Faulkner or Proust or Joyce or James, are registers of reason. For reading is reasoning, figuring things out through thoughts, making arrangements out of arrangements until we've understood a text so fully it is nothing but feeling and pure response, until its conceptual turns are like the reversals of mood in a marriage — petty, sad, ecstatic, commonplace, foreseeable, amazing.

In order to have this experience, however, one must learn to perform the text, say, sing, shout the words to oneself, give them, with *our* minds, *their* body. Otherwise the eye skates over every syllable like the speeder. There can be no doubt that often what we read should be skimmed, as what we are frequently asked to drink should be spilled. But the speeding reader is alone in another, less satisfactory way, one quite different from that of the reader who says the words to herself, because as we read we divide into a theater: There is the performer who shapes those silent sounds, moving the muscles of the larynx almost invisibly, and there is the listener who hears them said and who responds to their passion or their wisdom.

Such a reader sees every text as unique, greets every work as a familiar stranger. Such a reader is willing to allow another's words to become hers, his.

In the next moment, let us read a wine, since I promised I would talk 28 about drinking. We have prepared for the occasion, of course. The bottle has been allowed to breathe. Books need to breathe, too. They should be opened properly, hefted, thumbed. The paper, print, layout, should be appreciated. But now we decant the text into our wide-open and welcoming eyes. We warm the wine in the bowl of the glass with our hand. We let its bouquet collect above it just as the red of red roses seems to stain the air. We wade — shoeless, to be sure — through the color it has liquefied. We roll a bit of it about in our mouths. We sip. We savor. We say some sentences of Sir Thomas Browne: "We tearme sleepe a death, and yet it is waking that kils us, and destroyed those spirits which are the house of life. Tis indeed a part of life that best expresseth death, for every man truely lives so long as hee acts his nature, or someway makes good the faculties of himself. . . . "

Are these words not from a fine field, in a splendid year? There is, of course, a sameness in all these words: *life/death, man/nature.* We get the drift. But the differences! The differences make all the difference, the way nose and eyes and cheek bones form a face, the way a muscle makes emotion pass across it. It is the differences we read. Differences are not only identifiable, distinct; they are epidemic: The wine is light, perhaps, spicy, slow to release its grip upon itself, the upper thigh is widening wonderfully, the night air has hands, words fly out of our mouths like birds. "But who knows the fate of his bones," Browne says, "or how often he is to be buried."

Yet as I say his soul out loud, he lives again; he has risen up in me, and I can be, for him, that temporary savior that every real reader is, putting his words in my mouth; not nervously, notice, as though they were pieces of gum, but in that way that is necessary if the heart is to hear them. And though they are his words and his soul, then, that return through me, I am in charge. He has asked nothing of me; his words move because I move them. It is like cycling, reading is. Can you feel the air, the pure passage of the spirit past the exposed skin?

So this reading will be like living, then — the living each of you will be off in a moment to be busy with, not always speedily, I hope, or in the continuous anxiety of consequence, the sullenness of inattention, the annoying static of distraction. But it will be only a semblance of living — this living — nevertheless, the way unspoken reading is a semblance, unless, from time to time, you perform the outer world within. Because only in that manner can it deliver itself to us. As Rainer Maria Rilke once commanded: "Dance the taste of the fruit you have been tasting. Dance the orange." I should like to multiply that charge, even past all possibility. Speak the street to yourself sometimes, hear the horns in the forest, read the breeze aloud and make that inner wind yours, because, whether Nature, Man, or God has given us the text, we independently possess the ability to read, to read really well, and to move our own mind freely in tune to the moving world.

AFTERWORD

Reading Henry James aloud — William H. Gass says somewhere — is the only way to read him. In his Paris Review *interview Gass praises the poet Rilke for copying his poems "in his beautiful hand" to send to a friend "because that was the poem, not the printed imitation." The physical words — not their translation into abstractions of concept or summary — seize Gass as they seize word lovers always. "Writing by hand, mouthing by mouth: In each case you get a very strong physical sense of the emergence of language — squeezed out like a well-formed stool — what satisfaction! what bliss!"*

The metaphor of defecation is typical of Gass. Assault or hostility characterizes his interviews: "My work proceeds almost always from a sense of aggression. . . . I am in my best working mood when . . . very combative, very hostile." "I write because I hate. A lot. Hard. And if someone asks me the inevitable next dumb question, 'Why do you write the way you do?' I must answer that I wish to make my hatred acceptable because my hatred is much of me, if not the best part."

For a writer of Gass's temperament and genius, speed-reading is not only vulgar but a denial of the possibility of literature. If you speed-read Henry James you might as well be reading roadsigns. Half-witted people assume that you read literature for its "content" as if the physical words and their import could be separated like the wrapping from the package.

BOOKS AVAILABLE IN PAPERBACK

Fiction and the Figures of Life. Boston: David Godine. *Essays.*

Habitations of the Word. New York: Simon & Schuster-Touchstone. *Essays.*

In the Heart of the Heart of the Country and Other Stories. Boston: David Godine. *Short stories.*

Omensetter's Luck. New York: New American Library. *Novel.*

On Being Blue: A Philosophical Inquiry. Boston: David Godine. *Nonfiction.*

The World Within the Word. Boston: David Godine. *Nonfiction.*

STEPHEN JAY
GOULD

S TEPHEN JAY GOULD (b. 1941), whose essays delight and instruct the
nonscientist in the byways of natural history, dedicated Ever Since Darwin
(1977) to his father, "who took me to see the tyrannosaurus when I was five."
Maybe the child's visit to a museum formed the whole life.

Gould is a paleontologist who teaches geology, biology, and history of science at
Harvard University. After graduating from Antioch College in 1963, he took his
Ph.D. at Columbia University. He is an evolutionist. He writes that his essays
"range broadly from planetary and geological to social and political history, but they
are united . . . by the common thread of evolutionary theory — Darwin's version."
Author of a long book called Ontogeny and Phylogeny (1977) and of The
Mismeasure of Man (1981), which attacks methods of quantifying intelligence, he
has collected three volumes of brief scientific essays mostly from his column, "This
View of Life," in Natural History magazine. Ever Since Darwin was the first
collection, and he followed it with The Panda's Thumb (1980), Hen's Teeth and
Horse's Toes (1983), and The Flamingo's Smile (1985), from which we take the
essay printed here. In 1987 he collected his book reviews and miscellaneous writing
in An Urchin in the Storm: Essays About Books and Ideas. Among other
honors he has won a National Book Award and become a MacArthur Prize fellow.

Writing in the New York Times Book Review *about three great scientific essayists (T. H. Huxley, J. B. S. Haldane, and P. B. Medawar), Gould listed the qualities he admired in terms that we can apply to Gould himself: "All write about the simplest things and draw from them a universe of implications. . . . All maintain an unflinching commitment to rationality amid the soft attractions of an uncritical mysticism. . . . All demonstrate a deep commitment to the demystification of science by cutting through jargon; they show by example rather than exhortation that the most complex concepts can be rendered intelligible to everyone."*

Early in the 1980s Gould was diagnosed to suffer from mesothelioma, a form of cancer which usually — as he quickly discovered by research — terminates its victim in about eight months. Gould's case was discovered early and proved amenable to treatment. "I simply had to see my children grow up," he said, "and it would be perverse to come this close to the millennium and then blow it." During months of grave illness, weight loss, and debilitating chemotherapy, Gould continued teaching and writing. He appears completely recovered.

In one of Gould's essays he writes, "I have never been able to raise much personal enthusiasm for disembodied theory. Thus, when I wish to explore the explanatory power of evolutionary theory . . . , I write about apparent oddities resolved by Darwin's view — dwarf male anglerfishes parasitically united with females, wasps that paralyze insects to provide a living feast for their larvae, young birds that kill their siblings by simply pushing them outside a ring of guano." Although Gould may choose these "oddities" for their explanatory function, the reader glimpses in his writing, alongside the enthusiastic explainer, a five-year-old who looks with joy and wonder at the immense skeleton of a dinosaur.

Sex, Drugs, Disasters, and the Extinction of Dinosaurs

Science, in its most fundamental definition, is a fruitful mode of inquiry, not a list of enticing conclusions. The conclusions are the consequence, not the essence.

My greatest unhappiness with most popular presentations of science concerns their failure to separate fascinating claims from the methods that scientists use to establish the facts of nature. Journalists, and the public, thrive on controversial and stunning statements. But science is, basically, a way of knowing — in P. B. Medawar's apt words, "the art of the soluble." If the growing corps of popular science writers would focus on *how* scientists develop and defend those fascinating claims, they would make their greatest possible contribution to public understanding.

Consider three ideas, proposed in perfect seriousness to explain that greatest of all titillating puzzles — the extinction of dinosaurs. Since these three notions invoke the primally fascinating themes of our culture — sex, drugs, and violence — they surely reside in the category of fascinating claims. I want to show why two of them rank as silly speculation, while the other represents science at its grandest and most useful.

Science works with testable proposals. If, after much compilation and scrutiny of data, new information continues to affirm a hypothesis, we may accept it provisionally and gain confidence as further evidence mounts. We can never be completely sure that a hypothesis is right, though we may be able to show with confidence that it is wrong. The best scientific hypotheses are also generous and expansive: they suggest extensions and implications that enlighten related, and even far distant, subjects. Simply consider how the idea of evolution has influenced virtually every intellectual field.

Useless speculation, on the other hand, is restrictive. It generates no testable hypothesis, and offers no way to obtain potentially refuting evidence. Please note that I am not speaking of truth or falsity. The speculation may well be true; still, if it provides, in principle, no material for affirmation or rejection, we can make nothing of it. It must simply stand forever as an intriguing idea. Useless speculation turns in on itself and leads nowhere; good science, containing both seeds for its potential refutation and implications for more and different testable knowledge, reaches out. But, enough preaching. Let's move on to dinosaurs, and the three proposals for their extinction.

1. Sex: Testes function only in a narrow range of temperature (those of mammals hang externally in a scrotal sac because internal body temperatures are too high for their proper function). A worldwide rise in temperature at the close of the Cretaceous period caused the testes of dinosaurs to stop functioning and led to their extinction by sterilization of males.
2. Drugs: Angiosperms (flowering plants) first evolved toward the end of the dinosaurs' reign. Many of these plants contain psychoactive agents, avoided by mammals today as a result of their bitter taste. Dinosaurs had neither means to taste the bitterness nor livers effective enough to detoxify the substances. They died of massive overdoses.
3. Disasters: A large comet or asteroid struck the earth some 65 million years ago, lofting a cloud of dust into the sky and blocking sunlight, thereby suppressing photosynthesis and so drastically lowering world

temperatures that dinosaurs and hosts of other creatures became extinct.

Before analyzing these three tantalizing statements, we must establish a basic ground rule often violated in proposals for the dinosaurs' demise. *There is no separate problem of the extinction of dinosaurs.* Too often we divorce specific events from their wider contexts and systems of cause and effect. The fundamental fact of dinosaur extinction is its synchrony with the demise of so many other groups across a wide range of habitats, from terrestrial to marine.

The history of life has been punctuated by brief episodes of mass extinction. A recent analysis by University of Chicago paleontologists Jack Sepkoski and Dave Raup, based on the best and most exhaustive tabulation of data ever assembled, shows clearly that five episodes of mass dying stand well above the "background" extinctions of normal times (when we consider all mass extinctions, large and small, they seem to fall in a regular 26-million-year cycle). The Cretaceous debacle, occurring 65 million years ago and separating the Mesozoic and Cenozoic eras of our geological time scale, ranks prominently among the five. Nearly all the marine plankton (single-celled floating creatures) died with geological suddenness; among marine invertebrates, nearly 15 percent of all families perished, including many previously dominant groups, especially the ammonites (relatives of squids in coiled shells). On land, the dinosaurs disappeared after more than 100 million years of unchallenged domination.

In this context, speculations limited to dinosaurs alone ignore the larger phenomenon. We need a coordinated explanation for a system of events that includes the extinction of dinosaurs as one component. Thus it makes little sense, though it may fuel our desire to view mammals as inevitable inheritors of the earth, to guess that dinosaurs died because small mammals ate their eggs (a perennial favorite among untestable speculations). It seems most unlikely that some disaster peculiar to dinosaurs befell these massive beasts — and that the debacle happened to strike just when one of history's five great dyings had enveloped the earth for completely different reasons.

The testicular theory, an old favorite from the 1940s, had its root in an interesting and thoroughly respectable study of temperature tolerances in the American alligator, published in the staid *Bulletin of the American Museum of Natural History* in 1946 by three experts on living and fossil reptiles — E. H. Colbert, my own first teacher in paleontology; R. B. Cowles; and C. M. Bogert.

The first sentence of their summary reveals a purpose beyond alligators: "This report describes an attempt to infer the reactions of extinct reptiles, especially the dinosaurs, to high temperatures as based upon reactions observed in the modern alligator." They studied, by rectal thermometry, the body temperatures of alligators under changing conditions of heating

8

and cooling. (Well, let's face it, you wouldn't want to try sticking a thermometer under a 'gator's tongue.) The predictions under test go way back to an old theory first stated by Galileo in the 1630s — the unequal scaling of surfaces and volumes. As an animal, or any object, grows (provided its shape doesn't change), surface areas must increase more slowly than volumes — since surfaces get larger as length squared, while volumes increase much more rapidly, as length cubed. Therefore, small animals have high ratios of surface to volume, while large animals cover themselves with relatively little surface.

Among cold-blooded animals lacking any physiological mechanism for keeping their temperatures constant, small creatures have a hell of a time keeping warm — because they lose so much heat through their relatively large surfaces. On the other hand, large animals, with their relatively small surfaces, may lose heat so slowly that, once warm, they may maintain effectively constant temperatures against ordinary fluctuations of climate. (In fact, the resolution of the "hot-blooded dinosaur" controversy that burned so brightly a few years back may simply be that, while large dinosaurs possessed no physiological mechanism for constant temperature, and were not therefore warm-blooded in the technical sense, their large size and relatively small surface area kept them warm.)

Colbert, Cowles, and Bogert compared the warming rates of small and large alligators. As predicted, the small fellows heated up (and cooled down) more quickly. When exposed to a warm sun, a tiny 50-gram (1.76-ounce) alligator heated up one degree Celsius every minute and a half, while a large alligator, 260 times bigger at 13,000 grams (28.7 pounds), took seven and a half minutes to gain a degree. Extrapolating up to an adult 10-ton dinosaur, they concluded that a one-degree rise in body temperature would take eighty-six hours. If large animals absorb heat so slowly (through their relatively small surfaces), they will also be unable to shed any excess heat gained when temperatures rise above a favorable level.

The authors then guessed that large dinosaurs lived at or near their optimum temperatures; Cowles suggested that a rise in global temperatures just before the Cretaceous extinction caused the dinosaurs to heat up beyond their optimal tolerance — and, being so large, they couldn't shed the unwanted heat. (In a most unusual statement within a scientific paper, Colbert and Bogert then explicitly disavowed this speculative extension of their empirical work on alligators.) Cowles conceded that this excess heat probably wasn't enough to kill or even to enervate the great beasts, but since testes often function only within a narrow range of temperature, he proposed that this global rise might have sterilized all the males, causing extinction by natural contraception.

The overdose theory has recently been supported by UCLA psychiatrist Ronald K. Siegel. Siegel has gathered, he claims, more than 2,000 records of animals who, when given access, administer various drugs to themselves

— from a mere swig of alcohol to massive doses of the big H. Elephants will swill the equivalent of twenty beers at a time, but do not like alcohol in concentrations greater than 7 percent. In a silly bit of anthropocentric speculation, Siegel states that "elephants drink, perhaps, to forget . . . the anxiety produced by shrinking rangeland and the competition for food."

Since fertile imaginations can apply almost any hot idea to the extinction of dinosaurs, Siegel found a way. Flowering plants did not evolve until late in the dinosaurs' reign. These plants also produced an array of aromatic, amino-acid-based alkaloids — the major group of psychoactive agents. Most mammals are "smart" enough to avoid these potential poisons. The alkaloids simply don't taste good (they are bitter); in any case, we mammals have livers happily supplied with the capacity to detoxify them. But, Siegel speculates, perhaps dinosaurs could neither taste the bitterness nor detoxify the substances once ingested. He recently told members of the American Psychological Association: "I'm not suggesting that all dinosaurs OD'd on plant drugs, but it certainly was a factor." He also argued that death by overdose may help explain why so many dinosaur fossils are found in contorted positions. (Do not go gentle into that good night.)

Extraterrestrial catastrophes have long pedigrees in the popular litera- 16 ture of extinction, but the subject exploded again in 1979, after a long lull, when the father-son, physicist-geologist team of Luis and Walter Alvarez proposed that an asteroid, some 10 km in diameter, struck the earth 65 million years ago (comets, rather than asteroids, have since gained favor. Good science is self-corrective).

The force of such a collision would be immense, greater by far than the megatonnage of all the world's nuclear weapons. In trying to reconstruct a scenario that would explain the simultaneous dying of dinosaurs on land and so many creatures in the sea, the Alvarezes proposed that a gigantic dust cloud, generated by particles blown aloft in the impact, would so darken the earth that photosynthesis would cease and temperatures drop precipitously. (Rage, rage against the dying of the light.) The single-celled photosynthetic oceanic plankton, with life cycles measured in weeks, would perish outright, but land plants might survive through the dormancy of their seeds (land plants were not much affected by the Cretaceous extinction, and any adequate theory must account for the curious pattern of differential survival). Dinosaurs would die by starvation and freezing; small, warm-blooded mammals, with more modest requirements for food and better regulation of body temperature, would squeak through. "Let the bastards freeze in the dark," as bumper stickers of our chauvinistic neighbors in sunbelt states proclaimed several years ago during the Northeast's winter oil crisis.

All three theories, testicular malfunction, psychoactive overdosing, and asteroidal zapping, grab our attention mightily. As pure phenomenology, they rank about equally high on any hit parade of primal fascination. Yet one represents expansive science, the others restrictive and untestable speculation. The proper criterion lies in evidence and methodology; we must probe behind the superficial fascination of particular claims.

How could we possibly decide whether the hypothesis of testicular frying is right or wrong? We would have to know things that the fossil record cannot provide. What temperatures were optimal for dinosaurs? Could they avoid the absorption of excess heat by staying in the shade, or in caves? At what temperatures did their testicles cease to function? Were late Cretaceous climates ever warm enough to drive the internal temperatures of dinosaurs close to this ceiling? Testicles simply don't fossilize, and how could we infer their temperature tolerances even if they did? In short, Cowles's hypothesis is only an intriguing speculation leading nowhere. The most damning statement against it appeared right in the conclusion of Colbert, Cowles, and Bogert's paper, when they admitted: "It is difficult to advance any definite arguments against this hypothesis." My statement may seem paradoxical — isn't a hypothesis really good if you can't devise any arguments against it? Quite the contrary. It is simply untestable and unusable.

Siegel's overdosing has even less going for it. At least Cowles extrapo- 20 lated his conclusion from some good data on alligators. And he didn't completely violate the primary guideline of siting dinosaur extinction in the context of a general mass dying — for rise in temperature could be the root cause of a general catastrophe, zapping dinosaurs by testicular malfunction and different groups for other reasons. But Siegel's speculation cannot touch the extinction of ammonites or oceanic plankton (diatoms make their own food with good sweet sunlight; they don't OD on the chemicals of terrestrial plants). It is simply a gratuitous, attention-grabbing guess. It cannot be tested, for how can we know what dinosaurs tasted and what their livers could do? Livers don't fossilize any better than testicles.

The hypothesis doesn't even make any sense in its own context. Angiosperms were in full flower ten million years before dinosaurs went the way of all flesh. Why did it take so long? As for the pains of a chemical death recorded in contortions of fossils, I regret to say (or rather I'm pleased to note for the dinosaurs' sake) that Siegel's knowledge of geology must be a bit deficient: muscles contract after death and geological strata rise and fall with motions of the earth's crust after burial — more than enough reason to distort a fossil's pristine appearance.

The impact story, on the other hand, has a sound basis in evidence. It can be tested, extended, refined, and, if wrong, disproved. The Alvarezes did not just construct an arresting guess for public consumption. They proposed their hypothesis after laborious geochemical studies with Frank Asaro and Helen Michael had revealed a massive increase of iridium in rocks deposited right at the time of extinction. Iridium, a rare metal of the platinum group, is virtually absent from indigenous rocks of the earth's crust; most of our iridium arrives on extraterrestrial objects that strike the earth.

The Alvarez hypothesis bore immediate fruit. Based originally on evidence from two European localities, it led geochemists throughout the world to examine other sediments of the same age. They found abnormally high amounts of iridium everywhere — from continental rocks of the western United States to deep sea cores from the South Atlantic.

Cowles proposed his testicular hypothesis in the mid-1940s. Where has it gone since then? Absolutely nowhere, because scientists can do nothing with it. The hypothesis must stand as a curious appendage to a solid study of alligators. Siegel's overdose scenario will also win a few press notices and fade into oblivion. The Alvarezes' asteroid falls into a different category altogether, and much of the popular commentary has missed this essential distinction by focusing on the impact and its attendant results, and forgetting what really matters to a scientist — the iridium. If you talk just about asteroids, dust, and darkness, you tell stories no better and no more entertaining than fried testicles or terminal trips. It is the iridium — the source of testable evidence — that counts and forges the crucial distinction between speculation and science.

The proof, to twist a phrase, lies in the doing. Cowles's hypothesis has generated nothing in thirty-five years. Since its proposal in 1979, the Alvarez hypothesis has spawned hundreds of studies, a major conference, and attendant publications. Geologists are fired up. They are looking for iridium at all other extinction boundaries. Every week exposes a new wrinkle in the scientific press. Further evidence that the Cretaceous iridium represents extraterrestrial impact and not indigenous volcanism continues to accumulate. As I revise this essay in November 1984 (this paragraph will be out of date when the book is published), new data include chemical "signatures" of other isotopes indicating unearthly provenance, glass spherules of a size and sort produced by impact and not by volcanic eruptions, and high-pressure varieties of silica formed (so far as we know) only under the tremendous shock of impact.

My point is simply this: Whatever the eventual outcome (I suspect it will be positive), the Alvarez hypothesis is exciting, fruitful science because it generates tests, provides us with things to do, and expands outward. We are having fun, battling back and forth, moving toward a resolution, and extending the hypothesis beyond its original scope.

As just one example of the unexpected, distant cross-fertilization that good science engenders, the Alvarez hypothesis made a major contribution to a theme that has riveted public attention in the past few months — so-called nuclear winter. In a speech delivered in April 1982, Luis Alvarez calculated the energy that a ten-kilometer asteroid would release on impact. He compared such an explosion with a full nuclear exchange and implied that all-out atomic war might unleash similar consequences.

This theme of impact leading to massive dust clouds and falling tem- 28
peratures formed an important input to the decision of Carl Sagan and a group of colleagues to model the climatic conseqences of nuclear holocaust. Full nuclear exchange would probably generate the same kind of dust cloud and darkening that may have wiped out the dinosaurs. Temperatures would drop precipitously and agriculture might become impossible. Avoidance of nuclear war is fundamentally an ethical and political imperative, but we must know the factual consequences to make firm judgments. I am heartened by a final link across disciplines and deep concerns — another criterion, by the way, of science at its best:[1] A recognition of the very phenomenon that made our evolution possible by exterminating the previously dominant dinosaurs and clearing a way for the evolution of large mammals, including us, might actually help to save us from joining those magnificent beasts in contorted poses among the strata of the earth.

AFTERWORD

Dinosaurs endure in the imagination. When Gould elsewhere deplores the boom in dinosaurs, he sounds like a romantic: "The problem now is there's no sense of wonder about dinosaurs. There's no mystery . . . they're on every street corner — I mean — dinosaurs are just a phase you go through, like firemen and policemen."

Happily Gould remains in his dinosaur phase. Much newspaper talk about dinosaurs concerns theories of their extinction, and Gould's theory here is one of many. I do not choose it because it proves its point, establishing at last the wording of the dinosaur's death certificate. I choose it for its spritely clear argument and its prose. Gould writes like a writer and thinks like a scientist.

Gould writes to present scientific thought: "My greatest unhappiness with most popular presentations of science concerns their failure to separate fascinating claims from the methods that scientists use to establish the facts of nature. . . . If the growing corps of popular science writers would focus on how *scientists develop and defend those fascinating claims, they would make their greatest possible contribution to public understanding."*

---

[1]This quirky connection so tickles my fancy that I break my own strict rule about eliminating redundancies from [this essay]. . . . — Gould's note.

BOOKS AVAILABLE IN PAPERBACK

Ever Since Darwin: Reflections in Natural History. New York: Norton. *Essays.*

The Flamingo's Smile: Reflections in Natural History. New York: Norton. *Essays.*

Hen's Teeth and Horse's Toes: Further Reflections in Natural History. New York: Norton. *Essays.*

The Mismeasure of Man. New York: Norton. *Nonfiction.*

Ontogeny and Phylogeny. Cambridge: Harvard University Press. *Nonfiction.*

The Panda's Thumb: More Reflections in Natural History. New York: Norton. *Essays.*

FRANCINE
DuPLESSIX GRAY

F RANCINE Du PLESSIX GRAY (b. 1930) came to the United States from
France when she was eleven. Her late introduction to English inspired her.
*"The challenge of a new language in one's adolescence! Think of Conrad — he was
eighteen or nineteen when he learned English. Learning a language beyond the
nursery years turns you into both a soldier and a lover."*

   *Novelist, journalist, essayist, Gray attended Bryn Mawr College for two years,
then Black Mountain College in North Carolina in the early fifties — a great
experimental school which included, among students and faculty, Robert Mother-
well, Charles Olson, Josef Albers, Merce Cunningham, Robert Rauschenberg, and
Robert Creeley. Her novels are* Lovers and Tyrants *(1976),* World Without End
(1981), and October Blood *(1985). She reported for UPI for a few years, worked
for* Art in America, *and has written articles for the* New Yorker, *the* New York
Review of Books, Vogue, Saturday Review, *and the* New Republic. Adam
and Eve in the City *(1987) collects her essays, including this one.*

   *Gray is the rare writer who delights in acknowledging the help of her editors,
especially when she writes journalism. "I love authority," she said in an interview
with* Contemporary Authors. *"I love to work with editors. . . . I love suggestions;*

I love being corrected and improved. I'll remain a perennial student until the day I die." It is possible that all *writers, on their most honest days, would admit to being perpetual students.*

Gray is married to a painter, has two children, and lives in Connecticut.

On Friendship

I saw Madame Bovary at Bloomingdale's the other morning, or rather, I saw many incarnations of her. She was hovering over the cosmetic counters, clutching the current issue of *Cosmopolitan*, whose cover line read "New Styles of Coupling, Including Marriage." Her face already ablaze with numerous products advertised to make her irresistible to the opposite sex, she looked anguished, grasping, overwrought, and terribly lonely. And I thought to myself: Poor girl! With all the reams of literature that have analyzed her plight (victimized by double standards, by a materialistic middle-class glutting on the excesses of romantic fiction), notwithstanding all these diagnoses, one fact central to her tragic fate has never been stressed enough: Emma Bovary had a faithful and boring husband and a couple of boring lovers — not so intolerable a condition — but she did not have a friend in the world. And when I think of the great solitude which the original Emma and her contemporaries exude, one phrase jumps to my mind. It comes from an essay by Francis Bacon, and it is one of the finest statements ever penned about the human need for friendship: "Those who have no friends to open themselves unto are cannibals of their own hearts."

In the past years the theme of friendship has been increasingly prominent in our conversations, in our books and films, even in our college courses. It is evident that many of us are yearning with new fervor for this form of bonding. And our yearning may well be triggered by the same disillusionment with the reign of Eros that destroyed Emma Bovary. Emma was eating her heart out over a fantasy totally singular to the Western world, and only a century old at that: the notion that sexual union between men and women who believe that they are passionately in love, a union achieved by free choice and legalized by marriage, tends to offer a life of perpetual bliss and is the most desirable human bond available on earth. It is a notion bred in the same frenzied climate of the romantic epoch that caused countless young Europeans to act like the characters of their contemporary literature. Goethe's *Werther* is said to have triggered hundreds of suicides. Numerous wives glutted on the fantasies of George Sand's heroines demanded separations because their husbands were unpoetic. And Emma Bovary, palpitating from that romantic fiction which precurses our current sex manuals in its outlandish hopes for the satiation of desire, muses in the third week of her marriage: Where is "the felicity, the passion, the intoxication" that had so enchanted her in the novels of Sir Walter Scott?

This frenzied myth of love which has also led to the downfall of Cleopatra, Juliet, Romeo, and King Kong continues to breed, in our time, more garbled thinking, wretched verse, and nonsensical jingles than any emotion under the sun: "All You Need Is Love," or as we heard it in our high-school days, "Tell me you'll love me forever, if only tonight." As Flaubert put it, we are all victims of romanticism. And if we still take for granted its cult of heterosexual passion, it is in part because we have been victimized, as Emma was, by the propaganda machine of the Western novel. It was the power and the genius of the novel form to fuse medieval notions of courtly love with the idealization of marriage that marked the rise of the eighteenth-century middle class. (By "romantic love," I mean an infatuation that involves two major ingredients: a sense of being "enchanted" by another person through a complex process of illusion, and a willingness to totally surrender to that person.)

One hardly needs a course in anthropology to realize that this alliance 4 of marriage and romantic love is restricted to a small segment of the Western world, and would seem sheer folly in most areas of this planet. The great majority of humans — be it in China, Japan, Africa, India, the Moslem nations — still engage in marriages prearranged by their elders or dictated by pragmatic reasons of money, land, tribal politics, or (as in the Socialist countries) housing shortages. Romantically motivated marriage as the central ingredient of the good life is almost as novel in our own West. In popular practice, it remained restricted to a narrow segment of the middle class until the twentieth century. And on the level of philosophical reflection, it was always friendship between members of the same sex, never any bonding of sexual affection, which from Greek times to the Enlightenment was held to be the cornerstone of human happiness. Yet this central role allotted to friendship for two thousand years has been progressively eroded by such factors as the nineteenth-century exaltation of instinct; science's monopoly on our theories of human sentiment; the massive eroticizing of society; and that twentieth-century celebration of the body that reaches its peak in the hedonistic solitude of the multiple orgasm.

To Aristotle, friendship can be formed only by persons of virtue: a man's capacity for friendship is the most accurate measure of his virtue; it is the foundation of the state, for great legislators care even more for friendship than they care for justice. To Plato, as we know, passionate affection untainted by physical relations is the highest form of human bonding. To Cicero, *Amicitia* is more important than either money, power, honors, or health because each of these gifts can bring us only one form of pleasure, whereas the pleasures of friendship are marvelously manifold; and friendship being based on equity, the tyrant is the man least capable of forming that bond because of his need to wield power over others. Montaigne's essay, along with Bacon's, is the most famous of many that glorify our theme in the Renaissance. And like the ancients, he stresses the advantages of friendship over any kind of romantic and physical attachment. Love for members of the opposite sex, in Montaigne's words, is "an impetuous and fickle flame, undulating and variable, a fever flame subject to fits and lulls." Whereas the fire of friendship produces "a general and universal warmth, moderate and even," and will always forge bonds superior to those of marriage because marriage's continuance is "constrained and forced, depending on factors other than our free will."

A century later, even La Rouchefoucauld, that great cynic who described the imperialism of the ego better than any other precursor of Freud, finds that friendship is the only human bond in which the tyrannical cycle of our self-love seems broken, in which "we can love each other even more than love ourselves." One of the last classic essays on friendship I can think of before it loses major importance as a philosophical theme is by Ralph Waldo Emerson. And it's interesting to note that by mid-nineteenth century, the euphoric absolutes which had previously described this form of bonding are sobered by many cautious qualifications. A tinge of modern pragmatism sets in. Emerson tends to distrust any personal friendship unless it functions for the purpose of some greater universal fraternity.

Yet however differently these thinkers focused on our theme, they all seemed to reach a consensus on the qualities of free will, equity, trust, and selflessness unique to the affection of friendship. They cannot resist comparing it to physical passion, which yearns for power over the other, seeks possession and the state of being possessed, seeks to devour, breeds on excess, can easily become demonic, is closely allied to the death wish, and is often a form of agitated narcissism quite unknown to the tranquil, balanced rule of friendship. And rereading the sagas of Tristan and Iseult, Madame Bovary, and many other romantic lovers, it is evident that their passions tend to breed as much on a masturbatory excitement as on a longing for the beloved. They are in love with love, their delirium is involved with a desire for self-magnification through suffering, as evidenced in Tristan's words, "Eyes with joy are blinded. I myself am the world." There is confrontation, turmoil, aggression, in the often militaristic language of romantic love: Archers shoot fatal arrows or unerring shafts; the male enemy presses, pursues, and conquers; women surrender after being besieged by amorous assaults. Friendship on the other hand is the most pacifist species in the fauna of human emotions, the most steadfast and sharing. No wonder then that the finest pacifist ideology in the West was devised by a religious group — the Quakers — which takes as its official name the Religious Society of Friends; the same temperate principle of fraternal bonding informs that vow demanded by the Benedictine Order — the Oath of Stability — which remains central to the monastic tradition to this day. No wonder, also, that the kind of passionate friendship shared by David and Jonathan has inspired very few masterpieces of literature, which seem to thrive on tension and illicitness. For until they were relegated to dissecting rooms of the social sciences, our literary views of friendship tended to be expressed in the essay form, a cool, reflective mode that never provided friendship with the motive, democratic, propagandistic force found by Eros in novel, verse, and stage. To this day, friendship totally resists commercial exploitation, unlike the vast businesses fueled by romantic love that support the couture, perfume, cosmetic, lingerie, and pulp-fiction trades.

One should note, however, that most views of friendship expressed in the past twenty centuries of Western thought have dealt primarily with the male's capacity for affection. And they tend to be extremely dubious about the possibility of women ever being able to enjoy genuine friendship with members of their own sex, not to speak of making friends with male peers. Montaigne expressed a prejudice that lasts well into our day when he wrote, "The ordinary capacity of women is inadequate for that communion and fellowship which is the nurse of that sacred bond, nor does their soul feel firm enough to endure the strain of so tight and durable a knot." It is shocking, though not surprising, to hear prominent social scientists paraphrase that opinion in our own decades. Konrad Lorenz and Lionel Tiger, for instance, seem to agree that women are made eminently unsociable by their genetic programming; their bondings, in Lorenz's words, "must be considered weak imitations of the exclusively male associations." Given the current vogue for sociobiology, such assertions are often supported by carefully researched papers on the courtship patterns of Siberian wolves, the prevalence of eye contact among male baboons, and the vogue for gangbanging among chimpanzees.

Our everyday language reflects the same bias: "Fraternity" is a word that goes far beyond its collegiate context and embraces notions of honor, dignity, loyalty. "Sorority" is something we might have belonged to as members of the University of Oklahoma's bowling team in the early 1950s. So I think it is high time that the same feminist perspective that has begun to correct the biases of art history and psychoanalysis should be brought to bear on this area of anthropology. We have indeed been deprived of those official, dramatically visible rites offered to men in pub, poolroom, Elks, hunting ground, or football league. And having been brought up in

8

235

a very male world, I'm ashamed to say it took me a decade of feminist consciousness to realize that the few bonding associations left to twentieth century women — garden clubs, church suppers, sewing circles (often derided by men because they do not deal with power) — have been activities considerably more creative and life-enhancing than the competition of the poolroom, the machismo of beer drinking, or the bloodshed of hunting.

Among both sexes, the rites and gestures of friendship seemed to have been decimated in the Victorian era, which brought a fear of homosexuality unprecedented in the West. (They also tended to decrease as rites of heterosexual coupling became increasingly permissive.) Were Dr. Johnson and James Boswell° gay, those two men who constantly exhibited their affection for each other with kisses, tears, and passionate embraces? I suspect they were as rabidly straight as those tough old soldiers described by Tacitus begging for last kisses when their legion broke up. Since Freud, science has tended to dichotomize human affection along lines of deviance and normalcy, genitality and platonic love, instead of leaving it as a graduated spectrum of emotion in which love, friendship, sensuality, sexuality, can freely flow into each other as they did in the past. This may be another facet of modern culture that has cast coolness and self-consciousness on our gestures of friendship. The 1960s brought us some hope for change, both in its general emotional climate and in our scientists' tendency to relax their definitions of normalcy and deviance. For one of the most beautiful signs of that decade's renewed yearning for friendship and community, particularly evident among the groups who marched in civil-rights or antiwar demonstrations, was the sight of men clutching, kissing, embracing each other unabashedly as Dr. Johnson and James Boswell.

Which leads me to reflect on the reasons why I increasingly turn to friendship in my own life: In a world more and more polluted by the lying of politicians and the illusions of the media, I occasionally crave to hear and to tell the truth. To borrow a beautiful phrase from Friedrich Nietzsche, I look upon my friend as "the beautiful enemy" who alone is able to offer me total candor. I look for the kind of honest friend Emma Bovary needed: one who could have told her that her lover was a jerk.

Friendship is by its very nature freer of deceit than any other relationship 12 we can know because it is the bond least affected by striving for power, physical pleasure, or material profit, most liberated from any oath of duty or of constancy. With Eros the *body* stands naked, in friendship our *spirit* is denuded. Friendship, in this sense, is a human condition resembling

---

Dr. Johnson and James Boswell   Samuel Johnson (1709–1784), quintessential English man of letters, whose fast friendship with James Boswell (1740–1795) resulted in Boswell's *Life of Samuel Johnson*, which immortalized Johnson as a brilliant, witty conversationalist.

what may be humanity's most beautiful and necessary lie — the promise of an afterlife. It is an almost celestial sphere in which we most resemble that society of angels offered us by Christian theology, in which we can sing the truth of our inner thoughts in relative freedom and abundance. No wonder then that the last contemporary writers whose essays on friendship may remain classics are those religiously inclined, scholars relatively unaffected by positivism or behaviorism, or by the general scientificization of human sentiment. That marvelous Christian maverick, C. S. Lewis, tells us: "Friendship is unnecessary, like philosophy, like art, like the universe itself (since God did not *need* to create). It has no survival value; rather it is one of those things that give value to survival." And the Jewish thinker Simone Weil focuses on the classic theme of free consent when she writes: "Friendship is a miracle by which a person consents to view from a certain distance, and without coming any nearer, the very being who is necessary to him as food."

The quality of free consent and self-determination inherent in friendship may be crucial to the lives of twentieth-century women beginning their vocations. But in order to return friendship to an absolutely central place in our lives, we might have to wean ourselves in part from the often submissive premises of romantic passion. I suspect that we shall always need some measure of swooning and palpitating, of ecstasy and trembling, of possessing and being possessed. But, I also suspect that we've been bullied and propagandized into many of these manifestations by the powerful modern organism that I call the sexual-industrial complex and that had an antecedent in the novels that fueled Emma Bovary's deceitful fantasies. For one of the most treacherous aspects of the cult of romantic love has been its complex idealization and exploitation of female sexuality. There is now a new school of social scientists who are militantly questioning the notion that Western romantic love is the best foundation for human bonding, and their criticism seems much inspired by feminist perspectives. The Australian anthropologist Robert Brain, for instance, calls romantic love "a lunatic relic of medieval passions . . . the handmaiden of a moribund capitalistic culture and of an equally dead Puritan ethic."

What exactly would happen if we women remodeled our concepts of ideal human bonding on the ties of friendship and abandoned the premises of enchantment and possession? Such a restructuring of our ideals of happiness could be extremely subversive. It might imply a considerable de-eroticizing of society. It could bring about a minor revolution against the sexual-industrial complex that brings billions of dollars to thousands of men by brainwashing us into the roles of temptress and seductress, and estranges us from the plain and beautiful Quaker ideal of being a sister to the world. How topsy-turvy the world would be! Dalliance, promiscuity, all those more sensationalized aspects of the Women's Movement that were once seen as revolutionary might suddenly seem most bourgeois and old-fashioned activities. If chosen in conditions of rigorous self-determination, the following values, considered up to now as reactionary, could suddenly become the most radical ones at hand: Virginity. Celibacy. Monastic communities. And that most endangered species of all, fidelity in marriage, which has lately become so exotically rare that it might soon become very fashionable, and provide the cover story for yet another publication designed to alleviate the seldom-admitted solitude of swinging singles: "Mick Jagger Is into Fidelity."

AFTERWORD

The classic essay takes a single topic for its title — "On Generosity," "Courage," "Old Age" — and meditates around and about it: reminiscing, quoting, generalizing, supplying anecdote and detail, running off on tangents. Both Cicero and Montaigne wrote on friendship. At the end of her first paragraph, Gray quotes another great essayist — quotation is characteristic of the classic essay — and continues citing the great in chronological order: Plato, Cicero, Montaigne, Bacon, La Rouchefoucauld, Emerson. . . .

Quotation makes a music of authority, and for the literary reader a reencounter with old friends. But there are dangers. Notice that for Gray every author quoted contributes to the structure of thought; none seems only decorative, pasted onto a structure to prettify it or disguise it. Sometimes an inexperienced writer uses quotations to pad an essay or merely to cover a shaky structure. Reading quotations without structural function, the reader leaps to the conclusion that the Reference Room bulks too large in the essay. Bartlett, Oxford, Penguin, and Mencken have supported many a diffident essayist and editorial writer.

At the start it seems that this essay might have been called "Against Love" rather than "On Friendship." Often it's bad tactics to praise hotdogs by slandering hamburgers, but maybe the name of LOVE is loud enough in the land so that Gray is shrewd to introduce friendship by knocking love off its pedestal.

VICKI
HEARNE

VICKI HEARNE teaches writing at Yale University. Most of her teaching life, she has worked with other species: Does experience of animal training modify the creative writing workshop?

Hearne has trained dogs in obedience and for hunting and tracking; she has also trained their owners. She has trained show horses, wolves, and one goat. Born (1946) in Texas, she grew up mainly in California, where she graduated from the University of California at Riverside and attended Stanford University on a writing fellowship. She has published two collections of poetry, Nervous Horses *(1980) and* In the Absence of Horses *(1984), and a novel,* The White German Shepherd *(1988). For a while she wrote a newspaper column about animals for the* Los Angeles Times, *and she has written essays for many magazines, especially* Harper's, *where "Consider the Pit Bull" originally appeared in a slightly earlier form. As an undergraduate she followed an interest in philosophy; her essays brim with allusion to Nietszche, Wittgenstein, and the contemporary philosopher Stanley Cavell. She married a philosopher who teaches at Yale and lives with him and her animals in Connecticut.*

Her Adam's Task *(1986), subtitled* Calling Animals by Name, *is a philosophical, combative, and learned account of horses and dogs with attention to the psychology and values of animals. A brilliant human mind encounters the minds of animals and tries not only to teach the animals but to learn from them — to hear, as she understands it, "the stories they tell."*

Consider the Pit Bull

Your goodness must have some edge to it — else it is none.
　　　　　　　　　　　　　　　　　– RALPH WALDO EMERSON

A disproportionately large number of pit bulls are able to climb trees.
　　　　　　　　　　　　　　　　　– RICHARD STRATTON

A few years back, when I was living in California, I happened to be looking for a working dog, by which I mean a dog bred to think and to do a job, not just to look pretty while the cameras snap. So I put the word out among the dog people I know. Poodles, bouviers des Flandres, and the like were pretty low on my list, since I am not fond of grooming (though I should say that Airedales, which need a lot of grooming, are always high on my list). Doberman pinschers and boxers were pretty high on the list, as were English bull terriers. I was really just waiting for a dog with genuine class to show up. I would have looked at a cocker spaniel if someone reliable had told me of a good one.

I heard, eventually, of a litter of puppies in which there was a promising little bitch. They were pit bulls, or what are commonly called pit bulls, though pit bulls are often called by other names, and other breeds are often misidentified as pit bulls — all this a result of newspaper and television and word-of-mouth horror stories about pit bulls, which is what *this* story is about. Anyway, fighting breeds, of which the pit bull is one, were also high on my list, and the pups were within my price range. So I went to take a look. The bitch puppy looked as good in the flesh as she had been made to look in the story I had heard about her. I bought her and named her Belle, a name that may sound fancy to Yankee ears, but a good old down-home name for a nice bitch. In Belle's eyes there was (and is) a certain quiet gleam of mischief and joy; more than that, she had a general air that made it clear that I was going to be dealing with her on *her* terms — and that one of these might be an impulse to make a fool of me.

Belle is mostly white, with some reddish brindle here and there, including, over one eye, a patch that sometimes gives her a raffish air but at other times, when she has her dignity about her (which is about 99 percent of the time), makes her look like the queen of an exotic and powerful nation. Except for that gleam in her eye, she is fairly typical of her breed in that she is very serious about whatever she happens to be doing. I've had her going on three years now, and the most violent thing she has done is this: one day, when her pillows were in the wash, she went about the house appropriating everyone else's pillows. Not *all* of the pillows; only the newer, plumper, more expensive ones. She was quite young when she did this. Maturity has brought with it a sense of the importance of respecting the property rights of others.

In James Thurber's day there were a lot of horror stories around about   4
bloodhounds, and he was exercised enough by these stories to write at least two pieces (including "Lo, Hear the Gentle Bloodhound!") defending these creatures. Of course no one these days believes bloodhounds eat up old ladies and nubile maidens. This, or something like it, is what people have come to believe about pit bulls, largely because of horror stories like the ones repeated on ABC's *20/20* one night last winter: "February 1984, Cleveland, Ohio. Police capture a pit bull terrier who attacked a two-year-old child at a bus stop. December 1984, Davie, Florida. This dog attacked a seven-week-old boy in his crib. The child later died. January 1985, Phoenix, Arizona. A fifty-year-old woman was attacked by her son's dogs when she tried to get into her own house."

These stories have a deceptively straightforward look about them; here, at least, it seems that we know what we're talking about. But it isn't at all clear what the stories are about (or *who* they are about), and I am exercised about this, and want to talk about the stories and about pit bulls.

A word about names. The French philosopher Jacques Derrida once remarked in a lecture about memory and mourning that we never know — that we die without being quite sure — what our proper names are. This is not always obvious to us, except perhaps in the case of some newlyweds. We do not generally feel puzzled or at a loss for an answer when someone asks, "What's your name?" The uncertainty Derrida spoke of is obvious, though, when we turn to the pit bull. There are a number of breeds that are related to the pit bull and are often confused with it. Among these are:

American pit bull dogs	Jack Russell terriers
English bull terriers	Staffordshire bull terriers
French bulldogs	Colored bull terriers
English bulldogs	

Often, in the horror stories published and broadcast and passed along in conversation, other breeds wholly unrelated to the pit bull are accused of being pit bulls. These include:

Doberman pinschers	Rottweilers
Boxers	Collies
Airedales	

I actually read a story about a "pit bull" who turned out to be a collie. 8
The dog was supposed to have hurt a baby; he had not, though he did
snap at the infant. When I protested to the newspaper editor that the dog
was plainly a collie, the reply was: "But it could have been a pit bull."

The dog I left off the list of genuine relatives of the pit bull is the
American Staffordshire terrier, which some American Staffordshire fanciers
say is the same breed as the pit bull, as do some serious pit bull people;
other members of both groups argue that the breeds are separate. If you
own a pit bull, or something like a pit bull, and are tired (as I am) of people
clutching their purses and babies and shying away from you whenever
they see your dog, just tell them that what you have is an American
Staffordshire terrier. Almost no one, so far as I know, is afraid of American
Staffordshire terriers.

As for the names of the actual dog under discussion, the possibilities
include:

Pit bull	American (pit) bull terrier
Pit bull terrier	American pit bull terrier
Bull terrier	American bulldog
American bull terrier	Bulldog

As to the history of the pit bull, it seems clear that at some point an
Englishman bred a terrier with what is often referred to as an English
bulldog. Involved in this history are bear baiting and bull baiting — especially the latter, as bulls were often baited with dogs before being killed as
a way of tenderizing the meat for human consumption. Dog fighting, to
the death in the pit, also figures in this history. If you were to try to write
an actual history of the breed, you would have to find out which if any of
the following names is a past name for the pit bull or an ancestor of the pit
bull. Some of these are now the names of definite breeds; others are *probably*
names for the pit bull that have passed out of use. Among these names
are:

Irish pit terrier	Bandog
Catch dog	Hog dog
Bear biter	Southern hound
Boar hound	Neopolitan mastiff
Bull biter	Dogue de Bordeaux
Mastiff	Olde bulldogge
Bull mastiff	Argentine dogo
Molossian	Tosa-inu
Bear dog	Colored bull terrier

The United Kennel Club in Kalamazoo, Michigan, after much debating 12 and many divorces, officially named the breed the American (pit) bull terrier. Affectionate owners call the dog simply pit. What pit bulls actually are, by the way, are bulldogs, though that is not the real name of the breed. And those dogs that *are* called bulldogs (including Handsome Dan, the mascot of the Yale football team) are not in fact bulldogs at all. They couldn't get a bull to behave if heaven depended on it for supper. (Still, I should say that Yale, in welcoming my pit bull, has warmed my heart.)

It was in the early 1970s that the first of the horror stories about pit bulls appeared. I didn't see the original one — a product of the inflamed mind of a Chicago journalist, I am told — but as the story was passed along and picked up and reprinted, polished, and "improved" by every paper in the country, as far as I could tell (I was doing some traveling then), I got to read it often. In its various versions, the tale tended to tell of what natural people-haters pit bulls are — preferring the flesh of elderly women and infants — and of what dog-haters "pit men" are, pit men being those who breed and handle dogs for organized pit fighting. (Staged dogfights are illegal in all fifty states, and moving dogs across state lines for the purpose of fighting is a federal offense. Fights are organized clandestinely throughout the country.)

At first, I was mildly amused and not especially worried by these stories; I have trained dogs professionally, I know many dog people, and at the time my life was in this world, in which there are no horror stories about pit bulls. Indeed, in this world, pit bulls are generally recognized as an amiable, easygoing lot. If pit bulls have a flaw in their relationship to people it is that they sometimes show a tendency toward reserve, a kind of aloofness that is a consequence of their being prone to love above all else reflection and meditation. Pit bulls — not all of them, but some — often hang back in social situations they don't understand.

Pit men, who breed and train their dogs to kill others for sport — the fighting-dog men who know what they are about, anyway — will tell you that a pit bull fighter is not a man-hating animal; in fact, a man-hating animal is not likely to survive in the pit, is apt to be a coward, a fear-biter rather than a tough, gamely fighter. In truth, there are very few biters among pit bulls.

You have to know this about fighting dogs, or hunting dogs who take 16 on opponents like mountain lions — any dog in whom the quality called gameness matters: in a true fighting dog there is no ill temper, no petty resentment. I once had an Airedale who was a visionary fighter, a veritable incarnation of the holy Law of the Jaw. (Never let go.) You could tell that Gunner was going into his fight mode by a certain precise and friendly wagging of the tail, a happy pricking of the ears, and a cheerful sparkle in the eye that quickly progressed to an expression of high trance. He was, when he wasn't fighting or thinking about fighting (he didn't think about it all of the time, only when it was appropriate), a dog of enormous charm and wit who never minded playing the fool.

One of the things he liked to do was to climb up the ladders of playground slides and then slide down, with a goofy, droll look in his eyes and his ears flying out. (He looked like a child playing at being an airplane.) His charm was often an annoyance: he always insisted on making an entrance and looking around happily for the cheering section. The only time I knew him to menace a human being happened when he was about a year old. It was late at night, and a man attacked me with a knife, a rather puny sort of knife. That man lost part of his nose and cheek and I don't know what else (it was dark).

Richard Stratton, in *The World of the American Pit Bull Terrier* and elsewhere, writes about the development of the horror stories and their consequences, one of which has been the impounding and in some cases the destruction of pit bulls and other dogs. In San Diego not long ago the good citizens saw to it that an entire line of dogs, on whose development the owner had spent decades, was killed. Later, a court ruled that the killing of the dogs had been illegal, but the corpses of the dogs appear not to have been impressed by this development. Stratton writes of how this peculiar form of "humania" has caught on around the country:

> In each case the approach was the same: the same stories as before were told, to which was added that certain states have very effective laws. Each state was assured that it was the center of dog fighting in America, and wasn't that a shameful "honor"? A news-media blitz characteristically preceded attempts at putting through legislation. In some states, penalties as high as ten years in prison were specified.

One of the standard elements in the horror stories is a gleeful account of how pit bull puppies are trained to be killers by starting them off on declawed kittens. The interesting thing here is that an authentic and intelligent admirer of good fighting dogs would find this an insult to the dogs and to the men who train them to fight — partly because most lovers of pit bulls are saps about animals of all sorts (often they hate hunting), and partly because they have a kind of Nietzschean sense of what counts as a worthy opponent (and kittens, declawed or otherwise, clearly are not). Someone like Richard Stratton would have deep contempt for anyone who would set a pit bull against a *dog* who was not a match. What Stratton and those like him say is roughly this: Look. We're talking about a dog who can stay the round with a porcupine. This dog doesn't need to practice on kittens. Which is to say, the charge of cruelty to kittens is secondary to a more serious charge: the insult to the nobility and courage of a breed.

It wasn't long after I got Belle, my pit bull, that she began to take an interest in the welfare and development of James, my year-old nephew. James would throw a plaything out of reach, and Belle would bring it back to him. James was entranced by this; soon he was spending most of his time throwing playthings out of reach. Belle, with a worried look about her, continued patiently to fetch them.

I must remind you of the seriousness of mind of this breed. It became clear after a short while that Belle was not just "playing fetch." Pit bulls are never just doing *anything*. Belle began bringing James her dumbbell, which I use in training her, and which is not a plaything in her mind; more than that, she began attempting to get him to handle it correctly. This was only natural: Belle's mother had been extremely devoted to the education of Belle and her litter-mates, and Belle takes her responsibilities seriously. She seems to feel that a necessary condition of fully developed humanhood is good dog-training skills; as I watched her trying to get James to hold the dumbbell properly, it dawned on me that she was trying to teach him to train *her*!

Belle's behavior with James is related to a standard pit bull trait — a trait, for that matter, standard to all gamely dogs. If purity of heart is to will one thing, as Kierkegaard said it was, then these dogs have purity of heart. A less generous way of putting it is to say that they have one-track minds. Bill Koehler, the father of my friend Dick Koehler and one of the grandest animal trainers the world will ever know, warns owners of such dogs not to play ball with them in the house except on the ground floor, because if the ball goes out the window, so does the dog.

I was talking to Dick Koehler one day about how nice it is to have Belle around, but how hard it is to explain *why*. Dick, a dog trainer like his father, said, "Yeah, it's hard to explain. They are so *aware*." And that's it, that's the quality Belle radiates quietly but unmistakably: awareness of all the shifting gestalts of the spiritual and emotional life around her. She spends a lot of her time just sitting and contemplating people and situations (which is one reason some people are afraid of her). Since in her case this awareness is coupled with a deep gentleness — no bull-in-the-china-shop routines once puppyhood was over — Dick has urged me not to have her spayed, for a while at least.

Dick thinks Belle might be a good "foundation dam" for a line of dogs bred to work with the handicapped. Which brings up another aspect of the horror stories: they tend to be told about just those breeds that are the best prospects for work with, say, the old, or those in wheelchairs. Some readers may remember the stories about German shepherds "turning on their masters" — dogs with whom the safety of the blind can be trusted! I think that the same qualities that make these breeds reliable companions for the more difficult-to-care-for members of our species inspire the horror stories. Belle's refusal to play with strangers who coo at her, which sometimes causes the strangers to fear her, is the quality that would make her reliable in a distracting situation if her quadriplegic master really needed her attentiveness.

Most dogs have an unusual amount of emotional courage in relationship to humans: they are willing and able to keep coming back; they have the heart to turn our emotional static back to us as clarity. But dogs who work with people with various disabilities, including the sort not always regarded as pathologies, such as an addiction to typewriters, need much more of this quality in order to do a proper job of being a dog. Someone who is, or who perceives himself to be, powerless will be querulous from time to time in his handling of a dog, and may occasionally be downright loony. The dog who can keep her cool and continue to do her job under such circumstances has to be more than just cuddly and agreeable, and certainly mustn't have any heart-tugging spookiness in her makeup; such a dog must be prepared to *think* and act in the absence of proper guidance from the master and (as in the case of guide dogs) even in the face of wrong guidance. For such a dog, love doesn't make a whole lot of sense outside the context of a discipline, a discipline in the older, fuller sense of that word, in which the context is the cosmos and not the classroom. What I am trying to say is, Real love has teeth. A dog with such a capacity to love is able to give the moral law to herself when her master (who, of course, runs the universe from the dog's point of view) fails to act on the law of being.

Pit bulls will often give themselves the moral law. One afternoon, while I was abstractedly working on something, I was startled into consciousness by Belle suddenly giving out, in place of the wimpy puppy-bark I had so far heard (she was about five months old at the time), a full-fledged, grown-up, I've-got-duties-around-here bark.

Investigation showed that the meter reader was going into the backyard by the side gate *without asking permission*. So I said, "What's up, Pup?" and put her on her leash and followed her outside to check the situation out. (This is part of the handling of a dog like Belle, a procedure designed to show respect for and encourage the dog's instinct to protect while making it clear that she must think and exercise judgment.) When we got outside I said, "Oh. That's just the meter reader, and you don't have to worry about him." Then, putting Belle on a "stand-for-examination" — an exercise in which the dog is not allowed to move toward or away from anyone or anything — I asked the meter reader to pet her.

He refused, saying that he was afraid of her. This worried me a bit, 28 since Belle was only a puppy, and while it wasn't too early in her career for her to be barking at strangers who enter the premises without asking permission, she was too young to be seriously menacing anyone. So I asked if she had ever tried to bite him, or whatever.

He said that Belle had never bothered him, but that he carried liver treats with him on his rounds in order to "make friends" with the dogs, and the only dog who had refused his liver treats had been Belle. No, ma'am, she didn't growl or anything, just turned her head away.

I refrained from telling him how rapidly anyone who offers a bribe to a pit bull sinks in the dog's estimation, really plummets; I simply suggested that in the future he knock on the front door when he came to read the meter and I would make sure the dog was in the house. After that Belle, understanding the situation, announced his arrival with two precise barks and otherwise seemed content to let him do his job — though she did keep an eye on him.

The meter reader incident filled me with dog-owner pride; but it also made me aware of the responsibility I had assumed in taking on a dog who needed no training to know a bribe when she saw one. I don't mean that I am afraid she is going to bite me, but that any unfairness or sloppiness in the way I handle her will be made known to me.

What Belle has is an ability to act with moral clarity, and this is a result of having qualities that have to do with real love, love with teeth. Do we tell horror stories about dogs because it is love that horrifies us?

Training Belle often seems astonishingly easy. This is not unusual with these dogs; I have friends with pit bulls who speak of having the sensation that they aren't so much training the dogs as reminding them of something. And yet there are people in other dog circles who wonder whether it is possible to train pit bulls (and dogs like them) at all. This is because these dogs are unresponsive to anything short of genuine training. Belle is as honest as daylight about her work, and because of that my training technique has had to improve a lot: she does not respond if I do something wrong. She is committed to her training, and she expects me to be; it is easy to mess these dogs up precisely because they know so much about how their training ought to go. Once I picked up Belle's leash and some other equipment, preparing to take her outside. But before I could get out the door, I got involved in a conversation — I got distracted. Belle barked three times, sharply, to remind me of my duties. It was a trivial conversation; she doesn't interrupt me when I'm giving my attention to something important.

When Belle was only a few months old I taught her that before she goes through any door to go outside, she must sit and wait for the release command. This was easy to do, as Belle takes to domestic order. Then I went out of town for a week, leaving Belle — with her new sit-and-wait discipline — in the care of a friend. My friend is a splendid woman, no two ways about it, but she never has seen the point of training the poor dogs (as she puts it), who would rather be left alone. When I got back I was told that Belle, no matter how full her bladder was, resisted going through the door. My friend would swing open the door and expect Belle to skip through — despite the fact that I had told her about Belle's command. My friend tried coaxing and cooing her through the door. Belle would lie down flat, ears and tail low and immobile — a melancholy imitation of the Rock of Gibraltar being her usual response to coaxing, flattery, and insults.

I didn't travel again until I felt Belle had a little more experience under her belt; maturity makes all of us less vulnerable to the various inconsistencies life brings. While she was still young, it was possible to break her heart — and a broken-hearted pit bull was not something I wanted to have around. My decision to stay home with Belle, by the way, was less a comment on my temperament than on hers — and on the way pit bulls inspire devotion. And this is why the ladies and gentlemen who want to exterminate pit bulls may win some battles but will never win the war.

Belle was still a puppy, and not a very big one — three months old, 36 maybe fifteen pounds — the first time I took her to the campus of the University of California at Riverside, where I was teaching. I went into the department office with Belle at heel, and one of the secretaries was so struck with terror that she couldn't speak. It was the horror stories, of course. A friend came in, assessed the situation, and asked the secretary, "What's wrong, Frieda?"

"Tha . . . tha . . . that . . . *dog!*"

"But it's only a puppy."

"That doesn't matter with these dogs. They're born killers."

Belle was by now looking at the secretary in uneasy puzzlement; just a 40 puppy, she didn't know anything about the horror stories. But now she had had her first lesson. I suspect that some pit bulls, once they come to grips with the horror stories, do start biting people who send out the wrong signals. Belle, as it happens, didn't start biting, and very few pit bulls do, but I wouldn't have blamed her if she had.

Anyway, for months, whenever Frieda's path and mine crossed on campus she would sidle along a wall, as far from Belle as she could get, or duck into the nearest doorway until we were safely past. Frieda would behave, in short, like a guilty woman; and dogs, like people, figure that behavior of this sort is suspicious. So Belle, because of the damned horror stories, is more wary than she would otherwise have been.

Then there are the horror stories about me: Belle is plainly the outward sign of my inner viciousness. Some of the expressions of this get back to me: "Oh yes. Vicki Hearne. She has a very repressive ideology. She keeps a pit bull, you know." Also: "Vicki is a threat to the collegiate atmosphere, with that dog of hers." This may be true, since I don't know what a collegiate atmosphere is. And of course there is: "She *delights* in harboring vicious animals."

In time, though, Belle herself began effecting changes in these stories. The serenity and sweetness she radiates is so strong that it can't help but be felt by all but the most distant of the tale-tellers. So recently what I have started hearing is, "Vicki, I don't know where you get off thinking that's a vicious dog. That dog wouldn't hurt a butterfly; a real patsy if I ever saw one!" Or: "Vicki likes to think she's tough, but I'll bet she can't bring herself to give a grade lower than B+, and just look at that mushy dog of hers!"

It is this, the way the horror stories can so easily flip over, that suggests 44 that we are on to something. "That dog wouldn't hurt a butterfly" and "born killer" are part of the same logical structure, the same story — an insight I owe largely to Stanley Cavell's *The Claim of Reason*, in which he writes:

> The role of Outsider might be played, say in a horror movie, by a dog, mankind's best friend. Then the dog allegorizes the escape from human nature (required in order to know of the existence of others) in such a way that we see the requirement is not necessarily for greater (super-human) intelligence. The dog sniffs something, a difference, something in the air. And it is important that we do not regard the dog as honest; merely as without decision in the matter. He is obeying his nature, as he always does, must.

It is important to tellers of dog horror stories that "we do not regard the dog as honest; merely as without decision in the matter." The dog has no moral dimension: *that* is the hidden and stinging part of the logic of these stories.

Consider the falseness of "wouldn't hurt a butterfly." As it happens, Belle would nail anyone who threatened me seriously, and right now. Notice that I said *seriously* — she wouldn't do anything to a guy who just grabbed my arm and wanted to talk. What I have been saying about this dog is that she has extraordinarily good judgment, which means that I do "regard the dog as honest," and not as "without decision in the matter." So, she is not obeying her nature in the way, say, that a falling stone is obeying its nature. She is not morally inert.

I would like to talk briefly about a painting titled *I'm Neutral, But Not Afraid of Any of Them*, dated 1914 and signed by Wallace Robinson. It depicts the heads of five dogs. From left to right are: English bulldog, German dachshund, American pit bull terrier, French bulldog, Russian wolfhound. Each dog is wearing the uniform of his country, and the pit bull, which not only is in the center but is also larger than the others, has an American flag tied sportively around his neck. It is the pit bull who is saying, "I'm neutral, but not afraid of any of them." This is plainly part of a story America was telling itself about the war in Europe. It was a story *about* Americans. In a tight spot, it was not such a bad story to be telling. The pit bull here, as in many other places (Thurber's tales and drawings, or Pete the Pup of *Our Gang*), is an emblem of what it used to be possible to think of as American virtues: independence, ingenuity, cooperation, a certain rakish humor, the refusal of the aristocratic pseudo-virtues of Europe.

These values and visions have failed; the new stories about pit bulls are also stories about Americans, about an America that seems to have gone out of its mind — about how skittish, and dangerously so, we have become. And it is not only in the "text" of the pit bull that this can be read. I am addicted to dog stories of all sorts — the most awful, sentimental children's tale will do. These stories have changed as radically as the stories about pit bulls. Most of the older dog stories were not written with Thurber's canny intelligence and humor, but in them there were generally children, and a dog, and the children learned from the dog's courage, loyalty, or wit how to clarify their own stances in the world. In the new sort of story, the initial situation is the same — the dog remains for the child the only point of emotional clarity in a shifting world. But today there is the possibility that halfway through the book the dog will be poisoned.

Dick Koehler and his father and hosts of other trainers, including the 48 monks of New Skete, a Franciscan order (see their book, *How to Be Your Dog's Best Friend*), speak contemptuously of the "humaniacs" who babble about "affection training" and the dog "who only needs understanding." These trainers' contempt for kindness is a Nietzschean maneuver; it is not kindness itself that is being refused, but rather the *word* "kind," because the word has become contaminated.

But "kind" is a good word, and I find myself wanting it back. I don't have room here to do a full job of reclaiming it, but I can at least recall that the word has a history. C. S. Lewis has more than once discussed the history of "kind"; this is from *The Discarded Image*:

> In medieval science the fundamental concept was that of certain sympathies, antipathies, and strivings inherent in matter itself. Everything has its right place, its home, the region that suits it, and, if not forcibly restrained, moves thither by a sort of homing instinct:
>
> > Every kindly thing that is
> > Hath a kindly stede there he

> May best in hit conserved be
> Unto which place everything
> Through his kindly enclyning
> Moveth for to come to.
>> (CHAUCER, *Hous of Fame*, II, 730 sq.)

Thus, while every falling body for us illustrates the "law" of gravitation, for them it illustrated the "kindly enclyning" of terrestrial bodies to their "kindly stede" the Earth, the center of the Mundus. . . .

What I would like to say is this: to be kind to a creature may mean being what we call harsh (though not cruel), but it always means respecting the *kind* of being the creature is, and the deepest kindness is the natural kind, in which your being is matched to the creature's, perhaps by a kindly inclining.

Understanding kindness in this way leads to an understanding that it is about as cruel to match pit bulls against each other in properly regulated matches as it is to take healthy greyhounds out for runs. In making that remark I do not imagine that I have settled the issue, only gestured at what a complicated matter it would be to raise it properly. And I don't intend to fight Belle, even though I understand that a breeding program managed by knowledgeable people who breed their fighters only from dogs showing gameness and stamina in properly managed pit fights can be as fine a thing as human beings are capable of.

Perhaps it is time for me to say emphatically that my praise of pit bulls should not be construed as advice that anyone should rush out and get one. They do like to fight other dogs, and they are, as you must realize by now, a tremendous spiritual responsibility. For example, once it turned out that I hadn't worked with Belle on retrieving for three days. I was lazing about, reading in bed, on the left side of the bed. Belle brought me her dumbbell and stared at me loudly. (Pit bulls can stare loudly without making a sound.) I said, "Oh, not now Belle. In a few minutes." She dumped the dumbbell on top of the book I was reading, put her paws upon the edge of the bed, and bit my hand, very precisely. She took the trouble to bite my *right* hand, even though my left one hung within easy reach. She bit, that is, the hand with which I throw the dumbbell when we are working. A gentle bite, I should say, but also just. An inherently excellent moment of exactitude: love with teeth.

Pit bulls give you the opportunity to know, should you want so terrible a knowledge, whether your relationships are coherent; whether your notion of love is a truncated, distorted, and free-floating bit of the debris of Romanticism or a discipline that can renew the resources of consciousness.

If you're ready for it, and can find a *real* dog trainer to help you figure out what you're doing, then go to. But be prepared. When these dogs are

251

in motion, they are awesome. Still, for most people, this awesomeness is not the most hazardous trait. There is something more subtle. If, for example, your boss comes over for dinner and coos at your dog or perhaps offers her an hors d'oeuvre, and the dog regards him impassively or turns away, the boss's feelings will be hurt, and your job may be in jeopardy. Moreover, if the boss later gets tipsy and tries to insult your dog, he will get the same treatment. And, be sure your spouse or lover is not the sort of person whose feelings will be so hurt. The dog, remember, has the power to compel your loyalty.

AFTERWORD

Hearne's eclectic and resourceful mind, alluding to philosophers and etymologies, pulls everything into her ken. If her account of her dog sounds too anthropomorphic to you, look at Adam's Task, *in which she includes a version of this essay; she anticipates such objections.* Adam's Task *is almost dialogue: Hearne takes constant, close account of opposing views.*

She makes much of the word kind *and its metamorphoses. Often we use the word as if it were as sugary as* sweet *or as characterless as* gentle; *to make her point she takes* kind *back to* species: *"to be kind to a creature may mean being what we call harsh (though not cruel), but it always means respecting the kind of being the creature is, and the deepest kindness is the natural kind, in which your being is matched to the creature's, perhaps by a kindly inclining."*

Hearne's diction mixes learning and informality, Kierkegaard with goofy. Her range is eccentric in essays and natural to speech. Her voice's identity lies not only in diction but in syntax. Often her sentences wander, a little loose, and can seem hard to follow. But the syntax, when it wanders or searches, mimics the mind's wandering search to discover. The apparently rough sentence turns out to be as careful as an apothegm because its ungainly movement imitates thought's hesitant and difficult approach to difficult solution.

BOOKS AVAILABLE IN PAPERBACK

Adam's Task: Calling Animals by Name. New York: Random House-Vintage. *Essays.*

In the Absence of Horses. Princeton: Princeton University Press. *Poetry.*

Nervous Horses. Austin: University of Texas Press. *Poetry.*

EDWARD
HOAGLAND

E *DWARD HOAGLAND (b. 1932) published his first novel two years after graduating from college. He spent a decade writing novels and short stories and more recently has concentrated on essays for* Harper's, *the* Atlantic, *and other magazines, editorials for the New York* Times, *and books of travel. His book-length journal of time spent in British Columbia is called* Notes from the Century Before *(1965).* African Calliope *(1979) is subtitled* A Journey to the Sudan, *and there are four essay collections —* The Courage of Turtles *(1971), from which we take the title essay,* Walking the Dead Diamond River *(1973),* Red Wolves and Black Bears *(1976), and* The Tugman's Passage *(1982) — as well as* The Edward Hoagland Reader *(1979), edited by Geoffrey Wolff. More recently, Hoagland published a novel,* Seven Rivers West *(1986), and a volume of his selected essays,* Heart's Desire *(1988).*

Hoagland worked with a traveling circus when he was young and later used the experience in a novel. Mostly he has worked as a writer. He returns to particular themes or topics: New York tugboats, tugboat captains, tugboat crews; animals; and life in the woods. He divides his time as well as his prose between Manhattan, where he lives with his family during the school year, and a small town in remote northern Vermont, where the Hoagland family spends its summers. Reading this author's essays, one flips back and forth between the wilderness of the north country and the wilderness of city streets.

Hoagland's work as an essayist is celebratory. He says somewhere that writers either "prefer subject matter that they rejoice in or subject matter they deplore and wish to savage with ironies. . . . I'm of the first type." He celebrates without heaping sugar on, and he is capable of irony, but joy is his major note — not merely joy in subject matter, writing happily about what makes you happy, but joy in the act of writing.

The Courage of Turtles

Turtles are a kind of bird with the governor turned low. With the same attitude of removal, they cock a glance at what is going on, as if they need only to fly away. Until recently they were also a case of virtue rewarded, at least in the town where I grew up, because, being humble creatures, there were plenty of them. Even when we still had a few bobcats in the woods the local snapping turtles, growing up to forty pounds, were the largest carnivores. You would see them through the amber water, as big as greeny wash basins at the bottom of the pond, until they faded into the inscrutable mud as if they hadn't existed at all.

When I was ten I went to Dr. Green's Pond, a two-acre pond across the road. When I was twelve I walked a mile or so to Taggart's Pond, which was lusher, had big water snakes and a waterfall; and shortly after that I was bicycling way up to the adventuresome vastness of Mud Pond, a lake-sized body of water in the reservoir system of a Connecticut city, possessed of cat-backed little islands and empty shacks and a forest of pines and hardwoods along the shore. Otters, foxes, and mink left their prints on the bank; there were pike and perch. As I got older, the estates and forgotten back lots in town were parceled out and sold for nice prices, yet, though the woods had shrunk, it seemed that fewer people walked in the woods. The new residents didn't know how to find them. Eventually, exploring, they did find them, and it required some ingenuity and doubling around on my part to go for eight miles without meeting someone. I was grown by now, I lived in New York, and that's what I wanted on the occasional weekends when I came out.

Since Mud Pond contained drinking water I had felt confident nothing untoward would happen there. For a long while the developers stayed away, until the drought of the mid-1960s. This event, squeezing the edges in, convinced the local water company that the pond really wasn't a necessity as a catch basin, however; so they bulldozed a hole in the earthen dam, bulldozed the banks to fill in the bottom, and landscaped the flow of water that remained to wind like an English brook and provide a domestic view for the houses which were planned. Most of the painted turtles of Mud Pond, who had been inaccessible as they sunned on their rocks, wound up in boxes in boys' closets within a matter of days. Their footsteps in the dry leaves gave them away as they wandered forlornly. The snappers and the little musk turtles, neither of whom leave the water except once a year to lay their eggs, dug into the drying mud for another siege of hot weather, which they were accustomed to doing whenever the pond got low. But this time it was low for good; the mud baked over them and slowly entombed them. As for the ducks, I couldn't stroll in the woods and not feel guilty, because they were crouched beside every stagnant pothole, or were slinking between the bushes with their heads tucked into their shoulders so that I wouldn't see them. If they decided I had, they beat their way up through the screen of trees, striking their wings dangerously, and wheeled about with that headlong, magnificent velocity to locate another poor puddle.

I used to catch possums and black snakes as well as turtles, and I kept dogs and goats. Some summers I worked in a menagerie with the big personalities of the animal kingdom, like elephants and rhinoceroses. I was twenty before these enthusiasms began to wane, and it was then that I picked turtles as the particular animal I wanted to keep in touch with. I was allergic to fur, for one thing, and turtles need minimal care and not much in the way of quarters. They're personable beasts. They see the same colors we do and they seem to see just as well, as one discovers in trying to sneak up on them. In the laboratory they unravel the twists of a maze with the hot-blooded rapidity of a mammal. Though they can't run as fast as a rat, they improve on their errors just as quickly, pausing at each crossroads to look left and right. And they rock rhythmically in place, as we often do, although they are hatched from eggs, not the womb. (A common explanation psychologists give for our pleasure in rocking quietly is that it recapitulates our mother's heartbeat *in utero*.)

Snakes, by contrast, are dryly silent and priapic. They are smooth movers, legalistic, unblinking, and they afford the humor which the humorless do. But they make challenging captives; sometimes they don't eat for months on a point of order — if the light isn't right, for instance. Alligators are sticklers too. They're like war-horses, or German shepherds, and with their bar-shaped, vertical pupils adding emphasis, they have the *idée fixe* of eating, eating, even when they choose to refuse all food and stubbornly die. They delight in tossing a salamander up toward the sky and grabbing him in their long mouths as he comes down. They're so eager that they get the jitters, and they're too much of a proposition for a casual aquarium like mine. Frogs are depressingly defenseless: that moist, extensive back, with the bones almost sticking through. Hold a frog and you're holding its skeleton. Frogs' tasty legs are the staff of life to many animals — herons, raccoons, ribbon snakes — though they themselves are hard to feed. It's not an enviable role to be the staff of life, and after frogs you descend down the evolutionary ladder a big step to fish.

Turtles cough, burp, whistle, grunt and hiss, and produce social judgments. They put their heads together amicably enough, but then one drives the other back with the suddenness of two dogs who have been conversing in tones too low for an onlooker to hear. They pee in fear when they're first caught, but exercise both pluck and optimism in trying to escape, walking for hundreds of yards within the confines of their pen, carrying the weight of that cumbersome box on legs which are cruelly positioned for walking. They don't feel that the contest is unfair; they keep plugging, rolling like sailorly souls — a bobbing, infirm gait, a brave, sea-legged momentum — stopping occasionally to study the lay of the land. For me, anyway, they manage to contain the rest of the animal world. They can stretch out their necks like a giraffe, or loom underwater like an apocryphal hippo. They browse on lettuce thrown on the water like a cow moose which is partly submerged. They have a penguin's alertness, combined with a build like a Brontosaurus when they rise up on tiptoe. Then they hunch and ponderously lunge like a grizzly going forward.

Baby turtles in a turtle bowl are a puzzle in geometrics. They're as decorative as pansy petals, but they are also self-directed building blocks, propping themselves on one another in different arrangements, before upending the tower. The timid individuals turn fearless, or vice versa. If one gets a bit arrogant he will push the others off the rock and afterwards climb down into the water and cling to the back of one of those he has bullied, tickling him with his hind feet until he bucks like a bronco. On the other hand, when this same milder-mannered fellow isn't exerting himself, he will stare right into the face of the sun for hours. What could be more lionlike? And he's at home in or out of the water and does lots of metaphysical tilting. He sinks and rises, with an infinity of levels to choose from; or, elongating himself, he climbs out on the land again to perambulate, sits boxed in his box, and finally slides back in the water, submerging into dreams.

I have five of these babies in a kidney-shaped bowl. The hatchling, who is a painted turtle, is not as large as the top joint of my thumb. He eats chicken gladly. Other foods he will attempt to eat but not with sufficient perseverance to succeed because he's so little. The yellow-bellied terrapin is probably a yearling, and he eats salad voraciously, but no meat, fish, or fowl. The Cumberland terrapin won't touch salad or chicken but eats fish and all of the meats except for bacon. The little snapper, with a black crenelated shell, feasts on any kind of meat, but rejects greens and fish. The fifth of the turtles is African. I acquired him only recently and don't know him well. A mottled brown, he unnerves the green turtles, dragging their food off to his lairs. He doesn't seem to want to be green — he bites the algae off his shell, hanging meanwhile at daring, steep, head-first angles.

The snapper was a Ferdinand until I provided him with deeper water. Now he snaps at my pencil with his downturned and fearsome mouth, his swollen face like a napalm victim's. The Cumberland has an elliptical red mark on the side of his green-and-yellow head. He is benign by nature and ought to be as elegant as his scientific name (*Pseudemys scripta elegans*), except he has contracted a disease of the air bladder which has permanently inflated it; he floats high in the water at an undignified slant and can't go under. There may have been internal bleeding, too, because his carapace is stained along its ridge. Unfortunately, like flowers, baby turtles often die. Their mouths fill up with a white fungus and their lungs with pneumonia. Their organs clog up from the rust in the water, or diet troubles, and, like a dying man's, their eyes and heads become too prominent. Toward the end, the edge of the shell becomes flabby as felt and folds around them like a shroud.

While they live they're like puppies. Although they're vivacious, they would be a bore to be with all the time, so I also have an adult wood turtle about six inches long. Her shell is the equal of any seashell for sculpturing, even a Cellini shell; it's like an old, dusty, richly engraved medallion dug out of a hillside. Her legs are salmon-orange bordered with black and protected by canted, heroic scales. Her plastron — the bottom shell — is splotched like a margay cat's coat, with black ocelli on a yellow background. It is convex to make room for the female organs inside, whereas a male's would be concave to help him fit tightly on top of her. Altogether, she exhibits every camouflage color on her limbs and shells. She has a turtleneck neck, a tail like an elephant's, wise old pachydermous hind legs, and the face of a turkey — except that when I carry her she gazes at the passing ground with a hawk's eyes and mouth. Her feet fit to the fingers of my hand, one to each one, and she rides looking down. She can walk on the floor in perfect silence, but usually she lets her shell knock portentously, like a footstep, so that she resembles some grand, concise, slow-moving id. But if an earthworm is presented, she jerks swiftly ahead, poises above it, and strikes like a mongoose, consuming it with wild vigor. Yet she will climb on my lap to eat bread or boiled eggs.

If put into a creek, she swims like a cutter, nosing forward to intercept a strange turtle and smell him. She drifts with the current to go downstream, maneuvering behind a rock when she wants to take stock, or sinking to the nether levels, while bubbles float up. Getting out, choosing her path, she will proceed a distance and dig into a pile of humus, thrusting herself to the coolest layer at the bottom. The hole closes over her until it's as small as a mouse's hole. She's not as aquatic as a musk turtle, not quite as terrestrial as the box turtles in the same woods, but because of her versatility she's marvelous, she's everywhere. And though she breathes the way we breathe, with scarcely perceptible movements of her chest, sometimes instead she pumps her throat ruminatively, like a pipe smoker sucking and puffing. She waits and blinks, pumping her throat, turning her head, then sets off like a loping tiger in slow motion, hurdling the jungly lumber, the pea vine and twigs. She estimates angles so well that when she rides over the rocks, sliding down a drop-off with her rugged front legs extended, she has the grace of a rodeo mare.

But she's well off to be with me rather than at Mud Pond. The other 12 turtles have fled — those that aren't baked into the bottom. Creeping up the brooks to sad, constricted marshes, burdened as they are with that box on their backs, they're walking into a setup where all their enemies move thirty times faster than they. It's like the nightmare most of us have whimpered through, where we are weighted down disastrously while trying to flee; fleeing our home ground, we try to run.

I've seen turtles in still worse straits. On Broadway, in New York there is a penny arcade which used to sell baby terrapins that were scrawled with bon mots in enamel paint, such as KISS ME BABY. The manager turned out to be a wholesaler as well, and once I asked him whether he had any larger turtles to sell. He took me upstairs to a loft room devoted to the turtle business. There were desks for the paper work and a series of racks that held shallow tin bins atop one another, each with several hundred babies crawling around in it. He was a smudgy-complexioned, serious fellow and he did have a few adult terrapins, but I was going to school and wasn't actually planning to buy; I'd only wanted to see them. They were aquatic turtles, but here they went without water, presumably for weeks, lurching about in those dry bins like handicapped citizens, living on gumption. An easel where the artist worked stood in the middle of the floor. She had a palette and a clip attachment for fastening the babies in place. She wore a smock and a beret, and was homely, short, and eccentric-looking, with funny black hair, like some of the ladies who show their paintings in Washington Square in May. She had a cold, she was smoking, and her hand wasn't very steady, although she worked quickly enough. The smile that she produced for me would have looked giddy if she had been happier, or drunk. Of course the turtles' doom was sealed when she painted them, because their bodies inside would continue to grow but their shells would not. Gradually, invisibly, they would be crushed. Around us their bellies

— two thousand belly shells — rubbed on the bins with a mournful, momentous hiss.

Somehow there were so many of them I didn't rescue one. Years later, however, I was walking on First Avenue when I noticed a basket of living turtles in front of a fish store. They were as dry as a heap of old bones in the sun; nevertheless, they were creeping over one another gimpily, doing their best to escape. I looked and was touched to discover that they appeared to be wood turtles, my favorites, so I bought one. In my apartment I looked closer and realized that in fact this was a diamond-back terrapin, which was bad news. Diamondbacks are tidewater turtles from brackish estuaries, and I had no sea water to keep him in. He spent his days thumping interminably against the baseboards, pushing for an opening through the wall. He drank thirstily but would not eat and had none of the hearty, accepting qualities of wood turtles. He was morose, paler in color, sleeker, and more Oriental in the carved ridges and rings that formed his shell. Though I felt sorry for him, finally I found his unrelenting presence exasperating. I carried him, struggling in a paper bag, across town to the Morton Street Pier on the Hudson. It was August but gray and windy. He was very surprised when I tossed him in; for the first time in our association, I think, he was afraid. He looked afraid as he bobbed about on top of the water, looking up at me from ten feet below. Though we were both accustomed to his resistance and rigidity, seeing him still pitiful, I recognized that I must have done the wrong thing. At least the river was salty, but it was also bottomless; the waves were too rough for him, and the tide was coming in, bumping him against the pilings underneath the pier. Too late, I realized that he wouldn't be able to swim to a peaceful inlet in New Jersey, even if he could figure out which way to swim. But since, short of diving in after him, there was nothing I could do, I walked away.

AFTERWORD

The New York Times *book critic, Christopher Lehmann-Haupt, reviewing essays by Edward Hoagland, noted: "The typical Hoagland essay announces its subject, broaches it, and at once collapses sideways into the author's delight and curiosity in things, catching us up so readily in its apparently free associations and random anecdotes that we quickly forget the starting point and hardly care to remember."*

"The Courage of Turtles" begins with one of the zaniest first sentences in literature: "Turtles are a kind of bird with the governor turned low." "Turtles are a kind of bird?" *"Wha — ?" Hoagland loves to break rules: You don't compare like with like; you don't compare turtles with birds, trucks with snowmobiles, but*

turtles with trucks. So Hoagland does it: ". . . with the governor turned low." The whole first paragraph is a marvel of quick motion, of surprises — and of joy in language. By the last sentence, turtles get themselves compared with "greeny wash basins."

Gretel Ehrlich writes about open places with a mad happy hurtle of description and information. With a narrower, not to say armored and shelled, subject, Hoagland's dense paragraphs accommodate a universe — from Vermont ponds to baby terrapins on Broadway. Watch his moves, which are as quick and skittery as a point guard's. "I've seen turtles in worse straits." (Note the pun.) "If put into a creek, she swims like a cutter. . . ." "The snapper was a Ferdinand. . . ." Then watch his exit — modulated, conclusive, final: "But since, short of diving in after him, there was nothing I could do, I walked away."

Time for grammar. This last complex sentence delays its main clause — its destination, its conclusion, its point — until the last three words. Beginning "But since," we know we are reading background or explanatory clauses, leading to a main clause, and so we lean forward in anticipation. Two brief phrases, including a subordinate clause — "since . . . there was nothing I could do" — fill out the background, allowing Hoagland to complete thought, sentence, and essay with a three-word main clause.

BOOKS AVAILABLE IN PAPERBACK

African Calliope: A Journey to the Sudan. New York: Penguin. *Nonfiction.*

Cat Man. New York: Arbor House. *Novel.*

The Circle Home. New York: Avon. *Novel.*

City Tales. Santa Barbara: Capra Press. *Short stories.*

The Courage of Turtles: Fifteen Essays by Edward Hoagland. San Francisco: North Point Press. *Essays.*

Notes From the Century Before: A Journal from British Columbia. San Francisco: North Point Press. *Nonfiction.*

Seven Rivers West. New York: Penguin. *Novel.*

The Tugman's Passage. New York: Penguin. *Essays.*

Walking the Dead Diamond River. San Francisco: North Point Press. *Essays.*

DIANE

JOHNSON

D IANE JOHNSON (b. 1934) took her B.A. at the University of Utah and her
Ph.D. at the University of California at Los Angeles. She now lives in
Berkeley, occasionally teaches at the University of California at Davis, and writes
novels, biographies, and essays. She is married to a pulmonologist and has four
children by an earlier marriage. In 1987 she was awarded a $250,000 Harold and
Mildred Strauss Living Award so that she can devote all her time to writing. The
latest of her six novels are Lying Low (1978) and Persian Nights (1987). She has
written a biography of mystery writer Dashiell Hammett. Her essays, mostly book
reviews enlarged by generality, appear in the New York Review of Books and
the New York Times Book Review. "Rape" comes from her essay collection
Terrorists and Novelists (1982), a title that expresses not only Diane Johnson's
range but also her desire to connect extremes of social reality and the printed page.

Johnson's prose, as in "Rape," creates reasonable discourse about subjects to
which reason is seldom applied. Sometimes we belittle the word intellectual, assuming that intellect is useful in evading or denying the emotional facts of life.
Sometimes we are right. But Johnson's intellect does its proper task, in a lucid

progress of good sentences that sort unpleasant matters into discernible units, subject to the clarification of mind. Biographer and novelist, as well as critic and essayist, she brings to her essays not only the orderly progress of ideas but story and image.

Rape

No other subject, it seems, is regarded so differently by men and women as rape. Women deeply dread and resent it to an extent that men apparently cannot recognize; it is perhaps the ultimate and essential complaint that women have to make against men. Of course men may recognize that it is wrong to use physical force against another person, and that rape laws are not prosecuted fairly, and so on, but at a certain point they are apt to say, "But what was she doing there at that hour anyway?" or "Luckily he didn't really hurt her," and serious discussion ceases.

Women sense — indeed, are carefully taught to feel — that the institution of rape is mysteriously protected by an armor of folklore, Bible tales, legal precedents, specious psychological theories. Most of all it seems protected by a rooted and implacable male belief that women want to be raped — which most women, conscientiously examining their motives, maintain they do not — or deserve to be raped, for violation of certain customs governing dress or behavior, a strange proposition to which women are more likely to accede.

While women can all imagine themselves as rape victims, most men know they are not rapists. So incidents that would be resented on personal grounds if happening to their "own" women do not have even the intrinsic interest for them of arguments on principle against military intervention in the political destiny of foreign nations, as in Vietnam, where the "rape" of that country was referred to in the peace movement and meant defoliation of crops. But unlike the interest in the political destiny of Vietnam, which greatly diminished when the danger to American males, via the draft, was eliminated, rape is an abiding concern to women.

Even if they don't think about it very much, most have incorporated 4 into their lives routine precautions along lines prescribed by the general culture. From a woman's earliest days she is attended by injunctions about strangers, and warnings about dark streets, locks, escorts, and provocative behavior. She internalizes the lessons contained therein, that to break certain rules is to invite or deserve rape. Her fears, if not entirely conscious, are at least readily accessible, and are continually activated by a vast body of exemplary literature, both traditional and in the daily paper. To test this, ask yourself, if you are a woman, or ask any woman what she knows about Richard Speck, the Boston Strangler, and "that thing that happened over on ——— Street last week," and you will find that she has considerable rape literature by heart.

It seems important, in attempting to assess the value or seriousness of Susan Brownmiller's polemic on rape (*Against Our Will*), to understand that there are really two audiences for it, one that will know much of what she has to say already, and another that is ill equipped by training or sympathy to understand it at all. This likely accounts for a certain unevenness of tone, veering from indignation to the composed deployment of statistics in the manner of a public debater. It is not surprising that women began in the past few years by addressing their complaints about rape to one another, not to men, and one infers that the subject is still thought to be of concern only to women. It remains to be seen what if any rhetorical strategies will prove to be of value in enlisting the concern of men.

That rape is aggressive, hostile, and intended to exact female submission, and that it is the extreme expression of underlying shared masculine attitudes, is, I think, most women's intuition of the subject, even women who have not been raped but who have tacitly accepted that this is how men are. Women who have in fact been raped (more than 255,000 each year) are certain of it after the indifference, disbelief, and brutality of police, doctors, judges, jurors, and their own families. That the actual rapists, making examples of a few women, in effect frighten and control all women seems obvious, even inarguable.

What is left to be explained, though neither Brownmiller nor Jean MacKellar, in another recent book on rape (*Rape: The Bait and the Trap*), can satisfactorily explain it, is what this primal drama of domination and punishment is about, exactly. Both books communicate an impression of an escalating conflict, with the increasing collective force of female anger and indignation about rape not only effecting some changes in judiciary and police procedures and even, perhaps, in popular attitudes, but also effecting an increase in anxiety about the subject, exemplified by the obligatory rape scenes in current movies and best sellers. Perhaps it is even female anger that is effecting an increase in rape itself, as if, whatever is at stake in this ancient hostility, it is now the rapist who has his back to the wall.

It is not too extreme to say that Brownmiller's book is exceedingly distressing, partly because it is exceedingly discouraging; it is a history of the failure of legal schemes and social sciences to improve society, at least society as viewed from a female perspective; it is the history of the failure of the social sciences even to address themselves to the peculiar mystery of male aggression toward those weaker than themselves. This failure seems in turn to demonstrate the powerlessness of human institutions before the force of patently untrue and sinister myths, whose ability to reflect, but also to determine, human behavior seems invincible. The disobedient Eve, the compliant Leda,° the lying wife of Potiphar° are still the keys to popular assumptions about women.

But Brownmiller's book is also distressing in another way that wicked myths and scary stories are distressing, that is, because they are meant to be. Here in one handy volume is every admonitory rape story you were ever told, horrifying in the way that propaganda is horrifying and also titillating just in the way that publishers hope a book will be titillating. Brownmiller is trapped in the fallacy of imitative form, and by the duplicitous powers of literature itself to contain within it its own contradictions, so that the exemplary anecdotes from Red Riding Hood to Kitty Genovese to the Tralala scene in *Last Exit to Brooklyn* must appeal at some level to the instincts they illustrate and deprecate. The book may be criticized for an emotional tone that is apparently impossible to exclude from an effective work on a subject so inaccessible to rational analysis. Because rape is an important topic of a potentially sensational and prurient nature, it is too bad that the book is not a model of surpassing tact and delicacy, unassailable learning and scientific methodology. Instead it is probably the book that was needed on this subject at this time, and may in fact succeed where reticence has failed to legitimate the fundamental grievance of women against men.

Much of the book is devoted to an attempt to locate in history the reasons for rape, but inquiry here is fruitless because though history turns up evidence, it offers little explanation. One learns merely that rape has been with us from earliest times, that it is associated variously with military policy, with ideas of property and possession (to rape someone's wife was interpreted as the theft of something from him), with interracial struggles and complicated tribal and class polarities of all kinds (masters and slaves, cowboys and Indians), with intrasexual power struggles, as in the rape of young or weak men in prison by gangs of stronger ones, and within families, by male relatives of young girls or children.

None of these patterns is, except in one respect, wholly consistent with the others, but viewed together they induce a kind of dispirited resignation to natural law, from which are derived the supposed constants of human nature, maybe including rape. The respect in which violations of conquered women in Bangladesh and of Indian (or white) women in pioneer America, or of men in prison, are alike is that they all dramatize

---

Leda Impregnated by Zeus, who came to her in the form of a swan.
Wife of Potiphar In Genesis, the wife of a wealthy Egyptian. She tries to seduce Joseph and, when she fails, accuses him of trying to seduce her.

some authority conflict. In war between groups of males, women are incidental victims and prizes, but in the back of the car the dispute arises between a man and a woman on her own behalf. The point at issue seems to be "maistrye," as the Wife of Bath° knew; and the deepest lessons of our culture have inculcated in both sexes the idea that he is going to prevail. This in turn ensures that he usually does, but the central question of why it is necessary to have male mastery remains unanswered, and perhaps unasked. Meantime, the lesson of history seems to elevate the right of the male to exact obedience and inflict punishment to the status of immutable law.

Anthropology seems to support this, too, despite Brownmiller's attempts to find a primitive tribe (the obligingly rape-free Arapesh) to prove otherwise. Rather inconsistently, she conjectures that the origin of monogamy lies in the female's primordial fear of rape and consequent willingness to attach herself to some male as his exclusive property. If this is so, it would be the only instance in which the female will has succeeded in dictating social arrangements. In any case, alternate and better hypotheses exist for the origin of the family, generally that it developed for the protection of the young. The insouciance of Brownmiller's generalizations invites cavil and risks discrediting her book, and with it her subject. Granting that a primitive tribe can be found to illustrate any social model whatever, one would like to know just what all the anthropological evidence about rape is. If rape is the primordial norm; if, as Lévi-Strauss° says, women were the first currency; if male humans in a state of nature run mad raping, unlike chimpanzees, who we are told do not, is rape in fact aberrant? Perhaps it is only abhorrent.

It seems evident that whatever the facts of our nature, it is our culture that leads women in some degree to collaborate in their own rape, an aspect of the matter that men seem determined to claim absolves *them* from responsibility. Perhaps this is implicit in the assumptions about male power they are heir to. But every woman also inherits assumptions about female submission. In even the simplest fairy tale, the vaguely sexual content of the punishment needs no elaboration: every woman darkly knows what really happened to Red Riding Hood in the woods — and to Grandmother, too, for that matter. Most women do not go into the woods alone, but the main point is that the form of the prohibition as it is expressed in most stories is not "Do not go into the woods lest you be raped," but "Obey me by not going into the woods or you *will* be raped."

Wife of Bath   A bawdy character in Chaucer's *Canterbury Tales*.
Lévi-Strauss   Claude Lévi-Strauss (b. 1908), French anthropologist.

Thus the idea of sexual punishment for disobedience is learned very early, and is accepted. Who has done this to you, Desdemona?° "Nobody; I myself, farewell," says Desdemona meekly as she dies. Everyone feels that Carmen,° that prick-tease, is "getting what she deserves," poor Lucrece's° suicide is felt to be both noble and tactful, maybe Anna Karenina's° too. So if a woman is raped, she feels, besides outrage, deep guilt and a need to find out what she has done "wrong" to account for it, even if her sin is only one of omission; for example, concerned citizens in Palo Alto were told a few days ago that "Sometimes women are raped because of carelessness."

To the extent that a woman can convince a jury that she was neither careless nor seductive, her attacker may be found guilty and she may be absolved from guilt, but more often in rape trials something is found in her behavior to "account" for her fate. The point is that whatever the circumstances of a rape, social attitudes and legal processes at the present time make the victim guilty of her own rape. Even the most innocent victim is likely to be told by her mother, "I told you never to walk home alone," and this is sometimes the attitude of an entire population, as in Bangladesh, where thousands of raped wives were repudiated by their husbands.

The unfortunate rape victim is in some ways worse off the more "feminine," the better socialized, she is, for she will have accepted normal social strictures: do not play rough, do not make noise or hit. Then she will be judged at the trial of her attacker on the extent to which she has struggled, hit, bitten (though she would not be expected to resist an armed robber). Not to struggle is to appear to want to be raped. In the courtroom men pretend not to understand the extent to which cultural inhibitions prevent women from resisting male force, even moral force, though in the parking lot they seem to understand it very well. 16

In the practical world, who are the rapists, who are the raped, what is to be done? It is here that Brownmiller's account is most interesting and most disturbing. Both Brownmiller and MacKellar agree on the statistical particulars: the rape victim is most likely a teen-aged black girl but she may be a woman of any age, and she will know her attacker to some extent in

---

Desdemona   In Shakespeare's play *Othello*, wife of the title character. She is murdered by Othello when he mistakenly believes that she was unfaithful to him.

Carmen   In the French tale and the opera by George Bizet, Carmen is a seductive Spanish gypsy who is stabbed by her jilted lover.

Lucrece   In Roman legend, Lucrece stabs herself after telling her father and her husband that she has been raped.

Anna Karenina   Anna Karenina, in Tolsoy's novel, commits suicide after her adulterous love affair goes awry.

about half of the cases. The rapist is the same sort of person as other violent offenders: young, uneducated, unemployed, likely black or from another deprived subculture; the rapist is *not* the shy, hard-up loner living with his mother, victim of odd obsessions; a quarter of all rapes are done in gangs or pairs.

The sociology of rapists has some difficult political implications, as Brownmiller, to judge from the care with which she approaches it, is well aware. She traces the complicated history of American liberalism and Southern racism which has led to the present pass, in which people who have traditionally fought for human freedom seem committed to obstructing freedom for women. Historically, she reminds us, the old left, and the Communist Party in particular.

> understood rape as a political act of subjugation only when the victim was black and the offender was white. White-on-white rape was merely "criminal" and had no part in their Marxist canon. Black-on-black rape was ignored. And black-on-white rape, about which the rest of the country was phobic, was discussed in the oddly reversed world of the Jefferson School as if it never existed except as a spurious charge that "the state" employed to persecute black men.

Meantime, circumstances have changed; folk bigotry, like folk wisdom, turns out to contain a half-truth, or grain of prescience; and the black man has taken to raping. Now

> the incidence of actual rape combined with the looming spectre of the black man as rapist to which the black man in the name of his manhood now contributes, must be understood as a control mechanism against the freedom, mobility, and aspirations of all women, white and black. The crossroads of racism and sexism had to be a violent meeting place. There is no use pretending it doesn't exist.

It is at this crossroads that the problem appears most complex and most insoluble. Not only rapists, but also people more suavely disguised as right-thinking, like the ACLU and others associated with the civil-rights movement, still feel that protection of black men's rights is more important than injustice to women, whether white or black. Black men and white women are in effect pitted against one another in such a way as to impede the progress of both groups, and in particular to conceal and perpetuate the specific victimization of black women. Various studies report that blacks do up to 90 percent of rapes, and their victims are 80 to 90 percent black women, who now must endure from men of their own race what they historically had to endure from whites. A black girl from the ages of ten to fifteen is twelve times more likely than others to be a victim of this crime.

In this situation, which will win in the long run, sexism or racism? Who 20 are the natural antagonists? It seems likely, on the evidence, that sexism, being older, will prevail.

The MacKellar/Amir book, a short, practical manual about rape, something to be used perhaps by jurors or counselors, gives a picture of the crime and of the rapist which is essentially the same as Brownmiller's. But MacKellar's advice, when compared with Brownmiller's, is seen to be overlaid by a kind of naive social optimism. What can women do? They can avoid hitchhiking; they can be better in bed: "if women were less inhibited with their men the sense of depravity that their prudishness inspires might be reduced," as if it were frustrated middle-class husbands who were out raping; authorities can search out those "many youngsters warped by a brutish home life [who] can still be recuperated for a reasonably good adult life if given therapy in time"; "Education. Education helps to reduce rape."

Maybe. But does any evidence exist to suggest that any of this would really help? Brownmiller has found none, but I suppose she would agree with MacKellar that for America's violent subcultures we must employ "the classical remedies of assimilating the people in these subcultures, economically and socially, in opportunities for education, jobs, and decent housing," and change the fundamental values of American society. "As long as aggressive, exploitive behavior remains the norm, it can be expected that individuals will make these errors and that the weaker members of society will be the victim."

Until aggressive, exploitive behavior is not the norm, a few practical measures are being suggested. The LEAA study, MacKellar, and Brownmiller are all in favor of prosecuting rape cases and of punishing rapists. Brownmiller feels the punishment should suit the crime, that it should be made similar to penalties for aggravated assault, which it resembles. MacKellar feels that the penalty should fit the criminal: "a nineteen-year-old unemployed black with a fourth-grade education and no father, whose uptight, superreligious mother has, after a quarrel, kicked him out of the home, should not be judged by the same standard nor receive the same kind of sentence as a white middle-aged used-car salesman, twice divorced, who rapes a girl he picks up at a newsstand during an out-of-town convention." She does not, by the way, say who should get the stiffer sentence, and I can think of arguments either way.

Both agree that corroboration requirements and courtroom questions 24 about a victim's prior sexual history should be eliminated, and in this the government-sponsored study for the Law Enforcement Assistance Administration (*Rape and Its Victims*) also agrees. At present the established view holds that whether or not a raped girl is a virgin or is promiscuous is germane to the issue of whether a forced act of sexual intercourse has occurred in a given case. This reflects the ancient idea that by violating male standards of female chastity, a woman forfeits her right to say no.

The LEAA study found that prosecutors' offices in general were doing little to urge the revision of outdated legal codes, and that the legal system is in fact impeding reform. It observes (in a nice trenchant style that makes better reading than most government reports) that

> since rapists have no lobby, the major opposition to reform measures can be expected from public defenders, the defense bar in general, and groups, such as the American Civil Liberties Union, that are vigilant with respect to the rights of criminal defendants.

The conclusion one cannot help coming to is that whatever is to be done about rape will have to be done by women primarily. Brownmiller feels that law enforcement must include 50 percent women. She finds it significant that whereas male law-enforcement authorities report 15 or 20 percent of rape complaints to be "unfounded," among the ones they actually bother to write down, women investigators find only 2 percent of such reports to be unfounded, exactly the number of unfounded reports of other violent crimes. Apparently the goal of male-female law enforcement is not without its difficulties; women police officers in Washington, D.C., recently have complained that their male patrol-car partners are attempting to force them to have sexual intercourse. Since these women are armed with service revolvers, we may soon see an escalation of what appears to be the Oldest Conflict.

MacKellar and the LEAA report both favor some sort of rape sentencing by degree, as in murder, with rape by a stranger constituting first-degree rape, and third degree taking cognizance of situations in which the victim may be judged to have shared responsibility for initiating the situation that led to the rape — for instance, hitchhiking. This is a compromise that would be unacceptable to feminist groups who feel that a woman is no more responsible for a rape under those circumstances than a man would be thought to be who was assaulted in the same situation.

It is likely that the concept of penalty by degree, with its concession to 28 history, will prevail here, but one sees the objection on principle. While men continue to believe that men have a right to assert their authority over women by sexual and other means, rape will continue, and this in turn suggests two more measures. One is control of pornography, which Brownmiller argues is the means by which the rape ethic is promulgated. In spite of objections about censorship and about the lack of evidence that pornography and violence are related, Brownmiller's argument here is a serious one. She also feels that women should learn self-defense, if only to give them increased self-confidence and awareness of their bodies. But it is easy to see that this is yet another way in which the female might be made to take responsibility for being raped. If a woman learns karate and is raped anyway, the question will become, why hadn't she learned it better?

Surely the definition of civilization is a state of things where the strong refrain from exercising their advantages over the weak. If men can be made to see that the abolition of sexual force is necessary in the long-term interest of making a civilization, then they may cooperate in implementing whatever measures turn out to be of any use. For the short term, one imagines, the general effect of female activism about rape will be to polarize men and women even more than nature has required. The cooperation of state authorities, if any, may ensue from their perception of rape, especially black-on-white rape, as a challenge to white male authority (as in the South). This in turn may produce an unlikely and ominous coalition of cops and feminists, and the generally severer prosecution and sentencing which we see as the current response to other forms of violent crime. But do we know that rapists will emerge from the prisons — themselves centers of homosexual rape — any less inclined to do it again?

Meantime, one feels a certain distaste for the congratulatory mood surrounding proposed law-enforcement reforms devoted entirely to making the crime less miserable for the victim while denying or concealing the complicity of so many men in its perpetuation. This implies a state of things worthy of a society described by Swift.°

AFTERWORD

"Rape" is an essay-review. A book review, narrowly conceived, tells us what's in a book and how good or bad it is. An essay-review — common in the New York Review of Books, *sometimes in the* New Yorker, *and in literary quarterlies — reports on a book but also assembles the essayist's own thoughts on the subject matter of the book. Sometimes an essayist-reviewer hardly touches on the book which is nominally the subject or dismisses it to substitute his or her own subjects. Some examples seem pure egotism, but the form — as Diane Johnson uses it — can be valuable: The reader gets two for the price of one.*

Notice how Diane Johnson, writing about outrage, avoids the language of outrage. In her opening paragraph she refers to actions — specific like Richard Speck's multiple murders, general like the quotidian omnipresence of rape — without using potent words, like outrage. *The acts named are sufficient; the rhetoric of outrage would obscure the thing itself. A rule of thumb: When a writer represents*

Swift   Jonathan Swift (1667–1745), English author best known for *Gulliver's Travels*, which satirically depicted the political and social structure of the day.

an action morally neutral, like a total eclipse of the sun, the writer's language may embody extremities of violence, ecstasy, and pain. When a writer deals with the morally evil, or with the saintly, understatement suffices; perhaps it is requisite.

BOOKS AVAILABLE IN PAPERBACK

Dashiell Hammett: A Life. New York: Fawcett Books. *Nonfiction*.

GARRISON
KEILLOR

GARRISON KEILLOR, born (1942) in Anoka, Minnesota, was the creator, host, and leading performer of A Prairie Home Companion. Saturdays from 1974 to 1987, National Public Radio featured Keillor's monologues about Lake Wobegon, a small Minnesota town compounded of memory, humor, and imagination, where Bob's Bank competed for attention with Bertha's Kitty Boutique. Four million people listened to A Prairie Home Companion broadcast over two hundred and sixty stations. When Keillor announced the end of the show, we endured a national day of mourning.

Cassettes from the show sell like Powdermilk Biscuits, and so do books by Garrison Keillor: Happy to Be Here (1981), from which we take "Shy Rights," Lake Wobegon Days (1985), and Leaving Home (1987). Growing up in Anoka, in a strict Plymouth Brethren sect, Keillor tried freelance writing when he was young, then moved to radio, which he had always loved, because he could not make a living as a writer. Of course radio turned around and made him a popular writer.

Radio is a superb medium for the good word, as television is not, because radio concentrates attention on the word without the distraction of visual images. For that matter, even without radio, we seem to reconnect literature with oral performance. *Public readings by poets and fiction writers have increased exponentially during the last twenty-five years.*

Leaving Home *collects thirty-six monologues from the radio show, stories that Keillor did not write down but improvised, now revised and altered into print for book publication. The radio show which brought them forth altered Keillor's life entirely and of course not entirely for the better. He became a celebrity, which meant that he was allowed no private life. When he stopped the show, he left Minnesota for Denmark, the provenance of his second wife, but soon the couple left Denmark and returned to the United States, not to Lake Wobegon but to Manhattan — "I find it dazzling" — where Keillor has a desk at the* New Yorker.

Shy Rights:
Why Not Pretty Soon?

Recently I read about a group of fat people who had organized to fight discrimination against themselves. They said that society oppresses the overweight by being thinner than them and that the term "overweight" itself is oppressive because it implies a "right" weight that the fatso has failed to make. Only weightists use such terms, they said; they demanded to be called "total" people and to be thought of in terms of wholeness; and they referred to thin people as being "not all there."

Don't get me wrong. This is fine with me. If, to quote the article if I may, "Fat Leaders Demand Expanded Rights Act, Claim Broad Base of Support," I have no objections to it whatsoever. I feel that it is their right to speak up and I admire them for doing so, though of course this is only my own opinion. I could be wrong.

Nevertheless, after reading the article, I wrote a letter to President Jimmy Carter demanding that his administration take action to end discrimination against shy persons sometime in the very near future. I pointed out three target areas — laws, schools, and attitudes — where shy rights maybe could be safeguarded. I tried not to be pushy but I laid it on the line. "Mr. President," I concluded, "you'll probably kill me for saying this but compared to what you've done for other groups, we shys have settled for 'peanuts.' As you may know, we are not ones to make threats, but it is clear to me that if we don't get some action on this, it could be a darned quiet summer. It is up to you, Mr. President. Whatever you decide will be okay by me. Yours very cordially."

I never got around to mailing the letter, but evidently word got around 4
in the shy community that I had written it, and I've noticed that most shy
persons are not speaking to me these days. I guess they think the letter
went too far. Probably they feel that making demands is a betrayal of the
shy movement (or "gesture," as many shys call it) and an insult to shy
pride and that it risks the loss of some of the gains we have already made,
such as social security and library cards.

Perhaps they are right. I don't claim to have all the answers. I just feel
that we ought to begin, at least, to think about some demands that we
might make if, for example, we *had* to someday. That's all. I'm not saying
we should make fools of ourselves, for heaven's sake!

Shut Up (A Slogan)

Sometimes I feel that maybe we shy persons have borne our terrible
burden for far too long now. Labeled by society as "wimps," "dorks,"
"creeps," and "sissies," stereotyped as Milquetoasts and Walter Mittys, and
tagged as potential psychopaths ("He kept pretty much to himself," every
psychopath's landlady is quoted as saying after the arrest, and for weeks
thereafter every shy person is treated like a leper), we shys are desperately
misunderstood on every hand. Because we don't "talk out" our feelings, it
is assumed that we haven't any. It is assumed that we never exclaim, retort,
or cry out, though naturally we do on occasions when it seems called for.

Would anyone dare to say to a woman or a Third World person, "Oh,
don't be a woman! Oh, don't be so Third!"? And yet people make bold
with us whenever they please and put an arm around us and tell us not to
be shy.

Hundreds of thousands of our shy brothers and sisters (and "cousins 8
twice-removed," as militant shys refer to each other) are victimized every
year by self-help programs that promise to "cure" shyness through hand-
buzzer treatments, shout training, spicy diets, silence-aversion therapy, and
every other gimmick in the book. Many of them claim to have "overcome"
their shyness, but the sad fact is that they are afraid to say otherwise.

To us in the shy movement, however, shyness is not a disability or
disease to be "overcome." It is simply the way we are. And in our own
quiet way, we are secretly proud of it. It isn't something we shout about
at public rallies and marches. It is Shy Pride. And while we don't have a
Shy Pride Week, we do have many private moments when we keep our
thoughts to ourselves, such as "Shy is nice," "Walk short," "Be proud —
shut up," and "Shy is beautiful, for the most part." These are some that I
thought up myself. Perhaps other shy persons have some of their own, I
don't know.

A "Number One" Disgrace

Discrimination against the shy is our country's number one disgrace in my own personal opinion. Millions of men and women are denied equal employment, educational and recreational opportunities, and rewarding personal relationships simply because of their shyness. These injustices are nearly impossible to identify, not only because the shy person will not speak up when discriminated against, but also because the shy person almost always *anticipates* being denied these rights and doesn't ask for them in the first place. (In fact, most shys will politely decline a right when it is offered to them.)

Most shy lawyers agree that shys can never obtain justice under our current adversary system of law. The Sixth Amendment, for example, which gives the accused the right to confront his accusers, is anti-shy on the face of it. It effectively denies shy persons the right to accuse anyone of anything.

One solution might be to shift the burden of proof to the defendant in   12
case the plaintiff chooses to remain silent. Or we could create a special second-class citizenship that would take away some rights, such as free speech, bearing arms, and running for public office, in exchange for some other rights that we need more. In any case, we need some sort of fairly totally new concept of law if we shys are ever going to enjoy equality, if indeed that is the sort of thing we could ever enjoy.

A Million-Dollar Ripoff

Every year, shy persons lose millions of dollars in the form of overcharges that aren't questioned, shoddy products never returned to stores, refunds never asked for, and bad food in restaurants that we eat anyway, not to mention all the money we lose and are too shy to claim when somebody else finds it.

A few months ago, a shy friend of mine whom I will call Duke Hand (not his real name) stood at a supermarket checkout counter and watched the cashier ring up thirty fifteen-cent Peanut Dream candy bars and a $3.75 copy of *Playhouse* for $18.25. He gave her a twenty-dollar bill and thanked her for his change, but as he reached for his purchases, she said, "Hold on. There's something wrong here."

"No, really, it's O.K.," he said.

"Let me see that cash register slip," she said.   16

"No, really, thanks anyway," he whispered. Out of the corner of his eye, he could see that he had attracted attention. Other shoppers in the vicinity had sensed that something was up, perhaps an attempted price-tag switch or insufficient identification, and were looking his way. "It's not for me," he pleaded. "I'm only buying this for a friend."

Nevertheless, he had to stand there in mute agony while she counted all of the Peanut Dreams and refigured the total and the correct change. (In fairness to her, it should be pointed out that Duke, while eventually passing on each copy of *Playhouse* to a friend, first reads it himself.)

Perhaps one solution might be for clerks and other business personnel to try to be a little bit more careful about this sort of thing in the first place. O.K.?

How About Shy History?

To many of us shys, myself included, the worst tragedy is the oppression of shy children in the schools, and while we don't presume to tell educators how to do their work, work that they have been specially trained to do, we do feel that schools must begin immediately to develop programs of shy history, or at the very least to give it a little consideration.

History books are blatantly prejudiced against shyness and shy person-hood. They devote chapter after chapter to the accomplishments of famous persons and quote them at great length, and say nothing at all, or very little, about countless others who had very little to say, who never sought fame, and whose names are lost to history.

Where in the history books do we find mention of The Lady in Black, Kilroy, The Unknown Soldier, The Forgotten Man, The Little Guy, not to mention America's many noted recluses?

Where, for example, can we find a single paragraph on America's hundreds of scale models, those brave men of average height whose job it was to pose beside immense objects such as pyramids and dynamos so as to indicate scale in drawings and photographs? The only credit that scale models ever received was a line in the caption — "For an idea of its size, note man (arrow, at left)." And yet, without them, such inventions as the dirigible, the steam shovel, and the swing-span bridge would have looked like mere toys, and natural wonders such as Old Faithful, the Grand Canyon, and the giant sequoia would have been dismissed as hoaxes. It was truly a thankless job.

Shys on "Strike"

The scale models themselves never wanted any thanks. All they wanted was a rope or device of some type to keep them from falling off tall structures, plus a tent to rest in between drawings, and in 1906, after one model was carried away by a tidal wave that he had been hired to pose in front of, they formed a union and went on strike.

Briefly, the scale models were joined by a contingent of shy artists' models who had posed for what they thought was to be a small monument showing the Battle of Bull Run only to discover that it was actually a large bas-relief entitled "The Bathers" and who sat down on the job, bringing the work to a halt. While the artists' models quickly won a new contract and went back to work (on a non-representational basis), the scale models' strike was never settled.

True to their nature, the scale models did not picket the work sites or negotiate with their employers. They simply stood quietly a short distance away and, when asked about their demands, pointed to the next man. A year later, when the union attempted to take a vote on the old contract, it found that most of the scale models had moved away and left no forwarding addresses.

It was the last attempt by shy persons to organize themselves anywhere in the country.

Now Is the Time, We Think

Now is probably as good a time as any for this country to face up to its 28 shameful treatment of the shy and to do something, almost anything, about it. On the other hand, maybe it would be better to wait for a while and see what happens. All I know is that it isn't easy trying to write a manifesto for a bunch of people who dare not speak their names. And that the shy movement is being inverted by a tiny handful of shy militants who do not speak for the majority of shy persons, nor even very often for themselves. This secret cadre, whose members are not known even to each other, advocate doing "less than nothing." They believe in tokenism, and the smaller the token the better. They seek only to promote more self-consciousness: that ultimate shyness that shy mystics call "the fear of fear itself." What is even more terrifying is the ultimate goal of this radical wing: They believe that they shall inherit the earth, and they will not stop until they do. Believe me, we moderates have our faces to the wall.

Perhaps you are saying, "What can *I* do? I share your concern at the plight of the shy and wholeheartedly endorse your two- (or three-) point program for shy equality. I pledge myself to work vigorously for its adoption. My check for ($10 $25 $50 $100 $———) is enclosed. In addition, I agree to (circulate petitions, hold fund-raising party in my home, write to congressman and senator, serve on local committee, write letters to newspapers, hand out literature door-to-door during National Friends of the Shy Drive)."

Just remember: You said it, not me.

AFTERWORD

All people think that they are shy; bold people tell themselves that they are good at hiding their shyness. Thus, I suppose, the famous radio star and author genuinely considers himself a shy person. At least a little bit. . . . Talking to four million people every week is a good way to disguise your shyness.

This essay is ironic in a gentle teasing way. It delights in using the clichés of current journalistic sociology — "target area," "not his real name."

It is diffidence, or lack of self-confidence, that Keillor embodies in the name of shyness. My favorite parts are the qualifications, beginning with the title: ". . . though of course this is only my own opinion. I could be wrong." "Whatever you decide will be okay by me." "I don't claim to have all the answers." "'Shy is beautiful, for the most part.'" "Perhaps other shy persons have some of their own, I don't know." ". . . in my own personal opinion."

The irony of mock-seriousness resembles Ian Frazier's "Dating Your Mom." Like Frazier, Keillor invents anecdotes, but we are never tempted to call this piece a short story. Keillor's made-up examples parody the factual details adduced in argument.

Tone is everything in an essay like Keillor's. He is a master of a consistent self-mockery which has its cake and eats it too: Who doesn't understand that this essay, for all its humor, is a plea for tolerance?

BOOKS AVAILABLE IN PAPERBACK

Happy to Be Here: Even More Stories and Comic Pieces. New York: Penguin.

Ten Years: The Official Souvenir Anniversary Program for a Prairie Home Companion. Minneapolis: Minnesota Public Radio. Nonfiction.

MAXINE HONG KINGSTON

MAXINE HONG KINGSTON *was born in California in 1940, the eldest of six children in a Chinese immigrant family. English is her second language, and only recently has she begun to dream in it. She grew up in the town of Stockton, in the San Joaquin Valley, where her family ran a laundry. Stockton's small Chinese population, most of whom came from a village called Sun Woi, regularly gathered at the laundry to tell stories. What the young child remembered became material for the adult writer.*

Kingston graduated from the University of California at Berkeley in 1962 and taught high school in California and Hawaii, where she has lived for many years. She has published poetry, stories, and articles in a variety of magazines — the New York Times Magazine, New West, Ms., *the* New Yorker, Iowa Review *— and has received extensive honors for her two books of reminiscence. This essay is the first chapter of* The Woman Warrior: Memoirs of a Girlhood Among Ghosts *(1975), which won the National Book Critics Award for Nonfiction. She followed it with* China Men *(1980), which received the American Book Award. From stories that an eldest child heard from her mother, and from the nostalgic ambience of a laundry in Stockton, Maxine Hong Kingston assembles narrative and* reminiscence that embody the collision and amalgamation of two cultures — the same combination that produced the author herself.

Writing as a member of a minority, Kingston has encountered a familiar problem: Some Chinese-Americans complain that she is unrepresentative of her cultural sources. She has replied: "When people criticize my work by saying that it does not reflect their experience, I hear an assumption that one of us — in this case, me — is expected to speak for all the rest. I don't think that is a good expectation. Each one of us has a unique voice, and no one else will see things exactly the way I do, or write about them the way I do." With her eye for particulars, with her intense feeling for family and for her family's alien America, she makes with her unique voice a special human reality.

An interviewer quoted Kingston to herself — "I have no idea how people who don't write endure their lives" — and asked for more. She answered, "When I said that, I was thinking about how words and stories create order. And some of the things that happen to us in life seem to have no meaning, but when you write them down you find the meanings for them; or, as you translate life into words, you force a meaning." One of the anomalies of the writer's life, heaven knows, is never to know whether you have discovered, or invented, the meaning you write down.

Maxine Hong Kingston is tale-teller for her tribe; she is shape-maker for herself and for all of us.

No Name Woman

"You must not tell anyone," my mother said, "what I am about to tell you. In China your father had a sister who killed herself. She jumped into the family well. We say that your father has all brothers because it is as if she had never been born.

"In 1924 just a few days after our village celebrated seventeen hurry-up weddings — to make sure that every young man who went 'out on the road' would responsibly come home — your father and his brothers and your grandfather and his brothers and your aunt's new husband sailed for America, the Gold Mountain. It was your grandfather's last trip. Those lucky enough to get contracts waved good-bye from the decks. They fed and guarded the stowaways and helped them off in Cuba, New York, Bali, Hawaii. 'We'll meet in California next year,' they said. All of them sent money home.

"I remember looking at your aunt one day when she and I were dressing; I had not noticed before that she had such a protruding melon of a stomach.

But I did not think, 'She's pregnant,' until she began to look like other pregnant women, her skirt pulling and the white tops of her black pants showing. She could not have been pregnant, you see, because her husband had been gone for years. No one said anything. We did not discuss it. In early summer she was ready to have the child, long after the time when it could have been possible.

"The village had also been counting. On the night the baby was to be 4 born the villagers raided our house. Some were crying. Like a great saw, teeth strung with lights, files of people walked zigzag across our land, tearing the rice. Their lanterns doubled in the disturbed black water, which drained away through the broken bunds. As the villagers closed in, we could see that some of them, probably men and women we knew well, wore white masks. The people with long hair hung it over their faces. Women with short hair made it stand up on end. Some had tied white bands around their foreheads, arms, and legs.

"At first they threw mud and rocks at the house. Then they threw eggs and began slaughtering our stock. We could hear the animals scream their deaths — the roosters, the pigs, a last great roar from the ox. Familiar wild heads flared in our night windows; the villagers encircled us. Some of the faces stopped to peer at us, their eyes rushing like searchlights. The hands flattened against the panes, framed heads, and left red prints.

"The villagers broke in the front and the back doors at the same time, even though we had not locked the doors against them. Their knives dripped with the blood of our animals. They smeared blood on the doors and walls. One woman swung a chicken, whose throat she had slit, splattering blood in red arcs about her. We stood together in the middle of our house, in the family hall with the pictures and tables of the ancestors around us, and looked straight ahead.

"At that time the house had only two wings. When the men came back, we would build two more to enclose our courtyard and a third one to begin a second courtyard. The villagers pushed through both wings, even your grandparents' rooms, to find your aunt's, which was also mine until the men returned. From this room a new wing for one of the younger families would grow. They ripped up her clothes and shoes and broke her combs, grinding them underfoot. They tore her work from the loom. They scattered the cooking fire and rolled the new weaving in it. We could hear them in the kitchen breaking our bowls and banging the pots. They overturned the great waist-high earthenware jugs; duck eggs, pickled fruits, vegetables burst out and mixed in acrid torrents. The old woman from the next field swept a broom through the air and loosed the spirits-of-the-broom over our heads. 'Pig.' 'Ghost.' 'Pig,' they sobbed and scolded while they ruined our house.

"When they left, they took sugar and oranges to bless themselves. They 8 cut pieces from the dead animals. Some of them took bowls that were not broken and clothes that were not torn. Afterward we swept up the rice and sewed it back up into sacks. But the smells from the spilled preserves lasted. Your aunt gave birth in the pigsty that night. The next morning when I went for the water, I found her and the baby plugging up the family well.

"Don't let your father know that I told you. He denies her. Now that you have started to menstruate, what happened to her could happen to you. Don't humiliate us. You wouldn't like to be forgotten as if you had never been born. The villagers are watchful."

Whenever she had to warn us about life, my mother told stories that ran like this one, a story to grow up on. She tested our strength to establish realities. Those in the emigrant generations who could not reassert brute survival died young and far from home. Those of us in the first American generations have had to figure out how the invisible world the emigrants built around our childhoods fit in solid America.

The emigrants confused the gods by diverting their curses, misleading them with crooked streets and false names. They must try to confuse their offspring as well, who, I suppose, threaten them in similar ways — always trying to get things straight, always trying to name the unspeakable. The Chinese I know hide their names; sojourners take new names when their lives change and guard their real names with silence.

Chinese-Americans, when you try to understand what things in you 12 are Chinese, how do you separate what is peculiar to childhood, to poverty, insanities, one family, your mother who marked your growing with stories, from what is Chinese? What is Chinese tradition and what is the movies?

If I want to learn what clothes my aunt wore, whether flashy or ordinary, I would have to begin, "Remember Father's drowned-in-the-well sister?" I cannot ask that. My mother has told me once and for all the useful parts. She will add nothing unless powered by Necessity, a riverbank that guides her life. She plants vegetable gardens rather than lawns; she carries the odd-shaped tomatoes home from the fields and eats food left for the gods.

Whenever we did frivolous things, we used up energy; we flew high kites. We children came up off the ground over the melting cones our parents brought home from work and the American movie on New Year's Day — *Oh, You Beautiful Doll* with Betty Grable one year, and *She Wore A Yellow Ribbon* with John Wayne another year. After the one carnival ride each, we paid in guilt; our tired father counted his change on the dark walk home.

Adultery is extravagance. Could people who hatch their own chicks and eat the embryos and the heads for delicacies and boil the feet in vinegar for party food, leaving only the gravel, eating even the gizzard lining — could such people engender a prodigal aunt? To be a woman, to have a daughter in starvation time was a waste enough. My aunt could not have been the lone romantic who gave up everything for sex. Women in the old China did not choose. Some man had commanded her to lie with him and be his secret evil. I wonder whether he masked himself when he joined the raid on her family.

Perhaps she encountered him in the fields or on the mountain where the daughters-in-law collected fuel. Or perhaps he first noticed her in the marketplace. He was not a stranger because the village housed no strangers. She had to have dealings with him other than sex. Perhaps he worked an adjoining field, or he sold her the cloth for the dress she sewed and wore. His demand must have surprised, then terrified her. She obeyed him; she always did as she was told. 16

When the family found a young man in the next village to be her husband, she stood tractably beside the best rooster, his proxy, and promised before they met that she would be his forever. She was lucky that he was her age and she would be the first wife, an advantage secure now. The night she first saw him, he had sex with her. Then he left for America. She had almost forgotten what he looked like. When she tried to envision him, she only saw the black and white face in the group photograph the men had had taken before leaving.

The other man was not, after all, much different from her husband. They both gave orders: she followed. "If you tell your family, I"ll beat you. I'll kill you. Be here again next week." No one talked sex, ever. And she might have separated the rapes from the rest of living if only she did not have to buy her oil from him or gather wood in the same forest. I want her fear to have lasted just as long as rape lasted so that the fear could have been contained. No drawn-out fear. But women at sex hazarded birth and hence lifetimes. The fear did not stop but permeated everywhere. She told the man, "I think I'm pregnant." He organized the raid against her.

On nights when my mother and father talked about their life back home, sometimes they mentioned an "outcast table" whose business they still seemed to be settling, their voices tight. In a commensal tradition, where food is precious, the powerful older people made wrongdoers eat alone. Instead of letting them start separate new lives like the Japanese, who could become samurais and geishas, the Chinese family, faces averted but eyes glowering sideways, hung on to the offenders and fed them leftovers. My aunt must have lived in the same house as my parents and eaten at an outcast table. My mother spoke about the raid as if she had seen it, when she and my aunt, a daughter-in-law to a different household, should not have been living together at all. Daughters-in-law lived with their husbands' parents, not their own; a synonym for marriage in Chinese is "taking a daughter-in-law." Her husband's parents could have sold her, mortgaged her, stoned her. But they had sent her back to her own mother and father, a mysterious act hinting at disgraces not told me. Perhaps they had thrown her out to deflect the avengers.

She was the only daughter; her four brothers went with her father, 20 husband, and uncles "out on the road" and for some years became western men. When the goods were divided among the family, three of the brothers took land, and the youngest, my father, chose an education. After my grandparents gave their daughter away to her husband's family, they had dispensed all the adventure and all the property. They expected her alone to keep the traditional ways, which her brothers, now among the barbarians, could fumble without detection. The heavy, deep-rooted women were to maintain the past against the flood, safe for returning. But the rare urge west had fixed upon our family, and so my aunt crossed boundaries not delineated in space.

The work of preservation demands that the feelings playing about in one's guts not be turned into action. Just watch their passing like cherry blossoms. But perhaps my aunt, my forerunner, caught in a slow life, let dreams grow and fade and after some months or years went toward what persisted. Fear at the enormities of the forbidden kept her desires delicate, wire and bone. She looked at a man because she liked the way the hair was tucked behind his ears, or she liked the question-mark line of a long torso curving at the shoulder and straight at the hip. For warm eyes or a soft voice or a slow walk — that's all — a few hairs, a line, a brightness, a sound, a pace, she gave up family. She offered us up for a charm that vanished with tiredness, a pigtail that didn't toss when the wind died. Why, the wrong lighting could erase the dearest thing about him.

It could very well have been, however, that my aunt did not take subtle enjoyment of her friend, but, a wild woman, kept rollicking company. Imagining her free with sex doesn't fit, though. I don't know any women like that, or men either. Unless I see her life branching into mine, she gives me no ancestral help.

To sustain her being in love, she often worked at herself in the mirror, guessing at the colors and shapes that would interest him, changing them frequently in order to hit on the right combination. She wanted him to look back.

On a farm near the sea, a woman who tended her appearance reaped a 24 reputation for eccentricity. All the married women blunt-cut their hair in flaps about their ears or pulled it back in tight buns. No nonsense. Neither style blew easily into heart-catching tangles. And at their weddings they displayed themselves in their long hair for the last time. "It brushed the backs of my knees," my mother tells me. "It was braided, and even so, it brushed the backs of my knees."

At the mirror my aunt combed individuality into her bob. A bun could have been contrived to escape into black streamers blowing in the wind or in quiet wisps about her face, but only the older women in our picture album wear buns. She brushed her hair back from her forehead, tucking the flaps behind her ears. She looped a piece of thread, knotted into a circle between her index fingers and thumbs, and ran the double strand across her forehead. When she closed her fingers as if she were making a pair of shadow geese bite, the string twisted together catching the little hairs. Then she pulled the thread away from her skin, ripping the hairs out neatly, her eyes watering from the needles of pain. Opening her fingers, she cleaned the thread, then rolled it along her hairline and the tops of her eyebrows. My mother did the same to me and my sisters and herself. I used to believe that the expression "caught by the short hairs" meant a captive held with a depilatory string. It especially hurt at the temples, but my mother said we were lucky we didn't have to have our feet bound when we were seven. Sisters used to sit on their beds and cry together, she said, as their mothers or their slave removed the bandages for a few minutes each night and let the blood gush back into their veins. I hope that the man my aunt loved appreciated a smooth brow, that he wasn't just a tits-and-ass man.

Once my aunt found a freckle on her chin, at a spot that the almanac said predestined her for unhappiness. She dug it out with a hot needle and washed the wound with peroxide.

More attention to her looks than these pullings of hairs and pickings at spots would have caused gossip among the villagers. They owned work clothes and good clothes, and they wore good clothes for feasting the new seasons. But since a woman combing her hair hexes beginnings, my aunt rarely found an occasion to look her best. Women looked like great sea snails — the corded wood, babies, and laundry they carried were the whorls on their backs. The Chinese did not admire a bent back; goddesses and warriors stood straight. Still there must have been a marvelous freeing of beauty when a worker laid down her burden and stretched and arched.

Such commonplace loveliness, however, was not enough for my aunt. She dreamed of a lover for the fifteen days of New Year's, the time for families to exchange visits, money, and food. She plied her secret comb. And sure enough she cursed the year, the family, the village, and herself.

Even as her hair lured her imminent lover, many other men looked at her. Uncles, cousins, nephews, brothers would have looked, too, had they been home between journeys. Perhaps they had already been restraining their curiosity, and they left, fearful that their glances, like a field of nesting birds, might be startled and caught. Poverty hurt, and that was their first reason for leaving. But another, final reason for leaving the crowded house was the never-said.

She may have been unusually beloved, the precious only daughter, spoiled and mirror gazing because of the affection the family lavished on her. When her husband left, they welcomed the chance to take her back

28

from the in-laws; she could live like the little daughter for just a while longer. There are stories that my grandfather was different from other people, "crazy ever since the little Jap bayoneted him in the head." He used to put his naked penis on the dinner table, laughing. And one day he brought home a baby girl, wrapped up inside his brown western-style greatcoat. He had traded one of his sons, probably my father, the youngest, for her. My grandmother made him trade back. When he finally got a daughter of his own, he doted on her. They must have all loved her, except perhaps my father, the only brother who never went back to China, having once been traded for a girl.

Brothers and sisters, newly men and women, had to efface their sexual color and present plain miens. Disturbing hair and eyes, a smile like no other, threatened the ideal of five generations living under one roof. To focus blurs, people shouted face to face and yelled from room to room. The immigrants I know have loud voices, unmodulated to American tones even after years away from the village where they called their friendships out across the fields. I have not been able to stop my mother's screams in public libraries or over telephones. Walking erect (knees straight, toes pointed forward, not pigeon-toed, which is Chinese-feminine), and speaking in an inaudible voice, I have tried to turn myself American-feminine. Chinese communication was loud, public. Only sick people had to whisper. But at the dinner table, where the family members came nearest one another, no one could talk, not the outcasts nor any eaters. Every word that falls from the mouth is a coin lost. Silently they gave and accepted food with both hands. A preoccupied child who took his bowl with one hand got a sideways glare. A complete moment of total attention is due everyone alike. Children and lovers have no singularity here, but my aunt used a secret voice, a separate attentiveness.

She kept the man's name to herself throughout her labor and dying; she did not accuse him that he be punished with her. To save her inseminator's name she gave silent birth. 32

He may have been somebody in her own household, but intercourse with a man outside the family would have been no less abhorrent. All the village were kinsmen, and the titles shouted in loud country voices never let kinship be forgotten. Any man within visiting distance would have been neutralized as a lover — "brother," "younger brother," "older brother" — one hundred and fifteen relationship titles. Parents researched birth charts probably not so much to assure good fortune as to circumvent incest in a population that has but one hundred surnames. Everybody has eight million relatives. How useless then sexual mannerisms, how dangerous.

As if it came from an atavism deeper than fear, I used to add "brother" silently to boys' names. It hexed the boys, who would or would not ask me to dance, and made them less scary and as familiar and deserving of benevolence as girls.

But, of course, I hexed myself also — no dates. I should have stood up, both arms waving, and shouted out across libraries, "Hey you! Love me back." I had no idea, though, how to make attraction selective, how to control its direction and magnitude. If I made myself American-pretty so that the five or six Chinese boys in the class fell in love with me, everyone else — the Caucasian, Negro, and Japanese boys — would too. Sisterliness, dignified and honorable, made much more sense.

Attraction eludes control so stubbornly that whole societies designed to organize relationships among people cannot keep order, not even when they bind people to one another from childhood and raise them together. Among the very poor and the wealthy, brothers married their adopted sisters, like doves. Our family allowed some romance, paying adult brides' prices and providing dowries so that their sons and daughters could marry strangers. Marriage promises to turn strangers into friendly relatives — a nation of siblings.

In the village structure, spirits shimmered among the live creatures, balanced and held in equilibrium by time and land. But one human being flaring up into violence could open up a black hole, a maelstrom that pulled in the sky. The frightened villagers, who depended on one another to maintain the real, went to my aunt to show her a personal, physical representation of the break she had made in the "roundness." Misallying couples snapped off the future, which was to be embodied in true offspring. The villagers punished her for acting as if she could have a private life, secret and apart from them.

If my aunt had betrayed the family at a time of large grain yields and peace, when many boys were born, and wings were being built on many houses, perhaps she might have escaped such severe punishment. But the men — hungry, greedy, tired of planting in dry soil, cuckolded — had had to leave the village in order to send food-money home. There were ghost plagues, bandit plagues, wars with the Japanese, floods. My Chinese brother and sister had died of an unknown sickness. Adultery, perhaps only a mistake during good times, became a crime when the village needed food.

The round moon cakes and round doorways, the round tables of graduated size that fit one roundness into another, round windows and rice bowls — these talismans had lost their power to warn this family of the law: a family must be whole, faithfully keeping the descent line by having sons to feed the old and the dead, who in turn look after the family. The villagers came to show my aunt and her lover-in-hiding a broken house. The villagers were speeding up the circling of events because she was too shortsighted to see that her infidelity had already harmed the village, that waves of consequences would return unpredictably, sometimes in disguise, as now, to hurt her. This roundness had to be made coin-sized so that she would see its circumference: punish her at the birth of her baby. Awaken

287

her to the inexorable. People who refused fatalism because they could invest small resources insisted on culpability. Deny accidents and wrest fault from the stars.

After the villagers left, their lanterns now scattering in various directions toward home, the family broke their silence and cursed her. "Aiaa, we're going to die. Death is coming. Death is coming. Look what you've done. You've killed us. Ghost! Dead ghost! Ghost! You've never been born." She ran out into the fields, far enough from the house so that she could no longer hear their voices, and pressed herself against the earth, her own land no more. When she felt the birth coming, she thought that she had been hurt. Her body seized together. "They've hurt me too much," she thought. "This is gall, and it will kill me." With forehead and knees against the earth, her body convulsed and then relaxed. She turned on her back, lay on the ground. The black well of sky and stars went out and out and out forever; her body and her complexity seemed to disappear. She was one of the stars, a bright dot in blackness, without home, without a companion, in eternal cold and silence. An agoraphobia rose in her, speeding higher and higher, bigger and bigger; she would not be able to contain it; there would be no end to fear.

Flayed, unprotected against space, she felt pain return, focusing her body. This pain chilled her — a cold, steady kind of surface pain. Inside, spasmodically, the other pain, the pain of the child, heated her. For hours she lay on the ground, alternately body and space. Sometimes a vision of normal comfort obliterated reality: she saw the family in the evening gambling at the dinner table, the young people massaging their elders' backs. She saw them congratulating one another, high joy on the mornings the rice shoots came up. When these pictures burst, the stars drew yet further apart. Black space opened.

She got to her feet to fight better and remembered that old-fashioned women gave birth in their pigsties to fool the jealous, pain-dealing gods, who do not snatch piglets. Before the next spasms could stop her, she ran to the pigsty, each step a rushing out into emptiness. She climbed over the fence and knelt in the dirt. It was good to have a fence enclosing her, a tribal person alone.

Laboring, this woman who had carried her child as a foreign growth that sickened her every day, expelled it at last. She reached down to touch the hot, wet, moving mass, surely smaller than anything human, and could feel that it was human after all — fingers, toes, nails, nose. She pulled it up on to her belly, and it lay curled there, butt in the air, feet precisely tucked one under the other. She opened her loose shirt and buttoned the child inside. After resting, it squirmed and thrashed and she pushed it up to her breast. It turned its head this way and that until it found her nipple. There, it made little snuffling noises. She clenched her teeth at its preciousness, lovely as a young calf, a piglet, a little dog.

She may have gone to the pigsty as a last act of responsibility: she would 44
protect this child as she had protected its father. It would look after her
soul, leaving supplies on her grave. But how would this tiny child without
family find her grave when there would be no marker for her anywhere,
neither in the earth nor the family hall? No one would give her a family
hall name. She had taken the child with her into the wastes. At its birth
the two of them had felt the same raw pain of separation, a wound that
only the family pressing tight could close. A child with no descent line
would not soften her life but only trail after her, ghostlike, begging her to
give it purpose. At dawn the villagers on their way to the fields would
stand around the fence and look.

Full of milk, the little ghost slept. When it awoke, she hardened her
breasts against the milk that crying loosens. Toward morning she picked
up the baby and walked to the well.

Carrying the baby to the well shows loving. Otherwise abandon it. Turn
its face into the mud. Mothers who love their children take them along. It
was probably a girl; there is some hope of forgiveness for boys.

"Don't tell anyone you had an aunt. Your father does not want to hear
her name. She has never been born." I have believed that sex was unspeakable and words so strong and fathers so frail that "aunt" would do my
father mysterious harm. I have thought that my family, having settled
among immigrants who had also been their neighbors in the ancestral land,
needed to clean their name, and a wrong word would incite the kinspeople
even here. But there is more to this silence: they want me to participate in
her punishment. And I have.

In the twenty years since I heard this story I have not asked for details 48
nor said my aunt's name; I do not know it. People who can comfort the
dead can also chase after them to hurt them further — a reverse ancestor
worship. The real punishment was not the raid swiftly inflicted by the
villagers, but the family's deliberately forgetting her. Her betrayal so mad-
dened them, they saw to it that she should suffer forever, even after death.
Always hungry, always needing, she would have to beg food from other
ghosts, snatch and steal it from those whose living descendants give them
gifts. She would have to fight the ghosts massed at crossroads for the buns
a few thoughtful citizens leave to decoy her away from village and home
so that the ancestral spirits could feast unharassed. At peace, they could
act like gods, not ghosts, their descent lines providing them with paper
suits and dresses, spirit money, paper houses, paper automobiles, chicken,
meat, and rice into eternity — essences delivered up in smoke and flames,
steam and incense rising from each rice bowl. In an attempt to make the
Chinese care for people outside the family, Chairman Mao encourages us
now to give our paper replicas to the spirits of outstanding soldiers and
workers, no matter whose ancestors they may be. My aunt remains forever
hungry. Goods are not distributed evenly among the dead.

My aunt haunts me — her ghost drawn to me because now, after fifty years of neglect, I alone devote pages of paper to her, though not origamied into houses and clothes. I do not think she always means me well. I am telling on her, and she was a spite suicide, drowning herself in the drinking water. The Chinese are always very frightened of the drowned one, whose weeping ghost, wet hair hanging and skin bloated, waits silently by the water to pull down a substitute.

AFTERWORD

This essay is more narrative than most; it is memoir or reminiscence with a wash of fiction. No one remembers conversations word for word; we are not tempted to believe that the young Maxine switched on a tape recorder whenever her mother spoke. In the act of writing memoir, we feel as if we were transcribing word for word conversations from twenty or forty years back. Upon reflection most of us will admit that phonographic reproduction by memory is most unlikely. We remember characteristic speech and particular plots; our imagination-memory mimics and we transcribe this mimickry. Out of my own memoir writing, I can testify to the conviction with which one writes and to the corroboration of survivors: One can catch the tone of the dead. But also: I have told anecdotes in which I have located a time and place exactly remembered in luminous detail — only to discover, by consulting incontrovertible evidence, that my memory was wrong. None of which expresses skepticism about the truth, or at least the validity, of Kingston's account.

BOOKS AVAILABLE IN PAPERBACK

China Men. New York: Ballantine. *Nonfiction.*

The Woman Warrior: Memoirs of a Girlhood Among Ghosts. New York: Random House-Vintage. *Nonfiction.*

MAXINE
KUMIN

MAXINE KUMIN (b. 1925) grew up in Philadelphia, where her father was the biggest pawnbroker in the city. She took her B.A. at Radcliffe College and for many years lived outside Boston, raising three children and writing. In 1963, she and her husband bought a hill farm in Warner, New Hampshire, and spent as much time there as they could manage, until in 1976 they moved up country for good. They raise horses, which they ride competitively; they raise sheep and vegetables for their table and chop their own wood.

Although Kumin has always been a poet, she has tried her hand at everything else. She wrote many juveniles beginning when her children were small. She has published four novels, a collection of short stories, and two volumes of essays — most recently In Deep *(1987), from which we take this journal. Her eight books of poems include* Up Country, *which won the Pulitzer Prize in 1973; her selected poems,* Our Ground Time Here Will Be Brief *(1982); and* The Long Approach *(1985).*

Up Country *came out of up country, like much of her work in all the genres. She writes well about the characters of the New Hampshire hills. Doubtless she is at her best writing about horses.*

Journal — Late Winter–
Spring 1978

13 February 1978　　Today, in the dying butternut tree that holds up the clothesline from which depend various suets and the main sunflower-seed feeder, an owl. Peterson's indicates it is a barred owl, not an unusual bird in these surroundings. He arrived, like a poem, unannounced. He squatted on the branch, puffed to an almost perfect roundness against the cold. His gray and brown and buff markings imitate the landscape of tree branch and caterpillar nest tatters against the snow. I could not, as the cliché has it, believe my eyes at first, and tried to make him into some recognizable artifact of nature — a clump of windblown leaves, for example. Like the notes for a poem, he would not go away but merely swelled there passively all through breakfast.

The squirrels did not show themselves, wisely. The chickadees are fearless, or at least know they have nothing to fear. The blue jays likewise. I note that our narrow-faced, downside-traveling nuthatches were absent all day.

14 February　　The owl is a Cheshire cat of an owl, noiselessly appearing, disappearing, flapping off soundlessly on immense wings, returning, higher up than before. He swivels his head almost 360 degrees, like a Japanese puppet-balloon held aloft on a stick. The face is infinitely old, infinitely wise, very catlike. When perched, no wings or claws are evident, lending him even more mystery than is warranted. Like the finished poem, he makes it all seem easy. Not since last winter's wild turkeys, not since last summer's swallow nestling sideshow on the front porch stringers, has there been better indoor viewing.

15 February　　This resident owl of ours, I muse on the third day of his tenure in the butternut, resembles nothing birdlike. Most of all he looks like a baseball pitcher in a tight spot, winding up, swiveling to check the runners at first and second, then . . . the balk. The old owls of my poems were of the furtive sort, night hooters. Whenever I did catch a daytime glimpse of them, they were in a hurry to get under cover and they seemed ragged, weary, diminished by a hard night's work. This one is larger than life-size. He has assumed the stature of a godhead in the birdfeeding zone, though today he and the squirrel eyed each other and nothing happened.

Perhaps the owl is full of his nightly mice? I noticed that the squirrel took care, while cleaning up the spilled sunflower husks, not to turn his back on the owl. Although only a small red squirrel, perhaps he is too large to tempt even an enlarged owl.

20 February   The filly these cold mornings canters in place in her stall. Too excited to tuck into her morning hay, she wants desperately to be let out, to run off some of that adolescent exuberance. Some days it is impossible to get a halter on her before her morning run. Today I unleashed her early and stood in the barn doorway to enjoy the aesthetics of her romp. The young horse is so improbably gracefully made; the body itself has not yet filled out, the legs are still disproportionately long. The extraordinarily high tail carriage, the whole plume of it arched over her back, and the floating suspended gait she displays at the trot, are inherited from her pure Arabian sire. It takes quite a lot of racing, dodging, cavorting, and bucking to get the morning kinks out. She can come to a dead stop from, say, thirty miles an hour. She can attain that speed in, say, three strides. What she does is harsher than ballet, and less controlled, something like dribbling down a basketball court, feinting, shooting, wheeling, back to the other end, and so on. The exultation I feel as I watch her move so freely and with such euphoria is a kind of glorying in effortlessness, no matter how much muscle is involved. She moves the way a poem ought to move, once it's crafted.

24 February   Putting in the spiles I lean on the brace and bit, having to use all my weight to keep the metal spiral angling upward into the tough tree. How astonishing, after the hole is bored, that the sap glistens, quivers, begins to run freely. To think that I have never seen or done this before! I am as captivated as the city child finding out where milk comes from.

We have cobbled a Rube Goldberg sort of contraption for boiling the sap down: an ancient kitchen sink for an evaporator, leftover bits of corrugated metal roofing to enclose the fire, a rack and grill from a long-abandoned fireplace gadget that was designed to throw heat back into the room but failed to do so to an appreciable degree, and two rusty pieces of stovepipe, one with a damper. Plus piles of trash wood, pine, primarily, which gives off too much pitch to be safe to burn indoors.

1 March   Although it is still too cold for any appreciable melt, one tree — we note that it's on higher ground than the others and thicker, too — is really running. The sap freezes almost as much as it drips, forming a great colorless cake of possibility. John Burroughs, quoted by the Nearings in their maple syrup text, says: "The first run, like first love, is always the best, always the fullest, always the sweetest."

How much still is dormant! And how the spirit yammers at the spirit hole, howling for spring to inch in. Now the horses are shedding, a gradual, indifferent sort of daily loss. Both Jack and the Boomer have grown an extra outer coat of coarse, short white guard hairs. These fly off in the slightest wind or are rubbed off, with grunts of horse pleasure, as they roll in the sun on the snow. Truffle, a mare of more refinement and considerable bloodlines, pure bay, has no such tough outer layer. Now that she is eight months pregnant she rolls only on one side, gets up, lies down anew to roll onto the other. Three months still to go. The foal will come at the end of May, in the full throat of spring.

Today I started half a dozen flats for the garden, of French celery and big-leaved basil, broccoli and cauliflower, and, optimistically because they always die of indoor wilt before it is time to set them out, some miniature hybrid tomatoes. Our bedroom is now crowded with trays hogging the available south light of two windows. Step stools, their step sides facing the windows, make ideal shelves on top of the counter that runs along the south wall. The secret is that I put some aged manure in the bottom of each tray. I hope it is sufficiently ancient so that it won't, at room temperature, begin to reek.

7 March   The chickadees have changed their tune and are now singing their mating song. Those same beggars who perched on my arm in January while I was filling their feeder now stay away most of the morning. They are citizens of independent means.

11 March   Everything is softening. The change, when it came, was direct, happened overnight. In spite of longing, reaching for it for weeks, we were still overtaken. The sap is running, a delightful chorus of plink-plinks in the sugarbush.[1] The horses are shedding apace. They itch enough to roll every morning now, all the guard hairs a drift of fuzz in the air, free to nesting birds for the taking.

The other night we did the barn chores together and stood a while enjoying Jack enjoying his hay. Wise old campaigner, he totes it by the mouthful to his water bucket and dunks as he crunches, not unlike the way our forebears crunched sugar lumps as they sucked up their tea. Soon the surface of Jack's water is a yellowish froth from the hayseeds. Alternately he sucks and chews, a moist rhythm.

13 March   The morning one is convinced it is spring there is a rising, manic elation for having outlasted the winter, for having come through, in

---

[1]In 1982, we converted to tubing.

Conrad's phrase, unscathed, with no bones broken. Last evening, at feeding time two crows went across the paddock cawing in midair, and I felt goosebumps rising at the nape of my neck. That crows know when to return! That ice will melt, snow cover shrink, days lengthen! Nothing is to be taken for granted after a winter of below-zero mornings, ice frozen in all the water buckets, the horses' nostrils rimmed with ice. After north winds that scour and cleanse and punish. After nights so cold the house clapboards crack and whine. Now the bad times ebb. The split wood lasted, we shall even have a cord or so to spare, as a hedge toward next winter. We calculated correctly on the hay, we congratulate ourselves on its quality, none of it dusty or moldy, enough of it so we can be generous. And Truffle now swelling and swelling, retreating more into herself, less sociable, more self-protective. In a few more weeks we will separate her, almost nine months of her eleven-month gestation now over.

15 March   Of mud, muck, and mire. Of the first, *The American Heritage Dictionary* says: "wet, sticky soft earth." Mire is deep, slimy soil or mud whereas muck is (1) "a moist, sticky mixture, especially of mud and filth," or, (2) "moist animal dung mixed with decayed matter and used as a fertilizer." Ergo, manure. Then there's *to muck about*, British, a synonym for puttering. To *muck up* is to mismanage, and the usage most common in these parts, *to muck out*, synonymous with *to redd up*, make tidy or clean, to put in order, usually before company comes, probably, says *The American Heritage* again, from ridden, to rid. Of mud, muck, and mire: they epitomize the general condition of the paddock at this season of steady, inexorable melt while our whole small world runs downhill, everything a rivulet.

The purest variety of mud squelches upward from the bases of the maple trees from which it is now necessary to gather sap twice a day. I carry ten gallons uphill twice a day. Mucking out, I displace and wheel off two barrowloads at a cleaning, I estimate forty pounds worth. This does not count wielding the ice chopper each morning to free the sliding barn doors which are kept shut[2] to discourage further inflowing of melt. What we want is outflow. We chip channels through the frozen barn floor, a tundra of semipermafrost, sawdust bedding, hay sprinklings, and manure, and build a dam across the inside lip to coax and cajole a downward, outward flow of what must necessarily all turn to water by May.

Life is hard, it says between my shoulderblades.

Every day the sap gets hauled uphill from twenty taps to metal trash barrels set in the snow at a point where the land thinks better of it and

---

[2]On grounds of poor pulmonary hygiene for the horses, we soon abandoned this practice.

levels off for a respite. The pioneers called these flat places "kiss-me-quicks," little plateaus where they could halt the team for a breather.

We boiled in our contraption for two windy days. It is sooty, cold, discouraging work, stoking and restoking the fire. At the end of each day we ladled the remaining four gallons into the canning kettle and set it indoors on the Jøtul overnight. Next morning I finished the syrup on the gas stove; it surpasses the fanciest grade triple-A boughten variety. Ours is even paler, purer, and has a buttery taste to it. We are full of grimy complacence. But what a lot of work! By rights maple syrup ought to cost five hundred dollars a gallon. Anything less is a swindle.

22 March   Statistics acquired at Saturday's all-day brood-mare clinic 20 run by the University of New Hampshire's extension service. The room was full of a hundred horse-proud people much like me. "Each stallion is a person," proclaimed the stud manager of Vermont's one Thoroughbred breeding farm. "The egg of the mare is about the size of a grain of sand, or one–two hundredth of an inch." She is born with approximately fifty thousand of them. A stallion will produce from seven to ten billion sperm per day. Five hundred million are sufficient for good fertilization. Exhaustion trials indicate that five or six mares per day are optimal, even for a young stud. The sperm is 1/2,000 of an inch in length. We saw many swimming about in slides projected on the screen.

"A mare," says the old-timey polo-playing vet, Stephen Roberts, "a mare is like a Vermonter: an animal that thinks otherwise."

A foal comes out into the air like a diver entering the water, in that position, front hooves on either side of cheek bones. The mare in labor can exert 170 pounds per square inch of pressure, so rotate a wrongly placed foal between contractions, otherwise you may get your arm broken. A lactating mare will yield up to 50 pounds of milk per day. The incidence of twinning is extremely rare, less than one percent of live births. Although twinning occurs in fifteen to twenty percent of conceptions, these almost invariably abort before the eighth month. Safe, viable births are rare with twins. One fetus ends up taking up most of the placental area. Even if she delivers two, the mare "hasn't the mentality," says Roberts, to take care of two and must be separated from them except at feeding time, for fear she'll step on one, sleep on one, forget one, and so on. Something new to worry about.

6 April   Of the Clivus Multrum and fruit flies, this note. The owners of Clivi Multra are not unlike Mercedes owners, which is to say, obsessed with the special nature of their possession. My cousin by marriage, the Mercedes owner, feels for his car the same affection I feel for my animals. He respects, even honors his machine's idiosyncrasies. The keeper of the

Clivus Multrum displays the same sort of bemused pride, but with more justification. These earth toilets, waterless, self-composting aerobic indoor privies, are the wave of the future, even though one New Hampshire town has vetoed the installation of any within its jurisdiction. Unquestionably, it is a better arrangement. Can one adjust after all these years of rigorous bathroom hygiene, years of the sound of the redemptive flush carrying off our wastes and gallons of precious water to the silent slanting cavern of fiberglass? I am uneasy squatting there. Our friends' Clivus, an hour north of us in true sugarbush country, has been in operation over a year now. They claim, indeed boast of success with it. Then over martinis they confess, as the Mercedes cousin might to an unidentifiable squeak, confess to an infestation in the Clivus of fruit flies.

I have sent away this day for a five-month supply of stingless hyme- 24 noptera, small, bite-free wasps that prey on the larvae of most of our common flies, stable flies, face flies, house flies, and so on. Fruit flies are also mentioned in the prospectus. One sprinkles the monthly shipment upon the manure pile or on fresh manure in the pasture (or down the Clivus, I should think) and nature, urged on a little, does the rest.

28 April　　No peepers yet. The trees are still bare though the lilacs are budding. Daffodils in bloom yesterday, willow showing yellow shoots, forsythia still without color. Such a slow season! Or is it the annual impatience? Nothing much above ground in the pastures, but the horses are full of vinegar so they must be getting some vitamins from the browse.

Coming back home from a week in Salt Lake City where spring abounded, skies were blue and weather balmy, is, contrary to expectation, not a downer. The secret knowledge that I'm to have two springs buoys me. It's enough to make one accept the Resurrection in all its dogmatic regalia. If ferns can, if the wake robin trillium can, if the coprinus mushroom on the manure pile can flourish so showily, then He is risen.

Our visiting mare, Shandy Dancer, all 16½ dapple gray Thoroughbred hands of her, arrived last Wednesday in the rain. Much confusion and outrage at first. Gentle Truffle took considerable umbrage at being turned out with this stranger and would at first not allow the new mare closer than a strong stone's throw. Boomerang, unused to strangers, responded in two ways. First, she made her jaw-clacking, lips-pulled-back submission gesture, the one that says, I am but a suckling foal, do not harm me. Then, perplexed as to gender and in the throes of her first heat, she flagged (raised her tail) and squirted urine. Jackanapes, king that he is, although gelded, strutted, bucked, shook his mighty neck, and tossed his head. The fence between the two sections of pasture, much of it my own handiwork, has given way in a few places. The rails are hemlock, the posts range from twelve to fourteen feet apart, and the span is too great to take the strain of all the rubbernecking going on between two sets of horses. Every morning I go out with my galvanized nails, hammer, and some short pieces of hemlock for mending. It's now a pretty patchy, poor-mouth sort of fence, but it's holding.

This morning we were remembering when Jack first came to live with 28 us and how he cowered, far from Elephant Child's hooves, meekly holding back till last by many lengths when the crew filed in for supper, or out of a morning. He knew his place in the pecking order. Now he is President for Life, a real banana republic–style dictator, and he keeps all the others in line. Oddly, he never kicks or nips Boomer. When he wants her to move on he pushes her forward with his lowered head, like a great hornless ox.

29 April This last week of April, all those little lurchings toward spring have landed us smack in the middle of the season. Pine siskins, crossbills, evening grosbeaks are back. Robins, redwing blackbirds, and cowbirds are back. The indefatigable barn swallows are back, swooping and diving hard for the first insects. My flats of tomatoes are now hardening out on the porch; they look healthy enough to flourish in the earth in a few more weeks. The broccoli and cauliflower have been transplanted into the cold frame where they seem to be standing still, sulking. All my winter dill died while I was in Utah. But the parsley we kept as a house pet right through from October is bushy and strong and as of today is back out of doors. Early peas are going in today.

Some few blackflies are abroad, particularly in the pasture when the wind dies. Just enough to remind us of the incursion to come. Just enough to make me want to press on with planting before they peak.

15 May Who can keep a journal past the first week of May? All in a one-day seizure, cattails, fiddlehead ferns, and nettles up for the picking. Nettle soup for supper. Three days later, marsh marigolds, which my neighbor Henry calls, as the British do, cowslips. The exquisite tedium of preparing the garden, plowing in last winter's manure, adding lime, destoning, smoothing with the patience if not the dexterity of frosting a cake. If you live with an engineer, you respectfully measure and line up your rows, keep a garden plan on graph paper and do your homework. Did I add half a day's labor to refurbish the fence of chicken wire, eight inches of which is buried to foil woodchucks, moles, voles, and mice? Meanwhile the air has filled with blackflies. Some days, if we dare to speak out of doors, we inhale them. Some days, like this one, a blessed breeze holds them hovering at bay.

May means grass, manna to the horses after a winter of hay. They set 32 about browsing with ferocious intensity. The tonic of spring juices creates a considerable amount of whinnying and squealing and racing, ruckus of the variety called horsing around. Everyone has lost his/her winter coat. The filly positively shines, like a simonized Jaguar. Truffle is ponderous and grave, she walks as though her feet hurt and perhaps they do, as she totes that heavy unborn foal from day to day.

Fulsome bird life. The feeder overcrowded with rose-breasted grosbeaks, purple finches, and half a dozen goldfinches queued up on the clothesline awaiting an opportunity. The swallows are nesting. They made their usual slapdash repairs to the nests over the brick terrace and once the eggs are hatched will shriek alarm and dive-bomb me if I dare to exit through the door. My peas are up, tentatively. The onions seem off to a strong start.

The peepers were later this year than any year I can remember. They did not give voice until May 8 and only this week have they found their true range. Once they're in full swing, it is deafening to walk by the lower pond at sunset. It is the purest form of noise pollution.

19 June I could not write this before today. It is three weeks since the morning I found Truffle's stillborn foal sprawled on its side in her stall, and Truffe lying quietly beside it, the placenta still trailing from her vagina. She had delivered it only moments before, a big, possibly too big, seal-brown filly, still warm to my touch, one eye glinting as if with life, the mouth slightly ajar so that its pink tongue, brilliantly pink in the graying five A.M. light, shone with the promise of life.

The vet came an hour later. He could find no cause but insisted it had never breathed. It had died either before or during its trip to the outside. I am not yet through blaming myself for not being there during Truffle's labor. She had shown no sign, no colostrum waxing on her teats, no restlessness the night before when at ten P.M. I made my final check of the barn. I remember that I felt her milk bag (for the hundredth time), felt her belly, and gave her a bit more hay. I go back and replay that day before, that evening before, I even replay the early dawn when I think now I heard a kick in the barn, a knock that might have been the portent. Had I dressed and gone to her stall then, had I waked fully and hurried out at that signal, we might have a healthy foal on the ground. These are the things I chew on, worrying them like the smooth gum space of an absent tooth.

We dug a grave behind the old chicken coop, dug and pickaxed and crowbarred away the stones, scooped and shoveled in a drench of early-morning, avid mosquitoes. Then we lifted the lovely heavy corpse into the wheelbarrow. The head lolled, hanging out, and I then cradled it and eased it back behind the rim of the barrow. I especially remember the little protective fuzz hairs that lined the ears, it was as perfectly made as that. We laid the foal in the earth and I got down beside it and folded the long legs in, tucking them back into fetal position, and then we shoveled the earth back over it and finally packed the top with stones so that nothing would disturb the grave.

It is already green there now.

A horse-friend from New York state writes me her condolences. She too has lost not one foal, but twin Thoroughbreds. "I would have spared you this shared experience if I could," she says. According to some astrological prognosticatory chart, we are both sixes on the scale. Sixes, Mary Beth writes, practice all their lives to die well, "act as Morticians of All Life and hold private burying rituals in their hearts."

So it is. So it has been. Truffle, two days later, was quite herself again. 40 Her milk never came in, so she was spared the discomfort of a swollen udder. She never grieved. She licked the dead foal when I came into her stall that morning. She nudged it once or twice with her muzzle, and when it did not respond, simply turned away.

O to turn away.

AFTERWORD

As athletes need to work out to keep in shape off-season, many writers keep journals when they are not consumed by a poem or a project. It keeps the word muscles active; and sometimes it provides a source for material. When writers publish their journals, some have been known to improve on the original. The most celebrated modern journalist is the French novelist André Gide. In his novel The Counterfeiters *a novelist character keeps a journal about a novel he is writing called* The Counterfeiters. *After he published the novel, Gide published the journal he kept while writing it. For a writer, nothing is real until it is written down.*

Kumin's journal has a quality that goes with the territory, alien to the essay proper, of ongoingness. *Journals are like news broadcasts. Eventually we may discern a structure of happenings, but as we read, the daily life simply* goes on. *The classical essay takes and makes its own time out of time; journals are present tense.*

Maxine Kumin's journal-essay is a triumph of attention, scrupulous seeing, and naming. The reader assents to its validity, swept by the fresh torrent of words. When the new grass comes in spring, the horses "set about browsing with a ferocious intensity." Then there's a playful sentence about playfulness: "The tonic of spring juices creates a considerable amount of whinnying and squealing and racing, ruckus of the variety called horsing around." This etymological conclusion is a happy stroke. Kumin shows happiness, in the horsing around of her own language — happiness which serves to render the end of her essay more powerful in its pain.

BOOKS AVAILABLE IN PAPERBACK

The Long Approach. New York: Penguin. *Poetry.*

The Microscope. New York: Harper & Row. *Children's poetry.*

Our Ground Time Here Will Be Brief. New York: Penguin. *Poetry.*

The Retrieval System. New York: Penguin. *Poetry.*

To Make a Prairie: Essays on Poets, & Country Living. Ann Arbor: University of Michigan Press. *Essays.*

BARRY
LOPEZ

*B*ARRY LOPEZ *lives in the Cascade Mountains of Oregon and writes full time*
— when he is not traveling in the Arctic Circle or the California desert
gathering material. Born in New York State (1945), he grew up largely in the San
Fernando Valley of California, went to Notre Dame University for his B.A., and
found Oregon when he did graduate work at the university.

Lopez first investigated wolves on a commission from Smithsonian *magazine.*
Living in the Arctic to attend to the society of wolves, he was attracted to the weird
landscape. "I was haunted. I had the same quickness of heart and very intense
feelings that human beings have when, in an utterly uncalculated way, they fall in
love." Of Wolves and Men *(1978), from which we take this excerpt, was followed*
by Arctic Dreams *in 1986. He is another American writer of natural history, a*
great tradition that includes Thoreau and John Burroughs, Peter Matthiessen,
Edward Abbey, Annie Dillard, John McPhee, and Edward Hoagland. Like some of
these writers he moves back and forth between natural history and fiction: Desert
Notes *(1976),* River Notes *(1979),* Winter Count *(1981).*

In essay or story, Lopez's language is meticulous and metaphorical. The critic
John Leonard put it: "A poet slips quietly out of Mr. Lopez's matter-of-fact prose,
like an eye on a long nerve-string."

Wolf Notes

Imagine a wolf moving through the northern woods. The movement, over a trail he has traversed many times before, is distinctive, unlike that of a cougar or a bear, yet he appears, if you are watching, sometimes catlike or bearlike. It is purposeful, deliberate movement. Occasionally the rhythm is broken by the wolf's pause to inspect a scent mark, or a move off the trail to paw among stones where a year before he had cached meat.

The movement down the trail would seem relentless if it did not appear so effortless. The wolf's body, from neck to hips, appears to float over the long, almost spindly legs and the flicker of wrists, a bicycling drift through the trees, reminiscent of the movement of water or of shadows.

The wolf is three years old. A male. He is of the subspecies *occidentalis*, and the trees he is moving among are spruce and subalpine fir on the eastern slope of the Rockies in northern Canada. He is light gray; that is, there are more blond and white hairs mixed with gray in the saddle of fur that covers his shoulders and extends down his spine than there are black and brown. But there are silver and even red hairs mixed in, too.

It is early September, an easy time of year, and he has not seen the 4 other wolves in his pack for three or four days. He has heard no howls, but he knows the others are about, in ones and twos like himself. It is not a time of year for much howling. It is an easy time. The weather is pleasant. Moose are fat. Suddenly the wolf stops in mid-stride. A moment, then his feet slowly come alongside each other. He is staring into the grass. His ears are rammed forward, stiff. His back arches and he rears up and pounces like a cat. A deer mouse is pinned between his forepaws. Eaten. The wolf drifts on. He approaches a trail crossing, an undistinguished crossroads. His movement is now slower and he sniffs the air as though aware of a possibility for scents. He sniffs a scent post, a scrawny blueberry bush in use for years, and goes on.

The wolf weighs ninety-four pounds and stands thirty inches at the shoulder. His feet are enormous, leaving prints in the mud along a creek (where he pauses to hunt crayfish but not with much interest) more than five inches long by just over four wide. He has two fractured ribs, broken by a moose a year before. They are healed now, but a sharp eye would notice the irregularity. The skin on his right hip is scarred, from a fight with another wolf in a neighboring pack when he was a yearling. He has not had anything but a few mice and a piece of arctic char in three days, but he is not hungry. He is traveling. The char was a day old, left on rocks along the river by bears.

The wolf is tied by subtle threads to the woods he moves through. His fur carries seeds that will fall off, effectively dispersed, along the trail some miles from where they first caught in his fur. And miles distant is a raven perched on the ribs of a caribou the wolf helped kill ten days ago, pecking like a chicken at the decaying scraps of meat. A smart snowshoe hare that eluded the wolf and left him exhausted when he was a pup has been dead a year now, food for an owl. The den in which he was born one April evening was home to porcupines last winter.

It is now late in the afternoon. The wolf has stopped traveling, has lain down to sleep on cool earth beneath a rock outcropping. Mosquitoes rest on his ears. His ears flicker. He begins to waken. He rolls on his back and lies motionless with his front legs pointed toward the sky but folded like wilted flowers, his back legs splayed, and his nose and tail curved toward each other on one side of his body. After a few moments he flops on his side, rises, stretches, and moves a few feet to inspect — minutely, delicately — a crevice in the rock outcropping and finds or doesn't find what draws him there. And then he ascends the rock face, bounding and balancing momentarily before bounding again, appearing slightly unsure of the process — but committed. A few minutes later he bolts suddenly into the woods, achieving full speed, almost forty miles per hour, for forty or fifty yards before he begins to skid, to lunge at a lodgepole pine cone. He trots away with it, his head erect, tail erect, his hips slightly to one side and out of line with his shoulders, as though hindquarters were impatient with forequarters, the cone inert in his mouth. He carries it for a hundred feet before dropping it by the trail. He sniffs it. He goes on.

The underfur next to his skin has begun to thicken with the coming of fall. In the months to follow it will becomes so dense between his shoulders it will be almost impossible to work a finger down to his skin. In seven months he will weigh less: eighty-nine pounds. He will have tried unsuccessfully to mate with another wolf in the pack. He will have helped kill four moose and thirteen caribou. He will have fallen through ice into a creek at twenty-two below zero but not frozen. He will have fought with other wolves.

He moves along now at the edge of a clearing. The wind coming down-valley surrounds him with a river of odors, as if he were a migrating salmon. He can smell ptarmigan and deer droppings. He can smell willow and spruce and the fading sweetness of fireweed. Above, he sees a hawk circling, and farther south, lower on the horizon, a flock of sharp-tailed sparrows going east. He senses through his pads with each step the dryness of the moss beneath his feet, and the ridges of old tracks, some his own. He hears the sound his feet make. He hears the occasional movement of deer mice and voles. Summer food.

Toward dusk he is standing by a creek, lapping the cool water, when a wolf howls — a long wail that quickly reaches pitch and then tapers, with several harmonics, long moments to a tremolo. He recognizes his sister. He waits a few moments, then, throwing his head back and closing his eyes, he howls. The howl is shorter and it changes pitch twice in the beginning, very quickly. There is no answer.

The female is a mile away and she trots off obliquely through the trees. The other wolf stands listening, laps water again, then he too departs, moving quickly, quietly through the trees, away from the trail he had been on. In a few minutes the two wolves meet. They approach each other briskly, almost formally, tails erect and moving somewhat as deer move. When they come together they make high squeaking noises and encircle each other, rubbing and pushing, poking their noses into each other's neck fur, backing away to stretch, chasing each other for a few steps, then standing quietly together, one putting a head over the other's back. And then they are gone, down a vague trail, the female first. After a few hundred yards they begin, simultaneously, to wag their tails.

In the days to follow, they will meet another wolf from the pack, a 12 second female, younger by a year, and the three of them will kill a caribou. They will travel together ten or twenty miles a day, through the country where they live, eating and sleeping, birthing, playing with sticks, chasing ravens, growing old, barking at bears, scent-marking trails, killing moose, and staring at the way water in a creek breaks around their legs and flows on.

AFTERWORD

This poet — "like an eye on a long nerve-string" — does not lack the sense of fact. Our excerpt comes early in Of Wolves and Men, *as the author captivates us by physical image and detail at the same time as he informs us. This prose blends poetry and exposition, not an easy task, and does the blending with apparent ease, so that the reader tastes evocative simile ("a bicycling drift through the trees, reminiscent of water or of shadows") together with encyclopedic fact (" . . . the subspecies* occidentalis, *and the trees he is moving among are spruce and subalpine fir . . . "). Movement between exposition and poetry is rapid and subtle; we take in both at once. Writers less adept at the mixture give us slabs of the one followed by slabs of the other, alternations hard to adjust to or digest. But Lopez blends: "A few minutes later he bolts suddenly into the woods, achieving full speed, almost forty miles per hour, for forty or fifty yards before he begins to skid, to lunge at a lodgepole pine cone. He trots away with it, his head erect, tail erect, his hips slightly to one side and out of line with his shoulders, as though hindquarters were impatient with forequarters, the cone inert in his mouth."*

BOOKS AVAILABLE IN PAPERBACK

Desert Notes: Reflections in the Eye of the Raven. New York: Avon. *Fictional narratives.*

Giving Birth to Thunder, Sleeping with His Daughter. New York: Scribner. *Nonfiction.*

Of Wolves and Men. New York: Scribner. *Nonfiction.*

River Notes: The Dance of the Herons. New York: Avon. *Fictional narratives.*

Winter Count. New York: Avon. *Short stories.*

ALISON
LURIE

ALISON LURIE (b. 1926) grew up in New York City and graduated from Radcliffe College. She has worked as a ghostwriter and librarian, raised three sons, and written six novels, most recently The War Between the Tates *(1974),* Only Children *(1979), and* Foreign Affairs *(1984). (All these titles are puns.) She is a professor of English at Cornell University, and she has been a Fellow of the Guggenheim and Rockefeller Foundations. She teaches part time and otherwise lives in London and in Key West.*

In the series "The Making of a Writer" in the New York Times Book Review, *Lurie remembered that as a child, certain she would grow up to be an old maid, she took to writing stories. "With a pencil and a paper, I could revise the world." A few years later, instead, she found herself married with two small children — and with two novels that publishers would not touch. She tried giving up writing, substituting a family life of tuna fish casseroles and playground excursions. But not writing did not satisfy her. She returned to it by way of the essay, making a memoir of a friend who died young, and then writing her third novel — which publishers touched and readers read.*

Alison Lurie's ironic fiction belongs with the work of modern English novelists like Evelyn Waugh, Nancy Mitford, and Anthony Powell. Her observation has been accused of wickedness; Gore Vidal called her "the Queen Herod of Modern Fiction." When she writes essays — often for the New York Review of Books — she brings her irony and humor with her. Henry James said that a novelist must be "one of those on whom nothing is lost." In her fiction, and in her observations on the clothes we wear, nothing is lost on Alison Lurie.

"Clothing as a Sign System" begins her book The Language of Clothes (1981), which is copiously illustrated. But without illustration, her prose supplies the pictures; and an overriding idea, using analogy as tracks for the train of thought, carries the reader to Alison Lurie's chosen destination.

Clothing as
a Sign System

For thousands of years human beings have communicated with one another first in the language of dress. Long before I am near enough to talk to you on the street, in a meeting, or at a party, you announce your sex, age, and class to me through what you are wearing — and very possibly give me important information (or misinformation) as to your occupation, origin, personality, opinions, tastes, sexual desires, and current mood. I may not be able to put what I observe into words, but I register the information unconsciously; and you simultaneously do the same for me. By the time we meet and converse we have already spoken to each other in an older and more universal tongue.

The statement that clothing is a language, though occasionally made with the air of a man finding a flying saucer in his backyard, is not new. Balzac, in *Daughter of Eve* (1839), observed that for a woman dress is "a continual manifestation of intimate thoughts, a language, a symbol." Today, as semiotics becomes fashionable, sociologists tell us that fashion too is a language of signs, a nonverbal system of communication. The French structuralist Roland Barthes, for instance, in "The Diseases of Costume," speaks of theatrical dress as a kind of writing, of which the basic element is the sign.

None of these theorists, however, have gone on to remark what seems obvious: that if clothing is a language, it must have a vocabulary and a grammar like other languages. Of course, as with human speech, there is not a single language of dress, but many: some (like Dutch and German) closely related and others (like Basque) almost unique. And within every language of clothes there are many different dialects and accents, some almost unintelligible to members of the mainstream culture. Moreover, as with speech, each individual has his own stock of words and employs personal variations of tone and meaning.

The vocabulary of dress includes not only items of clothing, but also hair styles, accessories, jewelry, make-up, and body decoration. Theoretically at least this vocabulary is as large as or larger than that of any spoken tongue, since it includes every garment, hair style, and type of body decoration ever invented. In practice, of course, the sartorial resources of an individual may be very restricted. Those of a sharecropper, for instance, may be limited to five or ten "words" from which it is possible to create only a few "sentences" almost bare of decoration and expressing only the most basic concepts. A so-called fashion leader, on the other hand, may have several hundred "words" at his or her disposal, and thus be able to form thousands of different "sentences" that will express a wide range of meanings. Just as the average English-speaking person knows many more words than he or she will ever use in conversation, so all of us are able to understand the meaning of styles we will never wear.

To choose clothes, either in a store or at home, is to define and describe ourselves. Occasionally, of course, practical considerations enter into these choices: considerations of comfort, durability, availability, and price. Especially in the case of persons of limited wardrobe, an article may be worn because it is warm or rainproof or handy to cover up a wet bathing suit — in the same way that persons of limited vocabulary use the phrase "you know" or adjectives such as "great" or "fantastic." Yet, just as with spoken language, such choices usually give us some information, even if it is only equivalent to the statement "I don't give a damn what I look like today." And there are limits even here. In this culture, like many others, certain garments are taboo for certain persons. Most men, however cold or wet they might be, would not put on a woman's dress, just as they would not use words and phrases such as "simply marvelous," which in this culture are considered specifically feminine.

Besides containing "words" that are taboo, the language of clothes, like speech, also includes modern and ancient words, words of native and foreign origin, dialect words, colloquialisms, slang, and vulgarities. Genuine articles of clothing from the past (or skillful imitations) are used in the same way a writer or speaker might use archaisms: to give an air of culture, erudition, or wit. Just as in educated discourse, such "words" are usually employed sparingly, most often one at a time — a single Victorian cameo or a pair of 1940s platform shoes or an Edwardian velvet waistcoat, never a complete costume. A whole outfit composed of archaic items from a single period, rather than projecting elegance and sophistication, will imply that

4

one is on one's way to a masquerade, acting in a play or film, or putting oneself on display for advertising purposes. Mixing garments from several different periods of the past, on the other hand, suggests a confused but intriguingly "original" theatrical personality. It is therefore often fashionable in those sections of the art and entertainment industry in which instant celebrities are manufactured and sold.

When using archaic words, it is essential to choose ones that are decently old. The sight of a white plastic Courrèges miniraincoat and boots (in 1963 the height of fashion) at a gallery opening or theater today would produce the same shiver of ridicule and revulsion as the use of words such as "groovy," "Negro," or "self-actualizing."

In *Taste and Fashion,* one of the best books ever written on costume, the late James Laver proposed a timetable to explain such reactions; this has come to be known as Laver's Law. According to him, the same costume will be

Indecent	10 years before its time
Shameless	5 years before its time
Daring	1 year before its time
Smart	
Dowdy	1 year after its time
Hideous	10 years after its time
Ridiculous	20 years after its time
Amusing	30 years after its time
Quaint	50 years after its time
Charming	70 years after its time
Romantic	100 years after its time
Beautiful	150 years after its time

Laver possibly overemphasizes the shock value of incoming fashion, which today may be seen merely as weird or ugly. And of course he is speaking of the complete outfit, or "sentence." The speed with which a single "word" passes in and out of fashion can vary, just as in spoken and written languages.

The appearance of foreign garments in an otherwise indigenous costume is similar in function to the use of foreign words or phrases in standard English speech. This phenomenon, which is common in certain circles, may have several different meanings.

First, of course, it can be a deliberate sign of national origin in someone who otherwise, sartorially or linguistically speaking, has no accent. Often this message is expressed through headgear. The Japanese-American lady in Western dress but with an elaborate Oriental hairdo, or the Oxford-educated Arab who tops his Savile Row suit with a turban, are telling us graphically that they have not been psychologically assimilated; that their ideas and opinions remain those of an Asian. As a result we tend to see the non-European in Western dress with native headgear or hairdo as dignified, even formidable; while the reverse outfit — the Oriental lady in a kimono and a plastic rain hat, or the sheik in native robes and a black bowler — appears comic. Such costumes seem to announce that their wearers, though not physically at ease in our country, have their heads full of half-baked Western ideas. It would perhaps be well for Anglo-American tourists to keep this principle in mind when traveling to exotic places. Very possibly the members of a package tour in Mexican sombreros or Russian bearskin hats look equally ridiculous and weak-minded to the natives of the countries they are visiting.

More often the wearing of a single foreign garment, like the dropping of a foreign word or phrase in conversation, is meant not to advertise foreign origin or allegiance but to indicate sophistication. It can also be a means of advertising wealth. When we see a fancy Swiss watch, we know that its owner either bought it at home for three times the price of a good English or American watch, or else he or she spent even more money traveling to Switzerland.

Casual dress, like casual speech, tends to be loose, relaxed, and colorful. 12 It often contains what might be called "slang words": blue jeans, sneakers, baseball caps, aprons, flowered cotton housedresses, and the like. These garments could not be worn on a formal occasion without causing disapproval, but in ordinary circumstances they pass without remark. "Vulgar words" in dress, on the other hand, give emphasis and get immediate attention in almost any circumstances, just as they do in speech. Only the skillful can employ them without some loss of face, and even then they must be used in the right way. A torn, unbuttoned shirt, or wildly uncombed hair, can signify strong emotions: passions, grief, rage, despair. They are most effective if people already think of you as being neatly dressed, just as the curses of well-spoken persons count for more than those of the customarily foul-mouthed.

Items of dress that are the sartorial equivalent of forbidden words have more impact when they appear seldom and as if by accident. The Edwardian lady, lifting her heavy floor-length skirt to board a train, appeared unaware that she was revealing a froth of lacy petticoats and embroidered black stockings. Similarly, today's braless executive woman, leaning over her desk at a conference, may affect not to know that her nipples show through her silk blouse. Perhaps she does not know it consciously; we are here in the ambiguous region of intention vs. interpretation which has given so much trouble to linguists.

In speech, slang terms and vulgarities may eventually become respectable dictionary words; the same thing is true of colloquial and vulgar fashions. Garments or styles that enter the fashionable vocabulary from a colloquial source usually have a longer life span than those that begin as vulgarities. Thigh-high patent leather boots, first worn by the most obvious variety of rentable female as a sign that she was willing to help act out certain male fantasies, shot with relative speed into and out of high fashion; while blue jeans made their way upward much more gradually from work clothes to casual to business and formal wear, and are still engaged in a slow descent.

Though the idea is attractive, it does not seem possible to equate different articles of clothing with the different parts of speech. A case can be made, however, for considering trimmings and accessories as adjectives or adverbs — modifiers in the sentence that is the total outfit — but it must be remembered that one era's trimmings and accessories are another's essential parts of the costume. At one time shoes were actually fastened with buckles, and the buttons on the sleeves of a suit jacket were used to secure turned-up cuffs. Today such buttons, or the linked brass rods on a pair of Gucci shoes, are purely vestigial and have no useful function. If they are missing, however, the jacket or the shoes are felt to be damaged and unfit for wear.

Accessories, too, may be considered essential to an outfit. In the 1940s 16 and 1950s, for instance, a woman was not properly dressed unless she wore gloves. Emily Post, among many others, made this clear:

> Always wear gloves, of course, in church, and also on the street. A really smart woman wears them outdoors always, even in the country. Always wear gloves in a restaurant, in a theatre, when you go to lunch, or to a formal dinner, or to a dance. . . . A lady never takes off her gloves to shake hands, no matter when or where. . . . On formal occasions she should *put gloves on* to shake hands with a hostess or with her own guests.

If we consider only those accessories and trimmings that are currently optional, however, we may reasonably speak of them as modifiers. It then becomes possible to distinguish an elaborately decorated style of dress from a simple and plain one, whatever the period. As in speech, it is harder to communicate well in a highly decorated style, though when this is done successfully the result may be very impressive. A costume loaded with accessories and trimmings can easily appear cluttered, pretentious, or confusing. Very rarely the whole becomes greater than its many parts, and the total effect is luxurious, elegant, and often highly sensual.

As writers on costume have often pointed out, the average individual above the poverty line has many more clothes that he needs to cover his body, even allowing for washing and changes of weather. Moreover, we often discard garments that show little or no wear and purchase new ones. What is the reason for this? Some have claimed that it is all the result of brainwashing by commercial interests. But the conspiracy theory of fashion change — the idea that the adoption of new styles is simply the result of a plot by greedy designers and manufacturers and fashion editors — has, I think, less foundation than is generally believed. Certainly the fashion industry might like us to throw away all our clothes each year and buy a whole new wardrobe, but it has never been able to achieve this goal. For one thing, it is not that the public will wear anything suggested to it, nor has it ever been true. Ever since fashion became big business, designers have proposed a bewildering array of styles every season. A few of these have been selected or adapted by manufacturers for mass production, but only a certain proportion of them have caught on.

As James Laver has remarked, modes are but the reflection of the manners of the time; they are the mirror, not the original. Within the limits imposed by economics, clothes are acquired, used, and discarded just as words are, because they meet our needs and express our ideas and emotions. All the exhortations of experts on language cannot save outmoded terms of speech or persuade people to use new ones "correctly." In the same way, those garments that reflect what we are or want to be at the moment will be purchased and worn, and those that do not will not, however frantically they may be ballyhooed.

In the past, gifted artists of fashion from Worth to Mary Quant have 20 been able to make inspired guesses about what people will want their clothes to say each year. Today a few designers seem to have retained this ability, but many others have proved to be as hopelessly out of touch as designers in the American auto industry. The classic case is that of the maxiskirt, a style which made women look older and heavier and impeded their movements at a time (1969) when youth, slimness, and energy were at the height of their vogue. The maxiskirt was introduced with tremendous fanfare and not a little deception. Magazines and newspapers printed (sometimes perhaps unknowingly) photos of New York and London street scenes populated with hired models in long skirts disguised as passers-by, to give readers in Podunk and Lesser Puddleton the impression that the capitals had capitulated. But these strenuous efforts were in vain: the maxiskirt failed miserably, producing well-deserved financial disaster for its backers.

The fashion industry is no more able to preserve a style that men and women have decided to abandon than to introduce one they do not choose to accept. In America, for instance, huge advertising budgets and the wholehearted cooperation of magazines such as *Vogue* and *Esquire* have not been able to save the hat, which for centuries was an essential part of everyone's outdoor (and often of their indoor) costume. It survives now mainly as a utilitarian protection against weather, as part of ritual dress (at formal weddings, for example), or as a sign of age or individual eccentricity.

As with speech, the meaning of any costume depends on circumstances. It is not "spoken" in a vacuum, but at a specific place and time, any change in which may alter its meaning. Like the remark "Let's get on with this damn business," the two-piece tan business suit and boldly striped shirt and tie that signify energy and determination in the office will have quite another resonance at a funeral or picnic.

According to Irving Goffman, the concept of "proper dress" is totally dependent on situation. To wear the costume considered "proper" for a situation acts as a sign of involvement in it, and the person whose clothes do not conform to these standards is likely to be more or less subtly excluded from participation. When other signs of deep involvement are present, rules about proper dress may be waived. Persons who have just escaped from a fire or flood are not censured for wearing pajamas or having uncombed hair; someone bursting into a formal social occasion to announce important news is excused for being in jeans and T-shirt.

In language we distinguish between someone who speaks a sentence 24 well — clearly, and with confidence and dignity — and someone who speaks it badly. In dress too, manner is as important as matter, and in judging the meaning of any garment we will automatically consider whether it fits well or is too large or too small; whether it is old or new; and especially whether it is in good condition, slightly rumpled and soiled or crushed and filthy. Cleanliness may not always be next to godliness, but it is usually regarded as a sign of respectability or at least of self-respect. It is also a sign of status, since to be clean and neat always involves the expense of time and money.

In a few circles, of course, disregard for cleanliness has been considered a virtue. Saint Jerome's remark that "the purity of body and its garments means the impurity of the soul" inspired generations of unwashed and smelly hermits. In the sixties some hippies and mystics scorned overly clean and tidy dress as a sign of compromise with the Establishment and too great an attachment to the things of this world. There is also a more widespread rural and small-town dislike of the person whose clothes are too clean, slick, and smooth. He — or, less often, she — is suspected of being untrustworthy, a smoothie or a city slicker.

In general, however, to wear dirty, rumpled, or torn clothing is to invite scorn and condescension. This reaction is ancient; indeed it goes back beyond the dawn of humanity. In most species, a strange animal in poor condition — mangy, or with matted and muddy fur — is more likely to be attacked by other animals. In the same way, shabbily dressed people are more apt to be treated shabbily. A man in a clean, well-pressed suit who falls down in a central London or Manhattan street is likely to be helped up sooner than one in filthy tatters.

At certain times and places — a dark night, a deserted alley — dirt and rags, like mumbled or growled speech, may be alarming. In Dickens's *Great Expectations* they are part of the terror the boy Pip feels when he first sees the convict Magwitch in the graveyard: "A fearful man, all in coarse grey, with a great iron on his leg. A man with no hat, and with broken shoes, and with an old rag tied round his head."

A costume not only appears at a specific place and time, it must be "spoken" — that is, worn — by a specific person. Even a simple statement like "I want a drink" or a simple costume — shorts and T-shirt, for example — will have a very different aspect in association with a sixty-year-old man, a sixteen-year-old girl, and a six-year-old child. But age and sex are not the only variables to be considered. In judging a costume we will also take into account the physical attributes of the person who is wearing it, assessing him or her in terms of height, weight, posture, racial or ethnic type, and facial features and expression. The same outfit will look different on a person whose face and body we consider attractive and on one whom we think ugly. Of course, the idea of "attractiveness" itself is not only subjective, but subject to the historical and geographical vagaries of fashion, as Sir Kenneth Clark° has demonstrated in *The Nude*. In twentieth-century Britain and America, for instance, weight above the norm has been considered unattractive and felt to detract from dignity and status; as Emily Post put it in 1922, "The tendency of fat is to take away from one's gentility; therefore, any one inclined to be fat must be ultra conservative — in order to counteract the effect." The overweight person who does not follow this rule is in danger of appearing vulgar or even revolting. In Conrad's *Lord Jim* the shame of the corrupt Dutch captain is underlined by the fact that, though grossly fat, he wears orange-and-green-striped pajamas in public.

In dress as in language there is a possible range of expression from the most eccentric statement to the most conventional. At one end of the spectrum is the outfit of which the individual parts or "words" are highly incongruent, marking its wearer (if not on stage or involved in some natural disaster) as very peculiar or possibly deranged. Imagine for instance a

---

Sir Kenneth Clark (1903–1983), British art historian and author of *Civilisation,* a history of Western civilization made into a television series. *The Nude: A Study in Ideal Form* (1956) is a historical study of the nude form in art.

transparent sequined evening blouse over a dirty Victorian cotton petticoat and black rubber galoshes. (I have observed this getup in real life; it was worn to a lunch party at a famous Irish country house.) If the same costume were worn by a man, or if the usual grammatical order of the sentence were altered — one of the galoshes placed upside down on the head, for example — the effect of insanity would be even greater.

At the opposite end of the spectrum is that costume that is the equivalent of a cliché; it follows some established style in every particular and instantly establishes its wearer as a doctor, a debutante, a hippie, or a whore. Such outfits are not uncommon, for as two British sociologists have remarked, "Identification with and active participation in a social group always involves the human body and its adornment and clothing." The more significant any social role is for an individual, the more likely he or she is to dress for it. When two roles conflict, the costume will either reflect the more important one or it will combine them, sometimes with incongruous effects, as in the case of the secretary whose sober, efficient-looking dark suit only partly conceals a tight, bright, low-cut blouse.

The cliché outfit may in some cases become so standardized that it is spoken of as a "uniform": the pin-striped suit, bowler, and black umbrella of the London City man, for instance, or the blue jeans and T-shirts of high-school students. Usually, however, these costumes only look like uniforms to outsiders; peers will be aware of significant differences. The London businessman's tie will tell his associates where he went to school; the cut and fabric of his suit will allow them to guess at his income. High-school students, in a single glance, can distinguish new jeans from those that are fashionably worn, functionally or decoratively patched, or carelessly ragged; they grasp the fine distinctions of meaning conveyed by straight-leg, flared, boot-cut, and peg-top. When two pairs of jeans are identical to the naked eye a label handily affixed to the back pocket gives useful information, identifying the garment as expensive (so-called designer jeans) or discount-department-store. And even within the latter category there are distinctions: in our local junior high school, according to a native informant, "freaks always wear Lees, greasers wear Wranglers, and everyone else wears Levis."

Of course, to the careful observer all these students are only identical 32 below the waist; above it they may wear anything from a lumberjack shirt to a lace blouse. Grammatically, this costume seems to be a sign that in their lower or physical natures these persons are alike, however dissimilar they may be socially, intellectually, or aesthetically. If this is so, the opposite statement can be imagined — and was actually made by my own college classmates thirty years ago. During the daytime we wore identical baggy sweaters over a wide variety of slacks, plaid kilts, full cotton or straight tweed or slinky jersey skirts, ski pants, and Bermuda shorts. "We're all

nice coeds from the waist up; we think and talk alike," this costume proclaimed, "but as women we are infinitely various."

The extreme form of conventional dress is the costume totally determined by others: the uniform. No matter what sort of uniform it is —
military, civil, or religious; the outfit of a general, a postman, a nun, a
butler, a football player, or a waitress — to put on such livery is to give up
one's right to act as an individual — in terms of speech, to be partially or
wholly censored. What one does, as well as what one wears, will be
determined by external authorities — to a greater or lesser degree, depending upon whether one is, for example, a Trappist monk, or a boy scout.
The uniform acts as a sign that we should not or need not treat someone
as a human being, and that they need not and should not treat us as one.
It is no accident that people in uniform, rather than speaking to us honestly
and straightforwardly, often repeat mechanical lies. "It was a pleasure
having you on board," they say; "I cannot give you that information"; or
"The doctor will see you shortly."

Constant wearing of official costume can so transform someone that it
becomes difficult or impossible for him or her to react normally. Dr. Grantly,
the archdeacon in Anthony Trollope's *The Warden* (1855), is pious and
solemn even when alone with his wife: "'Tis only when he has exchanged
that ever-new shovel hat for a tasselled nightcap, and those shining black
habiliments for his accustomed *robe de nuit*, that Dr. Grantly talks, and
looks, and thinks like an ordinary man."

To take off a uniform is usually a relief, just as it is a relief to abandon
official speech; sometimes it is also a sign of defiance. When the schoolgirls
in Flannery O'Connor's story "A Temple of the Holy Ghost" come home
on holiday, she writes that "They came in the brown convent uniforms
they had to wear at Mount St. Scholastica but as soon as they opened their
suitcases, they took off the uniforms and put on red skirts and loud blouses.
They put on lipstick and their Sunday shoes and walked around in the
high heels all over the house."

In certain circumstances, however, putting on a uniform may be a relief, 36
or even an agreeable experience. It can ease the transition from one role to
another, as Anthony Powell points out in *Faces in My Time* when he describes joining the British Army in 1939:

> Complete forgetfulness was needed of all that had constituted
> one's life only a few weeks before. This condition of mind
> was helped by the anonymity of uniform, something which
> has to be experienced to be appreciated; in one sense more
> noticeable off duty in such environments as railway carriages
> or bars.

It is also true that both physical and psychological disadvantage can be concealed by a uniform, or even canceled out; the robes of a judge or a surgeon may successfully hide a scrawny physique or fears of incompetence, giving him or her both dignity and confidence.

Unlike most civilian clothing, the uniform is often consciously and deliberately symbolic. It identifies its wearer as a member of some group and often locates him or her within a hierarchy; sometimes it gives information about his or her achievements, as do the merit badges of a scout and the battle ribbons of a general. Even when some details of an official costume are not dictated from above, they may by custom come to have a definite meaning. James Laver remarks that in Britain

> until quite recently it was still possible to deduce a clergyman's religious opinions from his neckwear. If you wore an ordinary collar with a white tie you were probably Low Church and Evangelical. If you wore any version of the Roman collar you displayed your sympathy with the . . . Oxford Movement.

It is likely that when they were first designed all uniforms made symbolic sense and were as easy to "read" as the outfit of a *Playboy* Bunny today. But official costume tends to freeze the styles of the time in which it was invented, and today the sixteenth-century uniforms of the guards at the Tower of London or the late-Edwardian morning dress of the butler may merely seem old-fashioned to us. Military uniforms, as James Laver points out, were originally intended "to impress and even to terrify the enemy" in hand-to-hand combat (just like the war whoops and battle cries that accompanied them), and warriors accordingly disguised themselves as devils, skeletons, and wild beasts. Even after gunpowder made this style of fighting rare, the desire to terrify "survived into modern times in such vestigial forms as the death's head on the hussar's headgear and the bare ribs of the skeleton originally painted on the warrior's body and later transformed into the froggings of his tunic."

The wearing of a uniform by people who are obviously not carrying out the duties it involves has often suggested personal laxity — as in the case of drunken soldiers carousing in the streets. In this century, however, it has been adopted as a form of political protest, and both men and women have appeared at rallies and marches in their Army, Navy, or police uniforms, the implied statement being "I'm a soldier, but I support disarmament/open housing/gay rights," etc. A related development in the 1960s was the American hippie custom of wearing parts of old Army uniforms — Civil War, World War I, and World War II. This military garb puzzled many observers, especially when it appeared in anti-Vietnam demonstrations. Others understood the implicit message, which was that the longhaired kid in the Confederate tunic or the Eisenhower jacket was not some kind of coward or sissy; that he was not against all wars — just against the cruel and unnecessary one he was in danger of being drafted into.

Between cliché and madness in the language of dress are all the known 40 varieties of speech: eloquence, wit, information, irony, propaganda, humor, pathos, and even (though rarely) true poetry. Just as a gifted writer combines unexpected words and images, risking (and sometimes briefly gaining) the reputation of being deranged, so certain gifted persons have been able to combine odd items of clothing, old and new, native and foreign, into a brilliant eloquence of personal statement. While other people merely follow the style of the age in which they live, these men and women transform contemporary fashion into individual expression. Some of their achievements are celebrated in the history of costume, but here, as in all the arts, there must be many unknown geniuses.

Unfortunately, just as there are more no-talent artists than there are geniuses, there are also many persons who do not dress very well, not because of lack of money but because of innate lack of taste. In some cases their clothes are merely monotonous, suggesting an uninteresting but consistent personality. Others seem to have a knack for combining colors, patterns, and styles in a way that — rightly or wrongly — suggests personal awkwardness and disharmony. In Henry James's *The Bostonians* (1886), the bad taste in clothes of the heroine, Verena Tarrant, foreshadows her moral confusion and her bad taste in men. Verena, who has bright-red hair, makes her first public appearance wearing "a light-brown dress, of a shape that struck [Basil Ransom] as fantastic, a yellow petticoat, and a large crimson sash fastened at the side; while round her neck, and falling low upon her flat young chest she had a double chain of amber beads." And, as if this were not enough, Verena also carried "a large red fan, which she kept constantly in movement."

Like any elaborate nonverbal language, costume is sometimes more eloquent than the native speech of its wearers. Indeed, the more inarticulate someone is verbally, the more important are the statements made by his or her clothes. People who are skilled in verbal discourse, on the other hand, can afford to be somewhat careless or dull in their dress, as in the case of certain teachers and politicians. Even they, of course, are telling us something, but they may not be telling us very much.

Men and women in uniform are not the only ones who wear clothes they have not selected themselves. All of us were first dressed in such garments, and often our late childhood and early adolescence were made stormy by our struggles to choose our own wardrobe — in verbal terms, to speak for ourselves. A few of us did not win this battle, or won only temporarily, and became those men (or, more rarely, women) most of whose clothes are selected by their wives, husbands, or mothers.

All of us, however, even as adults, have at some time been the grateful 44 or ungrateful recipients of garments bought by relatives or friends. Such a gift is a mixed blessing, for to wear clothes chosen by someone else is to accept and project their donor's image of you; in a sense, to become a ventriloquist's doll. Sometimes, of course, the gift may be welcome or flattering: the Christmas tie that is just right, the low-cut lace nightgown that encourages a woman of only moderate attractions to think of herself as a glamourpuss. Often, however, the gift is felt as a demand, and one harder to refuse because it comes disguised as a favor. When I was first married I dressed in a style that might be described as Radcliffe Beatnik (black jerseys and bright cotton-print skirts). My mother-in-law, hoping to remodel me into a nice country-club young matron, frequently presented me with tiny-collared, classically styled silk blouses and cashmere sweaters in white, beige, or pale green which I never wore and could not give away because they were monogrammed.

To put on someone else's clothes is symbolically to take on their personality. This is true even when one's motives are hostile. In Dickens's *Our Mutual Friend* (1864–65), the teacher Bradley Headstone disguises himself in "rough waterside second-hand clothing" and a "red neckerchief stained black . . . by wear" which are identical with those worn by Rogue Riderhood, so that Riderhood shall be blamed for the murder Headstone is planning to commit. In assuming this costume Headstone literally becomes just such a low, vicious, and guilty man as Riderhood.

In this culture the innocent exchange of clothing is most common among teenage girls, who in this way confirm not only their friendship but their identity, just as they do by using the same slang and expressing the same ideas. The custom may persist into adult life, and also occurs between lovers and between husband and wife, though in the latter case the borrowing is usually one-way. The sharing of clothes is always a strong indication of shared tastes, opinions, and even personality. Next time you are at a large party, meeting, or public event, look around the room and ask yourself if there is anyone present whose clothes you would be willing to wear yourself on that occasion. If so, he or she is apt to be a soul mate.

Perhaps the most difficult aspect of sartorial communication is the fact that any language that is able to convey information can also be used to convey misinformation. You can lie in the language of dress just as you can in English, French, or Latin, and this sort of deception has the advantage that one cannot usually be accused of doing it deliberately. The costume that suggests youth or wealth, unlike the statement that one is twenty-nine years old and has a six-figure income, cannot be directly challenged or disproved.

A sartorial lie may be white, like Cinderella's ball gowns; it may be various shades of gray, or it may be downright black, as in the case of the radical-hippie disguise of the FBI informant or the stolen military uniform of the spy. The lie may be voluntary, or it may be involuntary, as when a tomboy is forced into a velvet party dress by her parents. It may even be unconscious, as with the man who innocently wears a leather vest and boots to a bar patronized by homosexuals, or the American lady touring Scotland in a plaid she thought looked awfully pretty in the shop, but to which she has no hereditary right. If a complete grammar of clothing is ever written it will have to deal not only with these forms of dishonesty, but with many others that face linguists and semioticians:° ambiguity, error, self-deception, misinterpretation, irony, and framing.

Theatrical dress, or costume in the colloquial sense, is a special case of sartorial deception, one in which the audience willingly cooperates, recognizing that the clothes the actor wears, like the words he speaks, are not his own. Sometimes, however, what is only a temporary disguise for an actor becomes part of the everyday wardrobe of some members of the public. Popular culture, which has done so much to homogenize our life, has at the same time, almost paradoxically, helped to preserve and even to invent distinctive dress through a kind of feedback process. It is convenient for producers of films, TV programs, and commercials that clothes should instantly and clearly indicate age, class, regional origin, and if possible occupation and personality. Imagine that a certain costume is assigned to an actor representing a tough, handsome young auto mechanic, by a costume designer who has seen something like it in a local bar. Actual auto mechanics, viewing the program and others like it, unconsciously accept this outfit as characteristic; they are imitated by others who have not even seen the program. Finally the outfit becomes standard, and thus genuine.

Somewhere between theatrical costume and the uniform is ritual dress, the special clothing we adopt for the important ceremonies of our life: birth (the christening robe), college graduation, weddings, funerals, and other portentous occasions that also tend to involve ritual speech.

A more ambiguous sort of disguise is the costume that is deliberately chosen on the advice of others in order to deceive the beholder. For over a hundred years books and magazines have been busy translating the correct language of fashion, telling men and women what they should wear to

---

semioticians Philosophers who deal with the functions of signs and symbols in language.

seem genteel, rich, sophisticated, and attractive to the other sex. Journals addressed to what used to be called "the career girl" advised her how to dress to attract "the right kind of man" — successful, marriage-minded. Regardless of the current fashion, a discreet femininity was always recommended: soft fabrics and colors, flowers and ruffles in modest profusion, hair slightly longer and curlier than that of the other girls in the office. The costume must be neither too stylish (suggesting expense to the future husband) nor dowdy (suggesting boredom). Above all, a delicate balance must be struck between the prim and the seductive, one tending not to attract men and the other to attract the wrong kind. Times have changed somewhat, and the fashion pages of magazines such as *Cosmopolitan* now seem to specialize in telling the career girl what to wear to charm the particular wrong type of man who reads *Playboy,* while the editorial pages tell her how to cope with the resulting psychic damage.

Two recent paperbacks, *Dress for Success* and *The Woman's Dress for* 52 *Success Book,* by John T. Molloy, instruct businessmen and women on how to select their clothes so that they will look efficient, authoritative, and reliable even when they are incompetent, weak, and shifty. Molloy, who is by no means unintelligent, claims that his "wardrobe engineering" is based on scientific research and opinion polls. Also, in a departure from tradition, he is interested in telling women how to get promoted, not how to get married. The secret, apparently, is to wear an expensive but conventional "skirted suit" in medium gray or navy wool with a modestly cut blouse. No sweaters, no pants, no very bright colors, no cleavage, no long or excessively curly hair.

Anyone interested in scenic variety must hope that Molloy is mistaken; but my own opinion-polling, unfortunately, back him up. A fast-rising lady executive in a local bank reports to me — reluctantly — that "Suits do help separate the women from the girls — provided the women can tolerate the separation, which is another question altogether."

We put on clothing for some of the same reasons that we speak: to make living and working easier and more comfortable, to proclaim (or disguise) our identities, and to attract erotic attention. James Laver has designated these motives as the Utility Principle, the Hierarchical Principle, and the Seduction Principle. Anyone who has recently been to a large party or professional meeting will recall that most of the conversation that was not directed to practical ends ("Where are the drinks?" "Here is the agenda for this afternoon") was principally motivated by the Hierarchical or the Seduction Principle. In the same way, the clothes worn on that occasion, as well as more or less sheltering the nakedness of those present, were chosen to indicate their wearer's place in the world and/or to make him or her look more attractive.

The earliest utilitarian clothing was probably makeshift. Faced with extremes of climate — icy winters, drenching rainstorms, or the baking heat of the sun — men and women slung or tied the skins of animals around themselves; they fastened broad leaves to their heads as simple rain hats and made crude sandals from strips of hide or bark, as primitive tribes do today. Such protective clothing has a long history, but it has never acquired much prestige. The garment with a purely practical function is the glamourless equivalent of the flat, declarative sentence: "It's raining." "I'm working in the garden." But it is dificult, in costume as in speech, to make a truly simple statement. The pair of plain black rubbers which states that it is raining may also remark, "The streets are wet, and I can't afford to damage my shoes." If the streets are not in fact very wet, the rubbers may also declare silently, "This is a dull, timid, fussy person."

Sometimes, regardless of the weather, utility in itself is a minus quality. 56 The more water-repellent a raincoat is, ordinarily, the more it repels admiration — unless it is also fashionably colored or cut, or in some other way evidently expensive. Boots of molded synthetic leather that keep your feet warm and dry are thought to be less aesthetically pleasing than decorated leather ones which soon leak, and thus imply ownership of a car or familiarity with taxis.

Practical clothing usually seems most attractive when it is worn by persons who do not need it and probably never will need it. The spotless starched pinafore that covers a child's party dress or the striped overalls favored by some of today's college students look much more charming than they would on the housemaids and farmers for whom they were first intended.

This transformation of protective clothing into fashionable costume has a long history. As Rachel Kemper points out, the sort of garments that become fashionable most rapidly and most completely are those which were originally designed for warfare, dangerous work, or strenuous sports:

> Garments intended to deflect the point of a lance, flying arrows, or solar radiation possess a strange kind of instant chic and are sure to be modified into fashions for both men and women. Contemporary examples abound: the ubiquitous aviator glasses that line the rails of fashionable singles bars, perforated racing gloves that grip the wheels of sedate family cars, impressively complicated scuba divers' watches that will never be immersed in any body of water more challenging than the country-club pool.

Common sense and most historians of costume have assumed that the demands of either utility, status, or sex must have been responsible for the invention of clothing. However, as sometimes happens in human affairs, both common sense and the historians were apparently wrong: scholars have recently informed us that the original purpose of clothing was magical. Archaeologists digging up past civilizations and anthropologists studying primitive tribes have come to the conclusion that, as Rachel Kemper puts it, "Paint, ornament, and rudimentary clothing were first employed to attract good animistic powers and to ward off evil." When Charles Darwin visited Tierra del Fuego, a cold, wet, disagreeable land plagued by constant winds, he found the natives naked except for feathers in their hair and symbolic designs painted on their bodies. Modern Australian bushmen, who may spend hours decorating themselves and their relatives with patterns in colored clay, often wear nothing else but an amulet or two.

However skimpy it may be, primitive dress almost everywhere, like 60 primitive speech, is full of magic. A necklace of shark's teeth or a girdle of cowrie shells or feathers serves the same purpose as a prayer or spell, and may magically replace — or more often supplement — a spoken charm. In the first instance a form of *contagious* magic is at work: the shark's teeth are believed to endow their wearer with the qualities of a fierce and successful fisherman. The cowrie shells, on the other hand, work through *sympathetic* magic: since they resemble the female sexual parts, they are thought to increase or preserve fertility.

In civilized society today belief in the supernatural powers of clothing — like belief in prayers, spells, and charms — remains widespread, though we denigrate it with the name "superstition." Advertisements announce that improbable and romantic events will follow the application of a particular sort of grease to our faces, hair, or bodies; they claim that members of the opposite (or our own) sex will be drawn to us by the smell of a particular soap. Nobody believes those ads, you may say. Maybe not, but we behave as though we did: look in your bathroom cabinet.

The supernatural garments of European folk tales — the seven-league boots, the cloaks of invisibility, and the magic rings — are not forgotten, merely transformed, so that today we have the track star who can only win a race in a particular hat or shoes, the plain-clothes cop who feels no one can see him in his raincoat, and the wife who takes off her wedding ring before going to a motel with her lover. Amulets also remain very popular: circlets of elephant hair for strength and long life, copper bracelets as a charm against arthritis. In both cases what is operating is a form of magical thinking like that of the Australian aborigine: Elephants are strong and long-lived; if we constantly rub ourselves with their hair we may acquire these qualities. Copper conducts electricity, therefore it will conduct nerve impulses to cramped and unresponsive muscles, either by primitive contagious magic as with the elephant-hair bracelet, or by the modern contagious magic of pseudoscience: the copper "attracting and concentrating free-floating electrons," as a believer explained it to me.

Sympathethic or symbolic magic is also often employed, as when we hang crosses, stars, or one of the current symbols of female power and solidarity around our necks, thus silently involving the protection of Jesus, Jehovah, or Astarte. Such amulets, of course, may be worn to announce our allegiance to some faith or cause rather than as a charm. Or they may serve both purposes simultaneously — or sequentially. The crucifix concealed below the parochial-school uniform speaks only to God until some devilish human force persuades its wearer to remove his or her clothes; then it acts — or fails to act — as a warning against sin as well as a protective talisman.

Articles of clothing, too, may be treated as if they had mana, the impersonal supernatural force that tends to concentrate itself in objects. When I was in college it was common to wear a particular "lucky" sweater, shirt, or hat to final examinations, and this practice continues today. Here it is usually contagious magic that is at work: the chosen garment has become lucky by being worn on the occasion of some earlier success, or has been given to its owner by some favored person. The wearing of such magical garments is especially common in sports, where they are often publicly credited with bringing their owners luck. Their loss or abandonment is thought to cause injury as well as defeat. Actors also believe ardently in the magic of clothes, possibly because they are so familiar with the near-magical transforming power of theatrical costume. 64

Sometimes the lucky garment is believed to be even more fortunate when it is put on backwards or inside out. There may be different explanations of this belief. A student of my acquaintance, whose faded lucky sweat shirt bears the name of her high-school swimming team, suggests that reversing the garment places the printed side against her body, thus allowing the mana to work on her more directly.

Ordinarily, nonmagical clothes may also be worn inside out or reversed for magical reasons. The custom of turning your apron to change your luck after a series of household mishaps is widely known in both Britain and America; I have seen it done myself in upstate New York. Gamblers today sometimes turn their clothes before commencing play, and the practice was even more common in the past. The eighteenth-century British statesman Charles James Fox often sat at the gaming tables all night long with his coat turned inside out and his face blackened to propitiate the goddess of chance. Or perhaps to disguise himself from her; according to folk tradition, the usual explanation for the turning of garments is that it confuses demons. In blackface and with the elegant trimmings of his dress coat hidden, Fox was invisible to Lady Luck; the evil spirits that haunt housewives fail to recognize their intended victims and fly on to torment someone else.

At the other extreme from clothing which brings good luck and success is the garment of ill-omen. The most common and harmless version of this is the dress, suit, or shirt which (like some children) seems to attract or even to seek out dirt, grease, protruding nails, falling ketchup, and other hazards. Enid Nemy, who has written perceptively about such clothes for the New York *Times*, suggests that they may be lazy: "they'd just as soon rest on a hanger, or in a box — and they revolt when they're hauled into action." Or, she adds, they may be snobs, unwilling to associate with ordinary people. Whatever the cause, such accident-prone garments rarely if ever reform, and once one has been identified it is best to break off relations with it immediately. Otherwise, like accident-prone persons, it is apt to involve you in much inconvenience and possibly actual disaster, turning some important interview or romantic tryst into a scene of farce or humiliation. More sinister, and fortunately more rare, is the garment which seems to attract disasters to you rather than to itself. Ms. Nemy mentions an orange linen dress that apparently took a dislike to its owner, one Margaret Turner of Dover Publications. Orange clothes, as it happens, are likely to arouse hostility in our culture, but this dress seems to have been a special case. "Women friends seemed cattier, men seemed more aloof, and I'd get into bad situations with my boss," Ms. Turner reported. "And that wasn't all. I'd spill coffee, miss train connections, and the car would break down."

Even when our clothes are not invested with this sort of supernatural 68 power, they may have symbolic meanings that tend to increase with age. The man who comes home from work to discover that his wife has thrown out his shabby, stained tweed jacket or his old army pants is often much angrier than the situation seems to call for, and his anger may be mixed with depression and even fear. Not only has he lost a magical garment, he has been forced to see his spouse as in some real sense his enemy — as a person who wishes to deprive him of comfort and protection.

A pleasanter sort of magic occurs in the exchange of garments common among lovers. In the Middle Ages a lady would often give her kerchief or glove to a chosen knight. When he went into battle or fought in a tournament he would place it against his heart or pin it to his helmet. Today, probably because of the taboo against the wearing of female garments by men, the traffic is all one-way. The teenage girl wears her boyfriend's basketball jacket to school; the secretary who has spent the night impulsively and successfully at a friend's apartment goes home next morning with his London Fog raincoat over her disco outfit; and the wife, in a playful and affectionate mood, puts on her husband's red flannel pajama top. Often the woman feels so good and looks so well in the magical borrowed garment that it is never returned.

If the relationship sours, though, the exchange alters its meaning; the good spell becomes a curse. The magical article may be returned, often in poor condition: soiled or wrinkled, or with "accidental" cigarette burns. Or it may be deliberately destroyed: thrown in the trash, or even vindictively cut to shreds. An especially refined form of black magic is to give the garment away to the Salvation Army, in the hope that it will soon be worn by a drunken and incontinent bum — ideally, someplace where your former lover will see and recognize it.

As with the spoken language, communication through dress is easiest and least problematic when only one purpose is being served; when we wear a garment solely to keep warm, to attend a graduation ceremony, to announce our political views, to look sexy, or to protect ourselves from bad luck. Unfortunately, just as with speech, our motives in making any statement are apt to be double or multiple. The man who goes to buy a winter coat may simultaneously want it to shelter him from bad weather, look expensive and fashionable, announce that he is sophisticated and rugged, attract a certain sort of sexual partner, and magically infect him with the qualities of Robert Redford.

Naturally it is often impossible to satisfy all these requirements and make all these statements at once. Even if they do not contradict one another, the ideal garment of our fantasy may not be available in any of the stores we can get to, and if it is we may not be able to afford it. Therefore, just as with speech, it often happens that we cannot say what we really mean because we don't have the right "words." The woman who complains formulaically that she hasn't got anything to wear is in just this situation. Like a tourist abroad, she may be able to manage all right in shops and on trains, but she cannot go out to dinner, because her vocabulary is so limited that she would misrepresent herself and perhaps attract ridicule.

At present all these difficulties are compounded by contradictory messages about the value of dress in general. The Protestant ethic stressed modesty and simplicity of dress. Cleanliness was next to godliness, but finery and display were of the Devil, and the serious man or woman had no time for such folly. Even today to declare that one never pays much attention to what he or she is wearing is to claim virtue, and usually to receive respect. At the same time, however, we are told by advertisers and fashion experts that we must dress well and use cosmetics to, as they put it, liberate the "natural" beauty within. If we do not "take care of our looks" and "make the best of ourselves," we are scolded by our relatives and pitied by our friends. To juggle these conflicting demands is difficult and often exhausting.

When two or more wishes or demands conflict, a common psychological result is some disorder of expression. Indeed, one of the earliest theorists of dress, the psychologist J. D. Flügel, saw all human clothing as a neurotic

72

327

symptom. In his view, the irreconcilable emotions are modesty and the desire for attention:

> . . . our attitude towards clothes is *ab initio* "ambivalent," to use the invaluable term which has been introduced into psychology by the psychoanalysists; we are trying to satisfy two contradictory tendencies. . . . In this respect the discovery, or at any rate the use, of clothes, seems, in its psychological aspects, to resemble the process whereby a neurotic symptom is developed.

Flügel is considering only a single opposition; he does not even contemplate the neurotic confusion that can result when three or more motives are in conflict — as they often are. Given this state of things, we should not be surprised to find in the language of clothing the equivalent of many of the psychological disorders of speech. We will hear, or rather see, the repetitive stammer of the man who always wears the same jacket or pair of shoes whatever the climate or occasion; the childish lisp of the woman who clings to the frills and ribbons of her early youth; and those embarrassing lapses of the tongue — or rather of the garment — of which the classical examples are the unzipped fly and the slip that becomes a social error. We will also notice the signs of more temporary inner distress: the too-loud or harsh "voice" that exhausts our eye rather than our ear with glaring colors and clashing patterns, and the drab, colorless equivalent of the inability to speak above a whisper.

Dress is an aspect of human life that arouses strong feelings, some 76 intensely pleasant and others very disagreeable. It is no accident that many of our daydreams involve fine raiment; nor that one of the most common and disturbing human nightmares is of finding ourselves in public inappropriately and/or incompletely clothed.

For some people the daily task of choosing a costume is tedious, oppressive, or even frightening. Occasionally such people tell us that fashion is unnecessary; that in the ideal world of the future we will all wear some sort of identical jump suit — washable, waterproof, stretchable, temperature-controlled; timeless, ageless, and sexless. What a convenience, what a relief it will be, they say, never to worry about how to dress for a job interview, a romantic tryst, or a funeral!

Convenient perhaps, but not exactly a relief. Such a utopia would give most of us the same kind of chill we feel when a stadium full of Communist-bloc athletes in identical sports outfits, shouting slogans in unison, appears on TV. Most people do not want to be told what to wear any more than they want to be told what to say. In Belfast recently four hundred Irish Republican prisoners "refused to wear any clothes at all, draping themselves day and night in blankets," rather than put on prison uniforms. Even the offer of civilian-style dress did not satisfy them; they insisted on wearing their own clothes brought from home, or nothing. Fashion is free speech, and one of the privileges, if not always one of the pleasures, of a free world.

AFTERWORD

Lurie's title announces the analogy which her essay explores.

Logic tells us that analogy can be dangerous to clear thinking. When Plato wrote The Republic *he told us he constructed not a political system but an analogy to the human mind. This statement has not kept others from taking the analogy for the thing itself — and understanding* The Republic *as a model for republics. Oswald Spengler wrote* The Decline of the West *out of an analogy between political or cultural systems and living organisms. He begins by saying that civilizations are like organisms because each is born, grows mature, becomes old and feeble, and dies. Later he seems to argue in a circle, taking analogy as fact: Civilizations must die because, after all, they are organisms.*

Mostly we use analogy not as structure for a book or an essay but as an illustrative example incidental to exposition or argument. Remove the analogy and the house does not fall down, because analogy was not its foundation. Remove the analogy from Lurie and the house falls down. But who would want to remove the analogy? It works; it provides a continual, varying locus for witty and accurate observation. The secret of the long analogy is a comparison that can be sustained and that continually illuminates while it surprises.

BOOKS AVAILABLE IN PAPERBACK

Foreign Affairs. New York: Avon. *Novel.*

Imaginary Friends. New York: Avon. *Novel.*

The Language of Clothes. New York: Random House-Vintage. *Nonfiction.*

Love and Friendship. New York: Avon. *Novel.*

Nowhere City. New York: Avon. *Novel.*

Real People. New York: Avon. *Novel.*

JOHN
McPHEE

*J*OHN McPHEE *was born (1931) in Princeton, New Jersey, where he took his B.A. at the university and where he lives. He attended Cambridge University in England, wrote for television, worked on the staff of* Time, *and now writes regularly for the* New Yorker *magazine. His fist book was a profile of the Princeton University basketball player Bill Bradley, later a Rhodes scholar at Oxford, then a forward for the New York Knickerbockers, and now a U.S. senator from New Jersey. McPhee has written about the headmaster of a prep school, a desolate section of New Jersey, tennis, geology, Alaska, the Scottish Highlands, physics, and whitewater canoeing. His wide-ranging nonfiction books begin with* A Sense of Where You Are *(1965) and continue through many titles to his profile of the state of Alaska,* Coming into the Country *(1977), and recently a collection of miscellaneous pieces called* Table of Contents *(1985), which tells about bears, about doctors in rural family practice, about another John McPhee who is a bush pilot in Maine, about small hydroelectric plants, and about riding the boom extension.*

His work appeals to readers not because of his authority about a subject — like Lewis Thomas's in medicine and biology or John Kenneth Galbraith's in economics — but because readers trust him to collect ten thousand items of detail and to assemble this information into shapely paragraphs and impeccable sentences. Give him the materials of an improbable subject — oranges, pinball, birch bark canoes — and McPhee's carpentry will fashion a palace of pleasurable prose.

Headnotes about John McPhee are notoriously brief. Unlike most essayists (not only Dillard and Hoagland but Montaigne) McPhee enjoys remaining invisible and with few exceptions keeps his opinions to himself. There is not much to say about John McPhee; there is much to say about the books he signs with his name.

Riding the
Boom Extension

At the end of the day in slowly falling light a pickup truck with a camper rig came into Circle City, Alaska. It had a Texas license plate, and it drove to the edge of the Yukon River. Piled high on the roof were mining gear, camping gear, paddles, a boat, and a suction dredge big enough to suck the gold off almost anyone's capitol dome. To operate a suction dredge, swimmers move it from place to place on floats as it vacuums uncounted riches from the beds of streams. For the moment, though, no one was about to swim anywhere. In the gray of the evening, the Fahrenheit temperature was thirty-one degrees, smoke was blue above the cabins of the town, and the occupants of the pickup — having driven four thousand miles, the last hundred and twenty on an unpaved track through forests and over mountains — were not pausing long to stare at a firmly frozen river. May 4, 1980, 9 P.M., and the Yukon at Circle was white. The river had not yet so much as begun to turn gray, as it does when it nears breaking up.

There was a sign to read. "CIRCLE CITY, ESTABLISHED 1893. . . . MOST NORTHERN POINT ON CONNECTED AMERICAN HIGHWAY SYSTEM. . . . THE END OF THE ROAD." The new Dempster Highway, in Yukon Territory, runs a great deal farther north than this one, but the Dempster is in Canada and is therefore not American. The haul road that accompanies the Alyeska pipeline goes to and over the Brooks Range and quits at the edge of the Arctic Ocean, and if the haul road is ever opened to the public it will destroy Circle City's sign, but meanwhile the community maintains a certain focus on this moribund credential. Circle City was given its name in the mistaken belief that it was on the Arctic Circle, which is somewhere nearby. The town was established not as a gate to the Arctic, however, but as a result of the incontestable fact that it would stand beside the Yukon River. This was the trading port that supplied the Birch Creek mining district, which lies immediately to the south, and where the miners around the turn of the century working streams like Mammoth Creek and Mastodon Creek — in a country of mica schists and quartz intrusions, of sharp-peaked ridges, dendritic drainages, steep-walled valleys, and long flat spurs — washed out in their cleanups about a million ounces of gold. Circle was for a time the foremost settlement on the Yukon, and proclaimed itself "the largest log-cabin city in the world." It was served by woodburning stern-wheel steamers. They ran until the Second World War. In 1896, there were ten thousand miners out on the creeks of the district, with their small cabins, their caches. The resident population of Circle was twelve hundred, its all-time high. Works of Shakespeare were produced in the opera house. The town had a several-thousand-volume library, a clinic, a school, churches, music and dance halls, and so many whorehouses they may have outnumbered the saloons. A large percentage of these buildings have since fallen into the river. Circle is considerably smaller now and consists, in the main, of two rows of cabins, parallel to the Yukon and backed by a gravel airstrip. The center of commerce and industry includes the Yukon Trading Post ("SOUVENIRS, TIRE REPAIRS"), the Yukon Liquor Cache, and the Midnite Sun Cafe — names above three doors in one building. The cabins are inhabited by a few whites and for the most part by a group of Athapaskans who call themselves Danzhit Hanlaii, indicating that they live where the Yukon River comes out through mountains and begins its traverse of the vast savannas known as the Yukon Flats. Circle, Alaska 99733.

In a thousand miles of the upper Yukon, the largest vessel ever seen on the river in present times is the Brainstorm, a barge with a three-story white deckhouse, an orange hull; and on that chill May night a few weeks ago even the Brainstorm was disengaged from the river, and was far up on the bank, where it had been all winter, canting to one side in Circle City. To the suckers in their pickup from Texas, the appearance of the Brainstorm may have been one more suggestion that they had come a little early with their dredge. The pickup turned around, eventually, and moved slowly back into the forest.

If the arrival was untimely, the rig was nonetheless the first of a great 4 many like it that would come to the End of the Road in a summer of excited questing for gold. The price of one troy ounce had gone up so much over the winter that a new boom had come to a region whose economy has had no other history than booms. In Fairbanks, a hundred and sixty miles away, dealers in the goods of placer mining were selling their premises bare. Bulldozer parts were going like chicken livers — and whole bulldozers, too, many of them left over from the construction of the pipeline. Placer miners have recently discerned the hidden talents of AstroTurf. They use Astro-

Turf in sluice boxes — in much the way that the Greeks washed auriferous gravels over the unshorn hides of sheep. Gradually, the hides became extraordinarily heavy with arrested flecks of gold. They were burned to get the metal. What for the Greeks was Golden Fleece for us is AstroTurf. To be sure, the AstroTurf of Alaska is not the puny Easter-basket grass that skins the knees of Philadelphia Eagles. It is tough, tundric AstroTurf, with individualistic three-quarter-inch skookum green blades. In a cleanup, this advantageous material will yield its gold almost as readily as it has caught it. AstroTurf costs about four hundred dollars a roll. Sold out.

People from all over the Lower Forty-eight are fanning into the country north of Fairbanks. As they represent many states, they also represent many levels of competence. The new price of gold has penetrated deep into the human soul and has brought out the placer miner in the Tucson developer, the Denver lawyer, the carpenter of Knoxville, the sawyer of Ely, the merchant of Cleveland, the barber of Tenafly. Suction dredging is a small-time effort made by people without established claims, who move up and down streams sniping gold. The real earthmovers are the Cat miners, with their steel sluice boxes and their immense Caterpillar D8s and D9s. Some people named Green from Minnesota have shipped the family bulldozer to interior Alaska for five thousand five hundred dollars. There are a lot a new people in the country who know how to move gravel but will not necessarily know what to do with it when it moves. Whatever the level of their skills may be, the collective rush of suction dredgers and Cat miners is so numerous that, like the counterparts of the eighteen-nineties, most of them will inevitably go home with pockets innocent of gold. Gold is where you find it, though, and not all of it lies in the beds of creeks. Richard Hutchinson, who has been in the country for sixteen years, knows where the gold is now. He has struck it right here in Circle City.

Three years ago, Hutchinson went down to Fairbanks and returned with a telephone exchange in the back of his pickup. It had been in the Tanana Valley Clinic and was of a size that could deal with only about eighty individual lines, which had become too few for the expanding needs of the Tanana Valley Clinic but would be more than adequate for Circle City. Hutchinson prefers not to menion what he paid for it. He will say that he got it for "a song," but when asked he will not sing it. "The things is called a PABX. It was on its way to the dump. Luckily, I came along — the big boob at the right time. I got it for next to nothing." Hutchinson is a dust-kicking type, modest about himself and his accomplishments. He is big, yes, six feet one, and trim in form, with blue irises and blond hair, cut short in homage to the Marine Corps. But he is away from the mark when he calls himself a boob, as almost everyone in Circle will attest.

"He gave us lights."

"He gave us telephones."
8
"He did it all by himself."

Eight hours over the mountains he drove home with his PABX. A tall rectilinear box full of multicolored wires and wafery plates, it might have been a computer bought in an antique store in Pennsylvania. Hutchinson had no idea what its components were, what their purposes might be, or how to advance his new property into a state of operation. Remembering the extent of his knowledge of telephone technology at that time, he says, "I knew how to dial a number." There was a manual, but with its sequence charts and connecting schemes, its predetermined night answers and toll-diversion adapters, its spark-quench units and contact failures, the manual might as well have been for human sex. He had friends, though, who knew the system — telephone technicians and engineers, in Fairbanks, in Clear. They would give him his training, on the job. He emptied his tool shed and put the PABX in there. He strung wires. He sold subscriptions. In July, 1977, he opened his local service.

Carl Dasch was having none of it.

"Would you like a telephone, Carl?"
12
"No."

"A phone is a real convenience, Carl."

"When I say no, I don't mean yes."

Dasch, from Minnesota, has been in Alaska forty years and lives on a 16 pension from the First World War. He trapped for many seasons, and he used to take passengers on the river in his boat. He wears high black shoes and, as often as not, a black-and-red checkered heavy wool shirt. He has a full dark beard. He is solidly built, and looks much younger than his years. His cabin is small and is close to the river. "Why would I need a telephone? I can stand on the porch and yell at everyone here."

The village otherwise clamored for Hutchinson's phones. He soon had twenty subscribers. Albert Carroll, the on-again-off-again Indian chief, speaks for the whole tribe when he says, "I don't get out and holler the way we used to. I call from here to here. We stand in the window and look at each other and talk on the phone. I don't have to walk over next door and ask Anne Ginnis if she has a beer. I call her and tell her to bring it."

The wire cost Hutchinson a couple of thousand dollars. He already had the poles. In 1973, he bought a fifty-five-kilowatt generator and a seventy-five-kilowatt generator to bring light and power to the town. He went to Fairbanks and bought used telephone poles, which he set in holes he dug in frozen gravel, with an ice chisel, by hand. He strung his power line. "When I put it in, I couldn't wire a light fixture. It was comical." He sent away for *The Lineman's and Cableman's Handbook* and *The American Electrician's Handbook*. Before he was off page 1 he had almost everyone in town signed up for electricity. The only holdout was Carl Dasch. Soon there was a record-player in nearly every home. There would have been television everywhere, too, but television has yet to reach Circle City.

Hutchinson in his books learned how to install meters. His son, who is called Little Hutch, was five years old when the generators began to operate. He is now twelve and is the reader of the meters. A number of people in Circle have two Mr. Coffee coffeemakers, one for coffee and one for tea, which they brew in the manner of coffee. They have big freezers, in which king salmon are stacked like cordwood. Albert Carroll has at least three freezers, for his moose, ducks, fish, and geese. For four years, Carl Dasch observed all this without a kind word, but then one day he mentioned to Hutchinson that he wouldn't mind a little current after all. Hutchinson dropped whatever he was doing and went home for his wire, and Dasch was on line that day. Dasch has a small freezer, and a single forty-watt bulb that hangs from his cabin ceiling. With the capitulation of Carl Dasch, Hutchinson's electric monopoly became as complete as it ever could be, with a hundred per cent of the town subscribing.

At some point early in the history of the company, the thought occurred 20 to a number of customers that plugging in an electric heater would be, as one of them put it, "easier than going out and getting a log of wood." In various subtle ways, they brought heaters into Circle. They did not want Hutchinson to know. They did not understand the signficance of the numbers on his meters. Now there are not so many heaters in town. There are wringer-style electric washers but no dryers and no electric stoves, except at the school. The government and the pipeline are paying for the school. Hutchinson charges thirty-two cents a kilowatt hour for the first hundred kilowatt hours used each month, twenty-two cents through the second hundred, and seventeen cents after that — rates that are regulated by the Alaska Public Utilities Commission and are roughly double the rates in New Jersey. There are no complaints, and, according to one subscriber, complaints are unlikely from the present generation — "People remember what it was like to use kerosene lamps." In Hutchinson's electric-lighted home, an old Alaskan kerosene lamp is on display like a trophy: an instant antique, garlanded with plastic daisies.

For about a year and a half, the telephone customers of Circle Utilities, as Hutchinson has named his diversified company, had no one to call but themselves. That, however, was joy enough, and for five dollars a month they were on the telephone twenty-four hours a day, tattling, fighting, entertaining their neighbors. "It's almost like having TV," Hutchinson observed. "They're always on the phone, calling each other. Suddenly they can't live without it. A phone goes out and you ought to hear them squawk." From the beginning, he has been busy with his manual, practicing the art of repair. When conversations turn bellicose, people will rip phones off the wall. They shatter them on the floor. Albert Carroll, one winter night, opened the door of his wood stove and added his phone to the fire. Hutchinson makes cheerful rounds in his pickup, restoring service. The cost to him of a new telephone instrument is only twenty-eight dollars. He says, "Phones are cheap if you own the phone company."

At the end of 1978, RCA-Alascom and the Alaska Public Utilities Commission, the communications powers of Arctic America, completed a long series of discussions about Hutchinson, with the result that Circle City subscribers were let out of their closed circuit and into the telephone systems of the world. There is a white dish antenna outside the Circle City school, facing upward into the southeast toward a satellite in geosynchronous orbit more than twenty-two thousand miles high. When someone telephones a relative in Fort Yukon, which is the next town downriver (sixty miles), the call travels first to the dish antenna, and then up to the satellite, and then down to the Alascom earth station at Talkeetna (beyond the summits of the Alaska Range), and then back up to the satellite, and then down to Fort Yukon. The relative's voice reverses the caroms. The conversation travels ninety thousand miles in each direction, but the rate charge is reckoned by the flight of the crow: Circle City to Fort Yukon, forty-five cents for three minutes.

Alascom allows Hutchinson to keep about eighty per cent of the tolls. When someone at Alascom first acquainted Hutchinson with his nineteen-carat percentage, he could not believe what he was hearing.

"That's not right," he said.

"What? You want more?" said Alascom.

"No. That's too much," said Hutchinson.

And Alascom said, "Don't ever say it's too much."

Circle City people are running up phone bills above a hundred dollars a month, calling their kin in Fort Yukon. They call Metlakatla. They call Old Crow. They call Anchorage, Fairbanks, and Chalkyitsik. They call New York, Deadhorse, and San Jose. Albert Carroll's toll calls exceed fifteen hundred dollars a year. "When I'm drinking, I call my brothers in Fort Yukon and my sister in Florida," he says. "Before the telephone, I wrote letters. It took me two years to write a letter. Don't ever take the phone out of Circle City. It's our best resource." When it is suggested to the sometime chief that the dish antenna is drawing out of his pocket thousands of dollars that might otherwise be spent on something solider than words, he says, "Money is nothing. Easy come, easy go. I make good money trapping. I'm one-third partner in the Brainstorm."

Carroll is the captain of the Brainstorm. He goes to Black River, Coal Creek, Dawson, hauling diesel fuel and D8 Cats. He does not resemble

Lord Nelson.° He is short and sinewy, slight like a nail. With his dark felt eyebrows and black beard, his dark glasses and black visored cap, he is nearly illegible, but there is nothing enigmatic in his rapid flow of words. For the moment, he is not the chief. "Margaret Henry is the chief. But I'll straighten that out when I get good and ready," says Carroll. His wife, Alice Joseph, is the Health Aide in Circle, and school cook. "Her great-grandfather was Joe No. 6," he says, with evident pride. "I am Albert No. 1, you see — Albert Carroll Senior the First." The pelts of half a dozen ermine decorate their cabin wall. Hutchinson and Carroll used to trap together. Sometimes Hutchinson comes into Carroll's cabin, sees only one light on, and asks, "How am I going to make any money?" "He turns on every light there is, inside and out," Albert says. "If a bulb is missing, he'll go and get one."

Alice earns about fifteen thousand dollars a year. A doctor in Fairbanks calls her frequently to discuss the health of Circle. Last year, Albert trapped thirty lynx. A lynx skin was worth thirty-five dollars not long ago and was worth five hundred last year. Meanwhile, the State of Alaska has been making so much money from its one-eighth share of pipeline oil that the legislature is in a feeding frenzy. Pending court approval, Alaskans are to receive fifty dollars in 1980 for every year they have lived in Alaska since statehood. Alice and Albert Carroll will together get twenty-one hundred dollars. Next year, they will get twenty-two hundred, twenty-three hundred the year after that. The oil will last about twenty-five years. Easy come, easy go. The state will soon have a surplus in its treasury of nearly four billion dollars. It will cover many calls to Fort Yukon.

Circle is now a part of the Fairbanks and Vicinity Telephone Directory, wherein many businesses stand prepared to serve few people. There are five hundred yellow pages, a hundred white ones. The "vicinity" is about three hundred thousand square miles. It includes communities as far as six hundred miles from Fairbanks. One telephone book. One-tenth of the United States. Only eighteen towns are in the directory, because few villages have a Dick Hutchinson and telephones are little known in the bush. Circle, with its seventeen listings, is not the smallest community in the book. The Summit Telephone Company, of Cleary Summit, Alaska, lists seven subscribers. The Mukluk Telephone Company, an intercity conglomerate, has twenty-three listings in Teller (sixty miles north of Nome), thirty-two in Wales (on the Bering Strait), and fifty-six in Shishmaref (eighty miles

---

Lord Nelson Horatio Nelson (1758–1805), British naval hero whose fame rests on victories in the French Revolution and at Trafalgar.

up the coast from Wales). Up the Koyukuk, there are forty-one listed telephones in Bettles (Bettles Light & Power). Of course, there is no saying how many unlisted telephone numbers there might be in a given village. In Circle, there is one. Also, there are eight credit-card subscribers — trappers whose cabins are thirty, forty miles up the Yukon. They come into town and use other people's phones.

There is a shortwave transmitter in the Yukon Trading Post. People used 32 to come into the store and call Fairbanks, where they would be patched into the national telephone system. The charge was seven dollars and fifty cents to Fairbanks plus the toll from there. Hutchinson's rate charge for three minutes to Fairbanks is a dollar and ten cents. Two dollars and thirty-five cents to Anchorage. Of course, three minutes mean nothing to an Alaskan. They take three minutes just to say hello. When they talk, they talk. An encountered human being is like a good long read.

When the trappers come in from the country and appear over the riverbank, Hutchinson can be counted on to intercept them with their phone bills. Monthly statements are not mailed out in Circle. They are hand-delivered by Hutchinson in his Chevrolet pickup, a vehicle he starts with a hammer. In it is a gimballed cage in which a glass tumbler swings always level. Levi Ginnis, a hundred and ten dollars. Ruth Crow, a hundred and forty dollars. Albert Carroll, two hundred dollars. Helge Boquist's toll calls come to eight dollars and twenty-three cents. Helge is a Swede and he is married to an Athapaskan. Long since retired, he once worked Mastodon Creek. It is said that his Athapaskan relatives take advantage of his good nature, making free use of his telephone for long-distance calls. At eight dollars and twenty-three cents, he would seem to have the problem under control.

The Reverend Fred Vogel has a modest bill, too. Vogel is more or less a one-man denomination. He holds services in his cabin. The return address he send out with his mail is "Chapel Hill, Circle, Alaska." He has been in and out of Circle City for nearly thirty years. "He's all bent out of shape because the Episcopals give wine to kids during Communion," Hutchinson says. Once, when Vogel was off doing missionary work, he tried to close the Yukon Liquor Cache by mail from Liberia.

Calvary's Northern Lights Mission, of North Pole, Alaska, near Fairbanks, has a small outpost here in Circle — a young couple, who also have a low-toll phone bill. At its home base, the mission operates a fifty-thousand-watt radio station called KJNP — King Jesus North Pole. A great deal of bush communication is accomplished by a program called "Trapline Chatter" on KJNP — people announcing their travel plans and their babies, people asking favors or offering fragments of regional news, people begging and granting forgiveness. "Trapline Chatter" knits the lives of citizens of the bush, but its audience has declined in Circle City. As a result, Circle

City people are much less current with what is going on around the bush. What they know now is what has been said on their own telephones. And there are no party lines.

From time to time, a bill will become seriously overdue, the subscriber indefensibly delinquent. Hutchinson has yet to disconnect a phone. "I strap their lines," he says, which means that he takes a pair of pliers to the PABX and turns off their access to the satellite.

Gordon MacDonald's aggregate phone bill approaches five hundred dollars a month. He has two or three lines. Young and entrepreneurial, MacDonald and his wife, Lynne, own the Trading Post, the Liquor Cache, the Cafe, and a helicopter-and-fixed-wing flying service, which takes geologists into the country in a three-place Hiller for a hundred and fifty dollars an hour, or twice that in a five-place Hughes. MacDonald carries supplies to trappers in winter and to miners in summer. Hutchinson works for him as a part-time fixed-wing pilot. Certain trappers resist MacDonald, who has been in the country four years. They say that if he brings his geologists around their home streams they will open fire. "Just try that once" is MacDonald's response, "and a fifty-five-gallon drum filled with water will land on the roof of your cabin."

On billing days, Hutchinson does not call on Carl Dasch. Now and again, Hutchinson has renewed his attempts to sell Dasch a phone, but the prospect seems unlikely. "He knows it's no use," says Dasch. "I have no one to call." Living alone in his cabin, with his two rifles above his bed, Dasch has achieved a durable independence that he obviously enjoys. In the nineteen-seventies, Dasch's brother appeared one day in Circle. The two men had not seen each other in forty years. They had a pleasant conversation for fifteen or twenty minutes, and then Carl's brother went back down the road. The brother is dead now.

"This is a good country to get lost in if you want to get lost," says Carl.

"Yes, it is," Helge Boquist agrees. "One guy was lost here three months."

"That's a different kind of lost," says Carl Dasch.

Dasch went to Fairbanks last summer, and he has visited Anchorage. "Yes, I was in Anchorage just after the Second World War."

He has found much to interest him here in the country. He used to watch ornithologists from the Lower Forty-eight shooting peregrine falcons off the bluffs of the Yukon. "They were allowed to do this. It was a scientific deal. They wanted to see what the falcons had been eating. All they had to do was look at the bones in the nests to see what the falcons had been eating."

As advancing age increases his risks, would he not be reassured by having a telephone at hand?

"I'm a hard guy to convince. When I say no, I don't mean yes."

"What happens if you get sick, Carl?"

"If I get sick enough, I'll die, like everybody else."

Dasch's obstinance notwithstanding, Circle Utilities is in such robust 48
condition that Hutchinson has become deeply interested in the growth of
the town. This past school year, he was pleased to note five new first
graders. He referred to them as "future customers." Hutchinson is the town
welcome wagon. "Circle has plenty of capacity for expansion," he says. "I
think it could probably stand a hundred and fifty people and still be comfortable." The new census has amazed and gratified him. "The count was
eighty. That really surprised me. I thought there were sixty-five." To prepare himself for the demands of the future, he has bought a Pitman Polecat,
the classical truck of the telephone lineman, with a plastic bucket that can
lift him forty-one feet into the air and a big auger that can drill holes deep
in the ground. While Hutchinson is up in the bucket, Little Hutch is
operating the truck below, his hands flying to the levers of the pole-grabber,
the outriggers, the load line, the boom extension. It is Hutchinson's hope
that one day Little Hutch will inherit the place in the bucket.

Hutchinson's father was a Boston fireman, and Hutchinson grew up in
South Weymouth, Massachusetts, where he read a little less than he hunted
and fished. He learned offset printing in the Marine Corps, and had been
working for a job printer in Los Angeles when he first got into his pickup
and drove to Alaska. Unlike most people who experiment with Alaska, he
spent no time in Anchorage or Fairbanks but directly sought the country
of the upper Yukon. The year was 1964, and he was twenty-three. He lived
in the woods some miles from Circle. His adventure ended one day when,
just after killing a wolf, he tripped and accidentally shot himself in the leg.
After time in the hospital in Fairbanks, he went Outside to recover. It is a
measure of his affection for Alaska that he returned as soon as he could,
with intent to stay forever. He trapped from a cabin on Birch Creek and,
as the expression goes, made his groceries. He worked as "a flunky for a
biologist," live-trapping lynx, shooting them with tranquillizers, putting
radio collars around their necks, and then tracking their movements. He
worked in the Yukon Trading Post, and in Fairbanks printing *Jessen's Weekly*,
among other things, while assembling the capital to establish his utility.
His flight instruction was under the supervision of the late Don Jonz, who
was at the controls when the plane carrying Congressmen Hale Boggs and
Nick Begich disappeared over the Gulf of Alaska. Hutchinson has had a
commercial flying license since 1972. He also worked as a generator operator
on the construction of the Alyeska pipeline, making well over five thousand
dollars a month, at Franklin Bluffs and Prudhoe Bay, doing "seven twelves"
— twelve hours a day, seven days a week. Hutchinson's wife, Earla, thinks
more accurate translation of "seven twelves" would be "seven days a week,
twelve minutes a day," but Earla has the so-called work ethic deep in her
fabric. From Standish, Michigan, she came to Circle to teach in a Bible

school that was run by the Episcopal Church. The Hutchinsons have two children: Earl Francis (Little Hutch) and Krista, who is ten. For ten years, the family lived in a small cabin that had one bedroom. They now live in a handsome new house that stands eight feet in the air on steel poles like a giant cache. Last year, an ice jam on the Yukon at Circle backed up water until it went over the bank and flooded much of the town. The PABX telephone exchange stood boot-deep in water. So Hutchinson, later constructing his new home, backed the Pitman Polecat up to the site and planted his metallic stilts — ten feet into frozen ground. The house is all second floor — forty-two feet long, three bedrooms, galvanized roof. Temperatures in Circle reach seventy below zero. There's a foot of insulation in the elevated floor. Even the outhouse is raised off the ground on what appear to be short stilts. A chorus of sled dogs is chained in the yard.

Inside, Hutchinson sits back with a contented grin, a Calvert's-and-water. He listens to the static on his radio. "Music to my ears," he says. The static indicates that at least one long-distance telephone call is in progress in Circle City. It is an almost purring static. It stops when the parties hang up. The static caused by a local call is different. Local-call static is staccato, crackly, arrhythmic, and not particularly pleasing to Hutchinson's ears.

He wears a black-and-gold Ski-Doo cap, an elbow-patched canvas shirt, bluejeans, and L. L. Bean's shoepacs, which he calls "breakup boots." In his living room and kitchen, he is surrounded by mementos of life on the Yukon River: the locally obsolescent kerosene lantern, a wolverine pelt, a model of a log cabin (very much like the cabin the Hutchinsons lived in for so many years). There is a model dogsled and a model Yukon River fish wheel. A red fifty-five-gallon drum full of water stands beside the kitchen sink. It is the house water supply, and he fills it from a neighbor's well. There is a tall refrigerator-freezer, a microwave oven, an electric coffee-maker, an electric can opener, a toaster, a washing machine, an electric typewriter, an electric adding machine, and a Sears electric organ. Along a bookshelf are *Livingstone of the Arctic, Cultures of the North Pacific Coast, How to Select and Install Antennas, McGuffey's 5th Eclectic Reader*. Dick and Earla are partners in Circle Utilities, which earned for them about sixty-five thousand dollars last year. Earla now teaches in the public school. With her salary and his income from flying and trapping, their grand total has broken the six-digit barrier and gone into the proximate beyond. Hutchinson tugs apologetically at the visor of his Ski-Doo cap. He says, "Of course, that won't sound like much to people in the Lower Forty-eight."

Helge Boquist remembers that when he came here fifty years ago a 52 telephone line ran from Circle a hundred and sixty-five miles among miners out on the creeks. Galvanized wire went through the forest from tripod to tripod of spruce. It was an all-party line "with one long, three shorts, that sort of thing, a box on a wall with a crank," and everybody heard everybody else, from Circle to Ferry Roadhouse to Central to Miller House, and on Birch and Independence, Deadwood and Ketchum, Mammoth and Mastodon Creeks.

"Helge knows where gold still is," says Carl Dasch. "He should get a skookum young partner and go out there."

"Today, they get five hundred dollars for a teaspoonful of gold" is Boquist's comtemplative response. "And the old telephone wires that went out to the creeks are clotheslines now, here in Circle."

AFTERWORD

Twelve pages, fifty-four paragraphs. In some of his earlier work, John McPhee made paragraphs that were even longer — yet no one ever complains. His secret is the inventive fertility of his transitions. You always know where you are, like Bill Bradley on the basketball court. Short paragraphs give readers an excuse to let their attention wander. Lazy writers use short paragraphs when they know it's time to move from A to B but they don't know why or how. "Oh, well," they say, "I'll put in a paragraph, take a deep breath, and hope no one notices." McPhee on the other hand gently steers us, a touch on the elbow, from moment to moment through his crowded city square of detail and fact. Take any long paragraph by John McPhee — for instance, 2 or 49 — and look closely at the way he moves from point to point. He avoids obvious transitions; he plays the transition like a Stradivarius.

McPhee's essays are contemporary rather than classic. The old essay is opinionated, allusive, and subjective. McPhee satisfies the American or modern appetite for fact (instead of quotation from literature) and for detail, anecdote, and science (instead of opinion and reminiscence). His work is more like Time *or even the graphs and statistics of* USA Today *than it is like the old-fashioned Gretel Ehrlich or Samuel F. Pickering, Jr. Within this journalistic genre — the* New Yorker *calls such essays "fact pieces" —* John McPhee's *work is unique for the beauty of his prose.*

BOOKS AVAILABLE IN PAPERBACK

Annals of the Former World, 2 vols. New York: Farrar, Straus and Giroux. *Nonfiction.*

Basin and Range. New York: Farrar, Straus and Giroux. *Nonfiction.*

Coming into the Country. New York: Bantam. *Nonfiction.*

The Crofter and the Laird. New York: Farrar, Straus and Giroux. *Nonfiction.*

The Curve of Binding Energy: A Journey into the Awesome and Alarming World of Theodore B. Taylor. New York: Ballantine. *Nonfiction.*

The Deltoid Pumpkin Seed. New York: Farrar, Straus and Giroux. *Nonfiction.*

Encounters with the Archdruid. New York: Farrar, Straus and Giroux. *Nonfiction.*

Giving Good Weight. New York: Farrar, Straus and Giroux. *Nonfiction.*

The Headmaster: Frank L. Boyden of Deerfield. New York: Farrar, Straus and Giroux. *Nonfiction.*

Heirs of General Practice. New York: Farrar, Straus and Giroux. *Nonfiction.*

In Suspect Terrain. New York: Farrar, Straus and Giroux. *Nonfiction.*

The John McPhee Reader. New York: Farrar, Straus and Giroux. *Essays.*

Levels of the Game. New York: Farrar, Straus and Giroux. *Nonfiction.*

Oranges. New York: Farrar, Straus and Giroux. *Nonfiction.*

Pieces of the Frame. New York: Farrar, Straus and Giroux. *Nonfiction.*

The Pine Barrens. New York: Farrar, Straus and Giroux. *Nonfiction.*

La Place de la Concorde Suisse. New York: Farrar, Straus and Giroux. *Nonfiction.*

Riding the Boom Extension. Worcester: Metacom Press. *Nonfiction.*

Rising from the Plains. New York: Farrar, Straus and Giroux. *Nonfiction.*

A Roomful of Hovings and Other Profiles. New York: Farrar, Straus and Giroux. *Nonfiction.*

A Sense of Where You Are: A Profile of William Warren Bradley, 2nd ed., New York: Farrar, Straus and Giroux. *Nonfiction.*

The Survival of the Bark Canoe. New York: Farrar, Straus and Giroux. *Nonfiction.*

Table of Contents. New York: Farrar, Straus and Giroux. *Essays.*

JAN
MORRIS

*J*AN MORRIS *was born James Morris (1926) in Somerset, England, fought in World War II, graduated from Oxford University, fathered five children, and became a celebrated journalist at an early age, especially remembered for scooping Hillary and Tensing's ascent of Mount Everest in 1953.* Coronation Everest *(1958) followed, and then* The World of Venice *(1960) and* Cities *(1963). In 1964 James started to take hormone pills and in 1972 completed his transition into Jan by surgery. In her autobiography,* Conundrum *(1974), she remembered: "I was three or perhaps four years old when I realized that I had been born into the wrong body, and should really be a girl." As the most verbal of transsexuals, Jan Morris has much to say of this condition but in the end remains a conundrum.*

Her appearance altered — hair, skin, body contour — but prose style exists independent of secondary sexual characteristics. Jan Morris is prolific — somewhere she confesses to writing two thousand words a day; even with a five-day week, this makes more than half a million words a year — and her subjects range widely. She has written much about Islam, about Oxford, about the British Empire and the Victorian age, about Wales. But she followed Cities *with* Places *(1972), and it is*

as a travel writer, especially a reporter about cities, that Jan Morris is most known.
Manhattan *'45 (1987) is her most recent book. "City of* Yok" *appeared originally
in* Rolling Stone.

City of Yok
Istanbul, 1978

> In the late 1970s traditional Islam was enduring a period of violent
> discontent, powerfully affecting all the countries of the Middle East.
> Turkey, still largely Muslim, was no exception, and this portrait of
> Istanbul is colored by the sensations of unrest and uncertainty which
> dogged my explorations of old Byzantium.

The favorite epithet of Istanbul seems to be *yok*. I don't speak Turkish,
but *yok* appears to be a sort of general-purpose discouragement, to imply
that (for instance) it can't be done, she isn't home, the shop's shut, the
train's left, take it or leave it, you can't come this way, or there's no good
making a fuss about it, that's the way it is. *Yok* (at least in my interpretation)
is like *nyet* in Moscow, "Sorry luv" in London, or "Have a good day" in
New York. It expresses at once the good and the bad of Istanbul civic
philosophy: the bad, a certain prohibitive attitude to life, a lack of fizz or
obvious hopefulness, a forbidding fatalism, and an underlying sense of
menace; the good, an immense latent strength, an accumulated toughness
and stubbornness, which has enabled Istanbul to keep its personality intact,
if not its fabric, through 1,600 years of viciously variable fortune.

Istanbul is a traumatic kind of city. Standing as it does on the frontier
between Europe and Asia, it is like a man with a squint, looking east and
west at the same time; it is also a northern and a southern city, for immediately above it is the Black Sea, a cold Soviet lake, while almost in sight
to the south are the warm waters of the Mediterranean, waters of Homeric
myth and yearning.

Contemplating all this one evening, wondering about the meaning of
yok and looking at the famous view from a high vantage on Galata hill, I
found myself peculiarly disturbed by my thoughts. Morbid fancies assailed
me, and wherever I looked I seemed to see threatening images. Up the

Bosporus towards Russia, a mass of water traffic steamed or loitered between the green, villa-lined shores of the strait, but the ships did not have a cheerful air — they seemed balefully assembled, I thought, like a ragtag invasion fleet. To the south, the Sea of Marmara, which ought to have looked wine-dark and heroic, seemed instead bland, pallid, almost accusatory. Across the inlet of the Golden Horn the ridge of Stamboul, the original core of the city, was crowned in sunset with a splendid nimbus of domes, towers, and minarets, but its flanks of hills below seemed to be festering in the shadows, like a maggot heap beneath a throne.

I shook myself free of the obsession, and hurried down the hill for a   4
late tea; but *yok, yok, yok,* the birds seemed to be squawking, as they whirled beady-eyed above my head.

Istanbul leaves many of its visitors similarly unsettled, for it is not an easy place. It is one of the most obsessively fascinating of all cities, but indefinably deadening too; a gorgeous city, but unlovely; courteous, but chill. If you came to it by sea from the south, the classic way to come, you may sense these paradoxes almost from the start. The view from the Marmara is an unforgettable first prospect of a city, but its beauty is somehow unwelcoming. The tremendous skyline stands there, high above the sea, like a covey of watchtowers: one after another along the high Stamboul ridge, the pinnacles seem to be eyeing your approach suspiciously.

For Istanbul does possess, as you can feel from the deck of your ship, the arrogance of the very old: like the rudeness of an aged actor whose prime was long ago, whose powers have failed him, but who struts about still in cloak and carnationed buttonhole, snubbing his inferiors. Seen from the sea, Istanbul seems to be sneering from across the confluence of waters, the junction of the Marmara, Bosporus, and Golden Horn, which is its *raison d'être,* and all the caiques and motorboats and ferries seem to scuttle past it as though afraid of wounding comments.

It is only when you get closer that you realize the illusion of it, just as you observe, if he leans too close to you on the sofa, the creases of despair around the actor's mouth. Then that proud mass above the water dissolves into something crumblier and shabbier; the watchtowers lose some of their haughty command, the great sea wall of Stamboul is no more than a ruin, and it turns out that the passing boats are taking no notice of the city at all, but are simply impelled to and fro across the waterways, up and down the Golden Horn, zigzagging across the Bosporus, like so many mindless water insects.

For half the civilized world this was once *the* City, the ultimate —   8
Byzantium, Constantinople, the stronghold and repository of all that civilization had retrieved from the wreck of Rome. For the Turks it still is. It is no longer the political capital of Turkey, but it is much the greatest Turkish

city: the place where the money is made, the books are written, the place, above all, where the Turks see their own national character most faithfully mirrored or fulfilled. When I put myself into Istanbul's shoes that evening, I felt only some inkling of schizophrenia: when Turks do so, I am told, by immersing their imaginations in the history and spirit of the place, they feel most completely themselves.

I know of no other city that is so impregnated with a sense of fatefulness, and this is partly because few cities have been so important for so long. Constantine founded his capital, the New Rome, in A.D. 330, and there has not been a moment since when Istanbul was not conscious of its own mighty meaning. The successive dynasties that ruled the place competed with each other to proclaim its consequence. The Romans built their showy Hippodrome, adorning it with captured trophies and staging terrific chariot races beneath the golden horses of its tribune. The Greeks of Byzantium raised their marvelous cathedral, decorating it with precious frescoes and genuflecting in dazzling ritual before its jeweled reliquaries. The conquering Muslims of the Middle Ages commemorated themselves with mosques, schools, and caravanserais across the city, each larger, more pious, and more philanthropic than the last. The Ottomans built their vast Topkapi Palace, crammed with vulgar jewelry, where the ladies and eunuchs of the Seraglio gossiped life away in marble chambers, and the Sultans eyed their odalisques in exquisite pleasure kiosks above the sea. The mound of old Stamboul, the original Byzantium, is studded all over with monuments, so that every alleyway seems to lead to the courtyard of a stately mosque, a blackened obelisk or a triumphal column, a casket church of Byzantium, or at least a magnificent city wall.

But in between them all, under the walls, behind the churches, like a hideous carpet spreads the squalor of the centuries. It is as though these famous buildings were built upon a foundation of undisturbed muck — as though every scrap of rubbish, every gob of spittle, every bucket-load of ordure, has been stamped into the very substance of the place, never to be cleaned or scraped. When it rains, which it often does, the lanes are soon mucky: but it is not just mud that cakes your shoes, not plain earth lique-fied, but actually a glaucous composition of immemorial city excreta. The market streets of Istanbul are not exactly picturesque, if only because the citizenry is so drably dressed, in browns, grays, and grubby blacks, but they are vividly suggestive of unbroken continuity. The dark cluttered mass of the covered bazaars — the clamor of the market men — the agonizing jams of trucks, cars, horses and carts in the back-streets — the clatter of looms in half-derelict tenements — scuttling dogs and scavenging cats — bent-backed porters carrying beds or crates or carcasses — the click-clack of the man selling plastic clothes pegs, the toot-toot of the man selling wooden whistles, the ting-ting of the water seller with his tin cups —

listless detachment of coffee-shop men, oblivious over their cups and dominoes — stern, attention of policemen strutting through the shops — the shouts of itinerant greengrocers — the blare of pop music from the record stores — the glowering stone walls, the high towers above — the tumultuous odors of spice, coffee, raw meat, gasoline, sweat, mud — the sheer swell and flow and muddle of humanity there, seething through that urban labyrinth, makes one feel that nobody has ever left Istanbul, that nothing has ever been discarded, that every century has simply added its shambled quota to the uncountable whole, and made these streets a perpetual exhibition of what Istanbul was, is, and always will be.

Just as decomposing matter makes for fertile vegetation, so from the compost of Istanbul a timeless vigor emanates. Few cities move with such an intensity of effort, such straining virility. The generations of the dead are risen, to prod the living into life.

For yes, this is a vigor of the grave. These are bones rustling, and the 12 restless ferry-boats of Istanbul are so many funeral craft, carrying their complements of dead men to and fro between the railway stations. Though Istanbul is home to some three million souls, though its suburbs stretch far along the Marmara shore, deep into Thrace, up the Bosporus almost to the Black Sea, though there are few towns on earth so agitated and congested, still it sometimes feels like a tomb-city.

Of all the great Turkish despots, only Kemal Ataturk, the latest, rejected Constantinople as his capital. It was Ataturk who renamed the city Istanbul, and he had no sympathy, it seems, for its sedimented pride — he visited the city reluctantly during his years in office, though he died there in 1938. He was a futurist, a reformer, a secularist, and old Byzantium must have seemed the very negation of his aspirations. To this day Istanbul has never really absorbed his visionary ideas, or become a natural part of the Turkey he created.

Of course it has lost much of the Oriental quaintness that the great man so resented. No longer do the gaily skirted peasants swirl into the covered markets: gone are the tumbled wooden houses of tradition, and only a few of the old Ottoman love nests along the Bosporus, those tottering clapboard mansions that the romantic travelers used to relish, still stand frail and reproachful among the apartment blocks. Ring roads and flyovers have cut their statutory swaths through the slums and city ramparts. The obligatory international hotels ornament the best sites. Here and there one sees blighted enclaves of contemporary planning, blown by litter, stuck all over with peeling posters, invested with car parks and sad gardens.

But it is not really a modern city at all, not modern by taste or instinct, and it seems to reject transplants from our century. In the Municipal Museum (housed in a former mosque in the shadow of the Emperor Valens' great aqueduct) there is dimly displayed an American plan for a new bridge over the Golden Horn, with ceremonial approaches at either end. It is a lavish conception of spotless plazas and gigantic avenues, but it was doomed from the start, and survives only in an old brown frame upon a musty wall; even if it had been built, I do not doubt, long ago the mold of old Stamboul would have encroached upon its symmetries and rotted its high pretensions.

There can never be a fresh start in Istanbul. It is too late. Its successive 16 pasts are ineradicable and inescapable. I always stay at the Pera Palas Hotel on the Galata hill, almost the last of the old-school grand hotels to survive the invasion of the multinationals — a haven of potted plants, iron-cage elevators, ample baths with eagle feet. It has been halfheartedly modernized once or twice, but like Istanbul itself, it really ignores improvements and is settled complacently into its own florid heritage. My bedroom this time was Number 205, overlooking the Golden Horn. It was clean, fresh, and very comfortable — I love the hotel — but when, on my first morning, I lay flat on the floor to do my yoga, lo, from the deep recess beneath my double bed an authentic fragrance of the Ottomans reached me, dismissing the years and the vacuum cleaners alike: an antique smell of omelets and cigars, slightly sweetened with what I took to be attar of roses.

Something fibrous and stringy, like the inherited characteristics of a patrician clan, links the ages of Istanbul, and is as recognizable in its people today as a six-toed foot or albinism. For all its distracted air, in small matters at least Istanbul is a surprisingly reliable city. I never feel vulnerable to assault or robbery here, I seldom feel the need to check the bill, and even the most pestiferous of the local bravoes generally prove, if approached with sufficient firmness, dependable guides and advisers. *Yok* stands for rigidity, but for staunchness, too.

Istanbul has had to be staunch, to withstand the corrosions of time and retain its stature in the world. It has outlasted most of its rivals, after all, and generally wins its battles in the end. Scattered around Pera, the old foreigners' quarter of the city, are the former embassies of the powers, the nations of Europe that have periodically foreclosed Turkey as the bankrupt invalid of the Golden Horn. Nowadays, with the government in Ankara, they are mere consulates, but in their very postures you can still recognize the contempt with which their envoys and ambassadors, not so long ago, surveyed the pretensions of the Sublime Porte: the Russian embassy, like Tolstoy's estate behind its forecourt; the British a huge classical villa by the architect of the Houses of Parliament; the French with its private chapel in the garden; the Italian (once the Venetian) like a stately retreat upon the Brenta. They are still functioning, but they are half buried all the same in the debris of history, forlorn down messy cobbled alleyways or peering hangdog through their railings across the turmoil of the old Grand Rue.

Or take the Greek quarter across the Golden Horn. Here there stands the Patriarchate of the Greek Orthodox Church, the Vatican of Orthodox Christianity. Once it was an organization of immense power, attended by pilgrims and plenipotentiaries, surrounded by acolyte institutions, defying even the dominion of the Muslim caliphs down the road. Now it is pitifully diminished, an unobtrusive little enclave in a semi-slum, its ceremonial gateway symbolically painted black and welded shut forever: while on the hill behind it the huge Greek *lycée*, once aswarm with aspirants, now stands empty, shuttered, and despised.

Istanbul outlives all its challengers, reduced of course in worldly influ- 20 ence since the days of the Ottoman Empire, but hardly at all in self-esteem. Those powers and principalities have risen and fallen, some humiliated, some exalted, but the matter of Istanbul outlasts them all. This is a survivor city, essentially aloof to victory or defeat. The nearest a foreign enemy has come to assaulting Istanbul in our century was in 1915, when the armies of the Western alliance in the Great War, landing on the Gallipoli Peninsula some 150 miles to the south, tried to march north to the city. Supported by the guns of the most powerful battle fleet ever seen in the Mediterranean, they threw half a million of the world's finest infantry ashore on Turkish soil and expected to be at the Golden Horn within the month.

Though Istanbul was rigidly blockaded, though British and Australian submarines roamed the Marmara and bombarded the roads to the city, though a warship was torpedoed within sight of the sultan's palace, though the rumble of the battle shivered the minarets on the heights of Stamboul — still the enemy armies never advanced more than five miles from their beachheads.

Istanbul had said *yok*.

In theory this is a secular city, just as Turkey is a secular state. Ataturk decreed it so. In practice the voice of the muezzin rings out across the city, electronically amplified nowadays, almost as insistently as it did in the days of the caliphs, when this was the formal capital of all Islam. Like everything else in Istanbul, the faith proves irrepressible, and it remains the most potent single element, I suppose, in the personality of the place. I went one day to the Blue Mosque at the time of Friday prayers and positioned myself inside its great doorway — discreetly I hoped — to watch the faithful at their devotions. Not for long. A young man of distinctly unecumenical aspect rose from the back row of worshippers and approached me darkly. "Beat it," he said, and without a moment's hesitation, beat it I did.

The muezzin voices are voices from the glorious past, never silenced, 24 calling Istanbul always back again, home again to itself — back to the great days of the caliphs, the noble Ahmets, and the munificent Mehmets, back to the times when the princes of this city could build incomparable monuments of belief and generosity, high on their seven hills above the sea. Nobody has built in Istanbul like that since the end of the caliphate and its empire, just as nobody has given Istanbul a faith or a pride to call its own. Even the name of the place has lost its majesty. "Why did Constantinople get the works?" a popular song used to ask. "That's nobody's business but the Turks'": but the new name lacks the grand hubris of the old, and sends a *frisson*, I am afraid, down almost nobody's spine.

So many a patriot of this city looks back to Islam. The mosques are busy, the fanatics are aflame, regressive religion is one of the fiercest political movements in Istanbul. Though it used to be postulated that Turkish Islam, like capitalism, would wither away in time, the average age of that Blue Mosque congregation looked strikingly young to me. And though the veil has been officially forbidden for half a century now, women are going to the university these days with black scarves drawn pointedly around their faces. The activist Muslims of Istanbul look outside their own country for inspiration — to Iran, to Pakistan, to the Arab states, where militant Islam is on the march or already in power: and when they take to the streets, as they recently did, or engage in student skirmishes, or burn cars, or break windows, the newspapers are unable to define this heady amalgam of nostalgia and zealotry, and cautiously describe them as Idealists.

On the other side, now as always, are the leftists, by which the press means the heterogeneous mass of liberals, anarchists, hooligans, and real Communists, which roughly stands for change in an opposite direction. The longest graffito in the world is surely the one that somebody has painted along the whole expanse of the mole at the Kadiköy ferry station, containing in its message almost the entire idiom of the international Left, and leaving those with strong feelings about neo-Fascist hyenas with nothing much more to add. The leftists think of themselves as progressives, modernists, but they are really honoring a tradition older than Islam: for long before the caliphate was invented, the city crowd was a force in Byzantium. In those days the rival factions of the Blues and the Greens, originally supporters of competing charioteers in the Hippodrome, were infinitely more riotous than any soccer crowd today, and the great circuit of the racetrack, around whose purlieus the back-pack nomads now drink their mint tea in The Pub or the Pudding Shop, was the supreme arena of anarchy, the place where the frustration of the people found its ferocious release in bloodshed and insurrection.

Even now, I think, the quality of mercy is fairly strained in Istanbul, and the threat of public violence is always present. It is not so long since the mob, in its inherited and ineradicable suspicion of Greece, burned down half the covered bazaars of the city and destroyed everything Greek they could find. Step even now from a bus in Beyazit Square, on the Stamboul ridge, and you may find yourself looking straight down the gun barrel of a military patrol. Hang around long enough in Eminönü, by the waterfront, and you are sure to see somebody frog-marched off the scene by plain-clothes toughs or clapped into handcuffs by the implacable military police.

But you feel these antagonisms, this touch of the sinister, only so to speak by osmosis. The Turks are a courteous people, very kind to harmless strangers, and the ruthless side of their nature is generally masked. For that matter, nearly everything in Istanbul is blurred by its own congealment and decay. Cairo, Calcutta, Istanbul — these are the three great cities of the world where you may observe the prophecies of the doomwatch specialists apparently coming true. Chaos has not arrived yet, but it feels imminent enough. The ferry steamers seem to swirl around in a perpetual state of near collision. There is hardly room on the sidewalks for the press of people. Ever and again the city traffic, backed by some unseen mishap far away along the system, comes helplessly to a halt. The festering rubbish dumps of Stamboul seem to heave with incipient disease.

It has not happened yet. The ferry-boats generally evade each other in the end. The traffic does move again. The plague rats have not yet emerged from their garbage. But the suggestion is always there, the shadow of breakdown and anarchy: incubating, one feels, in the day-to-day confusion.

The sense of foreboding that characterizes Istanbul has a half-illusory quality, and seems to bewilder its citizens as it does its visitors. This is a city of theatrical hazards. Fires and earthquakes have periodically ravaged it. Empires have risen and fallen within its boundaries. There is a humped island called Yassiada, ten or so miles from Istanbul in the Marmara, which was pointed out to me one day as the place where Prime Minister Menderes was imprisoned after a military coup in 1960. It looked a nice enough place to me: a companionable little island, not at all remote, which looked as though it might have some agreeable bathing beaches. And what became of Menderes? I ignorantly asked my companion as our ship sailed by. "They killed him," he replied.

Now *that* hardly seemed real, on a blue and sunny day, on the deck of a pleasure-steamer, on a trip around the islands. Half fictional, half fact, a nebulous sense of menace informs the conversations of Istanbul. The foreign businessman has chill presentiments as he leans with his gin and tonic over his balcony by the Bosporus, watching a Russian cruise-ship sliding by, cabin lights ablaze and hammer-and-sickle floodlit, towards Odessa and the Motherland. "Something's going to happen. Something's going to crack . . . " The Turkish bank official, pausing didactically with your traveler's checks beneath his thumb, attributes the malaise to strategy. "Strategy is

the curse of Istanbul — it's where we live; we can never be left in peace."
The army colonel, over a drink at the Hilton, talks apocalyptically through
his mustache of conspiracies and conflicts. "I'll tell you quite frankly — and
the Americans know this well enough — the Greeks don't simply want
Cyprus for themselves, they don't simply want to make the Aegean a Greek
lake — *they want Istanbul itself!* They want to restore Byzantium!"

It is easy to feel perturbed in Istanbul. Every evening at the Pera Palas   32
a string trio plays, attentively listened to by the German package tourists
at their communal tables, and gives the place a comfortable, palm-court air.
Two elderly gentlemen in gypsy outfits are on piano and accordion, and
they are led by a romantic fiddler, adept at waltzes and polkas.

I was sitting there one evening when suddenly there burst into the
room, driving the trio from its podium and severely disconcerting the
Hausfraus, a team of ferocious Anatolian folk dancers, accompanied by a
young man with a reedy trumpet and an apparently half-crazed drummer.
The dancers were fairly crazed themselves. Apparently welded together
into a multicolored phalanx, they shrieked, they roared with laughter, they
leaped, they whirled, they waved handkerchiefs — a performance of furious
bravura, leaving us all breathless and aghast. They were like so many
houris, come to dance over the corpses on a battlefield.

They withdrew as abruptly as they had arrived, and in the stunned
hush that ensued I turned to the Americans at the next table. "My God,"
I said, "I'm glad they're on our side!" But a knowing look crossed the man's
face. "Ah, but *are* they?" he replied.

You can never be quite sure, with the Turks. They are nobody's satellites, and they habitually leave the world guessing. This does not make for
serenity, and Istanbul is not a blithe city. For foreigners it is a city, all too
often, of homesickness and bafflement, for Turks a city where life gets
tougher every day. I saw a protest demonstration one day clambering its
way up the hill towards the Hippodrome, on the Stamboul ridge, and never
did I see a demonstration so lacking in the fire of indignation. The hill is
very steep there, and the cheerleaders, men and women in antiphony,
found it hard to raise a response among their panting protégés: while
flanking the procession on either side, guns across their bellies, helmets
low over their foreheads, an escort of soldiers did their chesty best to keep
up. An armored car brought up the rear, flashing blue and white lights,
but even it found the progress heavy going.

More telling still perhaps, one day I walked up a hill on the Pera side   36
(every walk in Istanbul is up or down a hill) in the wake of a big brown
bear, chained to the staff of a lanky man in black. It was a dintinguished-
looking bear, lean and handsome, but it walked through Istanbul in movements of infinite melancholy and weariness, as though the day, the walk

up the hill, life itself would never end. I overtook it presently, and prodded by its master it stood on its hind legs for a moment to salute me as I passed: but it did so disdainfully, I thought, and somewhat *grandly*.

Istanbul indeed is nothing if not grand. It may not be exuberant, it is seldom funny, its humor running characteristically to not very prurient posters and bawdy badinage. It is hardly uplifting: sometimes, when I take the old funicular from Galata hill to the Golden Horn, I feel that its carriages, sliding into their narrow black tunnels, are plunging me into perpetual night. It is never optimistic: one feels that dire things may happen at any moment, and all too often they do, arrests, accidents, collapses, unidentified gunshots, and screaming sirens in the night being commonplaces of the city.

But grand, unquestionably. For all my unease in Istanbul, I greatly admire the place, and it is the grandeur that does it: not the grandeur of history or monument, but the grandeur of *yok*, the ornery strength and vigor that give a living dignity to its affairs. There is one incomparable vantage from which to observe this ironic vitality — the deck of one of the restaurant boats which are moored beside the Galata Bridge; and there at a typical Istanbul lunchtime — grayish, that is, with a warm breeze off the Bosporus to flutter the canvases — I will end my essay.

The setting down there is terrific. The bulk of Stamboul rises magnificently behind our backs, the iron-brown Galata hill is stacked across the Golden Horn, and to the east the ships pass to and fro along the wide expanse of the Bosporus. Everything is a little hazed, though: not merely by the cloud of spiced smoke in which the restaurateur is cooking our fish, on the open quayside by the boat, but by a kind of permanent opacity of life and light along the Golden Horn, through which everything moves powerfully but inexactly.

Those inescapable ferry-boats, for instance, twist and scuttle in a dream- 40 like frenzy, and across the bridge the traffic seems to lurch without pattern or priority. Peddlers, defying the massed tide of pedestrians like Californians wading into the surf, offer balloons, cutlery, incomprehensible household gadgets, and sizzling corn on the cob. Military policemen saunter watchfully by, eyes darting right and left for deserters or unsoldierly conduct. From their boats below the quay smoke-shrouded fishermen hand up chucks of grilled fish to their customers above, who sprinkle rough salt upon them from pots tied to the railings and wander off munching into the crowd. Lines of indistinguishable youths hang over their fishing rods beneath the bridge, and sometimes clouds of pigeons, suddenly emerging from their roosts in the dusty façade of the mosque at the end of the bridge, swoop across the scene like huge gray raindrops.

It is a wonderfully animated scene, but animated it seems by habit: numbly animated, passively animated, like a huge mechanical theater worked by the engines of history. Presently our food comes, with a chopped tomato salad on the side, a glass of beer, and some fine rough Turkish bread. "Oh," we may perhaps murmur, in our foreign way, "excuse me, but I wonder if we could possibly have some butter?" The waiter smiles, faintly but not unkindly. "*Yok*," he says, and leaves us to our victuals.

AFTERWORD

Somewhere Jan Morris says that she usually writes three drafts — which strikes me as an unusually low number for a writer of her skill; but newspaper training encourages clean copy. The first draft, she says, "is a sort of stream-of-consciousness affair." Although all writers have their differences, roughly speaking we can name two camps. Some writers like Morris need to scribble everything they know, fast, before they know what they know and can set it in order. Others prepare meticulous notes and even outlines, beginning a first draft only after much forethought. For Morris, as it were, forethought follows stream-of-consciousness: "The second draft is a sensible, no-nonsense tidying-up process," which doubtless includes cutting — of material that didn't develop or doesn't fit — and rearranging. The other sort of writer needs less rearranging or cutting. Morris's third phase sounds like fun: "The third," she says, "is when I try to make it sing and flow." Many competent journalists write carefully and informatively — thanks be to them — but few are able "to make it sing and flow."

"City of Yok*" comes from* Among the Cities *(1985) — another geography of pleasures — and it is beautifully made, with joy evident in the making. Notice the yok-structure. Did these bookends occur to Morris at the start, when she took notes in Istanbul? Or did it happen in the journey from draft one to draft two, stream-of-consciousness disciplined by the "sensible"? If we begin an essay reading "The favorite epithet of Istanbul seems to be yok," a sensible and friendly formal consciousness leads us to the ending: "The waiter smiles, faintly but not unkindly. 'Yok,' he says, and leaves us to our victuals."*

BOOKS AVAILABLE IN PAPERBACK

Destinations: Essays from Rolling Stone. New York: Oxford University Press. *Essays.*

Farewell the Trumpets: The Decline of an Empire. San Diego: Harcourt Brace Jovanovich. *Nonfiction.*

The Great Port: A Passage Through New York. New York: Oxford University Press. *Nonfiction.*

Heaven's Command: An Imperial Progress. San Diego: Harcourt Brace Jovanovich. *Nonfiction.*

Journeys. New York: Oxford University Press. *Nonfiction.*

The Matter of Wales: Epic Views of a Small Country. New York: Oxford University Press. *Nonfiction.*

Pax Britannica: The Climax of an Empire. San Diego: Harcourt Brace Jovanovich. *Nonfiction.*

The World of Venice. San Diego: Harcourt Brace Jovanovich. *Nonfiction.*

JOYCE CAROL OATES

*I*N 1986 SOMEONE COUNTED: *Joyce Carol Oates at thirty-eight had published sixteen novels, twelve collections of short stories, five books of poetry, and four essay collections — as well as uncollected book reviews, short stories, and plays. "Her idea of taking a break from the tension of writing novels," said the statistician, "is to write poetry and short stories." She also enjoys cooking, jogging, bicycling, playing the piano, and visiting New York City. She teaches at Princeton University and with her husband edits a press and a magazine, and yet she publishes more than a book a year.*

This prodigy was born in small-town upstate New York (1938) and published her first story in Mademoiselle *when she was still an undergraduate at Syracuse University. She took her M.A. at the University of Wisconsin and taught at the universities of Detroit and Windsor (Ontario) while she began to write and publish in earnest. Her third novel, called* them *(which is not a typographical error), won the National Book Award in 1970. Lately she has published a book of essays,* The Profane Art *(1983);* Last Days: Stories *(1984); and three novels in three years:* Solstice *(1985),* Marya: A Life *(1987), and* You Must Remember This *(1987).*

Almost from the start she has been criticized for writing too much. An Esquire critic titled his trashing *"Stop Me Before I Write Again." The charge is illogical: If you like what she writes, the more the better; if you don't like it, then you must have intrinsic reasons for disliking it. When I hear critics crying about quantity, I hear two things: They are lazy and they are envious.*

In an interview published by the Paris Review, *Oates speaks about suffering from periods of "inertia and depression" and about other times when she starts writing early, before breakfast, and delays breakfast until three in the afternoon. All writers, it has been suggested, are manic-depressive — which of course does not mean psychotic; many people with unusual volatility suffer not from delusions, which would be a thought disorder, but from a mood disorder. Balzac wrote long novels in twenty-hour days virtually without sleep, then sank into sloth and despair. Mania gives high energy; mania makes for clear seeing and for hard work. Someone has suggested that writers create while manic and while remembering depression. Surely the world of much fiction and poetry is dark enough.*

Oates's fiction describes a fallen world, and critics have found in it a Calvinist sense of total depravity. In The Contemporary Essay *many of our best writers, turning like Edward Abbey from a despised culture, find solace in the open spaces of the natural world. Not this writer. For Oates, the natural world is as fallen as anything; when Adam fell, and Eve, the garden also fell. "Against Nature" originally appeared in* Antaeus.

Against Nature

We soon get through with Nature. She excites an expectation which she cannot satisfy.

— THOREAU, *Journal*, 1854

Sir, if a man has experienced the inexpressible, he is under no obligation to attempt to express it.

— SAMUEL JOHNSON

The writer's resistance to Nature.

It has no sense of humor: in its beauty, as in its ugliness, or its neutrality, there is no laughter.

It lacks a moral purpose.

It lacks a satiric dimension, registers no irony.

Its pleasures lack resonance, being accidental; its horrors, even when premeditated, are equally perfunctory, "red in tooth and claw" et cetera.

It lacks a symbolic subtext — excepting that provided by man.

4

It has no (verbal) language.

It has no interest in ours.   8

It inspires a painfully limited set of responses in "nature-writers" — REVERENCE, AWE, PIETY, MYSTICAL ONENESS.

It eludes us even as it prepares to swallow us up, books and all.

* * *

I was lying on my back in the dirt-gravel of the towpath beside the Delaware-Raritan Canal, Titusville, New Jersey, staring up at the sky and trying, with no success, to overcome a sudden attack of tachycardia° that had come upon me out of nowhere — such attacks are always "out of nowhere," that's their charm — and all around me Nature thrummed with life, the air smelling of moisture and sunlight, the canal reflecting the sky, red-winged blackbirds testing their spring calls — the usual. I'd become the jar in Tennessee, a fictitous center, or parenthesis, aware beyond my erratic heartbeat of the numberless heartbeats of the earth, its pulsing pumping life, sheer life, incalculable. Struck down in the midst of motion — I'd been jogging a minute before — I was "out of time" like a fallen, stunned boxer, privileged (in an abstract manner of speaking) to be an involuntary witness to the random, wayward, nameless motion on all sides of me.

Paroxysmal tachycardia is rarely fatal, but if the heartbeat accelerates to   12
250–270 beats a minute you're in trouble. The average attack is about 100–150 beats and mine seemed so far to be about average; the trick now was to prevent it from getting worse. Brainy people try brainy strategies, such as thinking calming thoughts, pseudo-mystic thoughts, *If I die now it's a good death*, that sort of thing, *if I die this is a good place and a good time*, the idea is to deceive the frenzied heartbeat that, really, you don't care: you hadn't any other plans for the afternoon. The important thing with tachycardia is to prevent panic! you must prevent panic! otherwise you'll have to be taken by ambulance to the closest emergency room, which is not so very nice a way to spend the afternoon, really. So I contemplated the blue sky overhead. The earth beneath my head. Nature surrounding me on all sides, I couldn't quite see it but I could hear it, smell it, sense it — there is something *there*, no mistake about it. Completely oblivious to the predicament of the individual but that's only "natural" after all, one hardly expects otherwise.

When you discover yourself lying on the ground, limp and unresisting, head in the dirt, and helpless, the earth seems to shift forward as a presence; hard, emphatic, not mere surface but a genuine force — there is no other

---

tachycardia   Excessively rapid heartbeat.

word for it but *presence*. To keep in motion is to keep in time and to be stopped, stilled, is to be abruptly out of time, in another time-dimension perhaps, an alien one, where human language has no resonance. Nothing to be said about it expresses it, nothing touches it, it's an absolute against which nothing human can be measured. . . . Moving through space and time by way of your own volition you inhabit an interior consciousness, a hallucinatory consciousness, it might be said, so long as breath, heartbeat, the body's autonomy hold; when motion is stopped you are jarred out of it. The interior is invaded by the exterior. The outside wants to come in, and only the self's fragile membrane prevents it.

The fly buzzing at Emily's death.

Still, the earth *is* your place. A tidy grave-site measured to your size. Or, from another angle of vision, one vast democratic grave.

Let's contemplate the sky. Forget the crazy hammering heartbeat, don't 16 listen to it, don't start counting, remember that there is a clever way of breathing that conserves oxygen as if you're lying below the surface of a body of water breathing through a very thin straw but you *can* breathe through it if you're careful, if you don't panic, one breath and then another and then another, isn't that the story of all lives? careers? Just a matter of breathing. Of course it is. But contemplate the sky, it's there to be contemplated. A mild shock to see it so blank, blue, a thin airy ghostly blue, no clouds to disguise its emptiness. You are beginning to feel not only weightless but near-bodiless, lying on the earth like a scrap of paper about to be blown off. Two dimensions and you'd imagined you were three! And there's the sky rolling away forever, into infinity — if "infinity" can be "rolled into" — and the forlorn truth is, that's where you're going too. And the lovely blue isn't even blue, is it? isn't even there, is it? a mere optical illusion, isn't it? no matter what art has urged you to believe.

* * *

Early Nature memories. Which it's best not to suppress.

. . . Wading, as a small child, in Tonawanda Creek near our house, and afterward trying to tear off, in a frenzy of terror and revulsion, the sticky fat black bloodsuckers that had attached themselves to my feet, particularly between my toes.

. . . Coming upon a friend's dog in a drainage ditch, dead for several days, evidently the poor creature had been shot by a hunter and left to die, bleeding to death, and we're stupefied with grief and horror but can't resist sliding down to where he's lying on his belly, and we can't resist squatting over him, turning the body over . . .

. . . The raccoon, mad with rabies, frothing at the mouth and tearing at 20 his own belly with his teeth, so that his intestines spilled out onto the ground . . . a sight I seem to remember though in fact I did not see. I've been told I did not see.

* * *

Consequently, my chronic uneasiness with Nature-mysticism; Nature-adoration; Nature-as-(moral)-instruction-for-mankind. My doubt that one can, with philosophical validity, address "Nature" as a single coherent noun, anything other than a Platonic, hence discredited, isness. My resistance to "Nature-writing" as a genre, except when it is brilliantly fictionalized in the service of a writer's individual vision — Thoreau's books and *Journal,* of course — but also, less known in this country, the miniaturist prose-poems of Colette (*Flowers and Fruit*) and Ponge (*Taking the Side of Things*) — in which case it becomes yet another, and ingenious, form of storytelling. The subject is *there* only by the grace of the author's language.

Nature has no instructions for mankind except that our poor beleaguered humanist-democratic way of life, our fantasies of the individual's high worth, our sense that the weak, no less than the strong, have a right to survive, are absurd.

In any case, where *is* Nature? one might (skeptically) inquire. Who has looked upon her/its face and survived?

* * *

But isn't this all exaggeration, in the spirit of rhetorical contentiousness? Surely Nature is, for you, as for most reasonably intelligent people, a "perennial" source of beauty, comfort, peace, escape from the delirium of civilized life; a respite from the ego's ever-frantic strategies of self-promotion, as a way of insuring (at least in fantasy) some small measure of immortality? Surely Nature, as it is understood in the usual slapdash way, as human, if not dilettante, *experience* (hiking in a national park, jogging on the beach at dawn, even tending, with the usual comical frustrations, a suburban garden), is wonderfully consoling; a place where, when you go there, it has to take you in? — a palimpsest of sorts you choose to read, layer by layer, always with care, always cautiously, in proportion to your psychological strength?

Nature: as in Thoreau's upbeat Transcendentalist mode ("The indescribably innocence and beneficence of Nature, — such health, such cheer, they afford forever! and such sympathy have they ever with our race, that all Nature would be affected . . . if any man should ever for a just cause grieve"), and not in Thoreau's grim mode ("Nature is hard to be overcome but she must be overcome").

Another way of saying, not *Nature-in-itself* but *Nature-as-experience.*

The former, Nature-in-itself, is, to allude slantwise to Melville, a blankness ten times blank; the latter is what we commonly, or perhaps always,

24

mean when we speak of Nature as a noun, a single entity — something of ours. Most of the time it's just an activity, a sort of hobby, a weekend, a few days, perhaps a few hours, staring out of the window at the mind-dazzling autumn foliage of, say, Northern Michigan, being rendered speechless — temporarily — at the sight of Mt. Shasta, the Grand Canyon, Ansel Adams's West. Or Nature writ small, contained in the back yard. Nature filtered through our optical nerves, our "senses," our fiercely romantic expectations. Nature that pleases us because it mirrors our souls, or gives the comforting illusion of doing so. As in our first mother's awakening to the self's fatal beauty —

> I thither went
> With unexperienc't thought, and laid me down
> On the green bank, to look into the clear
> Smooth Lake, that to me seem'd another Sky.
> As I bent down to look, just opposite,
> A Shape within the watr'y gleam appear'd
> Bending to look on me, I started back,
> It started back, but pleas'd I soon return'd,
> Pleas'd it return'd as soon with answering looks
> Of sympathy and love; there I had fixt
> Mine eyes till now, and pin'd with vain desire.

— in these surpassingly beautiful lines from the Book IV of Milton's *Paradise Lost*.

Nature as the self's (flattering) mirror, but not ever, no never, Nature-in-itself. 28

* * *

Nature is mouths, or maybe a single mouth. Why glamorize it, romanticize it, well yes but we must, we're writers, poets, mystics (of a sort) aren't we, precisely what else are we to do but glamorize and romanticize and generally exaggerate the significance of anything we focus the white heat of our "creativity" upon . . .? And why not Nature, since it's there, common property, mute, can't talk back, allows us the possibility of transcending the human condition for a while, writing prettily of mountain ranges, white-tailed deer, the purple crocuses outside this very window, the thrumming dazzling "life-force" we imagine we all support. Why not.

Nature *is* more than a mouth — it's a dazzling variety of mouths. And it pleases the senses, in any case, as the physicists' chill universe of numbers certainly does not.

* * *

Oscar Wilde, on our subject: "Nature is no great mother who has borne us. She is our creation. It is in our brain that she quickens to life. Things are because we see them, and what we see, and how we see it, depends on the Arts that have influenced us. To look at a thing is very different from seeing a thing. . . . At present, people see fogs, not because there are fogs, but because poets and painters have taught them the mysterious loveliness of such effects. There may have been fogs for centuries in London. I dare say there were. But no one saw them. They did not exist until Art had invented them. . . . Yesterday evening Mrs. Arundel insisted on my going to the window and looking at the glorious sky, as she called it. And so I had to look at it. . . . And what was it? It was simply a very second-rate Turner, a Turner of a bad period, with all the painter's worst faults exaggerated and over-emphasized."

(If we were to put it to Oscar Wilde that he exaggerates, his reply might 32 well be: "Exaggeration? I don't know the meaning of the word.")

* * *

Walden, that most artfully composed of prose fictions, concludes, in the rhapsodic chapter "Spring," with Henry David Thoreau's comtemplation of death, decay, and regeneration as it is suggested to him, or to his protagonist, by the spectacle of vultures feeding off carrion. There is a dead horse close by his cabin and the stench of its decomposition, in certain winds, is daunting. Yet: ". . . the assurance it gave me of the strong appetite and inviolable health of Nature was my compensation. I love to see that Nature is so rife with life that myriads can be afforded to be sacrificed and suffered to prey upon one another; that tender organizations can be so serenely squashed out of existence like pulp, — tadpoles which herons gobble up, and tortoises and toads run over in the road; and that sometimes it has rained flesh and blood! . . . The impression made on a wise man is that of universal innocence."

Come off it, Henry David. You've grieved these many years for your elder brother John, who died a ghastly death of lockjaw, you've never wholly recovered from the experience of watching him die. And you know, or must know, that you're fated too to die young of consumption. . . . But this doctrinaire Transcendentalist passage ends *Walden* on just the right note. It's as impersonal, as coolly detached, as the Oversoul itself: a "wise man" filters his emotions through his brain.

Or through his prose.

* * *

Nietzsche: "We all pretend to ourselves that we are more simple-minded 36 than we are: that is how we get a rest from our fellow men."

* * *

Once out of nature I shall never take
My bodily form from any natural thing,
But such a form as Grecian goldsmiths make
Of hammered gold and gold enamelling
To keep a drowsy Emperor awake;
Or set upon a golden bough to sing
To lords and ladies of Byzantium
Of what is past, or passing, or to come.
— WILLIAM BUTLER YEATS, "Sailing to Byzantium"

Yet even the golden bird is a "bodily form taken from (a) natural thing." No, it's impossible to escape!

* * *

The writer's resistance to Nature.

Wallace Stevens: "In the presence of extraordinary actuality, conscious- 40
ness takes the place of imagination."

* * *

Once, years ago, in 1972 to be precise, when I seemed to have been another person, related to the person I am now as one is related, tangentially, sometimes embarrassingly, to cousins not seen for decades, — once, when we were living in London, and I was very sick, I had a mystical vision. That is, I "had" a "mystical vision" — the heart sinks: such pretension — or something resembling one. A fever-dream, let's call it. It impressed me enormously and impresses me still, though I've long since lost the capacity to see it with my mind's eye, or even, I suppose, to believe in it. There is a statute of limitations on "mystical visions" as on romantic love.

I was very sick, and I imagined my life as a thread, a thread of breath, or heartbeat, or pulse, or light, yes it was light, radiant light, I was burning with fever and I ascended to that plane of serenity that might be mistaken for (or *is*, in fact) Nirvana, where I had a waking dream of uncanny lucidity —

My body is a tall column of light and heat.

My body is not "I" but "it."   44

My body is not one but many.

My body, which "I" inhabit, is inhabited as well by other creatures, unknown to me, imperceptible — the smallest of them mere sparks of light.

My body, which I perceive as substance, is in fact an organization of infinitely complex, overlapping, imbricated structures, radiant light their manifestation, the "body" a tall column of light and blood-heat, a temporary agreement among atoms, like a high-rise building with numberless rooms, corridors, corners, elevator shafts, windows. . . . In this fantastical structure the "I" is deluded as to its sovereignty, let alone its autonomy in the (outside) world; the most astonishing secret is that the "I" doesn't exist! — but it behaves as if it does, as if it were one and not many.

In any case, without the "I" the tall column of light and heat would die, 48 and the microscopic life-particles would die with it . . . will die with it. The "I," which doesn't exist, is everything.

But Dr. Johnson is right, the inexpressible need not be expressed. And what resistance, finally? There is none.

* * *

This morning, an invasion of tiny black ants. One by one they appear, out of nowhere — that's their charm too! — moving single file across the white Parsons table where I am sitting, trying without much success to write a poem. A poem of only three or four lines is what I want, something short, tight, mean. I want it to hurt like a white-hot wire up the nostrils, small and compact and turned in upon itself with the density of a hunk of rock from the planet Jupiter. . . .

But here come the black ants: harbingers, you might say, of spring. One by one by one they appear on the dazzling white table and one by one I kill them with a forefinger, my deft right forefinger, mashing each against the surface of the table and then dropping it into a wastebasket at my side. Idle labor, mesmerizing, effortless, and I'm curious as to how long I can do it, sit here in the brilliant March sunshine killing ants with my right forefinger, how long I, and the ants, can keep it up.

After a while I realize that I can do it a long time. And that I've written 52 my poem.

AFTERWORD

This is the essay as notes toward a subject, discrete entries on a subject, paragraphs that could have been culled from a journal. It is fine to space your essay by a row of three asterisks, when you are Joyce Carol Oates and when the essay coheres — but a student should consult the instructor before using typographical devices to replace transitions.

Note how the beginnings of each separate passage, or summaries of each begin-ning, lay out the essay's structure: "The writer's [*meaning* My] resistance to Nature." / *Anecdote of tachycardia /* "Early Nature memories." / ". . . uneasiness with Nature-mysticism." / Imagined counterargument / Counter-counter number one / Counter-counter number two, Wilde /* Walden */ Nietzsche /Yeats / Stevens / Anecdote two, fever-dream / Antinatural climactic vision of ants.*

365

Note that, despite its episodic structure, this essay fulfills most of the expectations that the classic essay raises. It explores by reminiscence and allusion a single, general topic. At moments it includes narrative, like fiction; at others it includes the imagistic, or the apothegmatic, like poetry. Note also Oates's intellectual skepticism over the romantic inflation of nature. She manages to suggest, with a delicate stab of irony, that Thoreau's bad thinking comes not from deficiency of mind but from devotion to his own prose style.

BOOKS AVAILABLE IN PAPERBACK

Angel of Light. New York: Warner. *Novel.*

The Assassins. New York: Fawcett Books. *Novel.*

Bellefleur. New York: Dutton. *Novel.*

A Bloodsmoor Romance. New York: Warner. *Novel.*

Childwold. New York: Fawcett Books. *Novel.*

Crossing the Border. New York: Fawcett Books. *Short stories.*

Cybele. New York: Dutton. *Novel.*

Do With Me What You Will. New York. Fawcett Books. *Novel.*

Expensive People. New York: Fawcett Books. *Novel.*

The Fabulous Beasts: Poems. Baton Rouge: Louisiana State University Press. *Poetry.*

Invisible Woman. Princeton: Ontario Review. *Poetry.*

Last Days: Stories. New York: Dutton. *Short stories.*

Miracle Play. New York: Black Sparrow. *Play.*

Mysteries of Winterthurn. New York: Berkley Publishing Group. *Novel.*

New Heaven, New Earth: The Visionary Experience in Literature. New York: Fawcett Books, *Nonfiction.*

Night-Side. New York: Fawcett Books. *Short stories.*

The Profane Art: Essays and Reviews. New York: Persea Books. *Essays.*

Raven's Wing. New York: Dutton. *Novel.*

The Seduction and Other Stories. New York: Fawcett Books. *Short stories.*

A Sentimental Education: Stories. New York: Dutton. *Short stories.*

Son of the Morning. New York: Fawcett Books. *Novel.*

them. New York: Fawcett Books. *Novel.*

Three Plays. Princeton: Ontario Review. *Plays.*

The Triumph of the Spider Monkey. New York: Black Sparrow. *Novel.*

Unholy Loves. New York: Fawcett Books. *Novel.*

Where Are You Going, Where Have You Been? Stories of Young America. New York: Fawcett Books. *Short stories.*

CYNTHIA
OZICK

*R*AISED *IN THE BRONX (b. 1928), Cynthia Ozick took her B.A. at New
York University, went out to Ohio State University for her M.A., married a
lawyer, bore a daughter, and returned to live in New Rochelle. She is a novelist
and short-story writer, with a strong second calling in the essay. Her first novel
was* Trust *in 1966. More recently she published a book of short stories,* Levitation
(1982); an essay collection, Art and Ardor *(1983); and in the same year another
novel,* The Cannibal Galaxy. *Also in 1983 she was presented with one of the
Harold and Mildred Strauss Living Awards, thirty-five thousand dollars a year for
five years in support of her work. In 1987 she published* The Messiah of Stock-
holm, *only four years after her previous novel, which had come sixteen years after
her first. She also writes a monthly column for the* New York Times Book Review.
"The First Day of School" appeared in Harper's.

In an interview in Publishers Weekly, *Ozick discloses unusual habits. Most
writers as they get older tend to write early in the morning, when they feel their
energy highest. Cynthia Ozick writes late at night. She finishes when dawn arrives
with "the racket of those damn birds. . . . The depth of the night is guilt free,
responsibility free; nobody will telephone you, importune you, make any claims on*

368

*you. You own the world." She also acknowledges that "my first draft is the last."
But she defines "first draft" so that we understand her: A first draft can be the
product of much scratching around. "I must perfect each sentence madly before I
go on to the next," she says, because "at the end I want to be finished."*

The First Day of School:
Washington Square, 1946

This portion of New York appears to many persons the most delectable. It has a kind of established repose which is not of frequent
occurrence in other quarters of the long, shrill city; it has a riper,
richer, more honorable look than any of the upper ramifications of
the great longitudinal thoroughfare — the look of having had something of a social history.
                                — HENRY JAMES, *Washington Square*

I first came down to Washington Square on a colorless February morning
in 1946. I was seventeen and a half years old and was carrying my lunch
in a brown paper bag, just as I had carried it to high school only a month
before. It was — I thought it was — the opening day of spring term at
Washington Square College, my initiation into my freshman year at New
York University. All I knew of NYU then was that my science-minded
brother had gone there; he had written from the army that I ought to go
there too. With master-of-ceremonies zest he described the Browsing Room
on the second floor of the Main Building as a paradisal chamber whose
bookish loungers leafed languidly through magazines and exchanged high-
principled witticisms between classes. It had the sound of a carpeted Olym-
pian club in Oliver Wendell Holmes's Boston, Hub of the Universe, strewn
with leather chairs and delectable old copies of *The Yellow Book*.

On that day I had never heard of Oliver Wendell Holmes or *The Yellow
Book*, and Washington Square was a faraway bower where wounded birds
fell out of trees. My brother had once brought home from Washington
Square Park a baby sparrow with a broken leg, to be nurtured back to
flight. It died instead, emitting in its last hours melancholy faint cheeps,
and leaving behind a dense recognition of the minute explicitness of morality. All the same, in the February grayness Washington Square had the

allure of the celestial unknown. A sparrow might die, but my own life was luminously new: I felt my youth like a nimbus.

Which dissolves into the dun gauze of a low and sullen city sky. And here I am flying out of the Lexington Avenue subway at Astor Place, just a few yards from Wanamaker's, here I am turning a corner past a second-hand bookstore and a union hall; already late, I begin walking very fast toward the park. The air is smoky with New York winter grit, and on clogged Broadway a mob of trucks shifts squawking gears. But there, just ahead, crisscrossed by paths under high branches, is Washington Square; and on a single sidewalk, three clear omens — or call them riddles, intricate and redolent. These I will disclose in a moment, but before that you must push open the heavy brass-and-glass doors of the Main Building and come with me, at a hard and panting pace, into the lobby of Washington Square College on the earliest morning of my freshman year.

On the left, a bank of elevators. Straight ahead, a long burnished cor-   4
ridor, spooky as a lit tunnel. And empty, all empty. I can hear my solitary footsteps reverberate, as in a radio mystery drama: they lead me up a short staircase into a big dark ghost-town cafeteria. My brother's letter, along with his account of the physics and chemistry laboratories (I will never see them), has already explained that this place is called Commons — and here my heart will learn to shake with the merciless newness of life. But not today; today there is nothing. Tables and chairs squat in dead silhouette. I race back through a silent maze of halls and stairways to the brass-and-glass doors — there stands a lonely guard. From the pocket of my coat I retrieve a scrap with a classroom number on it and ask the way. The guard announces in a sly croak that the first day of school is not yet; come back tomorrow, he says.

A dumb bad joke: I'm humiliated. I've journeyed the whole way down from the end of the line — Pelham Bay, in the northeast Bronx — to find myself in desolation, all because of a muddle: Tuesday isn't Wednesday. The nimbus of expectation fades. The lunch bag in my fist takes on a greasy sadness. I'm not ready to dive back into the subway — I'll have a look around.

Across the street from the Main Building, the three omens. First, a pretzel man with a cart. He's wearing a sweater, a cap that keeps him faceless — he's nothing but the shadows of his creases — and wool gloves with the fingertips cut off. He never moves; he might as well be made of papier-mâché, set up and left out in the open since spring. There are now almost no pretzels for sale, and this gives me a chance to inspect the construction of his bare pretzel-poles. The pretzels are hooked over a column of gray cardboard cylinders, themselves looped around a stick, the way horseshoes drop around a post. The cardboard cylinders are the insides of toilet paper rolls.

The pretzel man is rooted between a Chock Full O' Nuts (that's the second omen) and a newsstand (that's the third).

The Chock Full: the doors are like fans, whirling remnants of conver-   8
sation. *She will marry him. She will not marry him.* Fragrance of coffee and hot chocolate. *We can prove that the senses are partial and unreliable vehicles of information, but who is to say that reason is not equally a product of human limitation?* Powdered doughnut sugar on their lips.

Attached to a candy store, the newsstand. Copies of *Partisan Review*: the table of the gods. Jean Stafford, Mary McCarthy, Elizabeth Hardwick, Irving Howe, Delmore Schwartz, Alfred Kazin, Clement Greenberg, Stephen Spender, William Phillips, John Berryman, Saul Bellow, Philip Rahv, Richard Chase, Randall Jarrell, Simone de Beauvoir, Karl Shapiro, George Orwell! I don't know a single one of these names, but I feel their small conflagration flaming in the gray street: the succulent hotness of their promise. I mean to penetrate every one of them. Since all the money I have is my subway fare — a nickel — I don't buy a copy (the price of *Partisan* in 1946 is fifty cents); I pass on.

I pass on to the row of houses on the north side of the square. Henry James was born in one of these, but I don't know that either. Still, they are plainly old, though no longer aristocratic: haughty last-century shabbies with shut eyelids, built of rosy-ripe respectable brick, down on their luck. Across the park bulks Judson Church, with its squat squarish bell tower; by the end of the week I will be languishing at the margins of a basketball game in its basement, forlorn in my blue left-over-from-high-school gym suit and mooning over Emily Dickinson:

> There's a certain Slant of light,
> Winter Afternoons —
> That oppresses, like the Heft
> Of Cathedral Tunes —

There is more I don't know. I don't know that W. H. Auden lives just down *there*, and might at any moment be seen striding toward home under his tall rumpled hunch; I don't know that Marianne Moore is only up the block, her doffed tricorn resting on her bedroom dresser. It's Greenwich Village — I know *that* — no more than twenty years after Edna St. Vincent Millay has sent the music of her name (her best, perhaps her only, poem) into these bohemian streets: bohemia, the honeypot of poets.

On that first day in the tea-leafed cup of the town I am ignorant,   12
ignorant! But the three riddle-omens are soon to erupt, and all of them together will illumine Washington Square.

Begin with the benches in the park. Here, side by side with students and their looseleafs, lean or lie the shadows of the pretzel man, his creased ghosts or doubles: all those pitiables, half-women and half-men, neither awake nor asleep; the discountable, the repudiated, the unseen. No more notice is taken of any of them than of a scudding fragment of newspaper in the path. Even then, even so long ago, the benches of Washington Square are pimpled with this hell-tossed crew, these Mad Margarets and Cokey Joes, these volcanic coughers, shakers, groaners, tremblers, droolers, blasphemers, these public urinators with vomitous breath and rusted teeth stumps, dead-eyed and self-abandoned, dragging their makeshift junkyard shoes, their buttonless layers of raggedy ratfur. The pretzel man with his toilet paper rolls conjures and spews them all — he is a loftier brother to these citizens of the lower pox, he is guardian of the garden of the jettisoned. They rattle along all the seams of Washington Square. They are the pickled city, the true and universal City-Below-Cities, the wolfish vinegar-Babylon that dogs the spittled skirts of bohemia. The toilet paper rolls are the temple columns of this sacred grove.

Next, the whirling doors of Chock Full O' Nuts. Here is the marketplace of Washington Square, its bazaar, its roiling gossip-parlor, its matchmaker's office and arena — the outermost wing, so to speak, evolved from the Commons. On a day like today, when the Commons is closed, the Chock Full is thronged with extra power, a cello making up for a missing viola. Until now, the fire of my vitals has been for the imperious tragedians of the *Aeneid*; I have lived in the narrow throat of poetry. Another year or so of this oblivion, until at last I am hammerstruck with the shock of Europe's skull, the bled planet of death camp and war. Eleanor Roosevelt has not yet written her famous column announcing the discovery of Anne Frank's diary. The term *cold war* is new. The Commons, like the college itself, is overcrowded, veterans in their pragmatic thirties mingling with the reluctant dreamy young. And the Commons is convulsed with politics: a march to the docks is organized, no one knows by whom, to protest the arrival of Walter Gieseking, the German musician who flourished among Nazis. The Communists — two or three readily recognizable cantankerous zealots — stomp through with their daily leaflets and sneers. There is even a Monarchist, a small poker-faced rectangle of a man with secretive tireless eyes who, when approached for his views, always demands, in perfect Bronx tones, the restoration of his king. The engaged girls — how many of them there seem to be! — flash their rings and tangle their ankles in their long New Look skirts. There is no feminism and no feminists: I am, I think, the only one. The Commons is a tide: it washes up the cold war, it washes up the engaged girls' rings, it washes up the several philosophers and the numerous poets. The philosophers are all existentialists; the poets are all influenced by *The Waste Land*. When the Commons overflows, the engaged girls cross the street to show their rings at the Chock Full.

Call it density, call it intensity, call it continuity: call it, finally, society. The Commons belongs to the satirists. Here, one afternoon, is Alfred Chester, holding up a hair, a single strand, before a crowd. (He will one day write stories and novels. He will die young.) "What is that hair?" I innocently ask, having come late on the scene. "A pubic hair," he replies, and I feel as Virginia Woolf did when she declared human nature to have "changed in or about December 1910" — soon after her sister Vanessa explained away a spot on her dress as "semen."

In or about February 1946 human nature does not change; it keeps on. 16 On my bedroom wall I tack — cut out from *Life* magazine — the wildest Picasso I can find: a face that is also a belly. Mr. George E. Mutch, a lyrical young English teacher still in his twenties, writes on the blackboard: "When lilacs last in the dooryard bloom'd," and "Bare, ruined choirs, where late the sweet birds sang," and "A green thought in a green shade"; he tells us to burn, like Pater, with a hard, gemlike flame. Another English teacher — older and crustier — compares Walt Whitman to a plumber; the next year he is rumored to have shot himself in a wood. The initial letters of Washington Square College are a device to recall three of the seven deadly sins: Wantonness, Sloth, Covetousness. In the Commons they argue the efficacy of the orgone box.° Eda Lou Walton, sprightly as a bird, knows all the Village bards, and is a Village bard herself. Sidney Hook is an intellectual rumble in the logical middle distance. Homer Watt, chairman of the English department, is the very soul who, in a far-off time of bewitchment, hired Thomas Wolfe.

And so, in February 1946, I make my first purchase of a "real" book — which is to say, not for the classroom. It is displayed in the window of the secondhand bookstore between the Astor Place subway station and the union hall, and for weeks I have been coveting it: *Of Time and the River.* I am transfigured; I am pierced through with rapture; skipping gym, I sit among morning mists on a windy bench a foot from the stench of Mad Margaret, sinking into that cascading syrup:

> Man's youth is a wonderful thing: It is so full of anguish and
> of magic and he never comes to know it as it is, until it is
> gone from him forever. . . . And what is the essence of that
> strange and bitter miracle of life which we feel so poignantly,
> so unutterably, with such a bitter pain and joy, when we are
> young?

---

orgone box   Invented by the Austrian psychiatrist and biophysicist Wilhelm Reich (1897–1957), the orgone box was supposed to restore human energy; it was declared a fraud.

Thomas Wolfe, lost, and by the wind grieved, ghost, come back again! In Washington Square I am appareled in the "numb exultant secrecies of fog, fog-numb air filled with solemn joy of nameless and impending prophecy, an ancient yellow light, the old smoke-ochre of the morning . . . "

The smoke-ochre of the morning. Ah, you who have flung Thomas Wolfe, along with your strange and magical youth, onto the ash-heap of juvenilia and excess, myself among you, isn't this a lovely phrase still? It rises out of the old pavements of Washington Square as delicately colored as an eggshell.

The veterans in their pragmatic thirties are nailed to Need; they have families and futures to attend to. When Mr. George E. Mutch exhorts them to burn with a hard, gemlike flame, and writes across the blackboard the line that reveals his own name,

> The world is too much with us; late and soon,
> Getting and spending, we lay waste our powers,

one of the veterans heckles, "What about getting a Buick, what about spending a buck?" Chester, at sixteen, is a whole year younger than I; he has transparent eyes and a rosebud mouth, and is in love with a poet named Diana. He has already found his way to the Village bars, and keeps in his wallet Truman Capote's secret telephone number. We tie our scarves tight against the cold and walk up and down Fourth Avenue, winding in and out of the rows of secondhand bookshops crammed one against the other. The proprietors sit reading their wares and never look up. The books in all their thousands smell sleepily of cellar. Our envy of them is speckled with longing; our longing is sick with envy. We are the sorrowful literary young.

Every day, month after month, I hang around the newsstand near the candy store, drilling through the enigmatic pages of *Partisan Review*. I still haven't bought a copy; I still can't understand a word. I don't know what cold war means. Who is Trotsky? I haven't read *Ulysses*; my adolescent phantoms are rowing in the ablative absolute with *pius* Aeneas. I'm in my mind's cradle, veiled by the exultant secrecies of fog.

Washington Square will wake me. In a lecture room in the Main Building, Dylan Thomas will cry his webwork syllables. Afterward he'll warm himself at the White Horse Tavern. Across the corridor I will see Sidney Hook plain. I will read the Bhagavad-Gita and Catullus and Lessing, and, in Hebrew, a novel eerily called *Whither*? It will be years and years before I am smart enough, worldly enough, to read Alfred Kazin and Mary McCarthy.

In the spring, all of worldly Washington Square will wake up to the luster of little green leaves.

AFTERWORD

The first day at college is a universal subject, though the particulars of Washington Square will clash with the particulars of Ann Arbor, Eugene, Tuscaloosa, and College Station — any college station.

Many of Ozick's essays are moral and even religious. This reminiscent piece is colored with a remembered past redolent of what's to come, the future nascent in the moment. In Art and Ardor Ozick had written: "The secrets that engage me — that sweep me away — are generally secrets of an inheritance: how the pear seed becomes a pear tree, for instance, rather than a polar bear. Ideas are emotions that penetrate the future of coherence — " This essay performs an odd trick. It tells of the future, of life after the first day, in a persistent series of negatives: "I did not know," "I had not read," "Later this or that will happen." The device collapses the years into the box of a narrow moment.

BOOKS AVAILABLE IN PAPERBACK

Art and Ardor: Essays. New York: Dutton. *Essays.*

Bloodshed: And Three Novellas. New York: Dutton, *Novellas.*

The Cannibal Galaxy. New York: Dutton. *Novel.*

Levitation: Five Fictions. New York: Dutton. *Short stories.*

The Pagan Rabbi: And Other Stories. New York: Dutton. *Short stories.*

Trust. New York: Dutton. *Novel.*

WALKER
PERCY

WALKER PERCY (b. 1916) was educated as a physician and completed his internship but became a novelist. (Maybe medical training is more useful than writers' workshops; the playwright and story writer Anton Chekhov studied to be a doctor; John Keats and William Carlos Williams were two doctors turned poets.) Born in Alabama, Percy took his B.A. at the University of North Carolina, then attended medical school at Columbia University, in New York City, where he also interned. He returned to reside in the South, where he lives in Covington, Louisiana, near New Orleans, the site of much of his fiction. ("I choose to live in a small town. One reason is that people here don't take writers very seriously and accordingly I don't either.") The most important biographical information about Walker Percy is his religion: He is a convert to Roman Catholicism, and his religious sensibility informs his imagination and his thought.

While interning after medical school he contracted tuberculosis. For two years he stayed in bed reading. Trying to return to medicine he suffered a relapse, and after a further period for recovery, he retired from medicine and began writing. He was middle-aged before he published his first novel, The Moviegoer, in 1961; it won the National Book Award, and Percy was immediately recognized as a major *contemporary novelist. Subsequent novels include* The Last Gentleman *(1966),* The Second Coming *(1980), and* The Thanatos Syndrome *(1987). In 1975 he published a book of essays,* The Message in the Bottle, *from which "The Loss of the Creature" is taken. The articles in that book appeared over twenty years, in literary quarterlies* (The Southern Review, Sewanee Review, Partisan Review) *and in philosophical journals* (Thought, The Journal of Philosophy, Philosophy and Phenomenological Research). *Few philosophers publish in literary quarterlies; few novelists publish in philosophical quarterlies. In 1983 Percy published* Lost in the Cosmos, *a collection of parodies and essays critical of contemporary society.*

In his author's note to The Message in the Bottle, *Percy refers to his "recurring interest" in "the nature of human communication." "The Loss of the Creature" begins with people naming something and continues by examining the relation of experience to the language by which we communicate experience. The loss that Percy describes is a psychic distance that civilization, or its development in our time, puts between reality and our mind's connection to reality. Before you read it, tuck away in your mind the author's subtitle for* The Message in the Bottle: How Queer Man Is, How Queer Language Is, and What One Has to Do with the Other.

The Loss of
the Creature

I

Every explorer names his island Formosa, beautiful. To him it is beautiful because, being first, he has access to it and can see it for what it is. But to no one else is it ever as beautiful — except the rare man who manages to recover it, who knows that it has to be recovered.

Garcia López de Cárdenas discovered the Grand Canyon and was amazed at the sight. It can be imagined. One crosses miles of desert, breaks through the mesquite, and there it is at one's feet. Later the government set the place aside as a national park, hoping to pass along to millions the experience of Cárdenas. Does not one see the same sight from the Bright Angel Lodge that Cárdenas saw?

The assumption is that the Grand Canyon is a remarkably interesting and beautiful place and that if it had a certain value P for Cárdenas, the same value P may be transmitted to any number of sightseers — just as Banting's discovery of insulin can be transmitted to any number of diabetics.

A counterinfluence is at work, however, and it would be nearer the truth to say that if the place is seen by a million sightseers, a single sightseer does not receive value P but a millionth part of value P.

It is assumed that since the Grand Canyon has the fixed interest value P, tours can be organized for any number of people. A man in Boston decides to spend his vacation at the Grand Canyon. He visits his travel bureau, looks at the folder, signs up for a two-week tour. He and his family take the tour, see the Grand Canyon, and return to Boston. May we say that this man has seen the Grand Canyon? Possibly he has. But it is more likely that what he has done is the one sure way not to see the canyon. 4

Why is it almost impossible to gaze directly at the Grand Canyon under these circumstances and see it for what it is — as one picks up a strange object from one's back yard and gazes directly at it? It is almost impossible because the Grand Canyon, the thing as it is, has been appropriated by the symbolic complex which has already been formed in the sightseer's mind. Seeing the canyon under approved circumstances is seeing the symbolic complex head on. The thing is no longer the thing as it confronted the Spaniard; it is rather that which has already been formulated — by picture postcard, geography book, tourist folders, and the words *Grand Canyon*. As a result of this preformulation, the source of the sightseer's pleasure undergoes a shift. Where the wonder and delight of the Spaniard arose from his penetration of the thing itself, from a progressive discovery of depths, patterns, colors, shadows, etc., now the sightseer measures his satisfaction *by the degree to which the canyon conforms to the preformed complex*. If it does so, if it looks just like the postcard, he is pleased; he might even say, "Why it is every bit as beautiful as a picture postcard!" He feels he has not been cheated. But if it does not conform, if the colors are somber, he will not be able to see it directly; he will only be conscious of the disparity between what it is and what it is supposed to be. He will say later that he was unlucky in not being there at the right time. The highest point, the term of the sightseer's satisfaction, is not the sovereign discovery of the thing before him; it is rather the measuring up of the thing to the criterion of the preformed symbolic complex.

Seeing the canyon is made even more difficult by what the sightseer does when the moment arrives, when sovereign knower confronts the thing to be known. Instead of looking at it, he photographs it. There is no confrontation at all. At the end of forty years of preformulation and with the Grand Canyon yawning at his feet, what does he do? He waives his right of seeing and knowing and records symbols for the next forty years. For him there is no present; there is only the past of what has been formulated and seen and the future of what has been formulated and not seen. The present is surrendered to the past and the future.

The sightseer may be aware that something is wrong. He may simply be bored; or he may be conscious of the difficulty: that the great thing yawning at his feet somehow eludes him. The harder he looks at it, the less he can see. It eludes everybody. The tourist cannot see it; the bellboy at the Angel Lodge cannot see it: for him it is only one side of the space he lives in, like one wall of a room; to the ranger it is a tissue of everyday signs relevant to his own prospects — the blue haze down there means that he will probably get rained on during the donkey ride.

How can the sightseer recover the Grand Canyon? He can recover it in 8 any number of ways, all sharing in common the stratagem of avoiding the approved confrontation of the tour and the Park Service.

It may be recovered by leaving the beaten track. The tourist leaves the tour, camps in the back country. He arises before dawn and approaches the South Rim through a wild terrain where there are no trails and no railed-in lookout points. In other words, he sees the canyon by avoiding all the facilities for seeing the canyon. If the benevolent Park Service hears about this fellow and thinks he has a good idea and places the following notice in the Bright Angel Lodge: *Consult ranger for information on getting off the beaten track* — the end result will only be the closing of another access to the canyon.

It may be recovered by a dialectical movement which brings one back to the beaten track but at a level above it. For example, after a lifetime of avoiding the beaten track and guided tours, a man may deliberately seek out the most beaten track of all, the most commonplace tour imaginable: he may visit the canyon by a Greyhound tour in the company of a party from Terre Haute — just as a man who has lived in New York all his life may visit the Statue of Liberty. (Such dialectical savorings of the familiar as the familiar are, of course, a favorite stratagem of the *New Yorker* magazine.) The thing is recovered from familiarity by means of an exercise in familiarity. Our complex friend stands behind the fellow tourists at the Bright Angel Lodge and sees the canyon through them and their predicament, their picture taking and busy disregard. In a sense, he exploits his fellow tourists; he stands on their shoulders to see the canyon.

Such a man is far more advanced in the dialectic than the sightseer who is trying to get off the beaten track — getting up at dawn and approaching the canyon through the mesquite. This stratagem is, in fact, for our complex man the weariest, most beaten track of all.

It may be recovered as a consequence of a breakdown of the symbolic 12 machinery by which the experts present the experience to the consumer. A family visits the canyon in the usual way. But shortly after their arrival, the park is closed by an outbreak of typhus in the south. They have the canyon to themselves. What do they mean when they tell the home folks of their good luck: "We had the whole place to ourselves"? How does one see the thing better when the others are absent? Is looking like sucking:

the more lookers, the less there is to see? They could hardly answer, but by saying this they testify to a state of affairs which is considerably more complex than the simple statement of the schoolbook about the Spaniard and the millions who followed him. It is a state in which there is a complex distribution of sovereignty, of zoning.

It may be recovered in a time of national disaster. The Bright Angel Lodge is converted into a rest home, a function that has nothing to do with the canyon a few yards away. A wounded man is brought in. He regains consciousness; there outside his window is the canyon.

The most extreme case of access by privilege conferred by disaster is the Huxleyan° novel of the adventures of the surviving remnant after the great wars of the twentieth century. An expedition from Australia lands in Southern California and heads east. They stumble across the Bright Angel Lodge, now fallen into ruins. The trails are grown over, the guard rails fallen away, the dime telescope at Battleship Point rusted. But there is the canyon, exposed at last. Exposed by what? By the decay of those facilities which were designed to help the sightseer.

This dialectic of sightseeing cannot be taken into account by planners, for the object of the dialectic is nothing other than the subversion of the efforts of the planners.

The dialectic is not known to objective theorists, psychologists, and the like. Yet it is quite well known in the fantasy-consciousness of the popular arts. The devices by which the museum exhibit, the Grand Canyon, the ordinary thing, is recovered have long since been stumbled upon. A movie shows a man visiting the Grand Canyon. But the moviemaker knows something the planner does not know. He knows that one cannot take the sight frontally. The canyon must be approached by the stratagems we have mentioned: the Inside Track, the Familiar Revisited, the Accidental Encounter. Who is the stranger at the Bright Angel Lodge? Is he the ordinary tourist from Terre Haute that he makes himself out to be? He is not. He has another objective in mind, to revenge his wronged brother, counterespionage, etc. By virtue of the fact that he has other fish to fry, he may take a stroll along the rim after supper and then we can see the canyon through him. The movie accomplishes its purpose by concealing it. Overtly the characters (the American family marooned by typhus) and we the onlookers experience pity for the sufferers, and the family experience anxiety for themselves; covertly and in truth they are the happiest of people and we are happy through them, for we have the canyon to ourselves. The movie cashes in on the recovery of sovereignty through disaster. Not only

16

Huxleyan   Referring to Aldous Huxley (1894–1963), an English writer best known for his novel *Brave New World* (1932), which depicts a scientific, mechanized utopia.

is the canyon now accessible to the remnant: the members of the remnant are now accessible to each other; a whole new ensemble of relations becomes possible — friendship, love, hatred, clandestine sexual adventures. In a movie when a man sits next to a woman on a bus, it is necessary either that the bus break down or that the woman lose her memory. (The question occurs to one: Do you imagine there are sightseers who see sights just as they are supposed to? a family who live in Terre Haute, who decide to take the canyon tour, who go there, see it, enjoy it immensely, and go home content? a family who are entirely innocent of all the barriers, zones, losses of sovereignty I have been talking about? Wouldn't most people be sorry if Battleship Point fell into the canyon, carrying all one's fellow passengers to their death, leaving one alone on the South Rim? I cannot answer this. Perhaps there are such people. Certainly a great many American families would swear they had no such problems, that they came, saw, and went away happy. Yet it is just these families who would be happiest if they had gotten the Inside Track and been among the surviving remnant.)

It is now apparent that as between the many measures which may be taken to overcome the opacity, the boredom, of the direct confrontation of the thing or creature in its citadel of symbolic investiture, some are less authentic than others. That is to say, some stratagems obviously serve other purposes than that of providing access to being — for example, various unconscious motivations which it is not necessary to go into here.

Let us take an example in which the recovery of being is ambiguous, where it may under the same circumstances contain both authentic and unauthentic components. An American couple, we will say, drives down into Mexico. They see the usual sights and have a fair time of it. Yet they are never without the sense of missing something. Although Taxco and Cuernavaca are interesting and picturesque as advertised, they fall short of "it." What do the couple have in mind by "it"? What do they really hope for? What sort of experience could they have in Mexico so that upon their return, they would feel that "it" had happened? We have a clue: Their hope has something to do with their own role as tourists in a foreign country and the way in which they conceive this role. It has something to do with other American tourists. Certainly they feel that they are very far from "it" when, after traveling five thousand miles, they arrive at the plaza in Guanajuato only to find themselves surrounded by a dozen other couples from the Midwest.

Already we may distinguish authentic and unauthentic elements. First, we see the problem the couple faces and we understand their efforts to surmount it. The problem is to find an "unspoiled" place. "Unspoiled" does not mean only that a place is left physically intact; it means also that it is not encrusted by renown and by the familiar (as in Taxco), that it has not been discovered by others. We understand that the couple really want to get at the place and enjoy it. Yet at the same time we wonder if there is not something wrong in their dislike of their compatriots. Does access to the place require the exclusion of others?

Let us see what happens. 20

The couple decide to drive from Guanajuato to Mexico City. On the way they get lost. After hours on a rocky mountain road, they find themselves in a tiny valley not even marked on the map. There they discover an Indian village. Some sort of religious festival is going on. It is apparently a corn dance in supplication of the rain god.

The couple know at once that this is "it." They are entranced. They spend several days in the village, observing the Indians and being themselves observed with friendly curiosity.

Now may we not say that the sightseers have at last come face to face with an authentic sight, a sight which is charming, quaint, picturesque, unspoiled, and that they see the sight and come away rewarded? Possibly this may occur. Yet it is more likely that what happens is a far cry indeed from an immediate encounter with being, that the experience, while masquerading as such, is in truth a rather desperate impersonation. I use the word *desperate* advisedly to signify an actual loss of hope.

The clue to the spuriousness of their enjoyment of the village and the 24 festival is a certain restiveness in the sightseers themselves. It is given expression by their repeated exclamations that "this is too good to be true," and by their anxiety that it may not prove to be so perfect, and finally by their downright relief at leaving the valley and having the experience in the bag, so to speak — that is, safely embalmed in memory and movie film.

What is the source of their anixety during the visit? Does it not mean that the couple are looking at the place with a certain standard of performance in mind? Are they like Fabre,° who gazed at the world about him with wonder, letting it be what it is; or are they not like the overanxious mother who sees her child as one performing, now doing badly, now doing well? The village is their child and their love for it is an anxious love because they are afraid that at any moment it might fail them.

We have another clue in their subsequent remark to an ethnologist friend. "How we wished you had been there with us! What a perfect goldmine of folkways! Every minute we would say to each other, if only you were here! You must return with us." This surely testifies to a generosity of spirit, a willingness to share their experience with others, not at all like their feelings toward their fellow Iowans on the plaza at Guanajuato!

Fabre Jean-Henri Fabre (1823–1915), French entomologist (a scientist who studies insects).

I am afraid this is not the case at all. It is true that they longed for their ethnologist friend, but it was for an entirely different reason. They wanted him, not to share their experience, but to certify their experience as genuine.

"This is it" and "Now we are really living" do not necessarily refer to 28 the sovereign encounter of the person with the sight that enlivens the mind and gladdens the heart. It means that now at last we are having the acceptable experience. The present experience is always measured by a prototype, the "it" of their dreams. "Now I am really living" means that now I am filling the role of sightseer and the sight is living up to the prototype of sights. This quaint and picturesque village is measured by a Platonic ideal of the Quaint and the Picturesque.

Hence their anxiety during the encounter. For at any minute something could go wrong. A fellow Iowan might emerge from a 'dobe hut; the chief might show them his Sears catalogue. (If the failures are "wrong" enough, as these are, they might still be turned to account as rueful conversation pieces: "There we were expecting the chief to bring us a churinga and he shows up with a Sears catalogue!") They have snatched victory from disaster, but their experience always runs the danger of failure.

They need the ethnologist to certify their experience as genuine. This is borne out by their behavior when the three of them return for the next corn dance. During the dance, the couple do not watch the goings-on; instead they watch the ethnologist! Their highest hope is that their friend should find the dance interesting. And if he should show signs of true absorption, an interest in the goings-on so powerful that he becomes oblivious of his friends — then their cup is full. "Didn't we tell you?" they say at last. What they want from him is not ethnological explanations; all they want is his approval.

What has taken place is a radical loss of sovereignty over that which is as much theirs as it is the ethnologist's. The fault does not lie with the ethnologist. He has no wish to stake a claim to the village; in fact, he desires the opposite: he will bore his friends to death by telling them about the village and the meaning of the folkways. A degree of sovereignty has been surrendered by the couple. It is the nature of the loss, moreover, that they are not aware of the loss, beyond a certain uneasiness. (Even if they read this and admitted it, it would be very difficult for them to bridge the gap in their confrontation of the world. Their consciousness of the corn dance cannot escape their consciousness of their consciousness, so that with the onset of the first direct enjoyment, their higher consciousness pounces and certifies: "Now you are doing it! Now you are really living!" and, in certifying the experience, sets it at nought.)

Their basic placement in the world is such that they recognize a priority 32 of title of the expert over his particular department of being. The whole horizon of being is staked out by "them," the experts. The highest satisfaction of the sightseer (not merely the tourist but any layman seer of sights) is that his sight should be certified as genuine. The worst of this impoverishment is that there is no sense of impoverishment. The surrender of title is so complete that it never even occurs to one to reassert title. A poor man may envy the rich man, but the sightseer does not envy the expert. When a caste system becomes absolute, envy disappears. Yet the caste of layman-expert is not the fault of the expert. It is due altogether to the eager surrender of sovereignty by the layman so that he may take up the role not of the person but of the consumer.

I do not refer only to the special relation of layman to theorist. I refer to the general situation in which sovereignty is surrendered to a class of privileged knowers, whether these be theorists or artists. A reader may surrender sovereignty over that which has been written about, just as a consumer may surrender sovereignty over a thing which has been theorized about. The consumer is content to receive an experience just as it has been presented to him by theorists and planners. The reader may also be content to judge life by whether it has or has not been formulated by those who know and write about life. A young man goes to France. He too has a fair time of it, sees the sights, enjoys the food. On his last day, in fact as he sits in a restaurant in Le Havre waiting for his boat, something happens. A group of French students in the restaurant get into an impassioned argument over a recent play. A riot takes place. Madame la concierge joins in, swinging her mop at the rioters. Our young American is transported. This is "it." And he had almost left France without seeing "it"!

But the young man's delight is ambiguous. On the one hand, it is a pleasure for him to encounter the same Gallic temperament he had heard about from Puccini° and Rolland.° But on the other hand, the source of his pleasure testifies to a certain alienation. For the young man is actually barred from a direct encounter with anything French excepting only that which has been set forth, authenticated by Puccini and Rolland — those who know. If he had encountered the restaurant scene without reading Hemingway, without knowing that the performance was so typically, charmingly French, he would not have been delighted. He would only have been anxious at seeing things get so out of hand. The source of his delight is the sanction of those who know.

This loss of sovereignty is not a marginal process, as might appear from my example of estranged sightseers. It is a generalized surrender of the horizon to those experts within whose competence a particular segment of

---

Puccini   Giacomo Puccini (1853–1924), Italian composer of emotional, somewhat melancholic operas.

Rolland   Romain Rolland (1866–1944), French author and playwright whose works depicted the contemporary French character.

the horizon is thought to lie. Kwakiutls are surrendered to Franz Boas;° decaying Southern mansions are surrendered to Faulkner and Tennessee Williams. So that, although it is by no means the intention of the expert to expropriate sovereignty — in fact he would not even know what sovereignty meant in this context — the danger of theory and consumption is a seduction and deprivation of the consumer.

In the New Mexican desert, natives occasionally come across strange- 36 looking artifacts which have fallen from the skies and which are stenciled: *Return to U.S. Experimental Project, Alamogordo. Reward.* The finder returns the object and is rewarded. He knows nothing of the nature of the object he has found and does not care to know. The sole role of the native, the highest role he can play, is that of finder and returner of the mysterious equipment.

The same is true of the layman's relation to *natural* objects in a modern technical society. No matter what the object or event is, whether it is a star, a swallow, a Kwakiutl, a "psychological phenomenon," the layman who confronts it does not confront it as a sovereign person, as Crusoe confronts a seashell he finds on the beach. The highest role he can conceive himself as playing is to be able to recognize the title of the object, to return it to the appropriate expert and have it certified as a genuine find. He does not even permit himself to see the thing — as Gerard Hopkins° could see a rock or a cloud or a field. If anyone asks him why he doesn't look, he may reply that he didn't take that subject in college (or he hasn't read Faulkner).

This loss of sovereignty extends even to oneself. There is the neurotic who asks nothing more of his doctor than that his symptoms should prove interesting. When all else fails, the poor fellow has nothing to offer but his own neurosis. But even this is sufficient if only the doctor will show interest when he says, "Last night I had a curious sort of dream; perhaps it will be significant to one who knows about such things. It seems I was standing in a sort of alley — " (I have nothing else to offer you but my own unhappiness. Please say that it, at least, measures up, that it is a *proper* sort of unhappiness.)

II

A young Falkland Islander walking along a beach and spying a dead dogfish and going to work on it with his jackknife has, in a fashion wholly unprovided in modern educational theory, a great advantage over the Scars-

---

Franz Boas German-born American anthropologist and ethnologist (1858–1942) whose fieldwork took place primarily in North America, Mexico, and Puerto Rico.

Gerard Hopkins Gerard Manley Hopkins (1844–1889), English poet noted for his innovative rhythms and his keen observation of the details of nature.

dale high-school pupil who finds the dogfish on his laboratory desk. Similarly the citizen of Huxley's *Brave New World* who stumbles across a volume of Shakespeare in some vine-grown ruins and squats on a potsherd to read it is in a fairer way of getting at a sonnet than the Harvard sophomore taking English Poetry II.

The educator whose business it is to teach students biology or poetry is 40 unaware of a whole ensemble of relations which exist between the student and the dogfish and between the student and the Shakespeare sonnet. To put it bluntly: A student who has the desire to get at a dogfish or a Shakespeare sonnet may have the greatest difficulty in salvaging the creature itself from the educational package in which it is presented. The great difficulty is that he is not aware that there is a difficulty; surely, he thinks, in such a fine classroom, with such a fine textbook, the sonnet must come across! What's wrong with me?

The sonnet and the dogfish are obscured by two different processes. The sonnet is obscured by the symbolic package which is formulated not by the sonnet itself but by the *media* through which the sonnet is transmitted, the media which the educators believe for some reason to be transparent. The new textbook, the type, the smell of the page, the classroom, the aluminum windows and the winter sky, the personality of Miss Hawkins — these media which are supposed to transmit the sonnet may only succeed in transmitting themselves. It is only the hardiest and cleverest of students who can salvage the sonnet from this many-tissued package. It is only the rarest student who knows that the sonnet must be salvaged from the package. (The educator is well aware that something is wrong, that there is a fatal gap between the student's learning and the student's life: The student reads the poem, appears to understand it, and gives all the answers. But what does he recall if he should happen to read a Shakespeare sonnet twenty years later? Does he recall the poem or does he recall the smell of the page and the smell of Miss Hawkins?)

One might object, pointing out that Huxley's citizen reading his sonnet in the ruins and the Falkland Islander looking at his dogfish on the beach also receive them in a certain package. Yes, but the difference lies in the fundamental placement of the student in the world, a placement which makes it possible to extract the thing from the package. The pupil at Scarsdale High sees himself placed as a consumer receiving an experience-package; but the Falkland Islander exploring his dogfish is a person exercising the sovereign right of a person in his lordship and mastery of creation. He too could use an instructor and a book and a technique, but he would use them as his subordinates, just as he uses his jackknife. The biology student does not use his scalpel as an instrument; he uses it as a magic wand! Since it is a "scientific instrument," it should do "scientific things."

The dogfish is concealed in the same symbolic package as the sonnet. But the dogfish suffers an additional loss. As a consequence of this double deprivation, the Sarah Lawrence student who scores A in zoology is apt to know very little about a dogfish. She is twice removed from the dogfish, once by the symbolic complex by which the dogfish is concealed, once again by the spoliation of the dogfish by theory which renders it invisible. Through no fault of zoology instructors, it is nevertheless a fact that the zoology laboratory at Sarah Lawrence College is one of the few places in the world where it is all but impossible to see a dogfish.

The dogfish, the tree, the seashell, the American Negro, the dream, are 44 rendered invisible by a shift of reality from concrete thing to theory which Whitehead° has called the fallacy of misplaced concreteness. It is the mistaking of an idea, a principle, an abstraction, for the real. As a consequence of the shift, the "specimen" is seen as less real than the theory of the specimen. As Kierkegaard° said, once a person is seen as a specimen of a race or a species, at that very moment he ceases to be an individual. Then there are no more individuals but only specimens.

To illustrate: A student enters a laboratory which, in the pragmatic view, offers the student the optimum conditions under which an educational experience may be had. In the existential view, however — the view of the student in which he is regarded not as a receptacle of experience but as a knowing being whose peculiar property it is to see himself as being in a certain situation — the modern laboratory could not have been more effectively designed to conceal the dogfish forever.

The student comes to his desk. On it, neatly arranged by his instructor, he finds his laboratory manual, a dissecting board, instruments, and a mimeographed list:

Exercise 22: Materials

1 dissecting board
1 scalpel
1 forceps
1 probe
1 bottle india ink and syringe
1 specimen of *Squalus acanthias*

Whitehead   Alfred North Whitehead (1861–1947), English mathematician and philosopher.
Kierkegaard   Sören Aabye Kierkegaard (1813–1855), Danish philosopher and theologian whose philosophy was based on faith and knowledge, thought and reality.

The clue to the situation in which the student finds himself is to be found in the last item: 1 specimen of *Squalus acanthias*.

The phrase *specimen of* expresses in the most succinct way imaginable the radical character of the loss of being which has occurred under his very nose. To refer to the dogfish, the unique concrete existent before him, as a "specimen of *Squalus acanthias*" reveals by its grammar the spoliation of the dogfish by the theoretical method. This phase, *specimen of*, example of, instance of, indicates the ontological status of the individual creature in the eyes of the theorist. The dogfish itself is seen as a rather shabby expression of an ideal reality, the species *Squalus acanthias*. The result is the radical devaluation of the individual dogfish. (The *reductio ad absurdum°* of White-head's shift is Toynbee's° employment of it in his historical method. If a gram of NaCl is referred to by the chemist as a "sample of" NaCl, one may think of it as such and not much is missed by the oversight of the act of being of this particular pinch of salt, but when the Jews and the Jewish religion are understood as — in Toynbee's favorite phrase — a "classical example of" such and such a kind of *Voelkerwanderung,°* we begin to suspect that something is being left out.)

If we look into the ways in which the student can recover the dogfish (or the sonnet), we will see that they have in common the stratagem of avoiding the educator's direct presentation of the object as a lesson to be learned and restoring access to sonnet and dogfish as beings to be known, reasserting the sovereignty of knower over known.

In truth, the biography of scientists and poets is usually the story of the discovery of the indirect approach, the circumvention of the educator's presentation — the young man who was sent to the *Technikum°* and on his way fell into the habit of loitering in book stores and reading poetry; or the young man dutifully attending law school who on the way became curious about the comings and goings of ants. One remembers the scene in *The Heart Is a Lonely Hunter°* where the girl hides in the bushes to hear the Capehart in the big house play Beethoven. Perhaps she was the lucky one after all. Think of the unhappy souls inside, who see the record, worry about scratches, and most of all worry about whether they are *getting it*, whether they are bona fide music lovers. What is the best way to hear

---

reductio ad absurdum A method of disproving a proposition by showing that it leads to an absurdity when carried to its logical conclusion.

Toynbee Arnold Toynbee (1889–1975), English historian, believed that history is shaped by spiritual rather than economic forces.

Voelkerwanderung Barbarian invasion.

Technikum Technical school.

The Heart Is a Lonely Hunter Novel (1940) by Carson McCullers (1917–1967).

Beethoven: sitting in a proper silence around the Capehart or eavesdropping from an azalea bush?

However it may come about, we notice two traits of the second situation: (1) an openness of the thing before one — instead of being an exercise to be learned according to an approved mode, it is a garden of delights which beckons to one; (2) a sovereignty of the knower — instead of being a consumer of a prepared experience, I am a sovereign wayfarer, a wanderer in the neighborhood of being who stumbles into the garden.

One can think of two sorts of circumstances through which the thing 52 may be restored to the person. (There is always, of course, the direct recovery: A student may simply be strong enough, brave enough, clever enough to take the dogfish and the sonnet by storm, to wrest control of it from the educators and the educational package.) First by ordeal: The Bomb falls; when the young man recovers consciousness in the shambles of the biology laboratory, there not ten inches from his nose lies the dogfish. Now all at once he can see it, directly and without let, just as the exile or the prisoner or the sick man sees the sparrow at his window in all its inexhaustibility; just as the commuter who has had a heart attack sees his own hand for the first time. In these cases, the simulacrum of everydayness and of consumption has been destroyed by disaster; in the case of the bomb, literally destroyed. Secondly, by apprenticeship to a great man: One day a great biologist walks into the laboratory; he stops in front of our student's desk; he leans over, picks up the dogfish, and, ignoring instruments and procedure, probes with a broken fingernail into the little carcass. "Now here is a curious business," he says, ignoring also the proper jargon of the specialty. "Look here how this little duct reverses its direction and drops into the pelvis. Now if you would look into a coelacanth, you would see that it — " And all at once the student can see. The technician and the sophomore who loves his textbooks are always offended by the genuine research man because the latter is usually a little vague and always humble before the thing; he doesn't have much use for equipment or the jargon. Whereas the technician is never vague and never humble before the thing; he holds the thing disposed of by the principle, the formula, the textbook outline; and he thinks a great deal of equipment and jargon.

But since neither of these methods of recovering the dogfish is pedagogically feasible — perhaps the great man even less so than the Bomb — I wish to propose the following educational technique which should prove equally effective for Harvard and Shreveport High School. I propose that English poetry and biology should be taught as usual, but that at irregular intervals, poetry students should find dogfishes on their desks and biology students should find Shakespeare sonnets on their dissecting boards. I am serious in declaring that a Sarah Lawrence English major who began poking about in a dogfish with a bobby pin would learn more in thirty minutes than a biology major in a whole semester; and that the latter upon reading on her dissecting board

> That time of year Thou may'st in me behold
> When yellow leaves, or none, or few, do hang
> Upon those boughs which shake against the cold —
> Bare ruin'd choirs where late the sweet birds sang.

might catch fire at the beauty of it.

The situation of the tourist at the Grand Canyon and the biology student are special cases of a predicament in which everyone finds himself in a modern technical society — a society, that is, in which there is a division between expert and layman, planner and consumer, in which experts and planners take special measures to teach and edify the consumer. The measures taken are measures appropriate to the consumer: The expert and the planner *know* and *plan,* but the consumer *needs* and *experiences.*

There is a double deprivation. First, the thing is lost through its packaging. The very means by which the thing is presented for consumption, the very techniques by which the thing is made available as an item of need-satisfaction, these very means operate to remove the thing from the sovereignty of the knower. A loss of title occurs. The measures which the museum curator takes to present the thing to the public are self-liquidating. The upshot of the curator's efforts are not that everyone can see the exhibit but that no one can see it. The curator protests: Why are they so indifferent? Why do they even deface the exhibit? Don't they know it is theirs? But it is not theirs. It is his, the curator's. By the most exclusive sort of zoning, the museum exhibit, the park oak tree, is part of an ensemble, a package, which is almost impenetrable to them. The archaeologist who puts his find in a museum so that everyone can see it accomplished the reverse of his expectations. The result of his action is that no one can see it now but the archaeologist. He would have done better to keep it in his pocket and show it now and then to strangers.

The tourist who carves his initials in a public place, which is theoretically 56 "his" in the first place, has good reasons for doing so, reasons which the exhibitor and planner know nothing about. He does so because in his role of consumer of an experience (a "recreational experience" to satisfy a "recreational need") he knows that he is disinherited. He is deprived of his title over being. He knows very well that he is in a very special sort of zone in which his only rights are the rights of a consumer. He moves like a ghost through schoolroom, city streets, trains, parks, movies. He carves his initials as a last desperate measure to escape his ghostly role of consumer. He is saying in effect: I am not a ghost after all; I am a sovereign person. And he establishes title the only way remaining to him, by staking his claim over one square inch of wood or stone.

Does this mean that we should get rid of museums? No, but it means that the sightseer should be prepared to enter into a struggle to recover a sight from a museum.

The second loss is the spoliation of the thing, the tree, the rock, the swallow, by the layman's misunderstanding of scientific theory. He believes that the thing is *disposed of* by theory, that it stands in the Platonic relation of being a *specimen of* such and such an underlying principle. In the transmission of scientific theory from theorist to layman, the expectation of the theorist is reversed. Instead of the marvels of the universe being made available to the public, the universe is disposed of by theory. The loss of sovereignty takes this form: As a result of the science of botany, trees are not made available to every man. On the contrary. The tree loses its proper density and mystery as a concrete existent and, as merely another *specimen of* a species, becomes itself nugatory.

Does this mean that there is no use taking biology at Harvard and Shreveport High? No, but it means that the student should know what a fight he has on his hands to rescue the specimen from the educational package. The educator is only partly to blame. For there is nothing the educator can do to provide for this need of the student. Everything the educator does only succeeds in becoming, for the student, part of the educational package. The highest role of the educator is the maieutic role of Socrates: to help the student come to himself not as a consumer of experience but as a sovereign individual.

The thing is twice lost to the consumer. First, sovereignty is lost: It is theirs, not his. Second, it is radically devalued by theory. This is a loss which has been brought about by science but through no fault of the scientist and through no fault of scientific theory. The loss has come about as a consequence of the seduction of the layman by science. The layman will be seduced as long as he regards beings as consumer items to be experienced rather than prizes to be won, and as long as he waives his sovereign rights as a person and accepts his role of consumer as the highest estate to which the layman can aspire. 60

As Mounier said, the person is not something one can study and provide for; he is something one struggles for. But unless he also struggles for himself, unless he knows that there is a struggle, he is going to be just what the planners think he is.

AFTERWORD

When Walker Percy writes novels he pursues thought by means of narrative and character which embody ideas and even a thesis, though the reader never sees these fictions as allegorical — ideas talking and wearing clothes — for Percy has the novelist's gift of bestowing life. Similarly his essays use fiction: all these imagined tourists, the imagined real Spanish discoverer, for that matter. If we know his novels, we can imagine a scene where a Percy protagonist visits the Grand Canyon, a chapter which would include the concepts of "The Loss of the Creature."

Although Percy like a modern philosopher resorts to mathematical technique — P for pleasure, or perhaps place — his thought is anecdotal and his philosophy reveals itself through imagined situations. For readers who prefer fiction to algebra, Percy's language makes its point. This essay should touch most immediately upon the college student, who has been trained in abstraction for at least six years and who undergoes during college a quantum leap in abstraction. As Percy says, the student has "a fight . . . on his hands to rescue the specimen from the educational package."

BOOKS AVAILABLE IN PAPERBACK

Lancelot. New York: Avon. *Novel.*

The Last Gentleman. New York: Avon. *Novel.*

Lost in the Cosmos. New York: Washington Square Press. *Essays.*

Love in the Ruins. New York: Avon. *Novel.*

The Message in the Bottle: How Queer Man Is, How Queer Language Is, and What One Has to Do with the Other. New York: Farrar, Straus and Giroux. *Essays.*

The Moviegoer. New York: Avon. *Novel.*

The Second Coming. New York: Washington Square Press. *Novel.*

SAMUEL F. PICKERING, Jr.

SAMUEL F. PICKERING, Jr., was born (1941) in Tennessee and took his B.A. at the University of the South. He took another B.A. at Cambridge University and a Ph.D. at Princeton. He now teaches at the University of Connecticut. As an academic he is a scholar of children's literature. As a writer he practices in the tradition of the informal essay and publishes his work in the Sewanee Review, Yankee, Reader's Digest, National Review, *and* Virginia Quarterly Review. *He collects these essays into books, among them* A Continuing Education *(1985), which contains "Occupational Hazard," and* The Right Distance *(1987).*

Occupational Hazard

Like the indiscretions of youth, some ailments are too boring to be bandied about in medical journals. While a thousand scalpels would leap from operating rooms to preserve the honor of cholera morbus, hardly a lancet would be raised in defense of tennis elbow or housewife's knee. Yet if such ailments do not inspire articles too profound for seriousness, a survey of academics from Maine to California would reveal that occupational hazards spare no named chair. In the paneled halls of ivy lurks pomposity.

Rarely fatal, the virus usually leads to a comfortable mental state in which the sufferer becomes inaccessible to thought. What the disease lacks in virulence, however, it makes up for in epidemic proportions. Even the brightest, blue-eyed, fit young instructor fresh from an exhilarating jog through graduate school eventually slows, swells, and sickens. No antidote has been found for the corrupting effects of being treated by undergraduates as one of the wise men of the ancient world. Slowly the belief that one is Delphic gets under the skin and becomes incurable.

But if medical science has found no vaccine for those sensations so warm to the ego, it has at least marked the stages of the disease's progress. Soon after his first book meets with friendly critical nods, the young assistant professor becomes susceptible. Giving the lie to the old adage that clothes make the man, the sufferer strides into pomposity's deceptive sartorial stage. Paunching slightly with confidence, he wraps himself in a tattered Afghan in the winter and lets his toes dangle through the slits of Rhodean sandals in the summer. When reversed his paisley tie delivers a full-fisted message, matched in its rough whimsicality only by the lavender shorts he wears to the President's tea party. To the outsider this would seem a young man on the way out. But to the cognoscenti, this is clearly a man on the way up. They know that it is only a short step from Afghan to Brooks Brothers. The paisley will be weeded out and Bronzini and Sulka will blossom in its place. The sandals will languish in the closet while those sweet harbingers of spring Whitehouse and Hardy wingtips will escort a new associate professor to that tenured land where Scotch and water purl against ice cubes like the Afton flowing gently to the sea.

Not long afterwards, our subject becomes "Guggenheimed" and flies 4 away for a year in the British Library. A penchant for Gauloises and Harvey's amontillado and the appearance, much anticipated, of the book mark the disease's inexorable progress. After the return from Bloomsbury, Vanity Fair prints of willowy John Whistler and languid Lord Leighton decorate the sufferer's office walls while the poster celebrating the annual rattlesnake roundup in Sweetwater, Texas, curls in the wastecan. In the classroom a great vowel shift occurs as our not-so-young young man sounds like he lost his youth on the playing fields of Eton or under the shadow of King's College Chapel. On the title page of the book, L. Stafford Brown rises like the phoenix from the ashes of Leroy Brown, Jr.

Alas, university life is imperfect. Unlike the happy bovine, the graying academic cannot forever graze in green pastures blissfully ruminating over the cud of learning long digested. Before our sufferer answers the great cattle call from above and assumes the mantle of a named chair, he becomes aware of his illness. While perusing the shelves of the bookstore and pondering a list of books to be read during summer vacation, he hears a student confuse him with Balaam's inelegant long-eared beast of burden. At a colleague's Christmas party, he harangues the pert helpmate of a junior member of the department with learned jocularity. Certain he had left her in the living room like Saul on the road to Damascus blinded by light, he returns from the Necessary House in time to hear her compare him to that befeathered creature whose cackling saved Rome from the Gauls. Awareness sweeps down upon him and he vows to take a cure.

Unfortunately diagnosis is easier than treatment. Several remedies are available; and although each may cause a temporary remission, none can completely eradicate the disease. First our sufferer grows long sideburns and begins frequenting the society of the young and ignorant. With enthusiastic joie de vivre, he puts off the old and selects a new wife from his seminar on the Age of Reason. Sadly he discovers that ignorance charms only at a distance and youth like okra rises on the cultivated stomach. The days when he could burst from bed to greet the sun like a morning glory are over. Before the bottoms of his jogging shoes wear thin, his wife decamps. The shoes join the sandals in the back of the closet, and our professor places his hopes for a cure in canine informality. When the leaves turn gold above the autumn mists, our professor comes to the office carrying a large blanket and leading a small dog. Alas, as little acorns grow into big oaks, so small dogs grow into large beasts. By the summer all the days are dog-days. And when Kim suddenly develops heartworms, the professor openly weeps but privately mixes a decanter of martinis.

Our sufferer's Indian summer of heartiness is over. Elevated to the department chair, he ignores the petty world scrabbling below and nods into graying dignity. Pomposity brooks opposition no longer, and the professor becomes a wonderful old boy in whose presence ideas flap heavily and fall to the ground like dying swans. Alumni recall his incompetence fondly. And when asked to speak at their annual dinner, he charms away fret from their busy lives by stumbling about sleepily. In his presence hardened men of the world drain their cups and recall that splendid time when they were boyish "Sons of old Cayuga."

On the campus stories describing his terse "ah ha's" and thoughtful "um's" abound. His enrollments swell as gentlemanly B's are bestowed with grand largesse. While students dream of girls as sugary as peppermint, the old boy puffs his pipe, rolls his *r*'s, and discusses the Immortal Bard's "Ring of Rightness." Time seems to doze until one long noon when pipe smoke gathers about the professor like cumulus clouds rolling to a storm. Suddenly there is a puff and he is gone. Some say he went above and now sits near the Great White Throne impatient to be promoted out of his number two wings and into number three wings. Some say he went to a warmer place. Others say he never left and that his spirit haunts the university waiting to capture a bushy-tailed young instructor.

Whatever the truth may be, the L. Stafford Brown Reading Room is dedicated at the next commencement. The walls of the room are paneled in rich walnut, rescued from a mildewing English country house. Large stuffed red leather chairs cluster here and there. Along one wall stands an 18th century mahogany and rosewood bookcase. On its shelves are the professor's collection of cream pitchers. From above the mantlepiece, a mantlepiece on which, it is rumored, Dr. Johnson once rested a weary elbow while expostulating with Boswell, stares the professor himself. He appears walking across the Cotswolds. Sheep frisk behind him while in his right hand, he carries *the book*. In his left he holds a pipe. There are always a few bleary-eyed students in the room. Soon it is known as the Cave of the Old Sleeper.

AFTERWORD

In the first two paragraphs, the beginning of the third, and occasionally after-ward, Pickering uses an analogy. It is not so distant a comparison as Lurie's treatment of clothes as language. In fact, it is a commonplace of speech to call something we don't like an illness. ("You're sick, sick, sick!") We call greed a plague, pride an affliction, diffidence a handicap; if we really dislike something we call it a cancer; we speak of people as paralyzed when they cannot make up their minds. Therefore the suggestion that academic pomposity is a physical affliction partakes of triteness; it would be a cliché, or a dead metaphor, simply to say that Professor X suffered from chronic attacks of self-inflation.

But Pickering brings the dead metaphor to life again, and Lazarus rises to walk in his shroud, because this writer expends energy and imagination extending the casual cliché by vivid details. Writers can always resuscitate clichés by diligence and wit. Analogy by its extension restores the life that repetition diminished or even deadened.

When you find a cliché in a draft, usually you do best to cross it out; sometimes you can do the opposite and expand it into vitality.

ALASTAIR
REID

ALASTAIR REID is a Scot, born (1926) in the small town of Whithorn, where his father was a minister. He served in the Royal Navy during World War II and published his first book of poems, To Lighten My House, *in 1953. In the essay collection where we found "Hauntings,"* Whereabouts: Notes on Being a Foreigner *(1987), Reid's theme is a multiplicity of places. His vocation has been restlessness; like the bee he has journeyed from flower to flower, and his garden has been the world: Manhattan, a remote Spanish village, an island in the West Indies, Latin America. He has taught briefly at American universities; he has worked on the staff of the* New Yorker — *many of the essays from* Whereabouts *first appeared in that magazine* — *he has written juveniles, he has translated much from the Spanish, and he has continued to write the poetry that was his first published writing.* Weathering: New and Selected Poems *came out in 1978.*

In 1984 Reid was the source of a moment's controversy. The journalistic air was dense with notions of fraud after a Pulitzer Prize winner was revealed to have fabricated the stories that won the prize. A reporter on the Wall Street Journal *alleged that Reid, in a* New Yorker *piece from Spain, had also invented characters and events — in effect had presented fiction as fact. The editor of the* New Yorker,

397

William Shawn, defended Reid, who had indeed disguised the provenance of certain political comments — during Franco's regime in Spain — to keep his friends out of jail.

Hauntings

My memory had always been to me more duffel bag than filing cabinet, but, even so, I have been fairly sure that if I rummaged enough I could come up with what I needed. Lately, though, certain things have caused me to apply my memory deliberately — to a place, a period in my life, to focus on it and recover it alive. One strong reason has been the death of friends, which shocks one through mourning into a ferocity of remembering, starting up a conversation in the memory in order to hear the dead voice talk, see the dead face come alive. The other impulse to put my memory in some kind of order came from a friend of mine with whom I have kept in written touch for thirty-odd years, who showed me a bulge in his ancient address book where he had had to paste in extra pages to contain more than forty permanent addresses for me since 1950, dotted all over Europe, Latin America, the United States. I looked long at them: French street names scrawled vertically in the margins; telephone numbers that rang very distant bells in my head — some of the places grown so faint that I had to focus hard, pluck at frail threads. I have never kept journals, but I have a jumble of old passports, diaries with little more than places and names, and a few cryptic notes meant to be instant sparks to the memory. Of late, I have taken to picking up threads and winding in, room by room, a house in Spain or an apartment in Geneva; then, with growing Nabokovian intensity, the picture above the fireplace, the sound of the front door closing behind. I have pursued my own chronology not so much to record it as to explore it. Remembering a particular house often brings back a predominant mood, a certain weather of the spirit. Sometimes, opening the door of a till-then-forgotten room brought on that involuntary shiver, that awed suspension. These sudden rememberings are gifts to writers, like the taste of the madeleine — for much of writing is simply finding ways of re-creating astonishments in words. But as I began to reel in my itinerant past I found that I was much less interested in recording it than in experiencing the sense it gave me of traveling in time, of making tangible a ghostly dimension; for an instance of remembering can, without warning, turn into a present moment, a total possession, a haunting.

Chronology can be a hindrance to remembering well: the assumption that individual lives have a design, a certain progression, persists in every-thing from obituaries to ear-written biographies of movie stars. A backward look, besides, is usually disposed to give past time a shape, a pattern, a set of explanations. Memory can be an agile and cunning editor; but if we use it instead as an investigative reporter it often turns up conflicting evidence, for we arrive as we age at a set of recountable versions (long and short) of our private time, a set of serviceable maps of the past to replace the yellowed photographs. If I look at my own time chart, it divides cata-clysmically into two parts, two contradictory modes of being. The first part, brief but everlasting, embraces the rural permanence I was born into in Scotland, articulated by the seasons, with the easy expectation that harvest followed harvest, that years repeated themselves with minor variations (growing being one of them), a time when I was wholly unaware of an outside world; the second part erupted with the Second World War, which obliterated the predictability of anything and severed all flow, all continuity. When I joined the Royal Navy, in the later years of the war, I was projected abruptly out of Scotland and to sea, on a series of small ships, around the Indian Ocean — endless ports of call that were all astonishments. It was never made clear to us where we were going, except to sea; so I learned to live by sea time, which is as close to a blank present as one can come. I also learned to live portably. We would move, on sudden orders, from ship to shore to ship, and what we could carry we could count on keeping; the rest was in the public domain. My personal possessions were not much more than a notebook or two; and, coming home after the war through the Suez Canal, I watched one of these notebooks slither from my fingers and shimmy its wavering way down in the lime green water. It was my first serious lesson in learning to shrug. When I got free of the service, I went back to Scotland to finish a degree at the University of St. Andrews, and then left, as I had long intended, taking as little as possible and making next to no plans.

Although I passed through Scotland irregularly in the next few decades, finding certain epiphanies in the moods of the place, reconnecting with friends and family, I felt firmly severed from it. It was less the past to me than the point of departure; and, besides, I had long disliked the abiding cloud of Calvinism that kept Scotland muffled, wary, resentful. An obli-gation of obedience was written into its educational system, which, when it came to imparting information, was certainly thorough, to use one of the Scots' favorite words; but during my school days if we made trouble or persistently misconstrued Greek irregular verbs our extended hand was struck a variable number of times with a thick leather strap, tongued at the end, called a tawse. The last time I was in Scotland, I discovered that the tawse was still in use. Put together a sniff of disapproval, a wringing of hands, a shaking of the head that clearly expects the worst, and you have some idea of how dire Scotland can be. All the other countries I have lived in have seemed comparatively joyful. The gloom, I hoped, would stay in Scotland and not follow me about. Certainly on these visits I felt no pull to stay. I had got used to the feeling of belonging nowhere, of being a foreigner by choice, entering a new country, a new language, in pursuit, almost, of anonymity and impermanence. Scotland seemed to have little to do with my present, and grew dimmer and dimmer in my memory.

In 1949, I first came to the United States, and it felt like immediate 4
liberation. I could sense the wariness in me melt, the native caution dwindle. Fluidity, it seemed to me, had replaced roots, and change fueled not a wringing of hands but a positive excitement. I taught for a few years, and then decided to live by writing — about the most portable of all occupations, and an always available pretext for traveling. I crossed, and crisscrossed, the Atlantic, mostly by sea, on the great ships that pulled out from the West Side piers in a regular booming of horns; and once crossed under sail. I discovered Spain and the Spanish language, which had far-flung geographical consequences for me, taking me as far as the tip of Chile. I had a number of friends with the same wandering disposition, who would turn up in some of the same places I had stumbled on, and with whom I often crossed paths. What we were all looking for was localities that moved to their own time, unmechanized villages, islands, isolated but not utterly, good places to work in, but with available distraction, refuges, our own versions of a temporary Garden of Eden, which had an illusion of permanence about them, however impermanent the stay. Work would quite often determine my movements; I found that a new place, in the energy of beginning, sharpened the attention. Some of these Edens were remote — a house, a garden, a village, perhaps — and, remembering them, I have to reach far, to remember a previous self. More than that, they are not separate in memory from the people I shared them with. They are places entwined with presences. Looking for temporary Edens is a perpetual lure certainly not confined to writers, who sooner or later discover that the islands of their existence are, in truth, the tops of their desks.

I had been back to Scotland quite often on brief visits, to see my parents as they grew old, into their eighties; but somehow I had never dwelt much on how I had got from there to wherever I was at the time. Then I spent the entire summer of 1980 in Scotland, on an escapade with my son and some friends, digging up a plastic box — a time capsule — that we had buried nine years previously, on the fringes of the golf course at St. Andrews. That summer, I spent a lot of time with my sister Kathleen, who had been my great ally in the turbulence of our growing up. Our parents were dead, and we had met only scantily in recent years, but as the deep green summer rained and rained we found ourselves almost involuntarily rummaging in the past as if it were a miscellaneous attic chest, startling ourselves at a remembered name, to a point at which we were mesmerized by remembering. We had photographs and documents that we had saved from clearing up our parents' papers, but we discovered that in the interaction of our memories we had much more. We re-created our parents from the point that we began, not in any systematic way but in flashes, days and seasons in a single vision. The rain watered my memory, and I found my whole abandoned beginning seeping slowly back, even into dreams.

I was born in a village called Whithorn, in the soft southwest of Scotland. It was my beginning; and, reaching back to it, I realize that for me it has remained in a time warp of its own — my personal Eden, in that although it was lost, the aura that comes back with remembering it stems from a time when house, family, garden, village, and friends were all I knew of the world, when everything had the glow of wholeness, when I had no idea of the passing of time except as anticipation. What I have discovered, too, are the contradictions — in many cases, our own mythifications of that time, the recountable, bookshelf version, which we put together to anchor the past in place. Even so, the myth is bound to predominate; we cannot become who we were or lose what we now know.

Whithorn lies close to the tip of one of the southern fingers of the part of Scotland known as Galloway: isolated, seldom visited, closer across the Irish Sea to Northern Ireland than it seems to the rest of Scotland; closer, too, to Ireland in the softness and cadence of its speech. It is rich, low-lying, carefully cultivated dairy country, with a few small fishing ports, and has a douce, mild climate, thanks to the proximity of the Gulf Stream, which has made certain Galloway gardens famous for their exotic transplantings. Whithorn was also a beginning for my parents. My father came from the midlands of Scotland, a member of the large and humorous family of a schoolmaster I never knew. My father had interrupted his divinity studies at Glasgow University to serve as a combatant in the First World War, and had been wounded in the Second Battle of the Somme; had married my mother, who had recently graduated as a doctor from Glasgow University; and had returned, with the war behind him, to pick up his existence. In 1921, he was chosen and ordained as Church of Scotland minister in Whithorn. The church stood on the site of Whithorn Priory, the first Christian settlement in Britain, founded on the arrival of St. Ninian, in the year 397, and a very early place of pilgrimage. It was my father's first charge, a village of some seven hundred, embracing the surrounding farms. My parents firmly took root there, my father healed over from the war, which nevertheless always troubled his memory, my mother had a house to turn into a household, and in later years they always spoke of these beginnings as a lucky time in their lives, for Galloway contains the kindliest of people in all that flinty country — all in all, a good place to begin in.

In shape, Whithorn looks much like a child's drawing of a village: built on a slope, it has a single main street — the houses on each side of it joined in a single façade, no two of them, however, exactly alike — which widens like a mandolin as it descends to a semblance of a square, where the shops cluster, where the bus pulls in. The street narrows again and runs to the bottom end of the village, where, in our day, the creamery and the railway station stood adjacent to each other. Every morning, the miniature beginnings of a train would start out from Whithorn: a wagonful of full milk churns from the creamery destined for Glasgow; a single passenger coach, occasionally carrying those who had business in the outside world. Whithorn was a place easy to learn by heart. All round it lay the farms and, beyond them, infinitely, the sea.

As minister, my father had the gift of the manse to live in (the houses of Scottish ministers are always called manses), and the manse in Whithorn was an outpost, set apart from the village. From the main street, under an old arch bearing Whithorn's coat of arms, a lane led, first, to the small white church that was my father's charge, surrounded by a well-kept graveyard, where we sometimes practiced our reading from the gravestones. The lane continued left past the church, crested a small rise, and ran down, over the trickle of a stream, to the white gates of the manse. A gravel drive led up to the manse, past a long, walled garden on the right; a semicircle of huge elm and beech trees faced the house from across the drive. Behind the house were stables and outhouses, and all around lay green fields. If you trudged across them, careful in summer to skirt the golden edges of standing oats and barley, you reached the sea — an irresistible pilgrimage.

The manse had the quality of certain Scottish houses — a kind of good sense realized in stone, made to last. There were ample rooms: attic rooms, where we children slept, and played on wet days, as we were born in turn; a study for my father, separated from the stepped-down kitchen by a long flagstone corridor, which led, through sculleries and pantries, to the garden. But it is a peopled place, not an empty house, in my memory. My eldest sister, Margaret, was born two years before my parents came to Whithorn; but there, in the house, my sister Kathleen, I, and my younger sister, Lesley, saw the light in that order, so that we became a tribe, and fell into the rhythms and ways of the place — a wondrous progression that I took in whole, with wide, unjudging eyes.

Whithorn was not at all well-to-do but thrived, rather, on the comfortable working equilibrium of that countryside. Some of its inhabitants went to sea, fishing, but most farmed; the creamery kept the dairy herds profitable; and the place had a kind of self-sufficient cheer that it needed, for it was truly at the end of a long, far line — it and its small seaport village, the Isle of Whithorn, a few miles beyond it, on the coast. There were not many comings and goings, and, so isolated, the people became their own sustenance, and had the warm grace of the countryside. Seven hundred people, if they do not actually know one another, know at least who everyone is. The village had the habit of churchgoing: besides my father, there was a United Free Church minister and a Catholic priest, shepherding even tinier flocks. The three of them became good friends. Like the doctor and the local solicitors, they had essential functions in the community. It was a harmonious place, with no sides, no sharp edges. My birth certificate bears the spidery signature of James J. Colquohoun, the local registrar, who had a head like a shriveled eagle and wore pince-nez, and who had memorized the local population and its ancestral connections so well that he often greeted people by reciting their family tree to them — or, at least, the lower branches.

The manse, the center of our world, hummed with our own lives. It 12 had the equilibrium that families often arrive at for a time before they break up into individual parts. Our household had its own modes and habits, which were set by the design of our parents' lives. Our parents fascinated us as children — during our growing, in particular — for, separately, they had natures about as opposite as seemed possible to us, yet they were never separate, and were noticeably devoted. My father, soft-spoken, gentle of manner, edging on shy, with a natural kindness and humor never far from his eyes, grew to be much liked in the place. When we walked with him, people would greet him warmly, and we would include ourselves by clutching at him. When we were assembled as a family, at meals, or on fire-circling evenings, he would question us, tease us, tell us stories; at other times he might take us, singly, on visits to farms; but often, poised at his desk reading, or sitting in an armchair with an unfixed gaze, he seemed to have pulled over him a quilt of silence, to be inhabiting an unreachable solitude. We grew used, also, to his different presences. On Sundays, he appeared in the pulpit, wearing his robes and a grave face, and we listened more than anything to the measured cadence of his pulpit voice. After church, except when it was raining, we waited for him in the garden, for he took a shortcut across the fields and dropped over the garden wall, returned from gravity into fatherhood, much to our relief.

My mother revered my father; and, as if to insure his chosen quiet, she forswore the practice of medicine and took over control of the house, the household, and us children, delegating us tasks according to our abilities. As with all houses in the country, there were endless chores, always a need of hands. The Church of Scotland paid its ministers very small stipends indeed, and although the manses were substantial houses, some of the more remote of them had fallen behind in time. We drew all our water from a hand pump — a domestic replica of the village pump — in the scullery off the kitchen. It was the obligation of the last pumper to leave behind three full buckets. The house was heated by coal fires and lit by oil lamps. These I would watch my father assemble on the lamp table, where he filled them, trimmed the wicks, and polished the funnels — a task I apprenticed myself to as soon as I could. We willingly ran on errands to the village like missions — for it was a common practice there to send notes by hand, using the mails only for letters to the world. When my two older sisters were in the village school, I inherited their task of walking across the fields to the creamery with a pitcher, to have it filled with still warm milk, and would wander home slowly by way of my private shrines.

My mother, whose father, younger sister, and brother were all doctors, showed no impulse to practice medicine. I suspect now that, having grown up in a medical household, tied always to one end of a wire of availability, she did not want ours to be so bound. But we got to know the local doctor well, and my mother would stand in for him when he was away, sometimes seeing his patients in the kitchen, which we would unclutter for the occasion. Neither was it uncommon for her to be summoned by an anxious knocking late at night when the doctor was out on call and could not be found. She did not, however, believe in sending out bills for any medical services, and never did. Added to that, my father's stipend was paid in part according to the old Scottish tithing system, whereby farmers who cultivated church land paid a tithe of their crop, or its market value, to help sustain the parish, so we had more than a passing interest in the harvest. As a consequence, our larder, with its long blue slate counter, was regularly replenished with fresh eggs, butter, oats, potatoes, game — the green abundance of that patiently farmed place. My father never carried money, nor did we, unless we were ordered to for something specific. At intervals, he paid all the bills at a stroke, totaling them carefully and going out the next day to the bank to take out the necessary sum. Occasionally, he would let us look at the notes before he paid them over, but I had not grasped the idea of money, and it did not interest us much — except for my sister Margaret, who was already plaguing us with knowing school airs.

My father's single obsession was with cars, and he drove very fast — this always surprised and delighted us — about the countryside, on his pastoral visits, in an ancient Fiat that looked half like a carriage. We had a network of friends on the surrounding farms, some of which were close enough for us, when we reached a certain age, to point ourselves like crows toward them, navigating the fields and stone dikes in between. I loved the days on the farm — the rituals of milking, still by hand; the work that changed according to season and weather — and I used to stay over at one farm, Broughton Mains, for haying in June, and for the golden weeks of harvest in late August: days we passed in the field, helping or playing;

days punctuated by the women bringing hampers of food they had spent the morning preparing; the fields orderly at the end of the day, the bound oats in their rows of standing clumps; days that felt like rites. After we had left Whithorn, I would go back to Broughton Mains for the peak of the harvest, immemorially, for there that drama of abundance crowned the whole year.

We spent as much as we could of the daylight of our lives then outdoors, the house a headquarters among the fields and climbable trees, or a shelter on days of rain or raw weather. Sometimes we would be recruited in a body to help in the garden — a string of small bearers, baskets of weeds on our heads. My world at that time embraced five villages, a dozen farms, a river, and three beaches, some houses we visited often, a countable number of friends we knew by name. We sailed sometimes on a fishing boat out of the Isle of Whithorn, and we often watched five or six local boats come in with their catches, sometimes with herring for the taking. My father preached there on odd Sunday evenings, in a small white church that protruded into the harbor, waves sometimes leaving their spray on its latticed windows during the service. Galloway mostly has soft winters and early springs, and we learned and looked for signs of growing, we followed the progress of the garden and the sown fields surrounding us, we eavesdropped on the farms, trying to pick up nuggets of country wisdom, and we practiced looking wisely at the sky.

From quite early on, our household grew its own legislative procedures when it came to deciding the shapes of days. Decisions, serious decisions, it was understood, lay with my father; but my mother was his plenipotentiary, and our initial dealings — from trivial to urgent — took place through her. She drove hard bargains, and sometimes we would waylay my father to appeal her rulings, for he was a natural peacemaker, patient in argument, attentive to language, and, we felt, fair. It was action my mother believed in, and if we wanted to talk to her it generally meant joining her in turning a small chaos of some kind into active order. She, too, had different manifestations. We overheard her at times talking to a patient — certain, quiet, reassuring. My father had a fair number of callers, and she had the skill of a diplomat in seeing that they did not consume his time. But when we wanted to talk to her it might involve holding a skein of wool for her to wind into a ball, or picking gooseberries by the basketful while we plied her with questions, which she answered crisply, her hands never still for a moment.

There is one period that I find comes back to me with particular clarity, but I am also aware of having mythified it: I had barely turned four; Margaret and Kathleen, in the turn of the years, were away all day at school; my sister Lesley, still a baby, slept in her pram most of the time outside the front door, which the swallows that nested in the stables every year swooped past all day long. The days then were my own, and I wandered on a long lead from the house, walking the flat-topped garden wall, damming the stream, skirting the bees, poking in the stables, and gravitating, in between quests, to the house. Outside, I was busy peopling my solitude, but when I came in I would find myself in the flagstone corridor, the steps down to the kitchen and my mother's domain at one end, the closed door to my father's study at the other. Some days, turning right, I would seek out my mother in the kitchen as she was baking, stocking the larder ahead of our appetites, and I would sit at a corner of the kitchen table, fascinated by the soft grain of its worn wood, while my mother, who, although she preferred working company, also liked company while she worked. I always took the opportunity to nudge her with questions, for I was extremely unclear about the obvious differences between the conditions of the visitors who came to see my father and those who on occasion would wait their turn to see my mother. When my father was talking with a parishioner in the front room, all that came through the closed door was a murmur of voices, but when my mother saw patients in the kitchen we heard, more than once, discomfiting cries from that end of the corridor. Were there some people who might call to see *both* my father and my mother? My mother avoided metaphysics, but she would give me occasional small seminars on things like the digestive system, or why we yawn — hardly the whole medical education I was keen to extract from her. Sometimes I would go with her on an errand to town, and she would explain to me who people were, what they did, their names — teaching me the village and its ways, for she had chosen to live within its particularities happily and actively, and she was the source of our tribal energies.

On other days, I would turn left along the corridor, open the door to my father's study, quietly, as I had learned to do, and find him at his desk, wreathed in smoke, a pool of concentration. He always took me in — he had his own quiet, and did not need silence — and sat me on a hassock by the stretch of bookshelves that held atlases, books with pictures, and an illustrated history of the First World War. This I would lug out, volume by voume, lying full length and gazing in incomprehension at the sepia photographs of blighted landscapes and the skeletons of buildings. Sometimes, when I had his attention, he would begin to explain the pictures to me, or show me on the map where he had been, where the battle lines met, but never for very long, for the subject frayed him. I remember sitting in that room of words and feeling islanded by not being able to read, for I felt that words were my father's business — his reading, his sermons, his writings, the fact that people came to him for his words. Even now, I am still pacing that corridor.

In that encapsulated world, I lived in complete innocence of time, except 20 that school was looming. I could not think of years as doing anything other than repeating themselves, nor did I want them to. But time did intrude, abruptly, into my wide-eyed world: we left Whithorn. My father accepted a call to a larger church, in Selkirk — a town in the Border district, much farther to the east, much larger, with working tweed mills, and set in rolling, forested sheep-farming country, crossed by rivers like the Tweed itself, salmon-famous. Needless to say, I had no voice in the moving, nor did I properly grasp its implications, for I had no idea what moving meant. I had not, after all, moved anywhere before. When we did move, time began for me, and Whithorn became my first loss. After a jolt of dislocation, I found myself in a place I could not recognize, full of strangers, everything to be learned again, and I begged my parents to go back. Bitterly, I mourned for Whithorn, in uncooperative silence, before I began to take a wary look around me. Selkirk was almost ten times as big as the village, and our house had a bigger garden, lawns, a small wood, more and grander rooms, hills to look at, even gaslight. It stood not far from the marketplace, which brimmed with shoppers and gossip; it had a telephone and a constancy of visitors; but I hung back from it, looking bewilderedly backward through the glass that had suddenly slid between me and a place that I had belonged to and that had also belonged to me. Leaving Whithorn was my first experience of acquiring a past; what I had left behind forever, I think, was the certainty of belonging — something I have never felt since.

What kept Whithorn alight and gave it an Edenic cast in my backward vision had to do with the natural world, the agrarian round, a way of life I had seen and felt as whole. From now on, these harmonies gave way to the human world, to other sets of rules and obligations, to a localism we were still strangers to, as we were to the different lilt in the voices. School began for me, and I did not find it an arrangement that I took to, except that I realized that if I were to go through with it I would know how to read at some point, and the books in my father's library would open and talk to me. As children, we were before long occupied in putting together new worlds of our own, making friends, laying down landmarks. In Scotland, the Border towns, ravaged across centuries by skirmishing with the English on both sides of the border, had an aggressive localism to them, something approaching a fortress mentality. Not to be born in Selkirk, we soon found out, amounted to an irremediable flaw; in the eyes of the staunchest locals we were naturally blighted, outsiders by definition — a tag I accepted quite happily, for I had come to much the same verdict about Selkirk.

Whereas Whithorn, with seven hundred people, had been a particularity, Selkirk, with around six thousand, remained an abstraction. Since it was bigger and much less remote — Edinburgh was not much over an hour away — many more things seemed to happen, and my parents' lives grew brisker; that made them less accidentally accessible to us. My father had a larger study, upstairs, with a window seat from which we could look south to the hazy blue of the Cheviot Hills, where the border with England lay. I laid an early claim to that seat as my reading post, and sometimes, struck book-deaf, I would have to be dragged from it, my eyes forcibly unfixed from the print. A large kitchen on the ground floor became a kind of operations room, which my mother ran just as energetically as she had run the smaller universe of Whithorn. Our household tasks multiplied, and the burden of a bigger garden spoiled my relations with the soil for a considerable time. With several doctors in the town, my mother gave almost no attention to medicine — at least, until the war loomed. My medical curiosity dried up for the time being; but my father, as if suddenly realizing my new literacy, decided to teach me Latin and Greek, for he had been a good classicist. He was patient and enthusiastic at the same time, and I was a diligent pupil, for I felt that these lessons were at last giving me entry into my father's province. When I came to take classics in school, I was well ahead, but I kept the fact secret, because it lightened the burden of the work we were always scrawling away at with inky fingers.

Where Whithorn had been purely a rural community, Selkirk had a different class structure, in part agricultural — a way of life we were in tune with, although after dairy farms I found sheep country dull and somnolent — and in part industrial, for the woollen mills were clustered in the valley along the River Ettrick, at the foot of the town, and sounded their sirens morning and evening. Mill owners, landowners, farm workers, mill workers — the town had an intricate hierarchy. Again, ministers, doctors, lawyers, by dint of their professions, moved easily across those class lines, but the town itself was stiff with them. We found ourselves referred to as the manse children, and a certain expectation of virtue was pinned to us with the phrase. As doctor's children, too, I suppose we were expected to be models of health. My mother was the most downright of doctors, and, I think, suspected the sick mostly of malingering. We certainly could not fool her with imaginary ills; but when she had to doctor one of us with any seriousness we saw her change, as my father did on Sundays, into someone serious and separate from us.

Margaret, my eldest sister, and Lesley, my youngest, formed a kind of parenthesis to our family. It was Kathleen and I, closest in age and temperament, who compared notes, speculated, pooled information; and it was with Kathleen that I shared my perplexities over religion, my father's domain. We were by now used to his transformations from old gardening clothes into the dark formality, clerical collar in place, tile hat in hand, that a wedding or a funeral demanded; but while in Whithorn churchgoing had seemed a cheerful family occasion, in Selkirk the lofty, well-filled church wore a kind of pious self-importance, and churchgoing took on a solemnity we had not bargained for. Saturday nights, we would get out of the way early, leaving my father settled in his study, hunched into the small hours over the bones of his sermon for the next day. On Sundays, he would appear for breakfast already shaved, dressed, and collared, and would set out for church ahead of us, leaving us to ready ourselves for the summoning of the church bell. The manse pew, where we were obliged to sit, was prominently placed, so my mother, who took appearances much more seriously than any of the rest of us, decreed that, barring emergencies like the Great Plague, three of the four of us would attend church with her every Sunday morning — in a rotation we sometimes used as a trading currency. Churchgoing was something I grew used to, letting my mind wander about in an uncontrolled mixture of attentions; but as I took in the bewildering anthology of human faces — I gazed as often as I dared at a man with white hair and a ginger mustache — I was listening in a subliminal way to the cadence of my father's voice, mesmerized by the sudden incandescence of a phrase, fascinated by the convoluted metrics of certain hymns, stirred by the grave measures of the liturgy, aware of language as a kind of spell, and astonished when, freed by a dismissive organ voluntary, the congregation made its way out into the unsanctified air, and all burst out talking at once, as though to make up for the imposed silence of church.

But to be left at home one Sunday out of four, to be alone, with the run of the house — that was the time we coveted. We were obliged only to keep an eye on whatever was simmering on the stove. We were expected to be chiseling away at homework. But the whole house was ours for a church-length, and we could open otherwise forbidden doors, drawers, and books, and play the piano without fear of being heard, although sometimes I would wander slowly from room to room just to take in the rarity of the silence. Everything had to be back in place before the gate clicked and the churchgoers tumbled in, smug with virtue but glad to be freed from the weight of it. Sunday lunches were events. More sumptuous than usual, they awaited my father's return, unrobed and predictably cheerful, for he had cleared what seemed to us his week's work — or, at least, its main hurdle — and the rest of the day lay ahead for us like a gift of time, before Monday dawned.

Kathleen and I at one point befriended Tom the Beadle, the church janitor, and, borrowing his keys, we would sometimes go exploring in the empty church: the halls underneath it, which smelled of musty stone; the cushioned vestry, where my father changed; up the back staircase into the church itself, and into the pulpit, where, however, we did not linger. In time, we learned to start the organ and play whatever scraps of music we had at our fingertips, but we were eventually banished by Tom, who feared, I think, that one day we would be tempted to pull the bell rope — his most public and audible formal duty. I feel that what perplexed us then was the sense, where religion was concerned, of having backstage connections. I realize now that I never felt a religious fervor: for me, the mysteries lay elsewhere. Very clearly, I had worked out the idea that God, in some inexplicable way, was my father's boss, and I saw church services from backstage as weekly programs with minor variations. Besides, my father was much less a religious thinker than an instinctive comforter and clarifier. I knew that he hid his shyness behind an assumed solemnity, and what concerned me most was that his parishioners saw and heard only his grave public self, not the person he changed into when he came back to us, teasing, telling stories, gloom gone. He never laid down laws, nor did we ever discuss religion: questions of doubt or belief did not trouble him, for he was less interested in religious dogma than in its human translation. For him, being a minister implied the same human practicality that was my mother's dimension. We used to suggest to them that they work as a team, but in fact they did just that. It was in his human form that we worshiped our father. His more formal self he left behind in the vestry, with his robes. He forgave us our irreverence — he abhorred piety and did not make us feel any obligation toward virtue. Our family image concerned my mother much more, but our natural anarchy prevailed. Their differences captivated us more and more. My father had infinite patience, my mother very little; and although she was as voluble as he was quiet, she never read, while I had entered a whole universe of reading, and my father would leave books lying about for me to discover. I always read during his sermons, a volume of Oxford *World Classics*, which were luckily bound like Bibles; my father, too shy to let me know that he knew and did not mind, always gave me a new *World Classic* for my birthday. Yet although I had moved into my father's domain of language, I still had a secret fixation on being a doctor — an unmentioned ambition I shelved once the war had begun, for medical students were exempted from military service and I had no wish to be.

Selkirk enclosed us in its rituals, Whithorn receded; and I suppose I began to think of it quite early as my childhood, my lost past, for the connections thinned and the haunting subsided in the frenzy of the present. I now think of that time in Selkirk, when the war loomed, as the beginning of disintegration — a movement from that once-glimpsed wholeness toward a splintering of time, the oncoming of many separations. We would never belong again, in that first sense. In Selkirk, I worked on farms in my vacations, and at a nearby grain mill with a waterwheel — the owner would give me work when I wanted it, and used to put away a part of my wages for me "just in case," as he would say. I haunted the green and bountiful countryside, but it did not haunt me back. Still, the town grew familiar, wearable, and the vast house enclosed us, although in increasingly separating solitudes, rooms of our own. I can remember those years most easily by the steady progression through school; but we were well aware of the slow edging into war, and then, during the Sunday-morning service, I remember Tom the Beadle suddenly entering the church and painfully climbing the pulpit steps to whisper in my father's ear, and then my father's quiet announcement that war had been declared.

The war disrupted ordinary human time. For anyone over fifty, it forms 28 a huge hinge in time. Nothing, we knew, would be the same again. Our childhood was over at a stroke. The town kept the skeleton of its old life going, but it became the center of a new and shifting one — troops passing through or stationed nearby, local people taking off into uniformed uncertainty, air-raid drills, austerities, school periods given over to cultivating an enormous food garden, my mother becoming attendant medical officer at a recruitment center, my father summoned to serve on a variety of committees, blackouts every evening. From that time on, throughout the war, I cannot put my memory in any presentable order, although I can pull back pieces and happenings in abundance. The impediment to memory, I suspect, is that none of that time was chosen time. In the service, we were moved about the world by decisions so anonymously distant from us that they might have been dice throws; and whatever happened — grotesque, exasperating, ludicrous, horrible as it may have been in its happening — soon receded into impermanence, because forgetting made the war much easier to survive than remembering. It scarcely arises now, either in memory or in dream, for I have instinctively enclosed it in a warp outside real time. It makes no more sense in the memory than it did in its nightmare reality.

The war dispirited my father, and he brooded more; but we were all so occupied then that we never stopped to take stock. The war sent us children in different directions and gave years time to pass. We did not project any future, but after that we met as a family only rarely or accidentally. I felt that my past had been wiped off the blackboard, and that only when the war was over could my chosen life begin. Whithorn, our early Eden, our world without end, our calendar of growing, had vanished forever; and when I went home on leave just before going overseas I realized that our family had changed from a whole into separate parts. The war aged my parents, and when it was over my father moved back to the kindlier west, to a village parish, even smaller than Whithorn but tuned to the seasonal round. When I visited my parents there, separate though we now were, in time, in place, in mind, I saw how close they were, and how the corridor that had preoccupied me with its polarities had been more an illusion of mine than anything else. What I inherited firmly from my father was the way he used time. Knowing what he had to do, he gave his days a shape of his own devising, for he was not bound by any timetable except on Sundays. Sitting at his desk in the evenings, he put his world in order. He owned his own time, and I wanted to do the same somehow. With my mother, I still argued, but we children had always had to bargain for time with her, because she had the kind of restless zeal that fumes at those who do not share it. I found among my father's papers a letter she had written to him when she was in her seventies, from an Edinburgh hospital during a brief stay, a love letter of such tenderness that it made me realize how close they had been, how dependent on each other, across what seemed to us the gulf of their difference.

After the war had cooled and subsided and I had separated myself from Scotland, my shifting life began — a long series of transitions. It was too late to return to the garden but not to inhabit temporary gardens. Of the string of houses and countries I inhabited, my memories are clearer — or, at least, clarifiable — since I can recall roughly why I was there, what I was doing, the people who came and went at the time. I still have many friends from those traveling years, and sometimes, scrambling about in the past, a friend and I will come up with something surprising and illuminating to both of us. My son and I, during our travels, spent three years at the end of the sixties living on an old Thames barge converted to a houseboat and moored in a line of others at Chelsea Reach, in London. Not long ago, we sat down and deliberately set about remembering. It was like dredging the Thames, for we recovered a lot of flotsam — sounds and sayings, the sway of the boat rising on the tide, the names and manners of our floating neighbors, incidents, accidents, the cast of characters who crossed our gangplank. We swamped ourselves with memory and returned to the present with a start.

Certain houses, however, retain in my memory a vividness that amounts to haunting — a mill where I once lived in the French Basque country, a street in Barcelona that became a warm locality, a courtyard in Chile that no longer exists, the stony house in the mountains in Spain that served as a retreat for more than twenty years, and that I have absorbed, stone by stone, to the point of being able to assume its silence in my mind. The addresses serve only as starting points: the places are there to wind in, when we have to recall them to clarify the present. But these houses were theaters for such a multiplicity of happenings, of human connections, of moods and modes, that they are mostly touchstones to memory, fixed points for it to start up from, because the houses have, for the most part, outlived our occupation of them. What I find my memory doing is reaching back, by way of place, to repeople past time, to recover lost presences, forgotten emotions. I think I remember more vividly through the ear than through the eye. If I can recover a voice, if I can fix the image and sound of someone talking, the atmospherics of place swim back with the sound, and the lost wavelengths reconnect themselves, across time, across absence, across loss. Voices remain living, and memory, for once, does not tamper with them. I can hear at will the measured phrasing of my father's pulpit voice, as I can the patient encouragement with which he led me through Tacitus, word by word.

I was with my father for the last month of his life in a thick green 32 summer, in the Border village he had come to rest in. Frail as he was, we would talk in the mornings, and it was to Whithorn that he always strayed, for it had remained his chosen place, the time of his life he liked to wander back to. He had once asked me, a year or two before, to take his ashes there when he died, and I had promised him solemnly that I would. The box of ashes sat in my desk drawer in London for over a year before I could make what is now a complicated journey back to that small, lost place; but I nodded to the box whenever I opened the drawer, and always felt the pull of memory, the trickle of forgotten details. I had negotiated for a small plot in the cemetery, and one Christmas I made the journey north. On a rainy, windswept morning, we buried the small box, attended by the incumbent minister and a small knot of aging parishioners, who remembered him and me. I called on those I still had attachments to, I walked the faint paths across fields more by instinct than anything else, I made a cursory visit to the manse. I did not stay long, for, inside, it had assumed the dimensions of other people — nothing to do with the images I carried. I did, however, verify that the corridor was not in fact endless but quite short, and found that the flagstones had given way to carpet. At twilight, coming back from a circuitous, meditative walk, I saw the manse light up suddenly in the early dusk, and it glowed through so many layers of time for me in that instant that it seemed like a ship that had been moored there forever, further back than I knew. I did not, however, decide to stay in Whithorn, although I felt myself no stranger.

There is a certain irresistibility about returning to past places: the visit may correct the memory or activate it, but it always carries an expectation of surprise. One fall during the sixties, I had to go unexpectedly to Edinburgh, and, seeing a bus that announced "SELKIRK" as its destination, I climbed aboard it, on a sudden whim, and was soon lumbering south, sparks flying in my memory as the countryside grew at first recognizable and then familiar. As I stepped down into the marketplace, several old films were all rolling at once in my head, and I made my way through a close toward the green back gate, latched on a spring, that I had shouldered open a thousand times. I sprang it open once more, to find not the cavernous house that had been our adolescent battleground, not the towering elm and the monumental beech hedge it had taken me two days to clip into shape, but nothing at all. Open air, bare ground, an idle bulldozer, and a man steadying a theodolite where the yew tree I used to hide myself in had stood. The man told me that within the year a whole housing scheme would take shape where our house once was. I did not go into the past with him. All I found was a surviving sliver of the garden wall, a thin,

teetering pillar of stone; but I left without taking even a piece as a touchstone.

> The house that shored my childhood up
> razed to the ground? I stood, amazed,
> gawking at a block of air,
> unremarkable except
> I had hung it once with crazy
> daywish and nightmare.
>
> Expecting to pass a wistful
> indulgent morning, I had sprung the gate.
> Facing me was a wood
> between which and myself
> a whole crow-gabled and slated
> mythology should have stood.
>
> No room now for the rambling
> wry remembering I had planned;
> nor could I replant
> that plot with a second childhood.
> Luck, to have been handed
> instead a forgettable element,
>
> and not to have had to meet
> regretful ghosts in rooms of glass.
> That house by now is fairytale
> and I can gloss it over
> as easily as passing
> clear through a wall.

My parents confessed later that they had not been able to bring themselves
to tell any of us about the removal of the house; but the disquiet, I suspect,
lay more with them, although Selkirk was a place they had never warmed
to, never gone back to. In a country like Scotland, where to endure is all,
razing an old house smacks of sacrilege, an insult to the past. Curiously, I
was not particularly disturbed by its absence. Physically, it no longer existed, true, and so could not contradict or confirm by its presence the mass
of memory it had generated. But I felt that if I were to apply my memory
patiently I could rebuild it, restore it, people it, putting together the enormous jigsaw puzzle of detail to arrive at the wholeness of a household.
But, as Borges reminds us often, forgetting is not only desirable but necessary; otherwise memory would overwhelm us. What haunts me most of
all, however, is that the house has not gone, nor have our memories been
wiped clean of it. All I would have to do is find the thread ends and slowly
reel it all in, from dark to light, as when, at the fall of dark, I would go
round the selfsame house from room to room carrying a lighted taper. I

would turn on the gas and hold the flame close to the mantle until it went
Plop! and lit up, opening my eyes to a room that no longer exists but is
there somewhere, should I ever want it back.

AFTERWORD

*To write is to remember. Even when you write an editorial about an issue of the
moment, you ransack your mind for details — out of experience, out of reading and
thinking — to support your argument. I say* ransack, *using a dead metaphor on
purpose: ransack as with a duffelbag? attic? junkyard or dump? filing cabinet? If a
filing cabinet is to be ransacked, it probably resembles a duffelbag.*

*If all writing uses memory, reminiscence multiplies memory by memory. Reid
identifies the intensity of these "Hauntings" by ascribing their* raison d'être *to the
death of friends — which may remind us that hauntings are achievements of the
dead. Then comes a phrase that exemplifies the power and skill of this writer —
three nouns and three prepositional phrases: "Through mourning into a ferocity of
remembering": How* ferocity *rises to a shout, centered between the whispers of*
mourning *and* remembering. *Reid's emotive, scrupulous language continues with
"starting up a conversation in the memory in order to hear the dead voice talk, see
the dead face come alive" — our desire for being haunted.*

*Although it is the "deaths of friends" that Reid mentions — and they are real
enough — surely by the end of this essay we understand that the deaths of fathers
are more to the point. "I was with my father for the last month of his life. . . ."
"The box of ashes sat in my desk drawer in London for over a year. . . ." This box
of ashes is metaphor (I don't mean it wasn't a box of ashes) for memory itself, and
the essay ends with a hymn to memory: "forgetting is not only desirable but
necessary; otherwise memory would overwhelm us. What haunts me" — this writer
knows what he says — "most of all, however, is that the house has not gone, nor
have our memories been wiped clean of it."*

ADRIENNE
RICH

*W*HEN ADRIENNE RICH (b. 1929) was a junior in college, the poet W. H.
Auden selected her first book of poems, A Change of World, for the Yale
Series of Younger Poets Award. It was published in 1951 as she graduated from
Radcliffe College, and a year later she became a Guggenheim Fellow. After six
further books of poems, including Diving into the Wreck, *which won the National*
Book Award in 1974, she published The Fact of a Doorframe: Poems Selected
and New, 1950–1984; *more recently she collected new poems in* Your Native
Land, Your Life *(1986).*

Rich's first prose book was Of Woman Born: Motherhood as Experience
and Institution *(1976), which she followed with an essay collection,* On Lies,
Secrets, and Silence *(1979), which reprinted "Taking Women Students Seriously,"*
a talk that Rich gave to the New Jersey College and University Coalition on Women's
Education. In 1986 she collected Blood, Bread, and Poetry: Selected Prose,
1979–1985. *At the time of her remarkable early success, she was widely praised as*
a talented young writer and sometimes criticized as conventional or even complacent.
In a long and gradual change, she has become a spokeswoman for the principled
anger of feminist outrage. No one of her talented generation of American writers
has taken so decisively radical a direction.

When she was still in her early twenties, she developed arthritis which, with some periods of remission, has afflicted her ever since and required many operations. She has three sons and was widowed in 1970. She has taught widely: Brandeis University, Douglass College of Rutgers University, and most recently Stanford University, where she is a professor of English and Feminist Studies.

Taking Women Students Seriously

I see my function here today as one of trying to create a context, delineate a background, against which we might talk about women as students and students as women. I would like to speak for a while about this background, and then I hope that we can have, not so much a question period, as a raising of concerns, a sharing of questions for which we as yet may have no answers, an opening of conversations which will go on and on.

When I went to teach at Douglass, a women's college, it was with a particular background which I would like briefly to describe to you. I had graduated from an all-girls' school in the 1940s, where the head and the majority of the faculty were independent, unmarried women. One or two held doctorates, but had been forced by the Depression (and by the fact that they were women) to take secondary school teaching jobs. These women cared a great deal about the life of the mind, and they gave a great deal of time and energy — beyond any limit of teaching hours — to those of us who showed special intellectual interest or ability. We were taken to libraries, art museums, lectures at neighboring colleges, set to work on extra research projects, given extra French or Latin reading. Although we sometimes felt "pushed" by them, we held those women in a kind of respect which even then we dimly perceived was not generally accorded to women in the world at large. They were vital individuals, defined not by their relationships but by their personalities; and although under the pressure of the culture we were all certain we wanted to get married, their lives did not appear empty or dreary to us. In a kind of cognitive dissonance, we knew they were "old maids" and therefore supposed to be bitter and lonely; yet we saw them vigorously involved with life. But despite their existence as alternate models of women, the *content* of the education they gave us in no way prepared us to survive as women in a world organized by and for men.

From that school, I went on to Radcliffe, congratulating myself that now I would have great men as my teachers. From 1947 to 1951, when I graduated, I never saw a single woman on a lecture platform, or in front of a class, except when a woman graduate student gave a paper on a special topic. The "great men" talked of other "great men," of the nature of Man, the history of Mankind, the future of Man; and never again was I to experience, from a teacher, the kind of prodding, the insistence that my best could be even better, that I had known in high school. Women students were simply not taken very seriously. Harvard's message to women was an elite mystification: we were, of course, part of Mankind; we were special, achieving women, or we would not have been there; but of course our real goal was to marry — if possible, a Harvard graduate.

In the late sixties, I began teaching at the City College of New York — 4 a crowded, public, urban, multiracial institution as far removed from Harvard as possible. I went there to teach writing in the SEEK° Program, which predated Open Admissions and which was then a kind of model for programs designed to open up higher education to poor, black, and Third World students. Although during the next few years we were to see the original concept of SEEK diluted, then violently attacked and betrayed, it was for a short time an extraordinary and intense teaching and learning environment. The characteristics of this environment were a deep commitment on the part of teachers to the minds of their students; a constant, active effort to create or discover the conditions for learning, and to educate ourselves to meet the needs of the new college population; a philosophical attitude based on open discussion of racism, oppression, and the politics of literature and language; and a belief that learning in the classroom could not be isolated from the student's experience as a member of an urban minority group in white America. Here are some of the kinds of questions we, as teachers of writing, found ourselves asking:

1. What has been the student's experience of education in the inadequate, often abusively racist public school system, which rewards passivity and treats a questioning attitude or independent mind as a behavior problem? What has been her or his experience in a society that consistently undermines the selfhood of the poor and the nonwhite? How can such a student gain that sense of self which is necessary for active participation in education? What does all this mean for us as teachers?

SEEK   Search for Education, Elevation, and Knowledge, a program with instruction by college teachers, artists, and writers.

2. How do we go about teaching a canon of literature which has consistently excluded or depreciated nonwhite experience?

3. How can we connect the process of learning to write well with the student's own reality, and not simply teach her/him how to write acceptable lies in standard English?

When I went to teach at Douglass College in 1976, and in teaching women's writing workshops elsewhere, I came to perceive stunning parallels to the questions I had first encountered in teaching the so-called disadvantaged students at City. But in this instance, and against the specific background of the women's movement, the questions framed themselves like this:

1. What has been the student's experience of education in schools which reward female passivity, indoctrinate girls and boys in stereotypic sex roles, and do not take the female mind seriously? How does a woman gain a sense of her *self* in a system — in this case, patriarchal capitalism — which devalues work done by women, denies the importance and uniqueness of female experience, and is physically violent toward women? What does this mean for a woman teacher?

2. How do we, as women, teach women students a canon of literature which has consistently excluded or depreciated female experience, and which often expresses hostility to women and validates violence against us?

3. How can we teach women to move beyond the desire for male approval and getting "good grades" and seek and write their own truths that the culture has distorted or made taboo? (For women, of course, language itself is exclusive: I want to say more about this further on.)

In teaching women, we have two choices: to lend our weight to the forces that indoctrinate women to passivity, self-depreciation, and a sense of powerlessness, in which case the issue of "taking women students seriously" is a moot one; or to consider what we have to work against, as well as with, in ourselves, in our students, in the content of the curriculum, in the structure of the institution, in the society at large. And this means, first of all, taking ourselves seriously: Recognizing that central responsibility of a woman to herself, without which we remain always the Other, the defined, the object, the victim; believing that there is a unique quality of validation, affirmation, challenge, support, that one woman can offer another. Believing in the value and significance of women's experience, traditions, perceptions. Thinking of ourselves seriously, not as one of the boys, not as neuters, or androgynes, but *as women*.

Suppose we were to ask ourselves, simply: What does a woman need to know? Does she not, as a self-conscious, self-defining human being, need a knowledge of her own history, her much-politicized biology, an awareness of the creative work of women of the past, the skills and crafts and techniques and powers exercised by women in different times and cultures, a knowledge of women's rebellions and organized movements against our oppression and how they have been routed or diminished? Without such knowledge women live and have lived without context, vulnerable to the projections of male fantasy, male prescriptions for us, estranged from our own experience because our education has not reflected or echoed it. I would suggest that not biology, but ignorance of our selves, has been the key to our powerlessness.

But the university curriculum, the high-school curriculum, do not provide this kind of knowledge for women, the knowledge of Womankind, whose experience has been so profoundly different from that of Mankind. Only in the precariously budgeted, much-condescended-to area of women's studies is such knowledge available to women students. Only there can they learn about the lives and work of women other than the few select women who are included in the "mainstream" texts, usually misrepresented even when they do appear. Some students, at some institutions, manage to take a majority of courses in women's studies, but the message from on high is that this is self-indulgence, soft-core education: the "real" learning is the study of Mankind.

If there is any misleading concept, it is that of "coeducation": that because women and men are sitting in the same classrooms, hearing the same lectures, reading the same books, performing the same laboratory experiments, they are receiving an equal education. They are not, first because the content of education itself validates men even as it invalidates women. Its very message is that men have been the shapers and thinkers of the world, and that this is only natural. The bias of higher education, including the so-called sciences, is white and male, racist and sexist; and this bias is expressed in both subtle and blatant ways. I have mentioned already the exclusiveness of grammar itself: "The student should test himself on the above questions"; "The poet is representative. He stands among partial men for the complete man." Despite a few halfhearted departures from custom, what the linguist Wendy Martyna has named "He-Man" grammar prevails throughout the culture. The efforts of feminists to reveal the profound ontological implications of sexist grammar are routinely ridiculed by academicians and journalists, including the professedly liberal *Times* columnist Tom Wicker and the professed humanist Jacques Barzun. Sexist grammar burns into the brains of little girls and young women a message that the male is the norm, the standard, the central figure beside which we are the deviants, the marginal, the dependent variables. It lays the foundation for androcentric thinking, and leaves men safe in their solipsistic tunnel-vision.

Women and men do not receive an equal education because outside the classroom women are perceived not as sovereign beings but as prey. The growing incidence of rape on and off the campus may or may not be fed by the proliferations of pornographic magazines and X-rated films available to young males in fraternities and student unions; but it is certainly occurring in a context of widespread images of sexual violence against women, on billboards and in so-called high art. More subtle, more daily than rape is the verbal abuse experienced by the woman student on many campuses — Rutgers for example — where, traversing a street lined with fraternity houses, she must run a gauntlet of male commentary and verbal assault. The undermining of self, of a woman's sense of her right to occupy space and walk freely in the world, is deeply relevant to education. The capacity to think independently, to take intellectual risks, to assert ourselves mentally, is inseparable from our physical way of being in the world, our feelings of personal integrity. If it is dangerous for me to walk home late of an evening from the library, *because I am a woman and can be raped,* how self-possessed, how exuberant can I feel as I sit working in that library? How much of my working energy is drained by the subliminal knowledge that, as a woman, I test my physical right to exist each time I go out alone? Of this knowledge, Susan Griffin° has written:

> . . . more than rape itself, the fear of rape permeates our lives. And what does one do from day to day, with *this* experience, which says, without words and directly to the heart, *your existence, your experience, may end at any moment.* Your experience may end, and the best defense against this is not to be, to deny being in the body, as a self, to . . . avert your gaze, make yourself, as a presence in the world, less felt.

Finally, rape of the mind. Women students are more and more often now reporting sexual overtures by male professors — one part of our overall growing consciousness of sexual harassment in the workplace. At Yale a legal suit has been brought against the university by a group of women demanding an explicit policy against sexual advances toward female students by male professors. Most young women experience a profound mixture of humiliation and intellectual self-doubt over seductive gestures by men who have the power to award grades, open doors to grants and graduate school, or extend special knowledge and training. Even if turned aside, such gestures constitute mental rape, destructive to a woman's ego. They are acts of domination, as despicable as the molestation of the daughter by the father.

Susan Griffin   Author of *Rape: The Power of Consciousness.*

But long before entering college the woman student has experienced 12
her alien identity in a world which misnames her, turns her to its own
uses, denying her the resources she needs to become self-affirming, self-
defined. The nuclear family teaches her that relationships are more important than selfhood or work; that "whether the phone rings for you, and
how often," having the right clothes, doing the dishes, take precedence
over study or solitude; that too much intelligence or intensity may make
her unmarriageable; that marriage and children — service to others — are,
finally, the points on which her life will be judged a success or a failure. In
high school, the polarization between feminine attractiveness and independent intelligence comes to an absolute. Meanwhile, the culture resounds
with messages. During Solar Energy Week in New York I saw young
women wearing "ecology" T-shirts with the legend: CLEAN, CHEAP, AND
AVAILABLE; a reminder of the 1960s antiwar button which read: CHICKS SAY
YES TO MEN WHO SAY NO. Department store windows feature female mannequins in chains, pinned to the wall with legs spread, smiling in positions
of torture. Feminists are depicted in the media as "shrill," "strident," "puritanical," or "humorless," and the lesbian choice — the choice of the
woman-identified woman — as pathological or sinister. The young woman
sitting in the philosophy classroom, the political science lecture, is already
gripped by tensions between her nascent sense of self-worth, and the
battering force of messages like these.

Look at a classroom: look at the many kinds of women's faces, postures,
expressions. Listen to the women's voices. Listen to the silences, the unasked questions, the blanks. Listen to the small, soft voices, often courageously trying to speak up, voices of women taught early that tones of
confidence, challenge, anger, or assertiveness, are strident and unfeminine.
Listen to the voices of the women and the voices of the men; observe the
space men allow themselves, physically and verbally, the male assumption
that people will listen, even when the majority of the group is female. Look
at the faces of the silent, and of those who speak. Listen to a woman
groping for language in which to express what is on her mind, sensing that
the terms of academic discourse are not her language, trying to cut down
her thought to the dimensions of a discourse not intended for her (*for it is
not fitting that a woman speak in public*); or reading her paper aloud at break-
neck speed, throwing her words away, deprecating her own work by a
reflex prejudgment: *I do not deserve to take up time and space.*

As women teachers, we can either deny the importance of this context
in which women students think, write, read, study, project their own
futures; or try to work with it. We can either teach passively, accepting
these conditions, or actively, helping our students identify and resist them.

One important thing we can do is *discuss* the context. And this need not
happen only in a women's studies course; it can happen anywhere. We

can refuse to accept passive, obedient learning and insist upon critical thinking. We can become harder on our women students, giving them the kinds of "cultural prodding" that men receive, but on different terms and in a different style. Most young women need to have their intellectual lives, their work, legitimized against the claims of family, relationships, the old message that a woman is always available for service to others. We need to keep our standards very high, not to accept a woman's preconceived sense of her limitations; we need to be hard to please, while supportive of risk-taking, because self-respect often comes only when exacting standards have been met. At a time when adult literacy is generally low, we need to demand more, not less, of women, both for the sake of their futures as thinking beings, and because historically women have always had to be better than men to do half as well. A romantic sloppiness, an inspired lack of rigor, a self-indulgent incoherence, are symptoms of female self-depre-cation. We should help our women students to look very critically at such symptoms, and to understand where they are rooted.

Nor does this mean we should be training women students to "think 16 like men." Men in general think badly: in disjuncture from their personal lives, claiming objectivity where the most irrational passions seethe, losing, as Virginia Woolf observed, their senses in the pursuit of professionalism. It is not easy to think like a woman in a man's world, in the world of the professions; yet the capacity to do that is a strength which we can try to help our students develop. To think like a woman in a man's world means thinking critically, refusing to accept the givens, making connections be-tween facts and ideas which men have left unconnected. It means remem-bering that every mind resides in a body; remaining accountable to the female bodies in which we live; constantly retesting given hypotheses against lived experience. It means a constant critique of language, for as Wittgenstein° (no feminist) observed, "The limits of my language are the limits of my world." And it means that most difficult thing of all: listening and watching in art and literature, in the social sciences, in all the descrip-tions we are given of the world; for the silences, the absences, the nameless, the unspoken, the encoded — for there we will find the true knowledge of women. And in breaking those silences, naming our selves, uncovering the hidden, making ourselves present, we begin to define a reality which resonates to *us*, which affirms *our* being, which allows the woman teacher and the woman student alike to take ourselves, and each other, seriously: meaning, to begin taking charge of our lives.

Wittgenstein   Ludwig Wittgenstein (1889–1951), philosopher noted for his theories on logic and on language.

AFTERWORD

When I talked about Margaret Atwood's lecture I mentioned the obligatory joke at the beginning of all lectures. Not for Adrienne Rich. As with the Atwood lecture, however, when we read this essay we should remain aware — in order to read well — that we read on the printed page a form of discourse created to be performed publicly, out of the mouth and with the gestures of the author. When Rich in the second paragraph puts "pushed" in quotation marks, she is not quoting anyone; these are tonal quotation marks, and good writers try to avoid them because although they ascribe tone they are unable to specify a particular tone. Often tonal quotation marks are apologetic: "I'm not sure of this word but I can't think of anything better." Here, if we imagine Rich as lecturer, we must try hearing the tone of voice in which she delivers "pushed."

Lectures are for hearing; essays are for reading with the eye. Yet when we read silently we still hear the writer's voice, especially when we find diction or rhythm expressive and idiosyncratic. When we listen to a lecture we are invited to see: Often a lecturer uses visual aids — graphs or charts or overhead projectors; it is often ignored that a lecturer's face, or hand gesturing, is another visual aid. I don't know how Rich, in her lecture, presented the material indented in paragraphs 4 and 5, but as we encounter it reading with our eyes it gives us visual messages — orderliness, periphrasis — even before we read it.

In her last paragraph Rich uses tonal quotes around "think like men" and it is easy enough to gauge the tone: "These words are quoted from others; I wouldn't have you think they are my own!"

BOOKS AVAILABLE IN PAPERBACK

Adrienne Rich's Poetry. New York: Norton. Poetry.

Blood, Bread, and Poetry: Selected Prose, 1979–1985. New York: Norton. Essays.

Diving Into the Wreck: Poems, 1971–72. New York: Norton. Poetry.

The Dream of a Common Language: Poems, 1974–1977. New York: Norton. Poetry.

The Fact of a Doorframe: Poems Selected and New, 1950–1984. New York: Norton. Poetry.

Leaflets: Poems, 1965–68. New York: Norton. Poetry.

Of Woman Born: Motherhood as Experience and Institution. New York: Norton. Nonfiction.

On Lies, Secrets, and Silence: Selected Prose, 1966–1978. New York: Norton. Essays.

Snapshots of a Daughter-In-Law. New York: Norton. *Poetry.*

A Wild Patience Has Taken Me This Far: Poems, 1978–1981. New York: Norton. *Poetry.*

Will to Change: Poems. New York: Norton. *Poetry.*

Your Native Land, Your Life: Poems. New York: Norton. *Poetry.*

RICHARD
RODRIGUEZ

*R*ICHARD RODRIGUEZ *was born (1944) in San Francisco, the son of Mexican immigrants. The family moved to Sacramento, where Rodriguez grew up speaking Spanish until he attended a Catholic school at the age of six. He delivered newspapers as a boy and worked as a gardener in the summer. He attended a Christian Brothers high school on a scholarship, then Stanford University for his B.A., and he did graduate work at Columbia University, the Warburg Institute in London, and the University of California at Berkeley. He took his Ph.D. in English Renaissance literature. He now works as a lecturer and educational consultant as well as a freelance writer.*

As an assimilated second-generation American, Rodriguez in his reminiscences — Hunger of Memory (1982) — argues against affirmative action and bilingual education. "The Achievement of Desire" is a chapter from Hunger of Memory, a personal narrative of Rodriguez's education away from his heritage, "separating me from the life I enjoyed before becoming a student." Unlike many members of American ethnic minorities, Rodriguez largely celebrates this separation. His work has been admired and denounced. While he tells his experiences of schooling, in a lucid progress of autobiographical exposition, he continually comments on his own story and reaches out for understanding by cross-cultural analogy to a book by an Englishman, separated as a "scholarship boy" from his working-class origins.

The Achievement of Desire

I stand in the ghetto classroom — "the guest speaker" — attempting to lecture on the mystery of the sounds of our words to rows of diffident students. "Don't you hear it? Listen! The music of our words. *'Sumer is i-cumen in. . . .'* And songs on the car radio. We need Aretha Franklin's voice to fill plain words with music — her life." In the face of their empty stares, I try to create an enthusiasm. But the girls in the back row turn to watch some boy passing outside. There are flutters of smiles, waves. And someone's mouth elongates heavy, silent words through the barrier of glass. Silent words — the lips straining to shape each voiceless syllable: *"Meet meee late errr."* By the door, the instructor smiles at me, apparently hoping that I will be able to spark some enthusiasm in the class. But only one student seems to be listening. A girl, maybe fourteen. In this gray room her eyes shine with ambition. She keeps nodding and nodding at all that I say; she even takes notes. And each time I ask a question, she jerks up and down in her desk like a marionette, while her hand waves over the bowed heads of her classmates. It is myself (as a boy) I see as she faces me now (a man in my thirties).

The boy who first entered a classroom barely able to speak English, twenty years later concluded his studies in the stately quiet of the reading room in the British Museum. Thus with one sentence I can summarize my academic career. It will be harder to summarize what sort of life connects the boy to the man.

With every award, each graduation from one level of education to the next, people I'd meet would congratulate me. Their refrain always the same: "Your parents must be very proud." Sometimes then they'd ask me how I managed it — my "success." (How?) After a while, I had several quick answers to give in reply. I'd admit, for one thing, that I went to an excellent grammar school. (My earliest teachers, the nuns, made my success their ambition.) And my brother and both my sisters were very good students. (They often brought home the shiny school tropies I came to want.) And my mother and father always encouraged me. (At every graduation they were behind the stunning flash of the camera when I turned to look at the crowd.)

As important as these factors were, however, they account inadequately 4 for my academic advance. Nor do they suggest what an odd success I managed. For although I was a very good student, I was also a very bad student. I was a "scholarship boy," a certain kind of scholarship boy. Always successful, I was always unconfident. Exhilarated by my progress. Sad. I became the prized student — anxious and eager to learn. Too eager, too anxious — an imitative and unoriginal pupil. My brother and two sisters enjoyed the advantages I did, and they grew to be as successful as I, but none of them ever seemed so anxious about their schooling. A second-grade student, I was the one who came home and corrected the "simple" grammatical mistakes of our parents. ("Two negatives make a positive.") Proudly I announced — to my family's startled silence — that a teacher had said I was losing all trace of a Spanish accent. I was oddly annoyed when I was unable to get parental help with a homework assignment. The night my father tried to help me with an arithmetic exercise, he kept reading the instructions, each time more deliberately, until I pried the textbook out of his hands, saying, "I'll try to figure it out some more by myself."

When I reached the third grade, I outgrew such behavior. I became more tactful, careful to keep separate the two very different worlds of my day. But then, with ever-increasing intensity, I devoted myself to my studies. I became bookish, puzzling to all my family. Ambition set me apart. When my brother saw me struggling home with stacks of library books, he would laugh, shouting: "Hey, Four Eyes!" My father opened a closet one day and was startled to find me inside, reading a novel. My mother would find me reading when I was supposed to be asleep or helping around the house or playing outside. In a voice angry or worried or just curious, she'd ask: "What do you see in your books?" It became the family's joke. When I was called and wouldn't reply, someone would say I must be hiding under my bed with a book.

(How did I manage my success?)

What I am about to say to you has taken me more than twenty years to admit: *A primary reason for my success in the classroom was that I couldn't forget that schooling was changing me and separating from the life I enjoyed before becoming a student.* That simple realization! For years I never spoke to anyone about it. Never mentioned a thing to my family or my teachers or class-mates. From a very early age, I understood enough, just enough about my classroom experiences to keep what I knew repressed, hidden beneath layers of embarrassment. Not until my last months as a graduate student, nearly thirty years old, was it possible for me to think much about the reasons for my academic success. Only then. At the end of my schooling, I needed to determine how far I had moved from my past. The adult finally confronted, and now must publicly say, what the child shuddered from knowing and could never admit to himself or to those many faces that smiled at his every success. ("Your parents must be very proud. . . .")

I

At the end, in the British Museum (too distracted to finish my disser- 8 tation) for weeks I read, speed-read, books by modern educational theorists, only to find infrequent and slight mention of students like me. (Much more is written about the more typical case, the lower-class student who barely is helped by his schooling.) Then one day, leafing through Richard Hoggart's *The Uses of Literacy*, I found, in his description of the scholarship boy, myself. For the first time I realized that there were other students like me, and so I was able to frame the meaning of my academic success, its consequent price — the loss.

Hoggart's description is distinguished, at least initially, by deep understanding. What he grasps very well is that the scholarship boy must move between environments, his home and the classroom, which are at cultural extremes, opposed. With his family, the boy has the intense pleasure of intimacy, the family's consolation in feeling public alienation. Lavish emotions texture home life. *Then*, at school, the instruction bids him to trust lonely reason primarily. Immediate needs set the pace of his parents' lives. From his mother and father the boy learns to trust spontaneity and non-rational ways of knowing. *Then*, at school, there is mental calm. Teachers emphasize the value of a reflectiveness that opens a space between thinking and immediate action.

Years of schooling must pass before the boy will be able to sketch the cultural differences in his day as abstractly as this. But he senses those differences early. Perhaps as early as the night he brings home an assignment from school and finds the house too noisy for study.

> He has to be more and more alone, if he is going to "get on."
> He will have, probably unconsciously, to oppose the ethos of
> the hearth, the intense gregariousness of the working-class
> family group. Since everything centres upon the living-room,
> there is unlikely to be a room of his own; the bedrooms are
> cold and inhospitable, and to warm them or the front room,
> if there is one, would not only be expensive but would require
> an imaginative leap — out of the tradition — which most
> families are not capable of making. There is a corner of the
> living-room table. On the other side Mother is ironing, the

wireless is on, someone is singing a snatch of song or Father says intermittently whatever comes into his head. The boy has to cut himself off mentally, so as to do his homework, as well as he can.[1]

The next day, the lesson is as apparent at school. There are even rows of desks. Discussion is ordered. The boy must rehearse his thoughts and raise his hand before speaking out in a loud voice to an audience of classmates. And there is time enough, and silence, to think about ideas (big ideas) never considered at home by his parents.

Not for the working-class child alone is adjustment to the classroom difficult. Good schooling requires that any student alter early childhood habits. But the working-class child is usually least prepared for the change. And, unlike many middle-class children, he goes home and sees in his parents a way of life not only different but starkly opposed to that of the classroom. (He enters the house and hears his parents talking in ways his teachers discourage.)

Without extraordinary determination and the great assistance of others 12 — at home and at school — there is little chance for success. Typically most working-class children are barely changed by the classroom. The exception succeeds. The relative few become scholarship students. Of these, Richard Hoggart estimates, most manage a fairly graceful transition. Somehow they learn to live in the two very different worlds of their day. There are some others, however, those Hoggart pejoratively terms "scholarship boys," for whom success comes with special anxiety. Scholarship boy: good student, troubled son. The child is "moderately endowed," intellectually mediocre, Hoggart supposes — though it may be more pertinent to note the special qualities of temperament in the child. High-strung child. Brooding. Sensitive. Haunted by the knowledge that one *chooses* to become a student. (Education is not an inevitable or natural step in growing up.) Here is a child who cannot forget that his academic success distances him from a life he loved, even from his own memory of himself.

Initially, he wavers, balances allegiance. ("The boy is himself [until he reaches, say, the upper forms] very much of *both* the worlds of home and school. He is enormously obedient to the dictates of the world of school, but emotionally still strongly wants to continue as part of the family circle.") Gradually, necessarily, the balance is lost. The boy needs to spend more and more time studying, each night enclosing himself in the silence permitted and required by intense concentration. He takes his first step toward academic success, away from his family.

---

[1]All quotations in this chapter are from Richard Hoggart, *The Uses of Literacy* (London: Chatto and Windus, 1957), chapter 10. [Author's note]

From the very first days, through the years following, it will be with his parents — the figures of lost authority, the persons toward whom he feels deepest love — that the change will be most powerfully measured. A separation will unravel between them. Advancing in his studies, the boy notices that his mother and father have not changed as much as he. Rather, when he sees them, they often remind him of the person he once was and the life he earlier shared with them. He realizes what some Romantics also know when they praise the working class for the capacity for human closeness, qualities of passion and spontaneity, that the rest of us experience in like measure only in the earliest part of our youth. For the Romantic, this doesn't make working-class life childish. Working-class life challenges precisely because it is an *adult* way of life.

The scholarship boy reaches a different conclusion. He cannot afford to admire his parents. (How could he and still pursue such a contrary life?) He permits himself embarrassment at their lack of education. And to evade nostalgia for the life he has lost, he concentrates on the benefits education will bestow upon him. He becomes especially ambitious. Without the support of old certainties and consolations, almost mechanically, he assumes the procedures and doctrines of the classroom. The kind of allegiance the young student might have given his mother and father only days earlier, he transfers to the teacher, the new figure of authority. "[The scholarship boy] tends to make a father-figure of his form-master," Hoggart observes.

But Hoggart's calm prose only makes me recall the urgency with which 16 I came to idolize my grammar school teachers. I began by imitating their accents, using their diction, trusting their every direction. The very first facts they dispensed, I grasped with awe. Any book they told me to read, I read — then waited for them to tell me which books I enjoyed. Their every casual opinion I came to adopt and to trumpet when I returned home. I stayed after school "to help" — to get my teacher's undivided attention. It was the nun's encouragement that mattered most to me. (She understood exactly what — my parents never seemed to appraise so well — all my achievements entailed.) Memory gently caressed each word of praise bestowed in the classroom so that compliments teachers paid me years ago come quickly to mind even today.

The enthusiasm I felt in second-grade classes I flaunted before both my parents. The docile, obedient student came home a shrill and precocious son who insisted on correcting and teaching his parents with the remark: "My teacher told us. . . ."

I intended to hurt my mother and father. I was still angry at them for having encouraged me toward classroom English. But gradually this anger was exhausted, replaced by guilt as school grew more and more attractive to me. I grew increasingly successful, a talkative student. My hand was raised in the classroom; I yearned to answer any question. At home, life was less noisy than it had been. (I spoke to classmates and teachers more often each day than to family members.) Quiet at home, I sat with my papers for hours each night. I never forgot that schooling had irretrievably changed my family's life. That knowledge, however, did not weaken ambition. Instead, it strengthened resolve. Those times I remembered the loss of my past with regret, I quickly reminded myself of all the things my teachers could give me. (They could make me an educated man.) I tightened my grip on pencil and books. I evaded nostalgia. Tried hard to forget. But one does not forget by trying to forget. One only remembers. I remembered too well that education had changed my family's life. I would not have become a scholarship boy had I not so often remembered.

Once she was sure that her children knew English, my mother would tell us, "You should keep up your Spanish." Voices playfully groaned in response. "¡*Pochos*!" my mother would tease. I listened silently.

After a while, I grew more calm at home. I developed tact. A fourth- 20 grade student, I was no longer the show-off in front of my parents. I became a conventionally dutiful son, politely affectionate, cheerful enough, even — for reasons beyond choosing — my father's favorite. And much about my family life was easy then, comfortable, happy in the rhythm of our living together: hearing my father getting ready for work; eating the breakfast my mother had made me; looking up from a novel to hear my brother or one of my sisters playing with friends in the backyard; in winter, coming upon the house all lighted up after dark.

But withheld from my mother and father was any mention of what most mattered to me: the extraordinary experience of first-learning. Late afternoon: In the midst of preparing dinner, my mother would come up behind me while I was trying to read. Her head just over mine, her breath warmly scented with food. "What are you reading?" Or, "Tell me all about your new courses." I would barely respond, "Just the usual things, nothing special." (A half smile, then silence. Her head moving back in the silence. Silence! Instead of the flood of intimate sounds that had once flowed smoothly between us, there was this silence.) After dinner, I would rush to a bedroom with papers and books. As often as possible, I resisted parental pleas to "save lights" by coming to the kitchen to work. I kept so much, so often, to myself. Sad. Enthusiastic. Troubled by the excitement of coming upon new ideas. Eager. Fascinated by the promising texture of a brand-new book. I hoarded the pleasures of learning. Alone for hours. Enthralled. Nervous. I rarely looked away from my books — or back on my memories. Nights when relatives visited and the front rooms were warmed by Spanish sounds, I slipped quietly out of the house.

It mattered that education was changing me. It never ceased to matter. My brother and sisters would giggle at our mother's mispronounced words. They'd correct her gently. My mother laughed girlishly one night, trying not to pronounce *sheep* as *ship*. From a distance I listened sullenly. From that distance, pretending not to notice on another occasion, I saw my father looking at the title pages of my library books. That was the scene on my mind when I walked home with a fourth-grade companion and heard him say that his parents read to him every night. (A strange-sounding book — *Winnie the Pooh*.) Immediately, I wanted to know, "What is it like?" My companion, however, thought I wanted to know about the plot of the book. Another day, my mother surprised me by asking for a "nice" book to read. "Something not too hard you think I might like." Carefully I chose one, Willa Cather's *My Ántonia*. But when, several weeks later, I happened to see it next to her bed unread except for the first few pages, I was furious and suddenly wanted to cry. I grabbed up the book and took it back to my room and placed it in its place, alphabetically on my shelf.

"Your parents must be very proud of you." People began to say that to me about the time I was in sixth grade. To answer affirmatively, I'd smile. Shyly I'd smile, never betraying my sense of the irony: I was not proud of my mother and father. I was embarrassed by their lack of education. It was not that I ever thought they were stupid, though stupidly I took for granted their enormous native intelligence. Simply, what mattered to me was that they were not like my teachers.

But, "Why didn't you tell us about the award?" my mother demanded, 24 her frown weakened by pride. At the grammar school ceremony several weeks after, her eyes were brighter than the trophy I'd won. Pushing back the hair from my forehead, she whispered that I had "shown" the *gringos*. A few minutes later, I heard my father speak to my teacher and felt ashamed of his labored, accented words. Then guilty for the shame. I felt such contrary feelings. (There is no simple road-map through the heart of the scholarship boy.) My teacher was so soft-spoken and her words were edged sharp and clean. I admired her until it seemed to me that she spoke too carefully. Sensing that she was condescending to them, I became nervous. Resentful. Protective. I tried to move my parents away. "You both must be very proud of Richard," the nun said. They responded quickly. (They were proud.) "We are proud of all our children." Then this afterthought: "They sure didn't get their brains from us." They all laughed. I smiled.

Tightening the irony into a knot was the knowledge that my parents were always behind me. They made success possible. They evened the path. They sent their children to parochial schools because the nuns "teach better." They paid a tuition they couldn't afford. They spoke English to us.

For their children my parents wanted chances they never had — an easier way. It saddened my mother to learn that some relatives forced their children to start working right after high school. To *her* children she would

433

say, "Get all the education you can." In schooling she recognized the key to job advancement. And with the remark she remembered her past.

As a girl new to America my mother had been awarded a high school diploma by teachers too careless or busy to notice that she hardly spoke English. On her own, she determined to learn how to type. That skill got her jobs typing envelopes in letter shops, and it encouraged in her an optimism about the possibility of advancement. (Each morning when her sisters put on uniforms, she chose a bright-colored dress.) The years of young womanhood passed, and her typing speed increased. She also became an excellent speller of words she mispronounced. "And I've never been to college," she'd say, smiling, when her children asked her to spell words they were too lazy to look up in a dictionary.

Typing, however, was dead-end work. Finally frustrating. When her youngest child started high school, my mother got a full-time office job once again. (Her paycheck combined with my father's to make us — in fact — what we had already become in our imagination of ourselves — middle class.) She worked then for the (California) state government in numbered civil service positions secured by examinations. The old ambition of her youth was rekindled. During the lunch hour, she consulted bulletin boards for announcements of openings. One day she saw mention of something called an "anti-poverty agency." A typing job. A glamorous job, part of the governor's staff. "A knowledge of Spanish required." Without hesitation she applied and became nervous only when the job was suddenly hers.   28

"Everyone comes to work all dressed up," she reported at night. And didn't need to say more than that her co-workers wouldn't let her answer the phones. She was only a typist, after all, albeit a very fast typist. And an excellent speller. One morning there was a letter to be sent to a Washington cabinet officer. On the dictating tape, a voice referred to urban guerrillas. My mother typed (the wrong word, correctly): "gorillas." The mistake horrified the anti-poverty bureaucrats who shortly after arranged to have her returned to her previous position. She would go no further. So she willed her ambition to her children. "Get all the education you can; with an education you can do anything." (With a good education *she* could have done anything.)

When I was in high school, I admitted to my mother that I planned to become a teacher someday. That seemed to please her. But I never tried to explain that it was not the occupation of teaching I yearned for as much as it was something more elusive: I wanted to *be* like my teachers, to possess their knowledge, to assume their authority, their confidence, even to assume a teacher's persona.

In contrast to my mother, my father never verbally encouraged his children's academic success. Nor did he often praise us. My mother had to remind him to "say something" to one of his children who scored some academic success. But whereas my mother saw in education the opportunity for job advancement, my father recognized that education provided an even more startling possibility: It could enable a person to escape from a life of mere labor.

In Mexico, orphaned when he was eight, my father left school to work 32 as an "apprentice" for an uncle. Twelve years later, he left Mexico in frustration and arrived in America. He had great expectations then of becoming an engineer. ("Work for my hands and my head.") He knew a Catholic priest who promised to get him money enough to study full time for a high school diploma. But the promises came to nothing. Instead there was a dark succession of warehouse, cannery, and factory jobs. After work he went to night school along with my mother. A year, two passed. Nothing much changed, except that fatigue worked its way into the bone; then everything changed. He didn't talk anymore of becoming an engineer. He stayed outside on the steps of the school while my mother went inside to learn typing and shorthand.

By the time I was born, my father worked at "clean" jobs. For a time he was a janitor at a fancy department store. ("Easy work; the machines do it all.") Later he became a dental technician. ("Simple.") But by then he was pessimistic about the ultimate meaning of work and the possibility of ever escaping its claims. In some of my earliest memories of him, my father already seems aged by fatigue. (He has never really grown old like my mother.) From boyhood to manhood, I have remembered him in a single image: seated, asleep on the sofa, his head thrown back in a hideous corpselike grin, the evening newspaper spread out before him. "But look at all you've accomplished," his best friend said to him once. My father said nothing. Only smiled.

It was my father who laughed when I claimed to be tired by reading and writing. It was he who teased me for having soft hands. (He seemed to sense that some great achievement of leisure was implied by my papers and books.) It was my father who became angry while watching on television some woman at the Miss America contest tell the announcer that she was going to college. ("Majoring in fine arts.") "College!" he snarled. He despised the trivialization of higher education, the inflated grades and cheapened diplomas, the half education that so often passed as mass education in my generation.

It was my father again who wondered why I didn't display my awards on the wall of my bedroom. He said he liked to go to doctors' offices and see their certificates and degrees on the wall. ("Nice.") My citations from school got left in closets at home. The gleaming figure astride one of my trophies was broken, wingless, after hitting the ground. My medals were placed in a jar of loose change. And when I lost my high school diploma, my father found it as it was about to be thrown out with the trash. Without telling me, he put it away with his own things for safekeeping.

These memories slammed together at the instant of hearing that refrain 36 familiar to all scholarship students: "Your parents must be very proud. . . ." Yes, my parents were proud. I knew it. But my parents regarded my progress with more than mere pride. They endured my early precocious behavior — both with what private anger and humiliation? As their children got older and would come home to challenge ideas both of them held, they argued before submitting to the force of logic or superior factual evidence with the disclaimer "It's what we were taught in our time to believe." These discussions ended abruptly, though my mother remembered them on other occasions when she complained that our "big ideas" were going to our heads. More acute was her complaint that the family wasn't close anymore, like some others she knew. Why weren't we close, "more in the Mexican style"? Everyone is so private, she added. And she mimicked the yes and no answers she got in reply to her questions. Why didn't we talk more? (My father never asked.) I never said.

I was the first in my family who asked to leave home when it came time to go to college. I had been admitted to Stanford, one hundred miles away. My departure would only make physically apparent the separation that had occurred long before. But it was going too far. In the months preceding my leaving, I heard the question my mother never asked except indirectly. In the hot kitchen, tired at the end of her workday, she demanded to know, "Why aren't the colleges here in Sacramento good enough for you? They are for your brother and sister." In the middle of a car ride, not turning to face me, she wondered, "Why do you need to go so far away?" Late at night, ironing, she said with disgust, "Why do you have to put us through this big expense? You know your scholarship will never cover it all." But When September came there was a rush to get everything ready. In a bedroom that last night I packed the big brown valise, and my mother sat nearby sewing initials onto the clothes I would take. And she said no more about my leaving.

Months later, two weeks of Christmas vacation: The first hours home were the hardest. ("What's new?") My parents and I sat in the kitchen for a conversation. (But, lacking the same words to develop our sentences and to shape our interests, what was there to say? What could I tell them of the term paper I had just finished on the "universality of Shakespeare's appeal"?) I mentioned only small, obvious things: my dormitory life; weekend trips I had taken; random events. They responded with news of their own. (One was almost grateful for a family crisis about which there was much to discuss.) We tried to make our conversation seem like more than an interview.

I I

From an early age I knew that my mother and father could read and write both Spanish and English. I had observed my father making his way through what, I now suppose, must have been income tax forms. On other occasions I waited apprehensively while my mother read onion-paper letters airmailed from Mexico with news of a relative's illness or death. For both my parents, however, reading was something done out of necessity and as quickly as possible. Never did I see either of them read an entire book. Nor did I see them read for pleasure. Their reading consisted of work manuals, prayer books, newspapers, recipes.

Richard Hoggart imagines how, at home, 40

> . . . [The scholarship boy] sees strewn around, and reads regularly himself, magazines which are never mentioned at school, which seem not to belong to the world to which the school introduces him; at school he hears about and reads books never mentioned at home. When he brings those books into the house they do not take their place with other books which the family are reading, for often there are none or almost none; his books look, rather, like strange tools.

In our house each school year would begin with my mother's careful instruction: "Don't write in your books so we can sell them at the end of the year." The remark was echoed in public by my teachers, but only in part: "Boys and girls, don't write in your books. You must learn to treat them with great care and respect."

OPEN THE DOORS OF YOUR MIND WITH BOOKS, read the red and white poster over the nun's desk in early September. It soon was apparent to me that reading was the classroom's central activity. Each course had its own book. And the information gathered from a book was unquestioned. READ TO LEARN, the sign on the wall advised in December. I privately wondered: What was the connection between reading and learning? Did one learn something only by reading it? Was an idea only an idea if it could be written down? In June, CONSIDER BOOKS YOUR BEST FRIENDS. Friends? Reading was, at best, only a chore. I needed to look up whole paragraphs of words in a dictionary. Lines of type were dizzying, the eye having to move slowly across the page, then down, and across. . . . The sentences of the first books I read were coolly impersonal. Toned hard. What most bothered me, however, was the isolation reading required. To console myself for the loneliness I'd feel when I read, I tried reading in a very soft voice. Until: "Who is doing all that talking to his neighbor?" Shortly after, remedial reading classes were arranged for me with a very old nun.

At the end of each school day, for nearly six months, I would meet with her in the tiny room that served as the school's library but was actually only a storeroom for used textbooks and a vast collection of *National Geographics*. Everything about our sessions pleased me: the smallness of the room; the noise of the janitor's broom hitting the edge of the long hallway outside the door; the green of the sun, lighting the wall; and the old woman's face blurred white with a beard. Most of the time we took turns. I began with my elementary text. Sentences of astonishing simplicity seemed to me lifeless and drab: "The boys ran from the rain . . . She wanted to sing . . . The kite rose in the blue." Then the old nun would read from her favorite books, usually biographies of early American presidents. Playfully she ran through complex sentences, calling the words alive with her voice, making it seem that the author somehow was speaking directly to me. I smiled just to listen to her. I sat there and sensed for the very first time some possibility of fellowship between a reader and a writer, a communication, never *intimate* like that I heard spoken words at home convey, but one nonetheless *personal*.

One day the nun concluded a session by asking me why I was so reluctant to read by myself. I tried to explain; said something about the way written words made me feel all alone — almost, I wanted to add but didn't, as when I spoke to myself in a room just emptied of furniture. She studied my face as I spoke; she seemed to be watching more than listening. In an uneventful voice she replied that I had nothing to fear. Didn't I realize that reading would open up whole new worlds? A book could open doors for me. It could introduce me to people and show me places I never imagined existed. She gestured toward the bookshelves. (Bare-breasted African women danced, and the shiny hubcaps of automobiles on the back covers of the *Geographic* gleamed in my mind.) I listened with respect. But her words were not very influential. I was thinking then of another consequence of literacy, one I was too shy to admit but nonetheless trusted. Books were going to make me "educated." *That* confidence enabled me, several months later, to overcome my fear of the silence.

In fourth grade I embarked upon a grandiose reading program. "Give 44 me the names of important books," I would say to startled teachers. They soon found out that I had in mind "adult books." I ignored their suggestion of anything I suspected was written for children. (Not until I was in college, as a result, did I read *Huckleberry Finn* or *Alice's Adventures in Wonderland*.) Instead, I read *The Scarlet Letter* and Franklin's *Autobiography*. And whatever I read I read for extra credit. Each time I finished a book, I reported the achievement to a teacher and basked in the praise my effort earned. Despite my best efforts, however, there seemed to be more and more books I needed to read. At the library I would literally tremble as I came upon whole shelves of books I hadn't read. So I read and I read and I read: *Great Expectations*; all the short stories of Kipling; *The Babe Ruth Story*; the entire first volume of the *Encyclopaedia Britannica* (A–ANSTEY); the *Iliad*; *Moby Dick*; *Gone with the Wind*; *The Good Earth*; *Ramona*; *Forever Amber*; *The Lives of the Saints*; *Crime and Punishment*; *The Pearl*. . . . Librarians who initially frowned when I checked out the maximum ten books at a time started saving books they thought I might like. Teachers would say to the rest of the class, "I only wish the rest of you took reading as seriously as Richard obviously does."

But at home I would hear my mother wondering, "What do you see in your books?" (Was reading a hobby like her knitting? Was so much reading even healthy for a boy? Was it the sign of "brains"? Or was it just a convenient excuse for not helping about the house on Saturday mornings?) Always, "What do you see . . . ?"

What *did* I see in my books? I had the idea that they were crucial for my academic success, though I couldn't have said exactly how or why. In the sixth grade I simply concluded that what gave a book its value was some major idea or theme it contained. If that core essence could be mined and memorized, I would become learned like my teachers. I decided to record in a notebook the themes of the books that I read. After reading *Robinson Crusoe*, I wrote that its theme was "the value of learning to live by oneself." When I completed *Wuthering Heights*, I noted the danger of "letting emotions get out of control." Rereading these brief moralistic appraisals usually left me disheartened. I couldn't believe that they were really the source of reading's value. But for many more years, they constituted the only means I had of describing to myself the educational value of books.

In spite of my earnestness, I found reading a pleasurable activity. I came to enjoy the lonely good company of books. Early on weekday mornings, I'd read in my bed. I'd feel a mysterious comfort then, reading in the dawn quiet — the blue-gray silence interrupted by the occasional churning of the refrigerator motor a few rooms away or the more distant sounds of a city bus beginning its run. On weekends I'd go to the public library to read, surrounded by old men and women. Or, if the weather was fine, I would take my books to the park and read in the shade of a tree. A warm summer evening was my favorite reading time. Neighbors would leave for vacation and I would water their lawns. I would sit through the twilight on the front porches or in backyards, reading to the cool, whirling sounds of the sprinklers.

I also had favorite writers. But often those writers I enjoyed most I was 48 least able to value. When I read William Saroyan's *The Human Comedy*, I was immediately pleased by the narrator's warmth and the charm of his story. But as quickly I became suspicious. A book so enjoyable to read couldn't be very "important." Another summer I determined to read all the novels of Dickens. Reading his fat novels, I loved the feeling I got — after the first hundred pages — of being at home in a fictional world where I knew the names of the characters and cared about what was going to happen to them. And it bothered me that I was forced away at the conclusion, when the fiction closed tight, like a fortune-teller's fist — the futures of all the major characters neatly resolved. I never knew how to take such feelings seriously, however. Nor did I suspect that these experiences could be part of a novel's meaning. Still, there were pleasures to sustain me after I'd finish my books. Carrying a volume back to the library, I would be pleased by its weight. I'd run my fingers along the edge of the pages and marvel at the breadth of my achievement. Around my room, growing stacks of paperback books reenforced my assurance.

I entered high school having read hundreds of books. My habit of reading made me a confident speaker and writer of English. Reading also enabled me to sense something of the shape, the major concerns, of Western thought. (I was able to say something about Dante and Descartes and Engels and James Baldwin in my high school term papers.) In these various ways, books brought me academic success as I hoped that they would. But I was not a good reader. Merely bookish, I lacked a point of view when I read. Rather, I read in order to acquire a point of view. I vacuumed books for epigrams, scraps of information, ideas, themes — anything to fill the hollow within me and make me feel educated. When one of my teachers suggested to his drowsy tenth-grade English class that a person could not have a "complicated idea" until he had read at least two thousand books, I heard the remark without detecting either its irony or its very complicated truth. I merely determined to compile a list of all the books I had ever read. Harsh with myself, I included only once a title I might have read several times. (How, after all, could one read a book more than once?) And I included only those books over a hundred pages in length. (Could anything shorter be a book?)

There was yet another high school list I compiled. One day I came across a newspaper article about the retirement of an English professor at a nearby state college. The article was accompanied by a list of the "hundred most important books of Western Civilization." "More than anything else in my life," the professor told the reporter with finality, "these books have made me all that I am." That was the kind of remark I couldn't ignore. I clipped out the list and kept it for the several months it took me to read all of the titles. Most books, of course, I barely understood. While reading Plato's *Republic*, for instance, I needed to keep looking at the book jacket comments to remind myself what the text was about. Nevertheless, with the special patience and superstition of a scholarship boy, I looked at every word of the text. And by the time I reached the last word, relieved, I convinced myself that I had read *The Republic*. In a ceremony of great pride, I solemnly crossed Plato off my list.

III

The scholarship boy pleases most when he is young — the working-class child struggling for academic success. To his teachers, he offers great satisfaction; his success is their proudest achievement. Many other persons offer to help him. A businessman learns the boy's story and promises to underwrite part of the cost of his college education. A woman leaves him her entire library of several hundred books when she moves. His progress is featured in a newspaper article. Many people seem happy for him. They marvel. "How did you manage so fast?" From all sides, there is lavish praise and encouragement.

In his grammar school classroom, however, the boy already makes 52 students around him uneasy. They scorn his desire to succeed. They scorn him for constantly wanting the teacher's attention and praise. "Kiss Ass," they call him when his hand swings up in response to every question he hears. Later, when he makes it to college, no one will mock him aloud. But he detects annoyance on the faces of some students and even some teachers who watch him. It puzzles him often. In college, then in graduate school, he behaves much as he always has. If anything is different about him it is that he dares to anticipate the successful conclusion of his studies. At last he feels that he belongs in the classroom, and this is exactly the source of the dissatisfaction he causes. To many persons around him, he appears too much the academic. There may be some things about him that recall his beginnings — his shabby clothes; his persistent poverty; or his dark skin (in those cases when it symbolizes his parents' disadvantaged condition) — but they only make clear how far he has moved from his past. He has used education to remake himself.

It bothers his fellow academics to face this. They will not say why exactly. (They sneer.) But their expectations become obvious when they are disappointed. They expect — they want — a student less changed by his schooling. If the scholarship boy, from a past so distant from the classroom, could remain in some basic way unchanged, he would be able to prove that it is possible for anyone to become educated without basically changing from the person one was.

Here is no fabulous hero, no idealized scholar-worker. The scholarship boy does not straddle, cannot reconcile, the two great opposing cultures of his life. His success is unromantic and plain. He sits in the classroom and offers those sitting beside him no calming reassurance about their own lives. He sits in the seminar room — a man with brown skin, the son of working-class Mexican immigrant parents. (Addressing the professor at the head of the table, his voice catches with nervousness.) There is no trace of his parents' accent in his speech. Instead he approximates the accents of teachers and classmates. Coming from *him* those sounds seem suddenly odd. Odd too is the effect produced when *he* uses academic jargon — bubbles at the tip of his tongue: "*Topos* . . . negative capability . . . vegetation imagery in Shakespearean comedy." He lifts an opinion from Coleridge, takes something else from Frye or Empsom or Leavis. He even repeats exactly his professor's earlier comment. All his ideas are clearly borrowed. He seems to have no thought of his own. He chatters while his listeners smile — their look one of disdain.

When he is older and thus when so little of the person he was survives, the scholarship boy makes only too apparent his profound lack of *self-confidence*. This is the conventional assessment that even Richard Hoggart repeats:

> [The scholarship boy] tends to over-stress the importance of examinations, of the piling-up of knowledge and of received opinions. He discovers a technique of apparent learning, of the acquiring of facts rather than of the handling and use of facts. He learns how to receive a purely literate education, one using only a small part of the personality and challenging only a limited area of his being. He begins to see life as a ladder, as a permanent examination with some praise and some further exhortation at each stage. He becomes an expert imbiber and doler-out; his competence will vary, but will rarely be accompanied by genuine enthusiasms. He rarely feels the reality of knowledge, of other men's thoughts and imaginings, on his own pulses. . . . He has something of the blinkered pony about him. . . .

But this is criticism more accurate than fair. The scholarship boy is a very bad student. He is the great mimic; a collector of thoughts, not a thinker; the very last person in class who ever feels obliged to have an opinion of his own. In large part, however, the reason he is such a bad student is because he realizes more often and more acutely than most other students — than Hoggart himself — that education requires radical self-reformation. As a very young boy, regarding his parents, as he struggles with an early homework assignment, he knows this too well. That is why he lacks self-assurance. He does not forget that the classroom is responsible for remaking him. He relies on his teacher, depends on all that he hears in the classroom and reads in his books. He becomes in every obvious way the worst student, a dummy mouthing the opinions of others. But he would not be so bad —

nor would he become so successful, a *scholarship* boy — if he did not accurately perceive that the best synonym for primary "education" is "imitation."

Those who would take seriously the boy's success — and his failure — 56 would be forced to realize how great is the change any academic undergoes, how far one must move from one's past. It is easiest to ignore such considerations. So little is said about the scholarship boy in pages and pages of educational literature. Nothing is said of the silence that comes to separate the boy from his parents. Instead, one hears proposals for increasing the self-esteem of students and encouraging early intellectual independence. Paragraphs glitter with a constellation of terms like *creativity* and *originality*. (Ignored altogether is the function of imitation in a student's life.) Radical educationalists meanwhile complain that ghetto schools "oppress" students by trying to mold them, stifling native characteristics. The truer critique would be just the reverse: not that schools change ghetto students too much, but that while they might promote the occasional scholarship student, they change most students barely at all.

From the story of the scholarship boy there is no specific pedagogy to glean. There is, however, a much larger lesson. His story makes clear that education is a long, unglamorous, even demeaning process — *a nurturing never natural to the person one was before one entered a classroom.* At once different from most other students, the scholarship boy is also the archetypal "good student." He exaggerates the difficulty of being a student, but his exaggeration reveals a general predicament. Others are changed by their schooling as much as he. They too must re-form themselves. They must develop the skill of memory long before they become truly critical thinkers. And when they read Plato for the first several times, it will be with awe more than deep comprehension.

The impact of schooling on the scholarship boy is only more apparent to the boy himself and to others. Finally, although he may be laughable — a blinkered pony — the boy will not let his critics forget their own change. He ends up too much like them. When he speaks, they hear themselves echoed. In his pedantry, they trace their own. His ambitions are theirs. If his failure were singular, they might readily pity him. But he is more troubling than that. They would not scorn him if this were not so.

I V

Like me, Hoggart's imagined scholarship boy spends most of his years in the classroom afraid to long for his past. Only at the very end of his schooling does the boy-man become nostalgic. In this sudden change of heart, Richard Hoggart notes:

He longs for the membership he lost, "he pines for some
Nameless Eden where he never was." The nostalgia is the
stronger and the more ambiguous because he is really "in
quest of his own absconded self yet scared to find it." He both
wants to go back and yet thinks he has gone beyond his class,
feels himself weighted with knowledge of his own and their
situation, which hereafter forbids him the simpler pleasures
of his father and mother. . . .

According to Hoggart, the scholarship boy grows nostalgic because he
remains the uncertain scholar, bright enough to have moved from his past,
yet unable to feel easy, a part of a community of academics.

This analysis, however, only partially suggests what happened to me in 60
my last year as a graduate student. When I traveled to London to write a
dissertation on English Renaissance literature, I was finally confident of
membership in a "community of scholars." But the pleasure that confidence
gave me faded rapidly. After only two or three months in the reading room
of the British Museum, it became clear that I had joined a lonely community.
Around me each day were dour faces eclipsed by large piles of books. There
were the regulars, like the old couple who arrived every morning, each
holding a loop of the shopping bag which contained all their notes. And
there was the historian who chattered madly to herself. ("Oh dear! Oh!
Now, what's this? What? Oh, my!") There were also the faces of young
men and women worn by long study. And everywhere eyes turned away
the moment our glance accidentally met. Some persons I sat beside day
after day, yet we passed silently at the end of the day, strangers. Still, we
were united by a common respect for the written word and for scholarship.
We did form a union, though one in which we remained distant from one
another.

More profound and unsettling was the bond I recognized with those
writers whose books I consulted. Whenever I opened a text that hadn't
been used for years, I realized that my special interests and skills united
me to a mere handful of academics. We formed an exclusive — eccentric!
— society, separated from others who would never care or be able to share
our concerns. (The pages I turned were stiff like layers of dead skin.) I
began to wonder: Who, besides my dissertation director and a few faculty
members, would ever read what I wrote? And: Was my dissertation much
more than an act of social withdrawal? These questions went unanswered
in the silence of the Museum reading room. They remained to trouble me
after I'd leave the library each afternoon and feel myself shy — unsteady,
speaking simple sentences at the grocer's or the butcher's on my way back
to my bed-sitter.

Meanwhile my file cards accumulated. A professional, I knew exactly
how to search a book for pertinent information. I could quickly assess and

summarize the usability of the many books I consulted. But whenever I started to write, I knew too much (and not enough) to be able to write anything but sentences that were overly cautious, timid, strained brittle under the heavy weight of footnotes and qualifications. I seemed unable to dare a passionate statement. I felt drawn by professionalism to the edge of sterility, capable of no more than pedantic, lifeless, unassailable prose.

Then nostalgia began.

After years spent unwilling to admit its attractions, I gestured nostal- 64 gically toward the past. I yearned for that time when I had not been so alone. I became impatient with books. I wanted experience more immediate. I feared the library's silence. I silently scorned the gray, timid faces around me. I grew to hate the growing pages of my dissertation on genre and Renaissance literature. (In my mind I heard relatives laughing as they tried to make sense of its title.) I wanted something — I couldn't say exactly what. I told myself that I wanted a more passionate life. And a life less thoughtful. And above all, I wanted to be less alone. One day I heard some Spanish academics whispering back and forth to each other, and their sounds seemed ghostly voices recalling my life. Yearning became preoccupation then. Boyhood memories beckoned, flooded my mind. (Laughing intimate voices. Bounding up the front steps of the porch. A sudden embrace inside the door.)

For weeks after, I turned to books by educational experts. I needed to learn how far I had moved from my past — to determine how fast I would be able to recover something of it once again. But I found little. Only a chapter in a book by Richard Hoggart. . . . I left the reading room and the circle of faces.

I came home. After the year in England, I spent three summer months living with my mother and father, relieved by how easy it was to be home. It no longer seemed very important to me that we had little to say. I felt easy sitting and eating and walking with them. I watched them, nevertheless, looking for evidence of those elastic, sturdy strands that bind generations in a web of inheritance. I thought as I watched my mother one night: Of course a friend had been right when she told me that I gestured and laughed just like my mother. Another time I saw for myself: My father's eyes were much like my own, constantly watchful.

But after the early relief, this return, came suspicion, nagging until I realized that I had not neatly sidestepped the impact of schooling. My desire to do so was precisely the measure of how much I remained an academic. *Negatively* (for that is how this idea first occurred to me): My need to think so much and so abstractly about my parents and our relationship was in itself an indication of my long education. My father and mother did not pass their time thinking about the cultural meanings of their experience. It was I who described their daily lives with airy ideas. And yet, *positively*: The ability to consider experience so abstractly allowed me to shape into desire what would otherwise have remained indefinite, meaningless longing in the British Museum. If, because of my schooling, I had grown culturally separated from my parents, my education finally had given me ways of speaking and caring about the fact.

My best teachers in college and graduate school, years before, had tried 68 to prepare me for this conclusion, I think, when they discussed texts of aristocratic pastoral literature. Faithfully, I wrote down all that they said. I memorized it: "The praise of the unlettered by the highly educated is one of the primary themes of 'elitist' literature." But, "the importance of the praise given the unsolitary, richly passionate and spontaneous life is that it simultaneously reflects the value of a reflective life." I heard it all. But there was no way for any of it to mean very much to me. I was a scholarship boy at the time, busily laddering my way up the rungs of education. To pass an examination, I copied down exactly what my teachers told me. It would require many more years of schooling (an inevitable miseducation) in which I came to trust the silence of reading and the habit of abstracting from immediate experience — moving away from a life of closeness and immediacy I remembered with my parents, growing older — before I turned unafraid to desire the past, and thereby achieved what had eluded me for so long — the end of education.

AFTERWORD

Rodriguez's essay is memoir and it is argument, addressing issues of education by means of personal experience. The writer who speaks on public issues from private or personal experience projects an authority that separates him from the theorist. Anecdote and detail, remembered, not invented or found in library research, gives argument the edges of reality and candor.

When we argue from our lives our authority is real but it is narrow. We run the risk of special pleading, of generalizing from the particular. Aware of this potential limitation, Rodriguez adds the library to the autobiography. When we find by research the testimony of others, to support the testimony of reminiscence, we are luckiest and most effective if the supporting material is unlike our own; as in metaphor or analogy, the best comparison combines least likely with most apt.

The English scholarship boy does not at first sight resemble the Mexican-American. At second sight, or rather with the careful parallelism (and scrupulous avowal of difference) shown by the essayist, the likeness of the unlike compels the reader's acquiescence.

Rodriguez uses Hoggart structurally, leaving him and coming back to him. The essay's power comes from memory's anecdote and detail — with the support of historical background supplied from reading.

PHYLLIS
ROSE

*P*HYLLIS ROSE *was born (1942) in New York and graduated from Radcliffe College, took her M.A. at Yale University, but returned to the Charles River for her Ph.D. at Harvard University. She taught briefly at Harvard and Yale before settling down to teach at Wesleyan University in Middletown, Connecticut, where she is a professor of English. She wrote a biography of Virginia Woolf,* Woman of Letters *(1978), but her best-known book is the wonderful anatomy of five Victorian marriages,* Parallel Lives *(1983). In it she recounts the marriages of five writers and their spouses; the writers are John Locke, George Eliot, Thomas Carlisle, John Ruskin, and Charles Dickens. Three of the five marriages were never consummated. In the only good marriage of the five — George Eliot (Mary Ann Evans) and George Henry Lewes — the two were not married.*

Phyllis Rose is currently working on Jazz Cleopatra, *a biography of the singer Josephine Baker. In addition she writes essays and reviews for the New York* Times, *the* Atlantic, *and the Washington* Post. *This terrible essay appeared in the* ATLANTIC.

Tools of Torture:
An Essay on
Beauty and Pain

In a gallery off the rue Dauphine, near the *parfumerie* where I get my massage, I happened upon an exhibit of medieval torture instruments. It made me think that pain must be as great a challenge to the human imagination as pleasure. Otherwise there's no accounting for the number of torture instruments. One would be quite enough. The simple pincer, let's say, which rips out flesh. Or the head crusher, which breaks first your tooth sockets, then your skull. But in addition I saw tongs, thumb-screws, a rack, a ladder, ropes and pulleys, a grill, a garrote, a Spanish horse, a Judas cradle, an iron maiden, a cage, a gag, a strappado, a stretching table, a saw, a wheel, a twisting stork, an inquisitor's chair, a breast breaker, and a scourge. You don't need complicated machinery to cause incredible pain. If you want to saw your victim down the middle, for example, all you need is a slightly bigger than usual saw. If you hold the victim upside down so the blood stays in his head, hold his legs apart, and start sawing at the groin, you can get as far as the navel before he loses consciousness.

Even in the Middle Ages, before electricity, there were many things you could do to torment a person. You could tie him up in an iron belt that held the arms and legs up to the chest and left no point of rest, so that all his muscles went into spasm within minutes and he was driven mad within hours. This was the twisting stork, a benign-looking object. You could stretch him out backward over a thin piece of wood so that his whole body weight rested on his spine, which pressed against the sharp wood. Then you could stop up his nostrils and force water into his stomach through his mouth. Then, if you wanted to finish him off, you and your helper could jump on his stomach, causing internal hemorrhage. This torture was called the rack. If you wanted to burn someone to death without hearing him scream, you could use a tongue lock, a metal rod between the jaw and collarbone that prevented him from opening his mouth. You could put a person in a chair with spikes on the seat and arms, tie him down against the spikes, and beat him, so that every time he flinched from the beating he drove his own flesh deeper onto the spikes. This was the inquisitor's chair. If you wanted to make it worse, you could heat the spikes. You could suspend a person over a pointed wooden pyramid and whenever he started to fall asleep, you could drop him onto the point. If you were Ippolito Marsili, the inventor of this torture, known as the Judas cradle, you could tell yourself you had invented something humane, a torture that worked without burning flesh or breaking bones. For the torture here was supposed to be sleep deprivation.

The secret of torture, like the secret of French cuisine, is that nothing is unthinkable. The human body is like a foodstuff, to be grilled, pounded, filleted. Every opening exists to be stuffed, all flesh to be carved off the bone. You take an ordinary wheel, a heavy wooden wheel with spokes. You lay the victim on the ground with blocks of wood at strategic points under his shoulders, legs, and arms. You use the wheel to break every bone in his body. Next you tie his body onto the wheel. With all its bones broken, it will be pliable. However, the victim will not be dead. If you want to kill him, you hoist the wheel aloft on the end of a pole and leave him to starve. Who would have thought to do this with a man and a wheel? But, then, who would have thought to take the disgusting snail, force it to render its ooze, stuff it in its own shell with garlic butter, bake it, and eat it?

Not long ago I had a facial — only in part because I thought I needed one. It was research into the nature and function of pleasure. In a dark booth at the back of the beauty salon, the aesthetician put me on a table and applied a series of ointments to my face, some cool, some warmed. After a while she put something into my hand, cold and metallic. "Don't be afraid, madame," she said. "It is an electrode. It will not hurt you. The other end is attached to two metal cylinders, which I roll over your face. They break down the electricity barrier on your skin and allow the moisturizers to penetrate deeply." I didn't believe this hocus-pocus. I didn't believe in the electricity barrier or in the ability of these rollers to break it down. But it all felt very good. The cold metal on my face was a pleasant change from the soft warmth of the aesthetician's fingers. Still, since Algeria° it's hard to hear the word "electrode" without fear. So when she left me for a few minutes with a moist, refreshing cheesecloth over my face, I thought, What if the goal of her expertise had been pain, not moisture? What if the electrodes had been electrodes in the Algerian sense? What if the cheesecloth mask were dipped in acid?

In Paris, where the body is so pampered, torture seems particularly sinister, not because it's hard to understand but because — as the dark side of sensuality — it seems so easy. Beauty care is among the glories of Paris.

Algeria   The French committed atrocities in the Algerian war for independence from France in the 1950s.

Soins esthétiques° include makeup, facials, massages (both relaxing and reducing), depilations (partial and complete), manicures, pedicures, and tanning, in addition to the usual run of *soins* for the hair: cutting, brushing, setting, waving, styling, blowing, coloring, and streaking. In Paris the state of your skin, hair, and nerves is taken seriously, and there is little of the puritanical thinking that tries to persuade us that beauty comes from within. Nor do the French think, as Americans do, that beauty should be offhand and low-maintenance. Spending time and money on *soins esthétiques* is appropriate and necessary, not self-indulgent. Should that loving attention to the body turn malevolent, you have torture. You have the procedure — the aesthetic, as it were — of torture, the explanation for the rich diversity of torture instruments, but you do not have the cause.

Historically torture has been a tool of legal systems, used to get information needed for a trial or, more directly, to determine guilt or innocence. In the Middle Ages confession was considered the best of all proofs, and torture was the way to produce a confession. In other words, torture didn't come into existence to give vent to human sadism. It is not always private and perverse but sometimes social and institutional, vetted by the government and, of course, the Church. (There have been few bigger fans of torture than Christianity and Islam.) Righteousness, as much as viciousness, produces torture. There aren't squads of sadists beating down the doors to the torture chambers begging for jobs. Rather, as a recent book on torture by Edward Peters says, the institution of torture creates sadists; the weight of a culture, Peters suggests, is necessary to recruit torturers. You have to convince people that they are working for a great goal in order to get them to overcome their repugnance to the task of causing physical pain to another person. Usually the great goal is the preservation of society, and the victim is presented to the torturer as being in some way out to destroy it.

From another point of view, what's horrifying is how easily you can persuade someone that he is working for the common good. Perhaps the most appalling psychological experiment of modern times, by Stanley Milgram, showed that ordinary, decent people in New Haven, Connecticut, could be brought to the point of inflicting (as they thought) severe electric shocks on other people in obedience to an authority and in pursuit of a goal, the advancement of knowledge, of which they approved. Milgram used — some would say abused — the prestige of science and the university to make his point, but his point is chilling nonetheless. We can cluck over torture, but the evidence at least suggests that with intelligent handling most of us could be brought to do it ourselves.

Soins esthétiques   Beauty treatments.

In the Middle Ages, Milgram's experiment would have had no point. It would have shocked no one that people were capable of cruelty in the interest of something they believed in. That was as it should be. Only recently in the history of human thought has the avoidance of cruelty moved to the forefront of ethics. "Putting cruelty first," as Judith Shklar says in *Ordinary Vices,* is comparatively new. The belief that the "pursuit of happiness" is one of man's inalienable rights, the idea that "cruel and unusual punishment" is an evil in itself, the Benthamite notion that behavior should be guided by what will produce the greatest happiness for the greatest number — all these principles are only two centuries old. They were born with the eighteenth-century democratic revolutions. And in two hundred years they have not been universally accepted. Wherever people believe strongly in some cause, they will justify torture — not just the Nazis, but the French in Algeria.

Many people who wouldn't hurt a fly have annexed to fashion the imagery of torture — the thongs and spikes and metal studs — hence reducing it to the frivolous and transitory. Because torture has been in the mainstream and not on the margins of history, nothing could be healthier. For torture to be merely kinky would be a big advance. Exhibitions like the one I saw in Paris, which presented itself as educational, may be guilty of pandering to the tastes they deplore. Solemnity may be the wrong tone. If taking one's goals too seriously is the danger, the best discouragement of torture may be a radical hedonism that denies that any goal is worth the means, that refuses to allow the nobly abstract to seduce us from the sweetness of the concrete. Give people a good croissant and a good cup of coffee in the morning. Give them an occasional facial and a plate of escargots. Marie Antoinette picked a bad moment to say "Let them eat cake," but I've often thought she was on the right track.

All of which brings me back to Paris, for Paris exists in the imagination of much of the world as the capital of pleasure — of fun, food, art, folly, seduction, gallantry, and beauty. Paris is civilization's reminder to itself that nothing leads you less wrong than your awareness of your own pleasure and a genial desire to spread it around. In that sense the myth of Paris constitutes a moral touchstone, standing for the selfish frivolity that helps keep priorities straight.

AFTERWORD

Phyllis Rose interrupts her research with personal anecdote and uses the first person. ("Not long ago I had a facial. . . .") In her historical exposition she sometimes uses the third person ("Stanley Milgram . . . showed that ordinary, decent people in New Haven, Connecticut . . .") but overwhelmingly she writes in the second person — a device (a torture?) seldom employed by an essayist.

Her you is relentless and devastating: "You don't need complicated machinery to cause incredible pain. If you want to saw your victim down the middle. . . ." "If you wanted to burn someone to death without hearing him scream, you could use a tongue lock. . . ." "You take an ordinary wheel, a heavy wooden wheel with spokes. You lay the victim on the ground with blocks of wood at strategic points under his shoulders, legs, and arms. You use the wheel to break every bone in his body." Syntactically innocent enough, in connection with torture the second person is an accusation that rises to a scream. Because in common usage — often in poetry — you is a mask of I, Rose does not let herself off the hook. (Note, please, the cliché or dead metaphor that comes to my mind.)

"The secret of torture, like the secret of French cuisine, is that nothing is unthinkable." The dark becomes darker when a candle is lit against it. Setting pain against pleasure, Paris against the instruments, Rose makes a casual irony which is all the more painful because of its casualness. When she continues, her language could apply to dead turkeys or live men, to lamb roasts or heretics: "Every opening exists to be stuffed, all flesh to be carved off the bone."

BOOKS AVAILABLE IN PAPERBACK

Parallel Lives: Five Victorian Marriages. New York: Random House. *Nonfiction.*

Woman of Letters: A Life of Virginia Woolf. San Diego: Harcourt Brace Jovanovich. *Nonfiction.*

SCOTT RUSSELL SANDERS

S COTT RUSSELL SANDERS teaches English at the University of Indiana and
writes science fiction, literary criticism, short stories, folklore, and essays;
therefore he publishes in the Georgia Review, Omni, North American Review,
and Isaac Asimov's Science Fiction Magazine. *Born in Tennessee (1945) he did*
his undergraduate work at Brown University, then took a Ph.D. at Cambridge
University where he was a Woodrow Wilson and a Danforth Fellow. Some of his
books are Fetching the Dead: Stories *(1984),* Wonders Hidden: Aububon's
Early Years *(1984), and* Hear the Wind Blow: American Folksongs Retold
(1985). This essay comes from The Paradise of Bombs *(1987), which he describes*
as "a collection of personal narratives about the culture of violence in America."

In a note that he wrote for Contemporary Authors, *Sanders spoke of the*
division, in his life and work, between the sciences and the arts. Clearly his science
fiction is one result; he has written a book about Audubon and plans to write
another. "In all of my work, regardless of period or style, I am concerned with the
ways in which human beings come to terms with the practical problems of living on
a small planet, in nature and in communities."

Doing Time in the Thirteenth Chair

The courtroom is filled with the ticking of a clock and the smell of mold. Listening to the minutes click away, I imagine bombs or mechanical hearts sealed behind the limestone walls. Forty of us have been yanked out of our usual orbits and called to appear for jury duty in this ominous room, beneath the stained-glass dome of the county courthouse. We sit in rows like strangers in a theater, coats rumpled in our laps, crossing and uncrossing our legs, waiting for the show to start.

I feel sulky and rebellious, the way I used to feel when a grade-school teacher made me stay inside during recess. This was supposed to have been the first day of my Christmas vacation, and the plain, uncitizenly fact is that I don't want to be here. I want to be home hammering together some bookshelves for my wife. I want to be out tromping the shores of Lake Monroe with my eye cocked skyward for bald eagles and sharp-shinned hawks.

But the computer-printed letter said to report today for jury duty, and so here I sit. The judge beams down at us from his bench. Tortoise-shell glasses, twenty-dollar haircut, square boyish face: although probably in his early forties, he could pass for a student-body president. He reminds me of an owlish television know-it-all named Mr. Wizard who used to conduct scientific experiments (Magnetism! Litmus tests! Sulphur dioxide!) on a kids' show in the 1950s. Like Mr. Wizard, he lectures us in slow, pedantic speech: trial by one's peers, tradition stretching back centuries to England, defendant innocent until proven guilty beyond a reasonable doubt, and so abundantly on. I spy around for the clock. It must be overhead, I figure, up in the cupola above the dome, raining its ticktocks down on us.

When the lecture is finished, the judge orders us to rise, lift our hands, and swear to uphold the truth. There is a cracking of winter-stiff knees as we stand and again as we sit down. Then he introduces the principal actors: the sleek young prosecutor, who peacocks around like a politician on the hustings; the married pair of brooding, elegantly dressed defense lawyers; and the defendant. I don't want to look at this man who is charged with crimes against the "peace and dignity" of the State of Indiana. I don't want anything to do with his troubles. But I grab an image anyway, of a squat, slit-eyed man about my age, mid-thirties, stringy black hair parted in the middle and dangling like curtains across his face, sparse black beard. The chin whiskers and squinted-up eyes make him look faintly Chinese, and faintly grimacing.

Next the judge reads a list of twelve names, none of them mine, and twelve sworn citizens shuffle into the jury box. The lawyers have at them, darting questions. How do you feel about drugs? Would you say the defendant there looks guilty because he has a beard? Are you related to any police officers? Are you pregnant? When these twelve have finished answering, the attorneys scribble names on sheets of paper which they hand to the judge, and eight of the first bunch are sent packing. The judge reads eight more names, the jury box fills up with fresh bodies, the questioning resumes. Six of these get the heave-ho. And so the lawyers cull through the potential jurors, testing and chucking them like two men picking over apples in the supermarket. At length they agree on a dozen, and still my name has not been called. Hooray, I think. I can build those bookshelves after all, can watch those hawks.

Before setting the rest of us free, however, the judge consults his list. "I am calling alternate juror number one," he says, and then he pronounces my name.

Groans echo down my inmost corridors. For the first time I notice a thirteenth chair beside the jury box, and that is where the judge orders me to go.

"Yours is the most frustrating job," the judge advises me soothingly. 8 "Unless someone else falls ill or gets called away, you will have to listen to all the proceedings without taking part in the jury's final deliberations or decisions."

I feel as though I have been invited to watch the first four acts of a five-act play. Never mind, I console myself: the lawyers will throw me out. I'm the only one in the courtroom besides the defendant who sports a beard or long hair. A backpack decorated with NO NUKES and PEACE NOW and SAVE THE WHALES buttons leans against my boots. How can they expect me, a fiction writer, to confine myself to facts? I am unreliable, a confessed fabulist, a marginal Quaker and Wobbly socialist, a man so out of phase with my community that I am thrown into fits of rage by the local newspaper. The lawyers will take a good look at me and race one another to the bench for the privilege of having the judge boot me out.

But neither Mr. Defense nor Mr. Prosecution quite brings himself to focus on my shady features. Each asks me a perfunctory question, the way vacationers will press a casual thumb against the spare tire before hopping into the car for a trip. If there's air in the tire, you don't bother about blemishes. And that is all I am, a spare juror stashed away in the trunk of the court, in case one of the twelve originals gives out during the trial.

Ticktock. The judge assures us that we should be finished in five days, just in time for Christmas. The real jurors exchange forlorn glances. Here I sit, number thirteen, and nobody looks my way. Knowing I am stuck here for the duration, I perk up, blink my eyes. Like the bear going over the mountain, I might as well see what I can see.

What I see is a parade of mangled souls. Some of them sit on the witness stand and reveal their wounds; some of them remain offstage, summoned up only by the words of those who testify. The case has to do with the alleged sale, earlier this year, of hashish and cocaine to a confidential informer. First the prosecutor stands at a podium in front of the jury and tells us how it all happened, detail by criminal detail, and promises to prove every fact to our utter satisfaction. Next, one of the defense attorneys has a fling at us. It is the husband of the Mr.-and-Mrs. team, a melancholy-looking man with bald pate and mutton-chop sideburns, deep creases in the chocolate skin of his forehead. Leaning on the podium, he vows that he will raise a flock of doubts in our minds — grave doubts, reasonable doubts — particularly regarding the seedy character of the confidential informer. They both speak well, without hemming and hawing, without stumbling over syntactic cliffs, better than senators at a press conference. Thus, like rival suitors, they begin to woo the jury. 12

At mid-morning, before hearing from the first witness, we take a recess. (It sounds more and more like school.) Thirteen of us with peel-away JUROR tags stuck to our shirts and sweaters retreat to the jury room. We drink coffee and make polite chat. Since the only thing we have in common is this trial, and since the judge has just forbidden us to talk about that, we grind our gears trying to get a conversation started. I find out what everybody does in the way of work: a bar waitress, a TV repairman (losing customers while he sits here), a department store security guard, a dentist's assistant, an accountant, a nursing home nurse, a cleaning woman, a caterer, a mason, a boisterous old lady retired from rearing children (and married, she tells us, to a school-crossing guard), a meek college student with the demeanor of a groundhog, a teacher. Three of them right now are unemployed. Six men, six women, with ages ranging from twenty-one to somewhere above seventy. Chaucer could gather this bunch together for a literary pilgrimage, and he would not have a bad sampling of smalltown America.

Presently the bailiff looks in to see what we're up to. She is a jowly woman, fiftyish, with short hair the color and texture of buffed aluminum. She wears silvery half-glasses of the sort favored by librarians; in the courtroom she peers at us above the frames with a librarian's skeptical glance, as if to make sure we are awake. To each of us she now gives a small yellow pad and a ballpoint pen. We are to write our names on the back, take notes on them during the trial, and surrender them to her whenever we leave the courtroom. (School again.) Without saying so directly, she lets us know that we are her flock and she is our shepherd. Anything we need, any yen we get for traveling, we should let her know.

I ask her whether I can go downstairs for a breath of air, and the bailiff answers "sure." On the stairway I pass a teenage boy who is listlessly polishing with a rag the wrought-iron filigree that supports the banister. Old men sheltering from December slouch on benches just inside the ground-floor entrance of the courthouse. Their faces have been caved in by disappointment and the loss of teeth. Two-dollar cotton work gloves, the cheapest winter hand-covers, stick out of their back pockets. They are veterans of this place; so when they see me coming with the blue JUROR label pasted on my chest, they look away. Don't tamper with jurors, especially under the very nose of the law. I want to tell them I'm not a real juror, only a spare, number thirteen. I want to pry old stories out of them, gossip about hunting and dogs, about their favorite pickup trucks, their worst jobs. I want to ask them when and how it all started to go wrong for them. Did they hear a snap when the seams of their life began to come apart? But they will not be fooled into looking at me, not these wily old men with the crumpled faces. They believe the label on my chest and stare down at their unlaced shoes.

I stick my head out the door and swallow some air. The lighted thermometer on the bank reads twenty-eight degrees. Schmaltzy Christmas organ music rebounds from the brick-and-limestone shopfronts of the town square. The Salvation Army bell rings and rings. Delivery trucks hustling through yellow lights blare their horns at jaywalkers. 16

The bailiff must finally come fetch me, and I feel like a wayward sheep. On my way back upstairs, I notice the boy dusting the same square foot of iron filigree, and realize that he is doing this as a penance. Some judge ordered him to clean the metalwork. I'd like to ask the kid what mischief he's done, but the bailiff, looking very dour, is at my heels.

In the hallway she lines us up in our proper order, me last. Everybody stands up when we enter the courtroom, and then, as if we have rehearsed these routines, we all sit down at once. Now come the facts.

The facts are a mess. They are full of gaps, chuckholes, switchbacks, and dead ends — just like life.

At the outset we are shown three small plastic bags. Inside the first is a wad of aluminum foil about the size of an earlobe; the second contains two white pills; the third holds a pair of stamp-sized, squarish packets of folded brown paper. A chemist from the state police lab testifies that he examined these items and found cocaine inside the brown packets, hashish inside the wad of aluminum foil. As for the white pills, they are counterfeits 20 of a popular barbiturate, one favored by politicians and movie stars. They're depressants — downers — but they contain no "controlled substances."

There follows half a day's worth of testimony about how the bags were sealed, who locked them in the narcotics safe at the Bloomington police station, which officer drove them up to the lab in Indianapolis and which drove them back again, who carried them in his coat pocket and who carried them in his briefcase. Even the judge grows bored during this tedious business. He yawns, tips back in his chair, sips coffee from a mug, folds and unfolds with deft thumbs a square of paper about the size of the cocaine packets. The wheels of justice grind slowly. We hear from police officers in uniform, their handcuffs clanking, and from mustachioed officers in civvies, revolvers bulging under their suitcoats. From across the court-room, the bailiff glares at us above her librarian's glasses, alert to catch us napping. She must be an expert at judging the degrees of tedium.

"Do you have to go back and be in the jail again tomorrow?" my little boy asks me at supper.

"Not jail," I correct him. "*Jury*. I'm in the jury."

"With real police?"   24

"Yes."

"And guns?"

"Yes, real guns."

On the second day there is much shifting of limbs in the jury box when 28 the confidential informer, whom the police call I90, takes the stand. Curly-haired, thirty-three years old, bear-built and muscular like a middle-range wrestler, slow of eye, calm under the crossfire of questions, I90 works — when he works — as a drywall finisher. (In other words, he gets plaster-board ready for painting. It's a dusty, blinding job; you go home powdered white as a ghost, and you taste the joint-filler all night.) Like roughly one-quarter of the construction workers in the county, right now he's unem-ployed.

The story he tells is essentially this: Just under a year ago, two cops showed up at his house. They'd been tipped off that he had a mess of stolen goods in his basement, stuff he'd swiped from over in a neighboring county. "Now look here," the cops said to him, "you help us out with some cases we've got going, and we'll see what we can do to help you when this here burglary business comes to court." "Like how?" he said. "Like tell us what you know about hot property, and maybe finger a drug dealer or so." He said yes to that, with the two cops sitting at his kitchen table, and — zap! — he was transformed into I90. (Hearing of this miraculous conversion, I am reminded of Saul on the road to Damascus, the devil's agent suddenly seeing the light and joining the angels.) In this new guise he gave information that led to several arrests and some prison terms, including one for his cousin and two or three for other buddies.

In this particular case, his story goes on, he asked a good friend of his where a guy could buy some, you know, drugs. The friend's brother led him to Bennie's trailer, where Bennie offered to sell I90 about any kind of drug a man's heart could desire. "All I want's some hash," I90 told him, "but I got to go get some money off my old lady first." "Then go get it," said Bennie.

Where I90 went was to the police station. There they fixed him up to make a "controlled buy": searched him, searched his car; strapped a radio transmitter around his waist; took his money and gave him twenty police dollars to make the deal. Back I90 drove to Bennie's place, and on his tail in an unmarked police car drove Officer B., listening over the radio to every burp and glitch sent out by I90's secret transmitter. On the way, I90 picked up a six-pack of Budweiser. ("If you walk into a suspect's house drinking a can of beer," Officer B. later tells us, "usually nobody'll guess you're working for the police.") Inside the trailer, the woman Bennie lives with was now fixing supper, and her three young daughters were playing cards on the linoleum floor. I90 bought a gram of blond Lebanese hashish from Bennie for six dollars. Then I90 said that his old lady was on him bad to get her some downers, and Bennie obliged by selling him a couple of 714's (the white pills favored by movie stars and politicians) at seven dollars for the pair. They shot the bull awhile, Bennie bragging about how big a dealer he used to be (ten pounds of hash and five hundred hits of acid a week), I90 jawing along like an old customer. After about twenty minutes in the trailer, I90 drove to a secluded spot near the L & N railroad depot, and there he handed over the hash and pills to Officer B., who milked the details out of him.

Four days later, I90 went through the same routine, this time buying 32 two packets of cocaine — two "dimes'" worth — from Bennie for twenty dollars. Inside the trailer were half a dozen or so of Bennie's friends, drinking whiskey and smoking pot and watching TV and playing backgammon and generally getting the most out of a Friday night. Again Officer B. tailed I90, listened to the secret radio transmission, and took it all down in a debriefing afterwards behind the Colonial Bakery.

The lawyers burn up a full day leading I90 through this story, dropping questions like breadcrumbs to lure him on, Mr. Prosecutor trying to guide him out of the labyrinth of memory and Mr. Defense trying to get him lost. I90 refuses to get lost. He tells and retells his story without stumbling, intent as a wrestler on a dangerous hold.

On the radio news I hear that U.S. ships have intercepted freighters bound out from Beirut carrying tons and tons of Lebanese hashish, the very same prize strain of hash that I90 claims he bought from Bennie. Not wanting to irk the Lebanese government, the radio says, our ships let the freighters through. Tons and tons sailing across the Mediterranean — into how many one-gram slugs could that cargo be divided?

Out of jail the defense lawyers subpoena one of I90's brothers, who is awaiting his own trial on felony charges. He has a rabbity look about him, face pinched with fear, ready to bolt for the nearest exit. His canary yellow T-shirt is emblazoned with a scarlet silhouette of the Golden Gate Bridge. The shirt and the fear make looking at him painful. He is one of seven brothers and four sisters. Hearing that total of eleven children — the same number as in my father's family — I wonder if the parents were ever booked for burglary or other gestures of despair.

This skittish gent tells us that he always buys his drugs from his brother, good old I90. And good old I90, he tells us further, has a special fondness for snorting cocaine. Glowing there on the witness stand in his yellow shirt, dear brother gives the lie to one after another of I90's claims. But just when I'm about ready, hearing all of this fraternal gossip, to consign I90 to the level of hell reserved by Dante for liars, the prosecutor takes over the questioning. He soon draws out a confession that there has been a bitter feud recently between the two brothers. "And haven't you been found on three occasions to be mentally incompetent to stand trial?" the prosecutor demands. 36

"Yessir," mutters the brother.

"And haven't you spent most of the past year in and out of mental institutions?"

"Yessir."

This second admission is so faint, like a wheeze, that I must lean forward to hear it, even though I am less than two yards away. While the prosecutor lets this damning confession sink into the jury, the rabbity brother just sits there, as if exposed on a rock while the hawks dive, his eyes pinched closed. 40

By day three of the trial, we jurors are no longer strangers to one another. Awaiting our entry into court, we exhibit wallet photos of our children, of nieces and nephews. We moan in chorus about our Christmas shopping lists. The caterer tells about serving 3,000 people at a basketball banquet. The boisterous old lady, to whom we have all taken a liking, explains how the long hairs on her white cats used to get on her husband's black suit pants until she put the cats out in the garage with heating pads in their boxes.

"Where do you leave your car?" the accountant asks.

"On the street," explains the lady. "I don't want to crowd those cats. They're particular as all get-out."

People compare their bowling scores, their insurance rates, their diets. 44

461

The mason, who now weighs about 300 pounds, recounts how he once lost 129 pounds in nine months. His blood pressure got so bad he had to give up dieting, and inside of a year he'd gained all his weight back and then some. The nurse, who wrestles the bloated or shriveled bodies of elderly paupers at the city's old folks' home, complains about her leg joints, and we all sympathize. The security guard entertains us with sagas about shoplifters. We compare notes on car wrecks, on where to get a transmission overhauled, on the outgoing college football coach and the incoming city mayor. We talk, in fact, about everything under the sun except the trial.

In the hall, where we line up for our reentry into the courtroom, a sullen boy sits at a table scrawling on a legal pad. Line after line he copies the same sentence: "I never will steal anything ever again." More penance. He's balancing on the first rung of a ladder that leads up — or down — to the electric chair. Somewhere in the middle of the ladder is a good long prison sentence, and that, I calculate, is what is at stake in our little drug-dealing case.

On the third day of testimony, we learn that I90 has been hidden away overnight by police. After he stepped down from the witness stand yesterday, Bennie's mate, Rebecca, greeted the informant outside in the lobby and threatened to pull a bread knife out of her purse and carve him into mincemeat. I look with new interest at the stolid, bulky, black-haired woman who has been sitting since the beginning of the trial right behind the defendant. From time to time she has leaned forward, touched Bennie on the shoulder, and bent close to whisper something in his good ear. She reminds me of the Amish farm wives of my Ohio childhood — stern, unpainted, built stoutly for heavy chores, her face a fortress against outsiders.

When Rebecca takes the stand, just half a dozen feet from where I sit in chair thirteen, I sense a tigerish fierceness beneath her numb surface. She plods along behind the prosecutor's questions until he asks her, rhetorically, whether she would like to see Bennie X put in jail; then she lashes out. God no, she doesn't want him locked away. Didn't he take her in when she had two kids already and a third in the oven, and her first husband run off, and the cupboards empty? And haven't they been living together just as good as married for eight years, except while he was in jail, and don't her three little girls call him Daddy? And hasn't he been working on the city garbage trucks, getting up at four in the morning, coming home smelling like other people's trash, and hasn't she been bagging groceries at the supermarket, her hands slashed with paper cuts, and her mother looking after the girls, all so they can keep off the welfare? Damn right she doesn't want him going to any prison.

What's more, Rebecca declares, Bennie don't deserve prison because 48 he's clean. Ever since he got out of the slammer a year ago, he's quit dealing. He's done his time and he's mended his ways and he's gone straight. What about that sale of cocaine? the prosecutor wants to know. It never happened, Rebecca vows. She was there in the trailer the whole blessed night, and she never saw Bennie sell nobody nothing, least of all cocaine, which he never used because it's too expensive — it'll run you seventy-five dollars a day — and which he never sold even when he was dealing. The prosecutor needles her: How can she remember that particular night so confidently? She can remember, she flares at him, because early that evening she got a call saying her sister's ten-year-old crippled boy was fixing to die, and all the family was going to the children's hospital in Indianapolis to watch him pass away. That was a night she'll never forget as long as she lives.

When I was a boy, my friends and I believed that if you killed a snake, the mate would hunt you out in your very bed and strangle or gnaw or smother you. We held a similar belief regarding bears, wolves, and mountain lions, although we were much less likely to run into any of those particular beasts. I have gone years without remembering that bit of child's lore, until today, when Rebecca's tigerish turn on the witness stand revives it. I can well imagine her stashing a bread knife in her purse. And if she loses her man for years and stony years, and has to rear those three girls alone, the cupboards empty again, she might well jerk that knife out of her purse one night and use it on something other than bread.

During recess, we thirteen sit in the jury room and pointedly avoid talking about the bread knife. The mason tells how a neighbor kid's Ford Pinto skidded across his lawn and onto his front porch, blocking the door and nosing against the picture window. "I took the wheels off and chained the bumper to my maple tree until his daddy paid for fixing my porch."

Everyone, it seems, has been assaulted by a car or truck. Our vehicular yarns wind closer and closer about the courthouse. Finally, two of the women jurors — the cigarillo-smoking caterer and the elderly cat lady — laugh nervously. The two of them were standing just inside the plate-glass door of the courthouse last night, the caterer says, when along came a pickup truck, out poked an arm from the window, up flew a smoking beer can, and then BAM! the can exploded. "We jumped a yard in the air!" cries the old woman. "We thought it was some of Bennie's mean-looking friends," the caterer admits. Everybody laughs at the tableau of speeding truck, smoking can, exploding cherry bomb, leaping jurors. Then we choke into sudden silence, as if someone has grabbed each of us by the throat.

Four of Bennie's friends — looking not so much mean as broken, like 52 shell-shocked refugees — testify on his behalf during the afternoon of day three. Two of them are out-of-work men in their twenties, with greasy hair to their shoulders, fatigue jackets, and clodhopper boots: their outfits and world-weary expressions are borrowed from record jackets. They are younger versions of the old men with caved-in faces who crouch on benches downstairs, sheltering from December. The other two witnesses are young women with reputations to keep up, neater than the scruffy men; gold crosses dangle over their sweaters, and gum cracks between crooked teeth. All four speak in muttered monosyllables and orphaned phrases, as if they are breaking a long vow of silence and must fetch bits and pieces of language from the archives of memory. They were all at Bennie's place on the night of the alleged cocaine sale, and they swear in unison that no such sale took place.

Officer B., the puppetmaster who pulled the strings on I90, swears just as adamantly that both the sales, of cocaine and of hash, *did* take place, for he listened to the proceedings over the radio in his unmarked blue Buick. He is a sleepy-eyed man in his mid-thirties, about the age of the informant and the defendant, a law-upholding alter ego for those skewed souls.

Double-chinned, padded with the considerable paunch that seems to be issued along with the police badge, Officer B. answers Mr. Prosecutor and Mr. Defense in a flat, walkie-talkie drawl, consulting a sheaf of notes in his lap, never contradicting himself. Yes, he neglected to tape the opening few minutes of the first buy, the minutes when the exchange of hashish and money actually took place. Why? "I had a suspicion my batteries were weak, and I wanted to hold off." And, yes, he did erase the tape of the debriefing that followed buy number one. Why? "It's policy to reuse the old cassettes. Saves the taxpayers' money." And, yes, the tape of the second buy is raw, indecipherable noise, because a blaring TV in the background drowns out all human voices. (Listening to the tape, we can understand nothing in the scrawking except an ad for the American Express Card.) The tapes, in other words, don't prove a thing. What it all boils down to is the word of the law and of the unsavory informer versus the word of the many-times-convicted defendant, his mate, and his friends.

Toward the end of Officer B.'s testimony, there is a resounding clunk, like a muffled explosion, at the base of the witness stand. We all jump — witness, judge, jury, onlookers — and only relax when the prosecutor squats down and discovers that a pair of handcuffs has fallen out of Officer B.'s belt. Just a little reminder of the law's muscle. All of us were envisioning bombs. When Officer B. steps down, the tail of his sportcoat is hitched up over the butt of his gun.

The arrest: A squad car pulls up to the front of the trailer, and out the 56 trailer's back door jumps Bennie, barefooted, wearing T-shirt and cut-off jeans. He dashes away between tarpaper shacks, through dog yards, over a stubbled field (his bare feet bleeding), through a patch of woods to a railroad cut. Behind him puffs a skinny cop (who recounts this scene in court), shouting, "Halt! Police!" But Bennie never slows down until he reaches that railroad cut, where he stumbles, falls, rolls down to the tracks like the sorriest hobo. The officer draws his gun. Bennie lifts his hands for the familiar steel cuffs. The two of them trudge back to the squad car, where Officer B. reads the arrest warrant and Bennie blisters everybody with curses.   .

The judge later instructs us that flight from arrest may be regarded as evidence, not of guilt but of *consciousness* of guilt. Oh ho! A fine distinction! Guilt for what! Selling drugs? Playing hooky? Original sin? Losing his job at Coca-Cola? I think of those bleeding feet, the sad chase. I remember a drunken uncle who stumbled down a railroad cut, fell asleep between the tracks, and died of fear when a train passed over.

On day four of the trial, Bennie himself takes the stand. He is shorter than I thought, and fatter — too many months of starchy jail food and no exercise. With exceedingly long thumbnails he scratches his jaw. When asked a question, he rolls his eyes, stares at the ceiling, then answers in a gravelly country voice, the voice of a late-night disk jockey. At first he is gruffly polite, brief in his replies, but soon he gets cranked up and rants in a grating monologue about his painful history.

He graduated from high school in 1968, worked eight months at RCA and Coca-Cola, had a good start, had a sweetheart, then the Army got him, made him a cook, shipped him to Vietnam. After a few weeks in the kitchen, he was transferred to the infantry because the fodder-machine was short of foot soldiers. "Hey, listen, man, I ain't nothing but a cook," he told them. "I ain't been trained for combat." And they said, "Don't you worry; you'll get on-the-job training. Learn or die." The artillery ruined his hearing. (Throughout the trial he has held a hand cupped behind one ear, and has followed the proceedings like a grandfather.) Some of his buddies got shot up. He learned to kill people. "We didn't even know what we was there for." To relieve his constant terror, he started doing drugs: marijuana, opium, just about anything that would ease a man's mind. Came home from Vietnam in 1971 a wreck, got treated like dirt, like a babykiller, like a murdering scumbag, and found no jobs. His sweetheart married an insurance salesman.

Within a year after his return he was convicted of shoplifting and bur- 60 glary. He was framed on the second charge by a friend, but couldn't use his only alibi because he had spent the day of the robbery in bed with a sixteen-year-old girl, whose father would have put him away for statutory rape. As it was, he paid out two years in the pen, where he sank deeper into drugs than ever before. "If you got anything to buy or trade with, you can score more stuff in the state prisons than on the streets of Indianapolis."

After prison, he still couldn't find work, couldn't get any help for his drug-thing from the Veterans' Administration, moved in with Rebecca and her three girls, eventually started selling marijuana and LSD. "Everytime I went to somebody for drugs, I got ripped off. That's how I got into dealing. If you're a user, you're always looking for a better deal."

In 1979 he was busted for selling hash, in 1980 for possessing acid, betrayed in both cases by the man from whom he had bought his stock. "He's a snitch, just a filthy snitch. You can't trust nobody." Back to prison for a year, back out again in December 1981. No jobs, no jobs, no damn jobs; then part-time on the city garbage truck, up at four in the morning, minus five degrees and the wind blowing and the streets so cold his gloves stuck to the trash cans. Then March came, and this I90 guy showed up, wanted to buy some drugs, and "I told him I wasn't dealing any more. I done my time and gone straight. I told him he didn't have enough money to pay me for no thirty years in the can." (The prosecutor bristles, the judge leans meaningfully forward: we jurors are not supposed to have any notion of the sentence that might follow a conviction on this drug charge.)

In his disk-jockey voice, Bennie denies ever selling anything to this I90 snitch. (He keeps using the word "snitch": I think of tattle-tales, not this adult betrayal.) It was I90, he swears, who tried to sell *him* the hash. Now the pills, why, those he had lying around for a friend who never picked them up, and so he just gave them to I90. "They was give to me, and so I couldn't charge him nothing. They wasn't for me anyway. Downers I do not use. To me, life is a downer. Just to cope with every day, that is way down low enough for me." And as for the cocaine, he never laid eyes on it until the man produced that little plastic bag in court. "I don't use coke. It's too expensive. That's for the bigwigs and the upstanding citizens, as got the money."

Sure, he admits, he ran when the police showed up at his trailer. "I'm flat scared of cops. I don't like talking to them about anything. Since I got back from Vietnam, every time they cross my path they put bracelets on me." (He holds up his wrists. They are bare now, but earlier this morning, when I saw a deputy escorting him into the courthouse, they were hand-cuffed.) He refuses to concede that he is a drug addict, but agrees he has a terrible habit, "a gift from my country in exchange for me going overseas and killing a bunch of strangers."

After the arrest, forced to go cold turkey on his dope, he begged the jail doctor — "He's no kind of doctor, just one of them that fixes babies" — to zonk him out on something. And so, until the trial, he has spent eight months drowsing under Valium and Thorazine. "You can look down your nose at me for that if you want, but last month another vet hung himself two cells down from me." (The other guy was a scoutmaster, awaiting trial for sexually molesting one of his boys. He had a record of severe depression dating from the war, and used his belt for the suicide.)

64

"The problem with my life," says Bennie, "is Vietnam." For a while after coming home, he slept with a knife under his pillow. Once, wakened suddenly, thinking he was still in Vietnam, he nearly killed his best friend. During the week of our trial, another Vietnam vet up in Indianapolis shot his wife in the head, imagining she was a gook. Neighbors got to him before he could pull out her teeth, as he used to pull out the teeth of the enemies he bagged over in Vietnam.

When I look at Bennie, I see a double image. He was drafted during the same month in which I, studying in England, gave Uncle Sam the slip. I hated that war, and feared it, for exactly the reasons he describes — because it was foul slaughter, shameful, sinful, pointless butchery. While he was over there killing and dodging, sinking into the quicksand of drugs, losing his hearing, storing up a lifetime's worth of nightmares, I was snug in England, filling my head with words. We both came home to America in the same year, I to job and family, he to nothing. Ten years after that homecoming, we stare across the courtroom at one another as into a funhouse mirror.

As the twelve jurors file past me into the room where they will decide on Bennie's guilt or innocence, three of them pat my arm in a comradely way. They withdraw beyond a brass-barred gate; I sit down to wait on a deacon's bench in the hallway outside the courtroom. I feel stymied, as if I have rocketed to the moon only to be left riding the ship round and round in idle orbit while my fellow astronauts descend to the moon's surface. At the same time I feel profoundly relieved, because, after the four days of testimony, I still cannot decide whether Bennie truly sold those drugs, or whether I90, to cut down on his own prison time, set up this ill-starred Bennie for yet another fall. Time, time — it always comes down to time: in jail, job, and jury box we are spending and hoarding our only wealth, the currency of days.

Even through the closed doors of the courtroom, I still hear the ticking 68 of the clock. The sound reminds me of listening to my daughter's pulse through a stethoscope when she was still riding, curled up like a stowaway, in my wife's womb. Ask not for whom this heart ticks, whispered my unborn daughter through the stethoscope: it ticks for thee. So does the courtroom clock. It grabs me by the ear and makes me fret about time — about how little there is of it, about how we are forever bumming it from one another as if it were cups of sugar or pints of blood ("You got a minute?" "Sorry, have to run, not a second to spare"). Seize the day, we shout, to cheer ourselves; but the day has seized us and flings us forward pell-mell toward the end of all days.

Now and again there is a burst of laughter from the jury room, but it is always squelched in a hurry. They are tense, and laugh to relieve the tension, and then feel ashamed of their giddiness. Lawyers traipse past me

467

— the men smoking, striking poses, their faces like lollipops atop their ties; the women teetering on high heels. The bailiff walks into our judge's office carrying a bread knife. To slice her lunch? As evidence against Rebecca? A moment later she emerges bearing a piece of cake and licking her fingers. Christmas parties are breaking out all over the courthouse.

Rebecca herself paces back and forth at the far end of my hallway, her steps as regular as the clock's tick, killing time. Her bearded and cross-wearing friends sidle up to comfort her, but she shrugs them away. Once she paces down my way, glances at the barred door of the jury room, hears muffled shouts. This she must take for good news, because she throws me a rueful smile before turning back.

Evidently the other twelve are as muddled by the blurred and contradictory "facts" of the case as I am, for they spend from noon until five reaching their decision. They ask for lunch. They ask for a dictionary. They listen again to the tapes. Sullen teenagers, following in the footsteps of Bennie and I90, slouch into the misdemeanor office across the hall from me; by and by they slouch back out again, looking unrepentant. At length the 300-pound mason lumbers up to the gate of the jury room and calls the bailiff. "We're ready as we're going to be." He looks bone-weary, unhappy, and dignified. Raising his eyebrows at me, he shrugs. Comrades in uncertainty.

The cast reassembles in the courtroom, the judge asks the jury for its 72 decision, and the mason stands up to pronounce Bennie guilty. I stare at my boots. Finally I glance up, not at Bennie or Rebecca or the lawyers, but at my fellow jurors. They look distraught, wrung-out and despairing, as if they have just crawled out of a mine after an explosion and have left some of their buddies behind. Before quitting the jury room, they composed and signed a letter to the judge pleading with him to get some help — drug help, mind help, any help — for Bennie.

The ticking of the clock sounds louder in my ears than the judge's closing recital. But I do, with astonishment, hear him say that we must all come back tomorrow for one last piece of business. He is sorry, he knows we are worn out, but the law has prevented him from warning us ahead of time that we might have to decide on one more question of guilt.

The legal question posed for us on the morning of day five is simple: Has Bennie been convicted, prior to this case, of two or more unrelated felonies? If so, then he is defined by Indiana state law as a "habitual offender," and we must declare him to be such. We are shown affidavits for those earlier convictions — burglary, sale of marijuana, possession of LSD — and so the answer to the legal question is clear.

But the moral and psychological questions are tangled, and they occupy the jury for nearly five more hours on this last day of the trial. Is it fair to sentence a person again, after he has already served time for his earlier offenses? How does the prosecutor decide when to apply the habitual offender statute, and does its use in this case have anything to do with the political ambitions of the sleek young attorney? Did Bennie really steal that $150 stereo, for which he was convicted a decade ago, or did he really spend the day in bed with his sixteen-year-old girlfriend? Did Vietnam poison his mind and blight his life?

Two sheriff's deputies guard the jury today; another guards me in my own little cell. The bailiff would not let me stay out on the deacon's bench in the hall, and so, while a plainclothes detective occupies my old seat, I sit in a room lined with file cabinets and stare out like a prisoner through the glass door. "I have concluded," wrote Pascal, "that the whole misfortune of men comes from a single thing, and that is their inability to remain at rest in a room." I agree with him; nothing but that cruising deputy would keep me here. 76

This time, when the verdict is announced, Rebecca has her daughters with her, three little girls frightened into unchildlike stillness by the courtroom. Their lank hair and washed-out eyes remind me of my childhood playmates, the children of dead-end, used-up West Virginia coalminers who'd moved to Ohio in search of work. The mother and daughter are surrounded by half a dozen rough customers, guys my age with hair down over their shoulders and rings in their ears, with flannel shirts, unfocused eyes. Doubtless they are the reason so many holstered deputies and upholstered detectives are patrolling the courthouse, and the reason I was locked safely away in a cell while the jury deliberated.

When the mason stands to pronounce another verdict of guilty, I glimpse what I do not want to glimpse: Bennie flinging his head back, Rebecca snapping hers forward into her palms, the girls wailing.

The judge accompanies all thirteen of us into the jury room, where he keeps us for an hour while the deputies clear the rough customers from the courthouse. We are not to be alarmed, he reassures us; he is simply being cautious, since so much was at stake for the defendant. "How much?" the mason asks. "Up to twenty-four years for the drug convictions, plus a mandatory thirty years for the habitual offender charges," the judge replies. The cleaning woman, the nurse, and the TV repairman begin crying. I swallow carefully. For whatever it's worth, the judge declares comfortingly, he agrees with our decisions. If we knew as much about this Bennie as he knows, we would not be troubled. And that is just the splinter in the brain, the fact that we know so little — about Bennie, about Vietnam, about drugs, about ourselves — and yet we must grope along in our ignorance, pronouncing people guilty or innocent, squeezing out of one another that precious fluid, time.

469

And so I do my five days in the thirteenth chair. Bennie may do as 80
many as fifty-four years in prison, buying his drugs from meaner dealers,
dreaming of land mines and of his adopted girls, checking the date on his
watch, wondering at what precise moment the hinges of his future slammed
shut.

AFTERWORD

*Use of the present tense is common, these days, both in essay and fiction. Many
times it seems only an affectation, not integral to the telling of a particular tale but
merely the fashion. The present tense can provide an artificial heightening of effect,
a technical urgency, playing the moment's tape. I suppose it comes from television,
as our brains turn into small Sonys: there is no past tense on the screen that alters
so rapidly before us, on which advertisers with fifty cuts in thirty seconds speed
epics into telegrams.*

*There are legitimate uses for the present tense. Talking about Kumin's journal
I spoke of its* ongoingness, *today's words written before tomorrow's aftermath.
Scott Russell Sanders's "Doing Time in the Thirteenth Chair," his essay on jury
duty, is indeed a "personal narrative about the culture of violence in America" —
and it is narrative first of all. We follow the story as it unfolds, gradually and
finally arriving at the moral of the story. The present tense allows us to understand
events as they happen, not from the perspective of a digested experience. The result
is not only a greater immediacy, which could be merely technical, but more intimacy
with the author's voice — as we learn with him and not just from him.*

BOOKS AVAILABLE IN PAPERBACK

Terrarium. New York: St. Martin's Press-Tor. *Novel.*

Wilderness Plots: Tales About the Settlement of the American Land. New York: William
Morrow. *Short stories.*

JONATHAN
SCHELL

*J*ONATHAN SCHELL *was born (1943) in New York, where he now lives and writes for the* New Yorker. *Schell attended Harvard University and the University of California at Berkeley; he did graduate work in Japan in Far Eastern history. Visiting Vietnam, he accompanied American soldiers in a helicopter raid against the Viet Cong that resulted in the destruction of a small village. His story of this action appeared first in the* New Yorker *and then as* The Village of Ben Suc *(1967), an early book on the Vietnam War. In* The Time of Illusion *(1976) he wrote about politics in America from 1969 through President Nixon's resignation in 1974. His most recent books are* America in Vietnam *(1987) and* History in Sherman Park: An American Family During the Reagan-Mondale Election *(1987).*

In The Fate of the Earth *(1982), Schell examines the prospects for nuclear war. When it was first serialized in the* New Yorker, *the book had an immediate influence on the movement for a nuclear freeze. "A Republic of Insects and Grass" comes from the opening section of* The Fate of the Earth. *Here it is Schell's self-appointed task to think about the unthinkable, to employ mind-numbing numbers without numbing the mind, to cite statistics almost impossible to imagine, yet through images and analogies to bring them into the reader's terrified comprehension.*

A Republic
of Insects and Grass

The "strategic" forces of the Soviet Union — those that can deliver nuclear warheads to the United States — are so far capable of carrying seven thousand warheads with an estimated maximum yield of more than seventeen thousand megatons of explosive power, and, barring unexpected developments in arms-controls talks, the number of warheads is expected to rise in the coming years. The actual megatonnage of the Soviet strategic forces is not known, and, for a number of reasons, including the fact that smaller warheads can be delivered more accurately, it is very likely that the actual megatonnage is lower than the maximum possible; however, it is reasonable to suppose that the actual megatonnage is as much as two-thirds of the maximum, which would be about eleven and a half thousand megatons. If we assume that in a first strike the Soviets held back about a thousand megatons (itself an immense force), then the attack would amount to about ten thousand megatons, or the equivalent of eight hundred thousand Hiroshima bombs. American strategic forces comprise about nine thousand warheads with a yield of some three thousand five hundred megatons. The total yield of these American forces was made comparatively low for strategic reasons. American planners discovered that smaller warheads can be delivered more accurately than larger ones, and are therefore more useful for attacking strategic forces on the other side. And, in fact, American missiles are substantially more accurate than Soviet ones. However, in the last year or so, in spite of this advantage in numbers of warheads and in accuracy, American leaders have come to believe that the American forces are inadequate, and, again barring unexpected developments in arms-control talks, both the yield of the American arsenal and the number of warheads in it are likely to rise dramatically. (Neither the United States nor the Soviet Union reveals the total explosive yield of its own forces. The public is left to turn to private organizations, which, by making use of hundreds of pieces of information that *have* been released by the two governments, piece together an over-all picture. The figures I have used to estimate the maximum capacities of the two sides are taken for the most part from tables provided in the latest edition of "The Military Balance," a standard yearly reference work on the strength of military forces around the world, which is published by a research institute in London called the International Institute for Strategic Studies.) The territory of the United States, including Alaska and Hawaii, is three million six hundred and fifteen thousand one hundred and twenty-two square miles. It contains approximately two hundred and twenty-five million people, of whom sixty per cent, or about a hundred and thirty-five million, live in various urban centers with a total area of only eighteen thousand square miles. I asked Dr. Kendall, who has done considerable research on the consequences of nuclear attacks, to sketch out in rough terms what the actual distribution of bombs might be in a ten-thousand-megaton Soviet attack in the early nineteen-eighties on all targets in the United States, military and civilian.

"Without serious distortion," he said, "we can begin by imagining that we would be dealing with ten thousand weapons of one megaton each, although in fact the yields would, of course, vary considerably. Let us also make the assumption, based on common knowledge of weapons design, that on average the yield would be one-half fission and one-half fusion. This proportion is important, because it is the fission products — a virtual museum of about three hundred radioactive isotopes, decaying at different rates — that give off radioactivity in fallout. Fusion can add to the total in ground bursts by radioactivation of ground material by neutrons, but the quantity added is comparatively small. Targets can be divided into two categories — hard and soft. Hard targets, of which there are about a thousand in the United States, are mostly missile silos. The majority of them can be destroyed only by huge, blunt overpressures, ranging anywhere from many hundreds to a few thousand pounds per square inch, and we can expect that two weapons might be devoted to each one to assure destruction. That would use up two thousand megatons. Because other strategic military targets — such as Strategic Air Command bases — are near centers of population, an attack on them as well, perhaps using another couple of hundred megatons, could cause a total of more than twenty million casualties, according to studies by the Arms Control and Disarmament Agency. If the nearly eight thousand weapons remaining were then devoted to the cities and towns of the United States in order of population, every community down to the level of fifteen hundred inhabitants would be hit with a megaton bomb — which is, of course, many, many times what would be necessary to annihilate a town that size. For obvious reasons, industry is highly correlated with population density, so an attack on the one necessarily hits the other, especially when an attack of this magnitude is considered. Ten thousand targets would include everything worth hitting in the country and much more; it would simply *be* the

United States. The targeters would run out of targets and victims long before they ran out of bombs. If you imagine that the bombs were distributed according to population, then, allowing for the fact that the attack on the military installations would have already killed about twenty million people, you would have about forty megatons to devote to each remaining million people in the country. For the seven and a half million people in New York City, that would come to three hundred megatons. Bearing in mind what one megaton can do, you can see that this would be preposterous overkill. In practice, one might expect the New York metropolitan area to be hit with some dozens of one-megaton weapons."

In the first moments of a ten-thousand-megaton attack on the United States, I learned from Dr. Kendall and from other sources, flashes of white light would suddenly illumine large areas of the country as thousands of suns, each one brighter than the sun itself, blossomed over cities, suburbs, and towns. In those same moments, when the first wave of missiles arrived, the vast majority of the people in the regions first targeted would be irradiated, crushed, or burned to death. The thermal pulses could subject more than six hundred thousand square miles, or one-sixth of the total land mass of the nation, to a minimum level of forty calories per centimeter squared — a level of heat that chars human beings. (At Hiroshima, charred remains in the rough shape of human beings were a common sight.) Tens of millions of people would go up in smoke. As the attack proceeded, as much as three-quarters of the country could be subjected to incendiary levels of heat, and so, wherever there was inflammable material, could be set ablaze. In the ten seconds or so after each bomb hit, as blast waves swept outward from thousands of ground zeros, the physical plant of the United States would be swept away like leaves in a gust of wind. The six hundred thousand square miles already scorched by the forty or more calories of heat per centimeter squared would now be hit by blast waves of a minimum of five pounds per square inch, and virtually all the habitations, places of work, and other manmade things there — substantially the whole human construct in the United States — would be vaporized, blasted, or otherwise pulverized out of existence. Then, as clouds of dust rose from the earth, and mushroom clouds spread overhead, often linking to form vast canopies, day would turn to night. (These clouds could blanket as much as a third of the nation.) Shortly, fires would spring up in the debris of the cities and in every forest dry enough to burn. These fires would simply burn down the United States. When one pictures a full-scale attack on the United States, or on any other country, therefore, the picture of a single city being flattened by a single bomb — an image firmly engraved in the public imagination, probably because of the bombings of Hiroshima and Nagasaki — must give way to a picture of substantial sections of the country being turned by a sort of nuclear carpet-bombing into immense infernal regions, literally tens of thousands of square miles in area, from which escape is impossible. In Hiroshima and Nagasaki, those who had not been killed or injured so severely that they could not move were able to flee to the undevastated world around them, where they found help, but in any city where three or four bombs had been used — not to mention fifty, or a hundred — flight from one blast would only be flight toward another, and no one could escape alive. Within these regions, each of three of the immediate effects of nuclear weapons — initial radiation, thermal pulse, and blast wave — would alone be enough to kill most people: the initial nuclear radiation would subject tens of thousands of square miles to lethal doses; the blast waves, coming from all sides, would nowhere fall below the overpressure necessary to destroy almost all buildings; and the thermal pulses, also coming from all sides, would always be great enough to kill exposed people and, in addition, to set on fire everything that would burn. The ease with which virtually the whole population of the country could be trapped in these zones of universal death is suggested by the fact that the sixty per cent of the population that lives in an area of eighteen thousand square miles could be annihilated with only three hundred one-megaton bombs — the number necessary to cover the area with a maximum of five pounds per square inch of overpressure and forty calories per centimeter squared of heat. That would leave nine thousand seven hundred megatons, or ninety-seven per cent of the megatonnage in the attacking force, available for other targets. (It is hard to imagine what a targeter would do with all his bombs in these circumstances. Above several thousand megatons, it would almost become a matter of trying to hunt down individual people with nuclear warheads.)

The statistics on the initial nuclear radiation, the thermal pulses, and [4] the blast waves in a nuclear holocaust can be presented in any number of ways, but all of them would be only variations on a simple theme — the annihilation of the United States and its people. Yet while the immediate nuclear effects are great enough in a ten-thousand-megaton attack to destroy the country many times over, they are not the most powerfully lethal of the local effects of nuclear weapons. The killing power of the local fallout is far greater. Therefore, if the Soviet Union was bent on producing the maximum overkill — if, that is, its surviving leaders, whether out of calculation, rage, or madness, decided to eliminate the United States not merely as a political and social entity but as a biological one — they would burst their bombs on the ground rather than in the air. Although the scope of severe blast damage would then be reduced, the blast waves, fireballs, and thermal pulses would still be far more than enough to destroy the country, and, in addition, provided only that the bombs were dispersed widely enough, lethal fallout would spread throughout the nation. The amount of radiation delivered by the fallout from a ground burst of a given size is still uncertain — not least because, as Glasstone notes, there has never been a "true land surface burst" of a bomb with a yield of over one kiloton. (The Bikini burst was in part over the ocean.) Many factors make for uncertainty. To mention just a few: the relative amounts of the fallout that rises into the stratosphere and the fallout that descends to the ground near the blast are dependent on, among other things, the yield of the weapon, and, in any case, can be only guessed at; the composition of the fallout will vary with the composition of the material on the ground that is sucked up into the mushroom cloud; prediction of the distribution of fallout by winds of various speeds at various altitudes depends on a choice of several "models"; and the calculation of the arrival time of the fallout — an important calculation, since fallout cannot harm living things until it lands near them — is subject to similar speculative doubts. However, calculations on the basis of figures for a one-megaton ground burst which are given in the Office of Technology Assessment's report show that ten thousand megatons would yield one-week doses around the country averaging more than ten thousand rems. In actuality, of course, the bombs would almost certainly not be evenly spaced around the country but, rather, would be concentrated in populated areas and in missile fields; and the likelihood is that in most places where people lived or worked the doses would be many times the average, commonly reaching several tens of thousands of rems for the first week, while in remote areas they would be less, or, conceivably, even nonexistent. (The United States contains large tracts of empty desert, and to target them would be virtually meaningless from any point of view.)

These figures provide a context for judging the question of civil defense. With overwhelming immediate local effects striking the vast majority of the population, and with one-week doses of radiation then rising into the tens of thousands of rems, evacuation and shelters are a vain hope. Needless to say, in these circumstances evacuation before an attack would be an exercise in transporting people from one death to another. In some depictions of a holocaust, various rescue operations are described, with unafflicted survivors bringing food, clothes, and medical care to the afflicted, and the afflicted making their way to thriving, untouched communities, where churches, school auditoriums, and the like would have been set up for their care — as often happens after a bad snowstorm, say. Obviously, none of this could come about. In the first place, in a full-scale attack there would in all likelihood *be* no surviving communities, and, in the second place, everyone who failed to seal himself off from the outside environment for as long as several months would soon die of radiation sickness. Hence, in the months after a holocaust there would be no activity of any sort, as, in a reversal of the normal state of things, the dead would lie on the surface and the living, if there were any, would be buried underground.

To this description of radiation levels around the country, an addition remains to be made. This is the fact that attacks on the seventy-six nuclear power plants in the United States would produce fallout whose radiation had much greater longevity than that of the weapons alone. The physicist Dr. Kosta Tsipis, of M.I.T., and one of his students, Steven Fetter, recently published an article in *Scientific American* called "Catastrophic Releases of Radioactivity," in which they calculate the damage from a one-megaton thermonuclear ground burst on a one-gigawatt nuclear power plant. In such a ground burst, the facility's radioactive contents would be vaporized along with everything nearby, and the remains would be carried up into the mushroom cloud, from which they would descend to the earth with the rest of the fallout. But whereas the fission products of the weapon were newly made, and contained many isotopes that would decay to insignificant levels very swiftly, the fission products in a reactor would be a collection of longer-lived isotopes (and this applies even more strongly to the spent fuel in the reactor's holding pond), since the short-lived ones would, for the most part, have had enough time to reduce themselves to harmless levels. The intense but comparatively short-lived radiation from the weapon would kill people in the first few weeks and months, but the long-lived radiation that was produced both by the weapon and by the power plant could prevent anyone from living on a vast area of land for decades after it fell. For example, after a year an area of some seventeen hundred square miles downwind of a power plant on which a one-megaton bomb had been ground-burst (again assuming a fifteen-mile-an-hour wind) would still be delivering more than fifty rems per year to anyone who tried to live there, and that is two hundred and fifty times the "safe" dose established by the E.P.A. The bomb by itself would produce this effect over an area of only twenty-six square miles. (In addition to offering an enemy a way of redoubling the effectiveness of his attacks in a full-scale holocaust, reactors provide targets of unparalleled danger in possible terrorist nuclear attacks. In an earlier paper, Tsipis and Fetter observe that "the destruction of a reactor with a nuclear weapon, even of relatively small yield, such as a crude terrorist nuclear device, would represent a national catastrophe of lasting consequences." It can be put down as one further alarming oddity of life in a nuclear world that in building nuclear power plants nations have opened themselves to catastrophic devastation and long-term contamination of their territories by enemies who manage to get hold of only a few nuclear weapons.)

If, in a nuclear holocaust, anyone hid himself deep enough under the earth and stayed there long enough to survive, he would emerge into a dying natural environment. The vulnerability of the environment is the last word in the argument against the usefulness of shelters: there is no hole big enough to hide all of nature in. Radioactivity penetrates the environment in many ways. The two most important components of radiation from fallout are gamma rays, which are electromagnetic radiation of the highest intensity, and beta particles, which are electrons fired at high speed from decaying nuclei. Gamma rays subject organisms to penetrating whole-body doses, and are responsible for most of the ill effects of radiation from fallout. Beta particles, which are less penetrating than gamma rays, act at short range, doing harm when they collect on the skin, or on the surface of a leaf. They are harmful to plants on whose foliage the fallout descends — producing "beta burn" — and to grazing animals, which can suffer burns as well as gastrointestinal damage from eating the foliage. Two of the most harmful radioactive isotopes present in fallout are strontium-90 (with a half-life of twenty-eight years) and cesium-137 (with a half-life of thirty years). They are taken up into the food chain through the roots of plants or through direct ingestion by animals, and contaminate the environment from within. Strontium-90 happens to resemble calcium in its chemical composition, and therefore finds its way into the human diet through dairy products and is eventually deposited by the body in the bones, where it is thought to cause bone cancer. (Every person in the world now has in his bones a measurable deposit of strontium-90 traceable to the fallout from atmospheric nuclear testing.)

Over the years, agencies and departments of the government have 8 sponsored numerous research projects in which a large variety of plants and animals were irradiated in order to ascertain the lethal or sterilizing dose for each. These findings permit the prediction of many gross ecological consequences of a nuclear attack. According to "Survival of Food Crops and Livestock in the Event of Nuclear War," the proceedings of the 1970 symposium at Brookhaven National Laboratory, the lethal doses for most mammals lie between a few hundred rads and a thousand rads of gamma radiation; a rad — for "roentgen absorbed dose" — is a roentgen of radiation that has been absorbed by an organism, and is roughly equal to a rem. For example, the lethal doses of gamma radiation for animals in pasture, where fallout would be descending on them directly and they would be eating fallout that had fallen on the grass, and would thus suffer from doses of beta radiation as well, would be one hundred and eighty rads for cattle; two hundred and forty rads for sheep; five hundred and fifty rads for swine; three hundred and fifty rads for horses; and eight hundred rads for poultry. In a ten-thousand-megaton attack, which would create levels of radiation around the country averaging more than ten thousand rads, most of the mammals of the United States would be killed off. The lethal doses for birds are in roughly the same range as those for mammals, and birds, too, would be killed off. Fish are killed at doses of between one thousand one hundred rads and about five thousand six hundred rads, but their fate is less predictable. On the one hand, water is a shield from radiation, and would afford some protection; on the other hand, fallout might concentrate in bodies of water as it ran off the land. (Because radiation causes no pain, animals, wandering at will through the environment, would not avoid it.)

The one class of animals containing a number of species quite likely to survive, at least in the short run, is the insect class, for which in most known cases the lethal doses lie between about two thousand rads and about a hundred thousand rads. Insects, therefore, would be destroyed selectively. Unfortunately for the rest of the environment, many of the phytophagous species — insects that feed directly on vegetation — which "include some of the most ravaging species on earth" (according to Dr. Vernon M. Stern, an entomologist at the University of California at Riverside, writing in "Survival of Food Crops"), have very high tolerances, and so could be expected to survive disproportionately, and then to multiply greatly in the aftermath of an attack. The demise of their natural predators the birds would enhance their success.

Plants in general have a higher tolerance to radioactivity than animals do. Nevertheless, according to Dr. George M. Woodwell, who supervised the irradiation with gamma rays, over several years, of a small forest at Brookhaven Laboratory, a gamma-ray dose of ten thousand rads "would devastate most vegetation" in the United States, and, as in the case of the pastured animals, when one figures in the beta radiation that would also be delivered by fallout the estimates for the lethal doses of gamma rays must be reduced — in this case, cut in half. As a general rule, Dr. Woodwell and his colleagues at Brookhaven discovered, large plants are more vulnerable to radiation than small ones. Trees are among the first to die, grasses among the last. The most sensitive trees are pines and the other conifers, for which lethal doses are in roughly the same range as those for mammals. Any survivors coming out of their shelters a few months after the attack would find that all the pine trees that were still standing were already dead. The lethal doses for most deciduous trees range from about two thousand rads of gamma-ray radiation to about ten thousand rads, with the lethal doses for eighty per cent of deciduous species falling between two thousand and eight thousand rads. Since the addition of the beta-ray burden could lower these lethal doses for gamma rays by as much as fifty per cent, the actual lethal doses in gamma rays for these trees during an attack could be from one thousand to four thousand rads, and in a full-scale attack they would die. Then, after the trees had died, forest fires would break out around the United States. (Because as much as three-quarters of the country could be subjected to incendiary levels of the thermal pulses, the sheer scorching of the land could have killed off a substantial part of the plant life in the country in the first few seconds after the detonations, before radioactive poisoning set in.) Lethal doses for grasses on which tests have been done range between six thousand and thirty-three thousand rads, and a good deal of grass would therefore survive, except where the attacks had been heaviest. Most crops, on the other hand, are killed by doses below five thousand rads, and would be eliminated. (The lethal dose for spring barley seedlings, for example, is one thousand nine hundred and ninety rads, and that for spring wheat seedlings is three thousand and ninety rads.)

When vegetation is killed off, the land on which it grew is degraded. And as the land eroded after an attack life in lakes, rivers, and estuaries, already hard hit by radiation directly, would be further damaged by minerals flowing into the watercourses, causing eutrophication — a process in which an oversupply of nutrients in the water encourages the growth of algae and microscopic organisms, which, in turn, deplete the oxygen content of the water. When the soil loses its nutrients, it loses its ability to "sustain a mature community" (in Dr. Woodwell's words), and "gross simplification" of the environment occurs, in which "hardy species," such as moss and grass, replace vulnerable ones, such as trees; and "succession" — the process by which ecosystems recover lost diversity — is then "delayed or even arrested." In sum, a full-scale nuclear attack on the United States would devastate the natural environment on a scale unknown since early geological times, when, in response to natural catastrophes whose nature has not been determined, sudden mass extinctions of species and whole ecosystems occurred all over the earth. How far this "gross simplification" of the environment would go once virtually all animal life and the greater part of plant life had been destroyed and what patterns the surviving remnants of life would arrange themselves into over the long run are imponderables; but it appears that at the outset the United States would be a republic of insects and grass.

AFTERWORD

One of the clichés in the literature of the bomb is "thinking about the unthinkable," a phrase which made the title of a book by Herman Kahn, who worked for a doomsday think tank.

We have similar problems with conceiving high numbers: If a debt of a thousand billion dollars is more than we can imagine, then a debt of a million billion is no larger: It also is "more than we can imagine." It also resembles the problem of the scream. A single terrifying cry in the night raises the hairs on our head; when screams become commonplace we no longer hear them — they become a Muzak of existence equal to sirens and slammed brakes, horn blowing and jackhammers. Yet the terror that produced the scream has not altered; our response has altered.

Schell understands. His solution is diligence, patience, doggedness, repetition, multiplication of the facts of terror. His strategy makes a war of attrition; our defenses are assaulted by the arrows and catapulted rocks of statistics, computations, and quantifications. Our harbors are blockaded; our aqueduct is ruptured; we are besieged by facts of research organized by passion and belief. Finally Schell's passion and belief shout louder even than his information, leaving us the image of our life destroyed or reduced to a remnant "republic of insects and grass."

BOOKS AVAILABLE IN PAPERBACK

Abolition. New York: Avon. *Nonfiction.*

The Fate of the Earth. New York: Avon. *Nonfiction.*

The Time of Illusion. New York. Random House-Knopf. *Nonfiction.*

ROBERT
STONE

ROBERT STONE *is another of our writers — Carver, Johnson, Ozick — to receive a Living Award from the Harold and Mildred Strauss Foundation. He was born in Brooklyn (1937) to a family of tugboat workers; his father left home when he was a baby; his mother taught school until she became schizophrenic, later worked as a chambermaid living with her son in rooming houses and welfare hotels until he was five and went to an orphanage. Educated in Catholic schools, he was a precocious reader, undertaking Thomas Carlyle's* The French Revolution *when he was only ten. In high school he won a short-story contest; he was expelled from high school before graduation. He spent three years in the navy, then took courses at NYU. In 1962 the first chapters of a novel won him a Stegner Fellowship in Creative Writing at Stanford University, where he met Ken Kesey and later Neal Cassady, Jack Kerouac, and Allen Ginsberg. He was a Merry Prankster with Ken Kesey on the cross-country bus ride described by Tom Wolfe in* The Electric Kool-Aid Acid Test.

Stone has written four novels: A Hall of Mirrors *(1967);* Dog Soldiers *(1974), winner of the National Book Award;* A Flag for Sunrise *(1981); and* Children of Light *(1986). This essay appeared in* Harper's.

A Higher Horror of the Whiteness: Cocaine's Coloring of the American Psyche

One day in New York last summer I had a vision near Saint Paul's Chapel of Trinity Church. I had walked a lot of the length of Manhattan, and it seemed to me that a large part of my time had been spent stepping around men who stood in the gutter snapping imaginary whips. Strangers had approached me trying to sell Elavil, an antidepressant. As I stood on Broadway I reflected that although I had grown to middle age seeing strange sights, I had never thought to see people selling Elavil on the street. Street Elavil, I would have exclaimed, that must be a joke!

I looked across the street from Saint Paul's and the daylight seemed strange. I had gotten used to thinking of the Wall Street area as a part of New York where people looked healthy and wholesome. But from where I stood half the men waiting for the light to change looked like Bartleby the Scrivener.° Everybody seemed to be listening in dread to his own heartbeat. They're all loaded, I thought. That was my vision. Everybody was loaded on cocaine.

In the morning, driving into Manhattan, the traffic had seemed particularly demonic. I'd had a peculiar exchange with a bridge toll taker who seemed to have one half of a joke I was expected to have the other half of. I didn't. Walking on Fourteenth Street, I passed a man in an imitation leopard-skin hat who was crying as though his heart would break. At Fourth Avenue I was offered the Elavil. Elavil relieves the depression attendant on the deprivation of re-refined cocaine — "crack" — which is what the men cracking the imaginary whips were selling. Moreover, I'd been reading the papers. I began to think that I was seeing stoned cops, stoned grocery shoppers, and stoned boomers. So it went, and by the time I got to lower Broadway I was concerned. I felt as though I were about to confront

---

Bartleby the Scrivener   The title character in a short story (1853) by Herman Melville, Bartleby is a Wall Street clerk without interest in his job and in life, who lapses into a state of extreme lethargy in which his only response becomes "I would prefer not to." Eventually he dies of starvation.

483

the primary process of hundreds of thousands of unsound minds. What I was seeing in my vision of New York as super-stoned Super City was cocaine in its role of success drug.

Not many years ago, people who didn't use cocaine didn't have to know much about it. Now, however, it's intruding on the national perception rather vigorously. The National Institute on Drug Abuse reported almost six million current users in 1985, defining a current user as one who took cocaine at least once in the course of the month preceding the survey. The same source in the same year reckoned that more than twenty-two million people had tried cocaine at least once during their lives.

So much is being heard about cocaine, principally through television, that even people who live away from the urban centers are beginning to experience it as a factor in their lives. Something of the same thing happened during the sixties, when Americans in quiet parts of the country began to feel they were being subjected to civil insurrection day in and day out.

One aspect that even people who don't want to know anything about cocaine have been compelled to recognize is that people get unpleasantly weird under its influence. The term "dope fiend" was coined for cocaine users. You can actually seem unpleasantly weird to yourself on coke, which is one of its greatest drawbacks.

In several ways the ubiquity of cocaine and its derivative crack have helped the American city to carry on its iconographic function as Vision of Hell. Over the past few years some of the street choreography of Manhattan has changed slightly. There seems to be less marijuana in the air. At the freight doors of garment factories and around construction sites people cluster smoking something odorless. At night in the ghettos and at the borders of ghettos, near the tunnels and at downtown intersections, an enormous ugly argument seems to be in progress. Small, contentious groups of people drift across the avenues, sometimes squaring off at each other, moving from one corner to the next, the conformations breaking up and re-forming. The purchase of illegal drugs was always a sordid process, but users and dealers (pretty much interchangeable creatures) used to attempt adherence to an idealized vision of the traffic in which smoothie dealt with smoothie in a confraternity of the hip. Crack sales tend to start with a death threat and deteriorate rapidly. The words "die" and "motherfucker" are among the most often heard. Petty race riots between white suburban buyers and minority urban sellers break out several times an hour. Every half block stand people in various states of fury, mindless exhilaration, and utter despair — all of it dreadfully authentic yet all of it essentially artificial.

On the day of my visionary walk through the city I felt beset by a drug I hadn't even been in the same room with for a year. New York always seems to tremble on the brink of entropy — that's why we love her even though she doesn't love us back. But that afternoon it felt as though white crystal had seeped through the plates and fouled the very frame of reference. There was an invisible whiteness deep down things, not just the glistening mounds in their little tricorn Pyramid papers tucked into compacts and under pocket handkerchiefs but, I thought, a metaphysical whiteness. It seemed a little out of place at first. I was not in California. I was among cathedrals of commerce in the midst of a city hard at work. I wondered why the sense of the drug should strike most vividly on Wall Street. It might be the shade of Bartleby, I thought, and the proximity of the harbor. The whiteness was Melvillean, like the whiteness of the Whale.

In the celebrated chapter on whiteness in *Moby-Dick*, Melville frequently mentions the Andes — not Bolivia, as it happens, but Lima, "the strangest saddest city thou canst see. . . . There is a higher horror in the whiteness of her woe." Higher horror seemed right. I had found a Lima of the mind.

"But not yet," Melville writes, "have we solved the incantation of this whiteness and learned why it appeals with such power to the soul . . . and yet should be as it is, the intensifying agent in things the most appalling to mankind . . . a dumb blankness full of meaning in a wide landscape of snows — a colorless all-color of atheism from which we shrink."

I was in the city to do business with some people who tend toward enthusiasms, toward ardor and mild obsession. Behind every enthusiasm, every outburst of ardor, every mildly obsessive response, I kept scouring the leprous white hand of narcosis. It's a mess when you think everybody's high. I liked it a lot better when the weirdest thing around was me.

We old-time pot smokers used to think we were cute with our instant 12 redefinitions and homespun minimalism. Our attention had been caught by a sensibility a lot of us associated with black people. We weren't as cute as we thought, but for a while we were able to indulge the notion that a small community of minds was being nurtured through marijuana. In a very limited way, in terms of art and music, we were right. In the early days we divided into two camps. Some of us were elitists who thought we had the right to get high because we were artists and musicians and consciousness was our profession and the rest of the world, the "squares," could go to hell. Others of us hoped the insights we got from using drugs like pot could somehow change the world for the better. To people in the latter camp, it was vaguely heartening when a walker in the city could smell marijuana everywhere. The present coke-deluded cityscape is another story.

Cocaine was never much to look at. All drugs have their coarse practicalities, so in the use of narcotics and their paraphernalia, dexterity and savoir-faire are prized. Coke, however, is difficult to handle gracefully. For one thing, once-refined cocaine works only in solution with blood, mucus, or saliva, a handicap to éclat that speaks for itself.

I remember watching an elegant and beautiful woman who was trying cocaine for the first time. The lady, serving herself liberally, had a minor indelicate accident. For a long time she simply sat there contentedly with her nose running, licking her lips. This woman was a person of such imposing presence that watching her get high was like watching an angel turn into an ape; she hung there at a balancing point somewhere midway along the anthropoid spectrum.

The first person I ever saw use cocaine was a poet I haven't seen for twenty-five years. It was on the Lower East Side, one night during the fifties, in an age that's as dead now as Agamemnon. Coltrane's "My Favorite Things" was on the record player. The poet was tall and thin and pale and self-destructive, and we all thought that was a great way to be. After he'd done up, his nose started to bleed. The bathtub was in the kitchen, and he sat down on the kitchen floor and leaned his head back against it. You had to be there.

Let me tell you, I honor that man. I honor him for his lonely independence and his hard outcast's road. I think he was one of the people who, in the fifties, helped to make this country a lot freer. Maybe that's the trouble. Ultimately, nothing is free, in the sense that you have to pay up somewhere along the line.

My friend the poet thought cocaine lived someplace around midnight that he was trying to find. He would not have expected it to become a commonplace drug. He would not have expected over 17 percent of American high school students to have tried it, even thirty years later, any more than he would have expected that one quarter of America's high school students would use marijuana. He was the wild one. In hindsight, we should have known how many of the kids to come would want to be the wild ones too.

A few weeks after my difficult day in the city I was sitting in my car in a New England coastal village leafing through my mail when for some reason I became aware of the car parked beside mine. In the front seat were two teenage girls whose tan summer faces seemed aglow with that combination of apparent innocence and apparent wantonness adolescence inflicts. I glanced across the space between our cars and saw that they were doing cocaine. The car windows were rolled up against the bay breeze. The drug itself was out of sight, on the car seat between them. By turns they descended to sniff. Then both of them sat upright, *bolt upright* might be the way to put it, staring straight ahead of them. They licked their fingers. The girl in the driver's seat ran her tongue over a pocket mirror. The girl beside her looked over at me, utterly untroubled by my presence; there was a six-inch length of peppermint-striped soda straw in her mouth. There are people I know who cannot remove a cigarette from its pack with someone

16

standing behind them, who between opening the seal and lighting up perform the most elaborate pantomimes of guilty depravity. Neither of these children betrayed the slightest cautious reflex, although we couldn't have been more than a few hundred yards from the village police station. The girl with the straw between her teeth and I looked at each other for an instant and I saw something in her eyes, but I don't know what it was. It wasn't guilty pleasure or defiance or flirtatiousness. Its intellectual aspect was crazy and its emotional valence was cold.

A moment later, the driver threw the car into reverse and straight into the path of an oncoming postal truck, which fortunately braked in time. Then they were off down the road, headed wherever they thought their state of mind might make things better. One wondered where.

Watching their car disappear, I could still see the moment of their highs. 20 Surfacing, they had looked frosted, their faces streaked with a cotton-candied, snotty sugary excitement, a pair of little girls having their afternoon at the fair, their carnival goodies, and all the rides in a few seconds flat. Five minutes from the parking lot, the fairy lights would be burned out. Their parents would find them testy, sarcastic, and tantrum prone. Unless, of course, they had more.

The destructiveness of cocaine today is a cause for concern. What form is our concern to take?

American politicians offer a not untypical American political response. The Democrats say they want to hang the dealers. The Republicans say they want to hang them and throw their bones to the dogs. Several individuals suggest that the military be used in these endeavors. Maybe all the partisan competition for dramatic solutions will produce results. Surely some of our politically inspired plans must work some of the time.

I was talking with a friend of mine who's a lawyer recently. Like many lawyers, she once used a lot of cocaine, although she doesn't anymore. She and I were discussing the satisfactions of cocaine abuse and the lack thereof, and she recounted the story of a stock-trading associate of hers who was sometimes guided in his decisions by stimulants. One day, all of his clients received telephone calls informing them that the world was coming to an end and that he was supervising their portfolios with that in mind. The world would end by water, said the financier, but the right people would turn into birds and escape. He and some of his clients were already growing feathers and wattles.

"Some gonna fly and some gonna die," the broker intoned darkly to his 24 startled customers.

We agreed that while this might be the kind of message you'd be glad to get from your Yaqui soothsayer, it hardly qualified as sound investment strategy. (Although, God knows, the market can be that way!)

"But sometimes," she said, "you feel this illusion of lucidity. Of excellence."

I think it's more that you feel like you're *about* to feel an illusion of lucidity and excellence. But lucidity and excellence are pretty hot stuff, even in a potential state, even as illusion. Those are very contemporary goals and quite different from the electric twilight that people were pursuing in the sixties.

"I thought of cocaine as a success drug," one addict is reported saying 28 in a recent newspaper story. Can you blame him? It certainly looks like a success drug, all white and shiny like an artificial Christmas morning. It glows and it shines just as success must. And success is back! The faint sound you hear at the edges of perception is the snap, crackle, and pop of winners winning and losers losing.

You can tell the losers by their downcast eyes bespeaking unseemly scruple and self-doubt. You can tell the winners by their winning ways and natty strut; look at them stepping out there, all confidence and hard-edged realism. It's a new age of vim and vigor, piss and vinegar and cocaine. If we work hard enough and live long enough, we'll all be as young as the President.

Meanwhile, behold restored as lord of creation, pinnacle of evolution and progress, alpha and omega of the rationalized universe, Mr. Success, together with his new partner and pal, Ms. Success. These two have what it takes; they've got heart, they've got drive, they've got aggression. It's a no-fault world of military options and no draft. Hey, they got it all.

Sometimes, though, it gets scary. Some days it's hard to know whether you're winning or not. You're on the go but so's the next guy. You're moving fast but so is she. Sometimes you're afraid you'd think awful thoughts if you had time to think. That's why you're almost glad there isn't time. How can you be sure you're on the right track? You might be on the wrong one. Everybody can't be a winner or there wouldn't be a game. "Some gonna fly and some gonna die."

Predestinarian religion generated a lot of useful energy in this republic. 32 It cast a long December shadow, a certain slant of light on winter afternoons. Things were grim with everybody wondering whether he was chosen, whether he was good enough, really, truly good enough and not just faking. Finally, it stopped being useful. We got rid of it.

It's funny how the old due bills come up for presentation. We had Faith and not Works. Now we've got all kinds of works and no faith. And people still wonder if they've got what it takes.

When you're wondering if you've got what it takes, wondering whether you're on the right track and whether you're going to fly, do you sometimes want a little pick-me-up? Something upbeat and cool with nice lines, something that shines like success and snaps you to, so you can step out there feeling aggressive, like a million-dollar Mr. or Ms.? And after that, would you like to be your very own poet and see fear — yes, I said fear — in a handful of dust? Have we got something for you! Something white.

On the New York morning of which I've spoken I beheld its whiteness. How white it really is, and what it does, was further described about 130 years ago by America's God-bestowed prophet, who delineated the great American success story with the story of two great American losers, Bartleby and Ahab. From *Moby-Dick:*

> And when we consider that . . . theory of the natural philos-
> ophers, that all other earthly hues — every stately or lovely
> emblazoning — the sweet tinges of sunset skies and woods;
> yea, and the gilded velvets of butterflies, and the butterfly
> cheeks of young girls; all these are but the subtle deceits, not
> actually inherent in substance, but only laid on from without;
> and when we proceed further, and consider that the mystical
> cosmetic which produces every one of her hues, the great
> principle of light, for ever remains white or colorless in itself,
> and if operating without medium upon matter, would touch
> all objects, even tulips and roses, with its own blank tinge —
> pondering all this, the palsied universe lies before us a leper;
> and like wilful travellers in Lapland, who refuse to wear col-
> ored and coloring glasses upon their eyes, so the wretched
> infidel gazes himself blind at the monumental white shroud
> that wraps all the prospect around him.

All over America at this moment pleasurable surges of self-esteem are 36 fading. People are discovering that the principal thing one does with cocaine is run out of it.

If cocaine is the great "success drug," is there a contradiction in that it brings such ruin not only to the bankers and the lawyers but to so many of the youngest, poorest Americans? I think not. The poor and the children have always received American obsessions as shadow and parody. They too can be relied on to "go for it."

"Just say no!" we tell them and each other when we talk about crack and cocaine. It is necessary that we say this because liberation starts from there.

But we live in a society based overwhelmingly on appetite and self-regard. We train our young to be consumers and to think most highly of their own pleasure. In this we face a contradiction that no act of Congress can resolve.

In our debates on the subject of dealing with drug abuse, one of the 40 recurring phrases has been "the moral equivalent of war." Not many of those who use it, I suspect, know its origin.

In 1910, the philosopher William James wrote an essay discussing the absence of values, the "moral weightlessness" that seemed to characterize modern times. James was a pacifist. Yet he conceded that the demands of battle were capable of bringing forth virtues like courage, loyalty, community, and mutual concern that seemed in increasingly short supply as the new century unfolded. As a pacifist and a moralist, James found himself in a dilemma. How, he wondered, can we nourish those virtues without having to pay the dreadful price that war demands? We must foster courage, loyalty, and the rest, but we must not have war. Very well, he reasoned, we must find the *moral equivalent of war*.

Against these drugs can we ever, rhetoric aside, bring any kind of real heroism to bear? When they've said no to crack, can we someday give them something to say yes to?

AFTERWORD

Robert Stone's best fiction is panicky, paranoid, violent, and druggy. As he lets us understand in the course of his essay, his experience of cocaine has not been entirely vicarious: "you have to pay up somewhere along the line."

The structure of Stone's essay is narrative, starting with an account which is also a vision of Manhattan; he later identifies it as a "Vision of Hell." He mixes anecdotes with information, slipping back and forth between statistics and stories.

This essay is allusive. Dante is alluded to, for anyone with a smattering of images from the Inferno. *The title of the essay refers to Melville, and in the second paragraph Stone mentions Bartleby, an emaciated clerk in a Melville story. From title through Bartleby, through later images of whiteness, Stone alludes to Melville without ascribing his source; then finally he refers openly to Melville, quotes him, and finds this great American writer a prophet of the white emptiness.*

Allusion here is structural, and yet the structure remains light because Stone does not insist upon it until he is ready to name and quote his author directly. Suppressing the ascription helps him establish a tone of the streets, rather than a tone of the library, until the library can speak to the streets.

BOOKS AVAILABLE IN PAPERBACK

Children of Light. New York: Ballantine. *Novel.*

Dog Soldiers. New York: Ballantine. *Novel.*

A Flag for Sunrise. New York: Ballantine. *Novel.*

A Hall of Mirrors. Boston: Houghton Mifflin. *Novel.*

PAUL
THEROUX

*P*AUL THEROUX *is an American who has lived in London for twenty years,*
when he has not been traveling around the world, by railroad whenever possible.
He was born (1941) in Medford, Massachusetts; he took his B.A. at the University
of Massachusetts, and he summers on Cape Cod. Among his six brothers and sisters
is another novelist, Alexander.

When he was young, Theroux taught in Africa and in the Far East, places that
turn up in his fiction and essays. As of 1986 he had published seventeen books of
fiction — novels and stories — including The Family Arsenal *(1976),* The
Mosquito Coast *(1982), and* O-Zone *(1986). Two of his most popular travel*
books have celebrated or memorialized railroad travel: The Great Railway Bazaar:
By Train Through Asia *(1975), and* The Old Patagonian Express: By Train
Through the Americas *(1979).* Sunrise with Seamonsters *(1985) collects essays*
written for magazines and newspapers, including "Mapping the World."

Theroux is a prolific writer, like most freelancers. He seems a restless man in
his work and in his peripatetic journeying. Critics compare him with other perpetual
exiles who take the world as their beat: Somerset Maugham, Graham Greene, V. S.
Naipaul.

Mapping the World

Cartography, the most aesthetically pleasing of the sciences, draws its power from the greatest of man's gifts — courage, the spirit of inquiry, artistic skill, man's sense of order and design, his understanding of natural laws, and his capacity for singular journeys to the most distant places. They are the brightest attributes and they have made maps one of the most luminous of man's creations.

But map-making also requires the ability to judge the truth of travelers' tales. Although Marco Polo's *Travels* allowed early European cartographers to give place-names and continental configurations to their maps, the book itself contained only a tiny sketch map and had many odd omissions (no Great Wall, no mention of tea). Columbus had the Latin version of 1483 among his belongings on his voyages westward — which was why, in Cuba in 1493, he sent a party of men searching the Cuban hinterland for the Great Khan, and on later voyages believed he was coasting past Indochina (it was Honduras) and about three weeks away from the Ganges. Columbus was not unique in his misapprehension: cartographic ignorance has been universal. There are the many maps of the Abyssinian kingdom of Prester John, and the maps which show California to be an island (this belief persisted throughout the seventeenth century). And it was only seventy or eighty years ago that the Chinese were finally satisifed that the world was round.

"It would seem as though cartography were an instinct implanted in every nation with any claim to civilization," the geographer Sir Alexander Hosie wrote. He had in mind a map of China, carved in stone, and discovered in the Forest of Tablets of Hsian, the capital of Shensi province. That stone map is dated in the year called *Fou Ch'ang*, 1137, but the Chinese had been making maps for centuries on wood, silk, and paper. The Chinese and the Romans were making maps of their respective known worlds at roughly the same tine. In 128 B.C., Chang Ch'ien, China's first historic traveler, returned home after having covered the immense distance to the Oxus (we know it as the Amu Darya) in Central Asia. Chang reported to the Emperor Wu on what he had seen, and the emperor named the mountains K'un-lun, where the Yellow River rose.

For the next thousand years, China was active — a nation of travelers, 4 warriors, conquerers, traders, and, inevitably, map-makers. What was the point of conquering if the subject lands were not then given a shape, and their rivers and households described on maps? The Chinese word for map, *t'u,* also means "plan," "chart," and "drawing." (Our own word *map* has Latin cousins meaning "napkin" and "sheet.") Chinese cartography could be ambitious. P'ei Hsiu (224–271), sometimes called the Father of Chinese Cartography, did a magnificent map of China in eighteen panels ("The Map of the Territory of the Tribute of Yu"), and codified map-making in Six Principles. His First Principle, an enormous contribution to the art, was *fen lu,* the grid system.

P'ei's successor was Chia Tan, whose masterpiece in 801 was "The Map of China and Barbarian Countries Within the Seas." Chia was working in the T'ang Dynasty (618–907), one of the most renowned in Chinese history. It was very much a map-making dynasty — it had imperial ambitions, pursuing a policy of conquest in the west and south. Chia was commissioned to make maps of the conquered territories. Subsequent maps of China for the following few hundred years were based on Chia's ninth century work.

China also exemplifies the way cartography can go into decline. As a nation craves silence and becomes xenophobic and inward-looking, demanding tribute instead of initiating trade, it loses the will to communicate with the world and begins to wither of its own egotism. The Chinese still continued to regard the world as flat and four-square (though they believed the sky to be round). One cannot attribute this to stubborn ignorance; after all, it took Europe a thousand years to accept the notion that the world was round.

Yet all of China's naive geocentricity can be seen in the outrage of the Imperial Court's scrutiny of a Jesuit map in which China was situated in the eastern corner. What was the Middle Kingdom doing on the far right? Father Matteo Ricci cleverly redrew his map by spinning his globe, so to speak, and placing the Celestial empire smack in the middle, with Europe in the distant west. That was in 1602. The Chinese accepted the priest's version of the world — it somewhat resembled their own — but they rejected his spherical projection.

When China lost interest in foreign countries her maps became inaccurate, not to say bizarre. These maps showed European countries and the United States and Africa as tiny islands and sandbars off the Middle Kingdom coast. Even in the mid-nineteenth century Chinese maps depicted the natives of these little islands as monstrous and one-eyed, and some were shown with holes through their stomachs for their convenient carrying on poles. Around the turn of the nineteenth century, the Chinese accepted that the world was round. It is possible, I think, to read in this acceptance of a new map a profound understanding of their place in the world.

Cartography has always required utter truthfulness — it is one of its most appealing features: crooked maps are worse than useless, and nothing dates more quickly than the political map ("German East Africa," "French

Indochina," "the Central African Empire," "Jonestown"). But until the recent past, maps have been more than scientific; they have depended on a high level of pictorial art — vivid imagery and lettering — and a style of labeling and a conciseness in description that is literary in the best sense.

Blaeu is the Rembrandt of geography. Most maps, even modern ones, are beautiful — beautiful in color and contour, and often breathtaking in their completeness. They can tell us everything, and the best ones, from the great periods of trade and exploration — our own is one such period — have always attempted to do this. In 500 B.C. Anaximander's successor, Hecataeus, made a disc-shaped map — it was a startling illumination. But maps specialize in such surprises.

Consider the Ortelius map of China of 1573 — "Regnum Chinae." It is full of fictitious lakes, but it accurately places rivers, mountains, and cities — enough to guide any explorer or trader to his destination. It also includes the westernmost portion of America ("America Pars") at 180° longitude, and it shows what we know as the Bering Sea. In vivid marginal pictures it tells us about the Far East — the Great Wall is drawn, a Chinese junk is rendered in perfect detail, a man is shown being crucified in Japan for being a Christian and keeping the faith (there is a warning in Latin). In a corner is a Chinese four-wheeled cart, powered by a sail, and this cart (so the inscription tells us) can also be used as a boat. The map is a masterpiece of practicality and imagination.

Cartography has the capacity to open up countries to world trade. For 12 example, throughout most of the nineteenth century it was recognized that a canal was needed in Central America to join the two great oceans. Mexico and most of the Central American countries were exhaustively mapped, and a dozen canals were proposed. These maps expressed hopes, promises, and fantasies. On a map by F. Bianconi in 1891, Honduras — which could not have been emptier — is shown as a teeming go-ahead republic. "Railways under construction," it says and you see hundreds and hundreds of miles of track, two lines from coast to coast. Who needs a canal with such trains! In the Mosquito jungle you have the impression of intense cultivation, and mining, and cattle-grazing. Honduras looks blessed — full of sarsparilla and sugar-cane, and iron, zinc, silver, and gold. The word "gold" appears on this map sixty-five times, in each spot where it apparently lies in the ground.

There were similar maps of Panama, and of course Panama won out. But a modern map of Honduras shows most of the cartographic detail in this hundred-year-old map to be unfulfilled promises. Anyone who looks at a lot of maps becomes highly suspicious of the designations "Proposed railway," "Road under construction," "Projected highway" — with dotted lines; or that other heart-sinker, "Site of proposed Hydro-electric Dam." These are not features which are found only on maps of Third World

Countries. "The M25 Ring-Road" is shown on some maps of Outer London, though the road has yet to be finished. The most ominous line on a map is the one labeled "Disputed boundary," and it makes one think that there are perhaps fifty versions of the world map, depending on your nationality. Israel has about four different shapes, and on some modern Arab maps it does not exist at all.

The map of the London Underground is by almost any standard a work of art — a squint turns it into late-Mondrian — but it also has great practical value. After ten years of residence in London I still have to consult this map every time I travel by tube: the underground system is too complex for me to hold in my head. The same goes for the New York subway, which is a problem for cartographers — at least three recent attempts have been made to map it so that it can be understood and used by a stranger. None has succeeded. It remains an intimidating map.

The map predates the book (even a fairly ordinary map may contain several books' worth of information). It is the oldest means of information storage, and can present the most subtle facts with great clarity. It is a masterly form of compression, a way of miniaturizing a country or society. Most hill-climbers and perhaps all mountaineers know the thrill at a certain altitude of looking down and recognizing the landscape that is indistinguishable from a map. The only pleasure I take in flying in a jet plane is the experience of matching a coastline or the contour of a river to the corresponding map in my memory. A map can do many things, but I think its chief use is in lessening our fear of foreign parts and helping us anticipate the problems of dislocation. Maps give the world coherence. It seems to me one of man's supreme achievements that he knew the precise shape of every continent and practically every river-vein on earth long before he was able to gaze at them whole from the window of a rocket-ship.

This sense of map-shapes is so strong it amounts almost to iconography. 16 The cartographer gives features to surfaces, and sometimes these features are resonant. It is easy to see a dependency in the way Sri Lanka seems to linger at the tip of India; Africa looks like one of its own paleolithic skulls; and some countries are, visibly, appendages. Who has looked upon Chile and not seen in it an austere narrowness, or smiled at Delaware, or wondered what Greenland is *for*? The shape of a country may condition our initial attitude towards it, though I don't think any conclusion can be drawn from the fact that Great Britain looks like a boy riding on a pig. And position matters, too. It does not surprise me that the Chinese called their country the Middle Kingdom. It is human to be geocentric. Every country, to its people, is a middle kingdom — zero longitude, where East and West begin. And what a shock it must be for the Pacific islander looking for his country for the first time on a world map, and not finding it, and having to be told that his great island is this tiny dot. The opposite is also remarkable. We have the word of many British people who have spoken of their pride at seeing the Empire verified in pink on a globe.

Maps have also given life to fiction. From *Gulliver's Travels* to *The Lord of the Rings*, novels have contained maps of their mythical lands. Thomas Hardy carefully drew a map so that his readers could understand his Wessex novels, and so did Norman Mailer when he published *The Naked and the Dead*. In these books the map came later, but there is an example of a fantasy map preceding a work of literature. Robert Louis Stevenson wrote,

> . . . I made the map of an island; it was elaborately and (I thought) beautifully coloured: the shape of it took my fancy beyond expression; it contained harbours that pleased me like sonnets; and with the unconsciousness of the pre-destined, I ticketted my performance *Treasure Island* . . . as I pored over my map of Treasure Island, the future characters in the book began to appear there visibly among imaginary woods; and their brown faces and bright weapons peeped out upon me from unexpected quarters, or they passed to and fro, fighting and hunting treasure. The next thing I knew I had some paper before me and was writing out a list of chapters . . .

I was delighted to find this example for Stevenson's cartographic inspiration, because for two years I worked on a novel — *The Mosquito Coast* — with a map of Central America next to my desk. When I was stuck for an idea, or when I wanted to reassure myself that my fictional settlements really existed, I studied this map.

Most novelists are map conscious, and all great novelists are cartographers. So are all true explorers, and the most intrepid travelers and traders. The real explorer is not the man who is following a map, but the man who is making one.

I do not think that it is profit alone, the desire for financial gain or celebrity, that animates such men. But it is a fact that the most commercial-minded countries have also been the most outward-looking. In the past, there were no trading nations that were not also the dedicated patrons of cartographers. Today, the proudest boast of any commercial enterprise is its illustration, with a map, of its influence and success. All maps are records of discovery; without fresh discoveries no new maps are possible. Our fastidious curiosity and our passionate business sense and even our anxieties have made ours a cartographic age.

Maps reflect the face of the land. They tell us most things but not 20 everything. Long ago, they were shorelines; and then they were riverbanks; and at last they were territories with a million features. But they have always been surfaces figured with routes and suggestions. To the most courageous and imaginative of us, these surfaces are eloquent, showing the way to new discoveries. In a sense, the world was once blank. And the reason cartography made it visible and glowing with detail was because man believed, and rightly, that maps are a legacy that allows other men and future generations to communicate and trade.

A good map is better than a guidebook: it is the ultimate tool of the man who wishes to understand a distant country. It can be merciless in its factuality. It can also tells us things that are unobtainable anywhere else.

About ten and a half years ago, in Singapore, I rented a house — sight-unseen — in the English county of Dorsetshire. I had been to England twice, but never to Dorset. The village, South Bowood, was not mentioned in any guidebook. What descriptions I came across were general and un-helpful. After a great deal of reading I still knew absolutely nothing of the place in which I was now committed to spend six months with my wife and two small children. I began to wonder if the place existed.

It was then that I found some Ordnance Survey Maps. The whole of Britain is scrupulously mapped. I had the correct sheet. I located South Bowood: it was a hamlet of about eight houses. Letters and symbols told me there was a public house down the road, and a mailbox, and a public telephone. The post office and school were a mile distant, and the nearest church was at Netherbury; but we would be on a hill, and there were meadows all around us, and footpaths, and not far from us the ruins of an Iron Age hill fort. The houses were small black squares, and at last, sitting there in the Singapore Library studying the map, I worked out which house would be ours. So I knew exactly where I was going, and all my fears vanished. With this map, I was prepared: without it, I would have been in darkness.

AFTERWORD

Many essays mix research, reminiscence, and idea. Proportions differ and struc-tures vary according to the subject and the writer's whim. Here research is a major ingredient; Theroux assembles diverse facts about maps and mapmaking, information that in the objective style of an encyclopedia would bore us to death. But with his journalistic licenses of wit and style — and with license not to footnote his sources — Theroux livens what he touches and writes an amusing essay which remains dense with information.

Dashes of reminiscence, later of speculation, add spice to the stew. Mostly he amuses us by moving rapidly, by choosing details that divert, and by varying the rhythm of his sentences. Paragraph 2 begins with a dozen words of topic sentence and then spins off into a complex sentence of thirty-eight words ending with a parenthesis. *(When we speak parenthetically, we drop the pitch of our voices.) Throughout this essay Theroux keeps changing rhythms and pitches; he varies his voice like a skilled actor reading a book out loud. After the parenthesis in paragraph 2 Theroux makes a still longer sentence, fifty-six words, parceled out by dashes and commas and parentheses into subgroups, easy to follow — but a long breath, a long whirl on this dance floor. Moving toward the paragraph's conclusion he diminishes into sentences of twenty-nine and twenty words, reversing the order of length that begins the paragraph, so that the last sentence seems rhythmically an echo of the first. This paragraph is a model of graceful, rhythmical, and even musical exposition.*

BOOKS AVAILABLE IN PAPERBACK

The Black House. New York: Washington Square Press. *Novel.*

The Consul's File. New York: Washington Square Press. *Novel.*

The Family Arsenal. New York: Washington Square Press. *Novel.*

Girls at Play. New York: Washington Square Press. *Novel.*

The Great Railway Bazaar. New York: Ballantine. *Nonfiction.*

Half Moon Street. New York: Washington Square Press. *Novel.*

The Kingdom by the Sea. New York: Washington Square Press. *Nonfiction.*

The London Embassy. New York: Washington Square Press. *Novel.*

The Mosquito Coast. New York: Avon. *Novel.*

O-Zone. New York: Ballantine. *Novel.*

The Old Patagonian Express. New York: Pocket Books. *Nonfiction.*

Picture Palace. New York: Pocket Books. *Novel.*

Saint Jack. New York: Washington Square Press. *Novel.*

Sunrise with Seamonsters. Boston: Houghton Mifflin. *Essays.*

LEWIS
THOMAS

*L*EWIS THOMAS *(b. 1913) grew up a doctor's son on Long Island, attended Princeton University, and took his M.D. at Harvard. For most of his life, he has practiced research in laboratories, more scientist than clinician, and served as administrator for medical schools and great hospitals. At present he is chancellor of Memorial Sloan-Kettering Cancer Center in New York City.*

For many years his publications were confined to medical journals and labored under titles like "The Physiological Disturbances Produced by Endotoxins" and "Reversible Collapse of Rabbit Ears after Intravenous Papain and Prevention of Recovery by Cortisone." Then, in 1975, he received not only a distinguished achievement award from Modern Medicine *but also a National Book Award in Arts and Letters; the National Book Award is not awarded for papers on the collapse of rabbit ears.*

Lewis Thomas's career as a prose stylist began with a series of columns written for the New England Journal of Medicine; *he also wrote a column for* Discovery, *a science magazine for a general audience. He has assembled three collections of essays:* The Lives of a Cell: Notes of a Biology Watcher *(1974);* The Medusa and the Snail *(1979), from which we take "The Tucson Zoo"; and* Late Night

Thoughts on Listening to Mahler's Ninth Symphony *(1984). In 1983 he published an autobiography called* The Youngest Science: Notes of a Medicine Watcher.

Reading the autobiography, Thomas's admirers were amused and unsurprised to discover a literary past. While he was intern and resident during the Depression in the 1930s, Thomas picked up pocket money by selling poems to the Atlantic Monthly, Harper's Bazaar, *and the old* Saturday Evening Post. *"Millennium" appeared in the* Atlantic *long before the atomic bomb fell on Hiroshima:*

> *It will be soft, the sound that we will hear*
> *When we have reached the end of time and light.*
> *A quiet, final noise within the air*
> *Before we are returned into the night.*
>
> *A sound for each to recognize and fear*
> *In one enormous moment, as he grieves —*
> *A sound of rustling, dry and very near,*
> *A sudden fluttering of all the leaves.*
>
> *It will be heard in all the open air*
> *Above the fading rumble of the guns,*
> *And we shall stand uneasily and stare,*
> *The finally forsaken, lonely ones.*
>
> *From all the distant secret places then*
> *A little breeze will shift across the sky,*
> *When all the earth at last is free of men*
> *And settles with a vast and easy sigh.*

Readers of The Youngest Science *learn how Thomas's enthusiasm for modern medicine and his scientific optimism take energy from recollecting his father's medical practice, at a time when doctors had little to offer patients except morphine and sympathy. His columns and essays usually report on medical and biological science in a writerly style, a human voice. Still, Thomas's gentle and personable prose serves the mind of a scientist; at times it almost turns on itself, or uses one side of itself to correct the other.*

The Tucson Zoo

Science gets most of its information by the process of reductionism, exploring the details, then the details of the details, until all the smallest bits of the structure, or the smallest parts of the mechanism, are laid out for counting and scrutiny. Only when this is done can the investigation be extended to encompass the whole organism or the entire system. So we say.

Sometimes it seems that we take a loss, working this way. Much of today's public anxiety about science is the apprehension that we may forever be overlooking the whole by an endless, obsessive preoccupation with the parts. I had a brief, personal experience of this misgiving one afternoon in Tucson, where I had time on my hands and visited the zoo, just outside the city. The designers there have cut a deep pathway between two small artificial ponds, walled by clear glass, so when you stand in the center of the path you can look into the depths of each pool, and at the same time you can regard the surface. In one pool, on the right side of the path, is a family of otters; on the other side, a family of beavers. Within just a few feet from your face, on either side, beavers and otters are at play, underwater and on the surface, swimming toward your face and then away, more filled with life than any creatures I have ever seen before, in all my days. Except for the glass, you could reach across and touch them.

I was transfixed. As I now recall it, there was only one sensation in my head: pure elation mixed with amazement at such perfection. Swept off my feet, I floated from one side to the other, swiveling my brain, staring astounded at the beavers, then at the otters. I could hear shouts across my corpus callosum, from one hemisphere to the other. I remember thinking, with what was left in charge of my consciousness, that I wanted no part of the science of beavers and otters; I wanted never to know how they performed their marvels; I wished for no news about the physiology of their breathing, the coordination of their muscles, their vision, their endocrine systems, their digestive tracts. I hoped never to have to think of them as collections of cells. All I asked for was the full hairy complexity, then in front of my eyes, of whole, intact beavers and otters in motion.

It lasted, I regret to say, for only a few minutes, and then I was back in 4 the late twentieth century, reductionist as ever, wondering about the details by force of habit, but not, this time, the details of otters and beavers. Instead, me. Something worth remembering had happened in my mind, I was certain of that; I would have put it somewhere in the brain stem; maybe this was my limbic system at work. I became a behavioral scientist, an experimental psychologist, an ethologist, and in the instant I lost all the wonder and the sense of being overwhelmed. I was flattened.

But I came away from the zoo with something, a piece of news about myself: I am coded, somehow, for otters and beavers. I exhibit instinctive behavior in their presence, when they are displayed close at hand behind glass, simultaneously below water and at the surface. I have receptors for this display. Beavers and otters possess a "releaser" for me, in the terminology of ethology, and the releasing was my experience. What was released? Behavior. What behavior? Standing, swiveling flabbergasted, feeling exultation and a rush of friendship. I could not, as the result of the trans-action, tell you anything more about beavers and otters than you already know. I learned nothing new about them. Only about me, and I suspect also about you, maybe about human beings at large: we are endowed with genes which code out our reaction to beavers and otters, maybe our reaction to each other as well. We are stamped with stereotyped, unalterable pat-terns of response, ready to be released. And the behavior released in us, by such confrontations, is, essentially, a surprised affection. It is compulsory behavior and we can avoid it only by straining with the full power of our conscious minds, making up conscious excuses all the way. Left to our-selves, mechanistic and autonomic, we hanker for friends.

Everyone says, stay away from ants. They have no lessons for us; they are crazy little instruments, inhuman, incapable of controlling themselves, lacking manners, lacking souls. When they are massed together, all touch-ing, exchanging bits of information held in their jaws like memoranda, they become a single animal. Look out for that. It is a debasement, a loss of individuality, a violation of human nature, an unnatural act.

Sometimes people argue this point of view seriously and with deep thought. Be individuals, solitary and selfish, is the message. Altruism, a jargon word for what used to be called love, is worse than weakness, it is sin, a violation of nature. Be separate. Do not be a social animal. But this is a hard argument to make convincingly when you have to depend on language to make it. You have to print up leaflets or publish books and get them bought and sent around, you have to turn up on television and catch the attention of millions of other human beings all at once, and then you have to say to all of them, all at once, all collected and paying attention: be solitary; do not depend on each other. You can't do this and keep a straight face.

Maybe altruism is our most primitive attribute, out of reach, beyond our control. Or perhaps it is immediately at hand, waiting to be released, disguised now, in our mind of civilization, as affection or friendship or attachment. I don't see why it should be unreasonable for all human beings to have strands of DNA coiled up in chromosomes, coding out instincts for usefulness and helpfulness. Usefulness may turn out to be the hardest test of fitness for survival, more important than aggression, more effective, in the long run, than grabbiness. If this is the sort of information biological science holds for the future, applying to us as well as to ants, then I am all for science.

One thing I'd like to know most of all: when those ants have made the Hill, and are all there, touching and exchanging, and the whole mass begins to behave like a single huge creature, and *thinks*, what on earth is that thought? And while you're at it, I'd like to know a second thing: when it happens, does any single ant know about it? Does his hair stand on end?

AFTERWORD

"Instead, me." Lewis Thomas makes a transition from observing the behavior of beavers and otters to observing the behavior of Lewis Thomas. He does it, elegantly, by means of a two-word sentence which follows a sentence of forty-two words and precedes a sentence of thirty-one words — providing rhythmic variation, simple sandwiched by complex. Of course the two-word sentence is incomplete; many teachers, for good reason, ask their students to avoid incomplete sentences until they approach the skillful control of a Lewis Thomas.

Really, the essayist has all along reported not on beavers or otters but on Lewis Thomas, for it was his "mechanistic and autonomic" reaction to the animals that he revealed, not the animals themselves. Thus the essay discovers, at the moment of this transition, that its subject is not what it thought its subject was: The essay's shape is the plot of its thought.

Perhaps "Instead, me" should be scrolled onto the essayist's coat of arms. Beginning with Montaigne, the essayist's subject has been me. *The assumption is implicit: If we understand one human being (possibly the one we stand closest to) we learn about all other human beings, for each man and woman potentially contains every man and woman. Lewis Thomas admires Montaigne and has written about the great inventor of the essay, who once said, "Each man bears the form of man's entire estate."*

BOOKS AVAILABLE IN PAPERBACK

Late Night Thoughts on Listening to Mahler's Ninth. New York: Bantam. *Essays.*

The Lives of a Cell: Notes of a Biology Watcher. New York: Penguin. *Essays.*

The Youngest Science: Notes of a Medicine Watcher. New York: Bantam. *Essays.*

CALVIN
TRILLIN

*C*ALVIN TRILLIN *was born (1935) in Kansas City, Missouri. He attended
    Yale University and worked as a reporter for* Time *magazine from 1960 to
1963, when he joined the staff of the* New Yorker. *His novel* Floater *(1980)
describes a hero who works for a magazine that sounds very much like* Time. *For
the* New Yorker *he has gone traveling; some of his reportage is collected in* U.S.
Journal *(1971). He writes a column for the* Nation, *more or less political, from
which he has collected* Uncivil Liberties *(1982),* With All Disrespect: More
Uncivil Liberties *(1985), and* If You Can't Say Something Nice *(1987). For
many readers, the essential Calvin Trillin is the man who celebrates eating, whom
Craig Claiborne — former food editor of the New York* Times *and author of
cookbooks — calls the "Homer, Dante, and Shakespeare of American food." His
finger-lickin' essays, mostly from the* New Yorker, *have been served up in three
courses:* American Fried *(1974),* Alice, Let's Eat *(1978), and* Third Helpings
*(1983). If Trillin is accurately dubbed the "Shakespeare of American food," he might
also be called the overeater's Woody Allen. "Health food," says Trillin, "makes me
sick."*

He is a comic writer who is not limited to the comic. U.S. Journal *is reportage,*

504

graceful and clear, from cities and towns all over the country. Killings (1984) collects a subcategory of these essays, sixteen Calvin Trillin essays on murder from the New Yorker. In these strangely nonviolent accounts of violence, the unusual or extreme event serves to show character, mores, culture — like "Rumors Around Town," which the New Yorker printed in 1986.

Rumors Around Town

The first headline in the *Junction City Daily Union* — "EMPORIA MAN FATALLY SHOT" — seemed to describe one of those incidents that can cause a peaceful citizen to shake his head and mumble something about how it's getting so nobody is safe anywhere. The Emporia man was Martin Anderson, a peaceful citizen who had a responsible job and a commission in the Army Reserve and a wife and four little girls. Early on a November evening in 1983, he was murdered by the side of State Highway 177, which cuts south from Manhattan through the rolling cattle-grazing land that people in Kansas call the Flint Hills. According to the newspaper story, the authorities had been told that Anderson was killed during a struggle with an unidentified robber. At the time of the murder, Anderson was on his way back to Emporia from Fort Riley, the infantry base that lies between Junction City and Manhattan. Apparently, the trip had been meant to combine some errands at the fort with an autumn drive through the Flint Hills. His wife was with him, and so were the little girls.

There is a special jolt to the headline "EMPORIA MAN FATALLY SHOT." For many Americans, Emporia, Kansas, conjures up the vision of a typical American town in the era when people didn't have to think about violent men bent on robbery — a town where neighbors drank lemonade on the front porch and kidded one another about their performances in the Fourth of July softball game. The vision grew out of the writings of William Allen White, the Sage of Emporia, who, as owner and editor of the *Emporia Gazette*, was widely thought of during the first forty years of this century as the national spokesman for the unadorned values of the American Midwest. The residents of Emporia in those days may have thought of their town as even more tranquil than its national reputation. What White had been looking for when he set out to buy a small-town newspaper, in 1895, was not a typical town but a college town — a place where his editorials could be understood and appreciated by "a considerable dependable minority of intelligent people, intellectually upper-middle class." Emporia, the

505

seat of Lyon County and a division point for the Santa Fe Railway and a
trading center for the surrounding farmland, had two colleges — the Kansas
State Normal School and a small Presbyterian liberal arts school called the
College of Emporia. During the years that people across the country thought
of Emporia as a typical midwestern town, its boosters sometimes spoke of
it as the Educational Center of the West, or even the Athens of Kansas.

In some ways, Emporia didn't change much after William Allen White
passed from the scene. The White family continued to own the *Gazette*.
Even now, Mrs. William L. White — the widow of the Sage's son, who
was an author and a foreign correspondent known into his seventies around
Emporia as Young Bill — comes in every day. Commercial Street still has
the look of the main trading street in a Kansas farm town — two-story
buildings separated by a slab of asphalt wide enough to accommodate angle
parking on both sides and four lanes of traffic. The College of Emporia
folded some years ago, though; its campus is now owned by a religious
cult called The Way. Although the Santa Fe's operation has been shrinking
in recent years, Emporia has, on the whole, become more of what was
called in White's day a lunch-bucket town. The construction of the Wolf
Creek nuclear power plant, forty miles to the southeast, brought a few
thousand construction workers to the area, and some of them remained
after the plant was completed. Although Kansas State Normal expanded as
it evolved first into Kansas State Teachers' College and then into Emporia
Kansas State College and then into Emporia State University, the largest
employer in town these days is not a college but a big meat-packing plant,
most of whose employees are not the sort of citizens who spend a lot of
their time perusing the editorial page. There is less talk than there once
was about Emporia's being the Athens of Kansas.

Still, a lot of people in Emporia lead an updated version of the peaceful   4
front-porch life that White portrayed, a life revolving around family and
church and school and service club and neighbors. The Andersons seemed
to lead that sort of life. When they walked into Faith Lutheran Church
every Sunday, the little girls wearing immaculate dresses that Lorna Anderson had made herself, they presented the picture of a wholesome,
attractive American family that a lot of people still have in mind when they
think of Emporia. Marty Anderson, a medical technologist, ran the laboratory at Newman Memorial County Hospital. He was on the board of
directors of the Optimist Club. His wife was working part time as secretary
of Faith Lutheran. She was a member of a social and service sorority called
Beta Sigma Phi, which used its annual Valentine's Day dance as a benefit
for the local hospitals. The Andersons were among the young couples who
saw one another at Optimist basketball games or church-fellowship meetings or Beta Sigma Phi socials — people who tended to recall dates by
saying something like, "Let's see, that was the year Jenny started nursery
school" or "I remember I was pregnant with Bobby."

Faith Lutheran Church is dominated by such families. It's a young church, in a former Assembly of God building on the West Side of Emporia, an area filled with split-level houses along blocks so recently developed that most of the trees are still not much higher than the basketball goals. Faith Lutheran was founded in 1982, when the one Missouri Synod Lutheran church in Emporia, Messiah Lutheran, decided that the way to expand was to ask for volunteers to form what was thought of as a "daughter congregation" on the West Side. Faith Lutheran grew so quickly that in October of 1982, just eight months after its founding, it was chartered as a separate congregation. The church — a pale brick building on a corner lot across the street from a school — turned out to be have been well placed, but the congregation had other advantages besides a fortunate location. The people who had volunteered to move from Messiah tended to be active young families with a strong interest in a range of church activities — what was sometimes called at Messiah "the early-service crowd." Thomas Bird, the minister who had been called from Arkansas to Messiah to lead the new undertaking, turned out to be a dynamic young pastor who fitted right in with his congregation. Tom Bird had been a long-distance runner at the University of Arkansas. He was married to his high school sweetheart, an astonishingly energetic young woman who had a master's degree in mathematics and managed to combine the responsibilities of a pastor's wife with some teaching at Emporia State. Like a lot of couples in the congregation, they had three small children and a small split-level and a swing set in the back yard.

The Missouri Synod is a particularly conservative branch of American Lutheranism. Tom Bird thought of himself as conservative in doctrinal and liturgical matters but flexible in dealing with the concerns of his congregation. Distinguishing Faith Lutheran from Missouri Synod churches more set in their ways — Messiah, for instance — he has said that he wanted his church to be more interested in people than in policies. Faith Lutheran lacked the stern, Germanic atmosphere sometimes associated with Missouri Synod churches. The attachment of some of the young West Side couples who soon joined the founders from Messiah was more demographic than liturgical. A lot of them were attracted by a friendly, almost familial bond among contemporaries who tended to be interested in the church volleyball team as well as the Bible classes. The Andersons, who had been active at First Presbyterian, were introduced to Faith when Lorna Anderson decided that its preschool, the Lord's Lambs, might be a convenient place for their two youngest children, twin girls. Eventually, Martin and Lorna Anderson found Faith Lutheran a comfortable place for the entire family. Lorna Anderson went to work half days as the church secretary. Marty Anderson put the pastor up for the Optimists.

A memorial service for Marty Anderson was held at Faith Lutheran. Tom Bird, Lorna Anderson's boss and friend as well as her pastor, was by her side. He could have been assumed to have sad cause for empathy. Only four months before, his own wife had died — killed, from what the authorities could ascertain by reconstructing the event, when her car missed a nasty curve next to the Rocky Ford Bridge, southeast of town, and plunged over an embankment into the Cottonwood River. On the day of Martin Anderson's memorial service, the sanctuary of Faith Lutheran Church was full. Tom Bird delivered the eulogy. The Optimists sat in the front rows.

The day before the memorial service, Susan Ewert, a friend of Lorna Anderson's from the Andersons' days at First Presbyterian, walked into the office of the *Emporia Gazette* first thing in the morning with an angry complaint. She said that the *Gazette* article reporting Martin Anderson's murder — a short Saturday-afternoon item that had been written near deadline on the strength of telephone conversations — implied that Lorna Anderson wasn't telling the truth about what had happened. The *Gazette*'s implication, according to Mrs. Ewert, had so disturbed Mrs. Anderson that her pastor, who was trying to console her, had found her nearly suicidal. The managing editor of the *Gazette*, Ray Call, said that the paper would be happy to give Mrs. Anderson the opportunity to tell her story in detail, and when the *Gazette* came out that afternoon, it carried a story headlined "MURDERED EMPORIAN'S WIFE RECALLS TERROR ON HIGHWAY."

Lorna Anderson's story was this: She was at the wheel of the family's van as it headed down 177 from Manhattan toward Emporia that evening. Apparently having eaten something in Manhattan that disagreed with her, she felt that she was about to be ill, so she stopped the car. As she got out, she took the keys with her — her husband had always insisted that she remove the keys any time she left the van — and then accidentally dropped them in the field at the side of the road. When her husband came out to help her look for them, he told her to return to the van and shine the headlights in his direction. While she was doing that, she heard someone say, "Where's your wallet?" She turned to see her husband hand his wallet to a masked man, who started shooting. Her husband fell to the ground. Then the man grabbed her, held the gun to her head, and pulled the trigger. The gun failed to fire. He fled into the darkness.

The story presented some problems. Would someone who was about to be ill really pull the keys out of a car parked on a deserted stretch of highway when her husband was sitting right in the front seat? What were the odds against a bandit's being on that stretch of highway when the Anderson's van stopped? The original item in the *Gazette* — an item that followed Lorna Anderson's account with the sentence "Officers are investigating the story" — had, in fact, reflected the skepticism of the Geary County officers who listened to the account the night of the murder. The implication of that skepticism was clear in a headline run by the *Junction*

City Daily Union the next day: "VICTIM'S WIFE AMONG SUSPECTS IN KILLING."
The *Emporia Gazette* was not as blunt, but that didn't mean an absence of
suspicion in Emporia. There were a lot of rumors around town.

Emporia, with a population of twenty-five thousand, is about the right
size for rumors. In a tiny town, people are likely to know firsthand what
is true and what isn't. In a large city, most of the population won't have
any connection at all with the people under discussion. In a place the size
of Emporia, though, people tend to have an uncle who knows the cousin
of someone through the Kiwanis, or a next-door neighbor who has the
word through a lawyer who has a kid in the same Boy Scout troop. The
Andersons had been in Emporia for only seven years — Marty Anderson
was from a small town south of Wichita, and his wife had grown up in
Hutchinson — but a lot of people knew someone who knew them. Just
about everybody had something to say about them.

Marty Anderson sounded like a person who had been both easy to like   12
and easy not to like. "He could be very aggravating, and the next minute
he could get you laughing," a fellow Optimist has said. The way Anderson
tried to get people laughing was usually through needling or practical jokes,
and in both forms he occasionally passed over the line from funny to mean.
Sometimes the object of the needling was his wife. He was a big man, more
than six feet tall, and not the sort of big man who slowed up coming into
second base for fear of bowling over a smaller player. At Newman Hospital,
he sometimes employed an army-sergeant manner that irritated people in
other departments, but the technologists who worked for him considered
him an essentially fair man who tried to run a meticulous laboratory.
Basically, they liked him. Outside the hospital, he was known as a man
who after quite a bit too much to drink at a party might decide to play a
prank that turned out not to have been such a good idea after all. His wife
was given to tearful recitals of how miserable life with Martin Anderson
could be, and some of the people who tried to be of comfort were told that
he beat her.

"Everybody was always comforting Lorna," a female associate of Martin
Anderson's said not long ago, putting a little twist on the word "comforting." Lorna Anderson cried easily. Until a couple of years before her husband's death, she had often phoned him at the lab, distraught and tearful,
but she was better known for seeking her comfort elsewhere. The Emporians of William Allen White's day could have described her with one
sentence: She had a reputation. A trim, dark-haired, pleasant-looking
woman of about thirty, she did not have the appearance of the town
bombshell. But there were women in Emporia — women who worked at
the hospital or were members of Beta Sigma Phi — who said that they
avoided parties where the Andersons were likely to be present because

they knew that before the evening was out Lorna Anderson would make a play for their husband. There were people in Emporia who said that a police investigation that included scrutiny of the Anderson's marriage had the potential of embarrassing any number of prominent business and professional men — men who had met Lorna Anderson when she worked at one of the banks or men who knew her through her work as local fund raiser for the American Heart Association or men who had simply run into her late in the evening at a place like the Continental Club of the Ramada Inn. Some people in Emporia — people who, say, worked with someone who knew someone connected with Faith Lutheran Church — were saying that Lorna Anderson's latest catch was Pastor Tom Bird. "Just after we got home from Marty's funeral, the phone rang," a colleague of Martin Anderson's recalled not long ago. "The person calling said there was a rumor that Lorna and Tom Bird had something to do with Marty's death."

Pastor Bird had been one of the people who were always comforting Lorna. Almost from the time she began working for the church, in early 1983, there were whispers in the congregation about the possibility that the pastor and his secretary had grown too close. After Sandra Bird's death, in July of 1983, Lorna Anderson was just one of a number of women from the congregation who concentrated on providing whatever support they could for the young pastor, but she was the only one whose relationship with Tom Bird continued to cause uneasiness in the congregation. The pastor of Messiah had spoken confidentially to Bird about what people were saying, and so had Faith's lay ministers — the equivalent of church elders in some Lutheran congregations. At one point, the lay ministers, intent on avoiding even the appearance of impropriety by the pastor, considered Lorna Anderson's resignation. Finally, it was agreed that she would remain church secretary but would limit her presence at the church to the hours that her job called for. Bird had assured the lay ministers that there was in fact no impropriety in his relationship with his secretary. She had a troubled marriage and a tendency to "spiral down," he told them, and he was only doing his best to counsel and support her. He continued to stand by her after Martin Anderson's death, and after suspicion was cast on her. He continued to stand by her when, only a couple of weeks after Anderson's death, Daniel Carter, an Emporia man who had been picked up by the Geary County authorities on a tip, said she had given him five thousand dollars to see that her husband was killed. Pastor Bird's support did not waver even when, shortly after Carter's arrest, Lorna Anderson herself was arrested for conspiracy to commit first-degree murder.

Lorna Anderson said she was innocent. Daniel Carter said he was guilty. He agreed to cooperate with the authorities investigating the role of Lorna Anderson and others in the plot.

"Do you recall when it was you first had occasion to meet her?" Steven 16
Opat, the Geary County attorney, asked during one of the times Carter
testified in court.

"Yes," Carter said. "I used to cut her hair."

That was at Mr. & Ms., on Commercial Street, in 1981. The relationship
was strictly business for about a year, Carter testified, and then there was
an affair, which lasted a few months, and then, in August of 1983, Lorna
Anderson asked him to find someone to get rid of her husband. By that
time, Carter was working on the construction crew at Wolf Creek, where
he presumably had a better chance of finding a hit man among his co-
workers than he would have had at the hairdresser's. The Geary County
authorities didn't claim that Carter had concocted a scheme that actually
resulted in the death of Martin Anderson. As they pieced the story together,
Carter took five thousand dollars from Lorna Anderson and passed it on
to Gregory Curry, his supervisor at Wolf Creek, who passed it on to a third
man, in Mississippi, who, perhaps realizing that nobody was in a position
to make a stink about having the money returned if services weren't rendered, didn't do anything.

That left the mystery of who killed Martin Anderson, which meant that
a number of investigators from the Geary County Sheriff's Office and the
Lyon County Sheriff's Office and the Kansas Bureau of Investigation were
still asking questions around Emporia — scaring up a covey of rumors with
each interview. When the next arrest came, though, it was not for murder
but for another plot, which nobody claimed had gone any further than talk.
On March 21, 1984, four and a half months after Martin Anderson's death,
the Lyon County attorney, Rodney H. Symmonds, filed charges against
Thomas Bird for criminal solicitation to commit first-degree murder. In an
affidavit filed at the same time, a KBI agent said that the prosecution was
acting largely on information it had received from an Emporia house builder
named Darrel Carter, Daniel Carter's older brother. Shortly after the arrest
of Daniel Carter, the affidavit said, Darrel Carter had gone to the authorities
to inform them that in May of 1983, three months before the plot his brother
had described, he, too, had been asked to help get rid of Martin Anderson.
According to the affidavit, Darrel Carter had gone to Faith Lutheran Church
one weekday morning at Lorna Anderson's request, and there had been
asked by Tom Bird if he would help in a murder scheme that was already
worked out. After Martin Anderson's death, the affidavit said, Darrel Carter
had got word that Tom Bird wanted to meet with him again in order to
"reaffirm their trust," but this time Carter had shown up wearing a hidden
transmitter provided by the Kansas Bureau of Investigation.

"Who would have thought that little old Emporia would have *two* hit 20
men?" a professor at Emporia State University has said. Even to people in
Emporia who had spent the months since Martin Anderson's death savor-

ing the ironies or embellishing the rumors, though, the idea of a minister plotting a murder scheme right in his own church was shocking. There was an accompanying shock in what the affidavit said about one of the possible murder plans that Bird was accused of presenting to Darrel Carter: "Bird told Carter he found a place with a bend in a road and a bridge outside of Emporia, which had an approximately fifty-foot drop-off to the river and that a person could just miss the curve, especially if the person were drunk, and go off down the embankment. Bird told Carter they were going to drug Marty, take him out there, and run the car off into the river."

Anyone who might have missed the implication of that could see it spelled out in the *Gazette's* coverage of Bird's arrest. "On July 17, Sandra Bird, Mr. Bird's wife, was found dead near the wreckage of her car that went off the road at the Rocky Ford Bridge southeast of Emporia," the *Gazette* said. "According to the accident report, Mrs. Bird had been driving northbound on the county road when the car apparently went off the roadway at the approach to the bridge and down a 65-foot embankment.

"An autopsy concluded that Mrs. Bird's death was accidental, caused by severe abdominal and chest injuries.

"Mr. Symmonds declined to comment on whether he considered Mrs. Bird's death to be accidental.

"'Whenever a person dies, it's always subject to further investigation,' he said." 24

Members of Faith Lutheran offered to post Tom Bird's bond. The church's attitude was summed up by the *Wichita Eagle* with the headline "CONGREGATION RALLIES AROUND PASTOR." There were people in the congregation who had been put out at Tom Bird at one time or another — he was known as someone who could be strong-willed about having things done his own way — but in general he was a popular figure. To people who might have expected a Missouri Synod Lutheran pastor to be a severe man on the lookout for sin, Tom Bird had always seemed accessible and informal and concerned. "We're going to stand behind him all the way," one young woman in the congregation told the reporter form Wichita. Faith Lutheran people spoke of Christian love and the American principle that a man is innocent until proved guilty. A lot of them considered the charge against Tom Bird a horrible mistake that would be straightened out at his first hearing. There were some people in the congregation, however, who believed that it would be inappropriate for Bird to continue in his pastoral duties as if nothing had happened, and there were a few who thought he should resign. Bird said that he had no intention of resigning or asking for a leave of absence. In a congregational meeting, a compromise was reached: it was decided that as a way of easing the pressure on Pastor Bird while he dealt with his defense, he could be relieved of preparing and delivering sermons while retaining his other pastoral duties. That arrangement was supposed to last until Bird's preliminary hearing. When the hearing was postponed for some weeks, Bird said that he would prefer to take the pulpit again, and the lay ministers, to the irritation of a few members who were outspokenly opposed to Pastor Bird's continued presence, agreed. On the Sunday that he preached his first sermon after his arrest, the worshipers emerging from the church after the service were greeted not only by their pastor but also by a couple of television crews and some out-of-town reporters.

In Bird's view, the presence of the press that Sunday effectively ended his ministry at Faith Lutheran by making it clear that the church would be no sanctuary from temporal concerns as long as Thomas Bird was its pastor. With or without television cameras at Sunday services, it was a hard time for Faith Lutheran. The atmosphere of relaxed fellowship that had attracted so many young families had turned tense. The effort of most members to withhold judgment meant that no one was quite certain of where anyone else stood. A few families had dropped out of the congregation, and some people came to church less often. "I didn't feel comfortable going to church," a member who was a strong supporter of Pastor Bird has said. "I felt people judging us as well as judging Tom." Faith members also felt some pressure from outside the church. The questions and remarks they heard from outsiders often seemed to carry the implication that the attitude of the congregation toward its pastor was naïve or silly. In the view of one Faith Lutheran member, "It got to be socially unacceptable to go to our church." In the days after Bird's return to the pulpit, it was clear from the pressure within the church not simply that he would no longer deliver sermons on Sundays but that he would have to resign. He delayed the announcement by several weeks in order to avoid going into his preliminary hearing carrying the burden of having resigned under pressure.

Bird had often expressed gratitude for the congregation's support, but even before his arrest he had written in a church newsletter that his reputation was being "sullied by the local gossips." Some of the people who thought the congregation had not been strong enough in its support believed that in the strained atmosphere that followed his arrest the pastor had reason to feel "unwelcome and unloved" in his own church. When he finally resigned, two months after his arrest, his farewell speech to the congregation was partly about such subjects as authentic Christian love and the purposes of the church, but it also included some rather bitter remarks about his treatment. "When I remained silent, I was judged to be unfair for not informing people; when I have spoken, I was judged to be defensive," he said. "When I looked depressed, I was judged to be full of self-pity; when I smiled and looked strong, I was judged to be failing to take matters seriously. When I acted timid, I was judged to be weak; when

I acted boldly, I was judged to be manipulating. When I was indecisive, I was judged to have lost my leadership capacity; when I acted decisively, I was judged to be using my position to railroad matters. To multiply the anguish of my predicament, I only hear these judgments second or third hand, so that I cannot share directly what is in my heart and my intentions to my accusers within the congregation."

By the time of Tom Bird's resignation, a folklorist at Emporia State who 28 is interested in the sort of jokes people tell was collecting Tom-and-Lorna jokes. The folklorist, Thomas Isern, believes that the range of humor in the mass media these days has forced folk humor to be scurrilous in order to remain folk humor, and scurrilous jokes flowed easily from a situation that included a couple of stock folklore characters — the preacher and the loose woman. The relationship between Tom Bird and Lorna Anderson was not the only subject of intense speculation in Emporia. A lot of people were talking about whether Sandra Bird's death had really been an accident. A couple of months after Bird's arrest, the *Gazette* reported that Sandra Bird's family, in Arkansas, had asked a Little Rock lawyer to supervise an investigation into the circumstances of her death. Once some doubt about the incident was made public, it became apparent that a number of people had at the time entertained doubts about whether Sandra Bird had simply missed a curve. A lot of people — neighbors, for instance, and people at Emporia State — had driven out to the Rocky Ford Bridge to have a look at the scene. What had given them pause was not any suspicion of Tom Bird but a feeling that the physical evidence didn't make sense. If Sandra Bird liked to take late-night drives by herself to unwind, as her husband had reported, why would she drive on the distinctly unrelaxing gravel road that approached the Rocky Ford Bridge? If the car was going so fast that it missed the curve at the bridge, which is the second half of an S curve, how did it negotiate the first half? If the car was going that fast, how come it wasn't more seriously damaged? It turned out that there had been people in Emporia who for months had not actually believed the official version of how Sandra Bird died. They thought that she might have committed suicide or that she might have been abducted in the parking lot at Emporia State, where she sometimes went late at night to use the computers, and murdered by her abductor.

By far the most popular topic for speculation, though, was what people in Emporia began to call simply the list. The prosecution, it was said, had a list of Emporia men who had been involved with Lorna Anderson. In some versions of the story, the *Gazette* had the list. In some versions, it was not a list but a black book. In some versions, the men who were on a list of potential witnesses for Lorna Anderson's trial had been informed of that by the prosecution so that they could break the news to their families themselves. The version of the list story some of the reporters on the *Gazette* liked best turned into one of the jokes that could be collected by Tom Isern:

A prominent businessman calls an acquaintance on the *Gazette* news staff and says nervously, "I have to know — does the *Gazette* have a list?"

"No," the *Gazette* reporter says in a soothing voice. "But we're compiling one."

Those people in Emporia who were counting on Lorna Anderson's trial 32 to end the suspense were in for a long wait. The case against her got tangled in any number of delays and legal complications. As it turned out, the first person to come to trial for plotting to murder Martin Anderson was Tom Bird. The defense asked for a change of venue, providing the court with the results of a survey indicating that the overwhelming majority of Emporia residents were familiar with the case. The motion was denied. In Kansas, there is a strong tradition against granting changes of venue even when there is wide community awareness of a case, and, as it happened, the survey indicated that a relatively small percentage of those who were familiar with the charges and the rumors had already made up their minds. But among the ones who had there was a strong indication of how Emporia opinion was running: out of thirty-nine people with firm opinions, thirty-two thought Tom Bird was guilty.

Bird's mother and his father, who is also a Lutheran minister, came up from Arkansas for the trial. So did Sandra Bird's father and mother and stepfather — who, it was noted around town, seemed to keep their distance from their former son-in-law during the proceedings. Reporters and television crews from Wichita and Topeka were in town; despite objections from the defense, a fixed television camera was permitted in the courtroom for the first time in Lyon County. There were members of Faith Lutheran who had come to testify for the defense and members who had come to testify for the prosecution and members who had come merely because, like most residents of Emporia, they were attracted by the prospect of seeing witnesses under oath clear up — or perhaps improve on — the rumors that had been going around town for eight months. The courtroom was jammed every day. "I've never been to anything like this before," one of the spectators told the *Gazette*. "I feel like I know them all; I've heard their names so many times."

The prosecution's case was based on the assumption that Tom Bird and Lorna Anderson had been lovers. According to the prosecutor, they wanted Marty Anderson out of the way, and they weren't interested in a less violent means of accomplishing that — divorce, for instance — because they also wanted the $400,000 in insurance money his death would bring. The prosecution's witnesses included the Anderson's insurance agent — he turned out to be the president of the Optimist Club — and a babysitter, who said that she once heard Lorna Anderson say on the telephone, "I cannot wait for Marty to die; I can't wait to count the green stuff." There was testimony from Faith Lutheran people who had been concerned that the pastor and his secretary were growing too close. "I saw a sparkle in their eyes when they talked to each other," said the preschool teacher, a young woman who under cross-examination acknowledged that she herself had wrestled with a crush on the pastor. "I felt electricity in the air." There was testimony from a development director of the Heart Association, who reduced the talk of electricity and eye-sparkling to more direct language; according to her testimony, Lorna Anderson had told her about having an affair with the pastor and had said that she was using Heart Association business as a cover for trysts in out-of-town motels. The Anderson's nine-year-old daughter, Lori, testified that she had seen her mother and Tom Bird hugging; Marty Anderson's brother and a KBI agent both testified that what Lori had said when she was first questioned was that she had seen her mother and Tom Bird kissing.

The prosecution's star witness was, of course, Darrel Carter. He testified that the meeting at the church in the spring of 1983 was not the first time Lorna Anderson had asked his help in killing her husband. She had first asked him a year or so before that, he said, at a time when the Andersons and the Carters knew each other casually from Beta Sigma Phi functions. "I was really kind of shocked to think that she would ask me that," Carter testified, "'cause Martin Anderson was a friend of mine." According to Carter's testimony, that friendship hadn't prevented him from having his own fling with Lorna some months later. To back up Carter's story of the meeting at Faith Lutheran, the prosecution called a couple of people he had mentioned the scheme to at the time. "I was doing a little work there one evening in my garage on an old Corvette that I'm restoring," one of them, a neighbor of Carter's, said in testimony that summoned up the traditional vision of summertime Emporia. "We visited about several things, which I can't tell you all they were, but the one that sticks in my mind right now is that he told me that someone had contacted him about killing someone."

What the defense asked the jury to do was to view Darrel Carter's testimony not as a story he had finally come forward with after his brother's arrest but as a story he had concocted in order to win some leniency for his brother — who had, in fact, been given probation, while Gregory Curry, his confederate in the scheme, was sentenced to prison. From that angle, the details that Darrel Carter knew could be seen as coming from police reports available to the defense in his brother's case. The similarity of the murder plan to the circumstances of Sandra Bird's death could be explained by the fact that when Carter concocted the story, he knew how Sandra Bird had died. The meeting at Faith Lutheran had indeed taken place, the defense said; its purpose was not to plot murder, though, but to explore the possibility of Faith youth-group members' working at Carter's fireworks stand in order to raise money for a trip to see the Passion Play in Eureka Springs, Arkansas. After Marty Anderson's death, Bird had indeed let it be known that he wanted to talk to Carter, the defense said, but that was because Susan Ewert, Lorna Anderson's friend, had told Bird that Carter was spreading rumors about him, and Bird wanted to put a stop to that. "I've heard enough rumors for sure," Bird could be heard saying on the tape. "Rumors are rampant."

During that conversation with Carter, in a bowling-alley parking lot, Bird made what the prosecution presented as incriminating remarks about the meeting at his church ("I just wanted to touch the bases and make sure that we just talked about possibly my youth group sellin' firecrackers for you") and about the murder of Martin Anderson ("Well, maybe we ought to be glad that we didn't follow through") and about how he felt about Anderson's death ("I ain't celebratin', but I ain't mournin', either"). Still, nothing on the tape was absolutely explicit, and Bird took the stand to provide a benign explanation for every remark — mostly based on the contention that what he and Carter hadn't followed through on was a plan to refer Lorna Anderson to an agency that assists battered wives. When the prosecution managed to bring into evidence two notes from Tom Bird that the police said they had found in Lorna Anderson's lingerie drawer, Bird said that they were meant simply to buck up Lorna's spirits and that such sentiments as "I love you so very much and that's forever" were expressions not of romantic attachment but of "authentic Christian love."

In describing his efforts to counsel Lorna Anderson, Bird admitted that, emotionally drained by his wife's death, he might have used bad judgment in providing the gossips with even the appearance of something worth gossiping about. In explaining why he had arranged the parking-lot meeting through a go-between, a woman he knew from an inquiry she had made about the Lord's Lambs preschool, he admitted a pressure tactic that some jurors might have considered un-Christian: he happened to know that the woman and Darrel Carter were having an affair, he testified, and he figured that making Carter aware of that knowledge might send "the message that everybody is capable of being a victim of rumors." But that was about all he admitted. Bird said that people who saw him hugging Lorna Anderson while comforting her might not have understood that standing across the room with consoling words would not have been "full communication." She had a "self-esteem problem" that required a lot of comforting, he said, and he had provided it as her pastor and her employer and her friend but not as her lover.

"If only he had admitted the affair," a remarkable number of people in Emporia said when talking about Tom Bird's trial for criminal solicitation.

The defense had insisted that the case amounted to a simple choice of whether to believe Tom Bird or Darrel Carter. In some ways, it was an unequal contest. Darrel Carter was nobody's idea of a model citizen. He did not claim that his response to having been asked to help murder a friend of his had included outrage or a telephone call to the authorities. He acknowledged — boasted about, the defense might have said — two affairs with married women while he was married himself. Someone who had hired him to build a house took the stand to say that he was "the biggest liar in ten counties." In contrast, several character witnesses testified that Tom Bird was a trustworthy, God-fearing man. "He is very conscious of the Word of God," the chairman of Faith Lutheran's board of lay ministers said, "and he is very deliberate in his close attention and following of the Word of God."

But practically nobody in Emporia believed Tom Bird when he said he 40 had not had an affair with Lorna Anderson. If only he had admitted the affair, people in Emporia said, the jury might have believed the rest of the story — or might at least have been understanding about what passion could have led him to do. The defense that Emporia people thought might have worked for Tom Bird amounted to a sort of Garden of Eden defense — a tragic twist on the jokes about the preacher and the loose woman. To some people in Emporia, it seemed that Tom Bird could have been presented as a vulnerable man who, at a particularly stressful time in his life, had been led by his passion for a temptress to do some things he came to regret, but who would never have conspired to break God's commandment against murder. A lot of people in Emporia, in other words, thought that Tom Bird's only hope was to repent. The people from Faith Lutheran who continued to believe in Pastor Bird right through the trial found that approach enraging. He could not repent, they said, for the simple reason that he had done nothing that required repentance. That, apparently, was not the view of the jury. Bird was found guilty of soliciting murder. He was sentenced to a term of two and a half to seven years in the Kansas State Penitentiary.

"Like most Emporians, we love a bit of juicy gossip now and then," an editorial in the *Gazette* said a month or so after Tom Bird's conviction. "But in recent weeks here, the saturation point for rumors has been reached and innocent people are being hurt." The *Gazette* mentioned some rumors about the possibility that "the defendant in a recent sensational trial had remarried." There were also further rumors about Lorna Anderson, who had moved back to Hutchinson, and about what might be revealed in her trial. Time had swollen accounts of the list. "At first the list was said to contain 20 names," the *Gazette* said. "Now the number has grown to 110 and includes 'bankers, lawyers, and other professional men.' This is a case of gross exaggeration." The *Gazette* thought it necessary to inform its readers that a professional man who had recently left town had not in fact fled because he was on the list and feared exposure.

The *Gazette* had begun a campaign to have the rumors surrounding Sandra Bird's death tested in a court of law. "Was it only coincidence that Mr. Bird's wife died in the manner and in the place that the minister had suggested for the murder of Mr. Anderson?" its editorial on the verdict in Tom Bird's trial asked. Two *Gazette* reporters, Roberta Birk and Nancy Horst, pounded away at the Sandra Bird case with stories carrying headlines like "CIRCUMSTANCES OF DEATH RAISE SUSPICIONS" and "TROOPER THOUGHT DEATH NOT ACCIDENT." The *Gazette* made a reward fund available for information on the case, and ran a series of stories about contributions to the fund from Sandra Bird's friends and family. In a sheriff's election that November, the *Gazette* editorialized against the incumbent partly on the ground that he had bungled the original investigation of Sandra Bird's death, and he was defeated. Eventually, Sandra Bird's body was exhumed, a second autopsy was performed, and a grand jury began investigating the case. In February of 1985, the grand jury handed up an indictment against Tom Bird for the murder of his wife.

The *Gazette*'s campaign angered the people in Emporia who continued to believe in Bird's innocence. In the months since the headline "CONGRE-GATION RALLIES AROUND PASTOR," of course, their ranks had suffered serious attrition. Some supporters had dropped away as they heard more and more about the relationship between Tom Bird and Lorna Anderson. A lot more had defected after the revelations of the trial or after the guilty verdict. But there remained people on the Faith Lutheran congregation who believed that the verdict was just wrong — a result of Darrel Carter's perfidy and the judge's perverse refusal to move the trial out of a community that had convicted Tom Bird before any witnesses took the stand. The Bird sup-porters who remained could point out inconsistencies in prosecution testi-mony. But basically they believed Bird was innocent partly because they thought he was incapable of the deeds he was accused of and partly because he said he was innocent. "He told me that he swears before God he's innocent," one of the lay ministers has said. "I have to believe him. I don't think he would say that if he were guilty."

Almost everybody else in Emporia tended to believe that Bird was guilty not only of plotting to kill Martin Anderson but also of murdering his own wife. According to a survey taken for Bird's lawyer to support a motion to move his murder trial out of Emporia, virtually everyone in town was familiar with the case, and more than 90 percent of those who had made up their minds about it believed that he was guilty. The motion was denied. Last July, the familiar cast of characters gathered once again in Lyon County District Court — Tom Bird and his parents, the family of Sandy Bird, the small band of Faith Lutheran members who remained loyal to Bird, County Attorney Rodney H. Symmonds, Darrel Carter, the TV crews from Topeka and Wichita. As the trial got under way, though, what most Emporia residents seemed to be discussing was not any revelation from the witness stand but news from Hutchinson that Lorna Anderson, whose trial was finally scheduled to begin later in the summer, had remarried. The bridegroom was a Hutchinson man named Randy Eldridge, someone she had known for years. In answer to reporters' questions, Eldridge said he believed that his new wife was innocent. She said that he was "a wonderful, Christian person" — someone who, it turned out, in his spare time was a member of a gospel-singing sextet. That fact and the rumors that both Eldridges were quite active in an Assembly of God church in Hutchinson had some people in Emporia concerned. It looked as if Lorna Anderson Eldridge might be planning to come to court as an upstanding Christian wife and mother who couldn't have had anything to do with plotting murder — and presumably the prosecution might attempt to destroy that picture of probity by calling to the stand any number of men from the list.

In Tom Bird's trial for murder, there was even more testimony about his relationship with his secretary than there had been in the previous trial. The prosecution called witnesses — Sandra Bird's mother among them — who testified that the pastor's wife had been so distraught over the relationship that she had been unable to eat. But a lot of the testimony was rather technical — testimony from pathologists and accident-reconstruction specialists — and there were days when finding a seat in the spectators' section was no problem. The prosecution called expert witnesses to testify that neither the injuries to Sandra Bird nor the damage to the car was consistent with an accident; the defense called expert witnesses to testify the opposite. By pointing out inconsistencies in Tom Bird's account of that evening and presenting some physical evidence, such as the presence of bloodstains on the bridge, the prosecutor suggested that Bird had beaten his wife, thrown her off the Rocky Ford Bridge, run their car off the embankment, and dragged her body over to it in order to create the appearance of an accident. The defense argued that inconsistencies were to be expected from a man who had been up half the night worrying about where his wife was and had had to start the day by telling his children that their mother was dead. Tom Bird was on trial not for how he ran his personal life, his lawyer said, but for the crime of murder, and "there's no evidence that a crime of any kind was committed." The testimony required twelve days. After that, the jury deliberated for six hours and found Tom Bird guilty of first-degree murder. He was sentenced to life in prison.

"Even a lot of people who thought he was guilty didn't think the trial proved it," a supporter of Bird's said not long ago. It is true, at least, that the prosecutor was not able to provide an eyewitness, as he had done in the criminal-solicitation case. It is also true that he went into the trial holding the advantage of Bird's conviction for plotting Martin Anderson's murder. Among people familiar with the case, it is taken for granted that without the earlier conviction Bird would never have been brought to trial for his wife's murder. Discussing the astonishing chain of events that transformed Tom Bird from a popular young minister to a lifer convicted of killing his wife, a lot of people in Emporia continue to say, "If only he had admitted the affair."

A month after Bird's second conviction, Lorna Anderson Eldridge sat in the same courtroom — neatly dressed, composed, almost cheerful — and said, "I believe it was in June 1983, Thomas Bird and I met with Darrel Carter at the Faith Lutheran Church. During that meeting we discussed various ways of murdering my husband, Martin Anderson." In a last-minute plea bargain, she had agreed to plead guilty to two counts of criminal solicitation to commit first-degree murder and to tell the authorities anything she knew about a case that had presumably already been decided — the death of Sandra Bird. In her plea, she said that Tom Bird had also been involved later in trying to hire a hit man through Danny Carter, and had, in fact, furnished the five thousand dollars. Lorna Eldridge's lawyer said she wanted to purge her soul. A month later, she was sentenced to a term of five and a half to eighteen years in state prison.

Her plea was a blow to those who had continued to believe in Tom 48 Bird, but it did not significantly reduce their ranks. At one point, one of them said not long ago, Bird had told his supporters, "There are very few left. They are falling away. And sooner or later you, too, will be gone." As it turned out, the people who had stuck with Tom Bird even through the murder trial did not fall away just because Lorna Anderson stated in open court that what the prosecution said about Tom Bird was true. They figured that she might be lying because she thought a plea bargain was in her best interest, or that she might be lying simply because she liked to lie. They continue to believe that someday something — a large criminal operation like a drug ring, perhaps — will come to light to explain events that the state has explained with accusations against Tom Bird. At times, they sound like early Christians who manage to shake off constant challenges to their faith. "Questions come up," one of them has said. "And I stop and think. But I always work it out." Tom Bird, when asked by a recent visitor to the Kansas State Penitentiary about the loyalty of his supporters, also explained their support in religious terms — as the action of Christians who understand that we are all sinners and that it is not our role to judge others. "They've grown in their faith," he said.

It is possible that the challenges to their faith in Tom Bird are not at an end. It is not known yet precisely what, if anything, Lorna Anderson Eldridge had to tell the prosecutors about the death of Sandra Bird. So far, nobody has been charged with the murder of Martin Anderson. In Geary County, though, investigators believe that they have made considerable progress. Presumably acting on information provided by Lorna Anderson Eldridge, the Geary County Sheriff's Office drained several farm ponds this fall and eventually found the gun it believes was used in the killing. It is said that the gun belonged to Martin Anderson. Shortly after the sheriff began draining farm ponds, Tom Bird was taken to Junction City from prison to answer questions. Each step in the investigation in Geary County set off ripples of speculation in Lyon County. Will Tom Bird be charged with another murder? Had one of the murder schemes already uncovered by the authorities resulted in Anderson's death after all? Or could it be that little old Emporia had *three* hit men?

To some extent, Lorna Anderson Eldridge's guilty plea meant that William Allen White's home town could get back to normal. Faith Lutheran Church, which had absorbed a fearful blow, has begun to recover. Nobody claims that it has regained the momentum of its early days, but the new pastor — another athletic and personable man with several children — believes that the church has come through its crisis into a period of consolidation. The Lord's Lambs preschool is back to its routine. So are the Optimist basketball games and the laboratory at Newman Hospital and the front page of the *Gazette*. Presumably, Mrs. Eldridge's guilty pleas brought a great sense of relief to those residents of Emporia who had reason to look with some trepidation on the prospect of her coming to trial. There was now less danger that what the *Gazette* called "the most sordid case in Emporia's history" would extend to sworn testimony about the sexual escapades of prominent citizens.

One change in Emporia is that two families are no longer there. The adults are dead or imprisoned, the chidren living in other cities. (The Anderson children have been adopted by Randy Eldridge; the Bird children are living in Arkansas with Tom Bird's parents, who are in the midst of a custody suit brought by the family of Sandra Bird.) Also, there are some people who believe that what happened to the Birds and the Andersons has to have changed what Emporians think of their town and their neighbors. People who have long taken the guilt of Tom Bird and Lorna Anderson for granted are still left with questions about how they could have brought themselves to do such awful deeds. Was Lorna Anderson a temptress who merely used Tom Bird to help get rid of her husband? Or did the death of Sandra Bird — perhaps caused by her husband in some fit of rage — lead inevitably to the death of Martin Anderson? If Tom Bird and Lorna Anderson were bound together, were they bound together by love or by guilty knowledge? Lately, there has been more talk in Emporia about the possibility that what happened can be explained through some sort of mental illness. In a 1984 story about the background of the Birds, Dana Mullin of the *Topeka Capital-Journal* reported that Tom Bird was once hospitalized with a severe heat stroke after a six-mile run in Arkansas and that such heat strokes have been known to cause brain damage. Putting that information together with some of the bizarre behavior attributed to Lorna Anderson even before her husband's death, some people in Emporia have theorized that perhaps Tom Bird and his secretary, who seemed so much like their neighbors, had mental difficulties that somehow meshed to result in deeds their neighbors consider unthinkable.

What was sordid about Emporia's most sordid case, of course, was not 52 simply the crimes but the lives they revealed — lives full of hatred and maybe wife beating and certainly casual, apparently joyless liaisons. (When Daniel Carter testified that his affair with Lorna Anderson had ended because she seemed to want more from him than he was willing to offer, the prosecutor asked what he had been willing to offer. "Nothing," Carter said.) Although the *Gazette* may have criticized rumors about a 110-man list as "a gross exaggeration," the prosecutors have never denied that a list, perhaps of more modest size, existed — assembled, it is assumed, in case the state of the Andersons' marriage became an issue. A jury had concluded that an Emporia minister beat his wife until she was unconscious or dead and threw her body off a bridge. A church secretary acknowledged involvement in plans to get rid of her husband, who was murdered virtually in front of their own children. What now seems remarkable about the outrageous rumors that gripped Emporia for so long is that so many of them turned out to be true.

AFTERWORD

There are styles that fly flags: idiosyncracy, wit, dazzling image, and triumphant metaphor, acrobatic feats on a high wire with no net. There are styles that hide themselves, pretending that they are not styles at all: "I am a glass of water; you aren't reading writing, you are looking at the thing that happens." Of course the style of stylelessness is another style — no better or worse, no easier or harder, than the style of style. When Trillin writes his Nation *columns, or when he writes about fast food in Kansas City, his humor depends on words that you look at; you see their texture, their roughness, their triteness, their wonderful inappropriateness. You know you are reading words when he writes about people who crave the hometown food of their geographically dispersed childhoods: "I have personally acted as a courier in bringing desperately craved burnt-almond chocolate ice cream from Will Wright's in Los Angeles to a friend who survived a Beverly Hills childhood and now lives in New York — living like a Spanish Civil War refugee who hates the regime but would give his arm for a decent bowl of gazpacho. I have also, in the dark of night, slipped into a sophisticated apartment in upper Manhattan and left an unmarked paper bag containing a powdered substance called Ranch Dressing — available, my client believes, only in certain supermarkets in the State of Oklahoma."*

But when he writes about murder, Trillin writes without irony. He would never use the parodistic *"available, my client believes, only . . . "* or the hyperbolic *"desperately craved."* He drops one voice and speaks with another. Even when he uses a cliché — what an ear for cliché Trillin has — he uses it without tone or without humor: *"The Emporians of William Allen White's day could have described her with one sentence: She had a reputation."* Here the euphemism is not comic but delicate, serving to speak not only of the woman described but of the people imagined describing her. The art of Trillin's comedy is personal; the art of this essay is to appear to stay out of it, to appear impartial.

Trillin's ear for language includes delight in the names of things. When Carter says that he used to cut hair, we don't need to know where he did it. But Trillin loves to tell us: *"That was at Mr. & Ms., on Commercial Street."* Other names of things: Continental Club, American Heart Association, Faith Lutheran Church, Optimist Club, Beta Sigma Phi, the Lord's Lambs.

Writing about the kind of murder case that Trillin writes about, his quiet, reticent, reportorial voice is exactly right. Out of the plainness of his language, as in understatements of enormity on other occasions, moral depravity writes itself quietly in huge red letters.

BOOKS AVAILABLE IN PAPERBACK

Alice, Let's Eat: Further Adventures of A Happy Eater. New York: Random House-Vintage. *Essays.*

American Fried: Adventures of a Happy Eater. New York: Random House-Vintage. *Essays.*

Killings. New York: Penguin. *Essays.*

Third Helpings. New York: Penguin. *Essays.*

Uncivil Liberties. New York: Penguin. *Essays.*

With All Disrespect: More Uncivil Liberties. New York: Penguin. *Essays.*

BARBARA W. TUCHMAN

WHEN WE CALL SOMEONE a historian these days, we usually mean a professor who teaches courses in a history department. Barbara W. Tuchman is a historian in an older sense: She studies the past, makes her own sense of things, and writes books to proclaim and defend her understanding. To work, she must study, consulting the documents assembled in archives and libraries. ("To an historian," she writes, "libraries are food, shelter, and even Muse.") She must take notes, follow clues, organize, make judgments, and write narrative that allows room for ideas and moral argument. By selection and organization of detail, she emphasizes particular themes and shows her interpretations.

Born in New York (1912), she graduated from Radcliffe College in 1933. Her early interests turned her Eastward, and she worked as a research assistant at the Institute of Pacific Relations. (Much later this interest found expression in her Stilwell and the American Experience in China, which won a Pulitzer Prize in 1971.) Later in the 1930s she wrote on politics for the Nation, the political magazine which her father owned. Then she worked as a journalist in London and wrote about the Spanish Civil War. After Pearl Harbor she took a job with the Office of War Information in Washington.

Perhaps because she matured in the 1930s as the world was heading toward World War II, she has always attended to the origins of war. Her first publishing success was The Guns of August *(1961), about the beginnings of World War I; subsequently* The Proud Tower *(1966) described that war's antecedents in European and in American history.* Practicing History *(1981) collects articles, reviews, and talks.* The March of Folly *(1984) assembles a rogue's gallery of misguided political leadership; her subtitle indicates her melancholy range:* From Troy to Vietnam.

When Tuchman writes about the fourteenth century in Europe, as she does in A Distant Mirror *(1978), she seems to leave modern history behind, but her theme is a six-hundred-year-old reflection. It is a commonplace that history repeats itself; Tuchman analyzing the fourteenth century writes by analogy about the twentieth. Her pursuit of this analogy is addressed to readers of her own time; she published it in 1973, during the Watergate scandal.*

History as Mirror

At a time when everyone's mind is on the explosions of the moment, it might seem obtuse of me to discuss the fourteenth century. But I think a backward look at that disordered, violent, bewildered, disintegrating, and calamity-prone age can be consoling and possibly instructive in a time of similar disarray. Reflected in a six-hundred-year-old mirror, a more revealing image of ourselves and our species might be seen than is visible in the clutter of circumstances under our noses. The value of historical comparison was made keenly apparent to the French medievalist, Edouard Perroy, when he was writing his book on the Hundred Years' War while dodging the Gestapo in World War II. "Certain ways of behaving," he wrote, "certain reactions against fate, throw mutual light upon each other."

Besides, if one suspects that the twentieth century's record of inhumanity and folly represents a phase of mankind at its worst, and that our last decade of collapsing assumptions has been one of unprecedented discomfort, it is reassuring to discover that the human race has been in this box before — and emerged. The historian has the comfort of knowing that man (meaning, here and hereafter, the species, not the sex) is always capable of his worst; has indulged in it, painfully struggled up from it, slid back, and gone on again.

In what follows, the parallels are not always in physical events but rather in the effect on society, and sometimes in both.

The afflictions of the fourteenth century were the classic riders of the 4
Apocalypse — famine, plague, war, and death, this time on a black horse.
These combined to produce an epidemic of violence, depopulation, bad
government, oppressive taxes, an accelerated breakdown of feudal bonds,
working class insurrection, monetary crisis, decline of morals and rise in
crime, decay of chivalry, the governing idea of the governing class, and
above all, corruption of society's central institution, the Church, whose loss
of authority and prestige deprived man of his accustomed guide in a darkening world.

Yet amidst the disintegration were sprouting, invisible to contemporaries, the green shoots of the Renaissance to come. In human affairs as in
nature, decay is compost for new growth.

Some medievalists reject the title of decline for the fourteenth century,
asserting instead that it was the dawn of a new age. Since the processes
obviously overlap, I am not sure that the question is worth arguing, but it
becomes poignantly interesting when applied to ourselves. Do *we* walk
amidst trends of a new world without knowing it? How far ahead is the
dividing line? Or are we on it? What designation will our age earn from
historians six hundred years hence? One wishes one could make a pact
with the devil like Enoch Soames, the neglected poet in Max Beerbohm's
story, allowing us to return and look ourselves up in the library catalogue.
In that future history book, shall we find the chapter title for the twentieth
century reading Decline and Fall, or Eve of Revival?

The fourteenth century opened with a series of famines brought on
when population growth outstripped the techniques of food production.
The precarious balance was tipped by a series of heavy rains and floods
and by a chilling of the climate in what has been called the Little Ice Age.
Upon a people thus weakened fell the century's central disaster, the Black
Death, an eruption of bubonic plague which swept the known world in the
years 1347–1349 and carried off an estimated one-third of the population in
two and a half years. This makes it the most lethal episode known to
history, which is of some interest to an age equipped with the tools of
overkill.

The plague raged at terrifying speed, increasing the impression of hor- 8
ror. In a given locality it accomplished its kill within four to six months,
except in larger cities, where it struck again in spring after lying dormant
in winter. The death rate in Avignon was said to have claimed half the
population, of whom ten thousand were buried in the first six weeks in a
single mass grave. The mortality was in fact erratic. Some communities
whose last survivors fled in despair were simply wiped out and disappeared
from the map forever, leaving only a grassed-over hump as their mortal
trace.

Whole families died, leaving empty houses and property a prey to looters. Wolves came down from the mountains to attack plague-stricken villages, crops went unharvested, dikes crumbled, salt water reinvaded and soured the lowlands, the forest crept back, and second growth, with the awful energy of nature unchecked, reconverted cleared land to waste. For lack of hands to cultivate, it was thought impossible that the world could ever regain its former prosperity.

Once the dark bubonic swellings appeared in armpit and groin, death followed rapidly within one to three days, often overnight. For lack of gravediggers, corpses piled up in the streets or were buried so hastily that dogs dug them up and ate them. Doctors were helpless, and priests lacking to administer that final sacrament so that people died believing they must go to hell. No bells tolled, the dead were buried without prayers or funeral rites or tears; families did not weep for the loss of loved ones, for everyone expected death. Matteo Villani, taking up the chronicle of Florence from the hands of his dead brother, believed he was recording the "extermination of mankind."

People reacted variously, as they always do: some prayed, some robbed, some tried to help, most fled if they could, others abandoned themselves to debauchery on the theory that there would be no tomorrow. On balance, the dominant reaction was fear and a desire to save one's own skin regardless of the closest ties. "A father did not visit his son, nor the son his father; charity was dead," wrote one physician, and that was not an isolated observation. Boccaccio in his famous account reports that "kinsfolk held aloof, brother was forsaken by brother . . . often times husband by wife; nay what is more, and scarcely to be believed, fathers and mothers were found to abandon their own children to their fate, untended, unvisited as if they had been strangers."

"Men grew bold," wrote another chronicler, "in their indulgence in 12 pleasure. . . . No fear of God or law of man deterred a criminal. Seeing that all perished alike, they reflected that offenses against human or Divine law would bring no punishment for no one would live long enough to be held to account." This is an accurate summary, but it was written by Thucydides about the Plague of Athens in the fifth century B.C. — which indicates a certain permanence of human behavior.

The nightmare of the plague was compounded for the fourteenth century by the awful mystery of its cause. The idea of disease carried by insect bite was undreamed of. Fleas and rats, which were in fact the carriers, are not mentioned in the plague writings. Contagion could be observed but not explained and thus seemed doubly sinister. The medical faculty of the University of Paris favored a theory of poisonous air spread by a conjunction of the planets, but the general and fundamental belief, made official by a papal bull, was that the pestilence was divine punishment for man's sins. Such horror could only be caused by the wrath of God. "In the year of our

Lord, 1348," sadly wrote a professor of law at the University of Pisa, "the hostility of God was greater than the hostility of men."

That belief enhanced the sense of guilt, or rather the consciousness of sin (guilt, I suspect, is modern; sin is medieval), which was always so close to the surface throughout the Middle Ages. Out of the effort to appease divine wrath came the flagellants, a morbid frenzy of self-punishment that almost at once found a better object in the Jews.

A storm of pogroms followed in the track of the Black Death, widely stimulated by the flagellants, who often rushed straight for the Jewish quarter, even in towns which had not yet suffered the plague. As outsiders within the unity of Christendom the Jews were natural persons to suspect of evil design on the Christian world. They were accused of poisoning the wells. Although the Pope condemned the attacks as inspired by "that liar the devil," pointing out that Jews died of plague like everyone else, the populace wanted victims, and fell upon them in three hundred communities throughout Europe. Slaughtered and burned alive, the entire colonies of Frankfurt, Cologne, Mainz, and other towns of Germany and the Lowlands were exterminated, despite the restraining efforts of town authorities. Elsewhere the Jews were expelled by judicial process after confession of well-poisoning was extracted by torture. In every case their goods and property, whether looted or confiscated, ended in the hands of the persecutors. The process was lucrative, as it was to be again in our time under the Nazis, although the fourteenth century had no gold teeth to rob from the corpses. Where survivors slowly returned and the communities revived, it was on worse terms than before and in walled isolation. This was the beginning of the ghetto.

Men of the fourteenth century were particularly vulnerable because of the loss of credibility by the Church, which alone could absolve sin and offer salvation from hell. When the papal schism dating from 1378 divided the Church under two popes, it brought the highest authority in society into disrepute, a situation with which we are familiar. The schism was the second great calamity of the time, displaying before all the world the unedifying spectacle of twin vicars of God, each trying to bump the other off the chair of St. Peter, each appointing his own college of cardinals, each collecting tithes and revenues and excommunicating the partisans of his rival. No conflict of ideology was involved; the split arose from a simple squabble for the office of the papacy and remained no more than that for the fifty years the schism lasted. Plunged in this scandal, the Church lost moral authority, the more so as its two halves scrambled in the political arena for support. Kingdoms, principalities, even towns, took sides, finding new cause for the endless wars that scourged the times.

The Church's corruption by worldliness long antedated the schism. By the fourteenth century the papal court at Avignon was called Babylon and rivaled temporal courts in luxury and magnificence. Its bureaucracy was enormous and its upkeep mired in a commercial traffic in spiritual things. Pardons, indulgences, prayers, every benefice and bishopric, everything the Church had or was, from cardinal's hat to pilgrim's relic, everything that represented man's relation to God, was for sale. Today it is the processes of government that are for sale, especially the electoral process, which is as vital to our political security as salvation was to the emotional security of the fourteenth century.

Men still craved God and spun off from the Church in sects and heresies, seeking to purify the realm of the spirit. They too yearned for a greening of the system. The yearning, and disgust with the Establishment, produced freak orders of mystics who lived in coeducational communes, rejected marriage, and glorified sexual indulgence. Passionate reformers ranged from St. Catherine of Siena, who scolded everyone in the hierarchy from the popes down, to John Wycliffe, who plowed the soil of Protestant revolt. Both strove to renew the Church, which for so long had been the only institution to give order and meaning to the untidy business of living on earth. When in the last quarter of the century the schism brought the Church into scorn and ridicule and fratricidal war, serious men took alarm. The University of Paris made strenuous and ceaseless efforts to find a remedy, finally demanding submission of the conflict to a supreme Council of the Church whose object should be not only reunification but reform.

Without reform, said the University's theologians in their letter to the popes, the damaging effect of the current scandal could be irreversible. In words that could have been addressed to our own secular potentate although he is — happily — not double, they wrote, "The Church will suffer for your overconfidence if you repent too late of having neglected reform. If you postpone it longer the harm will be incurable. Do you think people will suffer forever from your bad government? Who do you think can endure, amid so many abuses . . . your elevation of men without literacy or virtue to the most eminent positions?" The echo sounds over the gulf of six hundred years with a timeliness almost supernatural.

When the twin popes failed to respond, pressure at last brought about 20 a series of Church councils which endeavored to limit and constitutionalize the powers of the papacy. After a thirty-year struggle, the councils succeeded in ending the schism but the papacy resisted reform. The decades of debate only served to prove that the institution could not be reformed from within. Eighty years of mounting protest were to pass before pressure produced Luther and the great crack.

Despite the parallel with the present struggle between Congress and the presidency, there is no historical law that says the outcome must necessarily be the same. The American presidency at age two hundred is not a massive rock of ages embedded in a thousand years of acceptance as was the medieval Church, and should be easier to reform. One can wish for

Congress a better result than the councils had in the effort to curb the executive — or at least one can hope.

The more important parallel lies in the decay of public confidence in our governing institutions, as the fourteenth-century public lost confidence in the Church. Who believes today in the integrity of government? — or of business, or of law or justice or labor unions or the military or the police? Even physicians, the last of the admired, are now in disfavor. I have a theory that the credibility vacuum owes something to our nurture in that conspiracy of fables called advertising, which we daily absorb without believing. Since public affairs and ideas and candidates are now presented to us as a form of advertising, we automatically suspend belief or suspect fraud as soon as we recognize the familiar slickness. I realize, of course, that the roots of disbelief go down to deeper ground. Meanwhile the effect is a loss of trust in all authority which leaves us guideless and dismayed and cynical — even as in the fourteenth century.

Over that whole century hung the smoke of war — dominated by the Anglo-French conflict known to us, though fortunately not to them, as the Hundred Years' War. (With the clock still ticking in Indochina, one wonders how many years there are still to go in that conflict.) Fought on French soil and extending into Flanders and Spain, the Hundred Years' War actually lasted for more than a century, from 1337 to 1453. In addition, the English fought the Scots; the French fought incessant civil wars against Gascons, Bretons, Normans, and Navarrese; the Italian republics fought each other — Florence against Pisa, Venice against Genoa, Milan against everybody; the kingdom of Naples and Sicily was fought over by claimants from Hungary to Aragon; the papacy fought a war that included unbridled massacre to reconquer the Papal States; the Savoyards fought the Lombards; the Swiss fought the Austrians; the tangled wars of Bohemia, Poland, and the German Empire defy listing; crusades were launched against the Saracens, and to fill up any pauses the Teutonic Knights conducted annual campaigns against pagan Lithuania which other knights could join for extra practice. Fighting was the function of the Second Estate, that is, of the landed nobles and knights. A knight without a war or tournament to go to felt as restless as a man who cannot go to the office.

Every one of these conflicts threw off Free Companies of mercenaries, 24 organized for brigandage under a professional captain, which became an evil of the period as malignant as the plague. In the money economy of the fourteenth century, armed forces were no longer feudal levies serving under a vassal's obligation who went home after forty days, but were recruited bodies who served for pay. Since this was at great cost to the sovereign, he cut off the payroll as soon as he safely could during halts of truce or negotiation. Thrown on their own resources and having acquired a taste for plunder, the men-at-arms banded together in the Free Companies, whose savage success swelled their ranks with landless knights and squires and roving adventurers.

The companies contracted their services to whatever ruler was in need of troops, and between contracts held up towns for huge ransom, ravaged the countryside, and burned, pillaged, raped, and slaughtered their way back and forth across Europe. No one was safe, no town or village knew when it might be attacked. The leaders, prototypes of the *condottieri* in Italy, became powers and made fortunes and even became respectable like Sir John Hawkwood, commander of the famous White Company. Smaller bands, called in France the *tards-venus* (latecomers), scavenged like jackals, living off the land, plundering, killing, carrying off women, torturing peasants for their small horde of grain or townsmen for their hidden goods, and burning, always burning. They set fire to whatever they left behind, farmhouses, vineyards, abbeys, in a kind of madness to destroy the very sources off which they lived, or would live tomorrow. Destruction and cruelty became self-engendering, not merely for loot but almost one might say for sport. The phenomenon is not peculiar to any one time or people, as we know from the experience of our own century, but in the fourteenth century it seems to have reached a degree and extent beyond explanation.

It must be added that in practice and often personnel the Free Companies were hardly distinguishable from the troops of organized official wars. About 80 percent of the activity of a declared war consisted of raids of plunder and burning through enemy territory. That paragon of chivalry, the Black Prince, could well have earned his name from the blackened ruins he left across France. His baggage train and men-at-arms were often so heavily laden with loot that they moved as slowly as a woman's litter.

The saddest aspect of the Hundred Years' War was the persistent but vain efforts of the belligerents themselves to stop it. As in our case, it spread political damage at home, and the cost was appalling. Moreover it harmed the relations of all the powers at a time when they were anxious to unite to repel the infidel at the gates. For Christendom was now on the defensive against the encroaching Turks. For that reason the Church, too, tried to end the war that was keeping Europe at odds. On the very morning of the fatal battle of Poitiers, two cardinals hurried with offers and counter-offers between the two armed camps, trying in vain to prevent the clash. During periods of truce the parties held long parleys lasting months and sometimes years in the effort to negotiate a definitive peace. It always eluded them, failing over questions of prestige, or put off by the feeling of whichever side held a slight advantage that one more push would bring the desired gains.

All this took place under a code of chivalry whose creed was honor, loyalty, and courtesy and whose purpose, like that of every social code evolved by man in his long search for order, was to civilize and supply a pattern of rules. A knight's task under the code was to uphold the Church, defend his land and vassals, maintain the peace of his province, protect the weak and guard the poor from injustice, shed his blood for his comrade, and lay down his life if needs must. For the land-owning warrior class, chivalry was their ideology, their politics, their system — what democracy is to us or Marxism to the Communists.

Originating out of feudal needs, it was already slipping into anachronism by the fourteenth century because the development of monarchy and a royal bureaucracy was taking away the knight's functions, economic facts were forcing him to commute labor dues for money, and a rival element was appearing in the urban magnates. Even his military prowess was being nullified by trained bodies of English longbowmen and Swiss pikemen, nonmembers of the warrior class who in feudal theory had no business in battle at all.

Yet in decadence chivalry threw its brightest light; never were its ceremonies more brilliant, its jousts and tournaments so brave, its apparel so splendid, its manners so gay and amorous, its entertainments so festive, its self-glorification more eloquent. The gentry elaborated the forms of chivalry just *because* institutions around them were crumbling. They clung to what gave their status meaning in a desperate embrace of the past. This is the time when the Order of the Garter was founded by the King of England, the Order of the Star by the King of France, the Golden Fleece by the Duke of Burgundy — in deliberate imitation of King Arthur's Knights of the Round Table.

The rules still worked well enough among themselves, with occasional notorious exceptions such as Charles of Navarre, a bad man appropriately known as Charles the Bad. Whenever necessity required him to swear loyal reconciliation and fealty to the King of France, his mortal enemy, he promptly engaged in treacherous intrigues with the King of England, leaving his knightly oaths to become, in the White House word, inoperative. On the whole, however, the nobility laid great stress on high standards of honor. It was vis-à-vis the Third Estate that chivalry fell so far short of the theory. Yet it remained an ideal of human relations, as Christianity remained an ideal of faith, that kept men reaching for the unattainable. The effort of society is always toward order, away from anarchy. Sometimes it moves forward, sometimes it slips back. Which is the direction of one's own time may be obscure.

The fourteenth century was further afflicted by a series of convulsions 32 and upheavals in the working class, both urban and rural. Causes were various: the cost of constant war was thrown upon the people in hearth taxes, salt taxes, sales taxes, and debasement of coinage. In France the failure of the knights to protect the populace from incessant ravaging was a factor. It exacerbated the peasants' misery, giving it the energy of anger which erupted in the ferocious mid-century rising called the *Jacquerie*. Shortage of labor caused by the plague had temporarily brought higher wages and rising expectations. When these were met, especially in England, by statutes clamping wages at pre-plague levels, the result was the historic Peasants' Revolt of 1381. In the towns, capitalism was widening the gap between masters and artisans, producing the sustained weavers' revolts in the cloth towns of Flanders and major outbreaks in Florence and Paris. In Paris, too, the merchant class rose against the royal councillors, whom they despised as both corrupt and incompetent. To frighten the regent into submission, they murdered his two chief councillors in his presence.

All these struggles had one thing in common: they were doomed. United against a common threat, the ruling class could summon greater strength than its antagonists and acted to suppress insurrection with savagery equal to the fury from below. Yet discontent had found its voice; dissent and rejection of authority for the first time in the Middle Ages became a social force. Demagogues and determined leaders, reformers and agitators came to the surface. Though all were killed, several by mobs of their own followers, the uprisings they led were the beginning of modern, conscious, class war.

Meanwhile, over the second half-century, the plague returned with lesser virulence at intervals of every twelve to fifteen years. It is hardly to be wondered that people of the time saw man's fate as an endless succession of evils. He must indeed be wicked and his enemy Satan finally triumphant. According to a popular belief at the end of the century, no one since the beginning of the schism had entered Paradise.

Pessimism was a mark of the age and the *Danse Macabre* or Dance of Death its most vivid expression. Performed at occasions of popular drama and public sermons, it was an actual dance or pantomime in which a figure from every walk of life — king, clerk, lawyer, friar, goldsmith, bailiff, and so on — confronts the loathsome corpse he must become. In the accompanying verses and illustrations which have survived, the theme repeats itself over and over: the end of all life is putrefaction and the grave; no one escapes; no matter what beauty or kingly power or poor man's misery has been the lot in life, all end alike as food for worms. Death is not treated poetically as the soul's flight to reunion with God; it is a skeleton grinning at the vanity of life.

Life as well as death was viewed with disgust. The vices and corruptions 36 of the age, a low opinion of one's fellowmen, and nostalgia for the well-ordered past were the favorite themes of literary men. Even Boccaccio in his later works became ill-tempered. "All good customs fail," laments Christine de Pisan of France, "and virtues are held at little worth." Eustache Deschamps complains that "the child of today has become a ruffian. . . . People are gluttons and drunkards, haughty of heart, caring for nought, not honor nor goodness nor kindness . . ." and he ends each verse with the refrain, "Time past had virtue and righteousness but today reigns only vice." In England John Gower denounces Rome for simony, Lollards for heresy, clergy and monks for idleness and lust, kings, nobles, and knights for self-indulgence and rapine, the law for bribery, merchants for usury and fraud, the commons for ignorance, and in general the sins of perjury, lechery, avarice, and pride as displayed in extravagant fashions.

These last did indeed, as in all distracted times, reflect a reaching for the absurd, especially in the long pointed shoes which kept getting longer until the points had to be tied up around the knee, and the young men's doublets which kept getting shorter until they revealed the buttocks, to the censure of moralists and snickers of the crowd. Leaving miniskirts to the males, the ladies inexplicably adopted a fashion of gowns and posture designed to make them look pregnant.

Self-disgust, it seems to me, has reappeared in our time, not without cause. The succession of events since 1914 has disqualified belief in moral progress, and pollution of the physical world is our bubonic plague. Like the fourteenth century, we have lost confidence in man's capacity to control his fate and even in his capacity to be good. So we have a literature of the anti-hero aimlessly wandering among the perverse, absurd, and depraved; we have porn and pop and blank canvases and anti-music designed to deafen. I am not sure whether in all this the artists are expressing contempt for their fellowman or the loud laugh that bespeaks emptiness of feeling, but whatever the message, it has a faint ring of the *Danse Macabre*.

Historians until recently have hurried over the fourteenth century because like most people they prefer not to deal with failure. But it would be a mistake to imply that it was solid gloom. Seen from inside, especially from a position of privilege, it had beauties and wonders, and the ferment itself was exciting. "In these fifty years," said the renowned Comte de Foix to the chronicler Froissart in the year 1389, "there have been more feats of arms and more marvels in the world than in the three hundred years before." The Count himself, a famous huntsman, was known as Phoebus for his personal beauty and splendid court.

The streets of cities were bright with colored clothes: crimson fur-lined 40 gowns of merchants, parti-colored velvets and silks of a nobleman's retinue, in sky blue and fawn or two shades of scarlet or it might be the all-emerald liveries of the Green Count of Savoy. Street sounds were those of human voices: criers of news and official announcements, shopkeepers in their doorways and itinerant vendors crying fresh eggs, charcoal at a penny a sack, candlewicks "brighter than the stars," cakes and waffles, mushrooms, hot baths. Mountebanks entertained the public in the town square or village green with tricks and magic and trained animals. Jongleurs sang ballads of adventure in Saracen lands. After church on Sundays, laborers gathered in cookshops and taverns; burghers promenaded in their gardens or visited their vineyards outside the city walls. Church bells marked the eight times of day from Matins through Vespers, when shops closed, work ceased, silence succeeded bustle, and the darkness of unlit night descended.

The gaudy extravagance of noble life was awesome. Now and then its patronage brought forth works of eternal beauty like the exquisite illuminated Books of Hours commissioned by the Duc de Berry. More often it was pure ostentation and conspicuous consumption. Charles V of France owned forty-seven jeweled and golden crowns and sixty-three complete sets of chapel furnishings, including vestments, gold crucifixes, altarpieces, reliquaries, and prayer books. Jewels and cloth of gold marked every occasion and every occasion was pretext for a spectacle — a grand procession, or ceremonial welcome to a visiting prince, a tournament or entertainment with music, and dancing by the light of great torches. When Gian Galeazzo Visconti, ruler of Milan, gave a wedding banquet for his daughter, eighteen double courses were served, each of fish and meat, including trout, quail, herons, eels, sturgeon, and suckling pig spouting fire. The gifts presented after *each* course to several hundred guests included greyhounds in gem-studded velvet collars, hawks in tinkling silver bells, suits of armor, rolls of silk and brocade, garments trimmed with pearls and ermine, fully caparisoned warhorses, and twelve fat oxen. For the entry into Paris of the new Queen, Isabel of Bavaria, the entire length of the Rue St. Denis was hung with a canopy representing the firmament twinkling with stars from which sweetly singing angels descended bearing a crown, and fountains ran with wine, distributed to the people in golden cups by lovely maidens wearing caps of solid gold.

One wonders where all the money came from for such luxury and festivity in a time of devastation. What taxes could burned-out and destitute people pay? This is a puzzle until one remembers that the Aga Khan got to be the richest man in the world on the backs of the poorest people, and that disaster is never as pervasive as it seems from recorded accounts. It is one of the pitfalls for historians that the very fact of being on the record makes a happening appear to have been continuous and all-inclusive, whereas in reality it is more likely to have been sporadic both in time and place. Besides, persistence of the normal is usually greater than the effect of disturbance, as we know from our own times. After absorbing the daily paper and weekly magazine, one expects to face a world consisting entirely of strikes, crimes, power shortages, broken water mains, stalled trains, school shutdowns, Black Panthers, addicts, transvestites, rapists, and militant lesbians. The fact is that one can come home in the evening — on a lucky day — without having encountered more than two or three of these phenomena. This has led me to formulate Tuchman's Law, as follows: "The fact of being reported increases the *apparent* extent of a deplorable development by a factor of ten." (I snatch the figure from the air and will leave it to the quantifiers to justify.)

The astonishing fact is that except for Boccaccio, to whom we owe the most vivid account, the Black Death was virtually ignored by the great writers of the time. Petrarch, who was forty-four when it happened, mentions it only as the occasion for the death of Laura; Chaucer, from what I have read, passes it over in silence; Jean Froissart, the Herodotus of his time, gives it no more than one casual paragraph, and even that second Isaiah, the author of *Piers Plowman*, who might have been expected to make it central to his theme of woe, uses it only incidentally. One could argue that in 1348 Chaucer was only eight or nine years old and Froissart ten or eleven and the unknown Langland probably of the same vintage, but that is old enough to absorb and remember a great catastrophe, especially when they lived through several returns of the plague as grown men.

Perhaps this tells us that disaster, once survived, leaves less track than 44 one supposed, or that man's instinct for living pushes it down below the surface, or simply that his recuperative powers are remarkable. Or was it just an accident of personality? Is it significant or just chance that Chaucer, the greatest writer of his age, was so uncharacteristic of it in sanguine temperament and good-humored view of his fellow creatures?

As for Froissart, never was a man more in love with his age. To him it appeared as a marvelous pageant of glittering armor and the beauty of emblazoned banners fluttering in the breeze and the clear shrill call of the trumpet. Still believing, still enraptured by the chivalric ideal, he reports savagery, treachery, limitless greed, and the pitiless slaughter of the poor when driven to revolt as minor stumbles in the grand adventure of valor and honor. Yet near the end, even Froissart could not hide from himself the decay made plain by a dissolute court, venality in high places, and a knighthood that kept losing battles. In 1397, the year he turned sixty, the defeat and massacre of the flower of chivalry at the hands of the Turks in the battle of Nicopolis set the seal on the incompetence of his heroes. Lastly, the murder of a King in England shocked him deeply, not for any love of Richard II but because the act was subversive of the whole order that sustained his world. As in Watergate, the underside had rolled to the surface all too visibly. Froissart had not the heart to continue and brought his chronicle to an end.

The sad century closed with a meeting between King Charles VI of

France and the Emperor Wenceslaus, the one intermittently mad and the other regularly drunk. They met at Reims in 1397 to consult on means of ending the papal schism, but whenever Charles had a lucid interval, Wenceslaus was in a stupor and so the conference, proving fruitless, was called off.

It makes an artistic ending. Yet in that same year Johann Gutenberg, who was to change the world, was born. In the next century appeared Joan of Arc, embodying the new spirit of nationalism, still pure like mountain water before it runs downhill; and Columbus, who opened a new hemisphere; and Copernicus, who revolutionized the concept of the earth's relation to the universe; and Michelangelo, whose sculptured visions gave men a new status; in those proud, superb, unconquered figures, the human being, not God, was captain.

As our century enters its final quarter, I am not persuaded, despite the 48 signs, that the end is necessarily doom. The doomsayers work by extrapolation; they take a trend and extend it, forgetting that the doom factor sooner or later generates a coping mechanism. I have a rule for this situation too, which is absolute: you cannot extrapolate any series in which the human element intrudes; history, that is, the human narrative, never follows, and will always fool, the scientific curve. I cannot tell you what twists it will take, but I expect, that like our ancestors, we, too, will muddle through.

AFTERWORD

In this essay Tuchman uses a technique that can serve for exploration and exposition of many subjects. It resembles analogy, where X is continually discussed in terms of Y, although X and Y are as different as chickens and baseball. Tuchman's technique is parallelism: finding the similarities in dissimilar things (people, activities, arts, eras) of the same class. Parallelism is comparison and contrast, extended as analogy extends metaphor. One may parallel whole eras or statesmen of different eras; or two scientists or a scientist and an artist; or two sports or a sport and a different pastime.

When we speak of parallelism we speak of something large enough to shape a whole essay and important enough to render that shape significant. Parallelism without import makes for hollow essays, mere skeletal frames to hang details on. The rule of thumb, for successful parallelism, resembles the cases of analogy and metaphor: Comparisons that work best combine the greatest improbability with the greatest reality of resolution.

BOOKS AVAILABLE IN PAPERBACK

A Distant Mirror: The Calamitous Fourteenth Century. New York: Ballantine. *Nonfiction.*

The Guns of August. New York: Bantam. *Nonfiction.*

The March of Folly: From Troy to Vietnam. New York: Ballantine. *Nonfiction.*

Notes from China. New York: Macmillan-Collier. *Nonfiction.*

Practicing History: Selected Essays. New York: Ballantine. *Essays.*

The Proud Tower: A Portrait of the World Before the War, 1890–1914. New York: Ballantine. *Nonfiction.*

Stilwell and the American Experience in China, 1911–1945. New York: Bantam. *Nonfiction.*

The Zimmerman Telegram. New York: Ballantine. *Nonfiction.*

ALICE
WALKER

A LICE WALKER *was born (1944) in Georgia, the youngest of eight children in a sharecropping family. She attended Spelman College in Atlanta, then transferred to Sarah Lawrence College in New York City, from which she graduated. She returned to Georgia, working in the civil rights movement and beginning to write. She taught at Jackson State College and Tougalo College in Mississippi and at Wellesley College. Now, after many years in New York, she lives in San Francisco and teaches at the University of California at Berkeley. Her mother still lives in Georgia, where Alice Walker travels from California to visit her.*

Walker has received a grant from the National Endowment for the Arts and a fellowship from the Radcliffe Institute. She has published a biography of Langston Hughes for young people, three books of poems, two collections of short stories, and three novels. Her most recent novel, The Color Purple, *won the Pulitzer Prize and the American Book Award in 1983.*

She first collected essays (including the one that follows) in a volume called In Search of Our Mothers' Gardens *(1983) and in 1988 added* Living by the Word: Selected Writing, 1973–1989. *For Alice Walker's work, the most important source has been her relationship with her mother, as she believes it is for other black women writers. When Walker is interviewed — the success of* The Color Purple *brought Alice Walker's name to the forefront of literary attention — she returns often to the subject of mothers. In an article in* Ms. *magazine she recalls three gifts that her mother gave her despite poverty (her mother worked all day in affluent kitchens and earned less than twenty dollars a week): a sewing machine, so that the young daughter could make her own dresses for school; at high school graduation a suitcase for going away; and — not the least important for the young author — a typewriter.*

In Search of
Our Mothers' Gardens

I described her own nature and temperament. Told how they needed a larger life for their expression. . . . I pointed out that in lieu of proper channels, her emotions had overflowed into paths that dissipated them. I talked, beautifully I thought, about an art that would be born, an art that would open the way for women the likes of her. I asked her to hope, and build up an inner life against the coming of that day. . . . I sang, with a strange quiver in my voice, a promise song.

> – "Avey," JEAN TOOMER, *Cane*
> *The poet speaking to a prostitute who falls asleep while he's talking*

When the poet Jean Toomer walked through the South in the early twenties, he discovered a curious thing: black women whose spirituality was so intense, so deep, so *unconscious*, they were themselves unaware of the richness they held. They stumbled blindly through their lives: creatures so abused and mutilated in body, so dimmed and confused by pain, that they considered themselves unworthy even of hope. In the selfless abstractions their bodies became to the men who used them, they became more than "sexual objects," more even than mere women: they became "Saints." Instead of being perceived as whole persons, their bodies became shrines: what was thought to be their minds became temples suitable for worship. These crazy Saints stared out at the world, wildly, like lunatics — or quietly, like suicides; and the "God" that was in their gaze was as mute as a great stone.

Who were these Saints? These crazy, loony, pitiful women?

Some of them, without a doubt, were our mothers and grandmothers.

In the still heat of the post-Reconstruction South, this is how they 4
seemed to Jean Toomer: exquisite butterflies trapped in an evil honey,
toiling away their lives in an era, a century, that did not acknowledge them,
except as "the *mule* of the world." They dreamed dreams that no one knew
— not even themselves, in any coherent fashion — and saw visions no one
could understand. They wandered or sat about the countryside crooning
lullabies to ghosts, and drawing the mother of Christ in charcoal on courthouse walls.

They forced their minds to desert their bodies and their striving spirits
sought to rise, like frail whirlwinds from the hard red clay. And when those
frail whirlwinds fell, in scattered particles, upon the ground, no one
mourned. Instead, men lit candles to celebrate the emptiness that remained,
as people do who enter a beautiful but vacant space to resurrect a God.

Our mothers and grandmothers, some of them: moving to music not
yet written. And they waited.

They waited for a day when the unknown thing that was in them would
be made known; but guessed, somehow in their darkness, that on the day
of their revelation they would be long dead. Therefore to Toomer they
walked, and even ran, in slow motion. For they were going nowhere
immediate, and the future was not yet within their grasp. And men took
our mothers and grandmothers, "but got no pleasure from it." So complex
was their passion and their calm.

To Toomer, they lay vacant and fallow as autumn fields, with harvest 8
time never in sight: and he saw them enter loveless marriages, without joy;
and become prostitutes, without resistance; and become mothers of children, without fulfillment.

For these grandmothers and mothers of ours were not Saints, but Artists;
driven to a numb and bleeding madness by the springs of creativity in
them for which there was no release. They were Creators, who lived lives
of spiritual waste, because they were so rich in spirituality — which is the
basis of Art — that the strain of enduring their unused and unwanted talent
drove them insane. Throwing away this spirituality was their pathetic attempt to lighten the soul to a weight their work-worn, sexually abused
bodies could bear.

What did it mean for a black woman to be an artist in our grandmothers'
time? In our great-grandmothers' day? It is a question with an answer cruel
enough to stop the blood.

Did you have a genius of a great-great-grandmother who died under
some ignorant and depraved white overseer's lash? Or was she required to
bake biscuits for a lazy backwater tramp, when she cried out in her soul to
paint watercolors of sunsets, or the rain falling on the green and peaceful
pasturelands? Or was her body broken and forced to bear children (who
were more often than not sold away from her) — eight, ten, fifteen, twenty

children — when her one joy was the thought of modeling heroic figures of rebellion, in stone or clay?

How was the creativity of the black woman kept alive, year after year 12 and century after century, when for most of the years black people have been in America, it was a punishable crime for a black person to read or write? And the freedom to paint, to sculpt, to expand the mind with action did not exist. Consider, if you can bear to imagine it, what might have been the result if singing, too, had been forbidden by law. Listen to the voices of Bessie Smith, Billie Holiday, Nina Simone, Roberta Flack, and Aretha Franklin, among others, and imagine those voices muzzled for life. Then you may begin to comprehend the lives of our "crazy," "Sainted" mothers and grandmothers. The agony of the lives of women who might have been Poets, Novelists, Essayists, and Short-Story Writers (over a period of centuries), who died with their real gifts stifled within them.

And, if this were the end of the story, we would have cause to cry out in my paraphrase of Okot p'Bitek's great poem:

> O, my clanswomen
> Let us all cry together!
> Come,
> Let us mourn the death of our mother,
> The death of a Queen
> The ash that was produced
> By a great fire!
> O, this homestead is utterly dead
> Close the gages
> With *lacari* thorns,
> For our mother
> The creator of the Stool is lost!
> And all the young men
> Have perished in the wilderness!

But this is not the end of the story, for all the young women — our mothers and grandmothers, *ourselves* — have not perished in the wilderness. And if we ask ourselves why, and search for and find the answer, we will know beyond all efforts to erase it from our minds, just exactly who, and of what, we black American women are.

One example, perhaps the most pathetic, most misunderstood one, can provide a backdrop for our mothers' work: Phillis Wheatley, a slave in the 1700s.

Virginia Woolf, in her book *A Room of One's Own*, wrote that in order 16 for a woman to write fiction she must have two things, certainly: a room of her own (with key and lock) and enough money to support herself.

What then are we to make of Phillis Wheatley, a slave, who owned not even herself? This sickly, frail black girl who required a servant of her own at times — her health was so precarious — and who, had she been white, would have been easily considered the intellectual superior of all the women and most of the men in the society of her day.

Virginia Woolf wrote further, speaking of course not of our Phillis, that "any woman born with a great gift in the sixteenth century [insert "eighteenth century," insert "black woman," insert "born or made a slave"] would certainly have gone crazed, shot herself, or ended her days in some lonely cottage outside the village, half witch, half wizard [insert "Saint"], feared and mocked at. For it needs little skill and psychology to be sure that a highly gifted girl who had tried to use her gift of poetry would have been so thwarted and hindered by contrary instincts [add "chains, guns, the lash, the ownership of one's body by someone else, submission to an alien religion"], that she must have lost her health and sanity to a certainty."

The key words, as they relate to Phillis, are "contrary instincts." For when we read the poetry of Phillis Wheatley — as when we read the novels of Nella Larsen or the oddly false-sounding autobiography of that freest of all black women writers, Zora Hurston — evidence of "contrary instincts" is everywhere. Her loyalties were completely divided, as was, without question, her mind.

But how could this be otherwise? Captured at seven, a slave of wealthy, doting whites who instilled in her the "savagery" of the Africa they "rescued" her from . . . one wonders if she was even able to remember her homeland as she had known it, or as it really was. 20

Yet, because she did try to use her gift for poetry in a world that made her a slave, she was "so thwarted and hindered by . . . contrary instincts, that she . . . lost her health. . . ." In the last years of her brief life, burdened not only with the need to express her gift but also with a penniless, friendless "freedom" and several small children for whom she was forced to do strenuous work to feed, she lost her health, certainly. Suffering from malnutrition and neglect and who knows what mental agonies, Phillis Wheatley died.

So torn by "contrary instincts" was black, kidnapped, enslaved Phillis that her description of "the Goddess" — as she poetically called the Liberty she did not have — is ironically, cruelly humorous. And, in fact, has held Phillis up to ridicule for more than a century. It is usually read prior to hanging Phillis's memory as that of a fool. She wrote:

> The Goddess comes, she moves divinely fair,
> Olive and laurel binds her *golden* hair.
> Wherever shines this native of the skies,
> Unnumber'd charms and recent graces rise. [My italics]

It is obvious that Phillis, the slave, combed the "Goddess's" hair every morning; prior, perhaps, to bringing in the milk, or fixing her mistress's lunch. She took her imagery from the one thing she saw elevated above all others.

With the benefit of hindsight we ask, "How could she?"   24

But at last, Phillis, we understand. No more snickering when your stiff, struggling, ambivalent lines are forced on us. We know now that you were not an idiot or a traitor; only a sickly little black girl, snatched from your home and country and made a slave; a woman who still struggled to sing the song that was your gift, although in a land of barbarians who praised you for your bewildered tongue. It is not so much what you sang, as that you kept alive, in so many of our ancestors, *the notion of song*.

Black women are called, in the folklore that so aptly identifies one's status in society, "the *mule* of the world," because we have been handed the burdens that everyone else — *everyone* else — refused to carry. We have also been called "Matriarchs," "Superwomen," and "Mean and Evil Bitches." Not to mention "Castraters" and "Sapphire's Mama." When we have pleaded for understanding, our character has been distorted; when we have asked for simple caring, we have been handed empty inspirational appellations, then stuck in the farthest corner. When we have asked for love, we have been given children. In short, even our plainer gifts, our labors of fidelity and love, have been knocked down our throats. To be an artist and a black woman, even today, lowers our status in many respects, rather than raises it: and yet, artists we will be.

Therefore we must fearlessly pull out of ourselves and look at and identify with our lives the living creativity some of our great-grandmothers were not allowed to know. I stress *some* of them because it is well known that the majority of our great-grandmothers knew, even without "knowing" it, the reality of their spirituality, even if they didn't recognize it beyond what happened in the singing at church — and they never had any intention of giving it up.

How they did it — those millions of black women who were not Phillis   28 Wheatley, or Lucy Terry or Frances Harper or Zora Hurston or Nella Larsen or Bessie Smith; or Elizabeth Catlett, or Katherine Dunham, either — brings me to the title of this essay, "In Search of Our Mothers' Gardens," which is a personal account that is yet shared, in its theme and its meaning, by all of us. I found, while thinking about the far-reaching world of the creative black woman, that often the truest answer to a question that really matters can be found very close.

In the late 1920s my mother ran away from home to marry my father. Marriage, if not running away, was expected of seventeen-year-old girls. By the time she was twenty, she had two children and was pregnant with a third. Five children later, I was born. And this is how I came to know my mother: she seemed a large, soft, loving-eyed woman who was rarely impatient in our home. Her quick, violent temper was on view only a few times a year, when she battled with the white landlord who had the misfortune to suggest to her that her children did not need to go to school.

She made all the clothes we wore, even my brothers' overalls. She made all the towels and sheets we used. She spent the summers canning vegetables and fruits. She spent the winter evenings making quilts enough to cover all our beds.

During the "working" day, she labored beside — not behind — my father in the fields. Her day began before sunup, and did not end until late at night. There was never a moment for her to sit down, undisturbed, to unravel her own private thoughts; never a time free from interruption — by work or the noisy inquiries of her many children. And yet, it is to my mother — and all our mothers who were not famous — that I went in search of the secret of what has fed that muzzled and often mutilated, but vibrant, creative spirit that the black woman has inherited, and that pops out in wild and unlikely places to this day.

But when, you will ask, did my overworked mother have time to know 32 or care about feeding the creative spirit?

The answer is so simple that many of us have spent years discovering it. We have constantly looked high, when we should have looked high — and low.

For example: in the Smithsonian Institution in Washington, D.C., there hangs a quilt unlike any other in the world. In fanciful, inspired, and yet simple and identifiable figures, it portrays the story of the Crucifixion. It is considered rare, beyond price. Though it follows no known pattern of quiltmaking, and though it is made of bits and pieces of worthless rags, it is obviously the work of a person of powerful imagination and deep spiritual feeling. Below this quilt I saw a note that says it was made by "an anonymous Black woman in Alabama, a hundred years ago."

If we could locate this "anonymous" black woman from Alabama, she would turn out to be one of our grandmothers — an artist who left her mark in the only materials she could afford, and in the only medium her position in society allowed her to use.

As Virginia Woolf wrote further, in *A Room of One's Own*:   36

> Yet genius of a sort must have existed among women as it must have existed among the working class. [Change this to "slaves" and "the wives and daughters of sharecroppers."] Now and again an Emily Brontë or a Robert Burns [change this to "a Zora Hurston or a Richard Wright"] blazes out and proves its presence. But certainly it never got itself on to paper. When, however, one reads of a witch being ducked, of a woman possessed by devils [or "Sainthood"], of a wise woman selling herbs [our root workers], or even a very remarkable man who had a mother, then I think we are on the

track of a lost novelist, a suppressed poet, or some mute and
inglorious Jane Austen. . . . Indeed, I would venture to guess
that Anon, who wrote so many poems without signing them,
was often a woman. . . .

And so our mothers and grandmothers have, more often than not
anonymously, handed on the creative spark, the seed of the flower they
themselves never hoped to see: or like a sealed letter they could not plainly
read.

And so it is, certainly, with my own mother. Unlike "Ma" Rainey's
songs, which retained their creator's name even while blasting forth from
Bessie Smith's mouth, no song or poem will bear my mother's name. Yet
so many of the stories that I write, that we all write, are my mother's
stories. Only recently did I fully realize this: that through years of listening
to my mother's stories of her life, I have absorbed not only the stories
themselves, but something of the manner in which she spoke, something
of the urgency that involves the knowledge that her stories — like her life
— must be recorded. It is probably for this reason that so much of what I
have written is about characters whose counterparts in real life are so much
older than I am.

But the telling of these stories, which came from my mother's lips as
naturally as breathing, was not the only way my mother showed herself as
an artist. For stories, too, were subject to being distracted, to dying without
conclusion. Dinners must be started, and cotton must be gathered before
the big rains. The artist that was and is my mother showed itself to me
only after many years. This is what I finally noticed:

Like Mem, a character in *The Third Life of Grange Copeland,* my mother 40
adorned with flowers whatever shabby house we were forced to live in.
And not just your typical straggly country stand of zinnias, either. She
planted ambitious gardens — and still does — with over fifty different
varieties of plants that bloom profusely from early March until late November. Before she left home for the fields, she watered her flowers, chopped
up the grass, and laid out new beds. When she returned from the fields
she might divide clumps of bulbs, dig a cold pit, uproot and replant roses,
or prune branches from her taller bushes or trees — until night came and
it was too dark to see.

Whatever she planted grew as if by magic, and her fame as a grower of
flowers spread over three counties. Because of her creativity with her flowers, even my memories of poverty are seen through a screen of blooms —
sunflowers, petunias, roses, dahlias, forsythia, spirea, delphiniums, ver-
bena . . . and on and on.

And I remember people coming to my mother's yard to be given cuttings
from her flowers; I hear again the praise showered on her because whatever

rocky soil she landed on, she turned into a garden. A garden so brilliant with colors, so original in its design, so magnificent with life and creativity, that to this day people drive by our house in Georgia — perfect strangers and imperfect strangers — and ask to stand or walk among my mother's art.

I notice that it is only when my mother is working in her flowers that she is radiant, almost to the point of being invisible — except as Creator: hand and eye. She is involved in work her soul must have. Ordering the universe in the image of her personal conception of Beauty.

Her face, as she prepares the Art that is her gift, is a legacy of respect 44 she leaves to me, for all that illuminates and cherishes life. She has handed down respect for the possibilities — and the will to grasp them.

For her, so hindered and intruded upon in so many ways, being an artist has still been a daily part of her life. This ability to hold on, even in very simple ways, is work black women have done for a very long time.

This poem is not enough, but it is something, for the woman who literally covered the holes in our walls with sunflowers:

> They were women then
> My mama's generation
> Husky of voice — Stout of
> Step
> With fists as well as
> Hands
> How they battered down
> Doors
> And ironed
> Starched white
> Shirts
> How they led
> Armies
> Headragged Generals
> Across mined
> Fields
> Booby-trapped
> Kitchens
> To discover books
> Desks
> A place for us
> How they knew what we
> *Must* know
> Without knowing a page
> Of it
> Themselves.

Guided by my heritage of a love of beauty and a respect for strength — in search of my mother's garden, I found my own.

And perhaps in Africa over two hundred years ago, there was just such 48 a mother; perhaps she painted vivid and daring decorations in oranges and yellows and greens on the walls of her hut; perhaps she sang — in a voice like Roberta Flack's — *sweetly* over the compounds of her village; perhaps she wove the most stunning mats or told the most ingenious stories of all the village storytellers. Perhaps she was herself a poet — though only her daughter's name is signed to the poems that we know.

Perhaps Phillis Wheatley's mother was also an artist.

Perhaps in more than Phillis Wheatley's biological life is her mother's signature made clear.

AFTERWORD

Walker's writing is lyrical, metaphorical. She leaps from place to place, making images that carry feeling, seldom telling us the names of feelings unless image and metaphor have already established the emotion. For the reader timid about metaphor, her rapid improvisations may puzzle or confound; metaphor lovers luxuriate in her vigor, intelligence, and vivacity. Look at the fifth paragraph: Spirits leaving bodies turn into whirlwinds which exhaust themselves and become dust; by implication — "mourned" — they die. These whirlwind-spirits came from the bodies of women; when they die the men don't mourn them but worship the absence they left behind.

This thinking, not entirely logical, progresses by pictures and comparisons; it is the thinking of poetry.

BOOKS AVAILABLE IN PAPERBACK

The Color Purple. New York: Washington Square Press. *Novel.*

Good Night, Willie Lee, I'll See You in the Morning: Poems. San Diego: Harcourt Brace Jovanovich. *Poetry.*

Horses Make a Landscape Look More Beautiful: Poems. San Diego: Harcourt Brace Jovanovich. *Poetry.*

In Love and Trouble: Stories of Black Women. San Diego: Harcourt Brace Jovanovich. *Short stories.*

In Search of Our Mothers' Gardens: Womanist Prose. San Diego: Harcourt Brace Jovanovich. *Essays.*

Meridian. New York: Washington Square Press. *Novel.*

Once: Poems. San Diego: Harcourt Brace Jovanovich. *Poetry.*

Meridian. New York: Washington Square Press. *Novel*.

Revolutionary Petunias and Other Poems. San Diego: Harcourt Brace Jovanovich. *Poetry*.

The Third Life of Grange Copeland. San Diego: Harcourt Brace Jovanovich. *Novel*.

You Can't Keep a Good Woman Down: Stories. San Diego: Harcourt Brace Jovanovich. *Short stories*.

EUDORA
WELTY

EUDORA WELTY (b. 1909) published her Collected Stories *in 1980, bringing together 576 pages of the short fiction for which she is celebrated. Her short stories first appeared in magazines, often the literary quarterlies, and became regular features of annual collections of the best fiction from periodicals. Two of her most enduring stories are "Why I Live at the P.O.," which shows her comic genius, and "The Worn Path," which recounts the courage and perseverance of an old black woman.*

Among her novels are Delta Wedding *(1946),* Losing Battles *(1970), and* The Optimist's Daughter *(1972), which won the Pulitzer Prize. "The Little Store" comes from* The Eye of the Story *(1978), which is a collection of her essays, most on the art of fiction. In 1983 she delivered the William E. Massey Lectures at Harvard and a year later brought them out as a volume of recollections,* One Writer's Beginnings. *She has won the Gold Medal of the National Institute of Arts and Letters, the National Medal for Literature, and the Presidential Medal of Freedom.*

Born in Jackson, Mississippi, she still resides in Jackson, Mississippi. In this small town, her observation and imagination have found all the material they require.

When she writes an essay out of memory, as she does in "The Little Store," she brings to reminiscence the storyteller's skills of narration and use of significant detail. Maybe more important, she also brings the stylist's ear for rhythms of word and sentence that compel attention. Her gifts for evoking intimacy and cherished detail lead in the end to hints of the darker vision that underlies her best work.

The Little Store

Two blocks away from the Mississippi State Capitol, and on the same street with it, where our house was when I was a child growing up in Jackson, it was possible to have a little pasture behind your backyard where you could keep a Jersey cow, which we did. My mother herself milked her. A thrifty homemaker, wife, mother of three, she also did all her own cooking. And as far as I can recall, she never set foot inside a grocery store. It wasn't necessary.

For her regular needs, she stood at the telephone in our front hall and consulted with Mr. Lemly, of Lemly's Market and Grocery downtown, who took her order and sent it out on his next delivery. And since Jackson at the heart of it was still within very near reach of the open country, the blackberry lady clanged on her bucket with a quart measure at your front door in June without fail, the watermelon man rolled up to your house exactly on time for the Fourth of July, and down through the summer, the quiet of the early-morning streets was pierced by the calls of farmers driving in with their plenty. One brought his with a song, so plaintive we would sing it with him:

> "Milk, milk,
> Buttermilk,
> Snap beans — butterbeans —
> Tender okra — fresh greens . . .
> And buttermilk."

My mother considered herself pretty well prepared in her kitchen and pantry for any emergency that, in her words, might choose to present itself. But if she should, all of a sudden, need another lemon or find she was out of bread, all she had to do was call out, "Quick! Who'd like to run to the Little Store for me?"

I would.

4

She'd count out the change into my hand, and I was away. I'll bet the nickel that would be left over that all over the country, for those of my day, the neighborhood grocery played a similar part in our growing up.

Our store had its name — it was that of the grocer who owned it, whom I'll call Mr. Sessions — but "the Little Store" is what we called it at home. It was a block down our street toward the capitol and a half a block further, around the corner, toward the cemetery. I knew even the sidewalk to it as well as I knew my own skin. I'd skipped my jumping-rope up and down it, hopped its length through mazes of hopscotch, played jacks in its islands of shade, serpentined along it on my Princess bicycle, skated it backward and forward. In the twilight I had dragged my steamboat by its string (this was homemade out of every new shoebox, with candle in the bottom lighted and shining through colored tissue paper pasted over windows scissored out in the shapes of the sun, moon, and stars) across every crack of the walk without letting it bump or catch fire. I'd "played out" on that street after supper with my brothers and friends as long as "first-dark" lasted; I'd caught its lightning bugs. On the first Armistice Day° (and this will set the time I'm speaking of) we made our own parade down that walk on a single velocipede — my brother pedaling, our little brother riding the handlebars, and myself standing on the back, all with arms wide, flying flags in each hand. (My father snapped that picture as we raced by. It came out blurred.)

As I set forth for the Little Store, a tune would float toward me from the house where there lived three sisters, girls in their teens, who ratted their hair over their ears, wore headbands like gladiators, and were considered to be very popular. They practiced for this in the daytime; they'd wind up the Victrola, leave the same record on they'd played before, and you'd see them bobbing past their dining-room windows while they danced with each other. Being three, they could go all day, cutting in:

> "Everybody ought to know-oh
> How to do the Tickle-Toe
> (how to do the Tickle-Toe)" —

they sang it and danced to it, and as I went by to the same song, I believed it.

A little further on, across the street, was the house where the principal 8 of our grade school lived — lived on, even while we were having vacation. What if she would come out? She would halt me in my tracks — she had a very carrying and well-known voice in Jackson, where she'd taught almost everybody — saying "Eudora Alice Welty, spell OBLIGE." OBLIGE was the

---

the first Armistice Day   November 11, 1918, marked the end of World War I. Now celebrated as Veterans Day.

word that she of course knew had kept me from making 100 on my spelling exam. She'd make me miss it again now, by boring her eyes through me from across the street. This was my vacation fantasy, one good way to scare myself on the way to the store.

Down near the corner waited the house of a little boy named Lindsey. The sidewalk here was old brick, which the roots of a giant chinaberry tree had humped up and tilted this way and that. On skates, you took it fast, in a series of skittering hops, trying not to touch ground anywhere. If the chinaberries had fallen and rolled in the cracks, it was like skating through a whole shooting match of marbles. I crossed my fingers that Lindsey wouldn't be looking.

During the big flu epidemic he and I, as it happened, were being nursed through our sieges at the same time. I'd hear my father and mother murmuring to each other, at the end of a long day, "And I wonder how poor little *Lindsey* got along today?" Just as, down the street, he no doubt would have to hear his family saying, "And I wonder how is poor *Eudora* by now?" I got the idea that a choice was going to be made soon between poor little Lindsey and poor Eudora, and I came up with a funny poem. I wasn't prepared for it when my father told me it wasn't funny and my mother cried that if I couldn't be ashamed for myself, she'd have to be ashamed for me:

> There was a little boy and his name was Lindsey.
> He went to heaven with the influinzy.

He didn't, he survived it, poem and all, the same as I did. But his chinaberries could have brought me down in my skates in a flying act of contrition before his eyes, looking pretty funny myself, right in front of his house.

Setting out in this world, a child feels so indelible. He only comes to find out later that it's all the others along his way who are making themselves indelible to him.

Our Little Store rose right up from the sidewalk; standing in a street of 12 family houses, it alone hadn't any yard in front, any tree or flowerbed. It was a plain frame building covered over with brick. Above the door, a little railed porch ran across on an upstairs level and four windows with shades were looking out. But I didn't catch on to those.

Running in out of the sun, you met what seemed total obscurity inside. There were almost tangible smells — licorice recently sucked in a child's cheek, dill-pickle brine that had leaked through a paper sack in a fresh trail across the wooden floor, ammonia-loaded ice that had been hoisted from wet croker sacks and slammed into the icebox with its sweet butter at the door, and perhaps the smell of still-untrapped mice.

Then through the motes of cracker dust, cornmeal dust, the Gold Dust of the Gold Dust Twins that the floor had been swept out with, the realities emerged. Shelves climbed to high reach all the way around, set out with not too much of any one thing but a lot of things — lard, molasses, vinegar, starch, matches, kerosene, Octagon soap (about a year's worth of octagon-shaped coupons cut out and saved brought a signet ring addressed to you in the mail. Furthermore, when the postman arrived at your door, he blew a whistle). It was up to you to remember what you came for, while your eye traveled from cans of sardines to ice cream salt to harmonicas to flypaper (over your head, batting around on a thread beneath the blades of the ceiling fan, stuck with its testimonial catch).

Its confusion may have been in the eye of its beholder. Enchantment is cast upon you by all those things you weren't supposed to have need for, it lures you close to wooden tops you'd outgrown, boy's marbles and agates in little net pouches, small rubber balls that wouldn't bounce straight, frazzly kite-string, clay bubble-pipes that would snap off in your teeth, the stiffest scissors. You could contemplate those long narrow boxes of sparklers gathering dust while you waited for it to be the Fourth of July or Christmas, and noisemakers in the shape of tin frogs for somebody's birthday party you hadn't been invited to yet, and see that they were all marvelous.

You might not have even looked for Mr. Sessions when he came around 16 his store cheese (as big as a doll's house) and in front of the counter looking for you. When you'd finally asked him for, and received from him in its paper bag, whatever single thing it was that you had been sent for, the nickel that was left over was yours to spend.

Down at a child's eye level, inside those glass jars with mouths in their sides through which the grocer could run his scoop or a child's hand might be invited to reach for a choice, were wineballs, all-day suckers, gumdrops, peppermints. Making a row under the glass of a counter were the Tootsie Rolls, Hershey Bars, Goo-Goo Clusters, Baby Ruths. And whatever was the name of those pastilles that came stacked in a cardboard cylinder with a cardboard lid? They were thin and dry, about the size of tiddlywinks, and in the shape of twisted rosettes. A kind of chocolate dust came out with them when you shook them out in your hand. Were they chocolate? I'd say rather they were brown. They didn't taste of anything at all, unless it was wood. Their attraction was the number you got for a nickel.

Making up your mind, you circled the store around and around, around the pickle barrel, around the tower of Cracker Jack boxes; Mr. Sessions had built it for us himself on top of a packing case, like a house of cards.

If it seemed too hot for Cracker Jacks, I might get a cold drink. Mr. Sessions might have already stationed himself by the cold-drinks barrel, like a mind reader. Deep in ice water that looked black as ink, murky shapes that would come up as Coca-Colas, Orange Crushes, and various flavors of pop, were all swimming around together. When you gave the word, Mr. Sessions plunged his bare arm in to the elbow and fished out your choice, first try. I favored a locally bottled concoction called Lake's Celery. (What else could it be called? It was made by a Mr. Lake out of celery. It was a popular drink here for years but was not known universally, as I found out when I arrived in New York and ordered one in the Astor bar.) You drank on the premises, with feet set wide apart to miss the drip, and gave him back his bottle.

But he didn't hurry you off. A standing scales was by the door, with a   20 stack of iron weights and a brass slide on the balance arm, that would weigh you up to three hundred pounds. Mr. Sessions, whose hands were gentle and smelled of carbolic, would lift you up and set your feet on the platform, hold your loaf of bread for you, and taking his time while you stood still for him, he would make certain of what you weighed today. He could even remember what you weighed last time, so you could subtract and announce how much you'd gained. That was goodbye.

Is there always a hard way to go home? From the Little Store, you could go partway through the sewer. If your brothers had called you a scarecat, then across the next street beyond the Little Store, it was possible to enter this sewer by passing through a privet hedge, climbing down into the bed of a creek, and going into its mouth on your knees. The sewer — it might have been no more than a "storm sewer" — came out and emptied here, where Town Creek, a sandy, most often shallow little stream that ambled through Jackson on its way to the Pearl River, ran along the edge of the cemetery. You could go in darkness through this tunnel to where you next saw light (if you ever did) and climb out through the culvert at your own street corner.

I was a scarecat, all right, but I was a reader with my own refuge in storybooks. Making my way under the sidewalk, under the street and the street-car track, under the Little Store, down there in the wet dark by myself, I could be Persephone° entering into my six-month sojourn underground — though I didn't suppose Persephone had to crawl, hanging onto a loaf of bread, and come out through the teeth of an iron grating. Mother Ceres° would indeed be wondering where she could find me, and mad when she knew. "Now am I going to have to start marching to the Little Store for *myself?*"

I couldn't picture it. Indeed I'm unable today to picture the Little Store with a grown person in it, except for Mr. Sessions and the lady who helped

---

Persephone In Greek mythology, the daughter of Zeus and Demeter. She is abducted by Pluto to reign with him in the underworld for six months of every year.
Ceres The Roman name for Demeter, mother of Persephone.

him, who belonged there. We children thought it was ours. The happiness of errands was in part that of running for the moment away from home, a free spirit. I believed the Little Store to be a center of the outside world, and hence of happiness — as I believed what I found in the Cracker Jack box to be a genuine prize, which was as simply as I believed in the Golden Fleece.°

But a day came when I ran to the store to discover, sitting on the front   24 step, a grown person, after all — more than a grown person. It was the Monkey Man, together with his monkey. His grinding-organ was lowered to the step beside him. In my whole life so far, I must have laid eyes on the Monkey Man no more than five or six times. An itinerant of rare and wayward appearances, he was not punctual like the Gipsies, who every year with the first cool days of fall showed up in the aisles of Woolworth's. You never knew when the Monkey Man might decide to favor Jackson, or which way he'd go. Sometimes you heard him as close as the next street, and then he didn't come up yours.

But now I saw the Monkey Man at the Little Store, where I'd never seen him before. I'd never seen him sitting down. Low on that familiar doorstep, he was not the same any longer, and neither was his monkey. They looked just like an old man and an old friend of his that wore a fez, meeting quietly together, tired, and resting with their eyes fixed on some place far away, and not the same place. Yet their romance for me didn't have it in its power to waver. I wavered. I simply didn't know how to step around them, to proceed on into the Little Store for my mother's emergency as if nothing had happened. If I could have gone in there after it, whatever it was, I would have given it to them — putting it into the monkey's cool little fingers. I would have given them the Little Store itself.

In my memory they are still attached to the store — so are all the others. Everyone I saw on my way seemed to me then part of my errand, and in a way they were. As I myself, the free spirit, was part of it too.

All the years we lived in that house where we children were born, the same people lived in the other houses on our street too. People changed through the arithmetic of birth, marriage, and death, but not by going away. So families just accrued stories, which through the fullness of time, in those times, their own lives made. And I grew up in those.

But I didn't know there'd ever been a story at the Little Store, one that   28 was going on while I was there. Of course, all the time the Sessions family had been living right overhead there, in the upstairs rooms behind the little railed porch and the shaded windows; but I think we children never

---

Golden Fleece   In Greek mythology, the fleece of the golden ram, stolen by Jason and the Argonauts.

thought of that. Did I fail to see them as a family because they weren't living in an ordinary house? Because I so seldom saw them close together, or having anything to say to each other? She sat in the back of the store, her pencil over a ledger, while he stood and waited on children to make up their minds. They worked in twin black eyeshades, held on their gray heads by elastic bands. It may be harder to recognize kindness — or unkindness either — in a face whose eyes are in shadow. His face underneath his shade was as round as the little wooden wheels in the Tinker Toy box. So was her face. I didn't know, perhaps didn't even wonder: were they husband and wife or brother and sister? Were they father and mother? There were a few other persons, of various ages, wandering singly in by the back door and out. But none of their relationships could I imagine, when I'd never seen them sitting down together around their own table.

The possibility that they had any other life at all, anything beyond what we could see within the four walls of the Little Store, occurred to me only when tragedy struck their family. There was some act of violence. The shock to the neighborhood traveled to the children, of course; but I couldn't find out from my parents what had happened. They held it back from me, as they'd already held back many things, "until the time comes for you to know."

You could find out some of these things by looking in the unabridged dictionary and the encyclopedia — kept to hand in our dining room — but you couldn't find out there what had happened to the family who for all the years of your life had lived upstairs over the Little Store, who had never been anything but patient and kind to you, who never once had sent you away. All I ever knew was its aftermath: they were the only people ever known to me who simply vanished. At the point where their life overlapped into ours, the story broke off.

We weren't being sent to the neighborhood grocery for facts of life, or death. But of course those are what we were on the track of, anyway. With the loaf of bread and the Cracker Jack prize, I was bringing home the intimations of pride and disgrace, and rumors and early news of people coming to hurt one another, while others practiced for joy — storing up a portion for myself of the human mystery.

AFTERWORD

Criticizing writers whom we read in silence, often without moving our lips, we speak in metaphor of the author's voice, meaning the collective idiosyncrasies of a writer's style. In another metaphor, we sometimes call style the writer's signature.

The latter compares diction and syntax to the individual flourishes of handwriting; the former compares style to the characteristic noises of the human voicebox: accent, pitch, rhythm.

The more stylish the writer, the more do the words on the page control our hearing of them. And the best silent readers hear: *When I read poetry silently for an hour or two my throat gets tired from all that squeezing. Some prose — Henry James, Ernest Hemingway, Katherine Anne Porter, Eudora Welty — tires out the throat, or the tapping foot, as much as poetry does. Try out the pacing and pitch of Welty's long, idiomatic, characteristic first sentence: The first phrase so clearly* waits *for its attachment, you must pitch it high; the second phrase qualifies or tags the first, dangles from it attached by a thread; we drop the pitch of our voices to indicate that this phrase only specifies the one before it; the third phrase drops down even lower, maybe taxing the range of our pitch; here we learn further the identity of this place and receive important exposition in the guise of location.*

Then comes the main clause — "it was possible" *— and the sentence's conclusion, which gives us the* reason *the sentence started,* "Two blocks away from the Mississippi State Capitol." *Here in the main clause the voice finds its middle range: Here we find a main verb and a qualifying clause on the same pitch level: What kind of little pasture? The kind where you would keep a Jersey cow. These eighteen words, just before the end, are the meat and potato of the sentence and make sense of the earlier anticipatory phrases that kept us waiting. The sweetest measure of voice comes last, the dessert:* "which we did." *After the eighteen-word main clause, here is a comic three-word, three-syllable afterthought, plunk plunk plunk — as Welty with good-humored mimetic skill works on us with the rhythms of childhood.*

BOOKS AVAILABLE IN PAPERBACK

The Bride of Innisfallen and Other Stores. San Diego: Harcourt Brace Jovanovich. *Short stories.*

The Collected Stories of Eudora Welty. San Diego: Harcourt Brace Jovanovich. *Short stories.*

A Curtain of Green and Other Stories. San Diego: Harcourt Brace Jovanovich. *Short stories.*

Delta Wedding. San Diego: Harcourt Brace Jovanovich. *Novel.*

The Eye of the Story: Selected Essays and Reviews. New York: Random House-Vintage. *Essays.*

The Golden Apples. San Diego: Harcourt Brace Jovanovich. *Short stories.*

The Hitch-Hikers. New York: Dramatists Play. *Play.*

Losing Battles. New York: Random House-Vintage. *Novel.*

One Writer's Beginnings. New York: Warner. *Nonfiction*.

The Optimist's Daughter. New York: Random House-Vintage. *Novel*.

The Ponder Heart. San Diego: Harcourt Brace Jovanovich. *Novel*.

The Robber Bridegroom. San Diego: Harcourt Brace Jovanovich. *Novel*.

Thirteen Stories. San Diego: Harcourt Brace Jovanovich. *Short stories*.

The Wide Net and Other Stories. San Diego: Harcourt Brace Jovanovich. *Short stories*.

GEORGE F.
WILL

EORGE F. WILL *grew up in Illinois (b. 1941), where his father was a*
professor, and started by following in his father's footsteps. He attended
Oxford University after he graduated from Trinity College, then took his Ph.D. at
Princeton University and taught politics at Michigan State University. After a year
at the University of Toronto, he moved to Washington as an aide to Senator Gordon
Alcott of Colorado. He wrote regularly for the National Review *from 1972 to 1976*
and started his newspaper column, syndicated out of the Washington Post, *in 1974.*
In 1977 his columns won him a Pulitzer Prize. He appears frequently on television
and writes another column for Newsweek. *America's leading conservative jour-*
nalist remains unpredictable: It is not typical of conservatives to oppose prayer in
the schools.

Will has collected his columns in books: The Pursuit of Happiness and Other
Sobering Thoughts *(1979),* The Pursuit of Virtue and Other Tory Notions
(1972), and The Morning After *(1986), from which we take this essay. Other*
books include Statecraft as Soulcraft: What Government Does *(1983) and* The
New Season: A Spectator's Guide to the 1988 Election *(1987).*

Against
Prefabricated Prayer

I stand foursquare with the English ethicist who declared: "I am fully convinced that the highest life can only be lived on a foundation of Christian belief — or some substitute for it." But President Reagan's constitutional amendment concerning prayer in public schools is a mistake.

His proposal reads: "Nothing in this Constitution shall be construed to prohibit individual or group prayer in public schools or other public institutions. No person shall be required by the United States or by any state to participate in prayer." This would restore the *status quo ante* the 1962 Supreme Court ruling that public school prayers violate the ban on "establishment" of religion. The amendment would not settle the argument about prayer; it would relocate the argument. All 50 states, or perhaps all 3,041 county governments, or all 16,214 school districts would have to decide whether to have "voluntary" prayers. But the issue is not really voluntary prayers for individuals. The issue is organized prayers for groups of pupils subject to compulsory school attendance laws. In a 1980 resolution opposing "government authored or sponsored religious exercises in public schools," the Southern Baptist Convention noted that "the Supreme Court has not held that it is illegal for any individual to pray or read his or her Bible in public schools."

This nation is even more litigious than religious, and the school prayer issue has prompted more, and more sophisticated, arguments about constitutional law than about the nature of prayer. But fortunately Senator Jack Danforth is an ordained Episcopal priest and is the only person ever to receive degrees from the Yale Law School and the Yale Divinity School on the same day. Danforth is too polite to pose the question quite this pointedly, but the question is: Is public school prayer apt to serve authentic religion, or is it apt to be mere attitudinizing, a thin gruel of vague religious vocabulary? Religious exercises should arise from a rich tradition, and reflect that richness. Prayer, properly understood, arises from the context of the praying person's particular faith. So, Danforth argues, "for those within a religious tradition, it simply is not true that one prayer is as good as any other."

One person's prayer may not be any sort of prayer to another person [4] whose devotion is to a different tradition. To children from certain kinds of Christian families, a "nondenominational" prayer that makes no mention of Jesus Christ would be incoherent. The differences between Christian and

Jewish expressions of piety are obvious; the differences between Protestants and Roman Catholics regarding, for example, Mary and the saints are less obvious, but they are not trivial to serious religious sensibilities. And as Danforth says, a lowest-common-denominator prayer would offend all devout persons. "Prayer that is so general and so diluted as not to offend those of most faiths is not prayer at all. True prayer is robust prayer. It is bold prayer. It is almost by definition sectarian prayer."

Liturgical reform in the Roman Catholic and Episcopal churches has occasioned fierce controversies that seem disproportionate, if not unintelligible, to persons who are ignorant of or indifferent about those particular religious traditions. But liturgy is a high art and a serious business because it is designed to help turn minds from worldly distractions, toward transcendent things. Collective prayer should express a shared inner state, one that does not occur easily and spontaneously. A homogenized religious recitation, perfunctorily rendered by children who have just tumbled in from a bus or playground, is not apt to arise from the individual wills, as real prayer must.

Buddhists are among the almost 90 religious organizations in America that have at least 50,000 members. Imagine, Danforth urges, the Vietnamese Buddhist in a fourth-grade class in, say, Mississippi. How does that child deal with a "voluntary" prayer that is satisfactory to the local Baptists? Or imagine a child from America's growing number of Muslims, for whom prayer involves turning toward Mecca and prostrating oneself. Muslim prayer is adoration of Allah; it involves no requests and asks no blessing, as most Christian prayers do. Reagan says: "No one will ever convince me that a moment of voluntary prayer will harm a child . . ." Danforth asks: How is America — or religion — served by the embarrassment of children who must choose between insincere compliance with, or conscientious abstention from, a ritual?

In a nation where millions of adults (biologically speaking) affect the Jordache look or whatever designer's whim is *de rigueur,* peer pressure on children is not a trivial matter. Supporters of Reagan's amendment argue that a nine-year-old is "free" to absent himself or otherwise abstain from a "voluntary" prayer — an activity involving his classmates and led by that formidable authority figure, his teacher. But that argument is akin to one heard a century ago from persons who said child labor laws infringed the precious freedom of children to contract to work 10-hour days in coal mines.

To combat the trivializing of religion and the coercion of children who 8 take their own religious traditions seriously, Danforth suggests enacting the following distinction: "The term 'voluntary prayer' shall not include any prayer composed, prescribed, directed, supervised, or organized by an official or employee of a state or local government agency, including public school principals and teachers." When religion suffers the direct assistance of nervous politicians, the result is apt to confirm the judgment of the child who prayed not to God but for God because "if anything happens to Him, we're properly sunk."

It is, to say no more, curious that, according to some polls, more Americans favor prayers in schools than regularly pray in church. Supermarkets sell processed cheese and instant mashed potatoes, so many Americans must like bland substitutes for real things. But it is one thing for the nation's palate to tolerate frozen waffles; it is another and more serious thing for the nation's soul to be satisfied with add-water-and-stir instant religiosity. When government acts as liturgist for a pluralistic society, the result is bound to be a purée that is tasteless, in several senses.

AFTERWORD

Here is the essay as newspaper column, a form practiced also by Russell Baker.

The newspaper column is a small industry to itself. Many of us start every day with Ellen Goodman, Herb Caen, Art Buchwald, Jack Anderson, or Jimmy Breslin. When I started collecting material for this edition I expected to include several columnists — but it is part of the job description, for a columnist, to write for the moment; ephemerality is almost a virtue. George F. Will cements his daily observations into the foundation of a conservative citadel, which tends to give his columns more staying power.

There is also the grace and wit of his writing, which is allusive and dandified; some of his ideological enemies find him affected. He is quick on his feet and ironic in his manner. To counter the notion of a nine-year-old's voluntary prayer, he calls the argument "akin to one heard a century ago from persons who said child labor laws infringed the precious freedom of children to contract to work 10-hour days in coal mines."

Will ends with a tasteless analogy which bears rereading.

BOOKS AVAILABLE IN PAPERBACK

The Morning After: American Successes and Excesses. New York: Macmillan. *Essays.*

The Pursuit of Happiness and Other Sobering Thoughts. New York: Harper & Row. *Essays.*

The Pursuit of Virtue and Other Tory Notions. New York: Simon & Schuster-Touchstone. *Essays.*

Statecraft as Soulcraft: What Government Does. New York: Simon & Schuster-Touchstone. *Nonfiction.*

TOM
WOLFE

*T*OM WOLFE *(b. 1931), known as a master of the new journalism, is not to be confused with the novelist Thomas Wolfe (1900–1938), who wrote* Look Homeward, Angel. *The contemporary Tom Wolfe for decades was famous not for fiction but for essays that encroach upon fiction's territory; in 1987 he published his first novel,* The Bonfire of the Vanities, *and now he is famous for fiction too. For that matter he has published as an illustrator and exhibited his drawings in one-man shows. See also Guy Davenport; see John Berger.*

He was born in Virginia, attended Washington and Lee University, and received a Ph.D. in American Studies from Yale. Instead of turning professor, Wolfe became journalist, first as a reporter — he was Latin American correspondent for the Washington Post — *and then as a feature writer for magazines. The first examples of his hyperventilated prose style appeared in* Esquire *and in the New York* Herald Tribune's *Sunday magazine, called* New York. *He continued to write for* New York *when it survived the death of the newspaper, and for* Harper's *magazine as well.*

Wolfe's books began with The Kandy-Kolored Tangerine-Flake Streamline Baby *(1968), in which he examined facets of popular culture. The* Electric Kool-

Aid Acid Test *(1968) told of Ken Kesey's Merry Pranksters, dropouts, speed-freaks, and acid-heads of the 1960s.* The Pump House Gang *(1968) explored the California surfing culture, and* Radical Chic and Mau-mauing the Flak Catchers *(1970) discussed fashions in politics. Fashions in art and architecture occupied* The Painted Word *(1975) and* From Bauhaus to Our House *(1981).* The Right Stuff *(1979), which won an American Book Award for general nonfiction, was about the military test pilots who became the astronauts of the American space program, men accustomed to trying out experimental aircraft. Later it became a movie. In 1982 he published* The Purple Decade, *which collected essays from his earlier books.*

Wolfe is sometimes credited with inventing the new journalism; just as widely, critics deny him the credit or deny that this journalism is new. Surely Tom Wolfe's style is his own, and certain features are idiosyncratic — his frequent use of ellipses, his careening sentences and sentence fragments, his energetic use of slang, idiom, and professional jargon. Perhaps his major innovation has been the subjectivity of his reportage, his frequent attempts to enter the minds of his subjects as if they were characters in a novel and he the novelist who invented them. Whatever we decide about Wolfe's originality, we cannot deny his success. He has a genius for inventing phrases that quickly seem inevitable. Among his other gifts to the language, Tom Wolfe has contributed "radical chic," "the me-decade," and, most recently, "the right stuff."

He keeps on doing his journalism. This essay turned up in Popular Mechanics *in July 1986.*

Land of Wizards

The threat was delivered to Lemelson's lawyer. "Tell your client we're gonna bury him under a ton of paper." Lemelson wasn't too worried. He thought it was a figure of speech.

So the next day, Lemelson is in the courtroom, sitting at the plaintiff's table with his lawyer, waiting for the proceedings to begin. Lemelson is an inventor. He invented the automated warehouse, the automated machine shop, one of the first two industrial robots, several robot-vision machines, the drive mechanism of the audio cassette player, and 380 other things. He holds more patents than anybody except the great Edison himself and Edwin Land, inventor of the Polaroid camera. This causes him to be in courtrooms a great deal.

Many corporations manufacture his inventions, but not many mention it to him beforehand.

So it is on this particular day Jerome H. Lemelson is in a court of law   4
under the usual circumstances, charging a manufacturer with patent infringement. The lawyers for the manufacturer are right across from him at
the defendant's table. Between the two tables and the judge's bench is a
fifteen-foot stretch of floor.

The next thing Lemelson knows, the door to the courtroom opens, and
here comes a trucker's helper pushing a hand truck with archive boxes
piled from the fender on the bottom to the curve of the handles at the top.

An archive box is a box made of heavy cardboard with oak-grain patterns
printed on it to make it look like wood. On one end of the box is a little
metal frame that holds a card describing the contents. The box has a lid,
like a shoe box. Inside, there is room for a dozen reams of documents,
usually arranged in file folders with little tabs sticking up. However you
want to arrange it, you can get about forty pounds of paper into each box.

Fascinated, the way the chickadee is fascinated by the snake, Lemelson
watches as the trucker's helper begins unloading the boxes. He puts them
right on the floor between the tables and the judge's bench. One of the
lawyers is out there like a field commander, pointing to spots on the floor.
This one goes here. That one goes there. No sooner is that load arranged
than the courtroom door opens again, and here comes another teamster,
puffing and pushing a fresh load of archive boxes on a hand truck. Now
he's lugging his stack off the hand truck and putting it on the floor. The
door opens again. Here comes another yobbo pushing a hand truck with
archive boxes piled as tall as he is. You can hear the floor groaning from
the weight of the load as the wheels roll over the hardwood.

The field commander is out there, and the archive boxes are lining up   8
in rows like a tank formation. Lemelson's pale gray-blue eyes are the size
of radar dishes. He's speechless. The cargo humpers keep coming. Pretty
soon seventy or eighty square feet of floor is occupied by this squat battalion
of archive boxes. You don't have to be an engineering genius like Lemelson
to figure out that there is now a ton of paper sitting there. More than a
ton, perhaps a ton and a half.

"Well," Lemelson says to his lawyer, "at least it's not on top of me."

Neither of them laughed. They both had the feeling it was only a matter
of time. There was a judge but no jury. Apparently the ton of paper was
supposed to impress the judge and intimidate Lemelson.

Something impressed the judge; no question about that. Lemelson lost.
It wasn't even close.

He gritted his teeth and announced he was going to appeal. The next   12
message said: "O.K., go ahead. We'll search for evidence in Europe."

That meant they would send a lawyer to Europe to take depositions
from anybody they could find who had dealings with Jerome H. Lemelson
or his invention. Here you have the greatest device for generating paper
ever thought up by the legal profession: the deposition. All successful

inventors know about depositions. They learn to live with them the way one learns to live with arthritis.

A deposition is a pretrial maneuver in which lawyers take sworn testimony from people out of court, usually in somebody's office. A court reporter records the testimony on a stenotype machine and then types up a transcript. The number of pages of testimony that can come out of an hour of this is fabulous, and some depositions go on for a week. What might actually be divulged about Jerome H. Lemelson or his works on any of these thousands of pieces of paper was beside the point. The point was that Lemelson would have to hire a lawyer to represent his interests during each deposition, day after day, city after city, across the map of Europe. The sheets of paper would go into archive boxes, and every sheet meant another little hemorrhage in Lemelson's net worth.

This case began in the 1970s. It grinds on still. So far it has cost Lemelson $250,000 in lawyers' fees, and the meter is still ticking. It sounds like something from out of *Bleak House*, which Charles Dickens wrote in 1852 and 1853, but it is merely a typical episode in the life of an American inventor in the 1980s. Which is to say, it is the story of a man trying to dig his way out from under a ton of paper.

Is there any more feverish dream of glory in the world, outside of Islam, than the dream of being an inventor? Certainly not in the United States, and probably not in Japan or in any other industrial country. An invention is one of those superstrokes, like discovering a platinum deposit or a gas field or writing a novel, through which an individual, the hungriest loner, can transform his life, overnight, and light up the sky. The inventor needs only one thing, which is as free as the air: a terrific idea. 16

He doesn't need connections. The great American inventors of the past hundred years, the so-called age of technology, have not come from prominent families. They have not had money. They have not been part of the highly touted, highly financed research teams of industry and the universities. They have not been adept politically or socially. Many have been breathtakingly deficient in charm.

Thomas Edison was scarcely educated at all; three years in public school, and that was it. Alexander Graham Bell was a teacher who began his experiments, leading to the telephone, in the cellar of a house in Boston, where he rented a room. Steven Jobs and Steven Wozniak, of Apple Computer fame, were a pair of public high school A-V types. A-V types are audio-visual nerds who wear windbreakers, carry a lot of keys, and wire up directional mikes for the drama club. The Silicon Valley of California, center of the most spectacular new industry of the second half of the twentieth century, computers and semiconductors, is known as the Land of Nerd, the Planet of the Nerds, and the Emerald City of Nerdz. The centimillionaires of the Silicon Valley want nothing to do with the traditional

Society of nearby San Francisco. They can't get into Trader Vic's wearing their nerd shirts, which are short-sleeved white sport shirts with pencil guards on the pockets.

Wilbur and Orville Wright were regarded as two wet smacks who ran a bicycle repair shop in Dayton, Ohio, when they arrived at Kitty Hawk for their airplane experiment in 1903. Neither had graduated from high school. But theirs was the invention that dazzled Jerome H. Lemelson and thousands of other boys who were born in the early 1920s.

As a teenager, Lemelson was typical of the airplane "hobbyists," as they 20 were known, quiet boys who built gasoline-powered model airplanes, took them out in the fields, and flew them by wire or remote control. There were still a lot of open fields on Staten Island, where he grew up. His father was a doctor, a general practitioner, but Lemelson's passion was airplanes. During the Second World War he found his way into the engineering department of the Army Air Corps. After the war he earned a bachelor's degree in aeronautical engineering at New York University, then went to work at NYU for the Office of Naval Research's Project Squid. Project Squid was supposed to develop rocket and pulse jet engines.

One day in 1951, Lemelson took the subway over to the Arma factory in Brooklyn, which made control mechanisms for aircraft, to see a demonstration of a fully automatic, feedback-controlled metal lathe. "Feedback" was a hot new word in engineering circles. Nobody there on the work way at Arma took a second look at Jerome H. Lemelson. He was twenty-eight years old, neither fat nor thin, neither very tall nor very short, not bad looking and not Tyrone Power, either. He had a broad forehead, light brown curly hair, large eyes, and a long, straight nose. He was quiet, polite, reserved, and a typical hard-working young engineer, by the looks of him, if you looked at all.

Lemelson took more than a second look at the metal lathe, however. An ordinary metal lathe turned a metal rod while an operator shaved it down to whatever diameter or shape he wanted by adjusting a tool bit. In the case of the feedback-controlled lathe, the bit was controlled automatically by punch cards. The crowd murmured a lot as the bit rose and fell to unseen commands.

Lemelson began wondering how far you could take this idea of a programmed factory machine. Over the next three years he developed the designs for a "universal robot." The robot would have an arm with joints. It would rivet, weld, drill, measure, pick things up and move them. He drew up a 150-page patent application and submitted it to the U.S. Patent Office in Washington, D.C., on Christmas Eve, 1954. Unbeknownst to Lemelson, an inventor named George Devol had filed an application for a robot two weeks earlier. Theirs were the first industrial robots. As it turned out, both men had a long wait ahead of them.

In the meantime, Lemelson was already working on a second application 24 for an offshoot of the universal robot, a "flexible manufacturing system," which was the automated machine shop.

That same year, 1954, Lemelson married an interior decorator named Dolly Ginsberg. The first stop on their honeymoon was Bermuda. The second stop was the Willard Hotel in Washington because it happened to be across the street from the Search Room of the Patent Office. Lemelson was already deep in the grip of The Dream.

The Search Room was an enormous archive the size of Uline Arena, where the Washington Capitols, the professional basketball team, played their games. It was full of ancient wooden shelves and boxes, known as shoes, containing nearly 150 years' worth of patent documents. The spaces between the stacks of shelves were so narrow that the clerks had to shimmy past each other to fetch the shoes for people doing patent searches. This led to a lot of waiting and sighing. Dolly heard one patent lawyer complaining to another: "There ought to be some way to mechanize this place."

She happened to mention this to Lemelson. That started him off on another track, resulting in his "video filing system." The documents would be recorded on reels of videotape or magnetic tape. The average patent application was ten pages long. You could store 100,000 applications on just four reels of tape. You would look at them on a television screen in stop-frame pictures. (His conception of the stop-frame picture would lead, during the 1960s, to filmless photography, still pictures created from video images.)

Instead of having GS-8 civil servants shimmying between stacks of 28 shelves, you would press a few buttons and send a playback device along a track to a slot where the tape was. But how could the device connect with the tape and enable you to play it and wind it back and forth? Lemelson thought about that awhile and conceived of the mechanism that eventually became the core of the audio cassette player. He presented video filing and its components in a sixty-page patent application in 1955.

And he waited some more. Several years went by, and the Patent Office still had not issued any patents for all these brilliant ideas. Lemelson was now learning one of the facts of life about being an inventor in America. The first flash of genius lights up only a few yards of the road. The road is long and uphill.

More than once, he and Dolly had to fall back on her earnings as an interior decorator. There was only one way an inventor could make money rapidly without waiting for the patent process to go its course, and that was to design toys. In the case of a toy, you prudently filed for a patent but went ahead and sold the design immediately, if you could. Lemelson had an idea for a face-mask kit for children that would be printed on a cereal box. A child could cut out the pieces, assemble them in different combinations, and put on the mask. He filed for a patent and took his drawings to one of the cereal manufacturers. The company said it wasn't interested, and so he put the drawings away and forgot about them.

One day, three years later, he is in the grocery store, and there on the shelf is a cereal box with a face-mask kit on it. It's put out by the very people he showed his drawings to. He can't believe it. The way he sees it, he's staring at as blatant a case of patent infringement as you could imagine. He files suit. So now he's in court. It's a jury trial. The judge comes in, and he gives Lemelson and the lawyers a long look down his nose.

"This is a patent case," he says. He lets the term "patent case" hang in 32 the air for a moment, like a bad smell. "I have better things to do with my time than listen to patent cases. It is now ten-fifteen. You have until three o'clock this afternoon to complete your arguments."

Sure enough, at three o'clock on the dot he looks at his watch, stands up, and, without saying a word, walks out. Lemelson has an expert witness testifying for him at the time, and the fellow is sitting there on the stand with his mouth hanging open.

Then the judge pops back in. "Ladies and gentlemen of the jury, my apologies. I neglected to dismiss you. You are dismissed."

It turns out the case has been dismissed, too. Lemelson appeals, and a new trial is called — before the same judge, who summarily dismisses the suit, this time for good.

When Lemelson spoke of these things to other inventors, they smiled 36 without joy. He was just getting the picture. First, many American corporations, including many of the most respected, ignored patent rights without batting an eye. They didn't give you so much as a sporting wink. Second, the courts couldn't be bothered. Practically none of the judges who heard patent cases had any background in patent law, much less engineering. It was unfamiliar terrain, which seemed to make them irritable. On the one hand, they couldn't stand all these obsessive small-fry inventors, these parasites on the hide of Science, with their endless theories and their transducers and capacitive-sensitive relays and the rest of that paralyzing jargon. But on the other hand, if they, the judges, could understand an invention, then it must not be much of an invention. They had developed "the doctrine of obviousness." If an invention looked obvious, they declared the patent invalid.

The inventors kept ratings of the chances of having their patent rights upheld in the various federal jurisdictions. Back when Lemelson was starting out, your chances ran from zero in the Eighth Circuit, which covered most of the Midwest, to 45 percent in the South. The Second Circuit, covering New York, was rated about average, one chance in four.

But what about the operations? How could they get away with flouting the patent system and patent law? It was simple, the inventors told Lemelson. All that the corporations needed to overcome was their scruples, if any. In the United States, unlike Japan and parts of Europe, patent infringement was not considered a form of theft, so there were no criminal penalties. There were not even punitive damages in patent cases unless the inventory could prove "willful infringement." To avoid that, a manufacturer merely had to take the precaution of going to its own lawyer and having him write an opinion saying that such and such a product did not infringe upon any existing patents for such and such reasons. It didn't matter how cockeyed the reasons were. That was that lawyers were for.

Once the manufacturer had that document in hand, the worst that could have happened, even if the firm had been found guilty in court, was that the manufacturer would have had to pay the inventor the royalties he would have received if a license had been obtained. There were lawyers who would actually advise their corporate clients to ignore patents, calling it a no-risk strategy.

Just in case the inventor was new at this game, the manufacturer would let him know the odds, discreetly, or, if he looked a little thick, bluntly. To get a case as far as the trial stage was going to cost $40,000. Was he ready for that? To get a case through the trial and all the appeal stages — was he ready for $250,000? For good measure, the manufacturer usually added some variation of the theme, "We're gonna bury you under a ton of paper." If a corporation was big enough, it would threaten anybody, not merely little lone-wolf inventors but even another, smaller corporation. When J. Reid Anderson, the chief executive officer of Verbatim, a company specializing in computer storage devices, went to a big manufacturer complaining of patent infringement, he was told: "We have more patent attorneys than you have people in your company, and they are just sitting back waiting for someone to start a patent fight like this."

Lemelson's saving grace was that he was not a cynic. He didn't have a cynical or even a morbidly pessimistic bone in his body. Despite everything, he believed that it wasn't a bad world. His most important inventions had disappeared somewhere in the papyraphagous mew of the Patent Office. A manufacturer had just walked right over him, without stopping, and the court he had gone to for help hadn't even been able to hide its contempt for Jerome H. Lemelson. Moreover, he had just learned that this was the customary state of affairs for small-fries of his vocation.

But that was just what it was — a vocation, a calling. By now, Lemelson derived an aesthetic or spiritual — or some kind of — satisfaction that went beyond the money he wasn't making from inventing. He was irrepressible. He was thinking up new inventions at the rate of one a month, a pace that he managed to keep up for the next thirty years.

Once Lemelson had designed robots that did every imaginable industrial chore, he designed a robot that inspected what the other robots had done. He invented robot-vision or "image analysis" machines that could, among other things, detect diseased blood or tissue cells, such as cancer cells. He invented the "computer-controlled coordinate measuring machine," which would later be used to measure and align the tiles on the exterior of the space shuttles. He invented a computerized tourniquet that would allow a surgeon to perform an operation without stopping to turn valves to alter the flow of a patient's blood. He designed several systems for transfer of information between computers. He designed two laser-powered recording and reproduction systems, Lasercard and Videocard, to perform the computer functions now performed by floppy disks. He invented a widely used "automated teller machine" that scans credit cards and checks out their credit status. He invented both a cordless telephone and a cordless videophone.

At the same time, he was turning out toy and novelty designs. He designed the "watchpen," a ballpoint pen with a watch built into it. He invented the flexible-track car toy — one of the biggest-selling toys of all time — manufactured by at least five companies under different names, Hot Wheels being the best known. He invented the Velcro dart game, in which you throw a Velcro-covered ball, instead of a steel-tipped dart, at a Velcro-covered dart board. He invented the "printing putty toy," best known under the brand name Monster Print Putty, with which you can remove words and pictures from a newspaper and reprint them on another piece of paper. Lemelson was thinking up these things, doing the drawings, writing the descriptions, and dispatching them to the Patent Office so fast, his two sons called him The Blur.

During the early 1960s, when Lemelson was pushing forty, the patents finally started rolling in. First was his video filing system in 1961. Then the automated warehouse in 1962. In 1966, almost twelve years after he had submitted the application, his universal robot patent was issued. Devol's had come through five years earlier.

Lemelson closed his first major deal in 1964, selling an exclusive license for his automated warehouse system to a firm called Triax, but almost immediately he was up to his neck in lawsuits. Other firms, he and Triax charged, had already begun pirating the invention in violation of Triax's license. That litigation continues today, twenty-two years later.

In 1967, he sold an exclusive license to an English company, Molins, for the automated machine shop. In 1973, he made the best deal of his career, selling an exclusive license for his cassette drive mechanism to Sony. Sony sublicensed it to more than a hundred Japanese firms. Today, practically every audio cassette player on the market operates with the Lemelson drive.

None of this brought any dramatic improvement in Lemelson's style of 48
living. In 1959, after the birth of their second son, he and Dolly moved
from a garden apartment in Metuchen, New Jersey, looking out not onto a
garden but U.S. Route 1, to an eight-room house in Metuchen on a quarter
of an acre. It wasn't until 1985 that they moved to greener, grander scenery
in Princeton. No small part of the picture was the hundreds of thousands
of dollars that Lemelson was spending on legal fees, trying to deal with
American firms.

From the first, there were cases of what he regarded as the most arrant
infringement. It absolutely stupefied him. The retort of "go ahead and sue"
(. . . "and we'll bury you under a ton of paper") was standard practice.
Some firms were bluffing. If you brought suit, they would settle. But there
was only one way to find out, which was to sue. Other firms were not
bluffing. They would spend half a million dollars in legal fees to keep from
taking a license and paying royalties they knew wouldn't run over $150,000.
Lemelson couldn't figure these people out. He didn't know whether they
were trying to teach a lesson to other small-fry inventors — the lesson
being that Lemelson's legal bills were running well over $150,000 — or
whether these were displays of sheer competitive ego.

Sometimes the lawsuits sprang up on so many fronts, it was hard to
keep track of them. Lemelson found himself suing all the major manufacturers of the flexible-track car toy. These cases live on today. Some of the
suits turned ludicrous, but the laughs never came cheaply.

In one case, Lemelson was suing the U.S. government and two private
manufacturers over the same invention. He decided to abandon the case
against the government and grant it a license free of charge. The private
firms sought to block this move, apparently on the grounds that the government's acceptance of the license implied recognition of Lemelson's patent rights.

He ended up spending $18,000 in lawyers' fees to give the license away. 52

Lemelson was in noble, but expensive, company. Robert Goddard, now
called — officially, by the U.S. government — the father of American
rocketry, ran a lone-wolf rocket program west of nowhere in the New
Mexico desert in no small part to try to put an end to the pirating of his
patented inventions — chiefly by the U.S. government.

Fifteen years after his death, the government gave his wife $1 million
to settle his many claims of infringement. There was something melancholy
about this refrain of the widow and the million dollars.

One day Lemelson met a lawyer who had been in on the Armstrong
case. Edwin Armstrong was the inventor of FM, frequency modulation, the
greatest advance in broadcasting since the invention of the radio itself. In
1940, the Radio Corporation of America offered Armstrong a flat fee of $1
million for his FM patents. The lawyer had been in the room when Arm-

strong was handed the check. Armstrong looked at it and then, with great deliberation, tore it up and dropped the pieces on the floor.

In 1948, Armstrong sued RCA, Motorola, and several other corporations 56 for patent infringement. The lawyers rubbed their hands and licked their chops and started manufacturing a ton of paper. By the early 1950s, Armstrong was lamenting, "They will stall this along until I am dead or broke." It was the former. On the night of January 31, 1954, he jumped out the window of his Manhattan apartment ten stories above the East River. For some reason, he put on his overcoat, scarf, hat, and gloves before he jumped. Late that year, his widow accepted a million-dollar settlement. It was the merest fraction of what his invention had come to be worth.

Then there was the case of another loner, Gordon Gould, one of the three main holders of patents on the laser. Gould and Lemelson were about the same age. They had hit upon their major concepts at about the same time, the mid-1950s. Gould had been a thirty-six-year-old graduate student at Columbia University when what he called "the fire" first possessed him. He was the one who thought up the acronym LASER (for Light Amplification by Stimulated Emission of Radiation). For twenty-seven years he was embroiled in legal battles on two fronts, with the Patent Office and with laser manufacturers.

By the time a court ordered the Patent Office to grant him his key patents, Gould had retired. He was spending his golden years with his lawyers. He had twelve lawsuits going in the United States and Canada. His legal bills had come to $2.5 million, much of it paid for by a firm that would get 64 percent of his income — down the road — if he won the suits.

As for himself, Gould indicated in an interview, he was long past the stage of life in which the big money would interest him, even if it ever came.

Lemelson's problems were still more complicated, because he had so 60 many patents. He lived like a chess player who takes on forty opponents at once, walking from board to board, trying to keep straight in his mind what threats are coming up where.

Well, at least Lemelson had had enough victories to be able to keep breathing in the avalanche of paper and lawyers' bills. Very few independent inventors had the money even to get in the game.

In the late 1970s, it began to dawn on government statisticians that the United States was no longer the great world center of technological innovation. Over a single five-year stretch, 1971 to 1976, the number of American citizens receiving U.S. patents declined by 21 percent. The number of foreign citizens receiving U.S. patents increased by 16 percent. By 1979, about four of every ten new U.S. patents were going to foreigners. That year, the subject began to break out in the press. *Newsweek* ran a cover story titled "Innovation: Has America Lost Its Edge?" The conclusion was that it had lost it, or was losing it, to the Japanese. That was not news to Lemelson. The underlying problem, as he saw it, was the sad fate of the independent inventor.

By the late 1970s, the corporations had managed to create the impression that in the twentieth century the greatest technological innovations were no longer coming from the loners but from the corporate and university research teams. But this had never been true. Innovation and corporate research were very nearly a contradiction in terms; at bottom, the corporations were interested only in improvements in existing product lines. As for the universities, they actually looked down upon invention as an amateur pastime, despite the fact that much scientific study, especially in the area of electronics, was nothing more than the analysis of discoveries made by inventors.

In 1975, Lemelson was appointed to the Patent and Trademark Office 64 Advisory Committee. In July 1979, he testified at Senate hearings investigating what was beginning to be called "the innovation crisis." In a prepared statement, he said that corporations and the courts had combined to create an "antipatent philosophy" in the United States. "Company managers know that the odds of an inventor being able to afford the costly litigation are less than one in ten; and even if the suit is brought, four times out of five the courts will hold the patent invalid. When the royalties are expected to exceed the legal expense, it makes good business sense to attack the patent."

He contrasted this with the situation in Japan, where patent law was taken seriously, both morally and legally. "Although the majority of my income is derived from foreign licenses, I have *never* had to enforce a patent against a foreign infringer. I leave it to you to conclude the reason as to why the attitude is so different. My licensees have told me that they recognize the clear value of invention from an economic point of view. They feel that the United States has lived off the fat of its own technology for so long that we don't recognize that the consequence of the legal destruction of patents is a decline in innovation, a situation that is not within anyone's economic interest.

"What all this means to the inventor is that he either quits inventing or he licenses foreign."

One fine day a few months ago, Lemelson was in his New York office on Park Avenue, near Grand Central Terminal, talking to a reporter from a magazine. The two of them were sitting on a couch across from Lemelson's desk. The reporter had on a checked suit and a shirt collar like Herbert Hoover's. It looked about four inches high. Underneath his necktie you

could see a brass-plated collar button of the sort that went out forty-six
years ago. Lemelson's office, on the other hand, had a cool, immaculate,
low-slung, modern look in tones of beige, gray, taupe, and teak. Lemelson
himself was just as neatly composed. He was wearing a navy blazer, dark
gray pants, a blue shirt, and a sincere necktie. He was now sixty-two years
old and what remained of his curly hair was turning gray. But he was as
trim as a digital watch. That morning, as usual, he had run a mile and a
half and done forty push-ups, fifty sit-ups, and a hundred sidesaddle hops.
His face had the gaunt athletic look of those who stare daily down the bony
gullet of the great god Aerobics.

The reporter with the collar was wrapping his eyebrows around his nose   68
as he tried to think of the technical terms concerning Lemelson's inventions.
Lemelson listened patiently and sipped a glass of orange juice. Every now
and then, one of the two telephones on the desk would ring. Lemelson
would excuse himself and walk to the desk. One telephone had an ordinary
ring, and he would answer that one by saying hello. The other one rang
with an electronic burble. That one he would answer by saying, "Licensing
Management." Licensing Management Corp. was a firm he had created
chiefly to sell licenses for his own inventions to manufacturers.

"Licensing Management . . . Yes . . . This is Jerry Lemelson . . . Oh,
hi . . . No, I can't do it this week. I have three days of depositions coming
up."

The other telephone rings.

"Hello? . . . Oh, hi . . . Thursday of next week? I can't make it. I have
to be in Cleveland . . . What for? For a deposition."

It goes on like that.   72

"Hello? . . . Yes . . . Oh, hi . . . This afternoon? . . . I won't be here
that late. I have an appointment with my lawyer in half an hour."

Lemelson walks back to the couch. The reporter with the trick collar
says, "If you don't mind my asking, when do you . . . *invent*?"

"On the train."

"On the train?"   76

"On the train out to Princeton, where I live."

"On the train," the fellow with the collar repeats it, all the while staring
at him, apparently wondering if Lemelson is putting him on. But Lemelson
isn't the type.

Then the fellow says, "Your opponents say, or they imply, that you
make your money by filing lawsuits."

Not much ruffles Jerome H. Lemelson, but this gets under his skin.   80

"Who said that?"

"One of the lawyers."

Lemelson shakes his head. "Oh sure. They accuse me of being litigious.
But I've *lost* money on litigation. I've spent more than a million dollars on
it, and I don't even like to think about the time."

"Then why get involved in it?" 84

"*Why*? To protect my rights. What do you do when your rights are being violated? Lie down? Walk away? You show me a successful inventor who hasn't been a scrapper."

Then his expression changes. "I don't know if I should even stress this side of it. It all sounds so negative. I don't want to discourage inventors. I want to encourage them. I think we ought to have something like the National Inventors Council that we had during World War II. The government called upon our people for inventions to help win the war. They received four hundred thousand ideas during World War II alone, and over four thousand of them actually went into production, and they helped win the war. I'd like to see this type of thing revived to see if we can win the technological battle with the rest of the world."

He thinks a moment. "There's nothing wrong with our patent system itself. We just need to protect patents. And actually things are getting a little better. There's a new federal court for handling patent cases now, the court of appeals for the federal circuit, and the judges know patent law. Your chances are much better now. They're about fifty-fifty."

"If every opponent in every piece of litigation you have going right now 88 decided to settle in your favor, how much money would you receive?"

The thought of the corporations suffering this sudden mass attack of equity makes Lemelson laugh. "Millions. It won't turn out that way, of course.

"But I don't have any regrets. This has been a good life. I've been independent, and I've done exactly what I wanted to do."

The train to Princeton was fifteen or twenty minutes out of Penn Station, and everybody was settling into the dim blue haze of the car and the jouncing and bouncing. The roadbed was in a little better shape than it used to be. They were starting to replace the old wooden ties with concrete. It would be easy enough to invent better rail systems, and no doubt plenty of people had, but they would never be built, and so it wasn't worth thinking about.

A little more of the lurching there in the haze, a few more metal shrieks 92 from between the cars, and — bango! — it came to Lemelson, just like that. The drug delivery system, the whole thing — it all came to him while he was sitting there. For a long time he had been trying to think of a way to use drugs to treat a diseased area of the body without having to diffuse the chemicals and subject the entire body to their effects, as happens in chemotherapy. For people with certain forms of cancer, it would be a godsend. And now he had it! The time-release thing! The insertion system! All the parts were in place!

Lemelson reached into his briefcase and pulled out the pad he always kept on hand for such moments as these. He was aware for the first time of the man sitting next to him. The man looked like nothing more than a dead-average New Jersey commuter, but you never knew. You just never knew. Lemelson began writing it all down in a shorthand he had created for himself. The drug delivery. The time release. He was no longer aware of the haze and the motion of the car. He was soaring. It was like the beginning, once more, of a dream come true.

AFTERWORD

When James Joyce wrote the first sentence of his great short story "The Dead," *he misused a word. "Lily, the caretaker's daughter, was literally run off her feet."* *This* literally *has been commonplace for more than a century. The first* Oxford *English Dictionary citation comes from 1863 when a writer claimed that he "literally coined money." (He was not the master of the mint, nor was he a counterfeiter; he was only rich.) He used the dead metaphor "coined money" and tried to raise it from the dead by saying* literally.

When James Joyce did it, he used a device in fiction that Wolfe repeatedly uses in his nonfiction: He talked about a character, third person, in the language that the person would have used if the person were speaking; thus, Lily would (a little pretentiously) misuse literally *— and the solecism is characterization.*

In his next to last paragraph, Wolfe describes Lemelson sitting in the train from Penn Station to Princeton ". . . and — bango! — it came . . . just like that." In the last paragraph, still speaking of Lemelson in the third person, Wolfe enters his thoughts as he decides to conceal his script from a fellow passenger: "The man looked like nothing more than a dead-average New Jersey commuter, but you never knew. You just never knew."

BOOKS AVAILABLE IN PAPERBACK

Chip Carving: Hound Dogs, Racoon, Coon Hunter. West Chester: Schiffer. *Essays.*

The Electric Kool-Aid Acid Test. New York: Farrar, Straus & Giroux. *Nonfiction.*

From Bauhaus to Our House. New York: Pocket Books. *Nonfiction.*

In Our Time. New York: Farrar, Straus and Giroux. *Essays.*

The Kandy-Kolored Tangerine-Flake Streamline Baby. New York: Farrar, Straus & Giroux. *Essays.*

The Painted Word. New York: Bantam. *Nonfiction*.

The Pump House Gang. New York: Farrar, Straus & Giroux. *Essays*.

The Purple Decades: A Reader. New York: Berkley Publishing Group. *Essays*.

Radical Chic and Mau-Mauing the Flak Catchers. New York: Farrar, Straus and Giroux. *Essays*.

The Right Stuff. New York: Bantam. *Nonfiction*.

PAUL
ZWEIG

*P*AUL ZWEIG *was a poet born (1935) in New York, where he lived most of his adult life. He took his undergraduate degree at Columbia College, then did a Ph.D. at the University of Paris. He taught for many years at Queens College of the City University of New York. He translated and wrote much prose as well as poetry. Before he became ill, he published two books that have been called "cultural history"* — The Heresy of Self-Love *(1968) and* The Adventurer *(1974); two volumes of poems,* Against Emptiness *(1971) and* The Dark Side of the Earth *(1974); and a volume of memoirs,* Three Journeys *(1976).*

It was in 1978, when he was forty-three, that he discovered his lymphoma, which leukemia eventually complicated. He continued to write — a book about Walt Whitman and two books published posthumously: a book of poems called Eternity's Woods *(1985) and the memoir* Departures *(1986), from which we take "Transitions." He died at forty-nine in August 1984.*

Transitions

I've never been much good at transitions. Over the years, I have gone as if expelled, dragged, or broken from one life to another, never quite willing or knowing. It has been all zigzags, changes that sprang from nowhere and became irreversible, as if I had been shunted onto another plane of life, never choosing and never prepared. What I wanted was a limited existence: an enchanted ordinariness as an engineer, living in a tract house in Queens, or as an elementary school teacher in Brooklyn, living in a tenement, with a shopping street downstairs and the smell of food in the hallway. A life close to the center, undeviating and unproblematical; a sort of immortality. But then would come the dark shove, the loose wire in my genes, and I would start on some baffling new course: a marriage, a religious conversion, an obsession that filled my life with strangeness. Like the honeybee whose eccentric flight, full of swings and surprises, results from some twist in the bee's genetic grid, I too have apparently been programmed for fuzzy swoops and teeterings beyond reason.

Therefore I was prepared, if that is the word, when several years ago another sort of shove — even darker, more arbitrary — sent me reeling. Again I found myself in a new life, but one that would never become stale or overly familiar to me; that would always be new, always just discovered. This unexplored, unchosen life was the life of the dying — the life of all life, perhaps, but starker and more intense in my case. It is, most likely, my final incarnation, and I will never become tired of it, never leave it by the pratfall of a gene or the shove of an instinct.

I entered this life on a muggy May afternoon when a doctor, feeling my neck with a hard probing touch that I have gotten to know well, discovered a small, mobile lump at the base of my neck. Within an hour, I was getting my chest and belly X-rayed. The doctor was clipped and urgent. Although X-rays showed nothing, there would have to be a biopsy. The lump, buried in the soft tissue of my neck, was oblong and somewhat flaccid. A few days later, the surgeon — again the firm probing with both hands at the base of my neck — seemed undecided. The lump was so sleepy and obscure; but what the hell, let's do it. I remember the sizzling of the electric knife; the odor of burnt blood; the pushes and clips of the tools in the freshly opened slit. I lay there as if clubbed, not thinking, not thinking. Then the doctor lifted out the rubbery clot, dropped it into a container, and went down the hall to get a quick reading by the pathologist. The tissue is sliced and quick-frozen, and then given a preliminary look which must be confirmed later when the tissue has been appropriately dyed to emphasize the structure of the cells. He was back in a few minutes, looking old and heavy.

"There's something there," he said. "We'll have to wait for the slide to be sure." 4

Those were the words that swung me into my new life. I had walked into the outpatient operating room of the hospital young and immortal; death had been a neurotic tune I wrote about in poems. Now suddenly it was a heaviness that dragged my legs down, a mind that wanted to dissolve back into its spoonfuls of cells, and forget, forget. The slit in my neck was the latch, and now my mortality was seeping out, a thin, freezing gas that filled the operating room. I shivered amid the cutting tools and the bottles of disinfectant, and the doctor talking to me carefully, urgently. I heard what he said, watched his lips, but his words slid off my panic, powerless to reach me in my new life.

"Don't think of this as cancer," he said. "That's a terrifying word. You have a lymphoma. That's a *kind* of cancer, but it can be treated, kept under control; maybe cured. You're not dying. People do well with a lymphoma."

"Do well" is an oncologist's term that I have heard often since then. You're doing well. He did well. It's a term that must be listened to from the perspective of this new life. Its specific meaning is not "He's well now" but "He's well for the moment"; dying has stopped for a while; he will probably live for a long time. An oncologist's "long time" measures time in the new life. It may mean a few years, which is not bad, although possibly not comforting to a forty-seven-year-old man who still daydreams, at odd moments, of a long life.

For weeks after that my body was inspected for information I never 8 knew it contained. My urine and blood were analyzed; my bone marrow was biopsied. There were sonograms, nuclear scans and grams, X-rays. Incisions were made on the upper part of my feet, through which purple dye was injected into my lymph system. I spent a week in the hospital for some of these tests. I talked to hematologists, surgeons, oncologists, and just plain doctors. I talked to find out. I talked in the hope of hearing some word, some unintended phrase, maybe, that would release me, even for an hour, from the anxiety that spun itself into every corner of my body, deadening my face, giving a buzzing, flattened rhythm to all my thoughts. I felt like someone who had been thrown against an electric fence. Time had been cut off from before my face. The world was unchanged. The streets were full of cars and pedestrians; the sun still caught in the windows of buildings. The radio reported worldwide events. Everything was the same, but time had been removed. And without time, everything was unreal, but I was horribly real, oversized, bursting as a body bursts in a vacuum.

Listening to my doctor was delicate. I took in every shrug, every rise and fall of his voice. I weighed his words on a fine scale, to detect hope or despair. Then I called up another doctor, to hear how the words sounded in his voice. I triangulated and compared, all to find something that would shut off the terror for a while. It was as if there were a key buried in my psyche, and I had to feel around for it, probing in thick, dark waters, and then, not knowing what I'd found, finding it, then losing it again.

While my doctor gathered information, I spent my days walking. I preferred busy shopping streets: the lights and the shop windows, the double-parked cars, the people hurrying into and out of stores. There was energy, there was a present. My feelings would relax a little. I would become a temporary pedestrian, and forget my rarefied life where there was no time.

For months before all this started, my marriage had been in the process of breaking up. Already my wife was honing herself for her own version of a new life. Living with me was like being an old woman, used up, and yet she had hardly lived. It wasn't fair. For her, my lymphoma was the click of a jailer's cell closing upon her life. She boiled with guilty anger, and within a few days could hardly bear the sight of me. So I took long walks, to have something to do that kept me out of the house. Or I went to the playground with my three-year-old daughter and played in the sandbox, trying to imitate my daughter's innocence of time. In a peculiar way, my daughter and I were equals; neither of us had any time, and the irony was terrible, for I had lost mine and she hadn't acquired hers yet. Therefore we had each other. We had the work of filling a tomato-juice can with sand, had the slide polished by thousands of happy behinds. We had the soughing of the spring trees on Riverside Drive, the glow of new leaves, and the twisted, scaly trunks; the portable radios, large as suitcases, throbbing heavily as they went by; and the splintered benches, the yelps of the children, the mothers talking in their not-quite-designer jeans. My life had become a strategy for eluding terror.

It took a few weeks for the test results to be assembled. Then my doctor 12 gave me a course in cell biology as applied to a subclass of malignancy known as lymphoma, a cancer of the lymph system. There were various kinds of lymphoma, all more or less related, more or less combined in any single illness. A given biopsy slide was likely to show several of them, with a predominance of one or another. That is why lymphomas shift and change, speed up or slow down, mysteriously go into hiding, or explode in almost sudden death. They are related also to leukemia. All in all, it is a crowded picture, full of surprises, a little like life itself, but heated up and ominous. All of this was my doctor's way of telling me that he didn't know what was going to happen to me. My particular lymphoma was actually almost benign. Its cells were "well differentiated," their histology was "good." Words like "good" made my heart leap. Anything "good" was probably on my side. There began to be some time before me. Words like "years" were pronounced. There were other words too, but I heard them selectively. Well-differentiated lymphocytic lymphomas developed slowly, but they also tended to resist treatment. They were too benign to behave like cancer cells when they were treated with chemotherapy. Therefore, they came back. And one day, one year, the doctor could run out of treatments, and the sleepy, almost inadvertent disease would expand, like an elephant rolling over you, as if by accident, not knowing you were there, and almost saying, I'm sorry.

At the time I didn't hear all this. I wanted to be cured of terror even more than of the lymphoma, which I'd never seen or touched, and now accepted as an interpretation of pages full of computer letters, graphs, and a little box with glass slides in it, not as a physical fact which made my flesh more perishable.

In the end, my doctor chose a middle course. The tests had all been negative. The nodes scattered about in my lymphatic system were too small to register, even on the most sensitive tests; but that didn't mean they weren't there. The pattern of a lymphocytic lymphoma is to be scattered, not localized. A bone-marrow biopsy had disclosed a somewhat high level of lymphocytes that the pathologist called "compatible" with a lymphoma. "Compatible" is one of those cautious words doctors use to say they don't know. It meant that the lymphocytes were probably, but not definitely, connected to the lymphoma; on the other hand, they also could be normal for me. My doctor's decision was to treat with radiation, as a precautionary measure, the spot of my neck where the biopsy had been done, and not to treat the systemic disease, which was still more or less a fiction — an assemblage of data — even to him.

It was July by now, a hot, humid month. The leaves on the trees were heavy, almost flaccid. The radiologist's office was near Central Park. I went every morning at nine o'clock, and was marked with a purple paintbrush, to provide an accurate target for the machine. For twenty days, I received eight minutes and forty-seven seconds of radiation each day on my left shoulder and neck, including a small part of my jaw. The machine resembled a bulky mechanical eye that peered stolidly at the same spot on my body day after day, as if to be sure that it didn't miss anything. The radiologist's office was a warren of tiny dressing rooms, and larger rooms containing complicated machines: sonographs, gamma scanners, X-rays, hard-radiation machines. Eventually each of those machines had its turn with me, but now it was the silent, shadow-filled, almost empty room every morning, and the square, slightly battered bulk of the eye; eight minutes and forty-seven seconds of nothing, no touch, no sound. I lay on my back or stomach according to a schedule, and meditated, breathing evenly in and out. I felt solemn, detached, and then, as weeks passed, a little scared as my skin reddened, my saliva glands on that side of my mouth dried up, and the hair on my neck and jaw fell out.

Every morning, when my treatment was over, I walked to the boathouse 16 in Central Park, and had breakfast on the terrace overlooking the lake. The Central Park South skyline was reflected in the littered heavy shine of the water; the trees tossed their willow limbs in the gusts of breeze. There were always a few regulars at the café, with their shifts off, sunning themselves or doing exercises. The boathouse became my sanctuary. From its dazzled peacefulness, I could contemplate the ruins of my marriage. I could read and write, feeling myself sink into my new life, which now had some time. The terror of the previous weeks was gone. My doctor had dispelled it with his manic, speedy talk, his words like "good" histology, and his feeling that there was "time" to use chemotherapy "if" it became necessary. The implication was that there would be a next year and, surely, other years; that my "good" lymphoma might stay asleep "for a long time." The lymphoma was simply a darker, more underscored form of life, full of life's uncertainties but not a sentence, not a doom.

I didn't exactly relax. I lived in a heavy air, I swam in muted fright; and I came "home" to the boathouse every morning, to feel the hot stillness of summer, to read my books, and to escape my wife's irritation, which increased every day. I didn't want to think about her bitter voice, her resentment at the glaring light that had suddenly fallen upon me. I had become an emissary of mortality, a messenger from further along, outside the flimsy shelter of endlessness that we spin around us when we're lucky: a portable home, a little immortality, and then suddenly it collapses.

After sitting at the boathouse all morning, I walked home through the Rambles, my shoulder and neck in a state of angry sunburn. Sunlight filtered through the trees. Isolated men sat on benches with an air of melancholy expectation. There were brooks and bridges. It was a little world, strewn with crumpled bags and beer cans, the litter of a night's sexual encounters. The men on the benches resembled night birds who had forgotten to go home. I too was a passing solitude. Time had flowed back around me. Again, I was inside of life. I was freestanding, not thrust against a blankness.

Several times that month, my wife tried to leave me. Each time, my paper-thin peacefulness collapsed, and I came frantic, wild. The breakup of my marriage held an unreasoning terror for me. Perhaps I took it as a foreshadowing, a defeat that bespoke the unsayable defeat I tried to turn my mind from. We had been married for ten years, and for half of them things had been bad. My wife was a beautiful, slender woman, radiating calm and command. Her benign manner made her seem almost ethereal. But hard as it was to believe, this was purely theatrical; convincing, but simply a manner. In private, resentment boiled in her like life itself. Inside I feel like ashes, she would say, in rare moments of candor. I circled her bleakly, claiming to long for peace but drawn to the pitch of her nerves, which filled me with self-destructive bile. I felt like a man hanging from a cliff face. It was life on the edge, the loose wire in my genes. Our marriage had long since become Strindberg's dance of death, and we danced it like puppets; but now it was breaking up, for real death had come upon the scene and driven its neurotic imitators from the field.

When I was a boy, I used to wonder what would keep me from sinking   20 to the level of a bum on the street. Every tramp, every stinking hulk of a drunk, was a possible destiny. Later, I saw that it wasn't so easy to sink. You had to dive, you had to work your way down. Society buoyed you up to your level; family and friends, the structure of needs driven into your flesh and psyche, do not let themselves be easily betrayed. I hadn't thought of this other stripping down, the blow of destiny that thrust from within you and then, like a bolt falling from a cloud, from without you too. I was caught in this pincers now: stripped of time, stripped even of a home; afraid that the anguish breaking around my daughter would maim her in some way. For years I had been afraid that if my marriage broke up, I would lose my daughter. It had become an obsession; it summed up all the mysterious harm I felt my wife could do to me. More than once, I had seen murder in her eyes. Lying in our bed at night, I had felt like a naked target, waiting for her rage to solidify and become a weapon. Was the lymphoma her ultimate spell? The cellular substance of her wish for me? I shunned such thoughts, partly because they were self-serving and superstitious; partly because my doctors suspected that the lymphoma had been present in its sleepy state for a number of years; and partly because it meant that I had been defeated, bewitched, skewered on rage and resentment, outwitted. Strength against strength, my wife's tunnel vision of despair and accusation had been stronger than my contradictory soul with its compulsive large-mindedness, its play of feelings and knowledge.

A month later, the marriage was over. I had come alone to the house we owned in southern France. My wife had refused to come with me, and stayed in Paris with friends. I breathed the aromatic August air like a spiritual substance. The house is a low stone building, with a roof of rough red tiles, on a hilltop far from any road. The fields of barley and alfalfa had been harvested, and a swath of yellow stubble surrounded the house. Petunias splashed brightly in a stone basin. A little way down the hill, a walnut tree dangled its smoky limbs. I sat in front of the house and gazed at the hill crest across the valley or watched the sun ignite at dusk in plumes of red mist and cloud. The days creaked with cicadas. The nights were blocks of blankness, almost a burial, except for a veil of light spilling across

587

the sky, the Milky Way, and the bright nailheads of the largest stars. Every day I jogged down the dirt road into the valley, and walked back. Gradually, I increased the distance. It was a return among the living, a return to youth. Timidly, almost furtively — like Adam hiding his nakedness in the garden — I built the endlessness back around me. My saliva glands began to function again; the red square on my neck healed. One side of my jaw was still baby-smooth; I didn't have to shave it. It was my stigmata. But eventually that too became normal.

As days passed, it seemed that the house itself was healing me: its honey-colored stone walls and red, granular tiles; its days full of wind and somersaulting clouds. I thought of my grandparents' farm. The farm had been a model for my childhood love of empty places: the prairies, deserts, and forests I read about in my favorite books; any place where the claustrophobia of emotions was dissolved, where sheer emptiness made man small, as if my genes had conjured up primeval savannas as my true home. Now I had my own house in the woods; my own romantic emptiness that overlay the earlier memories and merged with them.

One day I telephoned my wife from a neighbor's house. No, she didn't want to come down; she also didn't want to live with me anymore. It took only a few words to establish this. The phone cracked against my ear in the long gaps between the few things we had to say to each other. Suddenly there was more room than I knew what to do with. As I climbed the steep path through the woods and crossed the harvested field to the house, I could hear the brittle stubble crunch under my feet. This was ground level: no family, a flimsy life. I hadn't become a derelict, but I had hit bottom in my own way.

I am sitting at my window, looking out over the Hudson. It is a scuffed blue-gray this morning, with patches of ripples and smoke melting into each other. The Palisades directly across from me are still speckled with points of light. At river level, the abandoned factories emerge faintly from the darkness as a slightly powdered gray. The river too is dark, almost an empty trough between its banks, which here are half a mile apart.

Now it is almost full daylight. I can see seagulls wheeling close to the near shore. From this height, they don't seem to be over the river, but on it, sliding and scooting on the surface like water flies.

The far end of my living room slants to the northwest. When the sun comes up eastward over the city — the slits of the streets and the dusty black squares of the rooftops, and beyond them, visible only if I lean my head out the window, the heavy metal arches of the Triborough Bridge — there is a fringing light along the window which lasts for only a few minutes. The imperfections in the glass are heightened, a milkiness veils the sleeve of emptiness: the river; the park on this side with its leafless knobs of trees, and its baseball fields which resemble large brown vulvas; the cliff on the other side, topped by the pale rectangles of condominiums; and closing it off to the north, like a musical instrument poised to produce a humming note, the George Washington Bridge.

When I lean up close to the window, I can see a few people down below waiting for the bus. On the square of pavement, between the soggy winter turf and the benches, they resemble a scattering of grains. There is a clarity in the scene, something unspoken. The sky is blue-white. Beyond the Palisades, the New Jersey hills form parallel pleats, broken here and there by the sharp outlines of factories, gas tanks, and distant neighborhoods which I will never visit, and whose names I will never know.

My living room with its five windows resembles a cage suspended from 28 the sky, looking out on space, on the low hum of the city. Below me, the bus opens its doors and inhales the scattered grains. This morning life is distant, a brightness rimming the city.

On several occasions I have thought of jumping — half flying — from my twenty-fourth-story window; not a thought really, a fleeting image of an action. Nothing I would do, but even the image of it has given my life a new vulnerability.

During the first years after my wife and I separated, there was in the struggle between us a flow of tension that seemed rarely to let me up for air. I felt that she was a tool of destruction swinging wildly at the core of my life. Wherever I looked, I stumbled over threads of her making: threats against me, against my daughter; thrills of anger that swept through the phone or down the stairs. At times, it seemed that the only avenue of escape was out of life. And the trough of the river, even-tempered and gladly indifferent, beckoned as a kind of heaven, a busy vacancy.

I've seen every kind of storm up here. The splats of thunder; the lightning crinkling in wide swaths over the Palisades; enormous thuds of wind, snaking the water in the toilet bowl, and drowning out the radio. Clouds sagged over the bridge; whitenesses of water skidded across the river, dashing up onto the highway, where cars crawled by with their headlights on, even in daylight. And the snowstorms in winter, wiping out space, crawling into my mind: a kind of death, a kind of giving up.

It is afternoon now. Reflected light from the river wavers over my wall 32 like a watermark. There is a peculiar solitude, a nothing spinning out spokes of attention. Soon the light will turn angry, and then begin to dim, contract to a purple disc sliding behind a cluster of high-rise buildings across the river. So much space, such a contraction of time, like a balloon shielding me from what I want to avoid, but which is closer to me than thought.

During these past few months, the lymphoma has wrapped its sluggish coils around me once again. In everything I do, there is an intensity, the tunnel vision of a man making an effort. Days pass when I don't even see the river, and then, suddenly, I am buoyed by a mysterious current, something unreasonable, something like hope, rising like heat from a sidewalk grating. I have learned how to navigate this foreshortened life of mine; to ruse with panic, duck under terror. My will has become a well-exercised muscle.

In November, I made one of my bimonthly visits to the doctor. It is a dimly lighted office piled with coats. People sit demurely and read magazines, or doze. There is not much talking. All of us are self-contained and casual as we wait for our blood test — the prick in the flesh of the fingertip, the small bead of blood, the glass siphon turning pink as the blood climbs inside it, the click of the counter whirring to its level. Then we are shepherded into small, bright consultation rooms with Daumier lithographs on the wall, and shelves full of barbarously named compounds which will weaken us and make us sick, loosen our hair, disrupt the lining of our stomach, thin out our bone marrow, cause a flulike arching of the muscles, but will do even more damage to those inconspicuous additions to our bodies, the nodes, tumors, and lymphocytes that gather within us to disrupt our organisms.

A year before, I had undergone a course of chemotherapy. Every few weeks, several large hypodermics of pink or transparent liquid had been injected into a vein on the inside of my elbow. There had been a cool rush in my arm and tongue; a lightheadedness; then I had gone into the bathroom and smoked a joint of marijuana to keep down the nausea. The result was a cool floating feeling, as I put my coat on and waited for a cab, then walked carefully to the elevator in my building, not jiggling or shaking. I felt breakable, as if the injection had turned me into glass. All day I would sit in my reading chair and listen to music or read a novel. This was not a day for thinking, not a day to measure my adequacy to the larger questions of life. Gradually I would get tired and nauseous. By the next morning, I would be sick and try to sleep it off. Then, hour by hour, the ashen feeling in my face would lessen, the wobbly numbness in my legs would vanish. The morning after that, I would go out running, as if I were acting out a private joke: the joke of health and youth, the joke of endlessness.

As months passed, the nodes in various parts of my body shrank, and 36 my blood count went down. My hair fell out, although I didn't become bald, only scalpy. I was hopeful and buoyant, proud that the chemotherapy didn't bother me too much. In the middle of it, I went to my house in France, and spent three weeks there. I felt that I was staring down death, although by then I already suspected that the treatment wasn't fully working. My hard little seeds had shrunk but not vanished. By this time, I knew enough about my illness to understand that those seeds would grow again, at a rate only they would determine. I knew that my doctor, for all his hard medical knowledge, observed my blood counts and my nodes as a witness to a mystery, ready to be surprised by variables that no instrument could measure. There were lymphomas that simmered for twenty years, others that "went sour" right away. The clock ticked, but no one could hear it. It was a subcase of the clock of life itself. In the four years since my lymphoma was diagnosed, my radiologist had died of a heart attack and the surgeon who had performed the lymphangiogram had drowned in a boating accident on Long Island Sound. Like me, they were young men. The fates had spun a short skein for them. And for me? Who can say? The bell curve does not favor me, but a bell curve is not destiny. Each year laboratories churn out results that may be altering the curve: new drugs, new regimens, entire new methods. Am I hopeful? Not exactly. I am trying to live until tomorrow, and then tomorrow.

Those three weeks at the house were a miracle. The winter trees resembled gray, upswept brushes; the fire grumbled all day in the fireplace. For four years I had been bending myself to a shorter arc of life. I wanted elbow room; I wanted an enlarged present, and I had managed by discipline and willpower, by selfishness, to thicken the everyday, attenuate the far-off. Normally we live in a double sphere of consciousness: a near shell reverberating with needs and hopes, full of urgency, heavy with the flesh of our lives; and a far, attenuated hood of thoughts and projects which spin us years into the future, where we pretend that there is time. The near shell is tribal and blood-real; the far, attenuated shell is glorious, flimsy; it is man's experiment with immortality, without which books would not be written and buildings would not be erected to last centuries. It is the lie of endlessness, the lie we spin out of ourselves like the "filament, filament" of the "patient spider" in Walt Whitman's poem, to give us time.

For three weeks at the house, I lived a purely tribal life. The days were empty and cold. I read long books by the fire, and felt thoughtless and happy as I jogged down the muddy road into the valley, past my neighbor's tobacco-drying shed, past the low, mossy roofs of the village, and then, laboriously, rasping and out of breath, up a long stony incline through the woods to my house. I felt that death could not harm me. I was neither young nor old. I was simply a man living alone in a stone house, surrounded by books, baking in the glowing heat of oak logs in the fireplace, feeling the sharp chill of black nights when I went outside to pee on the gravel, and heard the splatter of my urine mingling with the wind, and the reverberating hoot of an owl in the nearby woods.

Soon after that, my doctor decided to stop the chemotherapy. The most potent drug in the combination, Adriamycin, could damage my heart if more than a certain quantity was used over my lifetime. He had used about half of that, and wanted to save Adriamycin — a new kind of antibiotic which had been one of the important discoveries for cancer treatment in the 1970s — for another round of chemotherapy, "if" needed. A sonogram revealed a shadow persisting in my abdomen. No, I wasn't cured. The lymphoma had been ground down and compressed, but not extirpated. I was released into uncertainty. My outer shell of time had been broken; I would never give my thoughts to it again without an undercurrent of disbelief. Only tribal time was real to me, and tribal time was a kind of eternity. The gray smoky water of the river outside my window; the boys playing baseball on the large brown vulva that is the playing field in the park; my daughter's bony ballerina's grace, were real. Unreal were pension plans, and the conquering of cancer by the year 2000; unreal was my daughter as a young woman, a future I sometimes saw tentatively in her face. My daughter fluttered between the two times. Loving her drove holes in my body of time, and let in distance; distance that was denied me, distance I strove for and wished for without hoping, because hope devalued my one secure possession: the roomy present, which I savored best in the solitude that was the legacy of my childhood. My grandparents' farm, my house in France, my window overlooking the river.

Then, in November, came the visit to my doctor, to be palpated, X-rayed, to have my blood tested. These visits were never routine. I knew that when my doctor spoke, I would listen as to no one I had ever listened to in my life. He would push down at the base of my neck, probe under my arms and in my groin. He would feel at the margin of my rib cage on the right side and below my rib cage on the left side, for my liver and spleen. My doctor is a small, balding, energetic man. Over the years, we have gotten to know each other well. I've heard his jokes, listened to his fervent Zionism, his humorous indignation at divorce lawyers, and other favorite topics. There is a manic optimism about him, a speedy, sometimes angry intolerance. He doesn't like to answer questions, but he answers them, and I ask them. Too many of them. It is our joke. Even when I'm not sure if I want to know, I ask, and then sometimes I feel I know too much. I know how fundamentally helpless my doctor feels under his energetic manner. I know that all the clinical tests and the statistics still leave him face to face with luck every time he examines a patient in his confidence-giving little rooms. It boils down, finally, to intuition, and to ignorance. "I don't know" is the answer to many of my questions. I don't know how long you will live, if you will go into remission, if your disease will "go sour"; there are no signs, there is no text. I don't know how effective the latest combination of drugs will be; I don't know if the side effects in your case will be mild or severe; if, as a result of the treatment, you will get hepatitis, shingles, or pneumonia. To him as to me, my body reveals itself sporadically, at its own pace. From it he can derive sheets full of data on the level of trace minerals in a burnt sample of my hair; on my T cell, B cell, and lymphocyte counts, my red blood cells, my platelets, my sodium or glucose levels, my cholesterol. He can read my heartbeat on a graph, and my internal organs on an X-ray; test my urine; get the opinion of a pathologist on my bone marrow; perform biopsies. But finally he must say, "I don't know." And I've got to accept that my life is indeterminate; that my questions can receive only conditional answers; that no one can have the knowledge or the authority to make me safe again.

My doctor came into the consultation room holding my folder, thick with four and a half years' worth of data, including my latest platelet and white blood cell counts. He was subdued, almost casual, but he got to the point immediately without any jokes.

"I'm going to take a bone-marrow biopsy. We haven't done one in several years, and it's time to have a look. Your white count has been drifting up. I also can feel your spleen for the first time. It could be that something's up. The lymphoma may be changing over."

"Changing over" was an oncologist's phrase for something bad, that was clear.

"A lymphoma can start spilling lymphocytes into the blood," he ex- 44 plained, "and that may be happening here. But let's not jump to conclusions. I could be overreacting to a few numbers. Let's talk it over when we get some more data."

He brought in an apparatus equipped with a short hollow needle, anesthetized a patch of my hip, and drilled out a core sample of marrow. Despite the anesthetic, a deep, creaky pain radiated from the spot.

I felt heavy-headed and chilled as I sat on the examining table. Suddenly, all my philosophy had vanished. Again, time had been flung up close to me. I was not in remission and never had been. For months, under cover of my apparent good health, the disease had been heating up. My spleen had become a "bag full of lymphocytes," to use my doctor's phrase. When I got home, I felt under my arms, around my ribs, in my groin. There were small, inconspicuous lumps that probably hadn't been there before. I was sprouting, I was in flower. Almost immediately I began my panicky phone calls; to my doctor, first of all, in the hope that what he said would be less frightening than my imagination. This time, the truth itself was frightening. A lymphoma that "changes over" can "go sour" very quickly, or it can simmer gently. In the first case, I could be sick very soon, and he seemed almost surprised that I wasn't feeling the effects already. On the other hand, he said, that could be a good sign. I called the head of immunological oncology at the Sidney Farber Cancer Center in Boston, where I knew work was being done on a new approach to cancer treatment using something called monoclonal antibodies. I called a friend who knew doctors at Stanford who were also working with monoclonal antibodies. I called the National Cancer Institute in Washington, and spoke for an hour with a technician, who gave me all sorts of imprecise and reassuring information. I was plunged in a paradox. These monoclonal antibodies represented a radical new approach, and much of the research was being done on lymphoma. The whole field of cancer research was in an excitable state. Several lymphomas and leukemias had been traced to a virus. A type of cancer-stimulating gene, called on oncogene, had been discovered. Recombinant DNA was beginning to produce quantities of pure interferon that could represent a new form of treatment. The hope existed that malignancies could one day be turned off by genetic manipulation. Cheerful substances like vitamin A might have a normalizing effect on cancer cells. It was exciting, full of horizon. But my interest was peculiarly narrow and avid. I wanted to be saved, I wanted it now. But now there was nothing. My doctor, hardheaded, even conservative, under his manic ebullience, didn't get excited about anything that he couldn't use on the demure, patient people who sat in his waiting room. He was a pragmatist, the test was clinical usefulness.

Suddenly the wall had been shoved up close to me, and I felt bruised, as if I had been beaten with fists. Was it possible that my time was to be measured in months now, instead of years? I ran every day under the leafless November trees along Riverside Drive. The raw, moist air rasped in my lungs. The sunlight was thin, almost metallic. It was an absurd act, an act of faith, I suppose; or maybe an admission that I possessed no better kind of day than the ones I was living: teaching class, writing a book, caring for my daughter on the days that she was with me. For almost two years, I had been living with a woman, and from the start chemotherapy had been our companion, a third person that never left us alone. But now time had been brutally torn from me. I had been thrust far into the new life, where my friend couldn't follow me, where nobody could follow me. At times, while I waited for my doctor to assemble his information, it seemed to me that my fright was a way of drowning my aloneness. I had become a member of a heavy tribe, those who walked minute by minute into a blankness that ate the near distance, like the winter fog one year in Venice, unfurling in thick billows, until I walked in a blur of weight which made every step seem heavier, more obsessed. Now, too, space had clamped shut on me, except for sudden vanishing when the river, opening beyond the window, gave me room.

A week later, my doctor was ready to talk. My lymphoma had probably 48 "changed over" to something called a lymphosarcoma-cell leukemia. If so, this was a relatively infrequent occurrence, and he was not willing to predict what would happen next. On the other hand, looking over the flow chart of my visits to him during the past four years, he had noticed a slow upward drift of my white blood cell count all along. He had reread the original pathologist's report on my first bone-marrow biopsy, remarking a high level of lymphocytes, and remembered that a hematologist, at the time, had guessed that my lymphoma could well be accompanied by one of its near cousins, a chronic lymphocytic leukemia. By now I understood that these daunting terms — lymphoma, lymphosarcoma-cell leukemia, chronic lymphocytic leukemia — were not as definitive as they sounded. They were nets cast into a turmoil, freeze-frames of a complex flow. The conditions they referred to tended to blur into each other, and become each other. The immunological oncologists used other nomenclatures entirely, and the whole classificatory system for lymphomas was put in doubt by some scientists.

Medicine was still related to voodoo and witchcraft by one tenuous, life-giving link: it boiled down, finally, to educated guesses, habit, long practice, and clinical intuition. My doctor's knowledge, extensive and up-to-date as it was, provided him not with recipes but with a kind of yoga. In a given case, he absorbed the sheets of test results, the feel of the patient's body, the years of working through similar cases, exploring life at its extremity, life at its breaking point; and then he decided, the way a baseball player swings at a fast ball. It was disturbingly close to guesswork. In my case, it meant that what I wanted to know — live or die, now or later? — would emerge over time, as the blood tests accumulated, and my state of health spoke for itself.

I lived in a suspended breath. I waited — what else could I do? — and yet I could not bear to wait. I ran harder every day, and tugged at the exercise machines in the health club. My friend Vikki and I flew up to Boston, and I had bagfuls of blood extracted by the immunologists there. I saw another oncologist, who seemed grim about my prospects, frightening me to a new pitch of tension. I called my lawyer to get my will in order. I called my ex-wife, pleading with her to take good care of our daughter. I felt an incongruous need to finish the book I was working on. Did the world need another book? I knew that wasn't the question. I felt that writing was my best self. It was, internalized, the view from my window, or my stone house on a hilltop in southwestern France. It was the cohered tensions of living made deliberate and clear. Writing, I touched the roots of my life, as I did when Vikki and I made love, or when I spent an afternoon with my daughter. But writing was stronger, more sustaining than these. Every day, I spilled words onto my yellow pad, crossed out, inverted sentences, inserted new paragraphs on the back of the page. I raced my fountain pen from line to line, in erratic humps and jags. And this crabbed hieroglyphic, curling from top to bottom of the page, was my mind climbing quietly and privately to a plane of spirit that balanced above my sick body. There my limitations were acceptable; they were the language spoken by my pen, which drank at a deep source.

I saw that a writer's immortality exists in the moment of conception, in which language has seized hold of him, and not in the posterity which few of us believe in, in these days of nuclear shadow. A work is not a life, but writing is living, and now especially I wanted to live with all my might. I wanted to fight off the shrinking effect of fear. Therefore, I wrote my book, while I waited for the blood tests to speak. And gradually they spoke, in a temporary, self-revising idiom.

"At least your count isn't shooting through the roof," my doctor said, 52 "and that's good."

With chemotherapy the count began to come down, my nodes and spleen began to shrink again. I could see, as at the end of an alley, a brightness: the crisscrossing of passers-by, the honking and snoozing of cars; it was the bland ribbon of time that runs on, runs on.

Oh, yes, it is a flimsy ordinariness, an eroded shell. It is Vikki and her children, my daughter and me, at the Botanic Gardens, surprised by the pastel blossoms of the cherry trees like bursts of softness, in the chilly breeze of early April. It is cutting up parsnip roots, carrots, and broccoli for a stew; feeding the children, and then sitting in the high shadowy living room of Vikki's apartment late at night, reading or talking. It is the old dream of an enchanted ordinariness come true in snippets and jigsaw-puzzle fragments that don't last, but lasting isn't what's important now, as long as the puzzle is real. And then, every few weeks, it is the remembering again that I'm the loose piece, the medical case with the catheter in my arm, and the large hypodermics of clear fluid; the two days of homeopathic misery; the predictable weathering of the predictable storm, a man holding on; running under trees ready to thicken into spring; looking from my window, as now, on the rim of darkness over the Palisades, and the white street lamps of the road slanting to river level; the beige necklace of lights outlining the George Washington Bridge; the river, become a nothing of black and depth, almost unreal, like a fault line burst asunder into the earth's interior.

AFTERWORD

When Stanley Kunitz was a young poet, he imagined a dying writer taking notes on the experience. "Observe the wisdom of the Florentine / Who, feeling death upon him, scribbled fast / To make revision of a deathbed scene, / Gloating that he was accurate at last."

Normally writers talk more about dying when they are young and healthy than they do when they are old (Kunitz is well into his eighties now; what does he think of his youthful quatrain?), but the middle-aged Zweig, feeling death upon him, scribbled fast . . . as if the making of paragraphs might hold death off. At least it may distract the writer: Maybe this is a useful side to self-consciousness, to Walker

Percy's "*The Loss of the Creature.*" *It becomes useful to us, to understand out of Zweig's anxiety and dread and persistence how "the river, become a nothing of black and depth, almost unreal, like a fault line burst asunder into the earth's interior.*"

BOOKS AVAILABLE IN PAPERBACK

The Adventurer: The Fate of Adventure in the Western World. Princeton: Princeton University Press. *Nonfiction.*

Eternity's Woods. Middletown: Wesleyan University Press. *Poetry.*

The Heresy of Self-Love: A Study of Subversive Individualism. Princeton: Princeton University Press. *Nonfiction.*

Muktananda: Selected Essays. New York: Harper & Row. *Essays.*

Walt Whitman: The Making of the Poet. New York: Basic Books. *Nonfiction.*

To the Student

We regularly revise the books we publish in order to make them better. To do this we need to know what instructors and students think of the previous edition. At some point your instructor will be asked to comment on the second edition of *The Contemporary Essay*; now we would like to hear from you.

Please take a few minutes to complete this questionnaire and send it to Bedford Books of St. Martin's Press, 29 Winchester Street, Boston, Massachusetts 02116. We promise to listen to what you have to say. Thanks.

School _____

School location (city, state) _____

Course title _____ _____

Instructor's name _____

Please rate the selections.

	DEFINITELY KEEP	KEEP	DROP	NOT ASSIGNED
Abbey, "Aravaipa Canyon"	____	____	____	____
Atwood, "Canadian-American Relations"	____	____	____	____
Baker, "Through A Glass Darkly"	____	____	____	____
Baldwin, "If Black English Isn't a Language, Then Tell Me, What Is?"	____	____	____	____
Berger, "Her Secrets"	____	____	____	____
Berry, "Property, Patriotism, and National Defense"	____	____	____	____
Bly, "Chin Up in a Rotting Culture"	____	____	____	____

	DEFINITELY KEEP	KEEP	DROP	NOT ASSIGNED
Brodsky, "On Tyranny"	___	___	___	
Carver, "My Father's Life"	___	___	___	___
Cowley, "The View from 80"	___	___	___	___
Davenport, "Making It Uglier to the Airport"	___	___	___	___
Didion, "Holy Water"	___	___	___	___
Dillard, "Total Eclipse"	___	___	___	___
Ehrlich, "The Solace of Open Spaces"	___	___	___	___
FitzGerald, "Sun City — 1983"	___	___	___	___
Frazier, "Dating Your Mom"	___	___	___	___
Fussell, "Notes on Class"	___	___	___	___
Galbraith, "Corporate Man"	___	___	___	___
Gass, "Of Speed Readers and Lip-Movers"	___	___	___	___
Gould, "Sex, Drugs, Disasters, and the Extinction of Dinosaurs"	___	___	___	___
Gray, "On Friendship"	___	___	___	___
Hearne, "Consider the Pit Bull"	___	___	___	___
Hoagland, "The Courage of Turtles"	___	___	___	___
Johnson, "Rape"	___	___	___	___
Keillor, "Shy Rights: Why Not Pretty Soon?"	___	___	___	___

	DEFINITELY KEEP	KEEP	DROP	NOT ASSIGNED
Kingston, "No Name Woman"	___	___	___	___
Kumin, "Journal — Late Winter–Spring 1978"	___	___	___	___
Lopez, "Wolf Notes"	___	___	___	___
Lurie, "Clothing as a Sign System"	___	___	___	___
McPhee, "Riding the Boom Extension"	___	___	___	___
Morris, "City of *Yok*"	___	___	___	___
Oates, "Against Nature"	___	___	___	___
Ozick, "The First Day of School"	___	___	___	___
Percy, "The Loss of the Creature"	___	___	___	___
Pickering, "Occupational Hazard"	___	___	___	___
Reid, "Hauntings"	___	___	___	___
Rich, "Taking Women Students Seriously"	___	___	___	___
Rodriguez, "The Achievement of Desire"	___	___	___	___
Rose, "Tools of Torture"	___	___	___	___
Sanders, "Doing Time in the Thirteenth Chair"	___	___	___	___
Schell, "A Republic of Insects and Grass"	___	___	___	___
Stone, "A Higher Horror of the Whiteness"	___	___	___	___
Theroux, "Mapping the World"	___	___	___	___

	DEFINITELY KEEP	KEEP	DROP	NOT ASSIGNED
Thomas, "The Tucson Zoo"	——	——	——	——
Trillin, "Rumors Around Town"	——	——	——	——
Tuchman, "History as Mirror"	——	——	——	——
Walker, "In Search of Our Mothers' Gardens"	——	——	——	——
Welty, "The Little Store"	——	——	——	——
Will, "Against Prefabricated Prayer"	——	——	——	——
Wolfe, "Land of Wizards"	——	——	——	——
Zweig, "Transitions"	——	——	——	——

Any general comments or suggestions? _____

_____

_____

_____

_____

Name _____

Mailing Address _____

_____

Date _____

Resources for Teaching

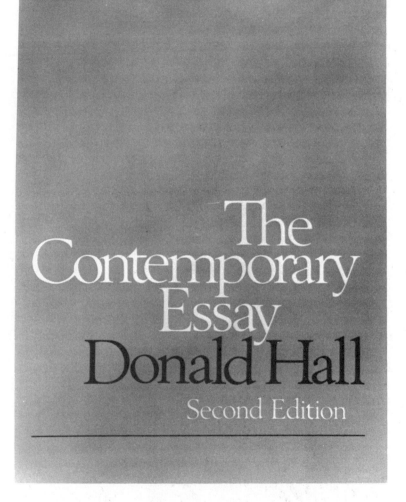

The
Contemporary
Essay
Donald Hall
Second Edition

Prepared by
Diane Elizabeth Young

Resources for Teaching

THE CONTEMPORARY ESSAY

Second Edition

by

Donald Hall

Prepared by

Diane Elizabeth Young
Stanford University

A Bedford Book
St. Martin's Press   •   New York

For information, write: St. Martin's Press, Inc.
175 Fifth Avenue, New York, NY 10010
Editorial Offices: Bedford Books of St. Martin's Press
29 Winchester Street, Boston, MA 02116

ISBN: 0-312-00347-1

Resources for Teaching

THE CONTEMPORARY ESSAY

Note to Instructors

The text selections in the second edition of *The Contemporary Essay* are rich enough to accommodate multiple approaches and interpretations, along with those Donald Hall presents in his Afterwords. Because of this and in response to suggestions from instructors who used the first edition, we chose not to limit instructors' options by including the conventional editorial apparatus in the text itself. We know, however, that some instructors appreciate such suggestions, and accordingly we've provided them here, where they can be used entirely at the instructor's discretion.

Resources for Teaching, prepared by Diane Elizabeth Young of Stanford University, provides commentaries, interpretations, and suggestions for teaching the works included in *The Contemporary Essay,* Second Edition. An entry appears for each selection in the text. These entires consist of Questions on Meaning, Questions on Strategy, Questions on Language, and at least two writing assignments for every essay. Each question is followed by a lengthy discussion, which includes advice about how to approach the selection, and suggests possible answers to the question. In addition, many entries discuss Donald Hall's Afterwords and ways these can be used to teach individual essays. No doubt some instructors will disagree with some of the entries — but those disagreements, too, will be springboards for class discussion.

The resources are arranged alphabetically by author, the order that the selections appear in the text. Following the title of each selection is the page number on which it appears in the text.

For instructors who want their students to have access to the questions (without answers), they are also available separately on 8-1/2-by-11-inch sheets for duplication. Instructors can order them from Bedford Books of St. Martin's Press, 29 Winchester Street, Boston, MA 02116.

Contents

EDWARD ABBEY

Aravaipa Canyon (p. 13)

Questions on Meaning

1.   Historically, the natural world was considered the Book of God, able to be read for its traces of the divine will. In the United States, this tradition of interpreting nature is most firmly found in the Puritan sermons, but it certainly continues into Hawthorne, Thoreau, Emerson, and Melville. Would you locate Edward Abbey in this tradition, despite the fact that in paragraph 12 he describes himself as an "apostate Presbyterian"? As such, why does he invest Aravaipa Canyon with religious qualities, describing it in the final paragraph as a place that is able to offer "redemption"? How do you reconcile this idea with paragraph 12, in which he sees nothing to inspire a frisson of "natural piety" in the pool's "inky" depths?

DISCUSSION: Abbey may have renounced his Presbyterianism, but only in the sense of it as an organized religion. He invests the canyon with religious qualities because he still, despite his renunciation, finds access to a spiritual world through nature. Nature, then, is able to offer some spiritual redemption. It is interesting that the inky depths, which might, in the history of literary tradition, stand as a very clear symbol of darkness and evil, don't carry any of those valences for Abbey. His essay suggests that his apostate Presbyterianism has lost one half of the equation offered by traditional religion — inherent evil is absent. Instead, the divine world, as reflected in nature, is completely good, and evil, far from existing in dark pools, is not present in nature at all. Rather, it seems to be found only in humans, and it finds clear expression in this essay in the extermination of the weakest of the Indians.

2.   In paragraph 11, the locusts interrupt with their "universal lament for mortality and time." Yet the canyon seems like nothing so much as a place out of time, a place that contains secret places, like Iceberg Canyon, "where the sun seldom shines." Is the whole canyon subject to "mortality and time"?

DISCUSSION: As the representation of the divine spirit, the canyon itself is immortal. And, of course, it is inanimate — rocks don't die. Those things that live in the canyon — the plants and the animals and the insects — do die, but the dead are replaced by the next generation. Mortality and time touch only the individuals, but the life of each species goes on.

Questions on Strategy

1.   Does showing us the surface of things let us glimpse the mystery they embody? Consider the final two paragraphs. What would this essay be about without them? Do they guide us to interpret in a certain way the world Abbey describes in such detail?

DISCUSSION: The final paragraphs certainly guide our interpretation of this essay, but earlier moments also suggest the mysteries of life that Abbey is trying to convey. In paragraph 14, for example, the mountain lion appears out of nowhere and then melts away, wraithlike. For Abbey, the wild cat inspires "wonder."

Questions on Language

1.   Abbey insists in paragraph 5 that "we are no more troubled by ancient history than are the mudsuckers in the pools. We prefer to enjoy the scenery." But the paragraph immediately preceding offers the bloody history of the white pioneers in Aravaipa Canyon. Is his statement about not caring true in the context of this essay? Why does he include the history at all?

DISCUSSION: *Despite Abbey's assertion in paragraph 5, the diction in paragraph 4 suggests another story: a group of "unarmed old men, women, children," "huddled," "exterminated," "death squad," "vigilante." These words clearly express the unequal combatants in the conflict, or, rather, the extermination. In his diction, Abbey is judging the whites. And the tone of the final sentence in paragraph 4 — "Since then those people have given us no back talk at all" — with its heavy irony, certainly seems to place Abbey's sympathies with the Apaches. Abbey returns to the subject in paragraph 15, when he compares the javelina, grazing in family bands, to the Apaches. They are equally "dangerous," ravening beasts who sink their tusks into "roots, tubers, the innards of barrel cactus" and feed on "grubs, insects, and carrion." And, in case we miss the point, he reminds us of the distinction between the Indians and the whites: the javelina, who represent the same peaceful characteristics as the Apaches, are "not so dangerous" as "us."*

2. Look at Abbey's diction throughout this essay. In an essay that is mainly description, how does the following sentence guide the reader toward a particular interpretation of the ideas Abbey sees in Aravaipa Canyon: "we pause to inspect a sycamore that seems to be embracing a boulder" (paragraph 13).

DISCUSSION: *The verb "embracing" is itself argument at the micro level. The guiding argument of the essay is the integrity, cohesion, and cyclical renewal of the natural world. The ideas in sentences support this thesis, and the individual words that make up the sentences support it at the smallest level.*

Writing Topics

1. Write an essay comparing "Aravaipa Canyon" to Annie Dillard's "Total Eclipse." How do they both use the natural world to comment on the human world?

2. Look at how Abbey, Didion, and Dillard press the concrete world into service. Write an essay in which you describe something in the natural world, rendering it visible to someone else. If your subject is a rose garden, for example, you will have to combine an exact eye — after all, to the uninitiated, roses all look the same — with a precise knowledge of where all the looking points. What makes your subject worth examining? Is the history of rose breeding meaningful in the history of humankind? For example, Napoleon spent an enormous amount of money running Malmaison, the estate where his wife, Empress Josephine, collected all the known rose varieties. Could you use roses to comment on the political life of Napoleon?

MARGARET ATWOOD

Canadian-American Relations:
Surviving the Eighties (p. 19)

Questions on Meaning

1. Atwood seems to be arguing that Canadian nationalism was crystallized by the growth of Canadian literary nationalism. Why does Harvard insist that its students read "reams and reams of second-rate" American literature (paragraph 30), and what does self-knowledge have to do with nationalism?

DISCUSSION: *Understanding what the citizens of one's country thought about and hoped for can lead to an understanding of what that country attempted to be: "the literature produced by a society has some connection with the society. It follows that by reading the literature you can get a bearing on the society" (paragraph 36). That understanding then allows one to make a "simple statement: we exist," in full comprehension of what that "we" refers to (paragraph 34).*

2.   Does Atwood think that nationalism is the answer in the 1990s and beyond?

DISCUSSION: In the close of the essay, Atwood advocates, implicitly, both a greater sensitivity to and an understanding of the differences between Canada and America. Earlier she asserts that "Canadians and Americans may look alike, but the contents of their heads are quite different" (paragraph 23). She attributes to Canadians a condition she calls "survivalism," the belief that survival means merely escaping with one's life (paragraph 36). Atwood interprets survivalism as an ethical stance in the world we share, since "where there seems to be increasingly less and less of more and more, it may be a more useful as well as a more ethical attitude toward the world than the American belief that there is always another horizon, a new frontier, that when you've used up what's in sight you only have to keep moving" (paragraph 38). She splits the world into two camps, "those countries that perform or tolerate political repression, torture and mass murder and those that do not." Therefore, individual cultural concerns, as perceived through "Canadian literature or even old American laundry lists," are no longer of paramount importance, whereas "the study of human aggression" is (paragraph 49). In the face of threats against the world as a whole, "there are values beyond national ones. Nobody owns the air; we all breathe it" (paragraph 51).

Questions on Strategy

1.   In the opening paragraphs (1–10) of the essay, Atwood talks about America's "unconscious imperialism," which stems, she says, from the way that Americans are accustomed to perceiving themselves in the world. How does she compare the Canadian national character with the American national character?

DISCUSSION: Notice Atwood's extensive use of metaphor. In paragraph 20, for instance, she writes: "Canadians live in a small house, which may be why they have their noses so firmly pressed to the windows, looking out." In contrast, all the Americans "can see is [their] own borders, and beyond that some wispy brownish fuzz that is barely worth considering. The Canadian experience was a circumference with no center, the American one a center which was mistaken for the whole thing" (paragraph 21).

2.   This essay includes an enormous range of topics; Atwood seems to wander, completely at her ease, through a critique of both the Canadian and the American national character, a thumbnail sketch of Canada's change from a British cultural colony to an American cultural colony, a brief history of historical education in Canada, and a short visit to Harvard-Radcliffe. What subject unites all these ideas?

DISCUSSION: In every case, Atwood is circling around the idea of nationalism, or the idea of one's country and one's history and its place in the world. The essay pulls all these ideas together at its end, with Atwood's plea for transcending nationalism for the common good: uniting together against violence and repression.

Questions on Language

1.   Speaking from the point of view of her ancestors, Atwood is making a funny point when she writes, "there had been a slight disagreement over who should rule [America] — divinely constituted law and order in the person of George III or a lot of upstart revolutionaries" (paragraph 1). What parts of this sentence make her family's historical perspective clear?

DISCUSSION: We know how her family interpreted the American Revolution through the use of modifiers: George III has "divinely constituted law and order" on his side, but the "upstart revolutionaries" have nothing. It's a way of arguing that loads the dice, since the descriptions of both the king and the revolutionaries are presented as factually true rather than stemming from opinion. This use of language is not an uncommon rhetorical technique, and it's not always put into humorous service. We see it when certain factions are described by a negative modifier — "strident" feminists, for example— that leaves no room for any dissenting opinion.

2.   How does Atwood implicitly convey the understanding of a young child in the following passage? "Canadian history was the explorers and was mostly brown and green, for all those trees. British history was kings and queens, and much more exciting, since you could use the silver and gold colored pencils for it" (paragraph 13).

DISCUSSION: This is history boiled down to the most basic concern: which story gets to be illustrated with the prettiest colors? Notice how diction can establish point of view, so that a sentence can intrinsically comment on the comprehension of the persona being described.

Writing Topics

1.   Reread the Afterword to this essay and write an essay that is to be delivered as a speech to your class. Use Atwood as your model; like her, you too will know your audience, and your essay will naturally be more immediate and relaxed than much of your other writing. Consider taking your home state as your subject, and develop your thesis by focusing on how your state's history was presented to you throughout grade school. How was your state presented in relation to your country and to other countries?

2.   One of Atwood's concerns is that whoever controls what is written, televised, or transmitted controls the culture (see paragraphs 45 and 46). Choose one specific medium and compare its effect on life today with its effect on life before you were born. For example, compare the way a certain product, perhaps cigarettes, was advertised in the sixties and in the eighties. Has the iconography of cigarette advertising changed? You know that there is a very strong cultural consensus against smoking now; is it reflected in a different presentation in advertising over the last twenty years?

RUSSELL BAKER

Through a Glass Darkly (p. 37)

Questions on Meaning

1.   Why would Baker choose this particular title?

DISCUSSION: The title is taken from 1 Corinthians 13:12: "For now we see through a glass, darkly; but then face to face: now I know in part; but then shall I know even as also I am known." The title is a comment on the subject of the piece, which is obscurantism.

Questions on Strategy

1. Why might Baker have decided to use the question and answer format?

DISCUSSION: The format mimics the interviewer getting the "definitive" answers from the authoritative interviewee. It's a format we are familiar with, especially in connection with politics and talk shows like Today *and even* Nightline. *Since we don't know who is asking the questions or who is supplying the answers, it also suggests the proliferation of clichés generated by a faceless and distant bureaucracy.*

Questions on Language

1. What is the difference between the final sentence and every other one?

DISCUSSION: The final sentence — and the title — are the only two places in the essay where we're given any historical location. They are also the only two places where we see Baker himself comment on the stuffing within his frame. Examine the answer to What is the Situation? *Notice how these answers could have been supplied in any time, in any country — yet they deny allegiance to any history.*

Writing Topics

1. Collect the literature from two organizations on opposite sides of an issue. Ignoring which group you personally favor, write an essay analyzing the rhetorical strategies they both employ that seem to obscure, rather than reveal, meaning.

2. RESEARCH: It's obvious that political speech is rife with the kinds of rhetorical strategies and language that Baker is lampooning here, but business has developed its own semiprivate jargon as well. Research some of the famous trials in which corporations have been defendants, such as the Love Canal trial, the exploding Pinto trial, or the DES trials. (Business schools, in some universities, might be able to give you references for your project.) In an essay, discuss what kind of language was used by participants in the trials. Compare the use of abstract and concrete diction. Try to interpret euphemism. How is language used to convey meaning in the documents you analyzed?

JAMES BALDWIN

If Black English Isn't a Language, Then Tell Me, What Is? (p. 41)

Questions on Meaning

1. What is Baldwin's definition of "a language"?

DISCUSSION: Baldwin describes language as being that which describes and controls circumstances; as being the expression of one's temporal identity; and as being a political instrument, means, and proof of power. As Hall points out, Baldwin defines a language through its purpose: "People evolve language in order to describe and thus control their circumstances, or in order not to be submerged by a reality that they cannot articulate" (paragraph 2). In this essay, Baldwin is not interested in participating in the various definitions of a language as they are generally acknowledged by a culture from which he and his race have been excluded. His definition is not a structural one, a list of features and rules that are unique to the language; in their stead, he does give a list of phrases that have been annexed by white English

5

Baldwin, *If Black English Isn't a Language* . . . (text pp. 41–46)

(paragraph 5). This is certainly a point on which his critics would attack him and his definition. Consider, however, historical precedent. Is it so easy to attack an idea because it rejects the general rules of the game and replaces them with its own rules? Look at Margaret Atwood's comment on nationalism and feminism: *"The cultural nationalism of the early '70s was not aggressive in nature. It was a simple statement: we exist. Such movements become militant only when the other side replies, in effect, No you don't. Witness feminism" (paragraph 34). Baldwin is asserting that black English says "we exist" and, in its very differences from white English,* "we exist in a different psychic reality from you." Why, then, he implies, should black English be spoken or judged according to the rules of another psychic reality, a different lifelong experience?

2.   Does any other language have, as its *raison d'être*, subversion?

DISCUSSION: In paragraph 6, Baldwin says that black English "permits the nation its only glimpse of reality." What does he mean by this? I think he means that through black English, the white people of America are confronted with the fact of what they have done to blacks; the very fact that black English is a language forces the whites to confront the knowledge of the horrific situations that have given rise to this necessity, this other tongue: "A language comes into existence by means of brutal necessity, and the rules of the language are dictated by what the language must convey" *(paragraph 7). Although Welsh and Gaelic preceded the subjection of their speakers, these languages now symbolize the identity of their speakers in opposition to the English.*

3.   Does language have to change if there is to be social change?

DISCUSSION: See paragraphs 7 and 10. What we know, historically, is that when social change occurs, language changes: the same consciousness that, in the thirties, could see only a lady reporter, for example, now sees many, and suddenly they are, most important, simply reporters. As our reality changes, our language changes. The example Baldwin gives is the creation of black English, born of the black diaspora.

Questions on Strategy

1.   In the opening paragraph, Baldwin rejects the claim that "the argument concerning . . . black English" has anything to do with "the question the argument supposes itself to be posing." Yet he doesn't define immediately what he sees as the real question. Where does he identify the question at issue, and why does he delay his answer for so long?

DISCUSSION: In the penultimate paragraph, Baldwin exposes the truth at the center of the argument: "It is not the black child's language that is in question, it is not his language that is despised: It is his experience." This framework, beginning with an implicit question and ending with an explicit answer, is the organizing principle of the entire essay; everything within the essay builds toward persuading the reader of the truth of the final statement.

Questions on Language

1.   The essay's final paragraph stands as a coda, a word derived from the Latin, meaning "tail," which in music is "a more or less independent passage concluding a composition" (*Random House College Dictionary*, rev. ed.). The final paragraph is one sentence long, but it is a complicated, passionate finale. Analyze the way Baldwin uses repetition in this sentence to create his supremely elegant indictment. In what rhetorical tradition might you locate this sentence?

DISCUSSION: The power of this sentence depends on repetition and syntactic replication. Look at the underlined phrases (emphasis added): "And, after all, finally, <u>in a country</u> with standards so untrustworthy, *a country that makes heroes of so many criminal mediocrities, a country unable to face why so many of the nonwhite are in prison, or on the needle, or standing, futureless, in the streets* — *it may very well be that both the child, and his elder, have concluded that they have nothing whatever to learn from the people of a country that has managed to learn so little."* This is highly formal writing, echoing both political rhetoric and liturgical syntax.

Writing Topics

1.   Write an autobiographical essay containing two anecdotes: you as the object of — or victim of — some form of prejudice and you as the subject of — or perpetrator of — some form of prejudice. Many of you will have encountered prejudice rarely. Think of prejudice in its widest sense, including feminism and nationalism. Some people have found that their "national character" has preceded them overseas, and have suffered from preconceived opinions. Based on reference to your personal stories, develop a theory of prejudice and how it works in society, which should make up about two-thirds of your paper.

2.   RESEARCH: The news has been full of stories about the resurgence of the neo-Nazi movement. Take this as your subject and develop your essay by focusing on one of the following ideas. Analyze the rhetoric these organizations use. Can you interpret their persuasive strategies? Research the history of these organizations. Look at the conflict between civil rights law in the United States, particularly involving free speech, and the self-proclaimed aims of a group like the Ku Klux Klan. How does a democratic society balance the right to free speech and the claims on its conscience made by the targets of these groups?

JOHN BERGER

Her Secrets (p. 47)

Questions on Meaning

1.   How does Berger introduce the subjects of secrets and language, specifically how language itself can be used to convey hidden meaning? Analyze the opening three paragraphs.

DISCUSSION: The opening paragraph ushers in the distinction between Berger and everyone else, everyone else belonging to the silent world; he knows about the "inevitability of death," and yet "nobody else [speaks] of it." This paragraph also sets up the idea of Berger's isolation: he learns about death on his own. The two succeeding paragraphs are about euphemisms, code words for things not spoken. In paragraph 2, Berger has a secret fear of death that can't be articulated. He tells us about his grandmother, who is described as having "passed over" and "being at rest" — code words for "dead." The secret question hiding behind his bland "See you in the morning!" is "You won't die in the night, will you?" And in the echoing, identical answer, he hears an implicit reassurance. The returning phrase gives the child a sense of promise; since they're both saying the same words, speaking the same language, they must mean the same thing — "The words promised that I would not (yet) be alone." By the end of the third paragraph we have learned everything the essay will go on to consider: secrets, code words, isolation, the vulnerability of language, and the attempt to use the weak tools of words to communicate across the abyss.

2.   Berger gives several definitions of a writer in this essay. In paragraph 8, a writer is "able to see to the horizon where, anyway, nothing is ever very distinct and all questions are open." A writer is "a person familiar with the secrets." In paragraph 15, he describes writers as "the secretaries of death." Donald Hall writes that Berger "makes the writer an emanuensis taking

7

down the spoken words of death the dictator." Death itself, Berger writes, is "the largest secret." What are the others, with which his mother believed the writer to be so familiar?

DISCUSSION: Berger writes that he "had to discover the existence of . . . death, poverty, pain (in others), sexuality" on his own and that he did discover them, "within the house or from its windows."

3.   With the knowledge discussed in question 2, he left home for good, "more or less prepared for the outside world, at the age of eight" (paragraph 10). He doesn't say another word about his departure. Why would a child leave home at eight years old? Why would such a child learn only of "pain (in others)," since one would imagine that he might find it in himself as well? Consider your answer in relation to Raymond Carver's "My Father's Life."

DISCUSSION: Both essayists keep crucial information suppressed in their essays; both seem to have allegiance to Berger's mother's principle "that events [carry] more weight than the self" (paragraph 10). We don't find out why Berger left home for good at the age of eight. Just as his mother "never spoke of these things," neither does he. The essay, in its withholding of information, reenacts the events of his own childhood, confronting the reader with what confronted him. Both John Berger and Raymond Carver talk about their parents as teachers, and both essays consider what their parents didn't teach them, what they had to learn on their own.

Questions on Strategy

1.   In paragraph 4, Berger says that he has no wish to write autobiography, that "orphan form" that "begins with a sense of being alone." His implicit definition of autobiography seems to be that it is a unique story of an individual experience that cannot be generalized, cannot contain just those "common moments" between the writer and others that he or she is so interested in. However, the opening two paragraphs and most of the rest of "Her Secrets" *are* autobiography. What do you think of his definition of autobiography, and in what genre would you place this essay? Discuss.

DISCUSSION: In the opening paragraph, Berger confides his childhood fears of his parents' death. He stresses that he came by the knowledge of death by himself — "nobody else spoke of it." Yet in the next paragraph, he immediately acknowledges the pervasiveness of this childhood nightmare, shared by "millions of other children." Berger has chosen to write an autobiography that does center on the common moments between people, a study of the parts of his life that are not private and unique but that reverberate with meaning for many others. Whereas you might argue that this essay redefines "autobiography" so that it becomes an inclusive term, you might, on the other hand, disagree with his definition of autobiography as an "orphan form."

2.   How would you describe the structure of this essay?

DISCUSSION: "Her Secrets" is split into two parts. In the first two-thirds, Berger tells of his childhood and describes his relationship with his mother. In the final third, he gives a scene of a day just before his mother's death in which he, Katya — who is his mother's granddaughter, the person the essay is dedicated to, and perhaps his own daughter — and his mother all appear. His mother talks about her death, saying that whether she is buried or cremated is not important to her (paragraph 34). "For the first time" she placed "the wrapped enigma between us" (paragraph 35). Death itself, and her own death, has been addressed, even if in such a small way. The essay does not end with the contemplation of death, however, but with a meditation on love. Berger repeats his mother's words: "Love . . . is the only thing that counts in this world." Like all the rest of the secrets, love itself remains unexplained.

Questions on Language

1. In the final paragraph, do you think that the comment about "real love" is meant to be transparently clear? Does Berger himself think that abstractions — death, pain, grief, love — convey the same things in each person?

DISCUSSION: Language itself is one of the subjects this essay considers. As a writer — someone who must have faith in words — Berger has an extraordinary feeling for the things that words are unable to capture. Ending the essay on his mother's words about "real love" and emphasizing that "she never added anything more" than "that simple adjective" seems to suggest that perfect knowledge of the great mysteries of life is beyond our reach but that contemplation of these secrets is essential.

Writing Topics

1. Write an essay comparing Berger's essay with Maxine Hong Kingston's "No Name Woman." Consider that both writers toss up the idea of "secrets" as if it were a ball, flashing and turning in the light, illuminating different parts of life. Both writers are interested in the idea of the unspoken and the codes we use to talk around something. Both writers are drawn to the enigma at the center of life.

2. Write an essay in which you, as a child, learn something about one of the secrets of life. Try to explain how language helped or hindered your knowledge, using the first three paragraphs of "Her Secrets" as a model.

WENDELL BERRY

Property, Patriotism, and National Defense (p. 54)

Questions on Meaning

1. As Donald Hall writes in the Afterword, Berry is putting forward a conservative argument yet comes up with what we would normally consider a liberal-progressive stance *against* nuclear weapons. This essay — which examines the ideas behind the words "national defense" — might also be challenging us to consider the ideas behind the words "progressive" and "conservative." Are these concepts, finally, as paradoxical as "national defense"?

DISCUSSION: Almost any call for nuclear disarmament can be said to be progressive to the degree that it wants the world to progress beyond the current state of affairs, or it can be considered conservative to the degree that it wants to conserve the world as it was before the appearance of those weapons. Major events in history, such as the American Revolution, have been termed "progressive" for their advocacy of change and "conservative" for their wish to preserve inalienable rights.

2. How would you describe Berry's vision of the future?

DISCUSSION: The most striking thing about Berry's advocacy of our return to the land is its nostalgia. His vision of the future is nothing so much as a return to the past. Is his vision possible or able to be achieved? Are there other visions that might not rely on having to return to what was?

3. How does Berry's vision support his case against nuclear weapons? Discuss.

DISCUSSION: Above all, Berry's vision grounds the distinction between natural and unnatural national defense. Berry concludes that sound national defense arises naturally from "widespread, settled, thriving local communities," which then "defend the country daily and hourly in all their acts by taking care of it, by causing it to thrive, by giving it the health and the satisfactions that make it worth defending, and by teaching these things to the young" (paragraph 33). From this "real national defense," military defense "would come . . . as if by nature" and would have no need to rely on nuclear weapons (paragraph 33).

Questions on Strategy

1. Think about arguing from definition. How does Berry use the concept of "national defense" to generate his argument?

DISCUSSION: Berry subverts the normal antagonisms that are expressed when we talk about national defense, in which one side usually pleads for less and the other for more. Rather, he steps in and says that "national defense" is no longer conceptually valid, that is, its definition makes no sense in our era. Throughout the first nine paragraphs, he tries to make the concept more and more concrete while actually exposing it as being progressively more abstract.

2. How is paragraph 5 organized?

DISCUSSION: Starting with "our nuclear weapons articulate a perfect hatred," Berry's list of paradoxes exposes the paradox of nuclear weaponry. Notice the balancing of antithetical points or opposites throughout the recitation: "innocent . . . guilty, . . . children . . . grown-ups, . . . Christian love and justice . . . perfect hatred and perfect injustice."

Questions on Language

1. Berry is obviously challenging the denotation and connotation of the word "defense" as we use it in "national defense." Are there other words that the history of civilization has called into question?

DISCUSSION: One obvious example might be "freedom," which always brings up questions of exactly what freedom means. Are we free today, or are we controlled by desire created by advertising? Does freedom coexist with society, or is only Rousseau's "natural man," living alone in the woods, truly free?

Writing Topics

1. Write an essay comparing Berry's piece with Atwood's "Canadian-American Relations: Surviving the Eighties." What are the paramount issues for each writer? What are their respective arguments against nuclear war? What solutions do they propose?

2. Write an essay in which you describe and support your vision of the future. As a starting point, consider whether your vision relies on the past, on whether it requires a renunciation of the past.

CAROL BLY

Chin Up in a Rotting Culture (p. 67)

Questions on Meaning

1.   Could you call the subject of this essay *denial*? In paragraph 4, how does Bly tell us that we are denying reality?

DISCUSSION: When Bly talks about the "surface life of America," she conjures up an image of bugs flitting about on the top of a pond. What she's writing about is the bottom of that pond, the cubic gallons of water and murk underneath the shining surface. In paragraph 4, she doesn't tell us directly that we're denying reality; rather, she concentrates on selling us by indirection; "we get to drive around in strong cars . . . although we are running out of fuel."

2.   What role do writers play in Bly's scenario?

DISCUSSION: Bly points to the poets — Nancy and Joe Paddock — and, by implication, the writers — herself — as the ones who, unlike the Chamber of Commerce, "worked to fasten together conscious and unconscious morality" (paragraph 12). But she seems to see writers only as pointers to the true heroes of our rotting culture. She wants the national grief expressed by being spoken, by choosing "five or six figures who have done marvelous service to the American people at large," people like Dr. Kelsey, who made it impossible to market thalidomide in this country (paragraphs 14–15).

Questions on Strategy

1.   Discuss the way Bly presents her subject, starting with her title.

DISCUSSION: Carol Bly's piece has great charm, much of it generated by the tension between the seriousness of the subject and the lightness of its presentation. Some, too, comes from the inherent contradictions in what she says. After reading the opening sentence, we might ask why rural Minnesotans would want to participate in our rotting national culture. Bly seduces us into reading her essay; the question to be asked is whether we would read it without her sparkling syntactic persuasion.

Questions on Language

1.   Consider the tone of this piece as a whole and the following sentence in particular. How would you describe the tone? "Killing and maiming people is something we must think about" (paragraph 17).

DISCUSSION: It's always hard to put your finger on tone, or what people mean when they speak about tone. This sentence combines two ways of thinking; it seems to be written in the high serious mode, like "drugs and teenage pregnancy are things we must think about." Then why is it funny? Bly's writing seems to take place in that gap between ideas that are so fundamental we all know them — obviously, killing and maiming people is something we must think about — and ideas that, just because of their unutterable truth, are never said aloud.

2.   The explanation for not building the floats — "It [grief over our rotting culture] gives us just enough general malaise so we don't get around to building forty-foot lutefisk floats" — is so bizarre as to be surreal (paragraph 10). How does this explanation work?

11

DISCUSSION: *"Lutefisk floats" — an intrinsically hilarious idea and phrase — carries a great deal of weight here; the unbuilt floats have to support all the unarticulated grief that Bly sees as being of crucial importance. Her insistence on locating the idea of grief in its absence of utterance determines her symbol for that absence; the symbol is something that does not, actually, exist. The floats are unbuilt.*

Writing Topics

1.   Choose a topic — such as the homeless, teenage suicides, alcoholism — that is difficult to talk about without pain. In an essay, can you induce people to read about a difficult, threatening, unpleasant subject by using Bly's strategy? Can you portray it lightly without gutting it?

2.   Write an essay that supports someone's nomination for the Carol Bly Award for American Hero of the Year. You must be clear about the ethics of the decision he or she made to qualify for this award.

JOSEPH BRODSKY

On Tyranny (p. 73)

Questions on Meaning

1.   Brodsky offers us a list of tyrants — Lenin, Hitler, Stalin, Mao, Castro, Qaddafi, Khomeini, Amin — and the mechanism that produces them. He does not, however, join the throng that explains their tyranny by revealing various frustrations these men suffered in their youth; neither Hitler's rejection from the art academy nor his missing testicle holds his interest. What does Brodsky see as the fundamental force behind the production of tyrants?

DISCUSSION: *Brodsky insists throughout this essay that tyranny is an inevitable consequence of what we might see as the Freudian compulsion to repeat. Rather than being an individual compulsion, however, he implies that it is a societal one, in which the community itself, acting as a doomed and single organism, endlessly reenacts the same destructive gestures. In paragraph 8, he writes, "The vehicle of a tyranny is a political party." In paragraph 10, he says that each new party is "created in the image of an old one, aping the existing structures." In paragraph 17, after the tyrant's death, the closed session will appoint a "new man" who "will differ from the old man only physically. . . . the closest thing we've got to resurrection." In paragraph 18, he offers that the party is a kind of pernicious but mindless conveyor belt that spits out tyrants like Detroit does cars.*

2.   Does Brodsky agree with the adage that people get the government they deserve? What does overpopulation have to do with tyranny?

DISCUSSION: *Brodsky does set the individualists and the masses in opposition. In paragraph 20, he writes that sheer numbers of people necessarily overcome the relatively few individualists. In paragraph 10, he criticizes the character of the masses and that of the tyrant: "The droning dullness of a party program and the drab, unspectacular appearance of its leaders appeal to the masses as their own reflection. In the era of overpopulation, evil (as well as good) becomes as mediocre as its subjects. To become a tyrant, one had better be dull." The characters of both are the same; a tyrant and his society are inextricably entwined. Again, Brodsky implies that tyranny is inevitable, that it is the undeniable progeny of a critical mass of numerical weight. "Presently," he writes, "the individualists quit laughing." What do you think of this symbiotic analysis?*

3.   In paragraph 3, Brodsky says that "politics is but geometrical purity embracing the law of the jungle." Does he mean to include all political parties in this assertion, including democracies?

DISCUSSION: *In paragraph 6, Brodsky returns to the topic of sheer numbers of human beings as being inherently dangerous to the individual virtues: "Today, every new sociopolitical setup, be it a democracy or an authoritarian regime, is a further departure from the spirit of individualism toward the stampede of the masses." And in paragraph 21, he insists that the "bureaucratization of individual existence starts* with thinking politics" *(emphasis added). He has previously defined a political party as "a fictitious reality invented by the mentally or otherwise employed " (paragraph 9). Certainly, a democracy seems vulnerable on the grounds of its size and on the grounds that its members are familiar with politically structured thought.*

Questions on Language

1.   Consider the following sentence from paragraph 14: "The average length of a good tyranny is a decade and a half, two decades at most." How would you describe the diction, and what is its effect?

DISCUSSION: *Brodsky tosses this sentence off casually, sounding as if he's describing the duration of a baseball game. The diction is colloquial, as it is in the following example: "Foreign doctors are flown in from abroad to fish your man out from the depths of senility to which he has sunk" (paragraph 14). As in Bly's "Chin Up in a Rotting Culture" we can see how much more effective relaxed, concrete diction can be than elevated, abstract language. Consider, too, Hall's Afterword and the importance he places on Brodsky's "imaged tyrant . . . a single evil old man."*

Writing Topics

1.   What is Brodsky advocating in this essay? Is he rejecting working and thinking within the political party system? Write an essay in which you discuss the alternative he holds out for escaping from what this essay says is inevitable — sooner or later, it seems, a democracy will become a tyranny.

2.   RESEARCH: It's very easy for us to identify tyrannies in other countries. Looking at the history of the United States, can you discuss someone who achieved tyrannical power? Do some research on the McCarthy hearings in the early 1950s. Was there a social mechanism that, in effect, generated the hearings?

RAYMOND CARVER

My Father's Life (p. 81)

Questions on Meaning

1.   How do you interpret the final stanza of Carver's poem (paragraph 29) in relation to the preceding ones?

DISCUSSION: *In "Photograph of My Father in His Twenty-Second Year," Raymond Carver addresses the reader until the last sentence, which makes up the final two and a half lines of the poem. There the orientation changes, and the author suddenly turns to his father in a direct address: "Father, I love you,/*

yet how can I say thank you, I who can't hold my liquor either / and don't even know the places to fish."
What is the son saying here? Consider the "yet how can I say thank you," which seems to indicate that
he cannot thank his father for teaching him: for he too is an alcoholic — "I who can't hold my liquor either"
— and his father didn't show him the "places to fish." It's not much of an inheritance that C. R. Carver
left his son, on the surface, and still Raymond's first words are "Father, I love you." The poem echoes the
balance between love and disappointment that Carver tries to express throughout the essay.

2. What does the closing line of the essay tell us about its subject?

DISCUSSION: In the closing paragraph, Carver says that he has lost his memory of the day of his father's
funeral. He thought he'd remember, but he "forgot it all." All the details are gone, but what is left is the
memory of hearing his and his father's name, Raymond, repeated all afternoon: "Raymond, these people
kept saying in their beautiful voices out of my childhood. Raymond." Hearing the name seems to tie
together, or give him back, all his childhood memories. Earlier in paragraph 27 Carver relates that he used
to examine his father's photograph as though it could convey some truth. He looked at it and tried "to
figure out some things about my dad, and maybe myself in the process. But [he] couldn't." The subject
of the essay is, of course, Carver's father, but as the poem articulates, the juxtaposition of this particular
father and son renders meaning to the now grown-up child. "My Father's Life" has as much about
Raymond Carver, Jr., in it as it does about Clevie Raymond Carver.

Questions on Strategy

1. How does Raymond Carver describe his life as he grew up?

DISCUSSION: Carver presents a series of small vignettes: his mother pouring whiskey down the sink
or diluting it; his mother finding lipstick and a lacy handkerchief in the car; his mother knocking out his
father with a colander. These scenes describe alcoholism, extramarital affairs, domestic violence. His
family had little money and less stability. But Carver presents this situation almost matter-of-factly,
omitting his reactions to, or feelings about, constant unpredictability. In paragraphs 22 and 23, he makes
two comments about his feelings. Seeing his father in the midst of his nervous breakdown, he thinks,
"What in hell is happening to my dad?" After six years of his father's illness, he says that "the word
sick was never the same for me again." Almost all of the hurt, betrayal, and confusion is left under the
surface of this essay, unspoken and only obliquely implied. Memoir, a French word, comes from the Latin
root meaning "memory." Of course, few of our childhood memories are uninterruptedly happy, but what
Carver gives us of his early life is almost relentlessly bleak.

Questions on Language

1. How does repetition work as a framing device in this essay? Consider the first and final
paragraphs.

DISCUSSION: Structurally, the final line refers back to the opening paragraph, in which the
relationship between the father and son is also addressed through the relationship between their names.

Writing Topics

1. In paragraph 27, Carver writes that his father died with things left unsaid. "I didn't have
the chance to tell him good bye, or that I thought he was doing great at his new job. That I was
proud of him for making a comeback." This is a sad and common reaction to someone's death.
Yet essayists often seem to take death as their subject and, through writing, make some peace
with, and some sense of, their past. Write an essay comparing "My Father's Life" with John
Berger's "Her Secrets." What would you identify as the two authors' different ways of looking
at their parents after their deaths?

2. Although this essay is titled "My Father's Life" and although it centers on the bond between father and son, it devotes a lot of time to Carver's mother. Discuss the ramifications of this in an essay. Why is Carver's mother in this essay? Look at the anecdotes of Carver's childhood, including the one where his mother tries a kind of magical water trick to draw out her husband's secrets (paragraph 16), and discuss what her function is in this essay. Why does Carver direct his attention to her, rather than his father, in these domestic scenes?

MALCOLM COWLEY

The View from 80 (p. 90)

Questions on Meaning

1. Death is often described as an enemy to be outwitted. Is death the enemy in this essay? Is death a *subject* in this essay?

DISCUSSION: One would certainly think that it would be hard to divorce the age of eighty from the idea of death. Look at the final two sentences: "[Yeats's] very last poem, and one of the best, is 'The Black Tower,' dated the 21st of that month. Yeats died a week after writing it." Where is the narrative emphasis in these two lines? Is it more important that he wrote a great poem or that he died? Is the emphasis in this essay on what one can accomplish in life or what one faces at the end of it?

2. How do you interpret the anecdote about Yeats's having new sex glands implanted (paragraphs 29–36)?

DISCUSSION: At first sight, this is a pathetic and ludicrous story. But Cowley doesn't look at what Yeats did in itself, but in what it gave him — a new perception of himself, not drained, not desperate, but rakish and dangerous and filled with the potential for new creation. Cowley takes not the conventional, but the longer, view. Cowley interprets a fact for us, so that we are guided to an unexpected conclusion about Yeats's operation (paragraph 37), just as we were, perhaps, in hearing Cowley's conclusions on death by tomahawk (paragraph 2). Even those facts that seem to do harm to a subject, like Yeats's having monkey glands implanted for testicles, are all radically changed by personal interpretation.

3. What are some of the cruelties our society inflicts on the aged? Why does Cowley choose such soft, relatively minor cruelties?

DISCUSSION: We hear of the initial embarrassment of being offered a seat on the bus, the humiliation of being dismissed as being too old to fight. With the information we get in the newspapers every day telling of old people being left in their own excrement in nursing homes, of having to buy dog meat for food, of being beaten by their "caretaking" sons and daughters, we know that the aging suffer much worse fates than being offered a seat on the bus. But Cowley's point is not that bad things happen to old people. His point is that in a way, it is horrible to be offered a seat on the bus — that is, to look like you need a seat, or, in fact, to need one because your body has become infirm.

Questions on Strategy

1. Would this essay be any different if it were written to a group of Cowley's peers?

DISCUSSION: *This might be a good opportunity to discuss a writer's audience and the different demands specific audiences have on what is written and how it is shaped. Notice how many anecdotes and stories Cowley uses rather than straight fact or statistics. In paragraph 4, Cowley sets himself up as a foreign correspondent, sending bulletins to the people back home so they, too, can imagine the reality of the country he's in. That other country, the age of eighty, is removed from the imaginative grasp of younger people. Compare paragraph 3 — the litany of facts on aging in America — with paragraphs 5 and 6, which give a litany of concrete examples of what it feels like to be old. The facts of paragraph 3 do not give the meaning of old age, but the anecdotes he tells do. Eighty-year-olds, surely, wouldn't have to be told in so many ways what it feels like to be that age. Cowley's essay seems to show very plainly the power of the story to illuminate experience.*

2. The conclusion to Cowley's first paragraph is certainly unexpected. Does Cowley's first paragraph exist only to shock, or is there some other rationale for this technique?

DISCUSSION: *In the first paragraph, we are stunned by the final sentence, but in the one following, Cowley interprets this method of death as being "quick and dignified" in contrast to the more subtle, protracted cruelties our society inflicts on the aged.*

3. Talking about the essay's tight structure, Hall writes that between the example of Gide and the concluding models of "triumph over the adversity of aging," Cowley inserts a series of "terrors and warnings. He uses a trinity of abstractions — avarice, untidiness, vanity — and specifies or particularizes by different methods — by example, by anecdote, and by allusion. "Cowley obviously hasn't fallen victim to this trinity, so why does he include it?

DISCUSSION: *This is a good example of how a personal essay has room for things that the writer himself hasn't experienced. The contrasting good and bad points of both old age and the elderly give Cowley's subject its authority; we are persuaded because he has painted all its dimensions. The strength of an essay, its persuasive power, rests on both the points that celebrate the subject and those that damn it.*

Questions on Language

1. The first paragraph of this essay is remarkably vivid and evocative. How does Cowley's diction contribute to this effect?

DISCUSSION: *The vividness of "The View from 80" owes a lot to diction, most remarkably in the opening paragraph. The birthday party has a list of familiar words related to such a social occasion — cards, "congratulation" or "condolence," catered food, cake, candles (notice the alliteration, adding to the lyricism of this passage) — followed immediately by the story of the Ojibwas' "deathday" party. It too has words that would not be out of place in any celebration — honor, feast, sang, song, danced. The final sentence, "While he was still singing, his son came from behind and brained him with a tomahawk," splits into two halves. The first phrase gives no indication of what is to follow, and the fact that it is his son who kills him makes the final clause even more shocking.*

Writing Topics

1. Adolescence is seen by many parents as a foreign country, dangerous and distant. Write an essay called "The View from 18," describing either what it is like, or, if you're older than eighteen, what you remember it as being like. Imagine you are addressing someone of your

parent's age, but someone who has no children. Can you remind them what it's like to be eighteen? No doubt your childless audience assumes that most parents overstress the difficulties of adolescence. Include interpreted anecdote to make your audience imaginatively realize the state of being eighteen. Examine how Cowley has not made this essay about himself. How can you give a representative image of life *in general* for eighteen-year-olds, many of whom are different from you? What are their strengths? Their weaknesses? What are the pitfalls they must guard against?

2.   Write an essay about being eighty. What would you like to be like? Do you know what you would like to have accomplished by then and what you hope your character will be?

GUY DAVENPORT

Making It Uglier to the Airport (p. 103)

Questions on Meaning

1.   Davenport's essay seems to identify esthetics as being the sign of a city's health as an organism. Why is this? How does he support this idea?

DISCUSSION: He begins the essay with an example that supports that thesis: the razed Old Stock Exchange in Chicago was important because the building itself symbolized Chicago's history, because it was an architectural landmark, and because its ornamentation could not be replaced. Sheer greed outweighed all this. Davenport's argument is that the spirit of a city is embodied in its overall design and in its buildings and that if people were considered as important as profit, a city would be rich with small neighborhoods — despite the "duplication of services" — and architectural playfulness solely for its celebration of the human spirit.

Questions on Strategy

1.   Discuss paragraph 8. How does Davenport implicitly place his anecdote in the category of the absurd?

DISCUSSION: Very simply, Davenport uses two writers, Gogol and Ionesco, as signifiers of the truly bizarre. Davenport writes, "I will not spin out the Gogolian scene that ensued, though it featured my being told that I didn't deserve to live in this country, my pointing out that I could scarcely leave it without a passport, and on around in circles that left the art of Gogol for that of Ionesco, until I got the State Department on the phone, and had my new passport, together with an apology, in three days." In "Her Secrets," John Berger does something similar: "If I were Aesop, I would say . . . my mother resembled the agouti" (paragraph 6). "Aesop" is used as shorthand, to signal quickly that Berger is making a moral point, an observation about his mother's character, her "prudence and persistence." A rather more complicated similarity is that both writers say, in effect, that they are not going to tell you something, and then both go ahead and say it. Berger is not Aesop, but he does compare his mother to a rodent. Davenport does not include every detail of the scene at the post office, but certainly enough to count as a story.

Questions on Language

1. How do Davenport's apothegms reinforce his thesis?

DISCUSSION: Davenport can be very succinct and direct, yet at the same time the apothegms that he uses are all metaphorical: "Money has no ears, no eyes, no respect; it is all gut, mouth, and ass" (paragraph 2); "all architects are now sculptors in ice (paragraph 3); "The automobile is an insect that eats cities, and its parking lots are a gangrene" (paragraph 5). Part of the reason for the vividness of these examples is that they are guided by Davenport's thesis. Architects can be many things, but they are only sculptors in ice when their creations are ephemeral rather than eternal; the Pyramids were not designed by "sculptors in ice." Just as he focuses on the fleeting rather than the enduring in his governing argument, so does he focus on the transient in his small metaphors. Even the tiniest pieces of the essay support the larger idea. In paragraph 12, he thinks about "buildings that ought to have existed for the fun of it" and he chooses a metaphor into which his thesis is compressed; because his argument is that cities should be organic, he chooses a phrase that uses natural images — "flowers" and "forest." Moreover, flowers are found with forests, so the images reinforce the integrity or coherence of the guiding idea. The result is "outrageous flowers for the granite forest."

Writing Topics

1. Davenport writes, "It is tempting to believe that New Burlington, Ohio, . . . went underwater because a society had emerged that is neurotic with idleness and pointlessness" (paragraph 14). In paragraph 25, he says that cities have changed because our "public lives are different: the automobile and airplane have made us nomads again. The city seems to be obsolete; a sense of community evaporates in all this mobility and stir." Yet, unlike many, he is not tempted to give us prescriptions for regaining what is lost — other than simple endurance. What is your experience of cities or even large towns? Do you think Davenport is indulging in simple nostalgia? It certainly doesn't seem that our lives are going to become more rooted and less frenetic. Write an essay in which you become a utopian, and describe what perfect city life would offer its inhabitants.

2. RESEARCH: In his discussions of scholarly works, Davenport has condensed a small historical study not only of the idea of the city but of the voices of those who live in it. Write a research paper on the idea of the university, using this essay as a model. As Davenport points out, you can take many different approaches. You can zone off the first ten years of development, study the changing history of coeducation, or perhaps interview the president of your university to find out what he or she understands the institution to represent.

3. RESEARCH: Write a research paper on one of the "postmodernist" architects, a group of people who, among other things, are attempting to include the history of a building or a city within a new structure. Take one of their buildings and attempt to analyze it as you would a painting; include a photocopy of the building you are critiquing. (The New York *Times* often carries an architectural column in the Sunday edition.) Choose from the architects Michael Graves, Robert Venturi, Charles Moore, Philip Johnson, Robert Stern, and Leon Krier. If your subject is Michael Graves, you might look at either the Humana Building in Pittsburgh, or the Portland Building in Portland, Oregon.

JOAN DIDION

Holy Water (p. 115)

Questions on Meaning

1. Barbara Grizutti Harrison, in the essay "Only Disconnect" in *Off Center* (New York: Playboy Paperbacks, 1980, p. 131), writes that Didion "chooses to regard a turbine with awe commensurate with that usually reserved for the contemplation of the ark of the covenant." In explaining Didion's fascination with and awe of water, how would you reply to Harrison's comment?

DISCUSSION: Didion says that one of her reasons for investing water with such power is that she is from an arid, vulnerable part of the world. It is also because of the terrific lengths to which we go in an attempt to control natural forces, the intricately calibrated systems we can set up to change nature. We can put monitors on the belly of the earth as we would on the belly of a pregnant woman, but they often tell us only how enormous the damage was after the earthquake struck.

2. Look at the parable offered in the second section, beginning with paragraph 4. Why would Didion use such an esoteric example as Peckinpah's enforced delay to illustrate the indirect effect that moving water has on our daily lives? What do you make of her saying, "This is a California parable, but a true one"?

DISCUSSION: The Peckinpah story is almost surreal. Didion often takes the extreme example — as Hall points out in his Afterword — to suggest the huge forces at play in the world. Even Sam Peckinpah, with his huge budget, his "gaffers, best boys, cameramen, assistant directors, script supervisors, stunt drivers," is unable to control the water; until "some grower" orders it, and "the agencies controlling the Colorado release it," Peckinpah's "desire" means nothing. Water is not free in the West, not at one's beck and call. Even when regulated by people instead of nature, it is still not subject to immediate desire.

Questions on Strategy

1. Comment on the construction of this essay.

DISCUSSION: This essay is divided into four parts. Didion ushers in the subject with the technological considerations of controlling huge amounts of water in different countries, which she develops into an overview of the Southern California water-moving system. The second section illustrates the indirect effect of moving water on our daily lives, albeit through the somewhat esoteric example of Sam Peckinpah's camera crew. The third section discusses human control of the natural world. The fourth section is truly a coda, in which Didion concludes that the great truth of the West is that it is the place where "the average annual rainfall drops below twenty inches." This very concrete appraisal is offered since the West is a place that "resists interpretation."

Questions on Language

1. How does Didion convey the sheer size of the water systems she is talking about?

DISCUSSION: Didion compiles lists of not only systems of water management but the areas they control. Much of her prose depends on accretion, which mimics the enormity of her subject: "in the waterworks themselves, in the movement of water through aqueducts and siphons and pumps and forebays and afterbays and weirs and drains, in plumbing on the grand scale" (paragraph 1). Repetition is also a frequent device; notice halfway through the first paragraph: "I know the data," "I know the difficulty," "I keep watch," "I can put myself to sleep," "I fall back on," "I replay a morning," "I remember," "I recall," "I recall."

Writing Topics

1. In the opening paragraph, Didion says that her "obsessive interest" is "not in the politics of water." She's making it very clear where she wants to focus her interest in this meditation, which certainly seems a fair privilege. Yet in paragraph 8, she asserts that a pool is "misapprehended as a trapping of affluence, real or pretended, and of a kind of hedonistic attention to the body." She resists this interpretation, saying instead that "actually a pool is . . . a symbol not of affluence but of order, of control over the uncontrollable." Certainly she is keeping to her thesis here, but what do you think of her rejection of the politics of water in this particular instance? Write an essay about a subject that is involved in the political realm — food, shelter, medicine — and look at it not from a political point of view. Will you have to concede the political valence of some points to allow your thesis to stand?

2. RESEARCH: "The apparent ease," Didion writes, "of California life is an illusion" (paragraph 9). California, of course, is not unique in its potential for natural disasters. All of us, to some degree, live a precarious life, subject to shattering by flood, fire, earthquake. Somewhere in this country, people can freeze to death if they get stranded outside in winter, people can die in tornadoes or hurricanes, people die of thirst in the desert. What is the most fundamental ecological weakness in your area of the country? Does your state or county need a finely tuned system, for example, to move snow? Research the mechanics of how one natural event is subject to control in your area.

ANNIE DILLARD

Total Eclipse (p. 122)

Questions on Meaning

1. In section II, Dillard describes the eclipse itself. The spectators attend, identically dressed "individualists," all expecting just another experience. "'Look at Mount Adams,' I said, and that was the last sane moment I remember" (paragraph 21). This line introduces the transformation of both the appearance and the reality of Dillard's world. Analyze her response in paragraphs 22–25. Why does she mention different centuries and countries?

DISCUSSION: The tintype of paragraph 22 is a photograph drained of life and significance; her own body is lost and replaced with one made of platinum and silver. Dillard becomes estranged from herself, so dislocated that she views herself from the perspective of a third person, filmed by an outside party. Her own century becomes lost to her; her distance from reality is measured by her feeling that she's in the Middle Ages. In paragraph 23, she is even farther removed. Her husband is far beyond her reach, seen "from the other side of death." Suddenly, Dillard merges with all the generations and generations of people who have ever been born and who have, in their turn, died. She has lost her place in the living world. Paragraph 24 locates Dillard in classical Greece, returns her to life without technology, science, or interpretation. It is even before Adam, by naming, brought the world into human history: "the river we called River." Paragraph 25 extinguishes the sun's light and, with it, life itself. "There was no world. We were the world's dead people." Dillard ends the eclipse section with "It was all over" because the eclipse had been endured to its conclusion and because the experience, at this point, has obliterated everything. In paragraph 37, she relives the eclipse and, with it, her own death and the death of everything mortal.

2.   Section III, after the eclipse, opens with her return to the metaphor she first introduced in paragraph 9: "Why burn our hands any more than we have to? But two years have passed; the price of gold has risen." Analyze what she's saying in paragraphs 9, 26, and the final sentence of 38.

DISCUSSION: *Dillard writes about the miner's journey into the center of the earth as a transforming experience. "When the miners return to the surface, their faces are deathly pale" (paragraph 9). The journey itself is fraught with mortal dangers; if the miners emerge, they bring gold with them. In section III, she is still recoiling from the overwhelming experience, overwhelming in that it obliterated her identity. The risk in mining gold is that you might die; the veins of gold are wedded to burning walls. But now two years have passed, giving her more time in which to interpret what happened, and she realizes that the gold — the meaning of the eclipse — has become more valuable. The value of what she's learned is now more important than the dangers she will face from reliving the experience. This essay is giving us the wealth of her knowledge "in a form that people can use" (paragraph 38).*

3.   Why does writing about an eclipse matter, when experiencing a nuclear war would have no meaning (paragraph 28)?

DISCUSSION: *In the eclipse, Dillard confronted the annihilation of the world as she knew it. But the eclipse was finite: it ended. She could make some sense of it and try to convey its meaning. A nuclear war would obliterate the "unified field," which is "our complex and inexplicable caring for each other, and for our life together here." A nuclear war has no meaning, finally, because it would kill everything sensate in the world. Meaning exists only if life exists.*

Questions on Strategy

1.   In the opening paragraph, Dillard describes herself before she experienced the eclipse. Look at her diction and syntax in the first lines. How does she begin this essay and why does she begin in that particular way?

DISCUSSION: *First consider the chronology. Dillard has experienced the eclipse by the time she writes, but she is writing about herself as though she has not yet lived through it. "Foreshadowing" is the easy answer, but look at the intensity of the description. She uses, like Didion, a great deal of repetition of both diction and syntax: "like dying," "that sliding down," "like the death of someone," "that sliding down," "the region of dread," "like slipping into fever," "falling down that hole in sleep." She is describing an external event — descending into the Yakima Valley — and the emotional experience of that event and, at the same time, suggesting the devastating power of what is yet to come.*

2.   Why does Dillard say that, in retrospect, she "watched the landscape innocently, like a fool, like a diver in the rapture of the deep who plays on the bottom while his air runs out" (paragraph 5)?

DISCUSSION: *When she drives into the Yakima Valley, Dillard has no idea of the enormity of the experience she is about to undergo. Like the diver, she is entranced with the appearance of the landscape and pays no attention to essential detail; every second brings the diver closer to distracted death, just as every second brings Dillard closer to that moment when she confronts her own death in the eclipse. This simile supports the essay's major theme and, like Davenport's use of apothegm, demonstrates how succinctly the argument can be articulated at the sentence level.*

21

Questions on Language

1. Like Berger, Dillard addresses the frailty of language itself, the difficulty of having language convey what we mean. In paragraph 7, among the other surreal objects in the hotel, she notices a sand bucket and a spade. How does she use these objects to further her thesis in the fourth section of the essay? See paragraph 42.

DISCUSSION: *In saying in paragraph 42,"The mind — the culture — has two little tools, grammar and lexicon: a decorated sand bucket and a matching shovel," Dillard is trying to show the frailty of words in the face of life. How much good would a sand bucket and shovel be against the force of a tidal wave on the Malibu coast? But with grammar and lexicon, "we try to save our very lives." In this essay, Dillard uses the eclipse to comment on the subject of meaning itself. The eclipse is something that defies complete explanation. Notice paragraph 31, in which she writes, "I assure you, if you send any shepherds a Christmas card on which is printed a three-by-three photograph of the angel of the Lord, the glory of the Lord, and a multitude of the heavenly host, they will not be sore afraid. More fearsome things can come in envelopes. . . . But I pray you will never see anything more awful in the sky." The gap between what we see, what we say, and what we mean is the size of the moon's shadow-cone.*

2. What is the major rhetorical device used in paragraph 37?

DISCUSSION: *In paragraph 37, the most extended passage on the meaning of the eclipse as the obliteration of all meaning, Dillard recites a litany of her central subjects: life/light/ death/dark, and memory. The repetition of key words creates something like an incantation, on which she closes the eclipse passage.*

Writing Topics

1. Many of the preceding questions, as well as Dillard's essay itself, address the deficiencies of language. Yet her essay is breathtaking and her writing here is magnificent. Describe something that seems, to you, outside the boundaries of language. Remember Dillard's own demand: the assignment is always a *brilliant* essay.

2. Write an essay comparing sections I and IV of "Total Eclipse." How does Dillard use the images she begins with? Who *are* those people in the hotel? Why does the clown have Rembrandt's eyes?

GRETEL EHRLICH

The Solace of Open Spaces (p. 135)

Questions on Meaning

1. The first seven paragraphs of this essay concentrate on the vastness of Wyoming, against which people are insignificant. How would you describe Ehrlich's relationship to the land?

DISCUSSION: *Although the comparison reduces humans to the size of a pinpoint, the relationship isn't adversarial. Rather, Ehrlich discovers the "absolute indifference" of the country to be steadying.*

2.   One of the subjects in FitzGerald's "Sun City—1983" is the peculiarly American compulsion to start life again from scratch, to reinvent oneself. How does Ehrlich deal with this idea?

DISCUSSION: In paragraph 8, Ehrlich gives a brief moment of autobiography. Symbolically, she was reborn when she moved to Wyoming: "I threw away my clothes and bought new ones; I cut my hair." She explicitly addresses the idea of starting over with nothing, in another place where her history has made no impression on this tabula rasa *that is Wyoming: "The arid country was a clean slate." And she addresses the historical manifestation of the same idea as it appealed in Wyoming's history to the settlers who, en masse, before the land was fenced in, had that "'anything is possible' fever" (paragraph 29). "The emptiness of the West," she writes, was "a geography of possibility" (paragraph 26). The Indians were at home in space, but for the "sodbusters who had arrived encumbered with families and ethnic pasts to be transplanted," it was "nightmarish" (paragraph 25). Yet, at the same time, Ehrlich points to vignettes in which history is still felt: "One friend told his wife on roundup to 'turn at the salt lick and the dead cow,' which turned out to be a scattering of bones and no salt lick at all" (paragraph 16). What used to be, in this passage, is as important as what is now.*

Questions on Strategy

1.   Much of this essay is concerned with the idea of space, of size, of the relationship between humans and the dwarfing land. How does this essay treat the topic of space to achieve closure?

DISCUSSION: In the final two paragraphs, Ehrlich takes up the idea of space as the presence, rather than the absence, of something. Space becomes the metaphor for a kind of wholeness or integrity, an inner balance that allows us to "accommodate intelligently any idea or situation." Instead of keeping that sustaining well of space inside us clear, we push it aside, fill it up, cloud it over. In its acute examination of the world, this entire essay reflects the "ability to see what is already there" (paragraph 42). Ehrlich's ending comments on her whole endeavor throughout this piece.

2.   How does Ehrlich differentiate urban life from ranch life in Wyoming?

DISCUSSION: Ehrlich describes "a person's life" in the language we usually use to talk about nature, as though it too were organic: "a slow accumulation of days, seasons, years, fleshed out by the generational weight of one's family and anchored by a land-bound sense of place" (paragraph 13). She slips into the beginning of the sentence a sly critique of urban life as "a series of dramatic events for which [a person] is applauded or exiled." One of the interesting, although implicit, differences that she suggests between city and country life is that the community in Wyoming is made up of known people who belong to known families: "private histories are largely public knowledge" (paragraph 12). People are known in a way that urban neighbors are not.

Questions on Language

1.   Ehrlich looks at a lot of physical detail in this essay, yet her description of the natural world changes. Consider paragraph 20. How would you describe her diction? Why is it appropriate to her subject?

DISCUSSION: The topic sentence sets the interpretation for the rest of the paragraph. "Spring weather," which is usually treated with all the surrounding metaphors of rebirth, is here "capricious and mean." Tornadoes are "elephant trunks" that "slurp everything up and leave." Even snowbanks "hiss and rot, viperous," like snakes. Rivers, far from being crystal clear and fed from mountain springs, "churn a milkshake brown" and then swallow whatever is in their path. Notice how Ehrlich, like Didion in "Holy Water," gives precise measurements of rainfall; in Wyoming, it's "less than eight inches." But water, unholy here, is somehow invested with flatness; it is life-giving, "like blood," but it doesn't create universal fecundity; its power is restricted to "festoon[ing] drab land with green veins."

23

FitzGerald, *Sun City* — 1983 (text pp. 146–187)

Writing Topics

1. Through her contemplation of the landscape, Ehrlich discovers something about living. Often, we come to know the world through watching what we love. In the book from which "Consider the Pit Bull" was taken (*Adam's Task: Calling Animals by Name*), Vicki Hearne writes that she knows the world through seeing dogs and horses and that someone familiar with buildings might know the world differently. Write an essay in which you pay close attention to something as Ehrlich and Hearne do in their writing.

2. RESEARCH: In this essay, Ehrlich uses the history of the Johnson cattle war (which was also the subject of Michael Cimino's film *Heaven's Gate*) to comment on the myth of the "egalitarian" West. Research the Johnson cattle war and write an essay comparing it with Ehrlich's account (paragraph 28). Are your conclusions the same?

FRANCES FITZGERALD

Sun City — 1983 (p.146)

Questions on Meaning

1. In *Cities on a Hill*, the book this essay was taken from, Frances FitzGerald examines four discrete communities — the homosexuals of The Castro in San Francisco, the fundamentalists of Liberty Baptist Church, the disciples of Rajneeshpuram, and the elderly of Sun City. All of them, in one way or another, are an "adaptation to the social transformation going on throughout the country." What are the two major social forces that bring the age-segregated community of Sun City into being?

DISCUSSION: *First, FitzGerald writes that this age group has never before existed in the form it takes today: "In the twentieth century the demographics . . . changed more than they had in the six previous centuries" (paragraph 5). In paragraph 11, she writes, "Americans now in their sixties and seventies are surely the first generation of healthy, economically independent retired people in history — and . . . they may well be the last one." Besides this enormous increase in longevity, Sun City reflects the changed relationship between parents and their adult children. No longer do aging parents expect their children to take care of them in their old age, and, concomitantly, no longer do they "speak as if their lives and their children's were intertwined" (paragraph 84). If anything, these elderly seem to disparage any lifelong bond with their children and their children's children: "A woman going north to be with her children and grandchildren is said to have 'gramma-itis'" (paragraph 84).*

2. In paragraph 58, FitzGerald writes that the Sun Citians "live in a town without any history on the edge of a social frontier, inventing a world for themselves." History and the idea of history seem central to this essay. How would you place FitzGerald's subjects in relationship to their past?

DISCUSSION: *In the introduction to* Cities on a Hill, *FitzGerald describes the members of all four communities as having "the extraordinary notion that they could start all over again from scratch. Uncomfortable with, or simply careless of, their own personal histories and their family traditions, they thought they could shuck them off and make new lives, new families, even new societies. They aimed to reinvent themselves" (p. 23). The Sun Citians, often at the instigation of the husband, decamped from their known neighborhoods and relocated where they knew no one. In this move, they seemed to shed their professional identities as well. "They have no jobs, no families around them, and not very much future," says FitzGerald (paragraph 42).*

24

3. What, then, makes up the life at Sun City? How do these people integrate their new lives with their old ones?

DISCUSSION: Very few people seem to have wanted to keep anything from their old lives. When Ronald Smith and his wife, Lora, "first arrived . . . they had dropped everything — had not even bothered to unpack — and had played golf solidly for two months" (paragraph 32). Their new lives are devoted to a kind of busyness in which reflection on the past has no part. Even their professions are lost to them, in that they were, more than anything, "a means of achieving a satisfactory private life" (paragraph 55) rather than being "socially necessary" (paragraph 58). "And even those who said they had liked their jobs seemed curiously detached from them: they had had jobs, but they had no work in the sense of lifelong interests" (paragraph 55). In paragraph 56, FitzGerald suggests that the two halves of their lives — pre- and post-retirement — are split because their worldview was not large enough to bridge the gap, even the gap between activities, so that "their philosophies, and, presumably, the beliefs they had grown up with, did not really support them in this enterprise of retirement."

Questions on Strategy

1. "Furthermore, the community they have chosen is already so homogeneous as to threaten the boundaries of the self," FitzGerald says in paragraph 42. What does she mean by this? How does she weave this idea into image?

DISCUSSION: The image she uses to convey this idea is that of the city's physical layout. "The streets curve around in maze fashion, ending in culs-de-sac or doubling back on themselves. There is no way in or out of Sun City Center except by the main road bisecting the town. The map, which looks like a child's board game . . . shows a vague area — a kind of no-man's land — surrounding the town. As the map suggests, there is nothing natural about Sun City Center. The lakes are artificial, and there is hardly a tree or a shrub or a blade of grass that has any correspondence in the world just beyond it." In paragraph 43, she writes, "The curving white streets . . . lead only back upon themselves, and since the land is flat they give no vistas on the outside world." The identical street layout mirrors its identical inhabitants. The Sun Citians are almost all white, almost all middle class or upper middle class, and they feel most comfortable being surrounded by versions of themselves: "That most Sun Citians have the same set of achievements and the same sort of prestige does not seem to worry them; indeed, the contrary is true" (paragraph 34).

2. The closing section of this essay, paragraphs 65–89, addresses the ideas of illness and death. How are Sun Citians approaching these states on their own?

DISCUSSION: In paragraph 85, FitzGerald writes that "Sun Citians have taken some steps to create a substitute for the extended family." These consist of neighbors, the churches, and nursing homes. It seems that their new extended families — consisting mainly of their peers — are replacing their own biological families. One of the symbolic ties between family members — money — is now redirected out of the blood family toward the surrogate family: "A sociologist studying retirement communities found that their members had a marked tendency to disinherit their children in favor of friends in the communities. Because these people did not appear to dislike or disapprove of their children, he called this phenomenon 'benevolent disinheritance'" (paragraph 84).

Questions on Language

1. In his Afterword, Hall writes that "FitzGerald as reporter keeps as clearly as she can to a tone of nonpartisan or objective description. She seems merely to tell us what is there: She quotes, she describes." Of course, Hall goes on to qualify this, by saying that there is a guiding intelligence behind what FitzGerald chooses to notice. Consider paragraph 46. Is FitzGerald merely describing or is she interpreting what she describes?

Frazier, *Dating Your Mom* (text pp. 188–191)

DISCUSSION: *Usually, describing adults — and not just adults, but what the Chinese call "elders" — as being childlike is a criticism, unless it is in a corny sentence that praises the "childlike sense of wonder they've managed to keep alive." FitzGerald, however, is not talking about any central and abiding awe they find in the mystery of life, but, rather, about their collections of stuffed animals. Her description suggests a characteristic that is inappropriate to the ideal quality associated with age: wisdom. "Eagerness to please" won't fill the bill. She goes on to develop this central immaturity in her subjects with their choice of place, which, with "warm air, the pastel colors, the arbitrary curving of the streets, the white plaster ducks," suggests nothing so much as a kind of stage set, vaguely reminiscent of Disneyland or Peter Pan's Island. Traditionally, children acknowledge life itself, and the absence of children symbolizes the absence of the Sun Citians' acknowledgment of their connection to the world itself.*

Writing Topics

1.   You have already analyzed the way that FitzGerald guides the reader to interpret what she shows in paragraph 46. Write a paper on where and how she makes judgments throughout the essay as a whole.

2.   Compare the Sun Citians' ideas on aging with those of Malcolm Cowley in "The View from 80."

3.   RESEARCH: Universities are, for the most part, age-segregated communities. Research the change in demographics that has occurred because people of college age are engaged in an activity separate from the outside world. What effect has absorption of young people in college, rather than in the work force, had on the greater society? What might the implications be?

IAN FRAZIER

Dating Your Mom (p. 188)

Questions on Meaning

1.   Donald Hall's Afterword suggests that, like Swift's essay, Ian Frazier's piece is satirizing the American male's psyche. What picture does Frazier paint of its condition?

DISCUSSION: *In a nutshell, Frazier is commenting on the fragility and immaturity of the male mind. This paradisaical relationship demands little effort: "you do not have to go to a party or a singles bar to meet [her], . . . you do not have to go to great lengths to get to know [her]" (paragraph 1). She — most probably — already likes you anyway. There is no competition, since "First, every woman, I don't care who she is, prefers her son to her husband. That is a simple fact" (paragraph 2).*

2.   Frazier insists that competing with one's father and leaving him single again would be no problem. What does the lack of guilt imply about the mind that conceived it as being okay?

DISCUSSION: *Frazier is demonstrating a mind that is entirely self-absorbed.*

Questions on Strategy

1.   The final two paragraphs push Frazier's argument to its limit. What is the logical outcome for a person who wants to participate in a romance with his mother?

DISCUSSION: The culmination of the romance is the return to symbiotic oneness. Frazier presents himself as a younger and younger child, a giant toddler. But he still has a final wish for regression back to absolute infancy, safe from everything, where his mother would stand between him and the world and even take charge of his bodily functions.

2.   How would you describe the point of view in this essay? Why does it change?

DISCUSSION: The first four paragraphs are written in the second person. Not until the final two paragraphs does Frazier shift into the first person, changing from advocating a relationship with one's mother to asserting his own place in such a relationship (paragraph 4). This collapse into "I" occurs exactly as he begins to describe the paradisaical infant-mother relationship.

Questions on Language

1.   In paragraph 3, Frazier says that many sons feel guilty about cutting out their dad. "They think, Oh, here's this kindly old guy who taught me how to hunt and whittle and dynamite fish." How does Frazier use diction to describe the father-son relationship?

DISCUSSION: Frazier is pressing this rhetorical technique into hilarious service by reducing the content of the relationship to trivialities; here, one's father does not teach anything of lasting value — there's certainly no sustaining intellectual or emotional bond produced by hunting and whittling and dynamiting fish. The same technique can be used toward other ends and is often employed, for instance, to describe the work of professors. You might think of it as persuasion through denigration.

2.   How does Frazier's prose style work to convey his absurd proposal?

DISCUSSION: Hall talks about how Frazier parodies pop jargon and self-help manual style in this piece. Frazier also keeps his prose absolutely deadpan. When he's walking the reader through the (self-help) "steps" to asking his mom out for a date, for example, he sounds comforting and familiar. "First, find a nice station on the car radio, one that she likes." Part of this satire's power comes from the disjunction between the ludicrous subject and the utterly ordinary way of talking about it.

Writing Topics

1.   Write a satire. Consider such topics as "Why You Should Raise Dogs Rather Than Children" or "Why the Lack of a College Education Should Be a Prerequisite for Political Office."

2.   Why would Frazier choose to make his points about male immaturity by pressing the Oedipal fantasy into service? Write an essay on the Oedipal fantasy, showing how it might or might not be particularly useful for demonstrating Frazier's thesis.

PAUL FUSSELL

Notes on Class (p. 192)

Questions on Meaning

1.   Why is class analysis the subject most likely to offend in America?

DISCUSSION: Fussell suggests that Americans hold two contradictory notions simultaneously: (1) that America has no class structure and (2) that everyone, no matter what his or her social class at birth, can, as the cliché has it, aspire to the presidency or move up in class. Both of these ideas, he writes, are myths: "Some people invite constant class trouble because they believe the official American publicity about these matters. The official theory, which experience is constantly disproving, is that one can earn one's way out of his original class" (paragraph 24). Even saying that one's birth class will determine one's adult social standing is profoundly unnerving when juxtaposed against the myth of democracy, which asserts equality for all. Fussell's assertion is that the truth is inequality in an alleged nation of equals.

2.   One reason that this essay might infuriate some people is its insistence on taste as a criterion of class standing. In paragraph 8, Fussell writes: "The top three classes invariably go in for hardwoods for doors and paneling; the Middle and High-Prole Classes, pine, either plain or 'knotty.' The knotty-pine 'den' is an absolute stigma of the Middle Class, one never to be overcome or disguised by temporarily affected higher usages." Whereas most people knowingly laugh at plastic-shrouded lampshades, one's taste in paneling might not be so obvious a class indicator. What is Fussell trying to say about taste? Consider paragraph 8 in terms of paragraph 25.

DISCUSSION: "Freedom and grace and independence" (paragraph 25) are the characteristics that for Fussell denote class standing. Freedom and independence are the antithesis of the knotty-pine den, simply because that specific rendition of a room is doing nothing so much as shouting its allegiance to a static and stereotypical idea of a version of success. A knotty-pine den is not chosen for its inherent beauty.

Questions on Strategy

1.   One of Fussell's strongest assertions is that the class system in America is as strong as it is in England, but in a different way. How does the way he writes this essay support that premise? Consider paragraphs 1–7.

DISCUSSION: Notice how Fussell labels and defines each class. In his essay, the labels, such as "Top Out-of-Sight" and "High-Proletarian," have an iron grip on the governing idea. Proletariat, for example, is a word taken from a class — the unpropertied — in rigidly hierarchical ancient Rome.

Questions on Language

1.   What criteria, according to Fussell, determine class? What is the most important criterion, and why? What is the guiding thesis of his discussion of language?

DISCUSSION: Taste determines class, as Fussell determines from his "façade study" in paragraphs 8–10. Freedom or autonomy, defined mainly by a lack of supervision in work, is offered in paragraph 11. Its subgroup, signs of "conspicuous waste," also proclaims economic freedom "in a social world where questions of unpayable medical bills or missed working days do not apply" (paragraph 15). Habits and attitudes are strong class indicators, including television watching (paragraph 12), the time at which dinner is eaten (paragraph 13), fatness or thinness (paragraph 14), and, most important, language (paragraphs 17–23). Language is able to signify psychological freedom; only those who are "socially secure risk nothing by calling a spade a spade" (paragraph 17). Fussell seems to be suggesting the same idea that Joan Didion put so elegantly in her essay "Slouching Towards Bethlehem": "The ability to think for one's self depends upon one's mastery of the language" (Slouching Towards Bethlehem, New York: Dell Publishing, 1968, p. 123). Fussell's thesis is not particularly clear, but in some places he does return to the guiding argument: "Their world of language is one containing little more than smokescreens and knowing innovations" (paragraph 18).

Writing Topics

1.   Write a paper on taste and its class associations. Go to that most uniform of places, the university dormitory. What decorations do people have on their walls? Do they denote intellectual curiosity and freedom or slavish adherence to the norm? Write an essay describing the reasons for displaying certain objects and categorizing the objects and the classes of people they represent.

2.   Write an essay in which you address Fussell's conclusions in paragraph 25. Do you agree with his governing criteria of "Freedom and grace and independence"? Why or why not? Would you look in the same places he does to find them?

3.   Consider Alison Lurie's essay "Clothing as a Sign System." How do her approaches to "reading" people's costumes relate to Fussell's efforts to define and use what he calls "façade conventions"? Look at the emphasis these authors give to language, not only as an indicator of types of people but also as a model for nonverbal communication. In an essay, discuss how language is essential to both Lurie's and Fussell's arguments.

JOHN KENNETH GALBRAITH

Corporate Man (p. 205)

Questions on Meaning

1.   What does Galbraith say "corporate man" has to give up?

DISCUSSION: The first thing that "corporate man" divests himself of is "the right to personal thought and expression" (paragraph 4). In addition, corporate man loses any public voice; outside of his own company — in the press, for instance — any comments he makes, which necessarily have his company as their subject, are entirely ignored or "subject . . . to a truly masterly condensation" (paragraph 5). In paragraph 7, Galbraith writes that corporate man will be able to make no contribution to what we generally acknowledge to be the life of ideas, or the creative life, which used to be the reason for attaining "a good income." But now, wealth can participate in artistic pursuits only by writing checks for them. Finally, corporate man (except, perhaps, Lee Iacocca) sacrifices his own identity. He is subsumed by the organizational machine (paragraph 9).

Galbraith, *Corporate Man* (text pp. 205–210)

Questions on Strategy

1.   What information about the essay's subject does the title give?

DISCUSSION: *Like "tool-using man," "corporate man" has an anthropological ring to it. It suggests that Galbraith is going to define the nature of corporate man, as though he were a separate subspecies of the human race. As Frances FitzGerald writes in her introduction to* Cities on a Hill, *the book from which "Sun City — 1983" was taken, her subjects had "kinship systems, customs, and rituals." Of course, Galbraith's inquiry is both limited in scope and satiric, but nonetheless he is examining the customs and rituals of the species corporate man.*

2.   How would you describe Galbraith's tone in his final paragraph?

DISCUSSION: *Galbraith's tone here is dry and saturnine. He seems to be mimicking the crisp summation of a business report, offering, finally, the pros and cons of corporate manhood. The satirical power of the fine line comes from what is crystal clear to Galbraith but is unconsidered by his subject, that is, the fact that corporate man has not done for himself what he would do for any business venture: he has never added up the gains against the losses. Galbraith's essay lists the characteristics of corporate man: rich, muzzled, creatively sterile, and anonymous. In saying "that to give up so much of the only life one is certain . . . to have is surely worth something," Galbraith, in a final irony, has turned the tables. Here he is corporate man's defender — since corporate man has never defended himself against his own indenture.*

Questions on Language

1.   In paragraph 7, Galbraith, referring to the graduates of the Harvard Business School, says: "They are an extremely bright and diverse convocation, with, as students go, exceptionally high standards of dress and personal hygiene." Describe what Galbraith achieves in this sentence.

DISCUSSION: *Galbraith damns Harvard Business School graduates with faint praise. The coupling of "Harvard" and "exceptionally high standards" sets up an expectation that these standards will have something to do with such things as mental acuity and intellectual rigor. But in the final phrase, he overturns our expectations by a description that would be appropriate, perhaps, for a prekindergarten class. He is using a very funny sentence to make an authorial judgment, and the graduates lose. As Hall says, "Galbraith bites where he wishes to bite."*

Writing Topics

1.   Write an essay in which you define and discuss satire, examining both Galbraith's "Corporate Man" and Ian Frazier's "Dating Your Mom."

2.   Can you write a serious rebuttal to a satire? On behalf of corporate men everywhere, take up Galbraith's claims and refute them as best you can. But first consider the function of satire and introduce your rebuttal by discussing the reason for Galbraith's endeavor.

Of Speed Readers and Lip-Movers (p. 211)

Questions on Meaning

1.   In this essay, Gass splits the world into two camps: the speed readers and the lip-movers. Himself a former speed reader — indeed, a member of a speed-reading team — he knows the difference between the two ways of approaching the world. What are the differences between speed readers and lip-movers?

DISCUSSION: Speed readers are looking only for "the inner core of meaning . . . the gist." They read "only for the most generalized, stereotyped sense" (paragraph 12). Speed readers "are persons consumed by consequences; they want to climax without crescendo." Only acquainted with simple passions, they merely want to get there (paragraph 21). The "jostle of images, this crazy collision of ideas — of landing strip, kernel, heart, guts, sex" — will be felt only by the lip-mover, the person reading slowly enough to perceive that the path to an idea itself contains that idea (paragraph 12).

Questions on Strategy

1.   Gass became a speed reader in school, joined a team sponsored by the school, and was tested in competitions with other schools. That means that people in charge of teaching him and his peers constructed this way of reading in an institution devoted to learning and rewarded children for it. On what grounds does Gass indict his teachers?

DISCUSSION: First he shows how he won competitions — by going, robotlike, for the obvious answer. In fact, he didn't even read the questions on Spengler's Decline of the West *but "simply encircled the gloomiest alternatives offered. Won in record time" (paragraph 15). The people who wrote the multiple-choice answers had themselves the most obvious interests and most literal ways of looking at the text: "There were many other mysteries, but not for these quiz masters who didn't even want to know the sexual significance of Cinderella's slipper, or why it had to be made of glass" (paragraph 15). He indicts his teachers as being undiscriminating, gluttonous consumers: "They told me that time was money. . . ." Turnover was topmost. What the world wanted me to get was the gist, but the gist was nothing but an idea of trade — an idea so drearily uniform and emaciated it might have modeled dresses" (paragraph 16).*

2.   In paragraph 1, Gass writes about "that silent pair of sisters, all spectacles and squints, who looked tough as German script and who hailed from Shaker Heights or some other rough neighborhood full of swift, mean raveners of text." Look at the final paragraph in this essay. How does it differ from the first paragraph and why?

DISCUSSION: This essay is divided into two parts. The first paragraph sets both the tone and subject for the first sixteen paragraphs. They are light, funny, witty, and anecdotal. They amuse us by showing the vulgarity of the speed-reading tests. The second fifteen paragraphs, on the other hand, turn to an examination of reading as it should be — serious and slow and full of wonder. Just as the lines quoted above are written in a style appropriate to their subject, so are the lines in the final paragraph written in a style appropriate to their subject: dense, allusive, and deeply thoughtful. We are not going to "get," as Gass would say, a line like "But it will be only a semblance of living — this living — nevertheless, the way unspoken reading is a semblance, unless, from time to time, you perform the outer world within" with the same ease we get the girls from Shaker Heights being "swift, mean raveners of text." "Performing the outer world within" is an idea that Gass has spent the entire essay leading up to, developing it in contrast to reading as a consumer activity. He uses Rilke to comment on the idea of "performing the outer world within," but being told to "Dance the orange" (paragraph 31) is not an idea immediately accessible. "There is no gist, no simple translation, no key concept that will unlock [such an idea]; actually, there is no lock, no door, no wall, no room, no house, no world" (paragraph 22). Its meaning will be found only by those who move their minds "freely in tune to the moving world" (paragraph 31).

Questions on Language

1. What trope is Gass using in paragraph 28? Samuel Johnson once wrote that a conceit, by violence, yokes two disparate ideas together. He was talking about metaphysical poetry, but how would you judge his remark in regard to Gass's work?

DISCUSSION: Gass, in comparing reading with drinking wine, has created an extended metaphor, or conceit, that runs throughout the paragraph. Consider his thesis about reading: it's something to be done slowly, to be savored; the journey is all. Drinking schnapps, for example, is done quickly, with the head thrown back, the liquor tossed into the mouth. Wine, on the other hand (especially red wine), is a liquor that demands slow familiarity. Red wine is the wine that "needs to breathe" to gain its full character. Books need to be approached slowly, even as objects, before we "decant the text into our wide-open and welcoming eyes." Look at the syntactical repetition in the next few lines: starting with "we decant," "We warm the wine," "We let its bouquet collect," "We wade," "We roll," "We sip," "We savor," and, finally, "We say some sentences of Sir Thomas Browne." Notice, too, that Gass is still sustaining the metaphor in the first sentence of paragraph 29, a nice example of a transition sentence: "Are these words not from a fine field, in a splendid year?" He's developed the idea of wine in the preceding paragraph into vineyard and vintage in its successor.

Writing Topics

1. Despite his title, William Gass is writing an essay "On Reading," just as Francine Du Plessix Gray writes "On Friendship." Write an essay in which you compare the ways in which Gass and Gray develop their topics. What arguments do they marshall to support their theses? Are their ideas, finally, persuasive?

2. Sometimes our strongest allegiances to books are formed when we first start reading. S. J. Perelman, for example, was so deeply affected by *Tarzan of the Apes* that, "subject only to the limitations of his physique and the topography of Rhode Island, he simply *became* Tarzan for a certain season of his life" (quoted in David Cowart, "The Tarzan Myth and Jung's Genesis of the Self," *Journal of American Culture* 2, 220). Write a paper that explores your most profound attachment to a specific book.

STEPHEN JAY GOULD

Sex, Drugs, Disasters,
and the Extinction of Dinosaurs (p. 221)

Questions on Meaning

1. What do you make of this essay's title? Is the subject of this essay the dinosaur's extinction?

DISCUSSION: Certainly, the title would lead one to believe that the dinosaurs are the real concern of this essay. It's a provocative title, deliberately designed to be enticing. As Gould writes, "these three notions invoke the primally fascinating themes of our culture." But against these primally fascinating themes Gould espouses rationalism and method. The dinosaurs and the various theories surrounding their extinction are only a vehicle through which Gould is able to demonstrate exactly how science is "a fruitful mode of inquiry" (paragraph 1). The true subject of this essay is the distinction between speculation and science.

2.   How does the Alvarez theory (paragraphs 19–20, 28–31) differ from the others?

DISCUSSION: Neither the testicular frying hypothesis nor the overdosing theory can be tested. There is not one single piece of physical evidence that could prove either one right or wrong, true or false. They will merely have to remain as "curious appendages," "untestable speculation." The Alvarez theory, on the other hand, pointed to a piece of evidence, an element — iridium — to test for, and a place to start testing: "extinction boundaries." Once the researchers had found iridium, they had uncovered "the crucial distinction between speculation and science" (paragraph 27).

Questions on Strategy

1.   After he summarizes the three theories in paragraph 9, Gould establishes a ground rule that all the theories of extinction must address: "*There is no separate problem of the extinction of dinosaurs.*" Why does he assert this so early in the paper?

DISCUSSION: After explaining, in brief, the theories he is going to analyze, Gould has to assert the death of the dinosaurs as part of a global phenomenon because it is the primary piece of evidence we have. To warrant consideration, any hypothesis must take into account not only the extinction of the dinosaurs but the concomitant mass dying of other species. If a theory is restricted solely to the dinosaurs and has no way of accounting for the death of other forms of life, it is not strong enough to embrace the phenomenon as a whole. Gould doesn't return to this essential premise until paragraph 23, when he finally refutes both Cowles's and Siegel's theories. But the reader needs this information early in the essay because, if its introduction were left until paragraph 23, Gould would be guilty of giving an essential piece of information far too late for us to consider when we are reading about the theories. It would be as if, in a mystery story, the murder was committed by someone who drowned his victim in a lake and in the final pages we discovered that the supposed murderer couldn't swim. You have to give your reader the essential information for him or her to be able to make informed judgments.

2.   One of the hardest paragraphs in any piece of writing is the conclusion. Look at Gould's concluding paragraph and discuss how it functions in this essay.

DISCUSSION: First, the conclusion mimics, in brief, the governing argument of the paper as a whole; just as the essay presents the definition of science as a way of knowing that works with testable proposals, so does the conclusion recapitulate this definition with an example. Because we know that the ancient asteroid made many forms of life insupportable on this earth, we can generalize from that situation to a comparable and current one. Here Gould is demonstrating a common admonition regarding a concluding paragraph: don't merely restate, but broaden your subject, draw inferences from your ideas that enter a larger sphere. The larger sphere that the extinction of the dinosaurs points to is the extinction of all our lives through nuclear winter. In his final sentence, notice how, despite the fact that he's talking about an abstraction—our own mass death—he presents it in terms of the memorable and concrete image taken from an earlier moment in the essay: we, too, could join the dinosaurs, entombed with them in their "contorted poses among the strata of the earth."

Questions on Language

1.   Describe Gould's writing style. Why is his essay written this way?

DISCUSSION: Gould is writing about science, and scientific writing is notorious for its abstract and distant style. Here, on the other hand, although the author is conveying a great deal of information, he is conveying it for the most part in colloquial language. Consider some of the diction in this essay: "the hypothesis of testicular frying" (paragraph 22), "one of history's five great dyings had enveloped the earth" (paragraph 11). Other colloquialisms Gould uses include: "hit parade" (paragraph 21), "zapping" (paragraphs 21 and 23), and "OD" (paragraph 23). "Testicular frying" is a memorably funny phrase, and yet it succinctly describes the theory. "Five great dyings" has the echoes of poetry reverberating behind it; one can hear Lucifer falling out of heaven and into hell in his "long day's dying" in Milton's Paradise Lost. *This essay is a good model for how to make a specialized subject available to a general audience.*

Writing Topics

1.   In paragraph 17 Gould writes that Ronald K. Siegel, the UCLA psychiatrist who thinks that elephants drink to forget, is exhibiting "a silly bit of anthropocentric speculation." What are the premises that Siegel's idea would depend on? Would it make a difference if he were interpreting the behavior of elephants in the wild rather than elephants in zoos? Write a paper in which you define "anthropocentric" theories of behavior and analyze Siegel's conclusions about elephants' drinking habits.

2.   Gather some science sections from newspapers. Compare two or three essays on science against Gould's opening criteria; do the articles fail "to separate fascinating claims from the methods that scientists use to establish the facts of nature" (paragraph 2)? In your paper, consider the newspaper articles from the viewpoint of how well they "focus on *how* scientists develop and defend" their claims (paragraph 2). You may want to use Gould's essay as a model against which to measure the science journalists.

FRANCINE Du PLESSIX GRAY

On Friendship (p. 231)

Questions on Meaning

1.   On what does Gray pin the blame for society's obsession with the primacy of romantic love?

DISCUSSION: In paragraphs 2 and 3, Gray presents the history of love as being a literary fantasy, one with tenacious roots in the "propaganda machine of the Western novel." "The power and the genius of the novel . . . fuse[d] medieval notions of courtly love with the idealization of marriage," giving rise to "the eighteenth-century middle class" and engendering an attitude to romantic love that has survived almost unchanged to modern times.

2.   Stephen Jay Gould's essay addresses the idea of "anthropocentrism" (paragraph 17). How does Gray see romantic love as an "ethnocentric" idea in the Western world?

DISCUSSION: In paragraph 4, Gray insists that only "a small segment" of people in the Western world believe fervently in the "alliance of marriage and romantic love." Here love is taken for granted as being the answer to happiness in life, and other cultures' marital arrangements are seen as mercenary or heartless. As a society, we don't examine the underpinnings of our beliefs and never think of romantic love as being a social construct, and a rather recent social construct at that. Gray lays out the two thousand years of human history against which she sets this new social idea: "from Greek times to the

Enlightenment," "it was always friendship between members of the same sex" that "was held to be the cornerstone of human happiness" (paragraph 4).

Questions on Strategy

1. Why is Gray's opening sentence provocative? How does it draw readers into the essay?

DISCUSSION: The most striking element of this sentence is the incongruous juxtaposition of a nineteenth-century French heroine and an American symbol of affluent consumerism: Bloomingdale's is just loaded with sign value. We don't expect this pairing, and the ideas it suggests promise an intriguing essay. Notice, too, the alliteration; "Bovary . . . Bloomingdale's" just sounds good.

2. In his Afterword, Hall writes, "Often it's bad tactics to praise hotdogs by slandering hamburgers." In this essay, how are the subjects love and friendship introduced? Does the introduction give us some idea of how Gray is going to handle her comparison?

DISCUSSION: Gray describes Madame Bovary and her modern counterparts as being "anguished, grasping, overwrought, and terribly lonely." The central description is that she is possessed by "a great solitude" (paragraph 1). This already suggests the boundaries against which Gray is going to locate love. In contrast, the only definition she gives of friendship is Bacon's reverse definition (paragraph 2); he is not defining friendship itself but is suggesting the desperate loneliness of being without friends. Friends, then, are those that relieve us of our "great solitude." By the end of the opening paragraph, Gray has given us the central category she is concerned with in this essay — solitude — and how, in regard to solitude, love and friendship are diametric opposites.

Questions on Language

1. Why, in paragraph 7, does Gray analyze the diction associated with love, but not that associated with friendship?

DISCUSSION: In paragraph 7 Gray is contrasting the turmoil of love with the steadiness of friendship. Physical passion is a necessary component to the ideal of romantic love, and, early in the paragraph, she shows its innate destructiveness. This theme is echoed in the diction we use to express the idea of love: "There is confrontation, turmoil, aggression, in the often militaristic language of romantic love: Archers shoot fatal arrows or unerring shafts." Inherent within the idea of love is the idea of war. The diction of love supports Gray's governing argument about love, just as the absence of a "language" of friendship, which doesn't inspire the same overwhelming emotion, supports her argument. Since literature is the primary vehicle of the romantic ideal, it seems clear that the novel hasn't inspired a similar "cult of friendship"; the novel itself is a form that thrives "on tension and illicitness."

2. Why, in paragraph 12, when Gray turns her focus solely on the idea of friendship, does she turn to religious thinkers rather than, say, scientists?

DISCUSSION: According to Gray, the idea of friendship does not include either great passion or great conflict. "With Eros the body stands naked, in friendship our spirit is denuded." She is interested in friendship as a spiritual condition, a condition that elevates us. The people she can turn to, then, are "those religiously inclined, . . . relatively unaffected by positivism or behaviorism, or by the general scientificization of human sentiment." Science is the great opposite of the spiritual realm, which has as its focus a global view, a unifying gaze.

35

Writing Topics

1. In this essay, Gray is arguing that friendship has historically been considered a male phenomenon, an emotional bond withheld from women because of an inherent female character weakness. On sheer anecdotal evidence, popular culture would have us believe that women are unable to be friends with one another. Write an essay discussing rites and gestures of friendship (see paragraph 10) in contemporary life, both male and female. Do you think that women's friendships are different from men's, and on what evidence do you support your argument? Finally, interview someone *who is not one of your friends* on the subject of friendship in his or her life — friendship with both members of the same sex and members of the opposite sex.

2. RESEARCH: Gray keeps returning to the idea of romantic love's medieval roots. Even in the penultimate paragraph, she quotes an anthropologist who calls love "a lunatic relic of medieval passions." Write a research paper in which you describe the phenomenon of courtly love and the reasons behind its enormous influence in its time and society.

VICKI HEARNE

Consider the Pit Bull (p. 239)

Questions on Meaning

1. Hearne writes that she was "exercised" enough about pit bull horror stories to offer a countering view. With what vision of the pit bull does she replace the most current and inflamed version? Look at paragraph 25.

DISCUSSION: *Hearne is most interested in the dog as a responsible moral agent, as an animal who is morally aware. A good pit bull, she argues, would be able "to give the moral law to herself when her master (who, of course, runs the universe from the dog's point of view) fails to act on the law of being." The central premise of this entire essay is that some dogs have the ability to envision a coherent universe and to insist on its remaining intact and perfectly balanced.*

2. Does Hearne address the idea of anthropomorphism in this essay? Consider such sentences as "If pit bulls have a flaw in their relationship to people it is that they sometimes show a tendency toward reserve, a kind of aloofness that is a consequence of their being prone to love above all else reflection and meditation" (paragraph 14) as well as the vignettes in the essay as a whole.

DISCUSSION: *What ways do we have to talk about animals? Anthropomorphizing animals means to invest them with human qualities. The opposite philosophical pole would probably be pure behaviorism, in which our only access to talking about animals would be to describe — but not interpret — their behavior. Those who would charge rampant anthropomorphism would also deny Hearne's essential premise, the one she repeatedly attempts to demonstrate throughout this article — that animals operate in a moral arena. "Consider the Pit Bull" does not explicitly address the ideas of anthropomorphism, but in its very interpretation of dogs' behavior it attempts to prove that the idea of anthropomorphizing an animal is itself anthropocentric; that is, believing that human beings have singular access to a spiritual and philosophical understanding of existence is supreme evidence of an overwhelming human ego.*

Questions on Strategy

1.   Why does Hearne, in paragraphs 6–12, present us with all the possible variants of words that might — or might not — refer to the pit bull?

DISCUSSION: One of Hearne's interests in this essay is defining what we mean when we use certain words. One of them is "dog," specifically "pit bull." Her whole essay is working toward a narrower and narrower definition of what she means by the words "pit bull," and her definition is not a common one.

2.   Hearne looks at the idea of pit bulls as "born killers" in the same section that she examines them as "the dog that wouldn't hurt a butterfly." Why is she coupling these two contradictory ideas from paragraphs 36 to 46?

DISCUSSION: Hearne insists that the opposite poles belong to a continuum of thought that has, at its heart, the idea that dogs are bereft of moral judgment, that is, that they are utterly deterministic organisms responding only to some inherent, fixed nature. The logic behind the statement "that dog wouldn't hurt a butterfly" is that never, no matter the provocation, would the dog attack. On the other hand, Hearne is attempting to illustrate that a dog is capable of using judgment to assess situations and distinguish between them appropriately, as Gunner did when he tore into Hearne's attacker.

Questions on Language

1.   In writing about dogs, Hearne invests them with enormous power: "Pit bulls give you the opportunity to know, should you want so terrible a knowledge, whether your relationships are coherent; whether your notion of love is a truncated, distorted, and free-floating bit of the debris of Romanticism or a discipline that can renew the resources of consciousness" (paragraph 54). Why does she use such language when talking about a dog? Consider some of the claims she's making in this passage.

DISCUSSION: Hearne's language never wavers from her premise; if her subject is the moral nature of the dog, she is going to use language proper to that moral sphere. In this passage, first, you have to decide whether Hearne is describing the dog as, essentially, a mirror, merely reflecting our own images, or as one-half of a reciprocal relationship that we engage in. From paragraph 54, we know that she is talking about dogs that are morally active (and remember paragraph 43: The dog "is not morally inert"). Belle reacted to Hearne's action or, more precisely, her absence of action, which was, as she lay in bed, a refusal to participate in an essential sphere of their relationship: training.

2.   Even though she is using language traditionally considered to be part of the highest human province, Hearne still insists, in her discussion of the word *kind*, that she is talking not about humans but about members of another species (paragraphs 49–52). How does she use this word to present an idea about fighting dogs?

DISCUSSION: In presenting a short history of the word kind, *Hearne is really arguing that every species has specific desires and needs. The parallel with the greyhounds suggests that fighting may be the only way to fulfill completely a certain part of a dog's nature. Cruelty, then, would be not allowing a dog to express its kind of nature, here described by "gameness and stamina" (paragraph 52). These particular words do not admit the traits of viciousness and cruelty.*

Writing Topics

1.   Write an essay discussing the importance of the two epigraphs: "Your goodness must have some edge to it — else it is none" and "A disproportionately large number of pit bulls are able to climb trees." How do these epigraphs usher in Hearne's subjects?

2. RESEARCH: In paragraph 48, Hearne writes about children's books, in which "the children learned from the dog's courage, loyalty, or wit how to clarify their own stances in the world." It sounds here as though Hearne is referring to animals as human exemplars, an idea that began to gain prominence at the end of the nineteenth century. Write a research paper in which you examine the representation of animals in the history of children's literature. For ideas, you might look at one or some of the following. Consider the history of *Black Beauty*, which was designedly didactic, and its relationship with the Royal Society for the Prevention of Cruelty to Animals. Or look at Harriet Ritvo's *The Animal Estate* and John Turner's *Animals, Pain and Humanity in the Victorian Age*. The representation of animals in literature has changed over the years, and you could contrast the Victorian view with the most modern books.

EDWARD HOAGLAND

The Courage of Turtles (p. 253)

Questions on Meaning

1. What is the world like for turtles, as Hoagland paints it? Compare the beginning of the essay with its end.

DISCUSSION: *In the opening pages, Hoagland relates the destruction of the turtles' Mud Pond. Since the local water company decided it was no longer necessary, the pond was bulldozed over and relandscaped into "a domestic view" for a subdivision. Some turtles ended up in the closets of the subdivision, and some, under the impression that this was jut another passing dry spell, dug deep and stayed there, entombed in mud. In the final two paragraphs, Hoagland shows us several hundred baby turtles who will die as their shells are decorated, and one turtle whom he mistakenly sends out to sea: "the waves were too rough for him, and the tide was coming in, bumping him against the pilings underneath the pier." They seem to be lumbering within an ever-contracting circle, revolving slowly in an increasingly dangerous world.*

2. This essay includes an enormous amont of minutely detailed description: "Baby turtles in a turtle bowl are a puzzle in geometrics. They're as decorative as pansy petals, but they are also self-directed building blocks" (paragraph 7). Yet we know that Hoagland sees their existence as being constantly threatened. Is this essay simply descriptive, or is it inherently persuasive?

DISCUSSION: *Nowhere in the essay does Hoagland stop and tell us to contribute to the Save the Turtles Fund. He's certainly not exhorting us to do something about their fragile ecology. Yet because of its descriptive power, this essay is persuasive; Hoagland shows us all the flashing facets of a world that most of us have seen nothing of before.*

Questions on Strategy

1. In the Afterword, Donald Hall writes that "Hoagland's dense paragraphs accommodate a universe — from Vermont ponds to baby terrapins on Broadway." Hoagland is focusing on turtles, but through them he can see many parts of the world, both animate and inanimate. What techniques does Hoagland use to get us from the turtles to "a universe" of other subjects? Consider especially paragraphs 10 and 11.

DISCUSSION: *Hoagland is depending on metaphors and similes. "She has a turtleneck neck, a tail like an elephant's, wise old pachydermous hind legs and the face of a turkey — except that when I carry her she gazes at the passing ground with a hawk's eyes and mouth." The first four phrases of the sentence liken the turtle to other creatures. Only the last phrase applies to the turtle's character; in comparing her to a hawk, Hoagland conveys an element of rapaciousness in the turtle's character. In describing the turtle, Hoagland has described a host of other creatures as well.*

2.   Usually, Hoagland's tone is extremely matter-of-fact, even when he's describing something painful. In his final paragraph, he describes the turtle he has thrown into the ocean as looking "afraid as he bobbed about on top of the water." Yet his final sentence — "But since, short of diving in after him, there was nothing I could do, I walked away" — as Hall says, is "modulated, conclusive, final." But is Hoagland always so matter-of-fact? Consider paragraph 12. How does it differ from the essay's final paragraph?

DISCUSSION: In paragraph 12, Hoagland describes the turtles left wandering and homeless after the destruction of Mud Pond. "It's like the nightmare most of us have whimpered through, where we are weighted down disastrously while trying to flee; fleeing our home ground, we try to run." The absolute vulnerability of the turtles has elicited explicit empathy from Hoagland, something he usually eschews. Suddenly, Hoagland sees these turtles as the characters that populate our human nightmares; suddenly, he identifies overtly with their loss.

Questions on Language

1.   After reading Vicki Hearne's "Consider the Pit Bull," you might be sensitive to moral language as applied to animals. What do you make of Hoagland's title? Is he really concerned with courage as a moral quality?

DISCUSSION: In contrast to Hearne's assertions about dogs, Hoagland might well agree with the statement "Turtles are morally inert." However, the same question comes up: how many ways do we have to talk about animals? In this essay, Hoagland seems to be using anthropomorphic language because of the turtles' difficult circumstances; from beginning to end, he describes their vanishing world. The trait that turtles exhibit that most affects him seems to be their persistence: "They don't feel that the contest is unfair; they keep plugging," and they live "on gumption" (paragraphs 6, 13). Nonetheless, Hoagland never implies that turtles make deliberate choices in their behavior, but rather that their instinct to just keep living exhibits courage enough.

2.   In paragraph 5, Hoagland writes: "[Snakes] are smooth movers, legalistic, unblinking, and they afford the humor which the humorless do. But they make challenging captives; sometimes they don't eat for months on a point of order — if the light isn't right, for instance." How does Hoagland thematically connect these two sentences?

DISCUSSION: He picks up on the word "legalistic" and extends its idea of hair-splitting precision into "point of order."

Writing Topics

1.   Write a paper analyzing paragraph 9. How does this paragraph support Hoagland's subject in this essay?

2.   Compare this essay with Barry Lopez's "Wolf Notes." In your essay, discuss the techniques each writer uses to connect the animal and the human world. What is essentially important to them about turtles and wolves? Do they see the same things in the natural world?

Rape (p. 261)

Questions on Meaning

1. In paragraph 2, Johnson addresses the "armor of folklore, Bible tales, legal precedents, specious psychological theories" that protect "the institution of rape." What does she mean by this? How is it possible to protect the institution of rape?

DISCUSSION: *Johnson is referring to the body of literature and law that protects the institution by blaming the victim. To blame the woman who is victimized by rape, one has to somehow locate the responsibility for being raped in some action that the woman did —or did not — make. Johnson mentions several literary characters who suffer this fate: "The disobedient Eve, the compliant Leda, the lying wife of Potiphar are still the keys to popular assumptions about women."*

2. Johnson builds her essay around book reviews. Does she agree with the books' conclusions?

DISCUSSION: *Johnson agrees with their conclusions only up to a certain point; for her, the books don't go far enough in the right direction. In that they all perceive rape in terms that disagree with the prevailing and passive societal understanding, she thinks they have value. However, Susan Brownmiller's book is marred by a kind of mimesis, in which she reflects the appeal "at some level to the instincts" that "myths and scary stories" both "illustrate and deprecate" (paragraph 9). Jean MacKellar's book is "overlaid by a kind of naive social optimism," which, in the final moments of her essay, Johnson says she does not share (paragraph 21). On the other hand, both books, along with an LEAA study, "agree that corroboration requirements and courtroom questions about a victim's prior sexual history should be eliminated" (paragraph 24). But neither Brownmiller nor MacKeller addresses the larger question; neither explains "what this primal drama of domination and punishment is about, exactly" (paragraph 7). The specific reasons why some men feel free to enact their own punitive fantasies, rendering women utterly submissive, is territory unexplored by the books she reviews.*

3. In paragraph 4, Johnson says that women's fears of rape "are continually activated by a vast body of exemplary literature, both traditional and in the daily paper." It's not surprising that the "Oldest Conflict," as Johnson puts it, is a traditional literary subject. Yet some of the literature belonging to high culture has some amazing views on rape. Consider this passage from Milton's "Comus" and locate its thesis in a traditional interpretation of a woman's responsibility for her own rape. A sister is going to be sent alone through the woods, and one brother worries: "Beauty . . . had need the guard / Of dragon-watch with unenchanted eye, To save her blossoms, and defend her fruit / From the rash hand of bold incontinence. / You may as well spread out the unsunned heaps / Of miser's treasure by an outlaw's den, / And tell me it is safe, as bid me hope / Danger will wink on opportunity, / And let a single helpless maiden pass / Uninjured in this wild surrounding waste" (lines 392–402). But no, his elder brother replies: "So dear to heaven is saintly chastity, / That when a soul is found sincerely so, / A thousand liveried angels lackey her, / Driving far off each thing of sin and guilt" (lines 452–455).

DISCUSSION: *"Comus" is not some aberrant poem, but a solid member of the literary canon. The first brother is worrying about the girl's vulnerability. He compares her to a heap of treasure placed next to an outlaw's den; it seems obvious to him that so desirable a thing will be stolen, just as it seems obvious that "a single helpless maiden" offers an easy target. The second brother scoffs. In his three short lines, he says that a sincerely chaste soul will be protected by the angels. In other words, only the unchaste are raped; the virtuous carry their own metaphysical protection. Thus, rape separates the chaste from the unchaste, and the women who are raped are themselves responsible for their attack. In Johnson's essay,* she relates similar, spurious beliefs: women are raped because they are out at the wrong time (paragraph 1); women are raped because they wear mini-skirts (interpreted as an "obvious" signal of desiring rape) (paragraph 2); women are raped because they are careless (paragraph 14); and women are raped because other women are sexually inhibited and their men are frustrated (paragraph 21).

Questions on Strategy

1. The conclusion of an essay that examines such an emotionally laden topic is often problematic. How would you describe Johnson's tone in the penultimate paragraph? How much weight do you think she gives her conclusions?

DISCUSSION: The final two paragraphs are permeated by a tone of resignation. Johnson has only perhaps the most admirable — but the most abstract — idea to turn to: a plea for civilized behavior. Yet she knows that appealing to inherent virtue is going to be of little use. Perhaps the coalition of cops and feminists along with severer sentences for rape will deter the rapists. Meanwhile, she feels "a certain distaste" for the current "congratulatory mood" over proposals that may help the victims but at the same time mask the role of male "complicity."

2. Consider the first and final paragraphs together. What does Johnson's essay charge men with?

DISCUSSION: The first paragraph charges men with an inability to empathize with or understand the deep dread and resentment women have of rape. The penultimate sentence in the final paragraph charges many men with complicity in the perpetuation of rape. They have failed "to address themselves to the peculiar mystery of male aggression toward those weaker than themselves" (paragraph 8). Instead, rape is considered primarily in light of the woman's role: what did she do to allow it to happen?

Questions on Language

1. Everyone knows the difference between active and passive construction. Passive construction says "the beaker was dropped on the floor," with no mention of who was responsible for dropping it. The major difference between the two is that active construction identifies the responsible agent and passive construction doesn't. In paragraph 14, residents of Palo Alto were told that "women are raped because of carelessness." Analyze the construction of this sentence and the underlying implications. In what kind of world-view does this statement make sense? How would you rewrite the sentence to identify the responsible agent?

DISCUSSION: "Women are raped because . . ." is really a form of shorthand. What is missing from this sentence is the responsible agent. Who rapes the women seems not to be the important question here. Rather, the sentence reflects the belief that the most important question is "What caused the opportunity for the rapist to rape"? The opportunity, of course, was created by women's carelessness. This sentence conjures up a vision of the world in which all women have to be charged with a kind of preternatural awareness, a world in which one slip in alertness shifts the responsibility from the attacker to the attacked. If the attacker weren't given any opportunity, there would be no rapes. A more accurate revelation of the moral agent would be found in a sentence like this: "Women are raped because someone rapes them."

Writing Topics

1. Consider paragraphs 17–20 and write a paper examining the collision of racism and sexism in rape. What does Johnson mean when she says "sexism . . . will prevail"?

2. In paragraph 13 Johnson argues that "our culture . . . leads women in some degree to collaborate in their own rape." Her example is the fairy tale "Little Red Riding Hood." Write a paper in which you analyze this fairy tale as a rape allegory. You might consider comparing some more modern versions with the Grimm version, titled in some translations "Little Red-Cap." How might such a fairy tale lead women to collaborate in their own rape?

GARRISON KEILLOR

Shy Rights: Why Not Pretty Soon? (p. 272)

Questions on Meaning

1. What are the "shy rights" that Keillor is so softly advocating?

DISCUSSION: Keillor wants to see shyness released from its pathological taxonomic category: "shyness is not a disability or disease to be 'overcome.' It is simply the way we are" (paragraph 9). Shyness should not be discriminated against on either a personal or a public level; to undo such discrimination would require major changes in the "current adversary system of law" (paragraph 11). Businesses should be more responsible and accurate since shy people are unable to assert themselves in the face of overcharges, shoddy products, return of a product for a refund, bad food, and lost money (paragraph 13). The lives of shy people should be represented in history (paragraph 20).

2. In paragraph 6, Keillor expresses frustration with the stereotypes associated with being shy. The worst one (far worse than being called a "dork," for example) is being "tagged" as a "potential psychopath": "'He kept pretty much to himself,' every psychopath's landlady is quoted as saying after the arrest, and for weeks thereafter every shy person is treated like a leper." This is hilarious, partly because of the firmness with which Keillor brings into being a new group — psychopaths' landladies (all their mothers must have kicked them out, since only psychopaths' landladies are ever interviewed by the press). But this humor has, at its heart, a deeply serious subject. What is the subject Keillor is addressing here? Can you give a parallel example?

DISCUSSION: The subject is stereotyping people. Stereotyping can be as simple as saying "all fat people are jolly," but it finds its most vicious voice in racism. Shy people have no physical marker of difference, but blacks are visibly the Other, especially to the white, middle-class, suburban community. Walking through this kind of neighborhood, blacks are often "tagged" as burglars or rapists, whereas a white man strolling down the street would usually be assumed to be going for a walk.

Questions on Strategy

1. In his unsent letter to Jimmy Carter, Keillor threatens that, if shy people don't get some action, "it could be a darned quiet summer" (paragraph 3). How might you describe the technique he's using here? How would you compare it to paragraph 19, in which he writes, "Perhaps one solution might be for clerks and other business personnel to try to be a little bit more careful about this sort of thing in the first place. O.K.?"

DISCUSSION: Very often, a writer can create humor by setting up an expectation and then supplying the reverse of that expectation. The normal pattern that Keillor is following in paragraph 3 is that of threatening violence — if you don't meet our demands, we'll riot — and inverting the promised outcome. By inverting it, by substituting being quiet for rioting, he's puncturing the balloon, a perfect example of ending not with a bang, but with a whimper. Perhaps most important, Keillor makes sure that his threat stays within the guiding thesis; since his persona is hallmarked by extreme diffidence, no threat could stay more perfectly in character. His gentle suggestion in paragraph 19 — try to be more careful — falls into the same category. No radical demand to fire the incompetent clerks, but rather a soft chiding that ends with the most assertive word this persona is capable of: "O.K.?"

2.   In paragraph 28, Keillor writes, "All I know is that it isn't easy trying to write a manifesto for a bunch of people who dare not speak their names. . . . This secret cadre, whose members are not known even to each other, advocate doing 'less than nothing.'" How can a cadre be composed of isolated strangers? What function do these inherent contradictions serve?

DISCUSSION: This passage depends on the idea of paradox. A manifesto is "a public declaration of intentions, opinions, objectives, or motives, as one issued by a government, sovereign, or organization" (Random House College Dictionary). A public declaration cannot be made by "a bunch of people who dare not speak their names." This small passage supports the guiding organization behind "Shy Rights"; the whole idea of rights being demanded by people who excommunicate one of their own for writing a letter, which was itself unsent, is paradoxical.

Questions on Language

1.   In the opening paragraph, Keillor writes that "the term 'overweight' itself is oppressive because it implies a 'right' weight that the fatso has failed to make." Of course, this is a funny point, and Keillor makes sure it's funny by using "fatso" at the end of the sentence. However, it's not completely unserious. What issue is Keillor addressing in this sentence?

DISCUSSION: Keillor is addressing a notion of language itself, language as it embodies ideas that inherently condemn some people as being inferior to the norm. Language can describe people not just as being the Other, but as being the Lesser. The "fat people" employ exactly the same tactics; in referring "to thin people as being 'not all there'" they are simply mimicking the same use of language.

2.   In his Afterword, Donald Hall says that his favorite parts of this essay are its qualifications. Analyze the qualifications in the following sentences: "Probably they feel that making demands is a betrayal of the shy movement (or 'gesture,' as many shys call it)" and "Hundreds of thousands of our shy brothers and sisters (and 'cousins twice-removed,' as militant shys refer to each other" (paragraphs 4 and 8).

DISCUSSION: In paragraph 4, the "shy movement" is reduced to a "gesture," a movement, presumably, being far too grand and sweeping for the shy to support. In paragraph 8, "shy brothers and sisters" seems to imply an embarrassing familiarity; "militant shys" are far more comfortable with distancing the relationship to "cousins twice-removed."

Writing Topics

1.   Write a short essay using Keillor's as your model. Notice how his humor never depends on sarcasm but rather depends on paradox and reversing expectations to make its points. The field of subjects is wide open.

2.   RESEARCH: Shy history is a wonderful paradox; Keillor wants people who are too frozen to ask for the correct change at the checkout counter to have their nonactions documented historically. But when he talks about how history, traditionally, has focused on "the accomplishments of famous persons" and overlooked "countless others who had very little to say, who never sought fame, and whose names are lost to history," he's actually getting very close

to a movement in historical studies that is gaining power — the study of ordinary men and women. Social historians are now writing what could be called the history of everyday life, based on people's diaries and letters. They are trying to fill in the great space that is left blank when only the most obvious or the grandest moments in history are documented. Write a research paper in which your subject is this kind of history. You could analyze the idea of social history, or you could write on some material in a library collection devoted to ordinary people's material. You might want to look at organizations that are collecting oral histories of people in a certain geographical area or field of interest.

MAXINE HONG KINGSTON

No Name Woman (p. 279)

Questions on Meaning

1. It becomes clear, when reading this essay, that Kingston herself does not know exactly what happened to her father's sister. This essay does not spring from her own memory, but her mother's — and her mother has not told her much. How are we to understand this imaginative re-creation? Does it give us truth or Maxine Hong Kingston's truth? What is the subject of this essay?

DISCUSSION: Like Malcolm Cowley, Kingston writes bulletins from another country. Yet her country seems so much more foreign than that of old age, run by secret charges and cryptic rituals, where much is hidden from utterance and where even what is spoken seems spoken in code. One of Kingston's jobs is to be our interpreter, so we can have free access to her mysterious memories. Yet even she does not seem to know everything, and what she does know includes acknowledged missing pieces. Her mother's story stretches over the first nine paragraphs and no longer. The essential facts are that No Name Woman killed her child and committed suicide. Everything else in Kingston's essay is her attempt to find a story that makes sense of the skeletal outline her mother gave her. Notice her two contradictory portraits of her father's sister, the No Name Woman of the title. In one vision, she is an active participant in her own fate, tempting men who should be thought of as brothers. In the other, and much stronger, vision she is a victim, commanded to lie down with the nameless rapist and "be his secret evil" (paragraph 15). The subject of the essay might be Kingston's attempt to consider the many possible stories it suggests and thus profoundly use its knowledge "to grow up on" (paragraph 10).

2. Maxine Hong Kingston's opening line is a powerful and fascinating beginning for an essay: "'You must not tell anyone,' my mother said, 'what I am about to tell you.'" She has been charged with obedient silence, and one of her essay's subjects is obedience. Yet, in it, she lays secrets bare, telling all to anyone who will read. What are her family's reasons for never speaking of No Name Woman? What are Kingston's reasons for "telling"?

DISCUSSION: Given in symmetry, charge and countercharge framing the essay, Kingston's reasons for breaking silence are offered in the final two paragraphs. Her family wishes to inflict eternal punishment on this nameless woman, so that "she should suffer forever, even after death." And Kingston herself is not merely writing this essay to lift that punishment, to exculpate her aunt. She too is afraid of this woman who "haunts" her, who does not "always mean [her] well." The essay is "telling on her," telling on someone who was herself drawn to violence, for in drowning herself she contaminates the drinking water. But telling her aunt's story might bring peace both to No Name Woman and to Kingston: her aunt will no longer have to snatch the gifts from other ghosts, since Kingston is devoting this essay to her, and Kingston might, through her essay, understand the truth of her family's story.

3.   The story of No Name Woman is, in many ways, so shocking, so foreign to middle-class American life, that it is tempting to assign blame to almost everyone. Is Kingston interested in assigning blame — to the rapist, to the villagers, to her family — in this essay? Consider her analysis of the proper version of the story in paragraphs 15, 16, and 19.

DISCUSSION: In these two paragraphs, Kingston tries to put what she knows of the story into the social context with the best "fit." Considering the social strictures governing Chinese women, Kingston seems persuaded that her aunt killed herself not over a lover but over a rapist. So she does seem to blame the rapist, but she doesn't blame the villagers for their terrifying raid or her family for their eternal punishment of No Name Woman. Rather than apportioning blame, this essay is an effort to understand the reasons behind their actions.

Questions on Strategy

1.   What does the final sentence — "The Chinese are always very frightened of the drowned one, whose weeping ghost, wet hair hanging and skin bloated, waits silently by the water to pull down a substitute" — mean? Does this sentence suggest any alternative to more violence?

DISCUSSION: Kingston says that she is "haunted" by her aunt, who doesn't always mean her well. Kingston is afraid of being her aunt's substitute, perhaps condemned, like her, for speaking of these matters. If the drowned have such power, consider the responsibility Kingston undertakes by bringing her aunt to life again in this essay. No Name Woman may be waiting "silently" by the well, but Kingston has given her back a voice. This sentence, and this essay as a whole, might suggest that speaking of these things could break the circle of violence that Kingston's essay relates. Getting the story right might help someone else avoid being "the drowned one."

Questions on Language

1.   Much of this essay's evocative power comes from its diction. What word or idea is Kingston defining in paragraph 15?

DISCUSSION: In writing that her family are people who "hatch their own chicks and eat the embryos and the heads for delicacies and boil the feet in vinegar for party food, leaving only the gravel, eating even the gizzard lining," Kingston defines the word "thrifty" — the opposite of extravagant. Her definition becomes a menu of the feast that can be made out of a chick, which has little meat on its bones: no thigh, no breast, no drumstick. But out of this tiny morsel, her family uses every bit, even the feet, even the gizzard lining. Notice how much more persuasive and comprehensive this description is than a simple defining word would be.

2.   There's a huge amount of violence rendered in this essay, both in the terrifying raid of the villagers and in the family's own violent reaction to their daughter's transgression. Both of these things are unarticulated, yet uttered in symbolic language. What does the raid symbolize?

DISCUSSION: Kingston gives us a rational reason for the raid: to symbolize how No Name Woman, in transgressing familial and sexual taboos, has broken the complete circle of harmonious village relations. The raid also symbolizes "No Name Woman's" total ostracization by the community.

Writing Topics

1.   Often, certain family members are held up as embodiments of moral tales. Kingston was raised on parables: "Whenever she had to warn us about life, my mother told stories that ran like this one, a story to grow up on. She tested our strength to establish realities. . . . Those of

45

us in the first American generations have had to figure out how the invisible world the emigrants built around our childhoods fit in solid America." Were any of your family members held up as lessons to you? Can you imagine telling your children stories about your own life to help them grow up?

2.   Find a newspaper account of a murder or a suicide. Taking just the bare facts of the case and knowing that you are not privy to what really happened, write an imaginative re-creation of what occurred to force the eventual outcome. Can you mediate between assigning blame and eliciting understanding?

MAXINE KUMIN

Journal —Late Winter–Spring 1978 (p. 291)

Questions on Meaning

1.   In his Afterword, Donald Hall writes that "Kumin's journal has a quality that goes with the territory ... of *ongoingness*. . . . Eventually we may discern a structure of happenings, but as we read the daily life simply *goes on*." Yet even this excerpt from Kumin's journal seems to have an obvious "structure of happenings." Compare the first and final journal entries.

DISCUSSION: The entry dated 13 February 1978 starts with a slight reference to death; the fourth word of the first sentence is "dying." The dying butternut tree is paired with the owl's arrival — new life — and this coupling begins the theme that is to be reintroduced in many different ways throughout this excerpt. The final entry deals with the arrival of the dead foal, so that structurally, the subject of the first sentence swells into an entire entry that closes Kumin's piece.

2.   If Kumin is simply noting the continuous unrolling of events, why does the journal contain a coherent skeleton, a skeleton consisting of the paired oppositions of life and death and the cycles and waves (of flies, of fiddlehead greens) of the seasons?

DISCUSSION: Kumin's subject is the natural world, an arena that has its own coherence, which is made up of a cycle moving through death and life. You might say that this subject is, itself, a subject of literature, so that the broad themes of life and death are the boundaries that hold the minutely examined detail. And if you give a writer any credence, you acknowledge that he or she is going to be attentive to coherence; even though the journal notes daily event, the writer's eye is attuned to what forms life, what repeating elements make up the different seasons.

Questions on Strategy

1.   Why is the final entry written in the past tense? How would you describe this entry, as "daily life simply [going] on" or as an "essay [that] takes and makes its own time out-of-time" (Afterword)?

DISCUSSION: The reason that Kumin is writing 19 June in the past tense is that she could not bear to write about the foal's death before some time had passed: "I could not write this before today" (paragraph 35). She has had time to reflect on the event and its meaning, which is going to have an effect on what she writes. The difference between this entry and most of the others is that it is a small essay, a small meditation on death that "takes and makes its own time out-of-time."

2.   What are some elements of closure in the final entry?

DISCUSSION: Elements of closure give a piece of writing its finished feeling. The subject of death might itself be considered an element of closure, since we associate death with finality. Rhetorically, opposition and repetition work to achieve closure. For example, in the first paragraph of the last entry, Kumin says she found Truffle's stillborn foal. Stillborn is just another word for dead, but a more precise word, in that it makes clear that the filly never lived outside the womb. The word itself, however, articulates "born" rather than "died." The foal was "still warm to my touch, one eye glinting as if with life, the mouth slightly ajar so that its pink tongue, brilliantly pink in the graying five a.m. light, shone with the promise of life" (paragraph 35). The underlined words falls into categories. Read as a list, they do not seem to indicate death, but its opposite. Life, or the appearance of life, is the thesis of this sentence, and to that end Kumin talks about the light qualities — "glinting," "brilliantly," "light," "shone" — and the colors — "pink" and, to intensify the idea, "brilliantly pink" against the one negative word, "graying," which, paradoxically, describes the color of the living world. So the first paragraph describes death as it mimics life. In the final few paragraphs, starting with "It is already green there now" (paragraph 38), Kumin addresses the idea of death as it affects her. The grave may have been covered with grass, the filly's death not touching the great indifference of nature, but Kumin cannot so easily move on. As a "Mortician of All Life" (paragraph 3), Kumin finds meaning in the foal's death, unlike Truffle, who, when the filly "did not respond, simply turned away" (paragraph 40), Kumin's vision adheres to the already passed event. Her final line, "O to turn away," picks up the preceding sentence and enlarges it; simply by adding "O to," Kumin invests the repeated phrase with the idea that, unlike the animal, she is unable to leave death behind, to leave the grieving for the "promise of life" present in the filly's still form.

Questions on Language

1.   In the entry of 14 and 15 February, notice how many metaphors and similes Kumin uses in a couple of paragraphs. Why? What is their function?

DISCUSSION: The owl is like "a Japanese puppet-balloon held aloft on a stick" (paragraph 3), "a baseball pitcher in a tight spot" (paragraph 4). These beautifully odd similes are trying to get at a physical description of the owl, to make the reader see what he or she cannot otherwise see. The other metaphors seem to be trying to describe not simply the appearance but the character and the attitude of the owl and the feeling he evokes in Kumin. Thus, the mystery of his silent arrivals and departures, making him "a Cheshire cat of an owl" (paragraph 3). Whereas in the first entry (13 February) Kumin writes, "He arrived like a poem, unannounced" (paragraph 1), in the second she compares him to a "finished poem" (paragraph 3) in that "he makes it all seem easy." In the first simile, the insistent demand of the poem is itself a visitation, as is this owl. In the second, the pure crafting of the poem, the use of mirrors and sleight of hand, hide the mechanics from sight, just as the owl's mechanical features, his wings and claws, are hidden from view. The poem returns again in the journal, when in the final line of 20 February, Kumin uses a filly's movement to describe the ideal muscular grace of the realized poem.

Writing Topics

1.   In 22 March, Kumin supplies a list of amazing facts, or the scientific view of the wonders of the natural world. In the middle of two long paragraphs, she drops in "'a mare' says the old-timey polo-playing vet, Stephen Roberts, 'a mare is like a Vermonter: an animal that thinks otherwise'" (paragraph 21). Why is this sentence here? How might you relate it to the final entry? In an essay, take this sentence and show how it might encompass the entirety of the natural world. How much control and authority does our human knowledge give us?

2.   Keep a journal for several weeks. After two weeks, take one of your daily entries and turn it into a small paper, an essay that "takes and makes its own time out-of-time." Hand in both

the journal entries (including the one from which you have developed a coherent whole) and the paper. Also hand in a small list of the subjects your journal keeps returning to and the broader thematic categories those subjects fall into, such as endings, beginnings, transitions.

BARRY LOPEZ

Wolf Notes (p. 302)

Questions on Meaning

1.   In paragraph 6, Lopez explains the ways in which the wolf is an important and integral part of the whole of the world he lives in. Could this wolf be any wolf?

DISCUSSION: The wolf here seems to stand as generic wolf, a representation for all wolves whose fur will disperse seed, leave carrion for the carrion eaters, and create dens that will be passed down to other animals.

2.   In the final sentence, how does the last phrase differ from the rest?

DISCUSSION: The long final sentence describes the general events of the wolves' lives as they age, such predictable and daily moments as eating and giving birth. The concluding phrase, however, doesn't "fit" precisely into the series. In finishing this excerpt by writing that the wolves will stare "at the way water in a creek breaks around their legs and flows on," Lopez returns to the idea suggested in his first sentence: "Imagine a wolf." This staring suggests an unknowable wolf, a wolf who could be thinking any thought but who is entranced by the mysterious details of life; if it's not too overstated, even a philosophical wolf. The essential mystery of the wolf, the imaginative idea of the wolf, returns to finish the essay.

Questions on Strategy

1.   Compare the narrator in the first two paragraphs with the narrator in the third paragraph. Compare paragraph 5 with paragraph 8. Considering the difficulty of watching a feral wolf for every moment for months or years, how are we supposed to understand this essay? Is it fact or imagination? Is it natural history or narrative?

DISCUSSION: The first sentence of this excerpt is "Imagine a wolf moving through the northern woods." After telling readers to imagine a wolf, Lopez imagines it for us. The wolf "appears, if you are watching, sometimes catlike or bearlike." Its movement appears effortless. Its body appears to float. The first two paragraphs are, in some ways, a conundrum. Who is watching this wolf? Lopez seems to be addressing the idea of fact and imagination in the sly phrase "if you are watching." In the third paragraph, there is a radical change from allusion and metaphor to concrete fact. "The wolf is three years old. A male. He is of the subspecies occidentalis," *Lopez states, with utter certainty. Suddenly, we are presented with the omniscient narrator, the narrator who has access to complete truth, the narrator who can know what the wolf has seen, what he's heard, what he feels like. This narrator even knows the hidden past: "two fractured ribs, broken by a moose a year before. They are healed now, but a sharp eye would notice the irregularity" (paragraph 5). In paragraph 8, the narrator's gaze is able to pierce the distant future: the wolf will weigh eighty-nine pounds, will have tried and failed to mate, will have helped kill an exact number of moose and caribou. The omniscient narrator has access to an exact future.*
*   This essay raises some fascinating questions about the effect of combining factual truth with imagined detail. The narrative flourishes — "Imagine a wolf" — suggest that Lopez is announcing that part of his work here seems to be extrapolated from fact rather than being fact itself, but the ramifications of a nonfictional piece of writing using fictional strategies (such as point of view) are profound. The*

questions this essay raises are questions of credibility, authority, and persuasiveness: does a "factual" piece become more persuasive of conveying truth when it uses fictional devices to render complete access to the life of the Other? Or does the use of fictional devices undermine the credibility of the world the writer perceives? Fiction, of course, has a long history of incorporating "factual" elements: think of the introduction to Nathaniel Hawthorne's The Scarlet Letter, for instance, where the author is trying to persuade the reader that the documents the story is based on were really found and really exist. But the reverse situation, in which factual works incorporate fictional elements, has not been attended to so closely, perhaps because writing that was perceived to be "scientific" and "objective" was not read as seriously by people who concentrated on canonical literature. English studies are beginning, however, to widen their gaze, and such books as Harriet Ritvo's The Animal Estate: The English and Other Creatures in the Victorian Age *(Cambridge: Harvard University Press, 1987) are looking at the fictional strategies inherent in nonfictional works.*

Questions on Language

1.   Describe the sentences in paragraph 4. Analyze the syntax. How do you interpret the change in syntax?

DISCUSSION: On the basis of sentence length, paragraph 4 can be divided into two parts. The first part opens and closes the paragraph and describes the wolf moving through the country; here, Lopez uses long, complex sentences. In the middle of the paragraph the syntax changes abruptly: "It is an easy time. The weather is pleasant. Moose are fat. Suddenly the wolf stops in mid-stride. A moment, then his feet slowly come alongside each other. He is staring into the grass. His ears are rammed forward, stiff. His back arches and he rears up and punches like a cat. A deer mouse is pinned between his forepaws. Eaten. The wolf drifts on." These short sentences signal a sudden change in attention, leading to the killing. The short sentences isolate one idea at a time: He stops. He puts his feet together. He stares at the grass. He rams his ears forward. All these actions are separate. In the actual killing, three movements are put together, joined by "and," a connective that gives equal importance to all three actions: "His back arches and he rears up and he pounces." These three components make up the killing moment. After that central act, the next sentences again describe one action each, until the wolf returns to traveling through the landscape and the syntax becomes wordier and more complex.

Writing Topics

1.   Write an essay beginning "Imagine a . . . " and fill in the animal. Most of us are familiar with domestic animals, dogs and cats, but we probably don't have the amount of factual knowledge about our animals that Lopez has about wolves. Research your animal and, using Lopez's essay as a model, write a short description.

2.   Choose a nonfictional essay not in this book and write an essay analyzing its narrative. How is the "story" told? Examine point of view. How does the perspective establish the narrator's own stance? Does the point of view have an effect on the factual truth of the narrative? If you're unsure where to start, consider something from the nineteenth century, perhaps an explorer's account; you might find something useful under the heading "Travel Literature" in the card catalog. Or read some of the essays in either *Writing Culture: The Poetics and Politics of Ethnography*, ed. James Clifford and George E. Marcus (Berkeley: University of California Press, 1986), or Hayden White's *Tropics of Discourse: Essays in Cultural Criticism* (Baltimore: Johns Hopkins University Press, 1978).

ALISON LURIE

Clothing as a Sign System (p. 307)

Questions on Meaning

1.   Lurie unifies her essay by a consistent use of analogy — a rhetorical technique by which a similarity between two different things provides the basis for an argument about both. This essay is about clothes and about language, but its thesis is that clothing *is* a language, "an older and more universal tongue" than that which we usually speak (paragraph 1). Lurie's essay argues that we're all adept at "reading" each other's clothes. What is the language of clothes?

DISCUSSION: *Lurie limits herself to a vocabulary, which is made up of the garments themselves, and a grammar, which consists of accessories, only modifiers. Necessarily, she adds the context: the situation in which the sentences are spoken also renders meaning. But in paragraphs 47 and 48, she addresses the obvious possibilities of duplicity in this nonverbal language, rendering our reading inaccurate. Aside from duplicity, there's the rather common phenomenon of a new language, or at least a new dialect, coming into being with each generation. But because almost all of us can "speak" the language of clothing, all of us are, to some extent, able to divine elements of personality or psychology from our reading. The language clothes speak is the language of personality.*

2.   When Lurie compares the uniform and the cliché outfit, she dwells much longer on the uniform (paragraphs 30–39). What are the essential similarities between the two and why does she scrutinize the uniform?

DISCUSSION: *The cliché outfit, like the uniform, is made up of a vocabulary validated by others; nothing much of personal eccentricity or whim is left to mar the safety of its surface. It is chosen to proclaim a "social role" played by its wearer, but it is chosen out of the wearer's free will, no matter how conventional that will might be (paragraph 30). The uniform, on the other hand, has its every detail decreed by others, and wearing it proclaims the surrender of free will: "to put on such a livery is to give up one's right to act as an individual" (paragraph 33). Lurie dwells long on this point because of the ramifications of donning a uniform; the individual, Lurie insists, is so captured by the symbolic power of his or her clothes that he or she becomes a nonperson, someone who "we should not or need not treat . . . as a human being, and [someone who] need not and should not treat us as one" (paragraph 33). The mechanical lies the uniform wearers utter are merely innocuous in this paragraph — "It was a pleasure having you on board"; "The doctor will see you shortly" — but the logical extension of Lurie's argument is that the uniform will make it equally easy to utter more powerful lies — My soldiers did not shoot your husband, for instance, or I don't know where your daughter is; she's probably run away from home. Lurie only implies a powerful indictment, suggesting that the uniform is made up of the stuff of nightmare.*

Questions on Strategy

1.   From paragraph 59 to 66, Lurie discusses the magical properties of clothing. How does she use the history of magical clothing and accessories to explain the contemporary world?

DISCUSSION: *This section is particularly interesting for its revelation of the perseverance of our belief in magic. Like happy and distant anthropologists, we might remark on the rather poignant charm of a shark's teeth necklace being donned to give its wearer "the qualities of a fierce and successful fisherman" (paragraph 60). It's rather another thing to see that we have, unwittingly, inherited the belief in contagious magic; copper bracelets were supposed to be the newest thing, and now Lurie reveals their ancient genealogy. The entire passage emphasizes the power of clothing, in a much more profound — if much less generally acknowledged — sense than the rest of the essay. The argument, up to now, has mainly concentrated on what most people "know" intuitively; if we stop to think while we're dressing or in analyzing someone else's dress, we realize that clothing is, for the most part, conscious speech. But here Lurie attaches clothing to the murky depths of the subconscious and manages to make hay of our self-conscious intellect.*

Questions on Language

1.   In some cases, Lurie personifies garments, granting them the ability to speak for them-selves, as she does when "the pair of plain black rubbers" says, "The streets are wet, and I can't afford to damage my shoes" (paragraph 55). What is she implying here about clothes and social status?

DISCUSSION: This is a point also made by Thorstein Veblen in Theory of the Leisure Class. *Basically, his argument states that there is an inverse proportion between one's social standing and the suitability of one's clothes for the natural world. In paragraph 56, for example, Lurie says that "the more water-repellent a raincoat is, ordinarily, the more it repels admiration — unless it is also fashionably colored or cut, or in some other way evidently expensive." But of course, a person's bank account — and often his or her social standing — is even more obvious if that person has no raincoat at all. Mink coats are admittedly warm, but they are usually worn not with leggings and fuzzy footwear but more often with nylons and thin-soled high heels, articles not designed for either comfort or warmth. The lack of utilitarian clothing, then, suggests a life in which one is cosseted and protected from the elements of the natural world that impinge upon the lives of other, poorer people.*

Writing Topics

1.   When Paul Fussell puts people into categories according to the clothes they wear, how is his argument similar to Lurie's and how is it different? Does one author seem more serious than the other? In an essay, describe the aspects of their styles that account for the differences in their relative seriousness.

2.   Study the window displays in some department stores. Notice how the clothing is presented. How lifelike are the mannequins? How are they posed? To what extent has the window dresser translated the clothes on display? Also study several magazines that carry fashion advertising (*Vogue, Glamour, Esquire,* New York *Times* Sunday fashion supplements). How do fashion photographers present the clothing of designers and manufacturers? Can we translate their images? Write an essay on the influence of display and advertising on the language of clothing.

JOHN MCPHEE

Riding the Boom Extension (p. 330)

Questions on Meaning

1.   In his Afterword, Donald Hall writes that "the old essay is opinionated" whereas "McPhee satisfies the American or modern appetite for fact." He goes on to tell us that the *New Yorker* calls such essays "fact pieces." Certainly, "Riding the Boom Extension" is packed with facts, but facts often suggest that writing is presenting sheer bald objective truth, which obviates any need for authorial interpretation. Is McPhee using facts to guide his readers to a certain judgment in this

piece? For example, in paragraphs 7–9 the townspeople testify in a reverent chorus to Hutch's virtues:

> "He gave us lights."
> "He gave us telephones."
> "He did it all by himself."

Does the narrator share their assessment?

DISCUSSION: There's a faint echo of "Let there be light" behind the three sentences quoted above, which invests Hutch with a kind of divine status. As Albert Carroll says in paragraph 28, "'Don't ever take the phone out of Circle City. It's our best resource.'" Notice the passive voice in the next sentence: "When it is suggested to the sometime chief that the dish antenna is drawing out of his pocket thousands of dollars that might otherwise be spent on something solider than words, he says . . ." Who suggests here that the telephone is the opposite of a good resource? We know it's not Hutch — "Sometimes Hutchinson comes into Carroll's cabin, sees only one light on, and asks, 'How am I going to make any money?' 'He turns on every light there is, inside and out,' Albert says. 'If a bulb is missing, he'll go and get one'. (paragraph 29) — and we can be sure it's not another subscriber to the phone service. It might be the lone holdout Carl Dasch, but it doesn't sound like him: 'Why would I need a telephone? I can stand on the porch and yell at everyone here'" (paragraph 16). It sounds like McPhee himself. Of course, that comment alone is not proof of the writer's judgment. McPhee writes the facts, but he writes the facts that cumulatively express what he sees as the truth of the entire situation, just as Frances FitzGerald does in "Sun City." In many cases, he doesn't have to comment; in paragraph 17, Carroll "speaks for the whole tribe when he says, 'I don't get out and holler the way we used to. I call from here to here. We stand in the window and look at each other and talk on the phone. I don't have to walk over next door and ask Anne Ginnis if she has a beer. I call her and tell her to bring it.'" This expression of the difference the telephone has made to Carroll's life seems obvious enough to stand alone.

2. The theme of money runs like a shining river throughout this essay. Why is McPhee so interested in money and in people's bank accounts?

DISCUSSION: In paragraph 20, McPhee tells us that the phone rates are "roughly double the rates in New Jersey." In paragraphs 23–28, he shows Hutch demurring at the eighty percent he's allowed to keep. Here, Hutch seems scandalized at the amount of profit, especially in comparison to Alascom, who seems the incarnation of the voice of greed — "Don't ever say it's too much" (paragraph 27). But Hutch doesn't turn the money down. In paragraph 30, McPhee writes: "The oil will last about twenty-five years. Easy come, easy go. The state will soon have a surplus in its treasury of nearly four billion dollars. It will cover many calls to Fort Yukon." McPhee's tone is so quiet that it's possible to glide right over the irony in these four lines. The chain of transformation changes oil — a nonrenewable resource (hear the echo of Carroll saying "[the phone is] our best resource") — into money into phone calls. From oil to ephemera: the spoken word.

Questions on Strategy

1. Carl Dasch emerges as an important person in this essay, mainly for his refusal to participate in the otherwise universal enthusiasms. Consider Carl's comments in paragraph 43: "He has found much to interest him here in the country. He used to watch ornithologists from the Lower Forty-eight shooting peregrine falcons off the bluffs of the Yukon. They were allowed to do this. It was a scientific deal. They wanted to see what the falcons had been eating. All they had to do was look at the bones in the nests to see what the falcons had been eating.'" Why does McPhee choose to include this paragraph, despite its very different subject?

DISCUSSION: In this paragraph, Carl addresses the issue of waste that runs throughout the essay. Unnecessarily killing the peregrines is another example of unreflective stupidity and ignorance. Whereas the explicit subject — the falcons — is different from the larger subject in this essay, Carl's interpretation reflects McPhee's interpretation of the Yukon's handling of its oil. Conservation and husbanding natural resources are much less important to both the government and the individual inhabitants of the Arctic as they are presented in "Riding the Boom Extension" than accruing enormous amounts of money. Remember McPhee's irony when he says, about the oil lasting twenty-five more years, "Easy come, easy go."

2.   The beginning of this essay, from paragraph 1 to 6, seems like a rather long introduction to the subject. Why does McPhee preface his portrait of Hutch and Circle City with such a beginning?

DISCUSSION: The first people we meet are the Texan suction dredgers, described as "the suckers" in paragraph 3. McPhee segues from the moment of their arrival to a history of Circle City and from that to a small description of Circle City now. But the suction dredgers personify both the past and the present of Circle City, "a region whose economy has had no other history than booms" (paragraph 4). The new price of gold has started another rush of opportunists and greed. Richard Hutchinson is tied to this frenzy in the last two lines of paragraph 6: "Richard Hutchinson, who has been in the country for sixteen years, knows where the gold is now. He has struck it right here in Circle City." By the end of the introduction, McPhee has set the context for his portrait of Hutch, and it is not a context in which heroism is measured by one's bank balance.

Questions on Language

1.   In paragraph 48, McPhee writes: "Hutchinson has become deeply interested in the growth of the town. This past school year, he was pleased to note five new first graders. He referred to them as 'future customers.' Hutchinson is the town welcome wagon." How do you interpret Hutch's comment?

DISCUSSION: When Hutch calls six-year-olds "future customers," he is seeing them solely in one specific context; although this interpretation makes it seem overstated, he is ignoring any human value they might have and instead is focusing on their money-making potential for his monopoly. This moment is typical of McPhee's style in the entire essay; he consistently buries moments that lead us to judgment, never hits the reader over the head with his interpretation, but rather lets the subjects speak for themselves. They speak enough, though, so that the judgment builds up and finally becomes inescapable.

Writing Topics

1.   Both McPhee's "Riding the Boom Extension" and FitzGerald's "Sun City" are about isolated communities, an idea that explicitly guides FitzGerald's interpretation of her subject city. Write an essay in which you compare these two essays. Does McPhee's essay address the idea of isolation in Circle City? Look at the moments in each piece of writing that guide the reader toward judgment. Do McPhee and FitzGerald use the same techniques? Are their judgments equally visible?

2.   Write an essay that focuses on a small community of people, such as a club or a newspaper office or a dorm room. Describe your subject — but to describe your subject as McPhee does here, you will also have to interpret your subject. The idea is to portray a small world that coheres in some way, which means you will have to develop an understanding of where you're leading the reader. The details you choose to relate should support your governing vision of that community.

JAN MORRIS

City of Yok (p. 344)

Questions on Meaning

1. Why does Morris title her piece "City of *Yok*"? What is she trying to do in this essay?

DISCUSSION: As she writes in the hilarious first paragraph, yok expresses two philosophies: "the bad, a certain prohibitive attitude to life, a lack of fizz or obvious hopefulness, a forbidding fatalism and an underlying sense of menace; the good, an immense latent strength, an accumulated toughness and stubbornness." This essay is attempting to portray those two philosophies as they are expressed by the city itself. The city is the character that Morris is trying to draw to life in these pages. Thus, the first sentence personifies the city: "The favorite epithet of Istanbul seems to be yok." In the usual course of things, Istanbul would be silent, and her inhabitants would speak. Not so in this essay.

2. In paragraph 11, Morris seems to be suggesting that Istanbul is about to undergo another period of change: "The generations of the dead are risen, to prod the living into life." Why does she, in the next paragraph, characterize this as "a vigor of the grave. These are bones rustling . . ."?

DISCUSSION: In paragraph 16, Morris returns to the same idea: "There can never be a fresh start in Istanbul. It is too late. Its successive pasts are ineradicable and inescapable." Even the new uprising of Islam is tied to "the days of the caliphs" (paragraph 23). The faith is ancient and "irrepressible, and it remains the most potent single element, I suppose, in the personality of the place." In paragraph 24, she locates Islam as an enormous nostalgic force, so that the "muezzin voices" insist always on a return, ever on a movement back into the ideal and golden past: "calling Istanbul always back again, home again to itself — back to the great days of the caliphs, the noble Ahmets and the munificent Mehmets, back to the times when the princes of this city could build incomparable monuments of belief and generosity, high on their seven hills above the sea." Notice how Morris emphasizes the controlling idea of nostalgia by using romantic diction; caliphs, nobles, princes, are located in a storybook place — high on their seven hills above the sea. It's fairy-tale language used to indicate a dream-vision.

Questions on Strategy

1. What is Morris doing in paragraph 6? What literary techniques does she use? How does the bear function in paragraph 36?

DISCUSSION: In paragraph 6, Morris makes the city's personification explicit, comparing Istanbul to "an aged actor whose prime was long ago, whose powers have failed him but who struts about still in cloak and carnationed buttonhole, snubbing his inferiors." The various metaphors and similes she uses throughout give different aspects of the personality of the city. The bear is almost a surreal detail, a bear invested with "infinite melancholy and weariness," a grand and somewhat disdainful bear. It suggests both the exotic nature of the surprises of life in Istanbul and its eccentric grandeur.

2. In attempting to convey the sense of a place, Morris is unable to say, "Istanbul is this. Istanbul is that." Instead, she has to come at the city obliquely and from all sides, sneaking up on her subject to reveal its personality. In paragraph 39, she suggests one reason for the impossibility of a direct view of the city. What is it?

DISCUSSION: Morris is talking about Istanbul's setting when she writes: "Everything is a little hazed, though; not merely by the cloud of spiced smoke in which the restaurateur is cooking our fish, on the open quayside by the boat, but by a kind of permanent opacity of life and light along the Golden Horn, through which everything moves powerfully but inexactly." This is a charge that clear interpretation is not easy to achieve in this city where the past is always in control; it seems the view of the present is inescapably occluded by the clouds of the past, and the view, in the final paragraph, is that of a "huge mechanical theater worked by the engines of history."

Questions on Language

1. Question 2 in "Questions on Meaning" discusses how the muezzin's cries conjure up a powerfully seductive vision from the past. Does Morris understand the new Islamic uprising in the terms the language she uses in paragraph 24 would suggest? Does the language change in paragraph 25?

DISCUSSION: *The nostalgia suggested by her diction in paragraph 24 is interpreted in the following paragraph, where Morris terms the new Islam a "regressive religion." Its new adherents are called "fanatics" who are "aflame." In paragraph 24, Morris allows us to understand the dream that the new generation of Islam harkens back to, but in paragraph 25 she gives us her own understanding of that dream, and it is devoid of the glory of the romantic past. In Islam's new incarnation, the ancient caliphs and princes and nobles and their "incomparable monuments of belief and generosity" are replaced by students and militants who "burn cars, or break windows."*

Writing Topics

1. In "History as Mirror," Barbara W. Tuchman discusses the similarities between the four-teenth and the twentieth centuries. Write an essay on the period when Islam was at its height, and compare it with Islam now. Would you agree with Morris's assessment of Islam in the past? See paragraph 24.) Now?

2. RESEARCH: Write an essay in which you try to convey the personality of a town or city. Using "City of *Yok*" as a model, include the past and the present of your subject. Try to sum up your city as succinctly as Morris does in her title.

JOYCE CAROL OATES

Against Nature (p. 357)

Questions on Meaning

1. How might Oates's paroxysmal tachycardia and the fever-dream, both given prominent positions in this essay, comment on her thesis?

DISCUSSION: *Both paroxysmal tachycardia and the fever-dream are fairly profound examples of moments when the intellect has lost its primacy, leaving the body supreme. In both cases, the body is not working properly (for when it's working properly, the mind is mostly unaware of it): the heart is pounding out of control and the body is burning up with fever, its invisible antibodies at war. Both episodes can be seen as the person being attacked by nature, being betrayed by her own body. Nature is the attacker. Notice that the strategies used by "brainy" people consist not of fighting against nature, of reasoning the heart out of its frightening urgency, but of acceding to the worst possibility it conjures up: "If I die now it's a good death" (paragraph 12).*

In the fever-dream, Oates loses her own sovereignty of self; in fact, she loses the idea of self utterly: "In this fantastical structure the 'I' is deluded as to its sovereignty, let alone its autonomy in the (outside) world; the most astonishing secret is that the 'I' doesn't exist! — but it behaves as if it does, as if it were one and not many" (paragraph 47). In paragraph 12, Oates comments not only on her own body — her own natural "world" — as attacker, but on surrounding nature as remaining distant, aloof, indifferent, "completely oblivious to the predicament of the individual."

2.   In his Afterword, Donald Hall mentions "Oates's intellectual skepticism over the romantic inflation of nature." Discuss this idea in reference to paragraphs 16 and 31.

DISCUSSION: At the end of paragraph 16, Oates turns to scientific truth to combat artistic truth, which is accused of inflating nature's importance: "And the lovely blue isn't even blue, is it? isn't even there, is it? a mere optical illusion, isn't it? no matter what art has urged you to believe." But her response is a conundrum, for whether an optical illusion or not, the blue sky is present to our universal perception. The truth — that the sky is not in fact blue but is invisible — is a truth that demands a leap of faith. In paragraph 31, the quotation Oates takes from Wilde turns the whole idea of art inside out. Wilde argues that Mrs. Arundel can see the sky only because poets and painters first showed it to her, but when he himself looks out at the view, he sees a very mediocre painting — nature as an inferior representation of Turner's art.

Questions on Strategy

1.   As the essay is structured, Oates sets up two definitions of nature, labeled in paragraph 26 *"Nature-in-itself"* and *"Nature-as-experience."* What definition is Oates most concerned with?

DISCUSSION: Nature-as-experience is developed as a counterargument, or the argument critics might hold up against her understanding. Oates, however, shrinks the definition from "a 'perennial' source of beauty, comfort, peace, escape from the delirium of civilized life" to a truncated, castrated version of nature: what gives us this sense of beauty, comfort, peace, and so on is not nature raw but nature tamed, in the suburban garden, on the well-marked hiking trail. This experience is of little dabs of nature doled out "in proportion to [one's] psychological strength," and there's something narcissistic about it: "Nature that pleases us because it mirrors our souls, or gives the comforting illusion of doing so" (paragraphs 24 and 27). This is not the Melvillean vision of nature that Oates is trying to address, a vision that can be described only by what it is not: "a blankness ten times blank" (paragraph 27).

2.   How do paragraphs 29 and 30 connect to the preceding section?

DISCUSSION: Oates is developing the idea of narcissism from paragraphs 27 and 28. Even our "high-cultural" tradition of nature worship is revealed to be a result of self-love; one of the things we love about nature is that we can impose our own opinions, beliefs, sensations on it with no backtalk. Our "white heat of . . . 'creativity'" first, nature second.

Questions on Language

1.   What do you make of the contrast between Thoreau's quotation in paragraph 33 and Oates's response to it? How would you describe the language used by each?

DISCUSSION: For all its formality, Thoreau's passage contains some interesting juxtapositions of "high" and colloquial diction: "that tender organizations can be so serenely squashed out of existence like pulp." Tadpoles are "gobbled up" in the same sentence that echoes Revelations: "sometimes it has rained flesh and blood!" The final sentence in the passage — "The impression made on a wise man is that of universal innocence" — has the effect of intellectually withdrawing from the squashing, the gobbling, and the pulp Thoreau has, immediately before, exulted in, and ends the passage with a rationalization whose effect is either shocking or smug, but certainly unexpected from the preceding lines.

Oates pops the pretension and distance of the final line with withering irony: "Come off it, Henry David" (paragraph 34). The following line, more a personal attack than anything, attempts to close the distance between Thoreau's rationalizing intelligence and his visceral experience of "nature-in-itself": "You've grieved these many years for your elder brother John, who died a ghastly death of lockjaw, you've never wholly recovered from the experience of watching him die." This is the pure personal voice here, the voice we hear on the streets, the voice undeceived by all the formal and polished prose we are given to admire in the classroom.

Writing Topics

1.   How do you interpret the opening section of this essay, entitled: "The writer's resistance to Nature"? Write an essay in which you locate the items on Oates's list in regard to her guiding definitions of "Nature-in-itself" and "Nature-as-experience." What is her main complaint?

2.   Write an essay defending the work of another nature writer from this book against Oates's charges. What does Annie Dillard's essay, for example, say to support or refute parts or the whole of Oates's argument? Abbey? Didion? Ehrlich? Hoagland? Lopez?

CYNTHIA OZICK

The First Day of School:
Washington Square, 1946 (p. 368)

Questions on Meaning

1.   What are the "three clear omens — or call them riddles, intricate and redolent" (paragraph 3)? How does Ozick interpret them?

DISCUSSION: The first omen is a pretzel man with a cart (paragraph 6). The second is a Chock Full O' Nuts coffee shop and the third is a newsstand (paragraph 7). Together, Ozick explains, "the three riddle-omens . . . will illumine Washington Square" (paragraph 12). Ozick suggests that while the pretzel man lives, "all those pitiables . . . the discountable, the repudiated, the unseen," will never be utterly forgotten. The pretzel man "conjures them all," for "he is the guardian of the garden of the jettisoned" (paragraph 13). On the other hand, Chock Full O' Nuts is the very opposite of the sacred; it is "the marketplace of Washington Square, its bazaar, its roiling gossip-parlor, its matchmaker's office and arena" — the social arena rather than the intellectual (paragraph 14). The newsstand sells Partisan Review, *whose writers create a "conflagration flaming in the gray street: the succulent hotness of their promise" (paragraph 9). But Ozick hasn't tasted their promise yet: "I still haven't bought a copy; I still can't understand a word. I don't know what cold war means. Who is Trotsky? I haven't read* Ulysses. . . . *I'm in my mind's cradle" (paragraph 20). The newsstand is Ozick's future.*

Questions on Strategy

1.   What tense is this essay written in? Where does it change? Why? What is the point of view?

DISCUSSION: Only the first two paragraphs are written in the past tense; with paragraph 3, the essay continues in the present. With the advent of the present tense, Ozick presents her protagonist, herself, in first person, but first person with a difference. "Here I am flying . . . here I am turning," she writes initially. She is pointing herself out, as though she were gesturing toward a character projected on a screen. Even the first line of paragraph 3 emphasizes this cinematic portrayal. "Which dissolves into the dun gauze of a low and sullen city sky" is not a sentence, but it might follow, as a clause, from the concluding sentence of paragraph 2, like this: "I felt my youth like a nimbus, which dissolves into the dun gauze of a low and sullen city sky." That haze of youth is dispersed into something darker, something concrete, and suddenly Ozick is center stage, in a particular location. After paragraph 2, Washington Square is no longer "the celestial unknown," but a place made up of small, known places: Lexington Avenue subway, Astor Place, the union hall, and the park.

2.   Discuss the last sentence of the essay. Why does Ozick end by shifting the focus of attention from herself to Washington Square?

DISCUSSION: The first sentence of the penultimate paragraph states the thesis of this essay: "Washington Square will wake me." The freshman who arrived early, knowing nothing, conscious of her own lacunae, is going to be shaken into alertness by Washington Square. The final sentence echoes that wakening, only changing its focus so that Washington Square becomes the awakened. What it wakens to, of course, is "the luster of little green leaves," the emblems of cyclical rebirth and renewal, pointing from past generations to future generations. In the final sentence, Ozick generalizes the particular experience she relates in this essay and points to its recurrence for many, many others, who will each, in their turn, share her unfurling from nascent bud into full consciousness.

Questions on Language

1.   Compare the diction and style in paragraphs 1 and 18.

DISCUSSION: The first few lines of "The First Day of School" are simple declarative sentences: "I first came down to Washington Square on a colorless February morning in 1946." The only descriptive word in the sentence is "colorless"; everything else relates pure fact. In contrast, paragraph 18 conveys the feeling and passion of Ozick's experiences in 1946. She begins the paragraph by reciting a phrase from Thomas Wolfe and uses that phrase to spring again into the feeling it first elicited. Her expression of that feeling is self-consciously "poetical," beginning with the "Ah": "Ah, you who have flung Thomas Wolfe, along with your strange and magical youth, onto the ash-heap of juvenilia and excess, myself among you, isn't this a lovely phrase still?" The beauty, not only of Wolfe's language but of one's own — repudiated — "strange and magical youth" is being addressed here, where Ozick reclaims the passion of her juvenile excess. The seduction of language and of learning is what Washington Square means to Ozick; the phrase, emblematic of her own past, "rises out of the old pavements . . . as delicately colored as an eggshell."

Writing Topics

1.   Ozick's writing is extremely evocative and allusive. Consider paragraph 8 and others like it: "The Chock Full: the doors are like fans, whirling remnants of conversation. *She will marry him. She will not marry him.* Fragrance of coffee and hot chocolate. *We can prove that the senses are partial and unreliable vehicles of information, but who is to say that reason is not equally a product of human limitation?* Powdered doughnut sugar on their lips." Why might she mention the fragrances? Whose voices is Ozick hearing? Write an essay in which you analyze Ozick's techniques for conjuring up memories of the past.

2.   As Donald Hall points out in his Afterword, "the first day at college is a universal subject." Go back further, to your first day of primary school or elementary or junior high or high school. You may not have experienced the power of Ozick's intellectual awakening at these various points, but you did enter a new world. Using Ozick's essay as a model, write one of your own in which you try to locate your own icons and anxieties from that time.

The Loss of the Creature (p. 376)

Questions on Meaning

1. In paragraph 28, Percy writes that the tourist's assessment of "this quaint and picturesque village is measured by a Platonic ideal of the Quaint and the Picturesque." In paragraph 4, he writes that the park planners have assumed that "the Grand Canyon has the fixed interest value P." In his essay, Percy argues against both those preformulated concepts, but what does he replace them with? Consider the answer Percy presents in paragraph 37.

DISCUSSION: The easy answer to this question is that Percy insists on a sovereign vision, a view that depends on oneself rather than on one's preformulated concepts. However, this answer begins to suggest the difficulty of the essay; if Percy is arguing against a "fixed interest value," how can he then insist on another interest value, an interest value labeled "sovereign" but one that still is a projected preformulation of interest on his part? Seeing the Grand Canyon with sovereign eyes would mean stepping out of one's culture and, almost, out of oneself. Is this even possible? In paragraph 37, Percy writes, "No matter what the object or event is, whether it is a star, a swallow, a Kwakiutl, a 'psychological phenomenon,' the layman who confronts it does not confront it as a sovereign person, as Crusoe confronts a seashell he finds on the beach." Here is a great paradox, for to convey his notion of sovereignty, Percy appropriates a character from Romanticism as articulated by Defoe — Robinson Crusoe. Percy's faith in the sovereign seems to be derived from a "symbolic package" that he accepts in its entirety. What makes his allegiance to Defoe's idea of Crusoe possible, a vision of Crusoe as representative of "authentic experience" itself, is Percy's own loss of sovereignty and his seduction by literary romanticism.

2. Percy focuses on the obscuring nature of the presentation, or representation, of things. "The sonnet is obscured by the symbolic package which is formulated not by the sonnet itself but by the *media* through which the sonnet is transmitted, the media which the educators believe for some reason to be transparent" (paragraph 41). We all have examples from our own lives for this idea — remembering the piano teacher rather than the music — but if Percy is saying that we annihilate the world through summation and theory, that we have to resist the compulsion to interpret examples and sum them up into concrete sentences, what is he saying about the possibility of communication? Compare Percy's implications with Richard Rodriguez's ideas in "The Achievement of Desire."

DISCUSSION: In some ways, this is a profoundly disturbing essay. Attending to the thing itself and noticing its richness of detail, rather than concentration on extrapolating a neat and tidy idea from the thing, seems to leave one in a box of profound isolation, where the possibility of communicating our experiences — except, as Percy does here, through allusion, accretion, indirection, and suggestion — is minimal. Yet, when you compare this essay with Rodriguez's "The Achievement of Desire," you find Rodriguez mourning his own imprisonment in the "symbolic package," reading only for the core nugget of accepted meaning and ignoring the value of his own critical intelligence and emotional engagement with the text or with the world. But the whole idea of the students' imprisonment in the symbolic package has a long history; John Dewey, for example, in the nineteenth century, worked to elevate experiential knowledge over rote memorization and packaged education.

Questions on Strategy

1. Percy's essay proceeds by accretion, piling example on example, illustration on illustration. Why does Percy provide such a stream of various scenarios throughout "The Loss of the Creature"? Why wouldn't just one example do for each point?

Percy, *The Loss of the Creature* (text pp. 376–392)

DISCUSSION: Each added example implies the difficulty of conveying the idea being addressed in its wholeness, so that the additions modify or add something to the previous ones. The thing Percy is attempting to address seems to be beyond words, a Platonic form itself, able to be glimpsed only in bits and pieces. Percy's cumulative examples resist the deliberate and definitive statement of meaning; in writing this essay, he has refused to translate his ideas into easily transferable, concrete blocks.

2.   We know from the headnote that Walker Percy is a highly educated man. What, then, might his reasons be for his own absence from this essay? Why doesn't he address his own education? What effect does his absence have on the essay as it stands?

DISCUSSION: Not including some autobiographical information about the process of his own education allows Percy to create an essay that is clearly ordered and comprehensible — although, as we've seen in other essays, the reverse argument doesn't hold. Including autobiography can make a subject clearer, as we see in Adrienne Rich's "Taking Women Students Seriously." However, in absenting himself from the same experiences his tourists and visitors undergo, Percy does give the impression that, whereas he has some kind of perfect access to this untranslatable mystery of being, everyone else does not. In fact, in this essay, no one has perfect knowledge except the author.

Questions on Language

1.   What does Percy mean when he writes: "As a result of the science of botany, trees are not made available to every man. On the contrary. The tree loses its proper density and mystery as a concrete existent and, as merely another *specimen of* a species, becomes itself nugatory" (paragraph 58). What tradition do such words as "concrete existent" belong to?

DISCUSSION: This quotation certainly echoes Wordsworth's line, "We murder to dissect" (see his poem "The Tables Turned"). Percy's whole essay insists that there is some kind of untransmittable knowledge and that to look in any formal way at anything is to kill whatever meaning it might have. The idea of the inchoate and unarticulable mystery of a thing being positively banished by address belongs to Romanticism as well as to the same place from which he takes his diction, the philosophical tradition of existentialism. Although he does mention Kierkegaard, a pre-existentialist, Percy's vocabulary and his ideas were used by, among others, Heidegger, Nietzsche, Sartre, and Simone de Beauvoir.

Writing Topics

1.   Write an essay in which you support Percy's refusal to cite his ideas in their historic and philosophical context. Why might his point be better made outside of that context? On the other hand, what impression does his insistence on standing alone create?

2.   In Annie Dillard's "Total Eclipse," she writes, "I assure you, if you send any shepherds a Christmas card on which is printed a three-by-three photograph of the angel of the Lord, the glory of the Lord, and a multitude of the heavenly host, they will not be sore afraid. More fearsome things can come in envelopes. More moving photographs than those of the sun's corona can appear in magazines. But I pray you will never see anything more awful in the sky" (paragraph 31). Dillard is addressing the idea of the thing itself being lost in representation, just as Percy argues in "The Loss of the Creature." Yet Dillard nonetheless tries to capture the eclipse in words. In an essay, discuss the techniques she uses to recover her subject.

3.   RESEARCH: Other writers have been thinking about this problem in other ways. Analyze Robert Haas's poem "Meditation at Lagunitas," in his book *Praise* (New York: Ecco Press, 1974). Haas begins by acknowledging the existence of the tradition he is working in: "All the new

thinking is about loss. / In this it resembles all the old thinking" (11.1–2). What are the speaker's reasons for acknowledging intellectual predecessors? Does the speaker, like Percy, believe that the recovery of the subject is possible yet inarticulate?

SAMUEL F. PICKERING, Jr.

Occupational Hazard (p. 393)

Questions on Meaning

1.   "Rarely fatal," Pickering writes, "the virus usually leads to a comfortable mental state in which the sufferer becomes inaccessible to thought" (paragraph 2). His diagnosis, however, becomes more particular. What arena of being becomes the most deformed by the disease?

DISCUSSION: *The virus in question accomplishes its end — making the sufferer inaccessible to thought — by attacking, through inflating, his ego. The professor refuses to restrain his pride with any intellectual humility; he is corrupted by failing to stop himself from basking in the glow from admiring undergraduates. (Perhaps if he spent more time talking to his colleagues, who, almost by definition, would not admire his every thought, the virus could be averted.) He generalizes from his classroom experience, in which he is supposed to be the most knowledgeable, to his total experience, in which he probably isn't, and "the belief that one is Delphic gets under the skin and becomes incurable" (paragraph 2).*

2.   Why are professors a particularly apt target for Pickering's satire?

DISCUSSION: *Pickering has chosen an excellent subject because overbearing ego is the exact opposite of intellectual rigor and what we, in Freshman Comp. courses, call "critical thinking." Ideas, supposed to be of paramount importance in the academy, demand primary allegiance; in shifting concentration to one's self, the professor betrays his own profession.*

Questions on Strategy

1.   In this essay, Pickering suggests that the professor has no authentic self or that the virus very quickly acts to make him replace himself with a new being. What are the symptoms?

DISCUSSION: *Pickering meticulously details the physical symptoms; clothes are described as the markers of the diagnosis, as though they were a spreading rash, changing color, changing shape, announcing the disease to anyone who has the eyes to read the body as pathological text. Just as Alison Lurie does, in "Clothing as a Sign System," Pickering interprets each article of clothing and each replacement of each article as it composes the vocabulary of the sentence: I am sick. The first stage affects eccentricity — the Afghan and sandals, the paisley tie and lavender shorts of paragraph 3 — the second, discernment and expense. He then begins to reinvent himself in earnest, redecorating his office in terms of its iconic value, changing his accent and his name. Pickering is showing us a social climber, but a social climber who aspires soley to the cultural heights. The cultural heights, unfortunately, are pathetic in their bland conformity. Each time the professor tries to change, his change is utterly predictable. Sporting sideburns and a new wife, supposedly indicative of renewal and rejuvenation, instead indicates a hackneyed last grab at youth. The acquisition of a dog signals the end is near; with the dog's death, the natural man publicly parades feeling but privately courts numbness. In every case, the symptoms are visible, since the professor's idea of reinvention belongs to the external, rather than the essential, world.*

Questions on Language

1. How does Pickering's subject affect his diction and style?

DISCUSSION: In describing the rampant pathogen of academia, Pickering's style engages in some, as yet unpurged, institutional illnesses: "While perusing the shelves of the bookstore and pondering a list of books to be read during summer vacation, he hears a student confuse him with Balaam's inelegant long-eared beast of burden" (paragraph 5). Saying "ass" would do, but professorial prose is notorious for its overabundance. The entire paragraph is poking fun at its own burden of Latinate words, its own refusal to speak directly, its insistence on literary, classical, and biblical allusion. (The medical model, of course, can be equally obscure to the uninitiated.)

Writing Topics

1. Write an essay in which you isolate the virus that affects doctors, lawyers, investment bankers, and so forth. Could the virus that affects professors have a more various pool of members than Pickering is aware of?

2. How would Paul Fussell analyze the professor? How would Alison Lurie? Discuss the professor in terms of "Notes on Class" and "Clothing as a Sign System." Or compare the portrait Pickering gives with that of "Corporate Man" by John Kenneth Galbraith. Do they use the same strategies? Which essay is a stronger condemnation of its subject?

ALASTAIR REID

Hauntings (p. 397)

Questions on Meaning

1. One subject that Reid returns to throughout this essay is time. He writes that remembering can turn the past into "a present moment, a total possession, a haunting" (paragraph 1). Caught up in a living memory, what significance does Whithorn have to him? Selkirk?

DISCUSSION: Whithorn belongs to an Eden that a younger Reid thought would be permanent, "articulated by the seasons, with the easy expectation that harvest followed harvest, that years repeated themselves with minor variations (growing being one of them), a time when [he] was wholly unaware of an outside world" (paragraph 2). Selkirk, in contrast to the lost world of nature, represents the social world, in which "other sets of rules and obligations" hold sway (paragraph 21). The move to Selkirk ushers in the Second World War, "which obliterated the predictability of anything and severed all flow, all continuity" (paragraph 2). Reid describes Whithorn as a paradise before the fall and says that "time began" for him when his family moved away: "leaving Whithorn was my first experience of acquiring a past." With its loss, he lost his "certainty of belonging" anywhere (paragraph 20). Even now, he things of "that time in Selkirk, when the war loomed, as the beginning of disintegration — a movement from that once-glimpsed wholeness toward a splintering of time, the oncoming of many separations" (paragraph 27).

2. In this essay, Reid uses his past memories to interpret his present, almost as a psychoanalyst would draw out the threads rooted in years past, or, as we mythologize our own pasts, from once-upon-a-time. He has compared his first life, in Whithorn, to Eden, but he also writes, "Looking for temporary Edens is a perpetual lure certainly not confined to writers, who sooner

or later discover that the islands of their existence are, in truth, the tops of their desks" (paragraph 4). This might be true for all writers, but there are recurring moments throughout "Hauntings" that give more specific reasons why writing might be Edenic for Reid in particular. What are they?

DISCUSSION: In paragraph 4, Reid begins with the most pragmatic, and perhaps least personal, reason for becoming a writer: "I taught for a few years, and then decided to live by writing — about the most portable of all occupations, and an always available pretext for traveling." Later, Reid talks about sitting in his father's study — "that room of words"— and "feeling islanded by not being able to read, for I felt that words were my father's business — his reading, his sermons, his writings, the fact that people came to him for his words. Even now, I am still pacing that corridor" (paragraph 19). Clearly, the world of language is identified as his father's world, and writing seems to be able to give him access to his father, to allow the child — and now the man — to touch his father's "unreachable solitude" (paragraph 12). And any variety of language would accomplish this feat of bridging the chasm; he writes that Latin and Greek "were at last giving me entry into my father's province" (paragraph 22). Even the spoken word is linked to his father, as in church, when he listens to his father's voice, he's "mesmerized by the sudden incandescence of a phrase, fascinated by the convoluted metrics of certain hymns, stirred by the grave measures of the liturgy, aware of language as a kind of spell" (paragraph 24). Even now, the spell of language conjures memory; Reid remembers "more vividly through the ear than through the eye. If I can recover a voice, if I can fix the image and sound of someone talking, the atmospherics of place swim back with the sound, and the lost wavelengths reconnect themselves, across time, across absence, across loss. Voices remain living, and memory, for once, does not tamper with them. I can hear at will the measured phrasing of my father's pulpit voice, as I can the patient encouragement with which he led me through Tacitus, word by word" (paragraph 31). What Reid is doing in this essay is what his father did in his study; just as his father used writing to "put his world in order," so does Reid order his own world in "Hauntings" (paragraph 29).

Questions on Strategy

1. Reid ends his essay with the image of a house that no longer stands. His poem makes us see, at once, the house and not the house: "The house that shored my childhood up" is now "a block of air." Why does his poem insist that it was "Luck, to have been handed instead / a forgettable element"?

DISCUSSION: The answer is not in the poem, but in the text of the essay. In the poem, he refers to the house as a "fairytale," as a part of his own mythology, his personal story of "once-upon-a-time." When he writes that he "can gloss it over / as easily as passing / clear through a wall," our interpretation depends on the way we read "gloss." Does it mean to slide over, which would suggest remythologizing it by not confronting the past truth it held for him? Or does he mean a literary gloss, a comment, an analysis of the house and its meaning? In either case, Reid says that both would be equally difficult; "passing / clear through a wall" is not an easy task. In the essay, he insists that he "was not particularly disturbed by its absence" (paragraph 33). Its nonexistence means that he cannot use it as a reality test, cannot use it to "contradict or confirm by its presence the mass of memory it had generated." His memory is powerful enough, alone, to restore the building whole, to piece it together and arrive at "wholeness." The thing that disturbs him much more than the house's absence is its presence: "What haunts me most of all, however, is that the house has not gone, nor have our memories been wiped clean of it" (paragraph 33). The past is always with us, and moving forty times in thirty years cannot eradicate our first beginnings.

Questions on Language

1. Reid writes "The rain watered my memory, and I found my whole abandoned beginning seeping slowly back, even into dreams" (paragraph 5). How do you analyze his diction?

DISCUSSION: *The idea Reid is addressing is the persistence of memory, and his diction inherently compares memory to something organic, suggesting that the landscape of memory is drought-tolerant; its flora will stay dormant until released into burgeoning growth by the rains.*

Writing Topics

1. Compare Reid's essay to another whose subject is memory, Kingston's "No Name Woman," perhaps, or Ozick's "The First Day of School." In an essay, consider whether each author has the same trust in memory. Do they mistrust their versions of events in the same ways and for the same reasons?

2. In "Her Secrets," John Berger's mother seems to be tied to writing in the same way Reid's father is. Write an essay in which you discuss the presence of Reid's mother in "Hauntings." Does she have the same totemic power that his father has for him? What does he learn from her?

ADRIENNE RICH

Taking Women Students Seriously (p. 416)

Questions on Meaning

1. In paragraph 2, Rich writes of the excellent teaching she was exposed to at Douglass College: "We were taken to libraries, art museums, lectures at neighboring colleges, set to work on extra research projects, given extra French or Latin reading." Yet, at the end of the paragraph she says "the *content* of the education . . . in no way prepared us to survive as women in a world organized by and for men." Since she was given the same education as — and better than in many cases — her male peers, what is the nature of her indictment?

DISCUSSION: *Rich addresses the idea of coeducation in paragraph 9, asserting that it is a fallacy to assume that "because women and men are sitting in the same classrooms, hearing the same lectures, reading the same books, performing the same laboratory experiments, they are receiving an equal education. They are not, first because the content of education itself validates men even as it invalidates women." The mechanics of male validation include "the exclusiveness of grammar" and what might be termed the annexation of history: "The 'great men' talked of other 'great men,' of the nature of Man, the history of Mankind, the future of Man" (paragraph 3). The annexation of history also refers to Rich's point 2 in paragraph 5, wherein she defines the body of traditional literature as a canon "which . . . consistently excluded or depreciated female experience, and which often expresses hostility to women and validates violence against us." Absorbing that canon uncritically, passively, and, generally, very quietly, is one of the problems. According to her argument, rote absorption and, following it, rote regurgitation, leave no room for women to "seek and write their own truths that the culture has distorted or made taboo" (point 3, paragraph 5). It's part of the same argument that Baldwin offers in "If Black English Isn't a Language, Then Tell Me, What Is?"*

2. The center of Rich's thesis is that women students are not taken seriously because women are not valued as highly as men in the whole of the culture. She defines our society as being one of "patriarchal capitalism" (point 1, paragraph 5). How does she interpret the traditionally accepted "woman's place" in this culture?

DISCUSSION: *Female passivity is at the heart of patriarchal capitalism. The primary tenet, "service to others," above all else, flows from essential acceptance of patriarchy. If girls are raised to become women who place primary importance on the happiness of others, they will never place "selfhood or work" above "relationships" (paragraph 12). If the energy required to sustain "intelligence or intensity" is measured against that required to sustain a marriage and children, the conditions against which a woman's life "will be judged a success or a failure," society is unfairly persuading women to give up their allegiance to themselves.*

Questions on Strategy

1.   This essay is split into two parts. It opens with autobiography and moves on to an analysis of the cultural constraints on women. Why might Rich decide to include her own story in "Taking Women Students Seriously"?

DISCUSSION: *The autobiography initially establishes Rich's unreflective acquiescence to the status quo. She had a good experience at Douglass, taught by "vital individuals, defined not by their relationships but by their personalities" (paragraph 2). She was happy going to college, "congratulating [herself] that now [she] would have great men as [her] teachers" (paragraph 3). Only at college did she realize that these great men didn't seem to believe in her potential with the same strength of her female teachers: "and never again was I to experience, from a teacher, the kind of prodding, the insistence that my best could be even better, that I had known in high school." It wasn't until Rich joined SEEK that she saw the parallels between the poor and the nonwhite and women. Her own experience was revealed to her by others. If white males occupy the center of concentration, then the poor and the nonwhite and women are all at the margins of that concentration.*

Questions on Language

1.   When Rich writes, "Feminists are depicted in the media as 'shrill,' 'strident,' 'puritanical,' or 'humorless,' and the lesbian choice — the choice of the woman-identified woman — as pathological or sinister," she is touching on the power of diction (paragraph 12). What is her implied argument?

DISCUSSION: *When was the last time you read a headline like "Thoughtful Feminists Conduct Seminar"? The diction Rich cites is predictable, and it reinforces a stereotype that offers no alternatives to anyone following feminist precepts. The words imply that one must be shrill, strident, puritanical, and humorless; there is no other way to be a feminist, for all feminists occupy only these modes of being, just as all lesbians, by definition, cannot be other than twisted and subversive.*

2.   In paragraph 1, Rich says, "and then I hope that we can have, not so much a question period, as a raising of concerns, a sharing of questions for which we as yet may have no answers, an opening of conversations which will go on and on." Why does she insist on redefining or reinterpreting the traditional question period?

DISCUSSION: *A question period implies an answer period. The traditional address of questions and answers leaves little room for raising those questions that have no easily limned replies, and Rich's redefinition, on a small level, duplicates the larger argument that her essay makes for inclusiveness rather than exclusiveness. This passage also suggests that she is attempting to break down the traditional voice of authority that the speaker holds; in changing her position from the Speaker-with-the-Voice-of-Truth to merely another member in the conversation, she is trying to replace the power dynamic that usually holds sway.*

Writing Topics

1. Compare Rich's essay with Diane Johnson's "Rape." Are their analyses of cultural pressure and its ramifications on women similar? How do they interpret society's estimate of female value?

2. Collect a series of modifiers from newspaper stories describing feminists and lesbians. Go to both right- and left-wing sources for the samples of diction. Write an essay analyzing the rhetorical strategies behind each side's presentation of its subjects. For example, if the women are described physically, consider the content of their descriptions. Look for the unacknowledged, or implicit, assumptions both made and conveyed about women through language.

3. RESEARCH: In paragraph 13, Rich writes: "Listen to the women's voices. Listen to the silences, the unasked questions, the blanks. Listen to the small soft voices, often courageously trying to speak up. . . . Listen to the voices of the women and the voices of the men." Anecdotal evidence has it that women speak unceasingly, especially in groups, which they dominate verbally. Scientific studies, however, have videotaped classroom behavior. (The education department of your school should be able to direct you to them.) Research the results of some of these studies and then conduct your own research. Choosing random classes, time the questions raised by each sex as well as the answers given to each sex. Who is talking more? Who is being responded to more? How do your conclusions fit with anecdotal evidence and how do you interpret your results?

RICHARD RODRIGUEZ

The Achievement of Desire (p. 426)

Questions on Meaning

1. Part of Rodriguez's argument in this essay depends on distinctions he makes between different kinds of learning. Throughout his career, he was awarded much praise for his scholarship. Why, then, does he find such fault with his own knowledge?

DISCUSSION: Rodriguez assesses his learning as being mimicry, the regurgitation of facts and other people's ideas. It is inauthentic because it didn't engage his own critical intelligence, elicit his own judgment, or generate his own passion: "Any book they told me to read, I read — then waited for them to tell me which books I enjoyed" (paragraph 16). Instead, reading became a way of becoming "learned" like his teachers, but only because each book gave him another nugget of information; "I simply concluded that what gave a book its value was some major idea or theme it contained" (paragraph 46). For Rodriguez, reading was an activity that "lacked a point of view," and so he read only "for epigrams, scraps of information, ideas, themes — anything to fill the hollow within me and make me feel educated" (paragraph 49). Yet it's clear that Rodriguez had a larger emotional and intellectual relationship with books and learning, but he distrusted his broader responses to fiction, not finding any way of incorporating them into his idea of what being "learned" meant. When reading Dickens, he writes, "it bothered me that I was forced away at the conclusion, when the fiction closed tight, like a fortune-teller's fist — the futures of all the major characters neatly resolved. I never knew how to take such feelings seriously, however. Nor did I suspect that these experiences could be part of a novel's meaning" (paragraph 48).

2. Rodriguez's central argument is that learning transforms *anyone* and that that transformation is profoundly disturbing — not just to Rodriguez, but to the world at large. The scholarship boy, he writes, "has used education to remake himself" (paragraph 52). And this "bothers his fellow academics," who would rather believe that "it is possible for anyone to become educated without basically changing the person one was" (paragraph 53). Why is this notion so disturbing, and what kind of transformation did Rodriguez undergo?

DISCUSSION: *Rodriguez disturbed his peers and professors because he embodied the idea that much of what passes for "'education' is 'imitation,'" that great academic success can be founded on a debased idea of knowledge (paragraph 55). Also, he reminded them of their own transformations, provided "no calming reassurance about their own lives," forced them to acknowledge their own grat change, the huge distance they have moved from their own past (paragraph 54 and 56). "Education," Rodriguez writes, is "a nurturing never natural to the person one was before one entered a classroom" (paragraph 57). In his education, Rodriguez became transformed and in his transformation became estranged from his own family and culture.*

Questions on Strategy

1. How does Rodriguez use his difficulties with learning to read to support his central thesis? How do paragraphs 41 43 connect with paragraphs 64 and 68?

DISCUSSION: *Rodriguez employs diction and imagery that augment the idea of learning as a transforming, and alienating, experience. Books themselves are presented as having personalities, being foreign, emphatically not his "*BEST FRIENDS*" (paragraph 41). Though books spoke to him, their sentences "were coolly impersonal. Toned hard" (paragraph 41). The impersonality of the written word was made stronger because reading required isolation, something Rodriguez tried to soften: "To console myself for the loneliness I'd feel when I read, I tried reading in a very soft voice." That image seems so poignant, conjuring up a vision of a small child, obviously sensitive to tone, trying to modify the coolness and foreignness of the books by replacing the hard effect of their words with the softer one of his own speech. The nun, of course, did exactly the same thing, coaxing life and immediacy out of the written word with her own voice: "Playfully she ran through complex sentences, calling the words alive with her voice, making it seem that the author somehow was speaking directly to me. I smiled just to listen to her. I sat there and sensed for the very firs time some possibility of fellowship between a reader and a writer, a communication, never intimate like that I heard spoken words at home convey, but one nonetheless personal" (paragraph 42). But reading by himself without the nun acting as intermediary between the book and the child — and, at the same time, creating a small society composed of the three of them still made Rodriguez "feel all alone — almost, I wanted to add but didn't, as when I spoke to myself in a room just emptied of furniture" (paragraph 43). The implicit metaphor — reading is being alone in an empty room — is Rodriguez's central thesis utterly compressed; the entire process of education moves him from a room furnished with his family and culture to a room barren of anything known, leaving him profoundly isolated, just as he found himself, decades later, in the British Museum, turning the book's pages, which were stiff, "like layers of dead skin" (paragraph 61). "The community of scholars" turns out to be "a lonely community," . . . "an exclusive — and eccentric! — society, separated from others who would never care or be able to share our concerns" (paragraphs 60 and 61). Yet reading, finally, saves Rodriguez, enabling him to put the two pieces of his life together. Hoggart's book (paragraph 8), quoted throughout "The Achievement of Desire," allows the author to admit and confront his desire for his past and his parents: "If, because of my schooling, I had grown culturally separated from my parents, my education finally had given me ways of speaking and caring about that fact" (paragraph 67).*

Questions on Language

1. What is the effect of Rodriguez's use of parentheses? Why isn't the information they contain allowed to stand in the body of the essay?

Rose, *Tools of Torture* (text pp. 448–453)

DISCUSSION: Reading the parentheses is like hearing another voice, a confiding voice that tells us the author's secret, unshared comment on the body of the text, or makes small jokes, adds emphasis, or creates quick character sketches. We have an instant portrait of "the historian who chattered madly to herself" when Rodriguez includes her panicky commentary: "('Oh dear! Oh! Now, what's this?' What? Oh, my!')" (paragraph 60). In paragraph 38, the parentheses contain bits of the conversation he and his parents do have as well as the unshared thoughts that the son cannot tell his mother and father: "The first hours home were the hardest. ('What's new?') My parents and I sat in the kitchen for a conversation. (But, lacking the same words to develop our sentences and to shape our interests, what was there to say? What could I tell them of the term paper I had just finished on the 'universality of Shakespeare's appeal'?)" The author, through parentheses, imitates, or portrays, the divided psychology of his subject in the very text of his essay. The two voices, one in parentheses, one not, are a way of realizing the divided worlds of the scholarship boy.

Writing Topics

1. In the introductory paragraph, Rodriguez talks to a class of students who have varying reactions to his words: "someone's mouth elongates heavy, silent words through the barrier of glass. Silent words — the lips straining to shape each voiceless syllable: "*Meet meee late errr.*" A young girl "keeps nodding and nodding at all that I say; she even takes notes." Which student were you? How did you learn to learn and what do you most vividly remember from your early schooling? Starting with one of Rodriguez's scenarios, perhaps reading the list of one hundred most important books, use his essay to write an essay of your own, explaining *your* education.

2. Write an essay interpreting Rodriguez's use of Hoggart's *The Uses of Literacy* (beginning in paragraph 8). Does Rodriguez use Hoggart's book "to acquire a point of view" (paragraph 49)? What is the alternative? How do you interpret the closing paragraphs of "The Achievement of Desire"?

3. Interpret Rodriguez's essay in the light of Walker Percy's "The Loss of the Creature." In your essay, consider whether Rodriguez, finally, agrees with Percy's assertions. Does Rodriguez's essay seem to owe allegiance to the idea that communication of more than Percy's "symbolic package" is possible?

PHYLLIS ROSE

Tools of Torture:
An Essay on Beauty and Pain (p. 448)

Questions on Meaning

1. What does Rose identify as the reason for "social and institutional" torture (paragraph 6)?

DISCUSSION: People will torture on behalf of the abstract virtue "the common good" (paragraph 7) or, as Rose writes, "the preservation of society (paragraph 6). In the Milgram experiment, the greater good was "the advancement of knowledge" (paragraph 7). Thus, both the legal system and the churches of various faiths have been able to press torture into their service; since they stood as emblems of the greatest good, their authority to persuade people to inflict great pain on others was authority that stemmed from good; inherent evil did not apply.

2. In her introductory paragraph, Rose writes "that pain must be as great a challenge to the human imagination as pleasure. Otherwise there's no accounting for the number of torture instruments." She describes in paragraph 2 the ends to which the human imagination is put in her graphic presentation of specific tortures. Yet while she's having her facial, in paragraph 4, she suddenly thinks, "What if the cheesecloth mask were dipped in acid?" What is the effect of this question?

DISCUSSION: In some way, the question refutes her assumption; torture does not seem to be a great challenge to the imagination. Simply inverting the idea of comfort — having a facial — to cruelty suggests the ease with which we can imagine creating pain. The human body is utterly vulnerable; if we look at it from a purely physical perspective, human beings are nothing but viscera in a sack that's shot through with nerve endings. Our bodies are opportunities for pain: "The human body is like a foodstuff, to be grilled, pounded, filleted. Every opening exists to be stuffed, all flesh to be carved off the bone" (paragraph 3). In paragraph 5, Rose capitulates to the insidious ease with which we can all imagine modes of torture: "In Paris, where the body is so pampered, torture seems particularly sinister, not because it's hard to understand but because — as the dark side of sensuality — it seems so easy." By this time, her essay has begun to develop pain as the simple reverse of pleasure.

Questions on Strategy

1. In her penultimate paragraph, Rose offers what appear to be jarringly inadequate substitutions for torture: "Give people a good croissant and a good cup of coffee in the morning. Give them an occasional facial and a plate of escargots." How do you interpret these contemporary replacements for the phrase "Let them eat cake"?

DISCUSSION: Although Rose's suggestions sound insubstantial, they are palpable in a way that "the nobly abstract" is not. Coffee and croissants are "the sweetness of the concrete" (paragraph 9), our immediate experience in everyday life. They stand as icons for life itself, redolent with sensual pleasure. In these icons, Rose is offering pleasure over pain, object over idea, and, finally, enjoyment over suffering. In the next paragraph, she reiterates that she offers these icons to all: "nothing leads you less wrong than your awareness of your own pleasure and a genial desire to spread it around."

Questions on Language

1. Look at Rose's opening sentence: "In a gallery off the rue Dauphine, near the *parfumerie* where I get my massage, I happened upon an exhibit of medieval torture instruments." This sentence grabs immediate attention. How does it do this?

DISCUSSION: The power of the sentence stems from its jarring juxtapositions. The heart of the sentence is the final clause: "I happened upon an exhibit of medieval torture instruments." It could have been preceded, simply, by "One day." After all, an exhibit of medieval torture instruments is not what we usually find in the general run of things; the view has a power all its own. But Rose increases that power by preceding the final clause with an introduction crammed with words suggesting culture and pleasure: "gallery," "rue Dauphine," "parfumerie," "massage." The ease and indulgence of France wafts from the page — and is brought up short, confronted by the shock of age-old torture. Not only does Rose hook the reader, compel his or her immediate attention, but she also, in one sentence, sets up the two subjects she's going to examine in the rest of the essay.

Writing Topics

1. Write an essay describing a time when you intentionally caused someone physical pain. What were your motivations? Or describe a time when someone intentionally caused you pain; consider his or her motivations. How do the dynamics in your essay correspond to those Rose describes?

2. RESEARCH: Consider Rose's prescription for discouraging torture: "Give people a good croissant . . . and a good cup of coffee, . . . an occasional facial and a plate of escargots" (paragraph 9). Write an essay discussing how effective such an approach might be. Find out what an organization devoted to the discouragement of torture (Amnesty International, for example) has to say about methods that might be used. Would you locate their methods in the abstract or the concrete world? How do they compare with Rose's suggestions?

3. RESEARCH: Michael Foucault has written on the history of torture in the first two chapters of his book *Discipline and Punish: The Birth of the Prison*, trans. Alan Sheridan (New York: Vintage Books, 1979). He adds another dimension to Rose's analysis of institutionalized torture, insisting on the spiritual office of purification it was believed to offer its victims. Write a paper addressing Foucault's work. You might consider interpreting Franz Kafka's "In the Penal Colony" in the light of *Discipline and Punish*.

SCOTT RUSSELL SANDERS

Doing Time in the Thirteenth Chair (p. 454)

Questions on Meaning

1. When Sanders is called for jury duty, he "feels sulky and rebellious," wanting to be "hammering together some bookshelves," and "out tromping the shores of Lake Monroe" (paragraph 2). When he is appointed the thirteenth juror, he feels "as though [he has] been invited to watch the first four acts of a five-act play" (paragraph 9). But a minute later, suddenly engaged, he changes his mind: "Like the bear going over the mountain, I might as well see what I can see" (paragraph 11). How does the resulting essay comment on the act of writing? How does writing comment on judgment?

DISCUSSION: *In paragraph 9, Sanders is sure he'll be rejected as the thirteenth juror: "How can they expect me, a fiction writer, to confine myself to facts? I am unreliable, a confessed fabulist, a marginal Quaker and Wobbly socialist, a man so out of phase with my community that I am thrown into fits of rage by the local newspaper." His writing seems aligned with his politics — in both, Sanders is the outsider, seeing things differently from most of the community. One of the subjects that Sanders is addressing is the problem of judgment. In court, the jurors are supposed to judge according to the facts of the case, but the facts seem problematical to Sanders: "The facts are a mess. They are full of gaps, chuckholes, switchbacks, and dead ends — just like life" (paragraph 19). Later, when Bennie is sentenced to fifty-four years in prison, the jurors cry, even though the judge agrees with their decisions. But for Sanders, the question of correct judgment seems unreachable: "And that is just the splinter in the brain, the fact that we know so little — about Bennie, about Vietnam, about drugs, about ourselves — and yet we must grope along in our ignorance, pronouncing people guilty or innocent, squeezing out of one another that precious fluid, time" (paragraph 79). In this essay, Sanders continually makes connections between people — between Bennie and Rebecca and the children, for example, between the old men who lost at life and the young men who are losing it. And although he recognizes the futility, in some sense, of trying to arrive at the truth of invisible events (like the drug sale, unrecorded, unseen by the jurors, like Vietnam and its effects on Bennie), Sanders, in writing "Doing Time in the Thirteenth Chair," is creating a coherent universe, an integrated and sustained meditation on different kinds of knowing. Sanders's specific kind of knowing is rooted in imagination; throughout the essay, he reflects on the unseen lives only suggested by the "muttered monosyllables and orphaned phrases" of those who testify, and in the end he himself is the trial's best witness (paragraph 52).*

2. Throughout the essay, Sanders seems to be focusing on one essential question he wants to answer, which has to do with the irrevocable step taken, leading a person from one life, irrecoverably, into another one. Where does he address this idea, and how might you explain his interest in it?

DISCUSSION: *In paragraph 15, Sanders wants to talk to the "old men sheltering from December . . . [whose] faces have been caved in by disappointment and the loss of teeth." He wants to "pry old stories out of them, gossip about hunting and dogs, about their favorite pickup trucks, their worst jobs. I want to ask them when and how it all started to go wrong for them. Did they hear a snap when the seams of their life began to come apart?" In paragraph 52, Sanders alludes to these men and these questions again, when he sees "four of Bennie's friends — looking not so much mean as broken, like shell-shocked refugees. . . . They are younger versions of the old men with caved-in faces who crouch on benches downstairs." And in the final phrase of the final sentence of the essay, Sanders closes by concentrating on this same essential moment: "Bennie may do as many as fifty-four years in prison, buying his drugs from meaner dealers, dreaming of land mines and of his adopted girls, checking the date on his watch, wondering at what precise moment the hinges of his future slammed shut." He uses a visual image to convey the increments of time that lead to any particular future: the boy copying lines for penance is "balancing on the first rung of a ladder that leads up — or down — to the electric chair. Somewhere in the middle of the ladder is a good long prison sentence" (paragraph 45). All these comments suggest that Sanders's vision of life is coherent, where the flow of events is a flow and where the past and the future have strong bonds. This insistence on coherence denies a life composed of a discrete and disjointed series of events, none of whose meaning impinges on other events. Yet he is fascinated with the breaking point, always attempting to discover whether the irrevocable moment is, in fact, able to be isolated and acknowledged or whether fixing its exact place is always beyond our knowledge.*

Questions on Strategy

1. Why does Sanders devote so much time to Rebecca? How does he present her? What does this tell us about his field of view?

DISCUSSION: *Rebecca isn't introduced until just over halfway through the essay, immediately after she has threatened a witness with a bread knife. She reminds Sanders "of the Amish farm wives of my Ohio childhood — stern, unpainted, built stoutly for heavy chores, her face a fortress against outsiders" (paragraph 46). In all descriptions of her, Sanders's diction refers to her character: "stolid," "bulky," "stern," "stoutly," "a fortress." The language imbues her with "a tigerish fierceness" (paragraph 47); she's capable of lashing out. Sanders follows her testimony with his childhood belief about a snake's gaining vengeance for its mate's death; it "would hunt you out in your very bed and strangle or gnaw or smother you. We held a similar belief regarding bears, wolves, and mountain lions" (paragraph 49). Notice that Sanders describes only one person as being able to conjure up such visions of the beast beneath the skin — a woman. Everyone else has been described, first in religious terms. (In the book* Women Who Kill, *Ann Jones discusses the phenomena of court reporters describing as "animals" women accused of murder. Perhaps Sanders is working from this tradition.) Here, though, it seems that Sanders is attempting to locate something essential about Rebecca that is not negative; her concentration is, literally, on survival, on life itself, and her chances of rearing her three girls, alone, "for years and stony years" (paragraph 49), lessen drastically with Bennie's incarceration. Rebecca's long testimony gives the bleak story of her past and future to which Sanders is completely sympathetic; in Bennie's loss, Rebecca and her three children will also be lost. The abstract virtue of justice is posed against Rebecca's precarious, precious, and concrete reality.*

Sanders, *Doing Time in the Thirteenth Chair* (text pp. 454–470)

Questions on Language

1. How does Sanders describe the various witnesses? Look at paragraph 12.

DISCUSSION: Before describing their physical appearances, which in many ways are striking enough, Sanders attends to their essential beingness: "What I see is a parade of mangled souls. Some of them sit on the witness stand and reveal their wounds; some of them remain offstage, summoned up only by the words of those who testify." In the final clause, he summons up a picture of wraiths, or specters, misty and unsubstantial until, like genies, they are fixed into a specific form by other witnesses. The diction "mangled souls . . . wounds" is religious, moral, and, in itself, a judgment; by addressing these people — most obviously seen as drug dealers and their cohorts — in religious terminology, Sanders is immediately acknowledging their fundamental importance, their inherent value. He sustains this diction and this viewpoint throughout "Doing Time in the Thirteenth Chair." In paragraph 29, referring to the petty thief's transformation into 190, he writes, "hearing of this miraculous conversion, I am reminded of Saul on the road to Damascus, the devil's agent suddenly seeing the light and joining the angels." But here he is being ironic, using the language of faith to describe dubious phenomena, immediately following the Saul and Damascus sentence with "In this new guise he gave information that led to several arrests and some prison terms, including one for his cousin and two or three for other buddies," juxtaposing faith and betrayal. In paragraph 36, Sanders is just about ready "to consign 190 to the level of hell reserved by Dante for liars," a drastic judgment that he is forced to rescind with the advent of the cross-examination.

Writing Topics

1. Write an essay in which you discuss whether Sanders writes from an objective or a subjective point of view. What *is* an objective point of view? A subjective one? How does the demand for factual presentation influence both the writer's assessment of the trial and the reader's assessment of the trial?

2. RESEARCH: Research a famous trial such as the Lizzie Borden case, in which Elizabeth Borden was accused of killing her parents with an ax. You will find collections of essays devoted to famous trials in the library and, often, the newspaper accounts of those trials on microfilm. In what kind of language is the accused described? On what aspect of the defendant does the diction concentrate? Write an essay interpreting the subject of the surrounding discourse; try to analyze how the accused is appropriated by language. If you can find descriptions of the same person written by different authors, see where they differ and what they have in common. Is there any implicit societal norm against which the accused is being measured?

3. RESEARCH: Find newspaper or magazine accounts of two contemporary murders, one committed by a man and the other by a woman. Is there a difference in the way they are described? What compels the writer's attention most strongly in each sex? Then find two newspaper accounts from fifty or one hundred years ago. Has the presentation of men and women who have committed the same crime changed? How has it remained the same? What aspects of the male and female compel the writer's attention most strongly in the historical accounts?

JONATHAN SCHELL

A Republic of Insects and Grass (p. 471)

Questions on Meaning

1. This essay falls into two parts. For the first six paragraphs Schell describes the damage that would be sustained by a nuclear attack on people, cities, and nuclear power plants. The rest of the essay, paragraphs 7–10, documents the effects on plants and animals, on all nonhuman life. In its "multiplication of the facts of terror," as Donald Hall writes, this essay is relentless. And Schell's facts, "the arrows and catapulted rocks of statistics, computations, and quantifications," range from the huge megatonnage directed at us to the smallest effects of that megatonnage. Besides trying to build up a definitive picture of the United States after a nuclear attack, what are some reasons for Schell's inclusion of such details as the lethal radiation dosages for spring barley seedlings?

DISCUSSION: Schell explains that the subjects of "numerous research projects . . . were irradiated-
. . . [to] permit the prediction of many gross ecological consequences of a nuclear attack" (paragraph 8).
That is the fact behind the research projects. But the comprehensiveness of such studies is astounding;
that there are people who are compiling the lethal radiation doses for every living thing, even something
as small as a barley seedling, gives pause and should raise profoundly disturbing questions in the reader's
mind. How widespread is this research? Considering what the studies have learned, it seems that there
is a small, mostly unknown, army of people investigating the effects of radiation. The question is, Does
this knowledge make us feel more, or less, secure? Are these studies, and the people involved in them,
simply taken for granted by the people who know what's going on? Is the vocabulary of lethal radiation
dose testing a familiar language for others? The information Schell gives should generate an enormous
shock for the reader, not the least of which should be caused by wondering why we are investigating the
subject in the first place. Is the "pure knowledge" produced by these studies going to be used to reassure
people that the United States, or any other country, could survive a nuclear holocaust? Are we
considering using this knowledge in "more completely" attacking others?

Questions on Strategy

1. Is Schell's position on nuclear arms explicit in his essay?

DISCUSSION: Schell never explicitly states that he is against the proliferation of nuclear arms or the
waging of nuclear war. However, his essay makes it impossible to infer that he supports either or believes
that nuclear war can be "limited." His tone throughout is quite objective, but the vision his essay unfolds
is one of horror. Furthermore, Schell concentrates on the long-term effects of nuclear energy, the fact that
we all have strontium-90 in our bones from previous nuclear testing and fallout (paragraph 7).

2. What is the effect of Schell's concentration on illustrating the force of the Soviet — rather than the American — nuclear arsenal?

DISCUSSION: First, Schell's focus locates the devastation at home, a recognizable place to which we all
have strong ties. Showing the same devastation wrought by the Americans on Russia would keep the
psychological effect of nuclear war in the distance; it would be something, like cancer, that happens to
other people. Schell's essay brings the nuclear war as close as possible, so the reader's imagination is forced
to confront the utter and terrible destruction of every city, town, person, tree, and spring wheat seedling.

Questions on Language

1. In paragraph 5, Schell writes, "In some depictions of a holocaust, various rescue operations are described, with unafflicted survivors bringing food, clothes, and medical care to the afflicted, and the afflicted making their way to thriving, untouched communities, where churches, school auditoriums, and the like would have been set up for their care — as often happens after a bad snowstorm, say." What is the effect of the final phrase in this sentence? How would you describe its tone?

DISCUSSION: The tone is wry and ironic. Schell's essay finds the reality of a nuclear holocaust to be so far from that of a bad snowstorm that the gulf between the two cannot be bridged. The depiction of the unafflicted helping the afflicted, in some untouched community, is ludicrous, and Schell is trying to convey its absurdity by placing the depiction in the context in which it belongs.

Writing Topics

1. Aside from their tremendous destructive potential, one of the worst effects of nuclear weapons may well be the anxiety, conscious and unconscious, that they cause in those aware of their dangers. Schell works hard to arouse these anxieties. Write an essay arguing that he is either part of the problem or part of the solution.

2. Schell's essay makes it clear that he has no illusions of America being able to survive a nuclear war. Collect some literature put out by those who do believe a nuclear war is survivable, and compare their rhetorical strategies with Schell's. Whose picture is more detailed? What kind of language and tone do the two opponents use? Do either include anecdote, or vignette, or scenario? Analyze whichever of these strategies is used. Who, finally, do you find more persuasive, and why?

3. RESEARCH: Schell's essay, in its compilation of facts, seems to imply that more people don't fear nuclear holocaust because they don't really know what it would mean. Yet there is a large body of material on nuclear war, including the novels *Riddley Walker* by Russell Hoban, *On the Beach* by Neville Shute, and *Fail-Safe* by Eugene Burdick and Harvey Wheeler and the popular movie *Dr. Strangelove*. There are other contemporary essays, like Ron Rosenbaum's "The Subterranean World of the Bomb" (in *The Literary Journalists*, ed. Norman Sims [New York: Ballantine Books, 1984]), that address the psychological aspects of the nuclear world. And we have eyewitness accounts by survivors of Hiroshima and Nagasaki who wrote on the nuclear catastrophes that destroyed their cities. Taking one of these or other sources, write a paper that offers some reasons for the persistence of the threat of nuclear war. Does the work you're analyzing put the major share of blame on general ignorance, or are there some other reasons?

ROBERT STONE

A Higher Horror of the Whiteness: Cocaine's Coloring of the American Psyche (p. 482)

Questions on Meaning

1. How does Stone use the color white to define and describe cocaine? Why does he repeatedly refer to Melville and allude to Dante?

DISCUSSION: *In* Moby Dick, *Melville's white whale was, for Ahab's symbolic imagination, evil itself. Stone is participating in this symbolic imagination by locating cocaine in the same context. In paragraph 8, Stone writes, "There was an invisible whiteness deep down things . . . a metaphysical whiteness. . . . The whiteness was Melvillean, like the whiteness of the Whale." In the next paragraph, Stone switches from the whale to the city of Lima, "the strangest saddest city thou canst see. . . . There is a higher horror in the whiteness of her woe." In paragraph 10, Stone cites thoughts on whiteness in Melville's* Moby Dick: *the whiteness has the extraordinary power of an incantation, compelling the soul; the whiteness itself is "the intensifying agent in things the most appalling to mankind." When Stone sees the teenage girls snorting coke in the car next to him, he glimpses something: "Its intellectual aspect was crazy and its emotional valence was cold" (paragraph 18).*

Throughout the essay, Stone shows the effects that cocaine has on people. In paragraph 7, he locates those effects in images from Dante's inferno: "At the freight doors of garment factories and around construction sites people cluster smoking something odorless. At night in the ghettos and at the borders of ghettos, near the tunnels and at downtown intersections, an enormous ugly argument seems to be in progress. Small, contentious groups of people drift across the avenues, sometimes squaring off at each other, moving from one corner to the next, the conformations breaking up and re-forming." He identifies cocaine, different from other, earlier drugs, as the responsible agent for this anarchic hell: "The purchase of illegal drugs was always a sordid process but users and dealers (pretty much interchangeable creatures) used to attempt adherence to an idealized vision of the traffic in which smoothie dealt with smoothie in a confraternity of the hip. Crack sales tend to start with a death threat and deteriorate rapidly. The words 'die' and 'motherfucker' are among the most often heard" (paragraph 7). There is no "idealized vision" in this exchange.

2. Stone devotes the final section of this essay to a meditation on how to channel one's concern about crack, which first entails locating reasons for the drug's enormous success. What are the reasons that Stone offers for the cocaine phenomenon? In what direction does he suggest we should channel our concern?

DISCUSSION: *Stone writes that "lucidity and excellence," the feelings that cocaine induces, "are pretty hot stuff, even in a potential state, even as illusion" (paragraph 27). The generation that's so attracted to these feelings of success is different from its predecessor, which pursued "the electric twilight." The cocaine generation seems to divide the world into two groups, winners and losers. The losers fall prey to "unseemly scruple and self-doubt," the archaic attributes of a world whose very language embraced moral scrutiny, especially moral scrutiny of the self (paragraph 29). Out of fashion now, the world recognizes only success's "natty strut," a "no-fault world" (paragraphs 29 and 30). In this world, self-scrutiny creeps in only in nightmares: "you're afraid you'd think awful thoughts if you had time to think. That's why you're almost glad there isn't time" (paragraph 31). In paragraph 32, Stone discusses the innate self-doubt and self-scrutiny of predestinarian religion that we've thrown out and replaced with the "pleasurable surges of self-esteem" (paragraph 36). In diametric opposition to a society guided by religious precepts, we have created a society "based overwhelmingly on appetite and self-regard" or, in other words, gluttony and pride, two of the seven deadly sins; "we train our young to be consumers and to think most highly of their own pleasure" (paragraph 39). The final line addresses the heart of the problem; we can "give them something to say yes to" only if our society nurtures some affirmative values, and affirmation, according to this essay, is not composed solely of success in economic terms. Stone does not make his suggestions explicit, finally, but he has led us to a point that inescapably implies that our world of winners and losers must be reversed, so that moral questioning is admired and self-scrutiny engaged in by winners.*

Questions on Strategy

1. Why does Stone locate his vision, in the opening sentence, near Saint Paul's Chapel of Trinity Church?

DISCUSSION: Churches are traditionally associated with religious visions, but of a different nature from the one that Stone describes. In the opening sentence, he sets up an expectation that he then reverses; Saint Paul's Chapel of Trinity Church, a symbol of faith, is juxtaposed against Dante's hell and Melville's evil. In one sense, however, his dark vision can be seen as religious, since hell and evil are recognized as being part of the religious arena.

Questions on Language

1. How do the Democrats and the Republicans participate in the street conversation about cocaine (paragraph 22)?

DISCUSSION: Both parties propose solutions that start with the same violence inherent in buying and selling cocaine. The Democrats or Republicans may not be using the same vocabulary — "die, motherfucker" — but they are definitely using the same language: "The Democrats say they want to hang the dealers. The Republicans say they want to hang them and throw their bones to the dogs" (paragraph 22). We know that this language, on the street, has not stopped the sale or use of cocaine; rather, it is the common argot. Why should the same language and the same sentiments stop the sale or use of cocaine just because it is spoken by politicians or the state? The vocabulary here reflects mimetic violence, the idea that violence conjures up violence. Its articulation by both those that use and those that want to eradicate the drug suggests that violence itself won't be able to break cocaine's stranglehold, for this is the very language that the drug itself speaks.

Writing Topics

1. The central section of this essay, from paragraph 12 to 24, is composed of quick portraits of people using cocaine. Why might Stone put these portraits in the center? Write an essay discussing the effect these anecdotal glimpses have. How do they connect to Stone's governing argument?

2. Write an essay comparing "A Higher Horror of the Whiteness" to Carol Bly's "Chin Up in a Rotting Culture." What ideas do these essays share? What aspects of society are they criticizing? What correctives do they suggest? Are there narrative similarities in the two essays?

PAUL THEROUX

Mapping the World (p. 491)

Questions on Meaning

1. As Theroux presents the subject, the great maps are associated with travel and trade. Why is this?

DISCUSSION: When countries are active and engaged in the world, their "travelers, warriors, conquerors, traders" inevitably become map-makers: "What was the point of conquering if the subject lands were not then given a shape, and their rivers and households described on maps?" (paragraph 4). "It is a fact," he writes, "that the most commercial-minded countries have also been the most outward-looking" (paragraph 19). Their maps, Theroux writes, "give the world coherence" (paragraph 15). They are also a valuable — and hereditable — piece of knowledge: "In a sense, the world was once blank. And the reason cartography made it visible and glowing with detail was because man believed, and rightly, that maps are a legacy that allows other men and future generations to communicate and trade" (paragraph 20). Maps filled in the blankness of the world so that successive generations were spared the difficulties of reinventing the wheel; with inherited maps, they started not from tabula rasa, not from ground zero, but from a coherent and accurate perspective of themselves in relation to others.

2.   In this essay, Theroux argues that maps are a way of knowing the map-makers' minds, an avenue of access to their idea of themselves in relation to others. How does he support this argument?

DISCUSSION: Theroux compares maps made during a country's periods of expansion and those made during periods of decline and discovers that the maps make a pictograph of the nation's psyche, almost as if the maps could attest to the country's psychology. For example, when China was active, her people made accurate maps of subjugated countries: "What was the point of conquering if the subject lands were not then given a shape, and their rivers and households described on maps?" (paragraph 4). Later, the nation withdrew from active trading, craving "silence and [becoming] xenophobic" (paragraph 6). Its ascending egotism was reflected in its maps: "When China lost interest in foreign countries her maps became inaccurate, not to say bizarre. These maps showed European countries and the United States and Africa as tiny islands and sandbars off the Middle Kingdom coast" (paragraph 8). China's geocentrism became reflected in its ethnocentrist map drawings: "Even in the mid-nineteenth century Chinese maps depicted the natives of these little islands as monstrous and one-eyed, and some were shown with holes through their stomachs for their convenient carrying on poles" (paragraph 8). The one-eyed monsters are the Other, inhabiting the terrible land of Not-Here. Depicting the Other with holes in their stomachs reflects a way of organizing the world only as it relates to oneself; if one sees the Other solely as prey, to be carried home in triumph, then the Other's physical properties must agree with one's vision, hence the handy holes. More modern examples are the Arab maps on which Israel "does not exist at all" (paragraph 13). This symbolic annihilation of a country reflects the Arabic desire to obliterate Israel.

Questions on Strategy

1.   Theroux ends on personal experience, something he has shied away from in the essay proper. What reasons does the essay suggest for this particular ending?

DISCUSSION: First, Theroux's ending recapitulates his argument through personal testimony, in that he himself has a vivid demonstration of how maps replace the "darkness" of dislocation and separation from the world with the light of knowledge. Second, his experience shows us the power of the map. From the Singapore Library, with a map, Theroux has the vision to see the most minute details of his new and unseen home in another country, is able to visualize the telephone and the pub, to imagine the meadows and the ruins. South Bowood was invisible in literature, unable to be captured or explained by the written word, but it was described, in precise detail, by the language of the map. The final paragraphs illustrate paragraph 20 exactly: "In a sense, the world was once blank" for Theroux, and "cartography made it visible and glowing with detail."

2.   How does Theroux control the comparisons he makes between paragraphs 9–11 and paragraphs 12–13?

DISCUSSION: Paragraphs 9-11 take as their subject cartography and truth, in which maps are accurate representations of both the geographic world and the cultural world. The Ortelius map of 1573 shows "in vivid marginal pictures . . . the Great Wall," a "Chinese junk," a "Chinese four-wheeled cart," and "a man . . . being crucified in Japan for being a Christian and keeping the faith (there is a warning in Latin)" (paragraph 11). Paragraphs 12–13 concern cartography and fantasy, in which maps are an attempt to persuade through the written symbol, possibly because the map might have the power to bring hope into reality: "On a map by F. Bianconi in 1891, Honduras — which could not have been emptier — is shown as a teeming go-ahead republic. . . . In the Mosquito jungle you have the impression of intense cultivation, and mining, and cattle-grazing. Honduras looks blessed — full of sarsparilla and sugar-cane, and iron, zinc, silver and gold. The word 'gold' appears on this map sixty-five times, in each spot where it apparently lies in the ground" (paragraph 12). Maps, then can be understood as the history of hopes and, in Panama's case, as the history of persuasion: "There were similar maps of Panama, and of course Panama won out" (paragraph 13).

Questions on Language

1. Either explicitly or implicitly, Theroux gives many definitions for the word "map" in his essay. Each definition of a map allows Theroux to look in a different direction. These cumulative definitions end in giving an exhaustive and definitive analysis of the map as well as guiding the structure of the essay. What are the definitions?

DISCUSSION: Maps are

> – *etymologically, plans, charts, or drawings (paragraph 4)*
> – *a "version of the world" (paragraph 7)*
> – *truth (paragraph 9)*
> – *hopes or fantasies (paragraph 12)*
> – *works of art (paragraph 14)*
> – *infinite complexity (paragraph 14)*
> – *the oldest means of information storage . . . a way of miniaturizing a country or society" (paragraph 15)*
> – *iconographic (paragraph 16)*
> – *the life of fiction (paragraph 17)*
> – *"records of discovery" (paragraph 19)*
> – *able to "reflect the face of the land" (paragraph 20)*
> – *"a legacy that allows other men and future generations to communicate and trade" (paragraph 20)*
> – *"the ultimate [tools] of the man who wishes to understand a distant country" (paragraph 21)*
> – *the light of knowledge, without which we would be "in darkness" (paragraph 23)*

Writing Topics

1. Locate an old map from any country, and write an essay that interprets it according to Theroux's argument. What does your map say about the map-makers' location of themselves in relation to others? What does it say about politics? Does your map seem to wish the world was a certain way, like the maps of Honduras and Panama?

2. RESEARCH: Theroux has interpreted the language of cartography similarly to the way in which Alison Lurie interprets the language of fashion. Write an essay about some other object or set of objects that in some manner recapitulate a history of the world or a part of the world. Could the language of household decoration of the fifties — the kidney-shaped coffee tables, the wire chairs, the colors turquoise and green — articulate something about America's psychological history? You might look at jewelry in a particular period, such as the Victorian age, to see what language it was thought to speak. What was mourning jewelry, for instance? What was it capable of expressing?

The Tucson Zoo (p. 499)

Questions on Meaning

1. What is it about the beavers and otters that attracts Thomas? How does his attraction comment on the introductory paragraph?

DISCUSSION: *In paragraph 2, Thomas identifies their life-charge as their special attribute; these animals are "more filled with life than any creatures [he has] ever seen before." And in paragraph 3 he exults in the wholeness, the completeness, the integrity of these animals, in "the full hairy complexity . . . of whole, intact beavers and otters in motion." The otters and beavers, which Thomas prizes just because of their wholeness, are presented in opposition to the practice of science itself, which "gets most of its information by the process of reductionism, exploring the details, then the details of the details, until all the smallest bits of the structure, or the smallest parts of the mechanisms, are laid out for counting and scrutiny (paragraph 1). The animals give Thomas such a vivid sense of their essential being that his view of them does "encompass the whole organism," despite the fact that he knows nothing of "the physiology of their breathing," is ignorant of "the coordination of their muscles, their vision, their endocrine systems, their digestive tracts" (paragraphs 1 and 3).*

2. How does Thomas generalize from his experience with the zoo animals?

DISCUSSION: *Thomas says that he is "coded . . . for otters and beavers," that he exhibits "instinctive behavior in their presence" (paragraph 5). The instinctive behavior that the animals release is "exultation and a rush of friendship." From this reaction to the aquatic animals, Thomas infers that all human beings are genetically programmed — "stamped with stereotyped, unalterable patterns of response" — to feel "a surprised affection" not just for otters, but for others.*

3. Thomas uses the ants as a positive symbol despite the popular perception of them as "crazy little instruments, inhuman, incapable of controlling themselves, lacking manners, lacking souls" (paragraph 6). The major charge against them, however, is that "they become a single animal," which is "a debasement, a loss of individuality, a violation of human nature, an unnatural act." Why does Thomas interpret this "violation" as being good?

DISCUSSION: *People who exhibit such loathing for ants cherish the separate ego, hold up individuality as the highest good, and view altruism as the greatest weakness. Thomas, on the other hand, thinks ants may stand as a hopeful symbol for our own evolution. The ants suggest that "usefulness may turn out to be the hardest test of fitness for survival, more important than aggression, more effective, in the long run, than grabbiness" (paragraph 8).*

Questions on Strategy

1. The introductory paragraph ends with the words "So we say," which have the effect of throwing Thomas's initial assertions into doubt. Why does he do this?

DISCUSSION: *Thomas's essay goes on to doubt his introductory statements in a particular way. He prepares the reader for a change in direction immediately, even though he doesn't declare his precise destination until halfway through paragraph 4, when he writes "Instead, me."*

2. "Left to ourselves," Thomas writes, "mechanistic and autonomic, we hanker for friends" (paragraph 5). What do these words imply about Thomas's position in the nature/nurture debate?

DISCUSSION: *If our genetic programming is one of fixed friendship, Thomas suggests that our social education, to overcome such an initially welcoming stance, must be both relentless and completely effective. By saying "left to ourselves," he is implicitly comparing innate attitudes to learned behavior; if friendliness is "compulsory," then racism, for instance, is the result of inculcated rationalization, a "straining with the full power of our conscious minds, making up conscious excuses all the way."*

3. How would you describe the way in which Thomas ends his essay? What are the reasons for the final vision?

DISCUSSION: *Thomas ends his essay with a vision of Platonic oneness as portrayed by the collective consciousness of the ants. He exploits what might ordinarily be considered repellent, that moment when "the whole mass begins to behave like a single huge creature" (paragraph 9). Rather than concentrating on the horrors of the dissolution of ego boundaries, he focuses on the unexplored territory of the new psychological state the ants participate in: "what on earth" would the mass ant think, and does each individual ant share in that thought? He doesn't know if each ant reacts to the phenomenon by having his "hair stand on end," but the final sentence certainly suggests that the mere consideration of such an event is exciting enough to make Thomas's hair prickle on his scalp.*

Questions on Language

1. In "The Tucson Zoo," Thomas presents a meditation on altruism, which is "jargon," or debased language, for "what used to be called love" (paragraph 7). What is the difference between the two words?

DISCUSSION: *Altruism is a word that accomplishes exactly what Thomas addresses in his opening paragraph; it's a narrowing of the word "love," a word produced "by the process of reductionism." The Stendahlian definition of "love," for example, refers to that moment of crystallization in which the beloved is invested with, and perceived as, perfection itself. Altruism, on the other hand, has been taken over by science to mean simply the unselfish devotion of self to others — even if they're not the perfect incarnation of the beloved.*

Writing Topics

1. Write an essay that presents the generally acknowledged attributes of various animals. Of course, these attributes are projected onto animals by human beings; the mechanistic and soulness aspects of the ants are probably not the ants' interpretation of themselves, if such a thing is possible. What do the negative and positive qualities with which we endow animals say about ourselves? What do we approve of in other species? Of what do we disapprove? In your essay, create an argument that interprets the value system we assign to the natural world.

2. Compare "The Tucson Zoo" with Margaret Atwood's "Canadian-American Relations: Surviving the Eighties." Where do the authors' viewpoints coincide? Does Atwood consider the psychology of altruism in her final paragraphs?

CALVIN TRILLIN

Rumors Around Town (p. 504)

Questions on Meaning

1. Why does Trillin devote paragraphs 2 – 4 to a description of Emporia and its citizens?

DISCUSSION: First, Trillin is trying to convey the disjunction between the setting and the act committed in that setting: "For many Americans, Emporia, Kansas, conjures up the vision of a typical American town in the era when people didn't have to think about violent men bent on robbery — a town where neighbors drank lemonade on the front porch and kidded one another about their performances in the Fourth of July softball game" (paragraph 2). This setting seems inappropriate to murder. Second, through this long and bucolic description, Trillin is attempting to set up a theme that he supports throughout the essay — appearance versus reality. He goes on to examine how external reality does not guarantee similarity between people; Tom Bird and his wife, "like a lot of couples in the congregation, . . . had three small children and a small split-level and a swing set in the back yard" (paragraph 5). In paragraph 44, for example, Lorna Anderson Eldridge takes on a new marriage and joins a new church and appears in court in her new incarnation, "as an upstanding Christian wife and mother who couldn't have had anything to do with plotting murder." Trillin emphasizes the disjunction between Lorna Anderson Eldridge's demeanor and psyche when he notes that she was "neatly dressed, composed, almost cheerful" when she confessed to a meeting in which "we discussed various ways of murdering my husband, Martin Anderson" (paragraph 47). Finally, "some people in Emporia" were forced to conclude that the only way to account for the murders was to assume that "Tom Bird and his secretary, who seemed so much like their neighbors, had mental difficulties that somehow meshed to result in deeds their neighbors consider unthinkable" (paragraph 51). Trillin addresses the unmasking of Bird and Lorna Anderson Eldridge when, in his final paragraph, he writes: "What was sordid about Emporia's most sordid case, of course, was not simply the crimes but the lives they revealed." The lives, so outwardly normal, were filled with "hatred and maybe wife beating and certainly casual, apparently joyless liaisons."

2. Why does Trillin call his piece "Rumors Around Town"? How does he treat the subject of rumors throughout the essay?

DISCUSSION: Trillin's title addresses one of his central concerns, a subject that he looks at again and again throughout his essay. In paragraph 11, Trillin shows how rumors are passed around: "in a place the size of Emporia . . . people tend to have an uncle who knows the cousin of someone through the Kiwanis, or a next-door neighbor who has the word through a lawyer who has a kid in the same Boy Scout troop." He himself uses the recapitulation of rumors to present information to the reader: "There were people in Emporia who said that a police investigation that included scrutiny of the Andersons' marriage had the potential of embarrassing any number of prominent business and professional men" (paragraph 13). In the following sentence, Trillin uses the present tense to introduce a rumor — and the conveyance of that rumor — that becomes central at Bird's trial: "Some people in Emporia — people who, say, worked with someone who knew someone connected with Faith Lutheran Church — were saying that Lorna Anderson's latest catch was Pastor Tom Bird" (paragraph 13). When the townspeople attend Bird's trial, they come because "they were attracted by the prospect of seeing witnesses under oath clear up — or perhaps improve on — the rumors that had been going around town for eight months" (paragraph 33). There is no mention of their wish to determine the truth of events, but rather merely a desire to judge them against the prevailing stories. But it seems, finally, that Trillin is not really condemning Emporia's citizens for their interest in the rumors, as we see when Trillin writes of the "people in Emporia who had spent the months since Martin Anderson's death savoring the ironies or embellishing the rumors" (paragraph 20). Certainly, he is addressing the siren call of the rumor, but, by juxtaposing it against the continuation of the sentence, which says that "the idea of a minister plotting a murder scheme right in his own church [is] shocking," he inverts the conventional view of rumor (paragraph 20). By the end of the essay, we discover that the murdering minister belongs to the realm of fact, so that fact far surpasses mere rumor in inherent evil. As Trillin states, so calmly, at the end of his essay, "what now seems remarkable about the outrageous rumors that gripped Emporia for so long is that so many of them turned out to be true" (paragraph 52).

Questions on Strategy

1.   In paragraph 5, Trillin describes Tom Bird: "He was married to his high school sweetheart, an astonishingly energetic young woman who had a master's degree in mathematics and managed to combine the responsibilities of a pastor's wife with some teaching at Emporia State." What is odd about this information when compared with paragraph 7? What might be Trillin's reasons for arranging his narrative in this way?

DISCUSSION: In paragraph 7, we find out that Sandy Bird is dead and has been for four months. She was "killed, from what the authorities could ascertain by reconstructing the event, when her car missed a nasty curve next to the Rocky Ford Bridge, southeast of town, and plunged over an embankment into the Cottonwood River." By withholding this information, and presenting it after he has made us believe that Sandy Bird is alive and well and practicing math, Trillin creates a real shock when he finally tells us she is dead. Furthermore, notice the context in which he tells us — we're at the funeral of murdered Marty Anderson. The two deaths are immediately connected in the reader's mind, although they are, as yet, linked by nothing but Trillin's authorial hand. As the essay continues, of course, the connection between the two deaths becomes more obvious.

2.   Describe some ways in which Trillin builds a portrait of Marty Anderson's character in paragraph 12.

DISCUSSION: Trillin describes Marty Anderson through the testimony of friends — "He could be very aggravating, and the next minute he could get you laughing" — followed by his own interpretation: "The way Anderson tried to get people laughing was usually through needling or practical jokes, and in both forms he occasionally passed over the line from funny to mean" (paragraph 12). When he writes, "He was a big man, more than six feet tall, and not the sort of big man who slowed up coming into second base for fear of bowling over a smaller player," Trillin compares, through a baseball metaphor, a big man who would check himself before he would cause even slight injury, with Martin Anderson, a big man who, although he fully recognizes his size and strength, is not unwilling to hurt others with it.

Questions on Language

1.   How do you interpret Tom Bird's analysis of his own words: "When the prosecution managed to bring into evidence two notes from Tom Bird that the police said they had found in Lorna Anderson's lingerie drawer, Bird said that they were meant simply to buck up Lorna's spirits and that such sentiments as 'I love you so very much and that's forever' were expressions not of romantic attachment but of 'authentic Christian love'" (paragraph 37)?

DISCUSSION: The first condemning thing about this note is its undeniable use of the personal pronoun "I," which suggests the expression of a personal, rather than a religious or institutional, sentiment. Someone needing reassurance of authentic Christian love might be more comforted by being told that God loves her and will love her forever, than by the fact of a particular individual's love. The argument could be posed that, as God's representative, a minister might say these words on behalf of God, but it seems more likely that a minister would like to make the distinction between divine love and earthly love clear. The lovely detail that Trillin makes sure to include is that the note was found in Anderson's lingerie drawer, which most of us would consider a context more suggestive of the carnal than of the divine.

Writing Topics

1. Other than the two or three paragraphs that Trillin devotes to describing both Martin Anderson and Sandy Bird, he almost leaves them out of this essay. Yet from their deaths arise the events he details in "Rumors Around Town." Write an essay discussing why Trillin chose not to exploit the sentiments conjured up by murder victims? Why did he choose to concentrate on the rather ugly parts of Martin Anderson's character in the little time he does address him?

2. Write an essay comparing the narrative strategy of this essay with Scott Russell Sanders's "Doing Time in the Thirteenth Chair." Both Trillin and Sanders are writing about events that were brought to trial, but Trillin does not focus on the trial in the way Sanders does. From what perspective does Sanders view his characters? How does it differ from Trillin's perspective? Does each write support the eventual verdict of his respective case?

BARBARA W. TUCHMAN

History as Mirror (p. 525)

Questions on Meaning

1. How does Tuchman interpret the fourteenth century? What does her interpretation imply about the twentieth century?

DISCUSSION: In "History as Mirror," although she documents the unremitting horrors of the fourteenth century, Tuchman sees in "the disintegration" the sprouts, "the green shoots of the Renaissance to come" (paragraph 5). Her essay addresses the idea of necessary decay — there has to be some great impetus, or "compost," for "new growth" (paragraph 5). Overall, her essay is interested in considering "the twentieth century's record of inhumanity and folly" against that of the fourteenth century's similar record because of the optimism it implies: "it is reassuring to discover that the human race has been in this box before — and emerged" (paragraph 2).

2. Tuchman gives us a comprehensive picture of the world's response to bubonic plague. What was the natural world's response to mass death? Since 1973, when this essay was written, we have witnessed the new plague of AIDS. Are we following the behavior of our historic predecessors in the face of plague? What is the difference between our knowledge of AIDS and the fourteenth century's knowledge of the black death?

DISCUSSION: In paragraph 9, the whole of the natural world seems to participate in the bubonic plague: "Wolves came down from the mountains to attack plague-stricken villages, crops went unharvested, dikes crumbled, salt water reinvaded and soured the lowlands, the forest crept back, and second growth, with the awful energy of nature unchecked, reconverted cleared land to waste." The world that human beings scrabbled out of the ground is recaptured by nature itself. In the fourteenth century, people mainly fled, leaving their mothers, fathers, husbands, wives, and children to die alone. "People reacted variously," Tuchman writes, "as they always do: some prayed, some robbed, some tried to help, most fled if they could, others abandoned themselves to debauchery on the theory that there would be no tomorrow. On balance, the dominant reaction was fear and a desire to save one's own skin" (paragraph 11).

Of course, no one knew what caused bubonic plague in the fourteenth century; its cause was an "awful mystery" (paragraph 13) and its transmission by fleas and rats unsuspected. In contrast, we have identified the virus that causes AIDS and we know that it is transmitted by sexual contact and infected needles. Yet, with all this knowledge, recognizing that a virus has nothing to do with "the wrath of God" (paragraph 13), our society has still reacted with unreasoning fear and horror, burning down the houses

83

of AIDS victims, evicting them from their homes, leaving them to die alone. One difference, however, between the two centuries, is that we do have an institutionalized system for protecting and helping AIDS victims, however unwieldy and slow it might be. And most of our population is better educated than most of the population in the fourteenth century, but the "gay-bashing" that has occurred in San Francisco, for example, has echoes of the pogroms suffered by the Jews of the fourteenth century (paragraph 15). The desire to find a scapegoat and punish him for somehow initiating plague seems to be still with us.

Questions on Strategy

1. Tuchman describes the Church as the institution that should have given the fourteenth century coherence and stability, but with its corruption came utter calamity. She locates the government in our more secular age as having the same function and writes, "Today it is the processes of government that are for sale, especially the electoral process, which is as vital to our political security as salvation was to the emotional security of the fourteenth century" (paragraph 17). How does Tuchman support her parallel?

DISCUSSION: Tuchman supports her parallel mainly through implication. In paragraph 19, she writes about the letters written to the popes in which the university theologians lamented, "Do you think people will suffer forever from your bad government? Who do you think can endure, amid so many abuses... your elevation of men without literacy or virtue to the most eminent positions?" Instead of citing exact correspondences in our time, Tuchman merely says "the echo sounds over the gulf of six hundred years with a timeliness almost supernatural." Of course, Watergate has receded a little by now, but consider the more recent Iran scandal and the numbers of indictments handed out to President Reagan's administration. The idea that Tuchman does address explicitly is the more general one of her governing argument: "The more important parallel lies in the decay of public confidence in our governing institutions, as the fourteenth-century public lost confidence in the Church" (paragraph 22).

Questions on Language

1. Tuchman uses many aphorisms in this essay, such as "guilt . . . is modern; sin is medieval" (paragraph 14). What does she mean by this? Find some other examples.

DISCUSSION: This aphorism alludes to the change in perspective between the medieval and the modern age. The idea of sin depends on the idea of a divine law, which is deliberately transgressed by the sinner. In the modern and more secular age, replacing sin with "guilt" implies simply a consciousness of doing wrong, but a wrong that cannot be so precisely measured. In paragraph 2, Tuchman writes, "man . . . is always capable of his worst," and in paragraph 31, "the effort of society is always toward order, away from anarchy." It is interesting to pair these two and discuss whether it is society's consciousness of "mankind at its worst" that brings order into being, or at least tries to prevent anarchy's predominance. Her final aphorism, on which she ends the essay, says, "You cannot extrapolate any series in which the human element intrudes; history, that is, human narrative, never follows, and will always fool, the scientific curve" (paragraph 48).

Writing Topics

1. Tuchman believes that "we have lost confidence in man's capacity to control his fate and even in his capacity to be good" (paragraph 38). She supports this claim by citing a list of cultural markers, such as "a literature of the anti-hero . . . porn and pop and blank canvases and anti-music designed to deafen." Do you agree with her interpretation of the art that upholds her argument? Write an essay in which you either support or refute her claim by using examples from modern novels, lyrics, and paintings.

2. In paragraph 18, Tuchman writes, "The yearning, and disgust with the Establishment, produced freak orders of mystics who lived in coeducational communes, rejected marriage, and glorified sexual indulgence." The scenario described took place in the fourteenth century, but communes, rejection of marriage, and sexual indulgence are by no means limited to that century. Joan Didion has argued that the members of any age marked by a spiritual vacuum find ways of creating their own systems of meaning. Think about the events and prevailing spiritual atmosphere of the past few years. Consider the current popularity of crystals as healing devices and the recent "harmonic convergence." Write an essay analyzing these phenomena. Do they seem to be inspired by "disgust with the Establishment" or other dynamics Tuchman discusses? In what ways are the prevailing social and moral climates similar? In what ways are they different?

ALICE WALKER

In Search of Our Mothers' Gardens (p. 540)

Questions on Meaning

1. In paragraph 12, Walker poses the central question of her essay: "How was the creativity of the black woman kept alive, year after year and century after century, when for most of the years black people have been in America, it was a punishable crime for a black person to read or write?" Walker herself is a writer, and if she'd been born a hundred years earlier she never would have been allowed access to written words. Why would access to written language have been a punishable crime? Are there any modern parallels?

DISCUSSION: *Written language, permanent, becomes an unavoidable fact, whereas oral language, ephemeral, can be more easily ignored. That writing was a crime testifies to the power of language, announcing that the written word is recognized in the way that the spoken word isn't. Writing was a criminal act because it was dangerous; it embodies thought that can be passed from person to person and considered and, finally, acted on; the written word reaches a larger audience. Communication among the members of any oppressed society is dangerous to the controlling members of that society, who fear and hate the ideas of those they oppress. Politically oppressive regimes often strip their opponents and critics of power by censoring their written words. Jacobo Timerman in Argentina was muzzled and tortured for what he managed to print; the Nigerian playwright Wole Soyinka was imprisoned without charge or trial for two years during the Nigerian Civil War. These are just two examples; such censorship takes place today, all over the world.*

2. There is an extremely high cultural value placed on language as a creative act. Without words, how did black women express their creativity?

DISCUSSION: *They used homely objects, close at hand, to speak for them, leaving their marks "in the only materials [they] could afford, and in the only medium [their positions] in society allowed [them] to use" (paragraph 35). the Smithsonian's quilt is made up of "bits and pieces of worthless rags," yet the story of the Crucifixion it portrays is ordered by "powerful imagination and deep spiritual feeling" (paragraph 34). Walker's own mother expressed her spirit and her creative need to interpret and order "the universe in the image of her personal conception of Beauty" through her garden (paragraph 43).*

Questions on Strategy

1. What does the epigraph, written by Jean Toomer, add to this essay? Why does Walker devote the first eight paragraphs of "In Search of Our Mothers' Gardens" to Toomer's perceptions?

DISCUSSION: *The epigraph addresses the central concern of Walker's essay— the lives of those who have no avenues through which to express themselves. Just as Toomer articulates the unspoken potential of the sleeping prostitute, so does Walker for all black women. The black women that Toomer saw — "exquisite butterflies trapped in an evil honey, toiling away their lives in an era, a century, that did not acknowledge them, except as 'the mule of the world'" (paragraph 4) — are those Walker both pays homage to and learns from.*

2. Considering the usual interpretation of Phillis Wheatley's work, why does Walker address her in this essay (beginning in paragraph 15)? How does she develop her argument regarding Wheatley?

DISCUSSION: *Walker tells us that Wheatley has been "held . . . up to ridicule for more than a century, [hanged] . . . as a fool" for praising her oppressors while writing on freedom and dignity (paragraph 22). Walker interprets the conditions of Wheatley's life that led her to choose the damning imagery of the Goddess with golden hair. By imaginatively entering Wheatley's situation — a child of seven, "a sickly little black girl, snatched from your home and country and made a slave" (paragraph 25) — Walker addresses the "contrary instincts" that came from her divided loyalties (paragraph 19). Wheatley was unable to perceive the tragedy of her own life and, perhaps, genuinely liked her kind mistress. Again, Wheatley drew her inspiration from what was close at hand, just like the quilt makers and the gardeners in the rest of the essay, turning to her mistress's golden hair as "the one thing she saw elevated above all others" (paragraph 23). Walker's essay rescues Wheatley from her traditional interpretation and finds much to praise in her ability and strength to keep alive "the notion of song" (paragraph 25).*

Questions on Language

1. In paragraph 5, Walker writes: "They forced their minds to desert their bodies and their striving spirits sought to rise, like frail whirlwinds from the hard red clay." What imagery does this simile depend on? How is it connected to the title?

DISCUSSION: *The simile depends on an image from the natural world, but this natural world is hard, arid, and barren. Rather than nourishing leaves and flowers and greenery, the "hard red clay" sends up only dusty and delicate whirlwinds, a form of life, but not a form we expect to be created by the earth. Later, in paragraph 8, Walker concentrates on life-giving sources that are unable to give life: "they lay vacant and fallow as autumn fields, with harvest time never in sight." These figures of speech invest the title of the essay with even greater poignancy, since they make clear that "our mothers' gardens" were created with great difficulty.*

Writing Topics

1. Write an essay explaining why it took Walker so long to recognize her own mother's creative voice. What are the cultural reasons that blinded her to acknowledging the role of her mother's garden? Examine those places in the essay that address, either explicitly or implicitly, what creative acts our society values.

2. Write an essay comparing "In Search of Our Mothers' Gardens" with James Baldwin's "If Black English Isn't a Language, Then Tell Me, What Is?" Can you connect the idea of writing as a punishable crime and the refusal to recognize black English as a language? What value does Walker place on writing? What emphasis does Baldwin give to creativity and its place in creating a language?

EUDORA WELTY

The Little Store (p. 551)

Questions on Meaning

1.   On her way to the Little Store, the young Eudora Welty describes an entire world, made up of such important landmarks as the house in which the three sisters dance all day to the "Tickle-Toe" song. What is the difference between this landmark and the next — the principal's house?

DISCUSSION: *Landmarks, for the young Welty, are not simply places where things are happening, but places where things could happen. Even though, in the particular trip the author is recounting, the principal does not emerge, the child's imagination encompasses the landmark's potential for what might happen: "What if she would come out? She would halt me in my tracks . . . saying 'Eudora Alice Welty, spell OBLIGE.' . . . She'd make me miss it again now, by boring her eyes through me from across the street. This was my vacation fantasy" (paragraph 8). The potential of landmarks is one reason for their importance to the girl; Lindsey's chinaberries "could have brought [her] down in my skates in a flying act of contrition before his eyes" (paragraph 10). Every landmark suggests a potential story, a narrative that might start in the same place but that could go in several directions.*

2.   In paragraph 28, Welty writes, "But I didn't know there'd ever been a story at the Little Store, one that was going on while I was there." Why didn't Welty know, and what function does the Monkey Man's appearance have in paragraph 25?

DISCUSSION: *Welty as a child was unable to see a story that didn't include her as a character. Even in the previous narratives that she concocted for the principal's house and Lindsey's house, Welty was a protagonist: "Everyone I saw on my way seemed to me then part of my errand" (paragraph 26). As the character in "The Little Store," she hadn't yet grown up enough to recognize that stories happen without our own participation; she was still limited to "what we could see within the four walls of the Little Store" (paragraph 29). And even then, she had been able to see only what related directly to herself, so that Mr. Sessions "had never been anything but patient and kind . . . [had] never once . . . sent you away" (paragraph 30). Mr. Sessions existed for young Welty only insofar as he presided over the grotto of delight that the store represented; her sense of the world and others was not yet large enough to wonder about his separate life and its personal relationships.*

The Monkey Man signals the change that is to come for Welty, forcing some incomplete knowledge on her: "But now I saw the Monkey Man at the Little Store, where I'd never seen him before. I'd never seen him sitting down. Low on that familiar doorstep, he was not the same any longer, and neither was his monkey. They looked just like an old man and an old friend of his that wore a fez, meeting quietly together, tired, and resting with their eyes fixed on some place far away, and not the same place" (paragraph 25). Although they haven't lost their "romance" for the young Welty, they've suffered some great and unknown change, just as the people in the Little Store are going to be transformed, from the known into the unfamiliar, and vanish.

Questions on Strategy

1.   "The Little Store" is an adult reminiscence of childhood experience, in which the perspective of the child jostles with that of the adult. Discuss the perspective in paragraphs 14, 15, and 17, and compare what is happening there to what is occurring in paragraph 2, with the various food suppliers.

DISCUSSION: *In paragraph 14, the child's eye travels "from cans of sardines to ice cream salt to harmonicas to flypaper." Welty has us looking over the child's shoulder here, but the adult perspective comments on the array of merchandise when she writes, "its confusion may have been in the eye of the* beholder" (paragraph 15). *In paragraph 17, the precision of the candy arrangements suggests the intense interest of the child in those arrangements, but Welty's adult memory comes up short over those "pastilles that came stacked in a cardboard cylinder with a cardboard lid." It's clearly the adult perspective when she muses "were they chocolate? I'd say rather they were brown. They didn't taste of anything at all, unless it was wood" (paragraph 17). In contrast, the child isn't interested in quality as much as she is in quantity: "Their attraction was the number you got for a nickel." In paragraph 2, the adult is not interpreting or commenting on the child's viewpoint as much. The young Eudora knows who Mr. Lemly is because he runs Lemly's Market and Grocery, but she knows the others only through what they sell. Thus, although an older Welty may know the "blackberry lady's" name, from the child's perspective she is defined through her most important attribute — selling blackberries. In paragraph 2, Welty is simply replicating the consciousness of the child.*

Questions on Language

1. What does Welty mean when she writes, "Setting out in this world, a child feels so indelible. He only comes to find out later that it's all the others along his way who are making themselves indelible to him" (paragraph 11)?

DISCUSSION: In the previous two paragraphs, the child has been conscious of being looked at, first by the principal, who might quiz her, and second by Lindsey, who might see her fall down ignominiously. The child, whose behavior is scrutinized by her parents, might feel that same scrutiny from the whole of her world and thus feel herself the indelible mark that can't be erased from anyone's consciousness. It might also suggest that the child feels utterly fixed, set, with suggestions of immortality and invulnerability — although the previous two paragraphs make the young Welty sound as though she's vulnerable in a certain way. Later, after growing up, Welty suggests that the former child realized how deeply she is affected by other people, that her younger feelings of being either scrutinized or intensely fixed have given way to her impressions of others, and that people are most deeply marked through their relationships with others.

Writing Topics

1. Welty closes her essay by saying, "We weren't being sent to the neighborhood grocery for facts of life, or death. But of course those are what we were on the track of, anyway. With the loaf of bread and the Cracker Jack prize, I was bringing home the intimations of pride and disgrace, and rumors and early news of people coming to hurt one another, while others practiced for joy — storing up a portion for myself of the human mystery." Write an essay in which you create, as Welty does here, the universe of a child who learns something about other people, even if the knowledge is merely an "intimation" of some great change.

2. In "Hauntings," Alastair Reid associates the two towns of his childhood with different kinds of knowledge, but he, like Welty, insists on the permanence of childhood memory. Write an essay comparing the ways in which each writer creates the universe of his or her childhood. How do the two writers convey the places they describe? Are they associated with senses like taste, smell, touch, and sight? What, in each essay, most captures the child's attention? How does each author show a child learning more about his or her world?

GEORGE F. WILL

Against Prefabricated Prayer (p. 561)

Questions on Meaning

1. Who do you think Will imagines his audience to be in this essay? What does his essay imply about his audience's understanding?

DISCUSSION: In "Against Prefabricated Prayer," Will seems to be addressing people who don't take their own religious traditions seriously, including President Reagan. Throughout the essay, he quotes from those who are deeply committed to religion and their faith's particular liturgical tradition. That both the Southern Baptists and Senator Danforth argue against prayer in schools should be persuasive evidence for some real doubts about its value. Those who most want school prayer, Will implies, are those who know the least about either faith or prayer, and thus those who would be content to both trivialize religion and coerce children who took "their own religious traditions seriously" (paragraph 8). The clear implication is that the appearance of devotion somehow has enormous sign value for this audience, that the appearance is more important than the thing itself.

2. How does Will interpret the idea of voluntary prayer as it is presented in Reagan's constitutional amendment: "Nothing in this Constitution shall be construed to prohibit individual or group prayer in public schools or other public institutions. No person shall be required by the United States or by any state to participate in prayer" (paragraph 2).

DISCUSSION: Will insists that the "issue is not really voluntary prayers for individuals." The context in which the amendment would operate is the school, which makes "the issue . . . organized prayers for groups of pupils subject to compulsory school attendance laws" (paragraph 2). Will interprets schoolchildren in this sentence as a captive group by definition. Their captivity, and concomittant lack of choice in the matter of prayer, is exacerbated by the psychological vulnerability of most small children: "peer pressure on children is not a trivial matter. Supporters of Reagan's amendment argue that a nine-year-old is 'free' to absent himself or otherwise abstain from a 'voluntary' prayer — an activity involving his classmates and led by that formidable authority figure, his teacher" (paragraph 7).

Questions on Strategy

1. The introductory sentence of "Against Prefabricated Prayer" is a quotation: "I stand foursquare with the English ethicist who declared: 'I am fully convinced that the highest life can only be lived on a foundation of Christian belief — or some substitute for it.'" Why does Will open the essay by declaring his personal beliefs?

DISCUSSION: First, Will's opening quotation allows us to understand from what ideological grounds he argues. Second, by presenting his personal convictions, he invests his objection to school prayer with more weight, since opposition is unexpected from his corner.

Questions on Language

1. In paragraph 5, Will writes that "collective prayer should express a shared inner state." How do the different languages of different prayers belonging to different faiths affect this shared inner state?

DISCUSSION: Mouthing sufficiently generic, nondenominational words is not going to create the conditions that lead to full body prostration and the adoration of Allah for a Muslim child. And a prayer "that makes no mention of Jesus Christ would be incoherent" to "certain kinds of Christian families" (paragraph 4). Any government-designed prayer will be unintelligible to at least a few members of the class, since the language of the different liturgies does not translate to other faiths; as Senator Jack Danforth says, "[True prayer] is almost by definition sectarian prayer" (paragraph 4). Will's argument implies that a group of people from different faiths are not going to be able to "express a shared inner state" simply by reciting the same words; their particular, complicated religious cosmologies are not addressed by using any old language; the idea of the divine for different people is inextricably linked to the specific language that encompasses their faith's understanding of divinity.

Writing Topics

1. Consider the following quotations: "It is, to say no more, curious that, according to some polls, more Americans favor prayers in schools than regularly pray in church" (paragraph 9). "How is America — or religion — served by the embarrassment of children who must choose between insincere compliance with, or conscientious abstention from, a ritual?" (paragraph 6). Write an essay in which you try to account for the beliefs expressed in both quotations: Why might Americans want schoolchildren to pray in school when they themselves don't pray in church? How is America or religion served by having schoolchildren pray? Do these beliefs reflect a notion that holds prayer as an incantation that, although it might be unable to reach God, has the power to rebound with beneficence on the person who prays? What is prayer associated with? Look at the iconography surrounding prayer, and examine the symbolic value of children praying.

2. Although Will cites the Southern Baptists as being against organized school prayer, other religious groups support the idea. Locate some of the proponents' literature and write an essay analyzing their reasons for supporting school prayer. Does Will's essay address all their concerns? Examine the diction and rhetorical strategies employed by the literature you find. What emotions are they appealing to? What is the foundation of their reasoning? Does their language invoke an implicit argument?

TOM WOLFE

Land of Wizards (p. 565)

Questions on Meaning

1. How does Wolfe describe inventors in this essay?

DISCUSSION: Wolfe's major point about inventors is their independence; they don't "need connections. The great American inventors of the past hundred years, the so-called age of technology, have not come from prominent families. They have not had money. They have not been part of the highly touted, highly financed research teams of industry and the universities. They have not been adept politically or socially. Many have been breathtakingly deficient in charm" (paragraph 17). Although, in the "late 1970s, the corporations had managed to create the impression that in the twentieth century the greatest technological innovations were no longer coming from the loners but from the corporate and university research teams," Wolfe argues that not only had this never been true, but both corporations and universities were antipathetic to inventors (paragraph 63). "Innovation and corporate research," he writes, "were very nearly a contradiction in terms; at bottom, the corporations were interested only in improvements in existing product lines. As for the universities, they actually looked down upon invention as an amateur pastime, despite the fact that much scientific study, especially in the area of electronics, was nothing more than the analysis of discoveries made by inventors" (paragraph 63).

2. In "Land of Wizards," American inventors face the triple-headed Goliath of corporations, government, and the courts. How do each of the three act to quash independent inventors?

DISCUSSION: *The corporations "ignored patent rights without batting an eye. They didn't give you so much as a sporting wink" (paragraph 36). It was economically advantageous for businesses to use inventions without paying royalties because "in the United States, unlike Japan and parts of Europe, patent infringement was not considered a form of theft, so there were no criminal penalties. There were not even punitive damages in patent cases unless the inventor could prove 'willful infringement'" (paragraph 38). If a corporation lost its case, the only damages it would be liable for would be that of paying the royalties it should have paid in the first place; ignoring patents was a "no-risk strategy" (paragraph 39). And, of course, the corporations had infinitely more lawyers and more money than single inventors, so suing for patent infringement could cost the inventor a quarter of a million dollars, when the royalties he could foresee in return would be far less than that: "[Corporations] would spend half a million dollars in legal fees to keep from taking a license and paying royalties they knew wouldn't run over $150,000" (paragraph 49). The U.S. government is indicted for the same theft; in paragraph 51, Lemelson is suing the government for patent infringement, and in the next two paragraphs, after deciding to "grant it a license free of charge," he ends up paying "$18,000 in lawyers' fees to give the license away" (paragraph 52). Robert Goddard, "the father of American rocketry," worked in intense isolation, "to try to put an end to the pirating of his patented inventions — chiefly by the U.S. government" (paragraph 53). And the courts, to judge from Lemelson's experience in paragraphs 32–35, "couldn't be bothered. Practically none of the judges who heard patent cases had any background in patent law, much less engineering. It was unfamiliar terrain, which seemed to make them irritable. On the one hand, they couldn't stand all these obsessive small-fry inventors, these parasites on the hide of Science, with their endless theories and their transducers and capacitive-sensitive relays and the rest of that paralyzing jargon. But on the other hand, if they, the judges, could understand an invention, then it must not be much of an invention. They had developed 'the doctrine of obviousness.' If an invention looked obvious, they declared the patent invalid" (paragraph 36).*

3. What is so important about the victimization of lone inventors? Why is Wolfe so interested in the rampant theft of their inventions, aside from exposing the unscrupulousness and immorality of the triple-headed Goliath?

DISCUSSION: *The effect of what could almost be termed a legally sanctioned conspiracy to defraud the small inventor is the loss of the technological edge for the entire country. Suddenly, in the 1970s, "it began to dawn on government statisticians that the United States was no longer the great world center of technological innovation" (paragraph 62). Whereas foreign corporations seem to "recognize the clear value of invention from an economic point of view," the United States, in their opinion, "has lived off the fat of its own technology for so long that we don't recognize that the consequence of the legal destruction of patents is a decline in innovation, a situation that is not within anyone's economic interest" (paragraph 65). Wolfe leaves us with a scene of Lemelson inventing a process by which such things as cancer therapy would be vastly improved, being far less invasive to and painful for the patient. The clear implication is that this invention, too, like the others, might be stolen. How soon will it be before Lemelson, and inventors like him, just stop? As Lemelson says, "What all this means to the inventor is that he either quits inventing or he licenses foreign" (paragraph 66).*

Questions on Strategy

1. In paragraphs 68–90, Lemelson is being interviewed by a reporter who is wearing "a checked suit and a shirt collar like Herbert Hoover's. It looked about four inches high. Underneath his necktie you could see a brass-plated collar button of the sort that went out forty-six years ago" (paragraph 67). Why does Wolfe describe the reporter's clothes in such detail? How does this help him enter the mind of his subject, Lemelson?

Wolfe, *Land of Wizards* (text pp. 565–580)

DISCUSSION: To be able to answer this question completely, the reader would benefit from knowing that Tom Wolfe is a sartorial dandy, the Beau Brummell of the modern age. These are exactly the clothes he would be wearing, and it seems that he's describing himself. His reasons for doing so might include sharing a private joke with the informed reader, allowing the reader to congratulate himself or herself for catching what's going on. It could also be that Wolfe is indulging in a bit of a joke at his own sartorial expense, rather ruefully confessing to his own love of dandyism. Most important, however, the reporter's objective description might include a teasing response to those critics who have charged him with being overintrusive; as Hall writes in his Foreword, the "subjectivity of his reportage" is his attempt "to enter the minds of his subjects as if they were characters in a novel and he the novelist who invented them." In this case, Wolfe describes himself objectively, without revealing the reporter as himself.

We can, however, talk about the effect this produces in his essay. When the reporter has apparently ended the interview and Lemelson boards the train to Princeton, the reader suddenly is granted access to the inventor's private thoughts: "For people with certain forms of cancer, it would be a godsend. And now he had it! The time-release thing! The insertion system! All the parts were in place!" (paragraph 92). This entrance into his subject's mind continues to the end of the essay. He switches to omniscient third-person reporting and throws all the emphasis on the subject's state of mind in the final paragraphs, so that Lemelson's excitement over his invention and his suspicion of his fellow passenger gains power.

Questions on Language

1. In paragraph 16, Wolfe writes: "Is there any more feverish dream of glory in the world, outside of Islam, than the dream of being an inventor? Certainly not in the United States, and probably not in Japan or in any other industrial country. An invention is one of those superstrokes, like discovering a platinum deposit or a gas field or writing a novel, through which an individual, the hungriest loner, can transform his life, overnight, and light up the sky. The inventor needs only one thing, which is as free as the air: a terrific idea" (paragraph 16). After reading the essay, how would you describe Wolfe's tone in this passage? Where does he address the dream again in "Land of Wizards"?

DISCUSSION: This passage is laden with irony. In his essay, Wolfe refutes almost every point made here: the inventors Wolfe presents are more likely to have jumped out of a window, robbed and penniless, than they are to have transformed their lives overnight. Far from lighting up the sky, they spend all their time in lawyers' offices and courtrooms. A terrific idea may be "as free as the air," but being credited with that idea could take hundreds of thousands of dollars and twenty years or more of the inventor's life. The only idea that Wolfe can salvage is the dream of the inventor, and we know that Lemelson, unlike many loners, is a remarkably tenacious and optimistic man. In paragraph 93, Wolfe closes the essay with Lemelson inventing on the train: "The drug delivery. The time release. He was no longer aware of the haze and the motion of the car. He was soaring. It was like the beginning, once more, a dream come true."

Writing Topics

1. In a way, although Wolfe is focusing on the obstacles faced by the small inventor, he's presenting, as he did with the astronauts in *The Right Stuff*, a kind of hero. Certainly, the inventor is an iconic figure in the American psyche. What is it about the inventor that elicits the nation's admiration? Does the inventor embody virtues that are specifically American? Does Wolfe address these ideas in this essay?

2. Write an essay analyzing Wolfe's narrative strategy, comparing it with Scott Russell Sanders's in "Doing Time in the Thirteenth Chair." To what degree does each author include himself in his essay? In what ways do the strategies of the two writers differ? Consider how Wolfe's approach might work in Sanders's essay and vice versa.

PAUL ZWEIG

Transitions (p. 581)

Questions on Meaning

1.   How does Zweig sustain the theme of time in this essay? How does his idea of time change after his diagnosis? What does he say is the usual view of time?

DISCUSSION: Immediately after his diagnosis, Zweig becomes alienated from the world: "Time had been cut off from before my face. The world was unchanged. The streets were full of cars and pedestrians; the sun still caught in the windows of buildings. The radio reported worldwide events. Everything was the same, but time had been removed. And without time, everything was unreal, but I was horribly real, oversized, bursting as a body bursts in a vacuum" (paragraph 8). He perceives the world, as, in a sense, being immortal, preferring scenes of energy and bustle in which "there was a present," which made him "forget [his] rarefied life where there was no time" (paragraph 10). His diagnosis gives him a strange new bond with his daughter, whose "innocence of time" — her intensity in the pure present — he tries to emulate. "In a peculiar way," he writes, "my daughter and I were equals; neither of us had any time, and the irony was terrible, for I had lost mine and she hadn't acquired hers yet. Therefore we had each other" (paragraph 11). Being in the natural world, especially at the boathouse in Central Park, gives him back his feeling of connection, returns him into the fold of the living: "Time had flowed back around me. Again, I was inside of life. I was freestanding, not thrust against a blankness" (paragraph 18). He discovers this feeling of continuity and potential at his house in France, where he builds "the endlessness back around [himself]" (paragraph 21). The huge view — "so much space" — from his New York apartment also contracts time, in that it intensifies the present, "like a balloon shielding me from what I want to avoid" — death itself (paragraph 32).

Zweig explicitly addresses his postdiagnosis attitude toward time in paragraph 37: "For four years I had been bending myself to a shorter arc of life. I wanted elbow room; I wanted an enlarged present, and I had managed by discipline and willpower, by selfishness, to thicken the everyday, attenuate the far-off." He analyzes the way people normally live, "in a double sphere of consciousness: a near shell reverberating with needs and hopes, full of urgency, heavy with the flesh of our lives; and a far, attenuated hood of thoughts and projects which spin us years into the future, where we pretend that there is time" (paragraph 37). Most of us live as though we are always going to live; "it is man's experiment with immortality, without which books would not be written and buildings would not be erected to last centuries. It is the lie of endlessness, the lie we spin out of ourselves like the 'filament, filament' of the 'patient spider' in Walt Whitman's poem, to give us time" (paragraph 37). For Zweig, living utterly in the present moment makes him feel that "death could not harm [him]" (paragraph 38). His daughter, because her very youth implies a future that he will not see, "[drives] holes in [his] body of time, and let[s] in distance; distance that was denied [him], distance [he] strove for and wished for without hoping, because hope devalued [his] one secure possession: the roomy present" (paragraph 39).

At the end of the essay, with his cancer in remission once again, Zweig concludes that the only thing of real importance in life is the moment, which is composed of daily ritual and pedestrian detail, "a flimsy ordinariness," made up of the cherry blossoms at the Botanic Gardens, "cutting up parsnip roots, carrots and broccoli for a stew; feeding the children, and then sitting in the high shadowy living room of Vikki's apartment late at night, reading or talking" (paragraph 54). These may be homey details, but they are the pieces of "the old dream of an enchanted ordinariness come true," a circumscribed and happy life that has continuity, even amidst its recognized brevity.

2.   Usually a writer is considered "immortal" because his or her words live on after death. How does Zweig understand the immortality of the writer?

DISCUSSION: For Zweig, having his words live on after his death is a doubtful proposition at best, "in these days of nuclear shadow" (paragraph 51). Instead, he sees that "a writer's immortality exists in the moment of conception, in which language has seized hold of him." For him "writing is living," touching "the roots of [his] life" (paragraphs 51 and 50).

Zweig, *Transitions* (text pp. 581–597)

Questions on Strategy

1. Zweig includes a portrait of his wife (soon to be ex-wife) that is far from flattering. Why might he have included those details about her? What effect does it give his essay?

DISCUSSION: In paragraph 17, Zweig writes that for his wife, he "had become an emissary of mortality, a messenger from further along, outside the flimsy shelter of endlessness that we spin around us when we're lucky: a portable home, a little immortality, and then suddenly it collapses." It is possible to hear an echo of the idea of "killing the messenger who brings bad news" behind this sentence, to think that part of his wife's anger comes out of fear and that for her, Zweig has become the embodiment of death. But a lot of what he tells us renders her unsympathetic: "For her, my lymphoma was the click of a jailer's cell closing upon her life. She boiled with guilty anger, and within a few days could hardly bear the sight of me" (paragraph 11). He is afraid that she will take his daughter, afraid she will attack him bodily: "Lying in our bed at night, I had felt like a naked target, waiting for her rage to solidify and become a weapon" (paragraph 20). He even succumbs to awarding her a complete and horrifying power, that of causing his cancer: "Was the lymphoma her ultimate spell? The cellular substance of her wish for me?" (paragraph 20). One of the reasons he tries to shun this thought is that it would mean that his "wife's tunnel vision of despair and accusation had been stronger than [his] contradictory soul with its compulsive large-mindedness, its play of feelings and knowledge" (paragraph 20). In this sentence, he presents himself with extreme sympathy, investing only his wife with virulent qualities — yet it's the "large-minded" soul who is creating this vituperative portrait. But he still wants her to be his wife, for without her he is left at "ground level: no family, a flimsy life" (paragraph 23). Yet even after she leaves, he still sees her as "a tool of destruction swinging wildly at the core of [his] life," tempting him to suicide (paragraph 30). Perhaps Zweig includes this portrait of his wife because he feels he is presenting a "truer" vision of life, in which family members fear and hate their terminally ill. Certainly, its effect on the essay is to make clear Zweig's almost desperate desire to have even the appearance of something substantial, a family, a bulwark against the solitude he contemplates in losing his family as well as his life.

Questions on Language

1. In paragraph 6, Zweig's doctor says, "Don't think of this as cancer . . . That's a terrifying word. You have a lymphoma." Why does he insist on using only an "approved" vocabulary?

DISCUSSION: The word cancer is terrifying because it is generally perceived to mean certain death. The doctor is addressing the power of language, and in replacing "cancer" with "lymphoma" he is trying to limit the psychological valences that the word conjures up. His admonition suggests that words really do have the power of spells and that part of the treatment of either cancer or lymphoma is psychological.

Writing Topics

1. Compare Zweig's "Transitions" with Annie Dillard's "Total Eclipse." How does each author understand such major subjects as time, immortality, writing, and death? What does each see as important in life?

2. In John Berger's "Her Secrets," the author describes autobiography as "that orphan form" that "begins with a sense of being alone" (paragraph 4). He implies that autobiography cannot capture the "common moments" that the majority of people share. In an essay, consider whether "Transitions" fits Berger's definition of autobiography. Does Zweig's testimony address a general world, or is it essentially the record of a private experience? In either case, what techniques does Zweig use to render his experience for his readers, and how successfully does he do so? How do his methods differ from Berger's?

Rhetorical Index

95

Comparison and Contrast

Definition

Description

Division and Classification

Example

Narration

Process Analysis